D1269628

THE
GREAT ALL-TIME
BASEBALL RECORD
BOOK

•

THE
GREAT ALL-TIME
BASEBALL RECORD
BOOK

●

JOSEPH L. REICHLER

Revised and Updated by

KEN SAMELSON

MACMILLAN PUBLISHING COMPANY   NEW YORK

MAXWELL MACMILLAN CANADA   TORONTO

MAXWELL MACMILLAN INTERNATIONAL

NEW YORK   OXFORD   SINGAPORE   SYDNEY

Macmillan Publishing Company
866 Third Avenue
New York, NY 10022

Maxwell Macmillan Canada, Inc.
1200 Eglinton Avenue East, Suite 200
Don Mills, Ontario M3C 3N1

Macmillan Publishing Company is part of the Maxwell Communication Group of Companies.

Reichler, Joseph L., 1915–1988
The great all-time baseball record book/by Joseph L. Reichler.—
Rev. and updated/by Ken Samelson.
p.   cm.
Includes index.
ISBN 0-02-603101-9
1. Baseball—United States—Records.   I. Samelson, Ken.
II. Title.
GV877.R39   1993   91-38197   CIP
796.357′021—dc20

Macmillan books are available at special discounts for bulk purchases for sales promotions, premiums, fund-raising, or educational use. For details, contact:
Special Sales Director
Macmillan Publishing Company
866 Third Avenue
New York, NY 10022

10   9   8   7   6   5   4   3   2   1

Printed in the United States of America

CONTENTS

●

ACKNOWLEDGMENTS

●

Since *The Great All-Time Baseball Record Book* was published in 1981, many revisions and additions have been made to its contents. I would like to thank the Society for American Baseball Research for their continuing efforts and for providing us with many of the updates in the book. Thanks go to SABR's Rich Topp, Bob McConnell, Bob Davids, David Vincent, Scott Flatow, Steve Nadel, Phil Goldberg, Al Blumkin, Dave Stephan, and Dave Zeman. Ross Adell, another SABR member, deserves my special thanks for his tireless research efforts. I would also like to thank Bill Deane of the National Baseball Library at the Hall of Fame for helping verify many of the records, Craig Barbarino of Major League Baseball, Bob Mecca of STATS, Inc., Andrew Attaway, and editor Jeanine Bucek, who got this project off the ground and directed this team effort.

KEN SAMELSON

LIST OF ABBREVIATIONS

●

League Abbreviations

A   American League (1901–present)
AA American Association (1882–91)
F   Federal League (1914–1915)
N   National League (1876–present)
P   Players' League (1890)
U   Union Association (1884)

Team Abbreviations

ALT	Altoona	MON	Montreal
ATL	Atlanta	NY	New York
BAL	Baltimore	NWK	Newark
BOS	Boston	OAK	Oakland
BKN	Brooklyn	PHI	Philadelphia
BUF	Buffalo	PIT	Pittsburgh
CAL	California	PRO	Providence
CHI	Chicago	RIC	Richmond
CIN	Cincinnati	ROC	Rochester
CLE	Cleveland	SD	San Diego
COL	Columbus	SEA	Seattle
DET	Detroit	SF	San Francisco
HAR	Hartford	STL	St. Louis
HOU	Houston	STP	St. Paul
IND	Indianapolis	SYR	Syracuse
KC	Kansas City	TEX	Texas
LA	Los Angeles	TOL	Toledo
LOU	Louisville	TRO	Troy
MIL	Milwaukee	WAS	Washington
MIN	Minnesota	WIL	Wilmington

Statistical Abbreviations

A	Assists	LH/RH	Left-Handed or
AB	At-Bats		Right-Handed
BB	Bases on Balls	LP	Losing Pitcher
1B	Singles or First Baseman	MVP	Most Valuable Player
2B	Doubles or Second	OF	Outfielder
	Baseman	Opp.	Opponent
3B	Triples or Third	P	Pitcher
	Baseman	Pct.	Percentage
C	Catcher	PO	Putouts
CF	Centerfielder	Pos.	Position
CG	Complete Games	R	Runs Scored
Cons.	Consecutive	RBI	Runs Batted In
Diff.	Difference	RF	Right Fielder
DP	Double Plays	RP	Runs Produced (Runs +
E	Errors		Runs Batted In − Home
ERA	Earned Run Average		Runs)
FA	Fielding Average	SB	Stolen Bases
G	Games	2nd	Finished Second
H	Hits	ShO	Shutouts
H/A	Home or Away	ShO L	Shutout Losses
HBP	Hit by Pitch	SO	Strikeouts
HR	Home Runs	SS	Shortstop
Inn.	Inning	SV	Saves
Inns.	Total Innings in Game	TB	Total Bases
IP	Innings Pitched	TC	Total Chances
L	Losses	W	Wins
LF	Left Fielder	WP	Winning Pitcher
		Yrs.	Years

In the tables a blank indicates a repeated name, team or date. If the number of innings is not listed, it is nine.

INTRODUCTION

●

This book began nearly fifty years ago.

On May 25, 1936, the headline in the *New York Sun* read, "Tony Lazzeri Bats in 11 Runs in a Game for the Yankees; Establishes New American League Record."

The newspaper account continued: "Lazzeri's output shattered an old AL record of 9 RBIs in a game last achieved by Jimmie Foxx, falling just one short of equaling the major league mark of 12 set by Jim Bottomley of the St. Louis Cardinals on September 16, 1924."

A detailed account of Lazzeri's collection of RBIs followed, but there was no further reference to the record. Who were the other American Leaguers to drive in 9 runs in a game? What about the National League? Did any National Leaguer ever drive in 11 runs—or 10 or 9?

A search through the available record books shed no additional light on the subject. They listed the RBI leaders in each league for a season, a game, an inning. But that was it. No top ten, no top five, no runner-up. The same was true for all the records listed in the existing books. For me, an avid young baseball fan, this was a tremendous disappointment. I was devoted to the game and looked upon the facts, the feats, and the figures—and the men who made them—as the lifeblood of baseball.

This event marked the beginning of a lifetime of research in the archives of baseball—a painstaking study of all box scores from the formation of the first major league more than a hundred years ago to the present. With the aid of microfilm, I carefully scanned weekly issues of *Sporting News, Sporting Life,* and *Sporting Times,* as well as daily newspapers from cities all over the United States, to track down and record individual and team efforts.

I soon expanded my records to include unusual, offbeat, and generally unrecorded facts and figures, such as the achievements of fathers and sons or of brothers, of lefty-righty pitching combinations, of sets of teammates. Most record books list all the men who pitched no-hitters, but I recorded who caught the games and who broke up the "almosts." Then there were the cycle hitters—players who have hit a single, double, triple, and home run in one game—and the iron men, the players and managers who have set the standards for longevity in a whole array of playing and pitching categories. I also gave special attention to rookies, to see how many players fulfilled the promise of noteworthy opening years.

The Great All-Time Baseball Record Book is the result of those years of research and record-keeping. Many of the records in this book have never before been compiled or published. Taken together, these records give both the casual fan and the professional a whole new look at the men who take the field every day to play our national sport.

This book boasts a thoroughness unparalleled in the annals of record books. Here the reader can study the records in depth. We all know Joe DiMaggio hit safely in 56 consecutive games; but this book lists all the players who have hit safely in more than 20. And you can find the runner-up to Jim Bottomley's 12 RBIs—a mark as yet unmatched: He is Phil Weintraub, who drove in 11 runs for the old New York Giants in 1944. The runners-up to Lazzeri in the American League are Norm Zauchin, Reggie Jackson, and Fred Lynn, all of whom have batted in 10 runs in one game.

Another indispensable asset this book offers is the breadth of the material, which allows for comparisons between players from all periods of baseball, including the long-neglected years before 1900. Every fan remembers not only the great stars but also the unsung heroes who lived in the shadows of their greater contemporaries and thus were never recognized for their true worth. In this book you can line the players up against the records themselves, eliminating the time factor, and evaluate an individual player's performance. You can compare today's stars to yesterday's greats and judge for yourself how they measure up.

A third feature of the book is the remarkable material it provides to the student of the game. Through the information furnished, the serious fan can note the home run explosion of the 1920s and 1930s, the remarkable increase in strikeouts in the 1950s and 1960s, the recent rediscovery of the stolen base, and the phenomenal growth of relief pitching in the 1970s. These changes reflect subtle differences in playing conditions (night baseball, jet travel, the extended season) and marked differences in how to build a winning club.

These pages contain a wonderful quantity of baseball information—the players who just missed the triple crown, the glorious runners-up who would have won a title in another year, the men who have won honors in both the AL and NL, the players who hung in long enough to make their marks, and the players who broke away to a great start but never reached the winner's circle. This is the heart of baseball, the goals that make each new season a new chance for every player to write his name in the record book.

It is my hope that, for the fan and the professional alike, this will be the most comprehensive book of its kind. The biographical material in it has been verified against *The Baseball Encyclopedia,* and all efforts were made to make *The Great All-Time Baseball Record Book* as accurate as humanly possible. Being human, we may have made mistakes. For the mistakes that may be listed, we apologize in advance; we are grateful for all corrections.

Above all, I want baseball fans to enjoy this book, to start arguments with it and settle them with it. Casey Stengel always said, ''You could look it up.'' Now you know where.

JOSEPH L. REICHLER

INDIVIDUAL BATTING RECORDS

●

Grand Slam Home Runs, AL

Player	Team	Date	Player	Team	Date
Herm McFarland	CHI	May 1, 1901	Jake Stahl	BOS	Aug 2, 1912
Dummy Hoy	CHI	May 1, 1901	Eddie Onslow	DET	Aug 22, 1912
Ducky Holmes	DET	Jun 17, 1901	Duffy Lewis	BOS	Oct 3, 1912
Jimmy Williams	BAL	Jun 18, 1901	Joe Jackson	CLE	May 11, 1913
Joe Yeager	DET	Jun 18, 1901	Sam Crawford	DET	Jun 11, 1913
Nap Lajoie	PHI	Jul 1, 1901	Birdie Cree	NY	Jul 11, 1913
	PHI	Jul 30, 1901	Roger Peckinpaugh	NY	Aug 22, 1913
Socks Seybold	PHI	May 1, 1902	Ty Cobb	DET	Sep 17, 1913
Deacon McGuire	DET	May 18, 1902	Walter Johnson	WAS	Jun 21, 1914
Nap Lajoie	CLE	Jun 24, 1902	Ray Demmitt	CHI	Jul 5, 1914
Harry Davis	PHI	Jul 8, 1902	Happy Felsch	CHI	Jun 18, 1915
Jimmy Collins	BOS	Jul 25, 1902	Frank Gilhooley	NY	May 31, 1916
Snake Wiltse	BAL	Aug 23, 1902	George Burns	DET	Jul 15, 1916
Erve Beck	DET	Aug 25, 1902	Rube Oldring	NY	Jul 27, 1916
John Anderson	STL	Sep 5, 1902	Joe Jackson	CHI	Jul 30, 1916
Herm McFarland	BAL	Sep 10, 1902	Elmer Smith	WAS	Aug 24, 1916
Hobe Ferris	BOS	Jun 5, 1903	Wally Schang	PHI	Sep 8, 1916
Fritz Buelow	DET	Sep 22, 1903	Marty Kavanagh	CLE	Sep 24, 1916
Harry Davis	PHI	May 6, 1904	Happy Felsch	CHI	Sep 30, 1916
John Ganzel	NY	Jun 16, 1904	Lee Gooch	PHI	Jun 17, 1917
Piano Legs Hickman	CLE	Jul 5, 1904	Ty Cobb	DET	Jun 30, 1917
Freddy Parent	BOS	Jul 8, 1904	Ping Bodie	PHI	Jun 30, 1917
Dave Fultz	NY	Jul 30, 1904	Wally Pipp	NY	Aug 17, 1917
Danny Murphy	PHI	Sep 19, 1904	Mike Menosky	WAS	Sep 29, 1917
Sam Crawford	DET	Jun 17, 1905	Happy Felsch	CHI	Jun 2, 1918
Joe Stanley	WAS	Sep 26, 1905	Jim Shaw	WAS	May 5, 1919
Frank LaPorte	NY	Oct 7, 1905	Babe Ruth	BOS	May 20, 1919
Cy Falkenberg	WAS	Jul 18, 1906	Eddie Collins	CHI	Jun 5, 1919
Charlie Jones	WAS	Aug 30, 1906	Babe Ruth	BOS	Jun 30, 1919
Frank LaPorte	NY	Sep 11, 1906		BOS	Jul 18, 1919
Nap Lajoie	CLE	Aug 29, 1907	Sammy Vick	NY	Aug 7, 1919
Germany Schaefer	DET	Jun 28, 1908	Harry Heilmann	DET	Aug 22, 1919
Danny Murphy	PHI	Jul 18, 1908	Babe Ruth	BOS	Aug 23, 1919
Hobe Ferris	STL	Aug 9, 1908	Ping Bodie	NY	Jun 3, 1920
Danny Murphy	PHI	Aug 20, 1908	Del Pratt	NY	Jun 4, 1920
Frank Baker	PHI	Apr 24, 1909	Stuffy McInnis	BOS	Jun 29, 1920
Kid Elberfield	WAS	April 20, 1910	Elmer Smith	CLE	Jun 29, 1920
Jake Stahl	BOS	Apr 21, 1910	Jack Tobin	STL	Jul 15, 1920
Donie Bush	DET	May 17, 1910	Joe Jackson	CHI	Jul 16, 1920
Lee Tannehill	CHI	Jul 31, 1910	Happy Felsch	CHI	Sep 13, 1920
Joe Jackson	CLE	May 7, 1911	George Uhle	CLE	Apr 28, 1921
Ty Cobb	DET	May 13, 1911	Bibb Falk	CHI	May 22, 1921
Ivy Olson	CLE	May 18, 1911	Howard Shanks	WAS	Jul 28, 1921
Harry Gessler	WAS	Jun 2, 1911	Bob Meusel	NY	Aug 9, 1921
Stuffy McInnis	PHI	Jun 24, 1911	Shano Collins	BOS	Aug 18, 1921
Roy Hartzell	NY	Jul 12, 1911	Tilly Walker	PHI	Sep 3, 1921
Frank LaPorte	STL	Aug 22, 1911	George Sisler	STL	Sep 16, 1921
Bud Ryan	CLE	May 12, 1912	Chick Fewster	NY	May 12, 1922
			Baby Doll Jacobson	STL	May 20, 1922

Grand Slam Home Runs, AL (*cont.*)

Player	Team	Date	Player	Team	Date
Tris Speaker	CLE	May 20, 1922	Babe Ruth	NY	Sep 24, 1925
Ken Williams	STL	May 29, 1922	Al Wingo	DET	May 5, 1926
Bobby Veach	DET	Jun 6, 1922	Tony Lazzeri	NY	May 18, 1926
Elmer Smith	BOS	Jun 8, 1922	Ken Williams	STL	Jun 17, 1926
George Sisler	STL	Jun 14, 1922	Sammy Hale	PHI	Jul 30, 1926
Bibb Falk	CHI	Jul 1, 1922	Bill Barrett	CHI	Aug 4, 1926
Babe Ruth	NY	Jul 6, 1922	Wally Schang	STL	Aug 15, 1926
Bobby Veach	DET	Jul 18, 1922	Joe Judge	WAS	Aug 30, 1926
Patsy Gharrity	WAS	Jul 26, 1922	Jack Tobin	BOS	Sep 12, 1926
Jack Tobin	STL	Aug 6, 1922	Babe Ruth	NY	Sep 25, 1926
Bobby LaMotte	WAS	Aug 23, 1922	Jack Tobin	BOS	Apr 23, 1927
Ken Williams	STL	Sep 5, 1922	Lou Gehrig	NY	May 7, 1927
Frank Brower	WAS	Sep 15, 1922	Wally Schang	STL	May 15, 1927
Wally Pipp	NY	May 14, 1923	Pat Collins	NY	Jun 13, 1927
Joe Connolly	CLE	Jun 6, 1923	Al Simmons	PHI	Jun 15, 1927
Tris Speaker	CLE	Jun 9, 1923	Lou Gehrig	NY	Jul 4, 1927
	CLE	Jun 30, 1923	Charlie Gehringer	DET	Jul 5, 1927
Patsy Gharrity	WAS	Jul 1, 1923	Bud Clancy	CHI	Jul 15, 1927
Everett Scott	NY	Jul 4, 1923	George Sisler	STL	Jul 18, 1927
Hank Severeid	STL	Jul 10, 1923	Tony Lazzeri	NY	Aug 24, 1927
Fred Haney	DET	Jul 11, 1923	Bill Barrett	CHI	Sep 6, 1927
Tris Speaker	CLE	Aug 11, 1923	Marty McManus	DET	Sep 17, 1927
Homer Summa	CLE	Oct 3, 1923	Babe Ruth	NY	Sep 27, 1927
Harvey Hendrick	NY	Oct 7, 1923		NY	Sep 29, 1927
Ike Boone	BOS	May 30, 1924	Joe Dugan	NY	May 4, 1928
Harry Hooper	CHI	Jun 16, 1924	Lou Gehrig	NY	May 11, 1928
Pat Collins	STL	Jun 16, 1924	Earle Combs	NY	May 20, 1928
Topper Rigney	DET	Jun 24, 1924	Sammy Hale	PHI	Jun 8, 1928
Harvey Hendrick	NY	Jul 10, 1924	Harry McCurdy	CHI	Jun 20, 1928
Bibb Falk	CHI	Jul 11, 1924	Bill Regan	BOS	Jun 23, 1928
Heinie Manush	DET	Jul 19, 1924	Larry Bettencourt	STL	Jun 26, 1928
Harry Hooper	CHI	Aug 27, 1924	Jackie Tavener	DET	Jul 16, 1928
Danny Clark	BOS	Sep 2, 1924	Al Simmons	PHI	Jul 25, 1928
Frank Ellerbe	CLE	Sep 11, 1924	Harry Heilmann	DET	Jul 26, 1928
Aaron Ward	NY	Sep 13, 1924	Al Simmons	PHI	Aug 9, 1928
Heinie Manush	DET	Sep 14, 1924	Jack Rothrock	BOS	Sep 3, 1928
Joe Judge	WAS	Apr 17, 1925	Bob Meusel	NY	Sep 9, 1928
Al Simmons	PHI	May 12, 1925	Harry Rice	DET	Sep 21, 1928
Ken Williams	STL	May 20, 1925	Al Simmons	PHI	Apr 27, 1929
Willie Kamm	CHI	May 28, 1925	Bob Meusel	NY	May 6, 1929
Joe Judge	WAS	Jun 13, 1925	Earl Averill	CLE	May 10, 1929
Ty Cobb	DET	Jun 15, 1925	Heinie Manush	STL	Jun 7, 1929
Bobby LaMotte	STL	Jun 18, 1925	Roy Johnson	DET	Jun 27, 1929
Pinky Hargrave	STL	Jul 2, 1925	Babe Ruth	NY	Jul 3, 1929
George Sisler	STL	Jul 11, 1925	Marty McManus	DET	Jul 8, 1929
Lou Gehrig	NY	Jul 23, 1925		DET	Jul 10, 1929
Spence Harris	CHI	Jul 28, 1925	Babe Ruth	NY	Aug 6, 1929

Grand Slam Home Runs, AL (*cont.*)

Player	Team	Date	Player	Team	Date
Babe Ruth	NY	Aug 7, 1929	Willie Kamm	CLE	Sep 18, 1932
Jack Rothrock	BOS	Aug 29, 1929	Jimmie Foxx	PHI	Sep 22, 1932
Lou Gehrig	NY	Sep 10, 1929		PHI	Sep 24, 1932
	NY	Sep 18, 1929	Red Ruffing	NY	Apr 14, 1933
Bob Fothergill	DET	May 7, 1930	Tony Lazzeri	NY	May 14, 1933
Lou Gehrig	NY	May 22, 1930	Bill Dickey	NY	May 27, 1933
Al Simmons	PHI	May 30, 1930	Art Jorgens	NY	Jun 10, 1933
Tony Lazzeri	NY	Jun 26, 1930	Heinie Manush	WAS	Jun 28, 1933
Jimmy Reese	NY	Jun 29, 1930	Dib Williams	PHI	Jul 22, 1933
Bill Dickey	NY	Jul 9, 1930	Jimmie Foxx	PHI	Aug 14, 1933
Harry Rice	NY	Jul 17, 1930	Red Kress	CHI	Aug 23, 1933
Jimmie Foxx	PHI	Jul 18, 1930	Jimmie Foxx	PHI	Apr 28, 1934
Dave Harris	WAS	Jul 19, 1930	Bill Knickerbocker	CLE	May 1, 1934
Liz Funk	DET	Jul 26, 1930	Bob Johnson	PHI	May 2, 1934
Lou Gehrig	NY	Jul 31, 1930	Zeke Bonura	CHI	May 8, 1934
Charlie Gehringer	DET	Aug 4, 1930	Lou Gehrig	NY	May 10, 1934
Dick Porter	CLE	Sep 1, 1930	Eddie Morgan	BOS	May 13, 1934
Earl Averill	CLE	Sep 17, 1930	Bucky Walters	BOS	May 13, 1934
Babe Ruth	NY	Sep 27, 1930	Lou Gehrig	NY	May 13, 1934
Lyn Lary	NY	May 9, 1931	Jimmy Dykes	CHI	May 21, 1934
Dib Williams	PHI	Jul 13, 1931	Bruce Campbell	STL	May 27, 1934
Earl Averill	CLE	Aug 14, 1931	Harlond Clift	STL	May 31, 1934
Babe Ruth	NY	Aug 20, 1931	Lou Gehrig	NY	Jun 10, 1934
Lou Gehrig	NY	Aug 29, 1931	Hal Trosky	CLE	Jun 14, 1934
	NY	Aug 31, 1931	Bob Boken	CHI	Jun 16, 1934
	NY	Sep 1, 1931	Heinie Manush	WAS	Jun 20, 1934
Bill Dickey	NY	Sep 17, 1931	Babe Ruth	NY	Jun 24, 1934
Jimmie Foxx	PHI	Sep 21, 1931	Al Simmons	CHI	Jun 27, 1934
Mickey Cochrane	PHI	Apr 21, 1932	Lou Gehrig	NY	Jul 5, 1934
Jimmy Dykes	PHI	May 10, 1932	Odell Hale	CLE	Jul 15, 1934
Jimmie Foxx	PHI	May 19, 1932	Pinky Higgins	PHI	Jul 15, 1934
Babe Ruth	NY	May 21, 1932	Bill Cissell	BOS	Jul 18, 1934
Lou Gehrig	NY	May 26, 1932	Jimmie Foxx	PHI	Aug 8, 1934
John Stone	DET	May 30, 1932	Hal Trosky	CLE	Sep 5, 1934
Tony Lazzeri	NY	Jun 3, 1932	Marty Hopkins	CHI	Sep 9, 1934
Eric McNair	PHI	Jun 11, 1932	Cliff Bolton	WAS	Sep 10, 1934
Mule Haas	PHI	Jun 20, 1932	Jimmie Foxx	PHI	Sep 19, 1934
Goose Goslin	STL	Jun 21, 1932	Hank Greenberg	DET	Sep 26, 1934
Mule Haas	PHI	Jun 27, 1932	Bob Johnson	PHI	Apr 19, 1935
Roy Johnson	BOS	Jun 27, 1932	Beau Bell	STL	Apr 21, 1935
Buddy Myer	WAS	July 1, 1932	Sammy West	STL	Apr 25, 1935
Jack Burns	STL	Jul 23, 1932	Frankie Crosetti	NY	Apr 26, 1935
Bill Dickey	NY	Aug 4, 1932	Earle Combs	NY	Apr 28, 1935
Lou Gehrig	NY	Sep 9, 1932	Hank Greenberg	DET	Apr 29, 1935
Bill Dickey	NY	Sep 10, 1932	Tony Lazzeri	NY	May 11, 1935
Dale Alexander	BOS	Sep 11, 1932	Ed Coleman	STL	May 25, 1935
Jimmy Dykes	PHI	Sep 14, 1932	Bruce Campbell	CLE	Jun 3, 1935

Grand Slam Home Runs, AL (*cont.*)

Player	Team	Date	Player	Team	Date
Bob Johnson	PHI	Jun 5, 1935	Joe DiMaggio	NY	Oct 3, 1937
Al Simmons	CHI	Jun 11, 1935	Chet Laabs	DET	Apr 25, 1938
	CHI	Jun 14, 1935	John Stone	WAS	May 5, 1938
Pete Fox	DET	Jun 14, 1935	Al Simmons	WAS	May 14, 1938
Hank Greenberg	DET	Jun 23, 1935	Rudy York	DET	May 16, 1938
Pete Fox	DET	Jun 30, 1935	Jeff Heath	CLE	May 19, 1938
Joe Kuhel	WAS	Jul 6, 1935	Rudy York	DET	May 22, 1938
Lou Gehrig	NY	Jul 7, 1935	Taffy Wright	WAS	May 26, 1938
Heinie Manush	WAS	Jul 26, 1935	Rudy York	DET	May 30, 1938
Lefty Grove	BOS	Jul 27, 1935	Jimmie Foxx	BOS	May 31, 1938
Jake Powell	WAS	Jul 28, 1935	Bob Johnson	PHI	Jun 1, 1938
George Selkirk	NY	Aug 10, 1935	Dario Lodigiani	PHI	Jun 9, 1938
Hal Trosky	CLE	Aug 19, 1935	Monty Stratton	CHI	Jun 10, 1938
Luke Sewell	CHI	Aug 20, 1935	Bob Johnson	PHI	Jun 12, 1938
Lou Gehrig	NY	Aug 21, 1935	Chet Laabs	DET	Jun 17, 1938
Joe Cronin	BOS	Sep 2, 1935	Al Simmons	WAS	Jun 26, 1938
Tony Lazzeri	NY	May 24, 1936	Bill Dickey	NY	Jul 1, 1938
	NY	May 24, 1936	Pete Fox	DET	Jul 2, 1938
Odell Hale	CLE	May 28, 1936	Jimmy Wasdell	WAS	Jul 10, 1938
Goose Goslin	DET	May 28, 1936	Bobby Doerr	BOS	Jul 15, 1938
Mickey Cochrane	DET	Jun 4, 1936	Hank Greenberg	DET	Jul 24, 1938
Mike Kreevich	CHI	Jun 7, 1936	Zeke Bonura	WAS	Jul 30, 1938
Bob Johnson	PHI	Jun 14, 1936	Red Kress	STL	Jul 31, 1938
Jake Powell	NY	Jun 24, 1936	Bob Johnson	PHI	Aug 3, 1938
Moose Solters	STL	Jun 28, 1936	Joe Cronin	BOS	Aug 5, 1938
Wes Ferrell	BOS	Aug 12, 1936	Jim Tabor	BOS	Aug 9, 1938
Lou Gehrig	NY	Aug 15, 1936	Buddy Myer	WAS	Aug 12, 1938
	NY	Sep 9, 1936	George Selkirk	NY	Aug 12, 1938
Bill Knickerbocker	CLE	Sep 9, 1936	Hank Greenberg	DET	Aug 19, 1938
Earl Averill	CLE	Apr 28, 1937	Lou Gehrig	NY	Aug 20, 1938
Hank Greenberg	DET	May 3, 1937	Jimmie Foxx	BOS	Aug 23, 1938
Moose Solters	CLE	May 29, 1937	Zeke Bonura	WAS	Aug 27, 1938
Gee Walker	DET	May 30, 1937	Rudy York	DET	Sep 3, 1938
Goose Goslin	DET	Jun 2, 1937	Sam Chapman	PHI	Sep 4, 1938
Hank Greenberg	DET	Jun 23, 1937	Pinky Higgins	BOS	Sep 4, 1938
Rudy York	DET	Jul 3, 1937	Harlond Clift	STL	Sep 18, 1938
Joe DiMaggio	NY	Jul 5, 1937	Birdie Tebbetts	DET	Sep 28, 1938
	NY	Jul 18, 1937	Jimmie Foxx	BOS	Oct 1, 1938
Lynn Nelson	PHI	Jul 21, 1937	Charlie Gehringer	DET	Apr 30, 1939
Sammy West	STL	Jul 25, 1937	Earle Brucker	PHI	May 7, 1939
Bill Dickey	NY	Aug 3, 1937	Rudy York	DET	May 14, 1939
	NY	Aug 4, 1937	Frankie Hayes	PHI	May 21, 1939
Zeke Bonura	CHI	Aug 8, 1937	Pete Fox	DET	Jun 8, 1939
Rudy York	DET	Aug 19, 1937	Frank Croucher	DET	Jun 10, 1939
Bob Johnson	PHI	Aug 29, 1937	Pete Fox	DET	Jun 15, 1939
Lou Gehrig	NY	Aug 31, 1937	Jim Tabor	BOS	Jul 4, 1939
Ben Chapman	BOS	Sep 21, 1937		BOS	Jul 4, 1939
Hal Trosky	CLE	Sep 21, 1937			

Grand Slam Home Runs, AL (*cont.*)

Player	Team	Date	Player	Team	Date
Schoolboy Rowe	DET	Jul 22, 1939	Frankie Crosetti	NY	Jun 10, 1941
Chet Laabs	STL	Jul 28, 1939	Rudy York	DET	Jun 17, 1941
Bobby Doerr	BOS	Aug 1, 1939	Charlie Keller	NY	Jun 19, 1941
Birdie Tebbetts	DET	Aug 5, 1939	Ben Chapman	CHI	Jun 22, 1941
Babe Dahlgren	NY	Aug 12, 1939	Jim Tabor	BOS	Jun 24, 1941
Hank Greenberg	DET	Aug 19, 1939	Joe Cronin	BOS	Jun 29, 1941
Ted Williams	BOS	Aug 19, 1939	Bobby Doerr	BOS	Jul 12, 1941
Joe Gordon	NY	Aug 23, 1939	Jimmy Bloodworth	WAS	Jul 19, 1941
Joe DiMaggio	NY	Aug 28, 1939	Jim Tabor	BOS	Jul 24, 1941
Ted Williams	BOS	Aug 29, 1939	Ted Williams	BOS	Jul 31, 1941
Ben Chapman	CLE	Apr 27, 1940	Benny McCoy	PHI	Jul 31, 1941
Lou Finney	BOS	May 11, 1940	Roy Cullenbine	STL	Jul 31, 1941
Jimmie Foxx	BOS	May 20, 1940	Harlond Clift	STL	Aug 17, 1941
	BOS	May 21, 1940	Sam Chapman	PHI	Aug 26, 1941
Zeke Bonura	WAS	May 30, 1940	Rudy York	DET	Aug 28, 1941
Jimmy Bloodworth	WAS	Jun 5, 1940	Dom DiMaggio	BOS	Sep 9, 1941
Roy Cullenbine	STL	Jun 8, 1940	Jimmie Foxx	BOS	Sep 14, 1941
Johnny Berardino	STL	Jun 18, 1940	Dom DiMaggio	BOS	Sep 24, 1941
Harlond Clift	STL	Jun 22, 1940	Charlie Keller	NY	Apr 21, 1942
Sam Chapman	PHI	Jun 26, 1940	Chet Laabs	STL	May 2, 1942
Hank Greenberg	DET	Jun 29, 1940	Buddy Blair	PHI	May 21, 1942
Roy Cullenbine	STL	Jun 30, 1940	Ted Williams	BOS	May 29, 1942
Taffy Wright	CHI	Jul 3, 1940	Joe Gordon	NY	Jun 7, 1942
Charlie Keller	NY	Jul 13, 1940	Tom Turner	CHI	Jun 24, 1942
Bobby Doerr	BOS	Jul 17, 1940	Chet Laabs	STL	Jul 15, 1942
Buddy Rosar	NY	Jul 18, 1940	Phil Rizzuto	NY	Jul 17, 1942
Bill Dickey	NY	Jul 24, 1940	Pinky Higgins	DET	Jul 30, 1942
Spud Chandler	NY	Jul 26, 1940	Charlie Keller	NY	Aug 12, 1942
Ken Keltner	CLE	Jul 31, 1940	Joe Gordon	NY	Sep 9, 1942
Joe DiMaggio	NY	Aug 13, 1940		NY	May 31, 1943
Ted Williams	BOS	Aug 15, 1940	Vince Castino	CHI	Jul 23, 1943
Jim Tabor	BOS	Aug 19, 1940	Rudy York	DET	Aug 12, 1943
Ken Keltner	CLE	Aug 20, 1940	Frank Skaff	PHI	Sep 27, 1943
George Selkirk	NY	Aug 21, 1940	Johnny Lindell	NY	Apr 25, 1944
Joe DiMaggio	NY	Aug 22, 1940	Frankie Hayes	PHI	May 15, 1944
Pinky Higgins	DET	Aug 24, 1940		PHI	May 24, 1944
Jimmie Foxx	BOS	Aug 25, 1940	Jimmy Outlaw	DET	May 28, 1944
Ray Mack	CLE	Sep 16, 1940	Al Unser	DET	May 31, 1944
Hank Greenberg	DET	Sep 18, 1940	Mark Christman	STL	Jun 3, 1944
Harlond Clift	STL	Sep 20, 1940	Jim Bucher	BOS	Jun 3, 1944
Joe DiMaggio	NY	Apr 20, 1941	Gene Moore	STL	Jun 11, 1944
Doc Cramer	WAS	Apr 20, 1941	Vern Stephens	STL	Jul 23, 1944
Frankie Hayes	PHI	Apr 23, 1941	Ken Keltner	CLE	Jul 25, 1944
Bob Johnson	PHI	May 1, 1941	Russ Derry	NY	Aug 13, 1944
Joe Cronin	BOS	May 14, 1941	Vern Stephens	STL	Aug 15, 1944
George Selkirk	NY	May 28, 1941	Frankie Crosetti	NY	Aug 19, 1944
Charlie Keller	NY	Jun 7, 1941	Ken Keltner	CLE	Aug 25, 1944

Grand Slam Home Runs, AL (*cont.*)

Player	Team	Date	Player	Team	Date
Dick Wakefield	DET	Sep 22, 1944	Yogi Berra	NY	Jul 30, 1947
Russ Derry	NY	Apr 17, 1945	Dom DiMaggio	BOS	Aug 19, 1947
Frankie Hayes	PHI	Apr 21, 1945	Sam Chapman	PHI	Sep 14, 1947
Russ Derry	NY	Apr 29, 1945	Jack Wallaesa	CHI	Sep 16, 1947
Vern Stephens	STL	May 18, 1945	Tom McBride	WAS	Apr 20, 1948
Paul Richards	DET	Jun 10, 1945	Ken Keltner	CLE	May 6, 1948
Mike Kreevich	STL	Jul 2, 1945	Carl Scheib	PHI	May 8, 1948
Harlond Clift	WAS	Jul 4, 1945	Lou Boudreau	CLE	May 31, 1948
Pat Seerey	CLE	Jul 13, 1945	Andy Anderson	STL	Jun 11, 1948
Zeb Eaton	DET	Jul 15, 1945	Billy Johnson	NY	Jun 19, 1948
Nick Etten	NY	Jul 21, 1945	Tommy Henrich	NY	Jun 23, 1948
Lou Finney	STL	Aug 1, 1945		NY	Jul 8, 1948
Pat Seerey	CLE	Aug 2, 1945	Hoot Evers	DET	Jul 18, 1948
George Binks	WAS	Aug 20, 1945	Bobby Doerr	BOS	Jul 19, 1948
Oris Hockett	CHI	Aug 27, 1945	Jim Hegan	CLE	Jul 21, 1948
Charlie Keller	NY	Sep 10, 1945	Joe DiMaggio	NY	Jul 22, 1948
Hank Greenberg	DET	Sep 30, 1945	Sam Chapman	PHI	Jul 27, 1948
Nick Etten	NY	May 2, 1946	Billy Goodman	BOS	Jul 29, 1948
Leon Culberson	BOS	May 7, 1946	Tommy Henrich	NY	Jul 30, 1948
Joe DiMaggio	NY	May 10, 1946	George Kell	DET	Jul 30, 1948
Johnny Berardino	STL	May 15, 1946	Don White	PHI	Aug 5, 1948
Ted Williams	BOS	May 18, 1946	Sam Chapman	PHI	Aug 11, 1948
Vern Stephens	STL	Jun 15, 1946	Tommy Henrich	NY	Aug 17, 1948
Pat Mullin	DET	Jun 24, 1946	Dom DiMaggio	BOS	Aug 20, 1948
Aaron Robinson	NY	Jul 11, 1946	Vern Stephens	BOS	Aug 21, 1948
Ted Williams	BOS	Jul 14, 1946	Birdie Tebbetts	BOS	Aug 29, 1948
Charlie Keller	NY	Jul 17, 1946	Joe DiMaggio	NY	Sep 10, 1948
Pat Seerey	CLE	Jul 19, 1946	Taffy Wright	CHI	Sep 15, 1948
Rudy York	BOS	Jul 27, 1946	Larry Doby	CLE	Sep 16, 1948
	BOS	Jul 27, 1946	Johnny Groth	DET	Apr 20, 1949
Pete Suder	PHI	Aug 1, 1946	Vern Stephens	BOS	Apr 23, 1949
Bobby Doerr	BOS	Aug 4, 1946	Johnny Groth	DET	Apr 28, 1949
Early Wynn	WAS	Sep 15, 1946	Ted Williams	BOS	May 1, 1949
Jeff Heath	STL	Apr 30, 1947	Vic Wertz	DET	May 15, 1949
Joe Gordon	CLE	May 3, 1947	Al Zarilla	BOS	May 30, 1949
Jack Wallaesa	CHI	May 4, 1947	Joe Gordon	CLE	Jun 14, 1949
Ted Williams	BOS	May 16, 1947	Elmer Valo	PHI	Jun 21, 1949
George Kell	DET	May 25, 1947	Sam Chapman	PHI	Jul 4, 1949
Joe DiMaggio	NY	Jun 1, 1947	Paul Campbell	DET	Jul 17, 1949
Jake Jones	BOS	Jun 15, 1947	Roy Sievers	STL	Jul 21, 1949
Bobby Doerr	BOS	Jun 21, 1947	Dizzy Trout	DET	Jul 28, 1949
Yogi Berra	NY	Jun 22, 1947	Yogi Berra	NY	Aug 5, 1949
Vern Stephens	STL	Jun 24, 1947	Johnny Lipon	DET	Aug 9, 1949
Ferris Fain	PHI	Jun 29, 1947	Sherry Robertson	WAS	Aug 10, 1949
Jeff Heath	STL	Jul 4, 1947	Vern Stephens	BOS	Aug 13, 1949
Phil Rizzuto	NY	Jul 13, 1947	Ferris Fain	PHI	Aug 21, 1949
Paul Lehner	STL	Jul 20, 1947	Vic Wertz	DET	Aug 24, 1949

Grand Slam Home Runs, AL (*cont.*)

Player	Team	Date	Player	Team	Date
Joe DiMaggio	NY	Sep 5, 1949	Clyde Vollmer	BOS	Jul 7, 1951
Pete Suder	PHI	Sep 18, 1949	Gus Zernial	PHI	Jul 12, 1951
Vern Stephens	BOS	Apr 21, 1950	Joe Collins	NY	Jul 13, 1951
Dick Kokos	STL	Apr 23, 1950	Cass Michaels	WAS	Jul 21, 1951
Gil Coan	WAS	May 3, 1950	Clyde Vollmer	BOS	Jul 28, 1951
	WAS	May 7, 1950	Charlie Maxwell	BOS	Aug 2, 1951
Ted Williams	BOS	May 11, 1950	Al Rosen	CLE	Aug 15, 1951
Roy Sievers	STL	May 14, 1950	Mike McCormick	WAS	Aug 24, 1951
Larry Doby	CLE	May 16, 1950	Yogi Berra	NY	Sep 14, 1951
Billy Johnson	NY	May 16, 1950	Tommy Byrne	STL	Sep 18, 1951
Sherm Lollar	STL	May 17, 1950	Luke Easter	CLE	Sep 29, 1951
Wally Moses	PHI	May 21, 1950	Faye Throneberry	BOS	Apr 17, 1952
Joe DiMaggio	NY	May 21, 1950	Don Lenhardt	BOS	Apr 19, 1952
Walt Dropo	BOS	May 25, 1950	Walt Dropo	BOS	May 2, 1952
Yogi Berra	NY	May 25, 1950	Faye Throneberry	BOS	May 4, 1952
Al Rosen	CLE	Jun 8, 1950	Harry Simpson	CLE	May 29, 1952
Don Lenhardt	STL	Jun 9, 1950	Don Lenhardt	BOS	Jun 2, 1952
Jim Hegan	CLE	Jun 18, 1950	Luke Easter	CLE	Jun 7, 1952
Dizzy Trout	DET	Jun 23, 1950	Don Lenhardt	DET	Jun 9, 1952
Billy Goodman	BOS	Jun 24, 1950	Sammy White	BOS	Jun 11, 1952
Al Rosen	CLE	Jun 25, 1950	Pat Mullin	DET	Jun 17, 1952
Walt Dropo	BOS	Jul 1, 1950	Joe Tipton	CLE	Jul 4, 1952
Ken Wood	STL	Jul 4, 1950	Hoot Evers	BOS	Jul 11, 1952
Saul Rogovin	DET	Jul 23, 1950	Gus Zernial	PHI	Jul 13, 1952
Sam Chapman	PHI	Aug 4, 1950	Eddie Joost	PHI	Jul 15, 1952
Ellis Kinder	BOS	Aug 6, 1950	Mickey Mantle	NY	Jul 26, 1952
Johnny Groth	DET	Aug 15, 1950	Steve Souchock	DET	Jul 26, 1952
Bobby Doerr	BOS	Aug 16, 1950	Mickey Mantle	NY	Jul 29, 1952
Vern Stephens	BOS	Aug 24, 1950	Gus Zernial	PHI	Aug 1, 1952
Clyde Vollmer	BOS	Aug 27, 1950	Dom DiMaggio	BOS	Aug 2, 1952
Ray Boone	CLE	Aug 27, 1950	Jackie Jensen	WAS	Aug 13, 1952
Johnny Hopp	NY	Sep 17, 1950	Luke Easter	CLE	Aug 20, 1952
Larry Doby	CLE	Sep 23, 1950	Gus Zernial	PHI	Aug 22, 1952
Joe Astroth	PHI	Sep 23, 1950	Al Rosen	CLE	Aug 27, 1952
Eddie Robinson	CHI	Sep 29, 1950	Don Kolloway	DET	Sep 3, 1952
Dale Mitchell	CLE	Apr 28, 1951	Johnny Mize	NY	Sep 7, 1952
Gil McDougald	NY	May 3, 1951	Dick Kryhoski	STL	Apr 25, 1953
Al Rosen	CLE	May 13, 1951	Al Rosen	CLE	Apr 26, 1953
Bud Stewart	CHI	May 18, 1951	Bob Porterfield	WAS	May 5, 1953
Dave Philley	PHI	May 18, 1951	Ray Boone	CLE	May 10, 1953
Al Rosen	CLE	May 19, 1951	Chico Carrasquel	CHI	May 12, 1953
Les Moss	BOS	May 22, 1951	Tommy Byrne	CHI	May 16, 1953
Ted Williams	BOS	May 27, 1951	Ray Boone	CLE	May 24, 1953
Lou Limmer	PHI	Jun 4, 1951	Bob Elliott	STL	May 28, 1953
Sam Mele	WAS	Jun 9, 1951	Larry Doby	CLE	Jun 4, 1953
Gus Zernial	PHI	Jun 15, 1951	Wayne Terwilliger	WAS	Jun 5, 1953
Al Rosen	CLE	Jun 23, 1951	Yogi Berra	NY	Jun 7, 1953

Grand Slam Home Runs, AL (*cont.*)

Player	Team	Date	Player	Team	Date
Sherm Lollar	CHI	Jun 13, 1953	Dave Philley	BAL	Aug 6, 1955
Jim Delsing	DET	Jun 13, 1953	Ralph Kiner	CLE	Aug 10, 1955
Mickey Mantle	NY	Jul 6, 1953	Jim Hegan	CLE	Aug 12, 1955
Sam Mele	CHI	Jul 8, 1953	Bob Kennedy	CHI	Aug 13, 1955
Al Rosen	CLE	Jul 16, 1953	Mickey Vernon	WAS	Aug 13, 1955
Ray Boone	CLE	Jul 19, 1953	Ted Williams	BOS	Aug 15, 1955
Gus Zernial	PHI	Aug 9, 1953		BOS	Aug 27, 1955
Ray Boone	DET	Aug 12, 1953	Grady Hatton	BOS	Aug 28, 1955
Vic Wertz	STL	Sep 4, 1953	Jim Dyck	BAL	Sep 13, 1955
Minnie Minoso	CHI	May 4, 1954	Gus Zernial	KC	Sep 14, 1955
Billy Shantz	PHI	May 9, 1954	Roy Sievers	WAS	Sep 16, 1955
Dave Philley	CLE	May 10, 1954	Gus Zernial	KC	Sep 18, 1955
George Strickland	CLE	May 14, 1954	Don Larsen	NY	Apr 22, 1956
Gus Zernial	PHI	May 26, 1954	Chico Carrasquel	CLE	Apr 26, 1956
Jackie Jensen	BOS	May 28, 1954	Pete Daley	BOS	May 20, 1956
Cass Michaels	CHI	May 28, 1954	Bill Tuttle	DET	May 20, 1956
Yogi Berra	NY	May 29, 1954	Eddie Robinson	NY	May 24, 1956
Ray Boone	DET	Jun 11, 1954	Bob Cerv	NY	May 25, 1956
Al Kaline	DET	Jun 11, 1954	Bob Kennedy	DET	Jun 1, 1956
Ferris Fain	CHI	Jun 16, 1954	Jim Hegan	CLE	Jun 2, 1956
Bill Glynn	CLE	Jul 5, 1954	Harmon Killebrew	WAS	Jun 21, 1956
Ted Lepcio	BOS	Jul 5, 1954	Jim Busby	CLE	Jul 5, 1956
Roy Sievers	WAS	Jul 5, 1954		CLE	Jul 6, 1956
Mickey Owen	BOS	Jul 19, 1954	Hank Bauer	NY	Jul 12, 1956
Harvey Kuenn	DET	Jul 20, 1954	Tito Francona	BAL	Jul 15, 1956
Bob Nieman	DET	Jul 29, 1954	Eddie Yost	WAS	Jul 21, 1956
Bob Kennedy	BAL	Jul 30, 1954	Mickey Mantle	NY	Jul 30, 1956
Phil Cavarretta	CHI	Aug 4, 1954	Harry Simpson	KC	Aug 11, 1956
Gil McDougald	NY	Aug 6, 1954	Rocky Colavito	CLE	Aug 16, 1956
Harry Agganis	BOS	Aug 15, 1954	Dick Williams	BAL	Aug 17, 1956
Bill Skowron	NY	Aug 17, 1954	Bobby Avila	CLE	Sep 14, 1956
Red Wilson	DET	Aug 29, 1954	Ray Boone	DET	Sep 18, 1956
Bobby Avila	CLE	Sep 17, 1954	Harry Simpson	KC	Sep 19, 1956
Walt Dropo	CHI	Apr 16, 1955	Charlie Maxwell	DET	Sep 24, 1956
George Kell	CHI	Apr 21, 1955	Roger Maris	CLE	Apr 18, 1957
Frank House	DET	Apr 27, 1955	Hank Bauer	NY	Apr 22, 1957
Irv Noren	NY	May 15, 1955	Walt Dropo	CHI	May 2, 1957
Vic Wertz	CLE	May 18, 1955	Jim Pisoni	KC	May 6, 1957
Mickey Mantle	NY	May 18, 1955	Hal Smith	KC	May 12, 1957
Norm Zauchin	BOS	May 27, 1955	Chico Carrasquel	CLE	May 21, 1957
Dave Pope	CLE	Jun 2, 1955	Walt Dropo	CHI	May 31, 1957
Jim Rivera	CHI	Jun 5, 1955	Rocky Colavito	CLE	Jun 25, 1957
Bob Nieman	CHI	Jun 12, 1955	Frank Malzone	BOS	Jun 29, 1957
Jackie Jensen	BOS	Jun 23, 1955	Jackie Jensen	BOS	Jun 30, 1957
	BOS	Jul 4, 1955	Bill Skowron	NY	Jul 14, 1957
Walt Dropo	CHI	Jul 7, 1955	Larry Doby	CHI	Aug 1, 1957
Ted Williams	BOS	Jul 31, 1955	Woodie Held	KC	Aug 11, 1957

Grand Slam Home Runs, AL (cont.)

Player	Team	Date	Player	Team	Date
Chico Carrasquel	CLE	Aug 15, 1957	Gene Stephens	BOS	Jul 13, 1959
Minnie Minoso	CHI	Aug 17, 1957	Minnie Minoso	CLE	Jul 23, 1959
Roy Sievers	WAS	Aug 18, 1957	Gene Woodling	BAL	Jul 27, 1959
Harry Simpson	NY	Aug 22, 1957	Roger Maris	KC	Jul 27, 1959
Vic Wertz	CLE	Sep 14, 1957	Faye Throneberry	WAS	Jul 27, 1959
Ted Williams	BOS	Sep 21, 1957	Vic Wertz	BOS	Aug 14, 1959
Roy Sievers	WAS	Sep 21, 1957	Woodie Held	CLE	Aug 22, 1959
Frank House	KC	Apr 21, 1958	Eddie Yost	DET	Aug 23, 1959
Mickey Vernon	CLE	Apr 25, 1958	Gus Triandos	BAL	Aug 24, 1959
Reno Bertoia	DET	May 7, 1958	Jim Lemon	WAS	Sep 5, 1959
Jackie Jensen	BOS	May 13, 1958	Johnny Callison	CHI	Sep 26, 1959
Ted Williams	BOS	May 22, 1958	Minnie Minoso	CHI	Apr 19, 1960
Jim Busby	BAL	May 26, 1958	Albie Pearson	BAL	Apr 24, 1960
Ray Boone	DET	Jun 5, 1958	Billy Klaus	BAL	Apr 24, 1960
Jackie Jensen	BOS	Jul 10, 1958	Lou Berberet	DET	Apr 24, 1960
Sherm Lollar	CHI	Jul 12, 1958	Earl Battey	WAS	Apr 26, 1960
Al Smith	CHI	Jul 18, 1958	Dick Williams	KC	May 10, 1960
Frank Malzone	BOS	Jul 18, 1958	Vic Wertz	BOS	May 10, 1960
Rocky Colavito	CLE	Jul 27, 1958	Rip Repulski	BOS	May 10, 1960
Ted Williams	BOS	Jul 29, 1958	Vic Power	CLE	May 22, 1960
Eddie Yost	WAS	Jul 30, 1958	Marv Throneberry	KC	May 30, 1960
Gus Triandos	BAL	Aug 2, 1958	Billy Gardner	WAS	Jun 2, 1960
Roger Maris	KC	Aug 3, 1958	Woodie Held	CLE	Jun 8, 1960
Sherm Lollar	CHI	Aug 9, 1958	Pumpsie Green	BOS	Jun 8, 1960
Roger Maris	KC	Aug 13, 1958	Jerry Lumpe	KC	Jun 24, 1960
Charlie Maxwell	DET	Sep 10, 1958	Jim Gentile	BAL	Jun 26, 1960
Rocky Colavito	CLE	Sep 12, 1958	Willie Tasby	BOS	Jul 3, 1960
Clint Courtney	WAS	Sep 13, 1958	Vic Wertz	BOS	Jul 10, 1960
Harry Chiti	KC	Sep 17, 1958	Yogi Berra	NY	Jul 16, 1960
Bill Skowron	NY	Apr 14, 1959	Norm Cash	DET	Jul 17, 1960
Woodie Held	CLE	Apr 14, 1959	Brooks Robinson	BAL	Jul 31, 1960
Bob Grim	KC	Apr 15, 1959	Camilo Pascual	WAS	Aug 14, 1960
Gus Triandos	BAL	Apr 21, 1959	Gus Triandos	BAL	Aug 21, 1960
Jim Lemon	WAS	May 2, 1959		BAL	Aug 25, 1960
Ted Lepcio	BOS	May 5, 1959	Vic Wertz	BOS	Aug 25, 1960
Bob Allison	WAS	May 6, 1959	Gene Woodling	BAL	Aug 31, 1960
Eddie Yost	DET	May 20, 1959	Al Kaline	DET	Sep 11, 1960
Preston Ward	KC	May 31, 1959	Marv Throneberry	KC	Sep 24, 1960
Rocky Colavito	CLE	Jun 13, 1959	Bob Allison	MIN	Apr 16, 1961
Minnie Minoso	CLE	Jun 14, 1959	Bill Skowron	NY	Apr 22, 1961
Rocky Bridges	DET	Jun 25, 1959	Bubba Phillips	CLE	Apr 24, 1961
Jackie Jensen	BOS	Jun 26, 1959	Dick Brown	DET	Apr 29, 1961
Harry Simpson	CHI	Jun 27, 1959	Marv Throneberry	KC	Apr 29, 1961
Al Smith	CHI	Jul 2, 1959	Mickey Mantle	NY	May 2, 1961
Charlie Maxwell	DET	Jul 2, 1959	Chuck Schilling	BOS	May 7, 1961
Bob Cerv	KC	Jul 3, 1959	Roy Sievers	CHI	May 7, 1961
Don Buddin	BOS	Jul 11, 1959	Jim Gentile	BAL	May 9, 1961

Grand Slam Home Runs, AL (cont.)

Player	Team	Date	Player	Team	Date
Jim Gentile	BAL	May 9, 1961	Gene Woodling	WAS	May 11, 1962
Billy Klaus	WAS	May 11, 1961	Vic Power	MIN	May 13, 1962
Dan Dobbek	MIN	May 19, 1961	Ed Charles	KC	May 26, 1962
Wes Covington	CHI	May 28, 1961	Pedro Ramos	CLE	May 30, 1962
Bob Cerv	NY	May 28, 1961	Yogi Berra	NY	Jun 23, 1962
Norm Cash	DET	May 30, 1961	Rocky Colavito	DET	Jun 26, 1962
Lee Thomas	LA	Jun 6, 1961	Lu Clinton	BOS	Jun 29, 1962
Al Smith	CHI	Jun 13, 1961	Don Dillard	CLE	Jul 4, 1962
Vic Wertz	BOS	Jun 15, 1961	Bob Allison	MIN	Jul 18, 1962
Jim Pagliaroni	BOS	Jun 18, 1961	Harmon Killebrew	MIN	Jul 18, 1962
Willie Tasby	WAS	Jun 18, 1961	Ken Hamlin	WAS	Jul 27, 1962
Roy Sievers	CHI	Jun 21, 1961	Bill Skowron	NY	Jul 31, 1962
Bob Allison	MIN	Jun 27, 1961	Bobby Richardson	NY	Aug 16, 1962
Harmon Killebrew	MIN	Jul 1, 1961	Charlie Maxwell	CHI	Aug 19, 1962
Jim Gentile	BAL	Jul 2, 1961	Bill Bruton	DET	Aug 19, 1962
Bob Allison	MIN	Jul 3, 1961	Mickey Mantle	NY	Aug 19, 1962
Julio Becquer	MIN	Jul 4, 1961	Boog Powell	BAL	Aug 21, 1962
Jim Gentile	BAL	Jul 7, 1961	Roger Maris	NY	Aug 21, 1962
Sherm Lollar	CHI	Jul 9, 1961	Steve Boros	DET	Aug 24, 1962
Ted Lepcio	MIN	Jul 13, 1961	Vic Power	MIN	Sep 19, 1962
Norm Cash	DET	Jul 17, 1961	Dave Nicholson	CHI	Apr 20, 1963
Johnny Blanchard	NY	Jul 21, 1961	Clete Boyer	NY	Apr 27, 1963
Bubba Phillips	CLE	Aug 3, 1961	George Thomas	LA	May 1, 1963
Gary Geiger	BOS	Aug 8, 1961	Woodie Held	CLE	May 2, 1963
Gene Green	WAS	Aug 12, 1961	Joe Pepitone	NY	May 2, 1963
Joe Koppe	LA	Aug 13, 1961	Don Lock	WAS	May 8, 1963
Bill Tuttle	MIN	Aug 13, 1961	Dick McAuliffe	DET	May 10, 1963
Carroll Hardy	BOS	Aug 25, 1961	Dick Stuart	BOS	May 15, 1963
Jake Wood	DET	Aug 28, 1961	Harmon Killebrew	MIN	May 24, 1963
Wayne Causey	KC	Aug 31, 1961	Vic Power	MIN	May 29, 1963
Lee Thomas	LA	Sep 5, 1961	Orlando Pena	KC	May 31, 1963
George Thomas	LA	Sep 9, 1961	Max Alvis	CLE	Jun 20, 1963
Al Smith	CHI	Sep 17, 1961	Don Zimmer	WAS	Jul 7, 1963
Jim Gentile	BAL	Sep 22, 1961	Lu Clinton	BOS	Jul 14, 1963
Floyd Robinson	CHI	Sep 22, 1961	Don Mincher	MIN	Jul 14, 1963
Jim King	WAS	Sep 23, 1961	Gus Triandos	DET	Jul 17, 1963
Leon Wagner	LA	Sep 28, 1961	George Alusik	KC	Jul 17, 1963
Buck Rodgers	LA	Sep 29, 1961	Norm Cash	DET	Jul 23, 1963
Walt Bond	CLE	Oct 1, 1961	Minnie Minoso	WAS	Jul 24, 1963
Carroll Hardy	BOS	Apr 11, 1962	Johnny Romano	CLE	Jul 28, 1963
Jim Landis	CHI	Apr 19, 1962	Felix Torres	LA	Jul 29, 1963
Lu Clinton	BOS	Apr 19, 1962	Fred Whitfield	CLE	Jul 31, 1963
Clete Boyer	NY	Apr 27, 1962	Johnny Blanchard	NY	Aug 15, 1963
Don Mincher	MIN	Apr 28, 1962		NY	Aug 22, 1963
	MIN	May 3, 1962	Ed Bressoud	BOS	Aug 22, 1963
Brooks Robinson	BAL	May 6, 1962	Don Zimmer	WAS	Aug 30, 1963
	BAL	May 9, 1962	Mike de la Hoz	CLE	Sep 1, 1963

Grand Slam Home Runs, AL (cont.)

Player	Team	Date	Player	Team	Date
Luis Aparicio	BAL	Sep 4, 1963	Tony Conigliaro	BOS	Jul 27, 1965
Dave Nicholson	CHI	Sep 6, 1963	Dick McAuliffe	DET	Aug 11, 1965
Harmon Killebrew	MIN	Sep 11, 1963	Don Demeter	DET	Aug 12, 1965
Dick Stuart	BOS	Apr 28, 1964	Tony Conigliaro	BOS	Aug 24, 1965
Earl Battey	MIN	May 1, 1964	Curt Blefary	BAL	Sep 5, 1965
Carl Yastrzemski	BOS	May 3, 1964	Chico Salmon	CLE	Sep 7, 1965
Leon Wagner	CLE	May 4, 1964	Horace Clarke	NY	Sep 21, 1965
Tony Oliva	MIN	May 7, 1964	Gates Brown	DET	Sep 21, 1965
Fred Whitfield	CLE	May 11, 1964	Dick Nen	WAS	Sep 23, 1965
Don Zimmer	WAS	May 14, 1964	Zoilo Versalles	MIN	Sep 30, 1965
Harmon Killebrew	MIN	May 17, 1964	Dick McAuliffe	DET	Apr 15, 1966
Manny Jimenez	KC	May 21, 1964	Bob Chance	WAS	Apr 17, 1966
Bobby Knoop	LA	May 23, 1964	Don Wert	DET	Apr 28, 1966
Pete Ward	CHI	May 23, 1964	Rico Petrocelli	BOS	May 8, 1966
Dick Stuart	BOS	May 24, 1964		BOS	May 17, 1966
Pete Ward	CHI	May 29, 1964	Jim King	WAS	May 28, 1966
Tony Conigliaro	BOS	Jun 3, 1964	Rocky Colavito	CLE	Jun 14, 1966
Dick Stuart	BOS	Jun 5, 1964	Tom McCraw	CHI	Jun 16, 1966
Nelson Mathews	KC	Jun 20, 1964	Willie Horton	DET	Jun 22, 1966
Dick McAuliffe	DET	Jun 23, 1964	Elston Howard	NY	Jun 24, 1966
Max Alvis	CLE	Jun 24, 1964	Joe Foy	BOS	Jun 26, 1966
Tom Tresh	NY	Jun 28, 1964	Boog Powell	BAL	Jul 6, 1966
Jerry McNertney	CHI	Jun 30, 1964	George Smith	BOS	Jul 10, 1966
Willie Smith	LA	Jul 2, 1964	Horace Clarke	NY	Jul 16, 1966
Lee Thomas	BOS	Jul 4, 1964	Norm Cash	DET	Jul 22, 1966
Pete Ward	CHI	Jul 12, 1964	Mickey Mantle	NY	Jul 23, 1966
Bob Tillman	BOS	Jul 18, 1964	Tom Tresh	NY	Jul 24, 1966
Rich Rollins	MIN	Jul 19, 1964	Fred Valentine	WAS	Jul 27, 1966
Nelson Mathews	KC	Aug 5, 1964	Jimmie Hall	MIN	Aug 2, 1966
Bob Tillman	BOS	Aug 21, 1964	Earl Wilson	DET	Aug 13, 1966
Don Mincher	MIN	Aug 23, 1964	Rich Rollins	MIN	Aug 23, 1966
Joe Pepitone	NY	Aug 29, 1964	Steve Whitaker	NY	Aug 28, 1966
Felix Mantilla	BOS	Apr 20, 1965	Harmon Killebrew	MIN	Sep 3, 1966
Camilo Pascual	MIN	Apr 27, 1965	Jim Fregosi	CAL	Sep 12, 1966
Costen Shockley	CAL	May 4, 1965	Jim Northrup	DET	Sep 15, 1966
Dick Green	KC	May 12, 1965	Don Mincher	MIN	Sep 23, 1966
Chuck Hinton	CLE	May 15, 1965	Ken McMullen	WAS	Apr 12, 1967
Fred Whitfield	CLE	May 16, 1965	Curt Blefary	BAL	Apr 28, 1967
Frank Howard	WAS	May 18, 1965	Dick Green	KC	Apr 29, 1967
Joe Pepitone	NY	May 24, 1965	Leon Wagner	CLE	May 17, 1967
Bill Freehan	DET	May 24, 1965	Jim Northrup	DET	May 17, 1967
Don Lock	WAS	Jun 12, 1965		DET	May 25, 1967
Mickey Mantle	NY	Jun 18, 1965	Frank Howard	WAS	May 30, 1967
Tom McCraw	CHI	Jun 28, 1965	John O'Donoghue	CLE	Jun 1, 1967
Clete Boyer	NY	Jul 10, 1965	Dick McAuliffe	DET	Jun 4, 1967
Mel Stottlemyre	NY	Jul 20, 1965	Curt Blefary	BAL	Jun 6, 1967
Johnny Romano	CHI	Jul 25, 1965	Rich Rollins	MIN	Jun 12, 1967

Grand Slam Home Runs, AL (*cont.*)

Player	Team	Date	Player	Team	Date
Joe Foy	BOS	Jun 20, 1967	Willie Horton	DET	Jun 21, 1969
Mike Epstein	WAS	Jun 24, 1967	Bob Oliver	KC	Jul 4, 1969
Rick Reichardt	CAL	Jun 25, 1967	Jay Johnstone	CAL	Jul 4, 1969
Norm Cash	DET	Jul 22, 1967	Fred Talbot	SEA	Jul 9, 1969
Joe Foy	BOS	Jul 23, 1967	Ken Harrelson	CLE	Jul 11, 1969
Paul Casanova	WAS	Jul 30, 1967	Willie Horton	DET	Aug 3, 1969
Rick Reichardt	CAL	Aug 23, 1967	Rich Reese	MIN	Aug 3, 1969
Tony Horton	CLE	Sep 8, 1967	Danny Cater	OAK	Aug 3, 1969
Don Buford	CHI	Sep 14, 1967	Don Mincher	SEA	Aug 11, 1969
Gary Peters	CHI	May 5, 1968	Carl Yastrzemski	BOS	Aug 19, 1969
Tom McCraw	CHI	May 7, 1968	Rico Petrocelli	BOS	Sep 1, 1969
Frank Fernandez	NY	May 16, 1968	Cesar Tovar	MIN	Sep 4, 1969
Jim Northrup	DET	May 17, 1968	Harmon Killebrew	MIN	Sep 7, 1969
Mickey Stanley	DET	Jun 2, 1968	Willie Horton	DET	Sep 13, 1969
Joe Pepitone	NY	Jun 5, 1968	Mike Epstein	WAS	Sep 14, 1969
Davey Johnson	BAL	Jun 5, 1968	Lee Maye	WAS	Sep 26, 1969
Russ Snyder	CHI	Jun 11, 1968	Brant Alyea	MIN	Apr 15, 1970
Ken Berry	CHI	Jun 15, 1968	Bill Voss	CAL	Apr 18, 1970
Jim Northrup	DET	Jun 24, 1968	Rick Renick	MIN	Apr 18, 1970
	DET	Jun 24, 1968	Ray Fosse	CLE	May 21, 1970
	DET	Jun 29, 1968	Rick Reichardt	WAS	May 24, 1970
Bill Voss	CHI	Jun 30, 1968	Roberto Pena	MIL	May 30, 1970
Tom Tresh	NY	Jul 27, 1968	Rico Petrocelli	BOS	Jun 7, 1970
Ron Hansen	WAS	Aug 1, 1968	Rich Reese	MIN	Jun 7, 1970
Ken Harrelson	BOS	Aug 4, 1968	Willie Horton	DET	Jun 9, 1970
Joe Foy	BOS	Aug 9, 1968	Rico Petrocelli	BOS	Jun 10, 1970
Pete Ward	CHI	Aug 20, 1968	Jim Northrup	DET	Jun 11, 1970
Dave McNally	BAL	Aug 26, 1968	Russ Snyder	MIL	Jun 12, 1970
Reggie Smith	BOS	Aug 29, 1968	Dick McAuliffe	DET	Jun 15, 1970
Joe Foy	BOS	Aug 31, 1968	Frank Fernandez	OAK	Jun 15, 1970
Don Buford	BAL	Sep 16, 1968	Merv Rettenmund	BAL	Jun 15, 1970
Frank Fernandez	NY	Apr 10, 1969	Mike Andrews	BOS	Jun 16, 1970
Bill Freehan	DET	Apr 10, 1969	Mike Epstein	WAS	Jun 18, 1970
Sal Bando	OAK	Apr 16, 1969	Tony Horton	CLE	Jun 21, 1970
Joe Pepitone	NY	Apr 17, 1969	Frank Robinson	BAL	Jun 26, 1970
Gerry Moses	BOS	Apr 20, 1969		BAL	Jun 26, 1970
Carl Yastrzemski	BOS	Apr 26, 1969	Rick Renick	MIN	Jun 30, 1970
Harmon Killebrew	MIN	Apr 29, 1969	Brooks Robinson	BAL	Jul 7, 1970
Rick Monday	OAK	Apr 30, 1969	Buddy Bradford	CLE	Jul 8, 1970
	OAK	May 10, 1969	Ted Kubiak	MIL	Jul 18, 1970
Rich Rollins	SEA	May 10, 1969	Ellie Hendricks	BAL	Jul 20, 1970
Carl Yastrzemski	BOS	May 18, 1969	Boog Powell	BAL	Jul 26, 1970
Mickey Stanley	DET	May 23, 1969	Vada Pinson	CLE	Jul 29, 1970
Bill Melton	CHI	May 24, 1969	Ed Herrmann	CHI	Aug 5, 1970
Jose Cardenal	CLE	May 30, 1969	Ed Kirkpatrick	KC	Aug 13, 1970
Carlos May	CHI	Jun 2, 1969	Jay Johnstone	CAL	Aug 25, 1970
Sal Bando	OAK	Jun 15, 1969	Don Buford	BAL	Aug 28, 1970

Grand Slam Home Runs, AL (cont.)

Player	Team	Date	Player	Team	Date
Ed Herrmann	CHI	Aug 29, 1970	Rico Petrocelli	BOS	Jul 2, 1972
Roy White	NY	Aug 30, 1970	Sal Bando	OAK	Jul 4, 1972
Tony Conigliaro	BOS	Sep 1, 1970	Rich Reese	MIN	Jul 9, 1972
Jim Price	DET	Sep 1, 1970	Bobby Darwin	MIN	Jul 10, 1972
Tony Conigliaro	BOS	Sep 4, 1970	Cookie Rojas	KC	Jul 12, 1972
Reggie Jackson	OAK	Sep 5, 1970	John Briggs	MIL	Jul 14, 1972
Brant Alyea	MIN	Sep 7, 1970	Terry Crowley	BAL	Jul 23, 1972
Leo Cardenas	MIN	Sep 15, 1970	Bobby Murcer	NY	Aug 4, 1972
Bill Melton	CHI	Apr 7, 1971	Rico Petrocelli	BOS	Aug 5, 1972
Luis Aparicio	BOS	Apr 10, 1971	Johnny Callison	NY	Aug 12, 1972
Willie Horton	DET	Apr 17, 1971	Reggie Smith	BOS	Aug 16, 1972
Bob Oliver	KC	Apr 19, 1971	Bill Freehan	DET	Aug 22, 1972
Dick Green	OAK	Apr 24, 1971	Bobby Grich	BAL	Aug 29, 1972
Roger Repoz	CAL	Apr 24, 1971	Boog Powell	BAL	Sep 13, 1972
Steve Dunning	CLE	May 11, 1971	John Mayberry	KC	Sep 20, 1972
Norm Cash	DET	May 23, 1971	Buddy Bradford	CHI	Oct 2, 1972
Paul Blair	BAL	Jun 5, 1971	Carlton Fisk	BOS	Apr 6, 1973
Bill Melton	CHI	Jun 15, 1971	Ken Henderson	CHI	Apr 12, 1973
Rick Reichardt	CHI	Jun 20, 1971	Danny Walton	MIN	Apr 17, 1973
Dick Billings	WAS	Jul 5, 1971	Ron Lolich	CLE	Apr 22, 1973
Curt Motton	BAL	Jul 10, 1971	Dave May	MIL	Apr 26, 1973
Brooks Robinson	BAL	Jul 18, 1971	Orlando Cepeda	BOS	May 2, 1973
Graig Nettles	CLE	Jul 20, 1971	Tommy Harper	BOS	May 13, 1973
Bobby Murcer	NY	Jul 25, 1971	Roy White	NY	May 20, 1973
Norm Cash	DET	Jul 29, 1971	Lou Piniella	KC	May 23, 1973
Sal Bando	OAK	Aug 4, 1971	Dick McAuliffe	DET	Jun 3, 1973
Mike Andrews	CHI	Aug 6, 1971	Darrell Porter	MIL	Jun 17, 1973
Bob Montgomery	BOS	Aug 9, 1971	Joe Lahoud	MIL	Jun 17, 1973
Roy Foster	CLE	Aug 21, 1971	Dick McAuliffe	DET	Jun 27, 1973
Ray Fosse	CLE	Aug 28, 1971	Bobby Darwin	MIN	Jun 29, 1973
Sal Bando	OAK	Aug 28, 1971	Bob Coluccio	MIL	Jul 7, 1973
Don Mincher	WAS	Aug 31, 1971	Bob Montgomery	BOS	Jul 8, 1973
Harmon Killebrew	MIN	Sep 3, 1971	Kurt Bevacqua	KC	Jul 9, 1973
Boog Powell	BAL	Sep 6, 1971	Gene Tenace	OAK	Jul 13, 1973
Jose Cardenal	MIL	Sep 8, 1971	Roy White	NY	Jul 20, 1973
Brooks Robinson	BAL	Sep 16, 1971	Jeff Burroughs	TEX	Jul 26, 1973
Carlos May	CHI	Sep 18, 1971	Bobby Grich	BAL	Jul 26, 1973
Boog Powell	BAL	Apr 21, 1972	George Scott	MIL	Jul 29, 1973
Buddy Bell	CLE	Apr 22, 1972	Jeff Burroughs	TEX	Jul 30, 1973
Mike Andrews	CHI	Apr 26, 1972		TEX	Aug 4, 1973
Ed Herrmann	CHI	Apr 30, 1972	Dick Green	OAK	Aug 5, 1973
Harmon Killebrew	MIN	May 28, 1972	Al Kaline	DET	Aug 15, 1973
Paul Schaal	KC	Jun 4, 1972	Tony Oliva	MIN	Aug 17, 1973
Rico Petrocelli	BOS	Jun 21, 1971	Deron Johnson	OAK	Aug 19, 1973
Carlos May	CHI	Jun 25, 1972	Joe Lahoud	MIL	Aug 22, 1973
Eric Soderholm	MIN	Jun 26, 1972	Paul Blair	BAL	Aug 26, 1973
Bill Freehan	DET	Jun 29, 1972	Earl Williams	BAL	Sep 3, 1973

Grand Slam Home Runs, AL (*cont.*)

Player	Team	Date	Player	Team	Date
Chris Chambliss	CLE	Sep 5, 1973	Nate Colbert	DET	Apr 12, 1975
Mickey Stanley	DET	Sep 8, 1973	Sal Bando	OAK	May 7, 1975
Dave May	MIL	Sep 9, 1973	Carl Yastrzemski	BOS	May 21, 1975
Gene Tenace	OAK	Sep 14, 1973	Dwight Evans	BOS	Jun 6, 1975
Joe Rudi	OAK	Sep 16, 1973	Bernie Carbo	BOS	Jun 9, 1975
Tommy Harper	BOS	Sep 24, 1973	Jim Sundberg	TEX	Jun 9, 1975
Frank Baker	BAL	Sep 28, 1973	Leroy Stanton	CAL	Jun 11, 1975
Carl Yastrzemski	BOS	Sep 28, 1973		CAL	Jun 15, 1975
Jeff Burroughs	TEX	Apr 9, 1974	Gorman Thomas	MIL	Jun 16, 1975
Don Money	MIL	Apr 10, 1974	Joe Rudi	OAK	Jun 18, 1975
Bernie Carbo	BOS	Apr 12, 1974	Roy Smalley	TEX	Jun 18, 1975
Bobby Darwin	MIN	Apr 14, 1974	Mike Cubbage	TEX	Jun 20, 1975
George Hendrick	CLE	Apr 28, 1974	Frank White	KC	Jun 25, 1975
Angel Mangual	OAK	May 19, 1974	Bill Melton	CHI	Jun 26, 1975
Paul Blair	BAL	May 21, 1974	Tony Oliva	MIN	Jun 29, 1975
Cookie Rojas	KC	May 28, 1974	Buddy Bell	CLE	Jul 5, 1975
Leron Lee	CLE	Jun 1, 1974	Ellie Hendricks	BAL	Jul 18, 1975
Dick Allen	CHI	Jun 4, 1974	Pat Kelly	CHI	Jul 19, 1975
Gene Tenace	OAK	Jun 5, 1974	Aurelio Rodriguez	DET	Jul 19, 1975
Ron Santo	CHI	Jun 8, 1974	Bill Stein	CHI	Jul 20, 1975
Bill Sudakis	NY	Jun 11, 1974	Tommy Davis	BAL	Jul 27, 1975
Eric Soderholm	MIN	Jun 14, 1974	Toby Harrah	TEX	Jul 29, 1975
Joe Rudi	OAK	Jun 15, 1974	Tommy Davis	BAL	Aug 1, 1975
John Briggs	MIL	Jun 20, 1974	Roy Howell	TEX	Aug 5, 1975
Darrell Porter	MIL	Jun 23, 1974	Joe Rudi	OAK	Aug 7, 1975
Rico Petrocelli	BOS	Jun 24, 1974	Rick Manning	CLE	Aug 29, 1975
John Lowenstein	CLE	Jun 24, 1974	Alan Ashby	CLE	Sep 28, 1975
Sal Bando	OAK	Jun 24, 1974	Rusty Staub	DET	Apr 27, 1976
Deron Johnson	MIL	Jun 27, 1974	Reggie Jackson	BAL	May 12, 1976
Juan Beniquez	BOS	Jun 29, 1974	Bobby Bonds	CAL	May 15, 1976
Rick Miller	BOS	Jul 7, 1974	Doug DeCinces	BAL	May 21, 1976
Graig Nettles	NY	Jul 9, 1974	Ken Singleton	BAL	May 22, 1976
Deron Johnson	MIL	Jul 21, 1974	Rick Manning	CLE	May 29, 1976
Jeff Burroughs	TEX	Aug 3, 1974	Kevin Bell	CHI	Jun 22, 1976
Boog Powell	BAL	Aug 13, 1974	Bobby Darwin	BOS	Jun 22, 1976
Gene Tenace	OAK	Aug 20, 1974	Toby Harrah	TEX	Jun 25, 1976
Vada Pinson	KC	Aug 21, 1974	Rod Carew	MIN	Jun 26, 1976
Larry Hisle	MIN	Aug 24, 1974		MIN	Jul 4, 1976
Joe Rudi	OAK	Aug 25, 1974	Ron Jackson	CAL	Jul 4, 1976
Bill Freehan	DET	Sep 8, 1974	Mike Cubbage	MIN	Jul 7, 1976
Phil Roof	MIN	Sep 8, 1974	Charlie Spikes	CLE	Jul 22, 1976
Darrell Porter	MIL	Sep 9, 1974	Leroy Stanton	CAL	Jul 25, 1976
Gorman Thomas	MIL	Sep 15, 1974	Butch Wynegar	MIN	Jul 30, 1976
Gene Tenace	OAK	Sep 24, 1974	Chris Chambliss	NY	Aug 7, 1976
Hal McRae	KC	Sep 26, 1974	Lee May	BAL	Aug 14, 1976
John Ellis	CLE	Sep 28, 1974	Reggie Jackson	BAL	Aug 14, 1976
Gene Tenace	OAK	Apr 9, 1975		BAL	Aug 22, 1976

Grand Slam Home Runs, AL (cont.)

Player	Team	Date	Player	Team	Date
Rod Carew	MIN	Sep 9, 1976	Rick Bosetti	TOR	May 7, 1978
Oscar Gamble	NY	Sep 10, 1976	Don Baylor	CAL	May 18, 1978
Graig Nettles	NY	Sep 29, 1976	Jim Spencer	NY	May 26, 1978
Joe Rudi	CAL	Apr 10, 1977	Billy Smith	BAL	Jun 2, 1978
Larry Hisle	MIN	Apr 24, 1977	Dick Davis	MIL	Jun 4, 1978
Jason Thompson	DET	Apr 27, 1977	Craig Reynolds	SEA	Jun 14, 1978
Bucky Dent	NY	May 3, 1977	Fred Stanley	NY	Jun 20, 1978
Lee May	BAL	May 4, 1977	Chris Chambliss	NY	Jun 23, 1978
John Grubb	CLE	May 6, 1977	Gary Alexander	CLE	Jun 24, 1978
Pat Kelly	BAL	May 8, 1977	Roy Smalley	MIN	Jun 25, 1978
Jim Spencer	CHI	May 14, 1977	Joe Rudi	CAL	Jun 27, 1978
Skip Jutze	SEA	May 17, 1977	John Hale	SEA	Jun 27, 1978
George Scott	BOS	May 22, 1977	Bob Stinson	SEA	Jun 29, 1978
Larry Hisle	MIN	May 25, 1977	Reggie Jackson	NY	Jun 30, 1978
Glenn Adams	MIN	Jun 26, 1977	Joe Rudi	CAL	Jul 6, 1978
Cecil Cooper	MIL	Jun 26, 1977	Buddy Bell	CLE	Jul 9, 1978
Hector Torres	TOR	Jun 27, 1977	Larry Milbourne	SEA	Jul 15, 1978
Jim Spencer	CHI	Jul 2, 1977	Doug DeCinces	BAL	Jul 25, 1978
Mike Jorgensen	OAK	Jul 2, 1977	Joe Rudi	CAL	Jul 26, 1978
Don Money	MIL	Jul 3, 1977	Rico Carty	TOR	Jul 31, 1978
Lee May	BAL	Jul 5, 1977	Bob Stinson	SEA	Aug 1, 1978
Don Baylor	CAL	Jul 27, 1977	Al Cowens	KC	Aug 6, 1978
Bernie Carbo	BOS	Aug 3, 1977	Mike Cubbage	MIN	Aug 8, 1978
Mike Cubbage	MIN	Aug 5, 1977	Tim Corcoran	DET	Aug 9, 1978
Ken Singleton	BAL	Aug 6, 1977	Leon Roberts	SEA	Aug 13, 1978
Rod Carew	MIN	Aug 12, 1977	Steve Kemp	DET	Aug 17, 1978
Milt May	DET	Aug 15, 1977	Lance Parrish	DET	Aug 21, 1978
Buddy Bell	CLE	Aug 22, 1977	Sixto Lezcano	MIL	Aug 24, 1978
Pat Kelly	BAL	Aug 29, 1977	Reggie Jackson	NY	Aug 25, 1978
Cliff Johnson	NY	Sep 4, 1977	Richie Zisk	TEX	Aug 25, 1978
Carlton Fisk	BOS	Sep 6, 1977	George Scott	BOS	Aug 29, 1978
Terry Crowley	BAL	Sep 9, 1977	Mitchell Page	OAK	Sep 8, 1978
Tom Grieve	TEX	Sep 10, 1977	Don Baylor	CAL	Sep 10, 1978
Jim Rice	BOS	Sep 11, 1977	Gary Roenicke	BAL	Sep 18, 1978
Tony Armas	OAK	Sep 23, 1977	Jason Thompson	DET	Sep 19, 1978
Reggie Jackson	NY	Sep 28, 1977	Ron Blomberg	CHI	Sep 19, 1978
Sixto Lezcano	MIL	Apr 7, 1978	Carl Yastrzemski	BOS	Apr 12, 1979
Cecil Cooper	MIL	Apr 7, 1978	Jay Johnstone	NY	Apr 14, 1979
Gorman Thomas	MIL	Apr 8, 1978	Don Baylor	CAL	Apr 21, 1979
Leon Roberts	SEA	Apr 9, 1978	Lee May	BAL	May 5, 1979
Rick Miller	CAL	Apr 12, 1978	Dan Meyer	SEA	May 7, 1979
Rusty Staub	DET	Apr 17, 1978	Joe Rudi	CAL	May 8, 1979
Amos Otis	KC	Apr 18, 1978	Jason Thompson	DET	May 20, 1979
Paul Dade	CLE	Apr 25, 1978	Andre Thornton	CLE	May 22, 1979
Eddie Murray	BAL	Apr 28, 1978	Dan Meyer	SEA	Jun 3, 1979
Willie Horton	CLE	May 3, 1978	Rick Burleson	BOS	Jun 4, 1979
Merv Rettenmund	CAL	May 6, 1978	Ben Oglivie	MIL	Jun 4, 1979

Grand Slam Home Runs, AL (*cont.*)

Player	Team	Date	Player	Team	Date
Dan Ford	CAL	Jun 8, 1979	Barry Bonnell	TOR	Apr 26, 1980
Jim Essian	OAK	Jun 10, 1979	Robin Yount	MIL	May 4, 1980
Willie Aikens	CAL	Jun 13, 1979	Otto Velez	TOR	May 4, 1980
Gary Allenson	BOS	Jun 13, 1979	Dave Roberts	TEX	May 14, 1980
Willie Aikens	CAL	Jun 14, 1979	Richie Hebner	DET	May 20, 1980
Dick Davis	MIL	Jun 15, 1979	Rick Cerone	NY	May 26, 1980
Bobby Bonds	CLE	Jun 17, 1979	Rick Peters	DET	May 27, 1980
Steve Kemp	DET	Jun 18, 1979	Tony Perez	BOS	Jun 6, 1980
Willie Horton	SEA	Jun 23, 1979	Tony Armas	OAK	Jun 11, 1980
Roy Howell	TOR	Jul 3, 1979	Reggie Jackson	NY	Jun 13, 1980
Cliff Johnson	CLE	Jul 3, 1979	Jose Morales	MIN	Jun 19, 1980
Wayne Nordhagen	CHI	Jul 4, 1979	Jim Gantner	MIL	Jun 23, 1980
Joe Rudi	CAL	Jul 7, 1979	Bo Diaz	CLE	Jul 1, 1980
Buddy Bell	TEX	Jul 14, 1979	Bobby Murcer	NY	Jul 4, 1980
Dave Edwards	MIN	Jul 15, 1979	Bump Wills	TEX	Jul 19, 1980
Willie Randolph	NY	Jul 21, 1979	Toby Harrah	CLE	Jul 20, 1980
Pat Kelly	BAL	Jul 23, 1979	Dan Graham	BAL	Jul 22, 1980
Joe Rudi	CAL	Jul 23, 1979	Joe Charboneau	CLE	Jul 24, 1980
John Lowenstein	BAL	Jul 24, 1979	Bobby Grich	CAL	Jul 29, 1980
Lee May	BAL	Jul 26, 1979	Terry Crowley	BAL	Aug 5, 1980
Rick Manning	CLE	Jul 29, 1979	Ruppert Jones	NY	Aug 12, 1980
Eddie Murray	BAL	Jul 31, 1979	Robin Yount	MIL	Aug 16, 1980
Toby Harrah	CLE	Aug 4, 1979	Gorman Thomas	MIL	Aug 18, 1980
John Wockenfuss	DET	Aug 8, 1979	Champ Summers	DET	Aug 28, 1980
Andre Thornton	CLE	Aug 23, 1979	Pat Kelly	BAL	Sep 10, 1980
Don Baylor	CAL	Aug 25, 1979	Bob Watson	NY	Sep 11, 1980
Willie Horton	SEA	Aug 25, 1979	Rob Wilfong	MIN	Sep 16, 1980
Doug DeCinces	BAL	Aug 26, 1979	Steve Kemp	DET	Sep 20, 1980
Oscar Gamble	NY	Aug 27, 1979	Ben Oglivie	MIL	Sep 26, 1980
Roy Howell	TOR	Aug 27, 1979	Eric Soderholm	NY	Sep 26, 1980
Andre Thornton	CLE	Sep 1, 1979	George Brett	KC	Sep 28, 1980
Rico Carty	TOR	Sep 7, 1979	Bobby Murcer	NY	Apr 9, 1981
Bobby Bonds	CLE	Sep 9, 1979	Brian Downing	CAL	Apr 9, 1981
Rick Dempsey	BAL	Sep 9, 1979	Jim Rice	BOS	Apr 12, 1981
Willie Montanez	TEX	Sep 12, 1979	Carlton Fisk	CHI	Apr 14, 1981
Wayne Gross	OAK	Sep 14, 1979	Roy Smalley	MIN	Apr 18, 1981
Leon Roberts	SEA	Sep 14, 1979	Paul Molitor	MIL	Apr 22, 1981
Bruce Bochte	SEA	Sep 26, 1979	Lenny Randle	SEA	Apr 27, 1981
Billy Smith	BAL	Sep 28, 1979	Roy Howell	MIL	May 28, 1981
Sixto Lezcano	MIL	Apr 10, 1980	Jerry Grote	KC	Jun 3, 1981
Cecil Cooper	MIL	Apr 11, 1980	Buddy Bell	TEX	Jun 7, 1981
Don Money	MIL	Apr 11, 1980	Frank White	KC	Aug 12, 1981
Jim Spencer	NY	Apr 13, 1980	Doug DeCinces	BAL	Aug 15, 1981
Jorge Orta	CLE	Apr 14, 1980	Eddie Murray	BAL	Aug 16, 1981
Jim Sundberg	TEX	Apr 14, 1980	Jeff Burroughs	SEA	Aug 24, 1981
Rusty Staub	TEX	Apr 19, 1980	Doug DeCinces	BAL	Aug 27, 1981
Al Oliver	TEX	Apr 26, 1980	Lenn Sakata	BAL	Sep 6, 1981

Grand Slam Home Runs, AL (*cont.*)

Player	Team	Date	Player	Team	Date
Eddie Murray	BAL	Sep 7, 1981	Cal Ripken	BAL	Sep 14, 1982
Dwayne Murphy	OAK	Sep 18, 1981	Carney Lansford	BOS	Sep 19, 1982
Gary Allenson	BOS	Sep 23, 1981	Gary Gaetti	MIN	Sep 19, 1982
Jerry Hairston	CHI	Oct 4, 1981	Orlando Mercado	SEA	Sep 19, 1982
Eddie Murray	BAL	Apr 5, 1982	Willie Aikens	KC	Sep 30, 1982
Amos Otis	KC	Apr 9, 1982	Rod Carew	CAL	Apr 9, 1983
Jesse Barfield	TOR	Apr 24, 1982	George Vukovich	CLE	Apr 9, 1983
Ron LeFlore	CHI	Apr 27, 1982	Fred Lynn	CAL	Apr 27, 1983
Roy Smalley	NY	May 1, 1982	Daryl Sconiers	CAL	Apr 27, 1983
Gary Ward	MIN	May 10, 1982	Barry Bonnell	TOR	May 1, 1983
Gary Roenicke	BAL	May 10, 1982	Tony Armas	BOS	May 7, 1983
Alan Trammell	DET	May 16, 1982	Dwayne Murphy	OAK	May 12, 1983
Jeff Burroughs	OAK	May 18, 1982	Daryl Sconiers	CAL	May 28, 1983
Jim Maler	SEA	May 22, 1982	Ellis Valentine	CAL	Jun 2, 1983
Graig Nettles	NY	May 28, 1982	Buck Martinez	TOR	Jun 5, 1983
Benny Ayala	BAL	May 29, 1982	Ron Jackson	CAL	Jun 6, 1983
Rick Miller	BOS	May 31, 1982	Davey Lopes	OAK	Jun 15, 1983
Bobby Murcer	NY	Jun 2, 1982	Don Baylor	NY	Jun 16, 1983
Kent Hrbek	MIN	Jun 10, 1982	Carney Lansford	OAK	Jun 29, 1983
Dan Ford	BAL	Jun 14, 1982	John Wockenfuss	DET	Jul 3, 1983
Steve Kemp	CHI	Jun 19, 1982	Ben Oglivie	MIL	Jul 4, 1983
Roy Smalley	NY	Jun 25, 1982	Lance Parrish	DET	Jul 10, 1983
Cecil Cooper	MIL	Jul 2, 1982	Cal Ripken	BAL	Jul 13, 1983
Larry Parrish	TEX	Jul 4, 1982	Bobby Grich	CAL	Jul 22, 1983
Hal McRae	KC	Jul 6, 1982	Steve Balboni	NY	Jul 26, 1983
Harold Baines	CHI	Jul 7, 1982	Lance Parrish	DET	Jul 29, 1983
Larry Parrish	TEX	Jul 7, 1982	Don Baylor	NY	Jul 31, 1983
	TEX	Jul 10, 1982	Joe Nolan	BAL	Aug 8, 1983
Harold Baines	CHI	Jul 11, 1982	Ken Griffey	NY	Aug 8, 1983
Fred Lynn	CAL	Jul 15, 1982	Tony Bernazard	SEA	Aug 13, 1983
Tom Brunansky	MIN	Jul 19, 1982	Juan Beniquez	CAL	Aug 17, 1983
Ben Oglivie	MIL	Jul 21, 1982	Jim Rice	BOS	Aug 20, 1983
Gary Gaetti	MIN	Jul 26, 1982	John Shelby	BAL	Aug 29, 1983
Dave Edler	SEA	Jul 27, 1982	Tom Brunansky	MIN	Sep 1, 1983
Andre Thornton	CLE	Jul 29, 1982	Ken Singleton	BAL	Sep 3, 1983
Alan Trammell	DET	Jul 30, 1982	Dwayne Murphy	OAK	Sep 3, 1983
Reggie Jackson	CAL	Aug 6, 1982	John Lowenstein	BAL	Sep 10, 1983
Terry Crowley	BAL	Aug 8, 1982	Willie Upshaw	TOR	Sep 11, 1983
Don Baylor	CAL	Aug 11, 1982	Gary Roenicke	BAL	Sep 13, 1983
Todd Cruz	SEA	Aug 15, 1982	Harold Baines	CHI	Sep 15, 1983
Tony Armas	OAK	Aug 21, 1982	Eddie Murray	BAL	Sep 18, 1983
Dave Henderson	SEA	Aug 22, 1982	Mike Fischlin	CLE	Sep 20, 1983
Joe Nolan	BAL	Aug 24, 1982	Alan Bannister	CLE	Sep 21, 1983
Eddie Murray	BAL	Aug 26, 1982	John Lowenstein	BAL	Sep 21, 1983
Brian Downing	CAL	Aug 31, 1982	Roy Howell	MIL	Oct 1, 1983
	CAL	Sep 6, 1982	Brian Downing	CAL	Apr 15, 1984
Dave Winfield	NY	Sep 13, 1982	Dave Kingman	OAK	Apr 16, 1984

Grand Slam Home Runs, AL (*cont.*)

Player	Team	Date	Player	Team	Date
Kent Hrbek	MIN	Apr 16, 1984	Howard Johnson	DET	Sep 25, 1984
Lloyd Moseby	TOR	Apr 20, 1984	Pat Tabler	CLE	Sep 25, 1984
Gary Pettis	CAL	Apr 28, 1984	Gorman Thomas	SEA	Apr 11, 1985
Julio Cruz	CHI	Apr 28, 1984	Dick Schofield	CAL	Apr 12, 1985
Alan Trammell	DET	May 8, 1984	Bill Schroeder	MIL	Apr 12, 1985
Larry Parrish	TEX	May 11, 1984	Phil Bradley	SEA	Apr 13, 1985
Andre Thornton	CLE	May 18, 1984	Fritz Connally	BAL	Apr 19, 1985
Pat Sheridan	KC	May 19, 1984	Marty Barrett	BOS	Apr 20, 1985
Dave Kingman	OAK	May 25, 1984	Ted Simmons	MIL	Apr 25, 1985
Wayne Gross	BAL	May 27, 1984	Steve Balboni	KC	Apr 30, 1985
Reggie Jackson	CAL	May 28, 1984	Brook Jacoby	CLE	May 7, 1985
Greg Luzinski	CHI	Jun 8, 1984	Gary Gaetti	MIN	May 8, 1985
	CHI	Jun 9, 1984	Don Baylor	NY	May 11, 1985
Gary Roenicke	BAL	Jun 17, 1984	Randy Bush	MIN	May 12, 1985
Eddie Murray	BAL	Jun 19, 1984	Ken Griffey	NY	May 14, 1985
Dave Kingman	OAK	Jun 20, 1984	Jerry Narron	CAL	May 15, 1985
Alvin Davis	SEA	Jun 23, 1984	Fritz Connally	BAL	May 17, 1985
Mike Hargrove	CLE	Jun 23, 1984	Ken Phelps	SEA	May 23, 1985
Carmen Castillo	CLE	Jul 1, 1984	Gary Ward	TEX	May 23, 1985
Jim Rice	BOS	Jul 4, 1984	Rich Gedman	BOS	Jun 1, 1985
Dwight Evans	BOS	Jul 5, 1984	Pat Tabler	CLE	Jun 8, 1985
Eddie Murray	BAL	Jul 7, 1984	Lance Parrish	DET	Jun 18, 1985
Dave Winfield	NY	Jul 16, 1984	Ernie Whitt	TOR	Jun 23, 1985
Alvin Davis	SEA	Jul 20, 1984	Ruppert Jones	CAL	Jun 25, 1985
Bill Buckner	BOS	Jul 21, 1984	Reggie Jackson	CAL	Jun 26, 1985
Randy Bush	MIN	Jul 28, 1984	Darrell Evans	DET	Jul 2, 1985
Frank White	KC	Aug 3, 1984	Harold Baines	CHI	Jul 2, 1985
Bill Buckner	BOS	Aug 7, 1984	Fred Lynn	BAL	Jul 6, 1985
Tony Armas	BOS	Aug 7, 1984	Carlton Fisk	CHI	Jul 8, 1985
Harold Baines	CHI	Aug 9, 1984	Eddie Murray	BAL	Jul 9, 1985
Joe Carter	CLE	Aug 12, 1984	George Bell	TOR	Jul 9, 1985
Don Slaught	TEX	Aug 16, 1984	Frank White	KC	Jul 10, 1985
Lance Parrish	DET	Aug 21, 1984	Don Baylor	NY	Jul 11, 1985
Chet Lemon	DET	Aug 26, 1984	Gary Roenicke	BAL	Jul 13, 1985
Buddy Bell	TEX	Aug 31, 1984	Kent Hrbek	MIN	Jul 18, 1985
Jim Presley	SEA	Aug 31, 1984		MIN	Jul 22, 1985
Ken Singleton	BAL	Sep 1, 1984	George Vukovich	CLE	Jul 23, 1985
Julio Franco	CLE	Sep 2, 1984	Eddie Murray	BAL	Jul 25, 1985
Mike Young	BAL	Sep 3, 1984	George Bell	TOR	Aug 2, 1985
Brett Butler	CLE	Sep 14, 1984	Darrell Evans	DET	Aug 4, 1985
Robin Yount	MIL	Sep 15, 1984	Bill Buckner	BOS	Aug 14, 1985
Lou Whitaker	DET	Sep 17, 1984	Cecil Cooper	MIL	Aug 15, 1985
Wayne Gross	BAL	Sept 17, 1984	Kent Hrbek	MIN	Aug 15, 1985
Mike Pagliarulo	NY	Sep 18, 1984	Dave Collins	OAK	Aug 17, 1985
Ken Singleton	BAL	Sep 20, 1984	Eddie Murray	BAL	Aug 26, 1985
George Brett	KC	Sep 21, 1984	Jack Howell	CAL	Aug 27, 1985
Darryl Motley	KC	Sep 24, 1984	Julio Franco	CLE	Aug 28, 1985

Grand Slam Home Runs, AL (cont.)

Player	Team	Date	Player	Team	Date
Mike Easler	BOS	Aug 31, 1985	Tony Armas	BOS	Aug 21, 1986
	BOS	Sep 2, 1985	Dick Schofield	CAL	Aug 29, 1986
Dave Kingman	OAK	Sep 10, 1985	Lloyd Moseby	TOR	Aug 31, 1986
Joe DeSa	CHI	Sep 13, 1985	Joe Carter	CLE	Sep 4, 1986
Steve Balboni	KC	Sep 20, 1985	Jim Rice	BOS	Sep 5, 1986
Bobby Grich	CAL	Sep 22, 1985	Pete Incaviglia	TEX	Sep 28, 1986
Jim Presley	SEA	Apr 8, 1986	Steve Lombardozzi	MIN	Oct 3, 1986
Brian Downing	CAL	Apr 11, 1986	Cory Snyder	CLE	Apr 9, 1987
Danny Tartabull	SEA	Apr 15, 1986	Joel Skinner	NY	Apr 14, 1987
Don Baylor	BOS	Apr 17, 1986	Bo Jackson	KC	Apr 14, 1987
Eddie Murray	BAL	Apr 19, 1986	Dwight Evans	BOS	Apr 15, 1987
Darrell Evans	DET	May 3, 1986	Tony Phillips	OAK	Apr 20, 1987
Wally Joyner	CAL	May 8, 1986	Matt Nokes	DET	Apr 30, 1987
Harry Spilman	DET	May 9, 1986	Doug DeCinces	CAL	May 3, 1987
Alvin Davis	SEA	May 9, 1986	Mike Pagliarulo	NY	May 8, 1987
Rick Dempsey	BAL	May 11, 1986	Fred Lynn	BAL	May 12, 1987
Frank White	KC	May 15, 1986	Don Mattingly	NY	May 14, 1987
Dave Winfield	NY	May 17, 1986	Tom Brunansky	MIN	May 20, 1987
Eddie Murray	BAL	May 18, 1986	Ellis Burks	BOS	May 25, 1987
Ernie Whitt	TOR	May 22, 1986	Tom Brookens	DET	May 29, 1987
Fred Lynn	BAL	May 23, 1986	Oddibe McDowell	TEX	Jun 1, 1987
Wade Boggs	BOS	May 25, 1986	Greg Walker	CHI	Jun 2, 1987
Dick Schofield	CAL	May 29, 1986	Pete O'Brien	TEX	Jun 5, 1987
Darnell Coles	DET	May 31, 1986	Tony Bernazard	CLE	Jun 10, 1987
Dave Kingman	OAK	Jun 3, 1986	Ellis Burks	BOS	Jun 10, 1987
George Bell	TOR	Jun 20, 1986	Marty Barrett	BOS	Jun 10, 1987
Joe Carter	CLE	Jun 20, 1986	George Bell	TOR	Jun 11, 1987
Greg Walker	CHI	Jun 23, 1986	Tim Laudner	MIN	Jun 14, 1987
Andre Thornton	CLE	Jul 2, 1986	Dick Schofield	CAL	Jun 14, 1987
Gary Gaetti	MIN	Jul 5, 1986	Bob Brower	TEX	Jun 21, 1987
George Hendrick	CLE	Jul 8, 1986	Willie Upshaw	TOR	Jun 23, 1987
Jim Sundberg	KC	Jul 11, 1986	Jim Rice	BOS	Jun 26, 1987
Jim Presley	SEA	Jul 17, 1986	Mike Stanley	TEX	Jun 27, 1987
Johnny Grubb	DET	Jul 23, 1986	Don Mattingly	NY	Jun 29, 1987
Rich Gedman	BOS	Jul 25, 1986	Dave Winfield	NY	Jun 29, 1987
Jim Traber	BAL	Jul 27, 1986	Wade Boggs	BOS	Jun 29, 1987
Brian Downing	CAL	Jul 31, 1986	Mike Stanley	TEX	Jul 3, 1987
Bob Boone	CAL	Jul 31, 1986	Cory Snyder	CLE	Jul 6, 1987
Pete Incaviglia	TEX	Aug 1, 1986	Don Mattingly	NY	Jul 10, 1987
Toby Harrah	TEX	Aug 6, 1986		NY	Jul 16, 1987
Larry Sheets	BAL	Aug 6, 1986	Mike Kingery	SEA	Aug 2, 1987
Jim Dwyer	BAL	Aug 6, 1986	Steve Kiefer	MIL	Aug 4, 1987
Darryl Motley	KC	Aug 10, 1986	Casey Parsons	CLE	Aug 6, 1987
Darrell Evans	DET	Aug 10, 1986	Sam Horn	BOS	Aug 10, 1987
Rich Gedman	BOS	Aug 10, 1986	Fred Lynn	BAL	Aug 13, 1987
Danny Tartabull	SEA	Aug 11, 1986	Devon White	CAL	Aug 17, 1987
Larry Herndon	DET	Aug 16, 1986	Rob Deer	MIL	Aug 19, 1987

Grand Slam Home Runs, AL (*cont.*)

Player	Team	Date	Player	Team	Date
Rob Deer	MIL	Aug 20, 1987	George Bell	TOR	Sep 4, 1988
Jamie Quirk	KC	Aug 22, 1987	Jesse Barfield	TOR	Sep 13, 1988
Don Baylor	BOS	Aug 23, 1987	Jim Rice	BOS	Sep 13, 1988
Frank White	KC	Aug 25, 1987	Jim Dwyer	MIN	Sep 15, 1988
George Bell	TOR	Aug 27, 1987	Jeffrey Leonard	MIL	Sep 18, 1988
Alvin Davis	SEA	Aug 28, 1987	Pete O'Brien	TEX	Sep 18, 1988
Kevin Seitzer	KC	Aug 30, 1987	Danny Tartabull	KC	Sep 20, 1988
Mike Pagliarulo	NY	Sep 4, 1987	Fred Lynn	DET	Sep 25, 1988
Darrell Evans	DET	Sep 5, 1987	Tony Fernandez	TOR	Apr 7, 1989
Mark Ryal	CAL	Sep 10, 1987	Ivan Calderon	CHI	Apr 8, 1989
Todd Benzinger	BOS	Sep 15, 1987	Carmen Castillo	MIN	Apr 11, 1989
Don Mattingly	NY	Sep 25, 1987	Steve Balboni	NY	Apr 14, 1989
Matt Nokes	DET	Sep 26, 1987	Jeffrey Leonard	SEA	Apr 14, 1989
Don Mattingly	NY	Sep 29, 1987	Bill Spiers	MIL	Apr 17, 1989
Danny Tartabull	KC	Oct 2, 1987	B. J. Surhoff	MIL	Apr 26, 1989
Devon White	CAL	Apr 12, 1988	Nick Esasky	BOS	Apr 28, 1989
Jesse Barfield	TOR	Apr 19, 1988	Rance Mulliniks	TOR	May 2, 1989
Cory Snyder	CLE	Apr 22, 1988	Mark McGwire	OAK	May 2, 1989
Joe Carter	CLE	Apr 22, 1988	Jeffrey Leonard	SEA	May 2, 1989
Mike Pagliarulo	NY	Apr 30, 1988	Dwight Evans	BOS	May 19, 1989
Rob Deer	MIL	May 1, 1988	Bill Schroeder	CAL	May 21, 1989
Alvin Davis	SEA	May 5, 1988	Matt Nokes	DET	May 29, 1989
Pat Sheridan	DET	May 6, 1988	Dan Gladden	MIN	May 31, 1989
Danny Tartabull	KC	May 15, 1988	Junior Felix	TOR	Jun 2, 1989
Gary Gaetti	MIN	May 22, 1988	Ernie Whitt	TOR	Jun 4, 1989
Mickey Brantley	SEA	May 28, 1988	Steve Finley	BAL	Jun 5, 1989
Gary Redus	CHI	May 31, 1988	Mark McGwire	OAK	Jun 9, 1989
Greg Gagne	MIN	Jun 3, 1988	Jim Dwyer	MIN	Jun 10, 1989
Gary Redus	CHI	Jun 4, 1988	Alvin Davis	SEA	Jun 15, 1989
Pat Sheridan	DET	Jun 8, 1988	Dwight Evans	BOS	Jun 17, 1989
Jay Buhner	NY	Jun 11, 1988	Mel Hall	NY	Jun 24, 1989
Tom Brookens	DET	Jun 14, 1988	Pat Borders	TOR	Jul 7, 1989
Ellis Burks	BOS	Jun 15, 1988	Terry Steinbach	OAK	Jul 16, 1989
Andy Allanson	CLE	Jun 19, 1988	Pete Incaviglia	TEX	Jul 17, 1989
Alan Trammell	DET	Jun 21, 1988	Fred McGriff	TOR	Jul 21, 1989
Daryl Boston	CHI	Jun 26, 1988	Lloyd Moseby	TOR	Jul 22, 1989
Rick Schu	BAL	Jul 2, 1988	Albert Belle	CLE	Jul 24, 1989
Terry Steinbach	OAK	Jul 2, 1988	Rob Deer	MIL	Jul 27, 1989
Bob Brower	TEX	Jul 3, 1988	Darnell Coles	SEA	Aug 5, 1989
Walt Weiss	OAK	Jul 10, 1988	Jim Eisenreich	KC	Aug 19, 1989
Brook Jacoby	CLE	Jul 15, 1988	Ellis Burks	BOS	Aug 27, 1989
Jose Cruz	NY	Jul 16, 1988	Ron Karkovice	CHI	Aug 27, 1989
Dave Winfield	NY	Jul 23, 1988	Daryl Boston	CHI	Sep 1, 1989
Ellis Burks	BOS	Jul 27, 1988	Glenallen Hill	TOR	Sep 1, 1989
Mike Greenwell	BOS	Aug 2, 1988	Dave Parker	OAK	Sep 6, 1989
Danny Tartabull	KC	Aug 11, 1988	Steve Lyons	CHI	Sep 9, 1989
Mark McGwire	OAK	Aug 11, 1988	Kent Hrbek	MIN	Sep 12, 1989

Grand Slam Home Runs, AL (cont.)

Player	Team	Date	Player	Team	Date
Bo Jackson	KC	Sep 27, 1989	Mike Gallego	OAK	May 31, 1991
George Bell	TOR	Apr 11, 1990	Dave Winfield	CAL	Jun 1, 1991
Brian Harper	MIN	May 5, 1990	Harold Baines	OAK	Jun 6, 1991
Gerald Perry	KC	May 8, 1990	Dante Bichette	MIL	Jun 6, 1991
Rey Palacios	KC	May 14, 1990	Brian Downing	TEX	Jun 7, 1991
Brian Giles	SEA	May 17, 1990	Pedro Munoz	MIN	Jun 12, 1991
Jose Canseco	OAK	May 22, 1990	Shane Mack	MIN	Jun 14, 1991
Wally Joyner	CAL	May 27, 1990	Joe Orsulak	BAL	Jun 16, 1991
Jay Buhner	SEA	Jun 1, 1990	Greg Vaughn	MIL	Jun 16, 1991
Cecil Fielder	DET	Jun 1, 1990	Robin Ventura	CHI	Jun 18, 1991
Lance Parrish	CAL	Jun 17, 1990	Kirk Gibson	KC	Jun 19, 1991
Terry Steinbach	OAK	Jun 20, 1990	Chris Hoiles	BAL	Jun 23, 1991
Darryl Hamilton	MIL	Jul 8, 1990	Frank Thomas	CHI	Jun 24, 1991
Phil Bradley	BAL	Jul 13, 1990	Harold Baines	OAK	Jun 29, 1991
Felix Jose	OAK	Jul 15, 1990	Max Venable	CAL	Jul 2, 1991
Alvin Davis	SEA	Jul 17, 1990	Rickey Henderson	OAK	Jul 4, 1991
Mike Devereaux	BAL	Jul 23, 1990	Jose Canseco	OAK	Jul 5, 1991
Julio Franco	TEX	Jul 31, 1990	Mike Macfarlane	KC	Jul 11, 1991
Lloyd Moseby	DET	Aug 2, 1990	Brian McRae	KC	Jul 14, 1991
Steve Buechele	TEX	Aug 3, 1990	Franklin Stubbs	MIL	Jul 15, 1991
Mike Macfarlane	KC	Aug 4, 1990	Todd Benzinger	KC	Jul 23, 1991
Cory Snyder	CLE	Aug 4, 1990	Ken Griffey, Jr.	SEA	Jul 23, 1991
Mitch Webster	CLE	Aug 10, 1990	Randy Milligan	BAL	Jul 23, 1991
Luis Polonia	CAL	Aug 14, 1990	Dwight Evans	BAL	Jul 26, 1991
Glenallen Hill	TOR	Aug 14, 1990	Ernest Riles	OAK	Jul 26, 1991
Mark McGwire	OAK	Aug 15, 1990	Ken Griffey, Jr.	SEA	Jul 30, 1991
Ron Karkovice	CHI	Aug 30, 1990	Carlos Quintana	BOS	Jul 30, 1991
Luis Rivera	BOS	Aug 31, 1990	Jack Clark	BOS	Jul 31, 1991
Mike Greenwell	BOS	Sep 1, 1990	Kent Hrbek	MIN	Jul 31, 1991
Harold Reynolds	SEA	Sep 5, 1990	Robin Ventura	CHI	Jul 31, 1991
Ruben Sierra	TEX	Sep 6, 1990	Mickey Tettleton	DET	Aug 11, 1991
Tony Fernandez	TOR	Sep 11, 1990	Danny Tartabull	KC	Aug 14, 1991
Sam Horn	BAL	Sep 14, 1990	Juan Gonzalez	TEX	Aug 18, 1991
Alvin Davis	SEA	Sep 18, 1990	Tom Brunansky	BOS	Sep 1, 1991
Cecil Fielder	DET	Sep 23, 1990	Shane Mack	MIN	Sep 2, 1991
Gary Gaetti	MIN	Sep 23, 1990	Ozzie Guillen	CHI	Sep 5, 1991
Alvin Davis	SEA	Sep 28, 1990	Dave Valle	SEA	Sep 6, 1991
Kelly Gruber	TOR	Sep 29, 1990	Reggie Jefferson	CLE	Sep 10, 1991
Gary Ward	DET	Oct 3, 1990	Jose Canseco	OAK	Sep 15, 1991
Jack Clark	BOS	Apr 8, 1991	Craig Grebeck	CHI	Sep 15, 1991
Sam Horn	BAL	Apr 15, 1991	Ken Griffey, Jr.	SEA	Sep 19, 1991
Rob Deer	DET	Apr 30, 1991	Bill Spiers	MIL	Sep 20, 1991
Kevin Romine	BOS	May 5, 1991	Matt Nokes	NY	Sep 23, 1991
Wally Joyner	CAL	May 10, 1991	Tim Spehr	KC	Sep 29, 1991
Milt Cuyler	DET	May 19, 1991	Cecil Fielder	DET	Oct 3, 1991
Pete Incaviglia	DET	May 20, 1991	Carlton Fisk	CHI	Oct 3, 1991
Kurt Stillwell	KC	May 25, 1991	B. J. Surhoff	MIL	Apr 8, 1992

Grand Slam Home Runs, AL (*cont.*)

Player	Team	Date
Dan Pasqua	CHI	Apr 11, 1992
Randy Milligan	BAL	Apr 17, 1992
Rafael Palmeiro	TEX	Apr 22, 1992
Tino Martinez	SEA	Apr 25, 1992
Mike Devereaux	BAL	May 1, 1992
Chris Hoiles	BAL	May 4, 1992
George Bell	CHI	May 5, 1992
Dave Winfield	TOR	May 7, 1992
Matt Nokes	NY	May 13, 1992
Franklin Stubbs	MIL	May 15, 1992
Mark Whiten	CLE	May 19, 1992
Ellis Burks	BOS	May 20, 1992
Gregg Jefferies	KC	May 20, 1992
Shane Mack	MIN	May 24, 1992
Danny Tartabull	NY	May 25, 1992
Kirby Puckett	MIN	May 29, 1992
	MIN	Jun 3, 1992
Sandy Alomar	CLE	Jun 3, 1992
Dean Palmer	TEX	Jun 4, 1992
Kevin Mitchell	SEA	Jun 4, 1992
Mickey Tettleton	DET	Jun 7, 1992
Milt Cuyler	DET	Jun 8, 1992
Leo Gomez	BAL	Jun 12, 1992
Wade Boggs	BOS	Jun 12, 1992
Mark McGwire	OAK	Jun 13, 1992
Steve Sax	CHI	Jun 16, 1992
Mike Devereaux	BAL	Jun 19, 1992
Cecil Fielder	DET	Jun 23, 1992
Bob Zupcic	BOS	Jun 30, 1992
Jay Buhner	SEA	Jul 3, 1992
George Bell	CHI	Jul 5, 1992
Albert Belle	CLE	Jul 8, 1992
Dean Palmer	TEX	Jul 9, 1992
Mike Stanley	NY	Jul 9, 1992
Bob Zupcic	BOS	Jul 10, 1992
Tom Brunansky	BOS	Jul 11, 1992
	BOS	Jul 27, 1992
Randy Ready	OAK	Jul 27, 1992
Brian Harper	MIN	Aug 1, 1992
Cecil Fielder	DET	Aug 1, 1992
Carney Lansford	OAK	Aug 7, 1992
Kirby Pucket	MIN	Aug 14, 1992
Edgar Martinez	SEA	Aug 19, 1992
Jose Canseco	OAK	Aug 20, 1992
John Valentin	BOS	Aug 22, 1992
Danny Tartabull	NY	Aug 26, 1992
Lou Whitaker	DET	Aug 29, 1992

Player	Team	Date
Kelly Gruber	TOR	Sep 1, 1992
Lee Stevens	CAL	Sep 4, 1992
Carlos Martinez	CLE	Sep 6, 1992
Ken Griffey, Jr.	SEA	Sep 8, 1992

Grand Slam Home Runs, NL

Player	Team	Date
Roger Connor	TRO	Sep 10, 1881
Harry Stovey	WOR	Sep 29, 1881
Curry Foley	BUF	May 19, 1882
	BUF	May 25, 1882
Larry Corcoran	CHI	Jun 20, 1882
Jim Lillie	BUF	Sep 3, 1883
Fred Pfeffer	CHI	Jun 21, 1884
Ned Williamson	CHI	Jul 4, 1884
Pete Hotaling	CLE	Aug 2, 1884
King Kelly	CHI	Aug 14, 1884
Alex McKinnon	NY	Aug 16, 1884
Charlie Bennett	DET	Sep 1, 1885
Mike Dorgan	NY	May 6, 1886
Paul Hines	WAS	Jun 7, 1886
Sid Farrar	PHI	Jun 29, 1886
Al Myers	KC	Aug 21, 1886
Ed Daily	PHI	Aug 30, 1886
Jimmy Ryan	CHI	Sep 8, 1886
John Morrill	BOS	May 17, 1887
Jack McGeachey	IND	Jun 18, 1887
Ned Hanlon	DET	Jul 27, 1887
Roger Connor	NY	Aug 19, 1887
Paul Hines	WAS	Aug 19, 1887
Pat Dealey	WAS	Oct 5, 1887
George Shoch	WAS	May 3, 1888
Ed Daily	WAS	Jul 12, 1888
Tom Brown	BOS	Aug 27, 1888
George Gore	NY	May 2, 1889
Jerry Denny	IND	May 4, 1889
Ad Gumbert	CHI	May 9, 1889
Sam Thompson	PHI	May 16, 1889
Charley Bassett	IND	Jun 6, 1889
Jack Glasscock	IND	Jun 20, 1889
Buck Ewing	NY	Jun 22, 1889
Jimmy Ryan	CHI	Aug 17, 1889
Joe Mulvey	PHI	Aug 19, 1889
Ned Hanlon	PIT	Aug 20, 1889
Monte Ward	NY	Sep 16, 1889
Howard Earl	CHI	May 8, 1890

Grand Slam Home Runs, NL

Player	Team	Date	Player	Team	Date
George Davis	CLE	May 30, 1890	Joe Kelley	BAL	Jun 25, 1894
Oyster Burns	BKN	Jun 5, 1890	Arlie Latham	CIN	Jul 4, 1894
Howard Earl	CHI	Jun 26, 1890	Lave Cross	PHI	Jul 7, 1894
Sam Thompson	PHI	Jul 16, 1890	Bid McPhee	CIN	Jul 19, 1894
Al Myers	PHI	Jul 21, 1890	Duke Farrell	NY	Jul 19, 1894
Tom Burns	CHI	Aug 16, 1890	Bug Holliday	CIN	Jul 27, 1894
Mal Kittridge	CHI	Aug 16, 1890	Walt Wilmot	CHI	Jul 29, 1894
Bob Allen	PHI	Aug 16, 1890	Duke Farrell	NY	Jul 30, 1894
Elmer Foster	CHI	Sep 8, 1890	Cap Anson	CHI	Aug 1, 1894
Chief Zimmer	CLE	Sep 18, 1890	Jimmy Bannon	BOS	Aug 6, 1894
Oyster Burns	BKN	May 1, 1891		BOS	Aug 7, 1894
George Gore	NY	Jun 12, 1891	Billy Nash	BOS	Aug 9, 1894
Tommy Tucker	BOS	Sep 9, 1891	Charlie Irwin	CHI	Aug 11, 1894
Joe Quinn	BOS	Sep 19, 1891	Eddie Burke	NY	Aug 21, 1894
Herman Long	BOS	Apr 12, 1892	Bill Shindle	BKN	Aug 24, 1894
Germany Smith	CIN	Apr 25, 1892	George Van Haltren	NY	Sep 3, 1894
Icebox Chamberlain	CIN	Apr 30, 1892	Sam Thompson	PHI	Sep 6, 1894
Perry Werden	STL	May 10, 1892	Heinie Reitz	BAL	Sep 30, 1894
Denny Lyons	NY	Jun 25, 1892	Tommy McCarthy	BOS	May 3, 1895
Lave Cross	PHI	Jul 6, 1892	Duff Cooley	STL	May 11, 1895
Charlie Comiskey	CIN	Jul 8, 1892	Ace Stewart	CHI	May 20, 1895
Bid McPhee	CIN	Jul 11, 1892	Doggie Miller	STL	May 26, 1895
Hugh Duffy	BOS	Jul 30, 1892	Billy Nash	BOS	Jun 4, 1895
Billy Hamilton	PHI	Aug 10, 1892	Hugh Duffy	BOS	Jun 10, 1895
Jimmy McAleer	CLE	Aug 11, 1892	Cupid Childs	CLE	Jun 15, 1895
Mike Tiernan	NY	Sep 9, 1892	Chief Zimmer	CLE	Jun 17, 1895
Kid Nichols	BOS	Sep 19, 1892	Ed McKean	CLE	Jun 17, 1895
Harry Stovey	BAL	Oct 12, 1892	Chief Zimmer	CLE	Jul 17, 1895
Bobby Lowe	BOS	May 11, 1893	Bobby Lowe	BOS	Aug 3, 1895
Bob Allen	PHI	Jun 13, 1893	Candy LaChance	BKN	Aug 24, 1895
Jesse Burkett	CLE	Jun 15, 1893	Jimmy Ryan	CHI	Aug 24, 1895
John McGraw	BAL	Jun 16, 1893	Eddie Burke	CIN	Aug 31, 1895
Bug Holliday	CIN	Jun 18, 1893	Charlie Abbey	WAS	Sep 16, 1895
Steve Brodie	STL	Jun 21, 1893	Arlie Latham	CIN	Sep 23, 1895
Jack Clements	PHI	Jun 22, 1893	John Anderson	BKN	Sep 27, 1895
George Van Haltren	PIT	Jul 8, 1893	Herm McFarland	LOU	May 5, 1896
Bill Lange	CHI	Jul 11, 1893	Lave Cross	PHI	May 5, 1896
Jack O'Connor	CLE	Jul 17, 1893	Bill Lange	CHI	May 18, 1896
Eddie Burke	NY	Jul 18, 1893	Jake Beckley	PIT	Jun 5, 1896
Mal Kittridge	CHI	Sep 3, 1893	Jake Stenzel	PIT	Jun 11, 1896
Parke Wilson	NY	Sep 5, 1893	Patsy Donovan	PIT	Jun 27, 1896
Jiggs Parrott	CHI	Sep 10, 1893	Ed Delahanty	PHI	Aug 19, 1896
Bug Holliday	CIN	Apr 20, 1894	Joe Kelley	BAL	Aug 26, 1896
Bobby Lowe	BOS	May 28, 1894	George Davis	NY	Aug 29, 1896
Harry Staley	BOS	May 28, 1894	George Van Haltren	NY	Sep 4, 1896
Farmer Vaughn	CIN	May 30, 1894	George Davis	NY	Sep 12, 1896
Jack O'Connor	CLE	Jun 1, 1894	Jack Boyle	PHI	Apr 29, 1897

Grand Slam Home Runs, NL (*cont.*)

Player	Team	Date	Player	Team	Date
Bones Ely	PIT	May 8, 1897	Jimmy Sheckard	BKN	Aug 17, 1903
Charlie Reilly	WAS	May 8, 1897	Jimmy Sebring	PIT	Aug 31, 1903
Steve Brodie	PIT	Jun 15, 1897	Dan McGann	NY	Sep 10, 1903
Jimmy Ryan	CHI	Jun 29, 1897	Art Devlin	NY	Apr 22, 1904
Bobby Wallace	CLE	Jul 14, 1897	Miller Huggins	CIN	May 10, 1904
Cupid Childs	CLE	Jul 28, 1897	Davy Jones	CHI	May 30, 1904
Hugh Duffy	BOS	Aug 19, 1897	Jack O'Neill	CHI	Aug 17, 1904
Chick Fraser	LOU	Aug 28, 1897	Dave Brain	STL	Aug 22, 1904
Chick Stahl	BOS	Sep 8, 1897	Bill Dahlen	NY	Aug 25, 1904
Jake Gettman	WAS	Sep 11, 1897	Red Dooin	PHI	Oct 1, 1904
Tuck Turner	STL	Oct 3, 1897	Bill Maloney	CHI	Jun 25, 1905
Bill Duggleby	PHI	Apr 21, 1898	Tommy Corcoran	CIN	Jul 5, 1905
Herman Long	BOS	May 12, 1898	Sam Mertes	NY	Jul 21, 1905
Hugh Duffy	BOS	Jun 8, 1898	Jim Delahanty	CIN	May 19, 1906
Honus Wagner	LOU	Jul 28, 1898	Ginger Beaumont	PIT	Jul 27, 1906
Jud Smith	WAS	Sep 6, 1898	Kitty Bransfield	PHI	Aug 18, 1906
Dan McGann	BAL	Sep 17, 1898	Johnny Bates	BOS	Oct 3, 1906
Jimmy Collins	BOS	Sep 29, 1898	Sammy Strang	NY	Oct 4, 1906
Kip Selbach	WAS	Sep 29, 1898	Patsy Flaherty	BOS	May 24, 1907
Candy LaChance	BKN	Oct 15, 1898	Tommy Leach	PIT	Aug 16, 1907
Pete Cassidy	WAS	Apr 28, 1899	John Ganzel	CIN	May 17, 1908
Willie Keeler	BKN	May 15, 1899	Johnny Kling	CHI	Jun 6, 1908
Elmer Flick	PHI	May 23, 1899	Johnny Kling	CHI	Sep 12, 1908
Lave Cross	STL	Jul 9, 1899	Honus Wagner	PIT	Jun 3, 1909
Bert Cunningham	LOU	Aug 2, 1899	Joe Delahanty	STL	Aug 25, 1909
Bill Everett	CHI	Aug 28, 1899	Chief Meyers	NY	Sep 11, 1909
Bert Cunningham	LOU	Sep 4, 1899	Beals Becker	BOS	Sep 13, 1909
Jake Beckley	CIN	Sep 9, 1899	Bill Collins	BOS	May 2, 1910
Jimmy Williams	PIT	Sep 26, 1899	Tommy Leach	PIT	Jul 21, 1910
Buck Freeman	WAS	Oct 12, 1899	Deacon Phillippe	PIT	Jul 22, 1910
Bill Keister	BAL	Oct 13, 1899	Sherry Magee	PHI	Aug 24, 1910
Fielder Jones	BKN	Apr 28, 1900	Dick Hoblitzell	CIN	Aug 26, 1910
Honus Wagner	PIT	Sep 22, 1901	Owen Wilson	PIT	Sep 13, 1910
John Ganzel	NY	Sep 22, 1901	Red Murray	NY	Sep 15, 1910
Joe Kelley	BKN	Sep 23, 1901	George Ferguson	BOS	Sep 22, 1910
Jimmy Sheckard	BKN	Sep 23, 1901	Beals Becker	NY	Sep 30, 1910
	BKN	Sep 24, 1901	Honus Wagner	PIT	May 4, 1911
Mike O'Neill	STL	Jun 3, 1902	Fred Beck	CIN	May 9, 1911
Frank Chance	CHI	Aug 4, 1902	Dick Egan	CIN	May 10, 1911
Wid Conroy	PIT	Aug 28, 1902	Eddie Grant	CIN	Jun 3, 1911
Frank Bonner	BOS	Apr 27, 1903	Wildfire Schulte	CHI	Jun 3, 1911
Roger Bresnahan	NY	Apr 28, 1903		CHI	Jul 4, 1911
Tommy Leach	PIT	Apr 30, 1903	Fred Luderus	PHI	Jul 6, 1911
Duff Cooley	BOS	May 23, 1903	Joe Tucker	CHI	Jul 15, 1911
Ginger Beaumont	PIT	Jul 10, 1903	Wildfire Schulte	CHI	Jul 18, 1911
Pat Moran	BOS	Aug 12, 1903	Tex Erwin	BKN	Jul 28, 1911
Joe Stanley	BOS	Aug 12, 1903	Wildfire Schulte	CHI	Aug 16, 1911

Grand Slam Home Runs, NL (*cont.*)

Player	Team	Date	Player	Team	Date
Tommy Leach	PIT	Sep 7, 1911	George Kelly	NY	Jun 28, 1920
Dick Hoblitzell	CIN	Sep 10, 1911	Ralph Miller	PHI	Apr 28, 1921
Vic Saier	CHI	Sep 21, 1911	Lee Meadows	PHI	Apr 28, 1921
Ben Houser	BOS	Oct 9, 1911	George Kelly	NY	Apr 30, 1921
Rube Ellis	STL	Apr 16, 1912		NY	May 12, 1921
Chief Meyers	NY	Jun 3, 1912	Hank Gowdy	BOS	Jun 12, 1921
Max Carey	PIT	Jun 25, 1912	Rogers Hornsby	STL	Jun 21, 1921
Owen Wilson	PIT	Jun 25, 1912	Frank Snyder	NY	Jul 9, 1921
Art Wilson	NY	Jul 1, 1912	Earl Smith	NY	Jul 13, 1921
Fred Luderus	PHI	Jul 6, 1912	Bob O'Farrell	CHI	Aug 6, 1921
Lee Magee	STL	Apr 20, 1913	George Kelly	NY	Aug 17, 1921
Joe Connolly	BOS	May 19, 1913	Dave Robertson	PIT	Aug 19, 1921
Vic Saier	CHI	May 25, 1913	Joe Schultz	STL	Aug 20, 1921
Larry Doyle	NY	Jun 26, 1913	Tony Boeckel	BOS	Aug 30, 1921
Bill Rariden	BOS	Jul 7, 1913	Hank Gowdy	BOS	May 13, 1922
Cy Williams	CHI	Aug 5, 1913	Irish Meusel	NY	Jun 12, 1922
Vic Saier	CHI	Sep 6, 1913	Kettle Wirtz	CHI	Jun 27, 1922
Rabbit Maranville	BOS	May 27, 1914	George Kelly	NY	Jul 8, 1922
Ed Konetchy	PIT	Aug 3, 1914	Jack Fournier	STL	Jul 21, 1922
Heinie Zimmerman	CHI	Aug 18, 1914	Johnny Mokan	PHI	Aug 8, 1922
George Burns	NY	Sep 3, 1914	Les Mann	STL	Aug 24, 1922
Rabbit Maranville	BOS	Sep 26, 1914	Rogers Hornsby	STL	Sep 15, 1922
George Cutshaw	BKN	Sep 28, 1914	Hack Miller	CHI	Sep 16, 1922
Possum Whitted	BOS	Oct 5, 1914	Jim Bottomley	STL	Apr 21, 1923
Hank Gowdy	BOS	Apr 29, 1915	Johnny Moken	PHI	Jun 4, 1923
Bob Bescher	STL	Jun 10, 1915	Stuffy McInnis	BOS	Jun 4, 1923
Honus Wagner	PIT	Jul 29, 1915	Reb Russell	PIT	Jun 8, 1923
Dots Miller	STL	Aug 27, 1915	Hack Miller	CHI	Jun 12, 1923
Gavvy Cravath	PHI	Sep 10, 1915	Bob O'Farrell	CHI	Jun 14, 1923
Dave Robertson	NY	Sep 19, 1915	Frank Snyder	NY	Jul 4, 1923
Red Smith	BOS	Aug 3, 1916	Russ Wrightstone	PHI	Jul 5, 1923
Sherry Magee	BOS	Sep 13, 1916	Pie Traynor	PIT	Jul 8, 1923
Bob Bescher	STL	Sep 14, 1916	Barney Friberg	CHI	Jul 15, 1923
Zack Wheat	BKN	Sep 16, 1916	Hod Ford	BOS	Jul 30, 1923
Marty Kavanaugh	STL	Sep 24, 1916	George Grantham	CHI	May 16, 1924
Benny Kauff	NY	Sep 28, 1916	Mule Watson	NY	Jun 8, 1924
Rogers Hornsby	STL	Jun 6, 1917	George Kelly	NY	Jun 14, 1924
Dave Robertson	NY	Jul 4, 1917	Joe Schultz	PHI	Jun 23, 1924
Marty Kavanagh	STL	Jun 4, 1918	George Harper	PHI	Jul 25, 1924
Fred Luderus	PHI	Jun 13, 1918	Jigger Statz	CHI	Aug 9, 1924
Max Flack	CHI	Jun 26, 1918	Jim Bottomley	STL	Aug 16, 1924
Rogers Hornsby	STL	Aug 18, 1918	Cy Williams	PHI	Sep 4, 1924
Edd Roush	CIN	Aug 19, 1918	George Kelly	NY	Sep 5, 1924
Irish Meusel	PHI	Aug 23, 1918	Travis Jackson	NY	Sep 5, 1924
Tommy Griffith	BKN	Jun 24, 1919		NY	Sep 6, 1924
Gene Paulette	PHI	Aug 11, 1919	Jim Bottomley	STL	Sep 16, 1924
Rogers Hornsby	STL	Sep 27, 1919	Walter Schmidt	PIT	Sep 16, 1924

Grand Slam Home Runs, NL (*cont.*)

Player	Team	Date	Player	Team	Date
Billy Southworth	NY	May 9, 1925	Wattie Holm	STL	Jun 2, 1928
Jimmy Ring	PHI	May 12, 1925	Del Bissonette	BKN	Jun 16, 1928
Eddie Brown	BKN	May 13, 1925	Charlie Hargreaves	PIT	Jun 17, 1928
Travis Jackson	NY	May 17, 1925	Bob O'Farrell	NY	Jun 25, 1928
George Harper	PHI	May 19, 1925	Paul Waner	PIT	Jun 29, 1928
Glenn Wright	PIT	May 27, 1925	Riggs Stephenson	CHI	Jul 3, 1928
Jim Bottomley	STL	Jun 2, 1925	Jack Cummings	NY	Jul 13, 1928
Zack Taylor	BKN	Jun 4, 1925	Clyde Beck	CHI	Jul 17, 1928
Kiki Cuyler	PIT	Jun 20, 1925	Les Bell	BOS	Sep 20, 1928
Pie Traynor	PIT	Jun 22, 1925	Shanty Hogan	NY	Sep 20, 1928
George Grantham	PIT	Jun 22, 1925	Harvey Hendrick	BKN	Sep 26, 1929
Lew Fonseca	PHI	Jun 27, 1925	Rogers Hornsby	CHI	Apr 17, 1929
Jim Bottomley	STL	Jun 28, 1925	Charlie Grimm	CHI	Apr 18, 1929
Jimmie Wilson	PHI	Jul 3, 1925	Bill Terry	NY	May 11, 1929
Cy Williams	PHI	Jul 18, 1925	Hack Wilson	CHI	May 17, 1929
Rogers Hornsby	STL	Jul 28, 1925	Chuck Klein	PHI	May 18, 1929
Cy Williams	PHI	Aug 21, 1925	Pat Crawford	NY	May 26, 1929
Zack Wheat	BKN	Aug 24, 1925	Taylor Douthit	STL	May 26, 1929
Mandy Brooks	CHI	Aug 25, 1925	Les Bell	BOS	May 26, 1929
George Harper	PHI	Aug 25, 1925	Rogers Hornsby	CHI	Jun 15, 1929
Jim Bottomley	STL	Sep 10, 1925	Spud Davis	PHI	Jun 15, 1929
Chicken Hawks	PHI	Sep 13, 1925	Hack Wilson	CHI	Jun 18, 1929
Cy Williams	PHI	Apr 15, 1926	George Grantham	PIT	Jun 21, 1929
Doc Farrell	NY	May 25, 1926	Phil Collins	PHI	Jun 23,1929
Gabby Hartnett	CHI	Jun 1, 1926	Denny Southern	PHI	Jun 26, 1929
Russ Wrightstone	PHI	Jun 14, 1926	Charlie Grimm	CHI	Jun 29, 1929
Rogers Hornsby	STL	Jun 23, 1926	Riggs Stephenson	CHI	Jul 1, 1929
Chuck Dressen	CIN	Aug 7, 1926	Adam Comorosky	PIT	Jul 4, 1929
Wally Pipp	CIN	Aug 11, 1926	Jim Bottomley	STL	Jul 6, 1929
Freddy Leach	PHI	Sep 6, 1926	Chick Hafey	STL	Jul 6, 1929
Cy Williams	PHI	Sep 8, 1926	Babe Herman	BKN	Jul 13, 1929
Pete Scott	CHI	Sep 11, 1926	Curt Walker	CIN	Jul 14, 1929
Bill Terry	NY	Apr 12, 1927	Chuck Klein	PHI	Jul 15, 1929
Russ Wrightstone	PHI	Apr 28, 1927	Rogers Hornsby	CHI	Jul 17, 1929
Chick Tolson	CHI	May 1, 1927	Bill Rhiel	BKN	Jul 23, 1929
Russ Wrightstone	PHI	May 14, 1927	Wally Roettger	STL	Jul 24, 1929
Pie Traynor	PIT	May 20, 1927	George Grantham	PIT	Jul 26, 1929
Cy Williams	PHI	May 20, 1927	Chuck Klein	PHI	Jul 26, 1929
George Kelly	CIN	May 20, 1927	Don Hurst	PHI	Jul 29, 1929
Les Bell	STL	May 25, 1927	Norm McMillan	CHI	Aug 26, 1929
Travis Jackson	NY	Jul 16, 1927	Kiki Cuyler	CHI	Sep 17, 1929
Freddy Leach	PHI	Jul 22, 1927	Babe Herman	BKN	Sep 17, 1929
George Harper	NY	Jul 31, 1927	Wally Berger	BOS	Apr 20, 1930
Rogers Hornsby	NY	Aug 12, 1927	Del Bissonette	BKN	Apr 21, 1930
Max Carey	BKN	Sep 14, 1927	Andy Reese	NY	Apr 27, 1930
Hack Wilson	CHI	Apr 19, 1928	Les Bell	CHI	Apr 29, 1930
Bill Terry	NY	May 29, 1928	Bill Walker	NY	May 5, 1930

Grand Slam Home Runs, NL (*cont.*)

Player	Team	Date	Player	Team	Date
Lance Richbourg	BOS	May 15, 1930	Fred Lindstrom	PIT	May 22, 1934
Charley Gelbert	STL	May 20, 1930	Leo Durocher	STL	Jun 14, 1934
Charlie Grimm	CHI	Jun 16, 1930	Lefty O'Doul	NY	Jun 17, 1934
Del Bissonette	BKN	Jul 9, 1930	Chuck Klein	CHI	Jun 22, 1934
Ethan Allen	NY	Jul 22, 1930	Joe Moore	NY	Jul 5, 1934
Wally Roettger	NY	Aug 21, 1930	Sam Leslie	BKN	Jul 6, 1934
Gabby Hartnett	CHI	Aug 22, 1930	Harlin Pool	CIN	Jul 8, 1934
Harry Heilmann	CIN	Aug 28, 1930	Roy Parmelee	NY	Jul 17, 1934
Tony Rensa	PHI	Sep 23, 1930	Marty McManus	BOS	Jul 25, 1934
Freddy Fitzsimmons	NY	May 10, 1931	Ernie Lombardi	CIN	Jul 31, 1934
Eddie Phillips	PIT	May 28, 1931	Danny Taylor	BKN	Apr 19, 1935
Gordon Slade	BKN	May 30, 1931	Lonny Frey	BKN	Apr 23, 1935
Johnny Frederick	BKN	Jun 29, 1931	Tommy Thompson	BOS	May 24, 1935
Rogers Hornsby	CHI	Jun 30, 1931	Wally Berger	BOS	May 29, 1935
Ethan Allen	NY	Jun 30, 1931	Ripper Collins	STL	Jun 2, 1935
Chick Hafey	STL	Aug 23, 1931	Johnny Vergez	PHI	Jun 21, 1935
Rogers Hornsby	CHI	Sep 13, 1931	Wally Berger	BOS	Jun 25, 1935
Vince Barton	CHI	Sep 27, 1931	Mel Ott	NY	Jul 7, 1935
Don Hurst	PHI	Apr 15, 1932	Danny Taylor	BKN	Jul 24, 1935
Johnny Vergez	NY	Apr 17, 1932	Gabby Harnett	CHI	Jul 27, 1935
Chuck Klein	PHI	Apr 29, 1932	Arky Vaughan	PIT	Aug 1, 1935
Hack Wilson	BKN	Jun 8, 1932	Wally Berger	BOS	Aug 11, 1935
Danny Taylor	BKN	Jun 11, 1932	Leo Durocher	STL	Aug 18, 1935
Pinky Whitney	PHI	Jun 15, 1932	Pie Traynor	PIT	Aug 26, 1935
Chuck Klein	PHI	Jun 23, 1932	Earl Grace	PIT	Aug 28, 1935
Fred Lindstrom	NY	Jul 15, 1932	Pepper Martin	STL	Aug 28, 1935
Tony Piet	PIT	Jul 28, 1932	Augie Galan	CHI	Sep 4, 1935
Chuck Klein	PHI	Aug 12, 1932	Paul Waner	PIT	Sep 11, 1935
Dutch Holland	BOS	Sep 11, 1932	Phil Cavarretta	CHI	May 16, 1936
Shanty Hogan	NY	Sep 17, 1932	Pinky Whitney	PHI	May 22, 1936
Joe Stripp	BKN	Sep 25, 1932	Sammy Byrd	CIN	May 23, 1936
Earl Grace	PIT	May 1, 1933	Al Hollingsworth	CIN	May 28, 1936
Arky Vaughan	PIT	May 1, 1933	Johnny Mize	STL	Jun 9, 1936
Chick Haley	CIN	May 12, 1933	Wally Berger	BOS	Jul 4, 1936
Spud Davis	PHI	May 13, 1933	Pepper Martin	STL	Jul 13, 1936
Hack Wilson	BKN	May 14, 1933	Hank Leiber	NY	Sep 17, 1936
Mel Ott	NY	May 19, 1933	Ripper Collins	STL	Sep 19, 1936
Homer Peel	NY	Jun 8, 1933	Jimmy Ripple	NY	Apr 30, 1937
Tony Cuccinello	BKN	Jun 23, 1933	Joe Medwick	STL	May 5, 1937
Johnny Vergez	NY	Jul 18, 1933	Frank Demaree	CHI	May 5, 1937
Babe Herman	CHI	Jul 20, 1933	Alex Kampouris	CIN	May 9, 1937
Harvey Hendrick	CHI	Jul 23, 1933	Dick Bartell	NY	May 20, 1937
Mel Ott	NY	Aug 5, 1933	Alex Kampouris	CIN	Jun 6, 1937
Gabby Harnett	CHI	Sep 23, 1933	Billy Herman	CHI	Jun 29, 1937
Wally Berger	BOS	Oct 1, 1933	Ray Mueller	BOS	Jul 21, 1937
Joe Medwick	STL	May 3, 1934	Chick Hafey	CIN	Jul 25, 1937
Tuck Stainback	CHI	May 18, 1934	Dolf Camilli	PHI	Jul 29, 1937

Grand Slam Home Runs, NL (*cont.*)

Player	Team	Date	Player	Team	Date
Elbie Fletcher	BOS	Jul 31, 1937	Rip Russell	CHI	Jul 5, 1940
Al Todd	PIT	Aug 10, 1937	Hank Leiber	CHI	Jul 19, 1940
Clay Bryant	CHI	Aug 28, 1937	Frank McCormick	CIN	Jul 21, 1940
Jim Bucher	BKN	Sep 3, 1937	Chet Ross	BOS	Aug 10, 1940
Eddie Wilson	BKN	Sep 12, 1937	Babe Young	NY	Aug 11, 1940
Dolf Camilli	PHI	Sep 23, 1937	Danny Litwhiler	PHI	Sep 2, 1940
Bucky Walters	PHI	Sep 29, 1937	Joe Medwick	BKN	Sep 6, 1940
Gene Moore	BOS	Apr 20, 1938	Bill Nicholson	CHI	Sep 7, 1940
Curt Davis	STL	Apr 26, 1938	Babe Young	NY	Sep 7, 1940
Arky Vaughan	PIT	Apr 27, 1938	Enos Slaughter	STL	Sep 15, 1940
Gene Moore	BOS	Apr 30, 1938	Babe Phelps	BKN	Sep 18, 1940
Harl Maggert	BOS	Apr 30, 1938	Don Manno	BOS	Sep 26, 1940
Harry Danning	NY	May 22, 1938	Johnny Rucker	NY	Sep 29, 1940
Augie Galan	CHI	May 24, 1938	Vince DiMaggio	PIT	Apr 17, 1941
Don Padgett	STL	Jun 3, 1938	Mel Ott	NY	Apr 18, 1941
Dolf Camilli	BKN	Jun 12, 1938	Harry Danning	NY	Apr 19, 1941
Johnny Rizzo	PIT	Jun 12, 1938	Dixie Walker	BKN	May 6, 1941
Hank Leiber	NY	Jun 17, 1938	Claude Passeau	CHI	May 19, 1941
Dick Bartell	NY	Jul 4, 1938	Bill Nicholson	CHI	May 21, 1941
Gus Mancuso	NY	Jul 4, 1938	Ernie Lombardi	CIN	May 22, 1941
Mel Ott	NY	Jul 17, 1938	Pete Reiser	BKN	May 25, 1941
Harry Craft	CIN	Aug 6, 1938	Bobby Bragan	PHI	Jun 1, 1941
Terry Moore	STL	Aug 23, 1938	Hank Leiber	CHI	Jun 10, 1941
Gabby Hartnett	CHI	Sep 14, 1938	Dom Dallessandro	CHI	Jul 5, 1941
Frank McCormick	CIN	May 7, 1939	Babe Young	NY	Jul 10, 1941
Cookie Lavagetto	BKN	May 28, 1939	Bill Nicholson	CHI	Jul 29, 1941
Augie Galan	CHI	Jun 22, 1939	Johnny Mize	STL	Aug 2, 1941
Al Lopez	BOS	Jul 2, 1939	Ken O'Dea	NY	Aug 4, 1941
Elbie Fletcher	PIT	Jul 2, 1939	Paul Waner	BOS	Aug 9, 1941
Don Padgett	STL	Jul 27, 1939	Harry Craft	CIN	Aug 24, 1941
Bily Myers	CIN	Jul 30, 1939	Dom Dallessandro	CHI	Aug 26, 1941
Hank Majeski	BOS	Aug 27, 1939	Eddie Joost	CIN	Sep 5, 1941
Elbie Fletcher	PIT	Sep 4, 1939	Bob Scheffing	CHI	Sep 20, 1941
Hank Leiber	CHI	Sep 12, 1939	Danny Litwhiler	PHI	Sep 21, 1941
Wally Berger	CIN	Sep 22, 1939	Willard Marshall	NY	Apr 15, 1942
Cookie Lavagetto	BKN	Sep 26, 1939	Al Glossop	PHI	Apr 20, 1942
	BKN	Apr 26, 1940	Ken O'Dea	STL	May 3, 1942
Bill Nicholson	CHI	Apr 26, 1940	Eddie Miller	BOS	May 3, 1942
Ernie Lombardi	CIN	May 1, 1940	Ray Lamanno	CIN	May 20, 1942
Elbie Fletcher	PIT	May 14, 1940	Gee Walker	CIN	May 27, 1942
Ival Goodman	CIN	May 17, 1940	Dixie Walker	BKN	May 31, 1942
Eddie Miller	BOS	May 30, 1940	Rip Russell	CHI	Jun 3, 1942
Pepper Martin	STL	Jun 28, 1940	Dom Dallessandro	CHI	Jun 21, 1942
Dixie Walker	BKN	Jun 29, 1940	Elbie Fletcher	PIT	Jul 11, 1942
Emmett Mueller	PHI	Jun 30, 1940	Mel Ott	NY	Aug 2, 1942
Jim Gleeson	CHI	Jun 30, 1940	Max West	STL	Aug 2, 1942
Pee Wee Reese	BKN	Jul 3, 1940	Dolph Camilli	BKN	Aug 3, 1942

Grand Slam Home Runs, NL (*cont.*)

Player	Team	Date	Player	Team	Date
	BKN	Aug 23, 1942	Walker Cooper	NY	Jun 2, 1946
Babe Young	NY	Sep 5, 1942	Frank Secory	CHI	Jun 6, 1946
Mel Ott	NY	Sep 19, 1942	Frank McCormick	PHI	Jun 7, 1946
Stan Musial	STL	Sep 22, 1942	Mickey Witek	NY	Jun 23, 1946
Schoolboy Rowe	PHI	May 2, 1943	Johnny Mize	NY	Jun 30, 1946
Phil Masi	BOS	May 16, 1943	Ron Northey	PHI	Jul 4, 1946
Hank Geary	PIT	Jun 6, 1943	Andy Seminick	PHI	Jul 17, 1946
Augie Galan	BKN	Jul 5, 1943	Jim Tabor	PHI	Aug 15, 1946
Frank McCormick	CIN	Jul 21, 1943	Ernie Lombardi	NY	Sep 6, 1946
Arky Vaughan	BKN	Jul 26, 1943	Bill Nicholson	CHI	Sep 16, 1946
Bill Baker	PIT	Jul 30, 1943	Bill Rigney	NY	Apr 18, 1947
Walker Cooper	STL	Aug 22, 1943	Bill Nicholson	CHI	Apr 20, 1947
Vince DiMaggio	PIT	Aug 22, 1943	Billy Cox	PIT	Apr 23, 1947
Howie Schultz	BKN	May 17, 1944	Johnny Mize	NY	May 23, 1947
Bill Nicholson	CHI	Jun 28, 1944	Pee Wee Reese	BKN	Jun 4, 1947
Gee Walker	CIN	Jul 4, 1944	Carl Furillo	BKN	Jun 22, 1947
Phil Weintraub	NY	Jul 18, 1944	Skeeter Newsome	PHI	Jun 27, 1947
Danny Litwhiler	STL	Jul 29, 1944	Wally Westlake	PIT	Jun 29, 1947
Bill Nicholson	CHI	Aug 16, 1944	Walker Cooper	NY	Jul 3, 1947
Jim Russell	PIT	Aug 20, 1944	Wally Westlake	PIT	Jul 15, 1947
Lennie Merullo	CHI	Aug 20, 1944	Bob Elliott	BOS	Jul 23, 1947
Ron Northey	PHI	Aug 25, 1944	Clyde Kluttz	PIT	Jul 24, 1947
Ernie Lombardi	NY	Sep 14, 1944	Hank Greenberg	PIT	Aug 3, 1947
Steve Mesner	CIN	Sep 27, 1944	Del Rice	STL	Aug 5, 1947
Dain Clay	CIN	Apr 17, 1945	Connie Ryan	BOS	Aug 9, 1947
Ernie Lombardi	NY	Apr 19, 1945	Howie Schultz	PHI	Aug 9, 1947
Phil Cavarretta	CHI	May 12, 1945	Augie Galan	CIN	Aug 11, 1947
Jimmie Foxx	PHI	May 18, 1945	Dixie Howell	PIT	Aug 13, 1947
Luis Olmo	BKN	May 18, 1945	Bruce Edwards	BKN	Aug 18, 1947
Vince DiMaggio	PHI	May 20, 1945	Eddie Miller	CIN	Aug 19, 1947
Luis Olmo	BKN	May 26, 1945	Stan Musial	STL	Aug 21, 1947
Vince DiMaggio	PHI	Jun 2, 1945	Eddie Waitkus	CHI	Aug 24, 1947
	PHI	Jun 27, 1945	Ron Northey	STL	Sep 3, 1947
Augie Bergamo	STL	Jul 4, 1945	Ox Miller	CHI	Sep 8, 1947
Butch Nieman	BOS	Jul 6, 1945	Cliff Aberson	CHI	Sep 9, 1947
Dixie Walker	BKN	Jul 8, 1945	Walker Cooper	NY	Apr 25, 1948
Johnny Hopp	STL	Aug 1, 1945	Wally Westlake	PIT	Apr 25, 1948
Bob Elliott	PIT	Aug 10, 1945	Preston Ward	BKN	Apr 29, 1948
Johnny Barrett	PIT	Aug 14, 1945	Joe Garagiola	STL	Apr 30, 1948
Paul Gillespie	CHI	Aug 15, 1945	Ralph Kiner	PIT	May 9, 1948
Pete Coscarart	PIT	Aug 21, 1945	Pee Wee Reese	BKN	May 9, 1948
Vince DiMaggio	PHI	Sep 1, 1945	Sid Gordon	NY	May 22, 1948
Andy Pafko	CHI	Sep 3, 1945	Grady Hatton	CIN	May 30, 1948
	CHI	Sep 23, 1945	Ron Northey	STL	May 30, 1948
Ralph Kiner	PIT	May 23, 1946	Enos Slaughter	STL	Jun 5, 1948
Buddy Blattner	NY	May 26, 1946	Sid Gordon	NY	Jun 6, 1948
Dick Sisler	STL	May 28, 1946	Hank Sauer	CIN	Jun 12, 1948

Grand Slam Home Runs, NL (*cont.*)

Player	Team	Date	Player	Team	Date
Jackie Robinson	BKN	Jun 24, 1948	Bobby Thomson	NY	May 6, 1950
Sid Gordon	NY	Jun 29, 1948	Ralph Kiner	PIT	May 6, 1950
Jim Russell	BOS	Jul 8, 1948		PIT	May 9, 1950
Stan Musial	STL	Jul 17, 1948	Rube Walker	CHI	May 18, 1950
Jeff Heath	BOS	Jul 18, 1948	Monte Irvin	NY	May 18, 1950
Frankie Baumholtz	CIN	Jul 25, 1948	Wally Westlake	PIT	May 23, 1950
Danny Murtaugh	PIT	Jul 25, 1948	Roy Smalley	CHI	May 26, 1950
Walker Cooper	NY	Jul 29, 1948	Andy Seminick	PHI	May 27, 1950
Del Rice	STL	Aug 14, 1948	Joe Garagiola	STL	May 28, 1950
Ron Northey	STL	Aug 21, 1948	Sid Gordon	BOS	Jun 1, 1950
Wally Westlake	PIT	Aug 26, 1948	Hank Thompson	NY	Jun 1, 1950
Ralph Kiner	PIT	Sep 11, 1948	Marty Marion	STL	Jun 1, 1950
Hank Sauer	CIN	Sep 16, 1948	Sid Gordon	BOS	Jun 3, 1950
Ralph Kiner	PIT	Apr 22, 1949	Roy Campanella	BKN	Jun 11, 1950
Eddie Miller	PHI	Apr 26, 1949	Gil Hodges	BKN	Jun 20, 1950
Pete Milne	NY	Apr 27, 1949	Jackie Robinson	BKN	Jun 24, 1950
Eddie Kazak	STL	May 9, 1949	Sibby Sisti	BOS	Jun 30, 1950
Gil Hodges	BKN	May 14, 1949	Willie Jones	PHI	Jul 2, 1950
Grady Hatton	CIN	May 18, 1949	Sid Gordon	BOS	Jul 4, 1950
Pete Reiser	BOS	May 28, 1949	Andy Seminick	PHI	Jul 4, 1950
Grady Hatton	CIN	Jun 12, 1949	Jack Phillips	PIT	Jul 8, 1950
Gil Hodges	BKN	Jun 12, 1949	Del Ennis	PHI	Jul 27, 1950
Joe Lafata	NY	Jun 21, 1949		PHI	Jul 30, 1950
Ralph Kiner	PIT	Jun 29, 1949	Wes Westrum	NY	Aug 2, 1950
Gene Hermanski	BKN	Jul 2, 1949	Don Mueller	NY	Aug 16, 1950
Monte Kennedy	NY	Jul 3, 1949	Walker Cooper	BOS	Aug 26, 1950
Walker Cooper	CIN	Jul 21, 1949	Wally Westlake	PIT	Sep 3, 1950
Gene Hermanski	BKN	Jul 28, 1949	Ron Northey	CHI	Sep 18, 1950
Bruce Edwards	BKN	Aug 7, 1949	Gil Hodges	BKN	Sep 20, 1950
Enos Slaughter	STL	Aug 8, 1949	Erv Palica	BKN	Sep 24, 1950
Jim Russell	BOS	Aug 17, 1949	Bob Elliott	BOS	Sep 27, 1950
Ron Northey	STL	Aug 29, 1949	Bobby Thomson	NY	Sep 27, 1950
Ralph Kiner	PIT	Sep 1, 1949	Monte Irvin	NY	Apr 19, 1951
Andy Seminick	PHI	Sep 3, 1949	Alvin Dark	NY	May 1, 1951
Tommy Glaviano	STL	Sep 4, 1949	Andy Pafko	CHI	May 3, 1951
Andy Pafko	CHI	Sep 4, 1949	Alvin Dark	NY	May 5, 1951
	CHI	Sep 9, 1949	Pee Wee Reese	BKN	May 6, 1951
Carl Furillo	BKN	Sep 11, 1949	Duke Snider	BKN	May 15, 1951
Ralph Kiner	PIT	Sep 13, 1949	Jack Cusick	CHI	May 18, 1951
Wally Westlake	PIT	Sep 18, 1949	Gil Hodges	BKN	May 22, 1951
Ron Northey	STL	Sep 18, 1949	Billy Cox	BKN	May 23, 1951
Ted Kluszewski	CIN	Sep 18, 1949	Connie Ryan	CIN	May 25, 1951
Tom Saffell	PIT	Sep 27, 1949	Granny Hamner	PHI	Jun 3, 1951
Ralph Kiner	PIT	Sep 30, 1949	Wes Westrum	NY	Jun 15, 1951
Sid Gordon	BOS	Apr 19, 1950	Willie Jones	PHI	Jun 19, 1951
Roy Campanella	BKN	Apr 21, 1950	Tommy Brown	PHI	Jun 21, 1951
Willie Jones	PHI	Apr 27, 1950	Earl Torgeson	BOS	Jun 30, 1951

Grand Slam Home Runs, NL (*cont.*)

Player	Team	Date	Player	Team	Date
Ralph Kiner	PIT	Jul 4, 1951	Gus Bell	CIN	May 4, 1953
Wes Westrum	NY	Jul 13, 1951	Ralph Kiner	CHI	Jun 14, 1953
Davey Williams	NY	Jul 13, 1951	Randy Jackson	CHI	Jun 19, 1953
Ralph Kiner	PIT	Jul 18, 1951	Del Rice	STL	Jun 23, 1953
Phil Cavarretta	CHI	Jul 29, 1951	Bobby Hofman	NY	Jun 25, 1953
Roy Campanella	BKN	Aug 5, 1951	Hank Thompson	NY	Jul 5, 1953
Randy Jackson	CHI	Aug 18, 1951	Preston Ward	PIT	Jul 7, 1953
Gus Bell	PIT	Aug 24, 1951	Monte Irvin	NY	Jul 8, 1953
Roy Campanella	BKN	Sep 3, 1951	Eddie Mathews	MIL	Jul 12, 1953
Gil Hodges	BKN	Sep 5, 1951	Gil Hodges	BKN	Jul 16, 1953
Wes Westrum	NY	Sep 11, 1951	Billy Cox	BKN	Jul 17, 1953
Willie Jones	PHI	Sep 21, 1951	Wayne Belardi	BKN	Jul 18, 1953
Johnny Pramesa	CIN	Sep 25, 1951	Daryl Spencer	NY	Jul 26, 1953
Ralph Kiner	PIT	Sep 30, 1951	Eddie Mathews	MIL	Jul 27, 1953
Hank Sauer	CHI	Apr 15, 1952	Steve Bilko	STL	Aug 2, 1953
Carl Furillo	BKN	Apr 19, 1952	Duke Snider	BKN	Aug 9, 1953
Ted Kluszewski	CIN	Apr 20, 1952		BKN	Aug 12, 1953
Red Schoendienst	STL	Apr 30, 1952	Andy Seminick	CIN	Aug 12, 1953
Joe Adcock	CIN	May 22, 1952	Bill Serena	CHI	Aug 14, 1953
Roy Campanella	BKN	May 23, 1952	Bobby Thomson	NY	Aug 16, 1953
Andy Seminick	CIN	May 24, 1952	Granny Hamner	PHI	Aug 31, 1953
Sam Jethroe	BOS	Jun 8, 1952	Preston Ward	PIT	Sep 2, 1953
Carl Furillo	BKN	Jun 8, 1952	Pee Wee Reese	BKN	Sep 9, 1953
Bobby Thomson	NY	Jun 16, 1952	Cal Abrams	PIT	Sep 20, 1953
Gus Bell	PIT	Jun 17, 1952	Jim Greengrass	CIN	Apr 15, 1954
Solly Hemus	STL	Jun 20, 1952	Gil Hodges	BKN	May 16, 1954
Hal Rice	STL	Jul 4, 1952	Hank Sauer	CHI	May 17, 1954
Mel Clark	PHI	Jul 15, 1952	Stan Musial	STL	May 21, 1954
Billy Johnson	STL	Jul 18, 1952	Whitey Lockman	NY	May 25, 1954
Pee Wee Reese	BKN	Jul 19, 1952	Walker Cooper	CHI	May 29, 1954
Andy Seminick	CIN	Jul 20, 1952	Eddie Mathews	MIL	Jun 2, 1954
Dee Fondy	CHI	Jul 22, 1952	Bobby Morgan	PHI	Jun 6, 1954
Hank Thompson	NY	Jul 26, 1952	Eddie Mathews	MIL	Jun 6, 1954
Dusty Rhodes	NY	Jul 31, 1952	Joe Adcock	MIL	Jun 8, 1954
Connie Ryan	PHI	Aug 2, 1952	Wes Westrum	NY	Jun 26, 1954
Gil Hodges	BKN	Aug 5, 1952	Alvin Dark	NY	Jul 10, 1954
Roy Campanella	BKN	Aug 7, 1952	Jim Command	PHI	Jul 11, 1954
Del Ennis	PHI	Aug 7, 1952	Walker Cooper	CHI	Jul 18, 1954
Earl Torgeson	BOS	Aug 11, 1952	Wally Moon	STL	Jul 24, 1954
Gil Hodges	BKN	Aug 31, 1952	Don Hoak	BKN	Aug 8, 1954
Hal Rice	STL	Sep 1, 1952	Carl Furillo	BKN	Aug 14, 1954
Andy Pafko	BKN	Sep 11, 1952	Clyde McCullough	CHI	Aug 17, 1954
Johnny Temple	CIN	Sep 12, 1952	Don Mueller	NY	Aug 20, 1954
Jim Greengrass	CIN	Sep 14, 1952	Del Ennis	PHI	Sep 1, 1954
Granny Hamner	PHI	Sep 23, 1952	Hank Thompson	NY	Sep 4, 1954
Frank Thomas	PIT	Apr 23, 1953	Bob Skinner	PIT	Sep 6, 1954
Daryl Spencer	NY	May 4, 1953	Whitey Lockman	NY	Sep 11, 1954

Grand Slam Home Runs, NL (*cont.*)

Player	Team	Date	Player	Team	Date
Bobby Hofman	NY	Sep 21, 1954	Willie Jones	PHI	Aug 1, 1956
Bobby Thomson	MIL	Apr 20, 1955	Ray Jablonski	CIN	Aug 2, 1956
Gene Freese	PIT	May 1, 1955	Chico Fernandez	BKN	Aug 4, 1956
Duke Snider	BKN	May 8, 1955	Ted Kazanski	PHI	Aug 8, 1956
Gene Freese	PIT	May 10, 1955	Ed Bailey	CIN	Aug 10, 1956
Ernie Banks	CHI	May 11, 1955	Wally Post	CIN	Aug 15, 1956
Carl Furillo	BKN	May 14, 1955	Gene Baker	CHI	Aug 23, 1956
Smoky Burgess	CIN	May 20, 1955	Bobby Thomson	MIL	Aug 23, 1956
Ernie Banks	CHI	May 29, 1955	Ed Bailey	CIN	Sep 11, 1956
Andy Seminick	PHI	Jun 2, 1955	Solly Hemus	PHI	Sep 14, 1956
Davey Williams	NY	Jun 4, 1955	Bill Bruton	MIL	Sep 23, 1956
Stan Lopata	PHI	Jun 12, 1955	Joe Adcock	MIL	Apr 26, 1957
Willie Mays	NY	Jun 29, 1955	Walt Moryn	CHI	Apr 30, 1957
Gene Baker	CHI	Jul 1, 1955	Don Hoak	CIN	May 8, 1957
Stan Musial	STL	Jul 9, 1955	Stan Musial	STL	May 26, 1957
Ernie Banks	CHI	Jul 17, 1955	Red Schoendienst	NY	May 28, 1957
Dusty Rhodes	NY	Jul 27, 1955	Bob Thurman	CIN	Jun 2, 1957
Wally Moon	STL	Jul 27, 1955	Bobby Thomson	MIL	Jun 11, 1957
Smoky Burgess	CIN	Jul 29, 1955	Harry Anderson	PHI	Jun 18, 1957
Bob Thurman	CIN	Jul 29, 1955	Wally Post	CIN	Jun 20, 1957
Ernie Banks	CHI	Aug 2, 1955	Andre Rodgers	NY	Jun 21, 1957
Gil Hodges	BKN	Aug 3, 1955	Wally Post	CIN	Jul 2, 1957
Del Crandall	MIL	Aug 17, 1955	Gil Hodges	BKN	Jul 18, 1957
Willie Jones	PHI	Aug 21, 1955	Carl Furillo	BKN	Jul 28, 1957
Wally Moon	STL	Aug 25, 1955	Joe Cunningham	STL	Jul 30, 1957
Del Crandall	MIL	Aug 26, 1955	Gil Hodges	BKN	Aug 1, 1957
Don Zimmer	BKN	Sep 9, 1955	Wes Covington	MIL	Aug 14, 1957
Del Crandall	MIL	Sep 11, 1955	Hank Aaron	MIL	Sep 24, 1957
Ernie Banks	CHI	Sep 19, 1955	Vada Pinson	CIN	Apr 18, 1958
Gus Bell	CIN	Sep 21, 1955	Johnny Logan	MIL	Apr 18, 1958
Johnny Logan	MIL	Sep 21, 1955	Willie Mays	SF	May 12, 1958
Ray Jablonski	CIN	Apr 19, 1956	Ken Boyer	STL	May 18, 1958
Stan Musial	STL	Apr 22, 1956	Johnny Temple	CIN	Jun 1, 1958
	STL	May 2, 1956	Frank Thomas	PIT	Jun 11, 1958
Ken Boyer	STL	May 5, 1956	Joe Adcock	MIL	Jun 11, 1958
Danny Kravitz	PIT	May 11, 1956	Hank Aaron	MIL	Jun 20, 1958
Duke Snider	BKN	May 13, 1956	Gus Bell	CIN	Jun 22, 1958
Ted Kluszewski	CIN	Jun 9, 1956	Gene Green	STL	Jun 28, 1958
Del Ennis	PHI	Jun 23, 1956	Hank Aaron	MIL	Jun 29, 1958
Wally Moon	STL	Jul 1, 1956	Lew Burdette	MIL	Jul 10, 1958
Monte Irvin	CHI	Jul 8, 1956	Dick Stuart	PIT	Jul 11, 1958
Joe Adcock	MIL	Jul 13, 1956	Ken Boyer	STL	Jul 16, 1958
Gene Baker	CHI	Jul 15, 1956	Del Ennis	STL	Aug 8, 1958
Carl Furillo	BKN	Jul 15, 1956	Frank Torre	MIL	Aug 17, 1958
Joe Adcock	MIL	Jul 19, 1956	Gil Hodges	LA	Aug 23, 1958
Bobby Thomson	MIL	Jul 25, 1956	Ed Bouchee	PHI	Aug 24, 1958
Roberto Clemente	PIT	Jul 25, 1956	Pete Whisenant	CIN	Aug 27, 1958

Grand Slam Home Runs, NL (*cont.*)

Player	Team	Date	Player	Team	Date
Bob Schmidt	SF	Aug 31, 1958	Willie Mays	SF	Aug 25, 1960
Rip Repulski	PHI	Sep 3, 1958	Vada Pinson	CIN	Sep 3, 1960
Eddie Kasko	STL	Sep 9, 1958	Eddie Kasko	CIN	Sep 13, 1960
Wally Post	PHI	Sep 9, 1958	Bobby Malkmus	PHI	Sep 15, 1960
Gene Freese	PHI	Apr 18, 1959	Bob Schmidt	SF	Sep 19, 1960
Eddie Mathews	MIL	Apr 24, 1959	Al Heist	CHI	Apr 15, 1961
Dick Groat	PIT	Apr 26, 1959	Daryl Spencer	STL	Apr 17, 1961
Ken Boyer	STL	May 9, 1959	Frank Howard	LA	Apr 29, 1961
Earl Averill	CHI	May 12, 1959	Billy Williams	CHI	May 2, 1961
Ernie Banks	CHI	May 13, 1959	Joe Adcock	MIL	May 4, 1961
Leon Wagner	SF	May 26, 1959	Willie Mays	SF	May 13, 1961
Bob Skinner	PIT	May 31, 1959	Felipe Alou	SF	May 15, 1961
Jackie Brandt	SF	Jun 26, 1959	Ernie Banks	CHI	May 28, 1961
Gene Freese	PHI	Jul 2, 1959	Tommy Davis	LA	Jun 2, 1961
Bill White	STL	Jul 5, 1959	Bill White	STL	Jun 5, 1961
Gene Freese	PHI	Jul 9, 1959	Lee Maye	MIL	Jun 9, 1961
Earl Averill	CHI	Jul 22, 1959	Billy Williams	CHI	Jun 16, 1961
Willie Jones	CIN	Jul 23, 1959	Stan Musial	STL	Jun 23, 1961
Bob Purkey	CIN	Aug 1, 1959	Jimmie Schaffer	STL	Jun 30, 1961
Ed Bouchee	PHI	Aug 9, 1959	Roberto Clemente	PIT	Jul 14, 1961
Alvin Dark	CHI	Aug 13, 1959	Ken Boyer	STL	Jul 25, 1961
Frank Robinson	CIN	Aug 13, 1959	Norm Larker	LA	Jul 26, 1961
George Crowe	STL	Aug 13, 1959	Orlando Cepeda	SF	Jul 29, 1961
Ernie Banks	CHI	Aug 29, 1959	Hank Aaron	MIL	Aug 2, 1961
Bobby Avila	MIL	Sep 9, 1959	Dick Stuart	PIT	Aug 3, 1961
Del Crandall	MIL	Sep 19, 1959	Julian Javier	STL	Aug 9, 1961
Hal Smith	STL	Sep 22, 1959	Don Drysdale	LA	Aug 9, 1961
Ernie Banks	CHI	Apr 14, 1960	Frank Thomas	MIL	Aug 23, 1961
Jimmie Coker	PHI	Apr 24, 1960	Vada Pinson	CIN	Aug 26, 1961
Johnny Roseboro	LA	Apr 29, 1960	Bobby Gene Smith	PHI	Aug 27, 1961
Roberto Clemente	PIT	May 1, 1960	Bill White	STL	Sep 4, 1961
Vada Pinson	CIN	May 8, 1960	Don Demeter	PHI	Sep 10, 1961
Frank Howard	LA	May 17, 1960	Willie Mays	SF	Sep 19, 1961
Ed Bailey	CIN	May 27, 1960	Orlando Cepeda	SF	Sep 24, 1961
Norm Sherry	LA	May 31, 1960	Roberto Clemente	PIT	Apr 10, 1962
Wally Moon	LA	Jun 4, 1960	Joe Adcock	MIL	Apr 12, 1962
Dutch Dotterer	CIN	Jun 10, 1960	Willie Mays	SF	Apr 28, 1962
Willie McCovey	SF	Jun 12, 1960	Don Demeter	PHI	May 11, 1962
Bob Skinner	PIT	Jun 16, 1960	Denis Menke	MIL	May 15, 1962
Dick Stuart	PIT	Jun 19, 1960	Lou Brock	CHI	May 20, 1962
Bob Skinner	PIT	Jul 6, 1960	Johnny Edwards	CIN	May 26, 1962
Joe Adcock	MIL	Jul 15, 1960	Jim Davenport	SF	Jun 1, 1962
Frank Howard	LA	Jul 28, 1960	Don Buddin	HOU	Jun 10, 1962
Tommy Davis	LA	Jul 30, 1960	Roy Sievers	PHI	Jun 15, 1962
Bill White	STL	Jul 31, 1960	Hank Aaron	MIL	Jun 15, 1962
Jerry Lynch	CIN	Aug 7, 1960	Roberto Clemente	PIT	Jun 15, 1962
Ron Santo	CHI	Aug 14, 1960	Hank Aaron	MIL	Jun 18, 1962

Grand Slam Home Runs, NL (*cont.*)

Player	Team	Date	Player	Team	Date
Norm Larker	HOU	Jun 20, 1962	Bill Virdon	PIT	Sep 1, 1963
Hank Foiles	CIN	Jun 24, 1962	Ron Santo	CHI	Sep 2, 1963
Ed Bailey	SF	Jun 26, 1962	Gordy Coleman	CIN	Sep 11, 1963
Eddie Mathews	MIL	Jul 2, 1962	Johnny Roseboro	LA	Sep 12, 1963
Willie Davis	LA	Jul 2, 1962	Billy Williams	CHI	May 1, 1964
Rod Kanehl	NY	Jul 6, 1962	Julian Javier	STL	May 15, 1964
Frank Robinson	CIN	Jul 8, 1962	Joe Torre	MIL	May 20, 1964
Hank Aaron	MIL	Jul 12, 1962	Jim Pagliaroni	PIT	May 26, 1964
Johnny Logan	PIT	Jul 16, 1962	Johnny Edwards	CIN	Jun 7, 1964
Joe Adcock	MIL	Jul 25, 1962	Bob Aspromonte	HOU	Jun 11, 1964
Frank Thomas	NY	Aug 1, 1962	Joey Amalfitano	CHI	Jun 12, 1964
Art Mahaffey	PHI	Aug 2, 1962	Willie McCovey	SF	Jun 22, 1964
Tommie Aaron	MIL	Aug 4, 1962	Joe Christopher	NY	Jun 26, 1964
Donn Clendenon	PIT	Aug 11, 1962	Bob Aspromonte	HOU	Jun 29, 1964
Fred Whitfield	STL	Aug 12, 1962	Pete Rose	CIN	Jul 18, 1964
Frank Robinson	CIN	Aug 13, 1962	Ken Boyer	STL	Jul 18, 1964
	CIN	Aug 20, 1962	Jerry Lynch	PIT	Jul 21, 1964
Eddie Kasko	CIN	Aug 22, 1962	Ken Boyer	STL	Jul 25, 1964
Don Demeter	PHI	Aug 30, 1962	Leo Cardenas	CIN	Jul 26, 1964
Bill Mazeroski	PIT	Sep 7, 1962	Johnny Callison	PHI	Aug 11, 1964
Carl Sawatski	STL	Sep 9, 1962	Jim Hickman	NY	Aug 19, 1964
Tommy Davis	LA	Sep 10, 1962	Gene Oliver	MIL	Aug 30, 1964
Nelson Mathews	CHI	Sep 16, 1962	Gus Triandos	PHI	Sep 5, 1964
Charlie James	STL	Sep 21, 1962	Willie Davis	LA	Sep 9, 1964
Ed Bailey	SF	Apr 10, 1963	Orlando Cepeda	SF	Sep 12, 1964
Johnny Edwards	CIN	Apr 17, 1963	Ernie Banks	CHI	Sep 27, 1964
Jim Hickman	NY	Apr 21, 1963	Ed Bailey	MIL	Oct 1, 1964
Bill White	STL	May 9, 1963	Tony Perez	CIN	Apr 13, 1965
Hank Aaron	MIL	May 18, 1963	Gordy Coleman	CIN	Apr 15, 1965
Tom Haller	SF	May 22, 1963	Dick Stuart	PHI	May 15, 1965
Roy Sievers	PHI	May 26, 1963	Eddie Mathews	MIL	May 20, 1965
Tim McCarver	STL	Jun 9, 1963	Andre Rodgers	PIT	May 23, 1965
Bob Aspromonte	HOU	Jun 11, 1963	Mack Jones	MIL	Jun 5, 1965
Bill White	STL	Jun 19, 1963	Vada Pinson	CIN	Jun 27, 1965
Tim Harkness	NY	Jun 26, 1963	Dick Allen	PHI	Jul 8, 1965
Jim Campbell	HOU	Jul 4, 1963	Johnny Callison	PHI	Jul 17, 1965
Ken McMullen	LA	Jul 4, 1963	Bob Bailey	PIT	Jul 20, 1965
Carl Willey	NY	Jul 15, 1963	Ed Bailey	CHI	Jul 22, 1965
Ron Fairly	LA	Jul 21, 1963	Willie Stargell	PIT	Jul 31, 1965
Bob Aspromonte	HOU	Jul 26, 1963	Jim Ray Hart	SF	Aug 15, 1965
Jim Hickman	NY	Aug 8, 1963	Tim McCarver	STL	Aug 16, 1965
Hank Aaron	MIL	Aug 14, 1963	Billy Williams	CHI	Aug 27, 1965
Roberto Clemente	PIT	Aug 22, 1963	Willie Stargell	PIT	Aug 28, 1965
Joe Torre	MIL	Aug 22, 1963	Dick Stuart	PHI	Sep 5, 1965
Frank Robinson	CIN	Aug 25, 1963	Willie McCovey	SF	Sep 10, 1965
Gene Oliver	MIL	Aug 28, 1963	Frank Bolling	MIL	Sep 22, 1965
Ellis Burton	CHI	Aug 31, 1963	Bob Gibson	STL	Sep 29, 1965

Grand Slam Home Runs, NL *(cont.)*

Player	Team	Date	Player	Team	Date
Willie McCovey	SF	Apr 27, 1966	Al McBean	PIT	Jul 28, 1968
Orlando Cepeda	STL	May 7, 1966	Norm Miller	HOU	Aug 10, 1968
Curt Flood	STL	May 25, 1966	Don Lock	PHI	Aug 14, 1968
Randy Hundley	CHI	Jun 8, 1966	Mike Shannon	STL	Aug 15, 1968
Hank Aaron	ATL	Jun 8, 1966	Dick Allen	PHI	Aug 26, 1968
Eddie Mathews	ATL	Jun 12, 1966	Art Shamsky	NY	Aug 30, 1968
Ed Bressoud	NY	Jul 3, 1966	Bill Sudakis	LA	Sep 9, 1968
Tony Cloninger	ATL	Jul 3, 1966	Jim Ray Hart	SF	Sep 19, 1968
	ATL	Jul 3, 1966	Ron Santo	CHI	Sep 25, 1968
Bill Mazeroski	PIT	Jul 8, 1966	Dick Allen	PHI	Sep 29, 1968
Jim Davenport	SF	Jul 8, 1966	Felix Millan	ATL	Apr 8, 1969
Joe Torre	ATL	Jul 19, 1966	Dal Maxvill	STL	Apr 14, 1969
Jimmie Coker	CIN	Jul 28, 1966	Andy Kosco	LA	Apr 15, 1969
Jim Ray Hart	SF	Aug 3, 1966	Mike Ryan	PHI	Apr 19, 1969
Bill White	PHI	Aug 3, 1966	Willie Stargell	PIT	Apr 22, 1969
Bob Aspromonte	HOU	Aug 11, 1966	Jack Hiatt	SF	Apr 25, 1969
Hawk Taylor	NY	Aug 17, 1966	Tim McCarver	STL	Apr 26, 1969
Vada Pinson	CIN	Aug 24, 1966	Hector Torres	HOU	Apr 27, 1969
Bob Aspromonte	HOU	Aug 26, 1966	Al Ferrara	SD	May 2, 1969
Bill Mazeroski	PIT	Sep 5, 1966	Ollie Brown	SD	May 3, 1969
Chuck Harrison	HOU	Sep 16, 1966	Dick Allen	PHI	May 8, 1969
Bob Bailey	PIT	Sep 19, 1966	Mack Jones	MON	May 10, 1969
Tony Gonzalez	PHI	Apr 15, 1967	Roberto Pena	SD	May 10, 1969
Willie McCovey	SF	Apr 22, 1967	Cleon Jones	NY	May 14, 1969
Jack Hamilton	NY	May 20, 1967	Al Oliver	PIT	May 21, 1969
Randy Hundley	CHI	May 20, 1967	Ernie Banks	CHI	May 24, 1969
Don Pavletich	CIN	Jun 11, 1967	Nate Colbert	SD	May 25, 1969
Willie Mays	SF	Jun 13, 1967	Doug Rader	HOU	May 27, 1969
Tim McCarver	STL	Jun 14, 1967	Randy Hundley	CHI	May 28, 1969
Clete Boyer	ATL	Jun 14, 1967	Jerry May	PIT	Jun 8, 1969
Bob Uecker	ATL	Jun 21, 1967	Roberto Clemente	PIT	Jun 11, 1969
Hank Aaron	ATL	Jun 27, 1967	Bob Tillman	ATL	Jun 24, 1969
Adolfo Phillips	CHI	Jul 13, 1967	John Briggs	PHI	Jun 28, 1969
Felipe Alou	ATL	Jul 17, 1967	Willie McCovey	SF	Jun 28, 1969
Tommy Davis	NY	Jul 19, 1967	Vic Davalillo	STL	Jul 2, 1969
Jack Hiatt	SF	Jul 31, 1967	Bob Burda	SF	Jul 9, 1969
Clete Boyer	ATL	Aug 29, 1967	Lee May	CIN	Jul 15, 1969
Cookie Rojas	PHI	Sep 10, 1967	Tony Gonzalez	ATL	Jul 18, 1969
Rick Joseph	PHI	Sep 16, 1967	Mack Jones	MON	Jul 26, 1969
Willie McCovey	SF	Sep 23, 1967	Denis Menke	ATL	Jul 30, 1969
	SF	Sep 27, 1967	Jimmy Wynn	HOU	Jul 30, 1969
Jim Davenport	SF	Apr 23, 1968	Tony Taylor	PHI	Aug 3, 1969
Willie McCovey	SF	May 4, 1968	Johnny Bench	CIN	Aug 13, 1969
Bobby Bonds	SF	Jun 25, 1968	Maury Wills	LA	Aug 16, 1969
Ernie Banks	CHI	Jul 7, 1968	Jim Hickman	CHI	Aug 23, 1969
Billy Williams	CHI	Jul 14, 1968	Willie McCovey	SF	Aug 26, 1969
Ron Fairly	LA	Jul 16, 1968	Hank Aaron	ATL	Aug 28, 1969

Grand Slam Home Runs, NL (*cont.*)

Player	Team	Date	Player	Team	Date
Jose Martinez	PIT	Sep 8, 1969	Bob Watson	HOU	Sep 7, 1970
Ron Swoboda	NY	Sep 13, 1969	Ramon Webster	SD	Sep 7, 1970
Orlando Cepeda	ATL	Sep 26, 1969	Lee May	CIN	Sep 10, 1970
Hank Aaron	ATL	Apr 10, 1970	Bob Watson	HOU	Sep 17, 1970
Ken Henderson	SF	Apr 14, 1970	Dick Dietz	SF	Sep 23, 1970
Bobby Tolan	CIN	Apr 14, 1970	Willie Mays	SF	Apr 8, 1971
Lee May	CIN	Apr 16, 1970	Roger Freed	PHI	Apr 11, 1971
Ron Hunt	SF	Apr 18, 1970	Tommie Agee	NY	Apr 24, 1971
Orlando Cepeda	ATL	Apr 23, 1970	Orlando Cepeda	ATL	May 9, 1971
Dick Dietz	SF	Apr 26, 1970	Dave Marshall	NY	May 11, 1971
Ron Santo	CHI	Apr 26, 1970	Doug Rader	HOU	May 16, 1971
Willie McCovey	SF	Apr 26, 1970	Nate Colbert	SD	Jun 6, 1971
Dave Marshall	NY	Apr 28, 1970	Bob Barton	SD	Jun 18, 1971
Rico Carty	ATL	Apr 30, 1970	John Bateman	MON	Jun 18, 1971
Willie Stargell	PIT	May 1, 1970	Deron Johnson	PHI	Jun 20, 1971
Willie McCovey	SF	May 10, 1970	Willie Stargell	PIT	Jun 20, 1971
Al Oliver	PIT	May 13, 1970	Earl Williams	ATL	Jun 20, 1971
Bob Bailey	MON	May 18, 1970	Willie McCovey	SF	Jul 21, 1971
Ken Henderson	SF	May 22, 1970	John Bateman	MON	Jul 25, 1971
Dick Allen	STL	Jun 2, 1970	Bill Buckner	LA	Jul 27, 1971
Doug Rader	HOU	Jun 4, 1970	Dave Kingman	SF	Jul 31, 1971
Rusty Staub	MON	Jun 6, 1970	Ken Boswell	NY	Aug 7, 1971
Joe Pepitone	HOU	Jun 10, 1970	Johnny Callison	CHI	Aug 18, 1971
Bob Robertson	PIT	Jun 13, 1970	Rusty Staub	MON	Aug 23, 1971
Ron Fairly	MON	Jun 18, 1970	Rick Wise	PHI	Aug 28, 1971
John Bateman	MON	Jul 2, 1970	Cesar Cedeno	HOU	Sep 2, 1971
Billy Williams	CHI	Jul 3, 1970	Willie Stargell	PIT	Sep 6, 1971
Ron Santo	CHI	Jul 6, 1970	Paul Popovich	CHI	Sep 11, 1971
Denis Menke	HOU	Jul 9, 1970	George Foster	CIN	Sep 16, 1971
Ron Swoboda	NY	Jul 9, 1970	Joe Hague	STL	Sep 24, 1971
Byron Browne	PHI	Jul 16, 1970	Dick Dietz	SF	Sep 26, 1971
Jim Hutto	PHI	Jul 19, 1970	Tommie Agee	NY	Apr 28, 1972
Lee May	CIN	Jul 20, 1970	Jimmy Wynn	HOU	May 1, 1972
Tom Haller	LA	Jul 22, 1970	Ted Simmons	STL	May 10, 1972
Ron Fairly	MON	Jul 25, 1970	Rusty Staub	NY	May 14, 1972
Orlando Cepeda	ATL	Jul 26, 1970	Dave Kingman	SF	May 22, 1972
Dick Allen	STL	Aug 1, 1970	George Foster	CIN	May 31, 1972
Tony Taylor	PHI	Aug 2, 1970	Hal McRae	CIN	Jun 1, 1972
Willie Davis	LA	Aug 5, 1970	Hank Aaron	ATL	Jun 10, 1972
Tony Perez	CIN	Aug 11, 1970	Ted Simmons	STL	Jun 10, 1972
Carl Taylor	STL	Aug 11, 1970	Clarence Gaston	SD	Jun 14, 1972
Joe Pepitone	CHI	Aug 14, 1970	Randy Hundley	CHI	Jun 20, 1972
Hal King	ATL	Aug 14, 1970	Luis Melendez	STL	Jun 24, 1972
Ed Spiezio	SD	Aug 18, 1970	Manny Sanguillen	PIT	Jun 25, 1972
Hal King	ATL	Sep 2, 1970	Willie McCovey	SF	Jul 2, 1972
Gene Alley	PIT	Sep 2, 1970	Tito Fuentes	SF	Jul 16, 1972
Mike Corkins	SD	Sep 4, 1970	Nate Colbert	SD	Aug 1, 1972

Grand Slam Home Runs, NL (*cont.*)

Player	Team	Date	Player	Team	Date
Willie Stargell	PIT	Aug 6, 1972	Merv Rettenmund	CIN	Apr 12, 1974
Garry Maddox	SF	Aug 15, 1972	Ron Fairly	MON	Apr 13, 1974
Darrell Evans	ATL	Sep 1, 1972	George Mitterwald	CHI	Apr 17, 1974
Nate Colbert	SD	Sep 7, 1972	Dave Concepcion	CIN	Apr 21, 1974
Johnny Bench	CIN	Sep 12, 1972	Hank Aaron	ATL	Apr 26, 1974
Jim Hickman	CHI	Sep 15, 1972	Nate Colbert	SD	May 17, 1974
Burt Hooton	CHI	Sep 16, 1972	Willie McCovey	SD	May 19, 1974
Chris Speier	SF	Sep 23, 1972	Milt May	HOU	May 23, 1974
Billy Williams	CHI	Sep 27, 1972	Hank Aaron	ATL	Jun 4, 1974
Jorge Roque	MON	Apr 12, 1973	Mike Lum	ATL	Jun 8, 1974
Chris Arnold	SF	May 1, 1973	Willie Stargell	PIT	Jun 9, 1974
Al Oliver	PIT	May 3, 1973	Cesar Cedeno	HOU	Jun 11, 1974
Rusty Staub	NY	May 3, 1973	Willie Davis	MON	Jun 11, 1974
Lee May	HOU	May 6, 1973	Jim Lonborg	PHI	Jun 24, 1974
Davey Johnson	ATL	May 8, 1973	Bob Bailey	MON	Jun 25, 1974
Willie Crawford	LA	May 25, 1973	Ron Fairly	MON	Jun 28, 1974
Tim McCarver	STL	Jun 2, 1973	Darrel Chaney	CIN	Jul 7, 1974
Tony Perez	CIN	Jun 2, 1973	Billy Williams	CHI	Jul 26, 1974
Luis Melendez	STL	Jun 13, 1973	Vic Correll	ATL	Jul 31, 1974
Darrell Evans	ATL	Jun 13, 1973	Bobby Bonds	SF	Aug 1, 1974
Dave Kingman	SF	Jun 17, 1973	Steve Yeager	LA	Aug 5, 1974
Mike Schmidt	PHI	Jun 19, 1973	Willie Montanez	PHI	Aug 6, 1974
Tommy Helms	HOU	Jun 21, 1973	Ted Simmons	STL	Aug 9, 1974
Ralph Garr	ATL	Jun 24, 1973	Joe Morgan	CIN	Aug 19, 1974
Cesar Cedeno	HOU	Jun 24, 1973	Carmen Fanzone	CHI	Aug 20, 1974
Mike Schmidt	PHI	Jun 27, 1973	Bill Madlock	CHI	Aug 28, 1974
Bobby Bonds	SF	Jun 29, 1973	Johnny Bench	CIN	Aug 31, 1974
Bob Bailey	MON	Jul 3, 1973	Richie Zisk	PIT	Sep 2, 1974
Willie Stargell	PIT	Jul 3, 1973	Gary Matthews	SF	Sep 3, 1974
Lee May	HOU	Jul 4, 1973	Dave Parker	PIT	Sep 8, 1974
John Boccabella	MON	Jul 6, 1973	Jerry Morales	CHI	Sep 8, 1974
Rick Monday	CHI	Jul 6, 1973	Darrell Evans	ATL	Sep 12, 1974
Hal King	CIN	Jul 9, 1973	Cesar Geronimo	CIN	Sep 12, 1974
Bob Bailey	MON	Jul 13, 1973	Johnny Bench	CIN	Sep 12, 1974
Bob Gibson	STL	Jul 26, 1973	Mike Lum	ATL	Sep 13, 1974
John Milner	NY	Jul 28, 1973	Jimmy Wynn	LA	Sep 15, 1974
Ed Goodson	SF	Aug 1, 1973	Steve Swisher	CHI	Sep 21, 1974
Jerry Grote	NY	Aug 15, 1973	Ken Singleton	MON	Sep 29, 1974
John Milner	NY	Aug 18, 1973	Jimmy Wynn	LA	Apr 16, 1975
Bill Robinson	PHI	Aug 19, 1973	Rusty Staub	NY	Apr 23, 1975
Bob Watson	HOU	Aug 20, 1973	Ken McMullen	LA	Apr 24, 1975
Rick Wise	STL	Aug 21, 1973	Mike Jorgensen	MON	May 6, 1975
Davey Johnson	ATL	Aug 26, 1973	Johnny Bench	CIN	May 7, 1975
Rusty Staub	NY	Aug 27, 1973	Vic Correll	ATL	May 20, 1975
Bobby Bonds	SF	Sep 3, 1973	Johnny Bench	CIN	May 26, 1975
Mike Jorgensen	MON	Sep 6, 1973	Willie McCovey	SD	May 30, 1975
Richie Zisk	PIT	Sep 23, 1973	Al Oliver	PIT	Jun 13, 1975

Grand Slam Home Runs, NL (cont.)

Player	Team	Date	Player	Team	Date
Jerry Martin	PHI	Jun 13, 1975	Randy Elliott	SF	May 13, 1977
Cliff Johnson	HOU	Jun 15, 1975	Gary Matthews	ATL	May 15, 1977
Dave May	ATL	Jun 17, 1975	Biff Pocoroba	ATL	May 17, 1977
Ron Cey	LA	Jun 18,1975	Mike Ivie	SD	May 20, 1977
Ted Simmons	STL	Jun 23, 1975	Dave Parker	PIT	May 22, 1977
Mike Ivie	SD	Jul 1, 1975	Ken Reitz	STL	May 27, 1977
Ron Fairly	STL	Jul 8, 1975	Johnny Bench	CIN	May 29, 1977
Tony Perez	CIN	Jul 18, 1975	Jack Clark	SF	May 30, 1977
George Foster	CIN	Aug 4, 1975	John Stearns	NY	Jun 1, 1977
Ted Simmons	STL	Aug 23, 1975	Jeff Burroughs	ATL	Jun 4, 1977
Champ Summers	CHI	Aug 23, 1975	Barry Bonnell	ATL	Jun 5, 1977
Dave Kingman	NY	Aug 24, 1975	Greg Luzinski	PHI	Jun 11, 1977
Pete LaCock	CHI	Sep 8, 1975	Larry Bowa	PHI	Jun 22, 1977
Tim Hosley	CHI	Sep 14, 1975	Steve Garvey	LA	Jun 22, 1977
Steve Yeager	LA	Sep 27, 1975	Willie McCovey	SF	Jun 27, 1977
Dave Winfield	SD	Apr 13, 1976	Ken Reitz	STL	Jun 28, 1977
Greg Luzinski	PHI	Apr 21, 1976	Mike Tyson	STL	Jul 5, 1977
Bobby Tolan	PHI	May 5, 1976	Tim McCarver	PHI	Jul 5, 1977
Ken Griffey	CIN	May 9, 1976	Dave Concepcion	CIN	Jul 6, 1977
Dave Winfield	SD	May 21, 1976	Don Stanhouse	MON	Jul 6, 1977
George Foster	CIN	May 23, 1976	Steve Henderson	NY	Jul 17, 1977
Bobby Murcer	SF	May 25, 1976	Gary Thomasson	SF	Jul 21, 1977
Willie Crawford	STL	May 28, 1976	Bill Robinson	PIT	Jul 28, 1977
Ron Cey	LA	Jun 7, 1976	Keith Hernandez	STL	Jul 29, 1977
Bill Madlock	CHI	Jun 18, 1976	Greg Luzinski	PHI	Jul 30, 1977
Tom Paciorek	ATL	Jun 22, 1976	Bill Robinson	PIT	Jul 30, 1977
Darrell Evans	SF	Jun 23, 1976	Willie McCovey	SF	Aug 1, 1977
Bombo Rivera	MON	Jun 26, 1976	Dave Kingman	SD	Aug 5, 1977
John Milner	NY	Jun 26, 1976	Frank Taveras	PIT	Aug 5, 1977
Bob Boone	PHI	Jun 27, 1976	Rod Gilbreath	ATL	Aug 12, 1977
John Milner	NY	Jul 1, 1976	Joe Morgan	CIN	Aug 14, 1977
Dick Allen	PHI	Jul 2, 1976	Art Howe	HOU	Aug 15, 1977
Joe Morgan	CIN	Jul 5, 1976	Richie Hebner	PHI	Aug 18, 1977
Ollie Brown	PHI	Jul 25, 1976	Dave Kingman	SD	Aug 21, 1977
Greg Luzinski	PHI	Aug 1, 1976	Steve Yeager	LA	Aug 22, 1977
Garry Maddox	PHI	Aug 3, 1976	Junior Moore	ATL	Aug 25, 1977
Willie Stargell	PIT	Aug 5, 1976	Steve Garvey	LA	Aug 28, 1977
Bob Watson	HOU	Aug 14, 1976	Keith Hernandez	STL	Sep 3, 1977
Joe Morgan	CIN	Sep 6, 1976	Bob Watson	HOU	Sep 4, 1977
Joe Ferguson	STL	Sep 15, 1976	Dusty Baker	LA	Sep 12, 1977
John Milner	NY	Sep 27, 1976	Keith Hernandez	STL	Sep 18, 1977
Wayne Garrett	MON	Sep 29, 1976	Larry Christensen	PHI	Sep 27, 1977
Doug Rader	SD	Sep 29, 1976	Johnny Bench	CIN	Sep 28, 1977
Jeff Burroughs	ATL	Apr 12, 1977	Steve Henderson	NY	Apr 9, 1978
Gene Tenace	SD	Apr 18, 1977	Bill Robinson	PIT	Apr 15, 1978
Ron Cey	LA	Apr 24, 1977	Bobby Murcer	CHI	Apr 26, 1978
	LA	May 5, 1977	Davey Johnson	PHI	Apr 30, 1978

Grand Slam Home Runs, NL (*cont.*)

Player	Team	Date	Player	Team	Date
Gary Carter	MON	May 3, 1978	Ray Knight	CIN	Jul 19, 1979
Rennie Stennett	PIT	May 21, 1978	Dave Concepcion	CIN	Jul 22, 1979
Mike Ivie	SF	May 28, 1978	Dusty Baker	LA	Jul 24, 1979
Davey Johnson	PHI	Jun 3, 1978	Keith Hernandez	STL	Jul 30, 1979
Dale Murphy	ATL	Jun 5, 1978	Greg Luzinski	PHI	Aug 5, 1979
Dave Kingman	CHI	Jun 6, 1978	John Milner	PIT	Aug 5, 1979
Biff Pocoroba	ATL	Jun 7, 1978	Derrel Thomas	LA	Aug 10, 1979
Larry Parrish	MON	Jun 9, 1978	Ed Ott	PIT	Aug 11, 1979
Dusty Baker	LA	Jun 12, 1978	Bruce Kison	PIT	Aug 26, 1979
John Milner	PIT	Jun 24, 1978	Davey Lopes	LA	Sep 2, 1979
Dave Rader	CHI	Jun 26, 1978	Barry Foote	CHI	Sep 9, 1979
Jack Clark	SF	Jun 27, 1978	Dave Cash	MON	Sep 16, 1979
Mike Ivie	SF	Jun 30, 1978	Mike Schmidt	PHI	Sep 19, 1979
Dale Murphy	ATL	Jul 2, 1978	Ron Cey	LA	Sep 25, 1979
Lee Mazzilli	NY	Jul 4, 1978	Steve Garvey	LA	Sep 28, 1979
Dave Winfield	SD	Jul 4, 1978	Dave Kingman	CHI	Apr 19, 1980
Davey Lopes	LA	Jul 6, 1978	Mike Schmidt	PHI	Apr 22, 1980
Bake McBride	PHI	Jul 8, 1978	Barry Foote	CHI	Apr 22, 1980
Warren Cromartie	MON	Jul 19, 1978	Junior Kennedy	CIN	May 3, 1980
George Foster	CIN	Jul 19, 1978	Ray Knight	CIN	May 13, 1980
Steve Garvey	LA	Jul 26, 1978	Darrell Evans	SF	May 17, 1980
John Milner	PIT	Aug 8, 1978	Barry Evans	SD	May 25, 1980
Reggie Smith	LA	Aug 16, 1978	George Foster	CIN	May 26, 1980
George Hendrick	STL	Aug 25, 1978	Dale Berra	PIT	Jun 1, 1980
Wayne Garrett	STL	Aug 31, 1978	Mike Jorgensen	NY	Jun 11, 1980
Rod Gilbreath	ATL	Sep 5, 1978	Jerry Martin	CHI	Jun 18, 1980
George Foster	CIN	Sep 11, 1978	Ray Knight	CIN	Jun 25, 1980
Phil Garner	PIT	Sep 14, 1978	Keith Moreland	PHI	Jun 30, 1980
	PIT	Sep 15, 1978	Cliff Johnson	CHI	Jul 12, 1980
Willie Stargell	PIT	Sep 30, 1978	Milt May	SF	Jul 18, 1980
Johnny Bench	CIN	Oct 1, 1978	Gary Carter	MON	Jul 21, 1980
Joe Ferguson	LA	Apr 6, 1979	Johnny Bench	CIN	Aug 8, 1980
George Foster	CIN	Apr 8, 1979	Cliff Johnson	CHI	Aug 8, 1980
Dave Concepcion	CIN	Apr 11, 1979	Jack Clark	SF	Aug 14, 1980
Garry Maddox	PHI	Apr 17, 1979	Dale Murphy	ATL	Aug 17, 1980
Dave Kingman	CHI	Apr 20, 1979	Cesar Cedeno	HOU	Aug 26, 1980
Roger Freed	STL	May 1, 1979	Jose Cruz	HOU	Sep 6, 1980
Gary Carter	MON	May 6, 1979	Leon Durham	STL	Sep 12, 1980
Gary Matthews	ATL	May 9, 1979	Ray Knight	CIN	Sep 16, 1980
John Milner	PIT	May 9, 1979	Johnny Bench	CIN	Sep 19, 1980
Barry Foote	CHI	May 15, 1979	Gary Carter	MON	Sep 19, 1980
Bill Buckner	CHI	May 17, 1979	Ted Simmons	STL	Sep 25, 1980
Ted Simmons	STL	Jun 11, 1979	Enrique Romo	PIT	Oct 1, 1980
Tony Scott	STL	Jun 13, 1979	Randy Bass	SD	Apr 12, 1981
Mike Vail	CHI	Jun 30, 1979	Billy North	SF	May 9, 1981
Terry Kennedy	STL	Jul 1, 1979	Dave Kingman	NY	May 25, 1981
Jeff Burroughs	ATL	Jul 13, 1979	Jerry Martin	SF	Jun 2, 1981

Grand Slam Home Runs, NL (*cont.*)

Player	Team	Date	Player	Team	Date
Ron Oester	CIN	Jun 2, 1981	Mike Schmidt	PHI	Jul 11, 1983
Keith Hernandez	STL	Jun 6, 1981	Kurt Bevacqua	SD	Jul 14, 1983
Andre Dawson	MON	Aug 13, 1981	Joe Lefebrve	PHI	Jul 20, 1983
Dave Kingman	NY	Aug 22, 1981	Ken Landreaux	LA	Jul 23, 1983
Mike Schmidt	PHI	Aug 23, 1981	Jeffrey Leonard	SF	Jul 24, 1983
Gary Carter	MON	Aug 25, 1981	Jason Thompson	PIT	Jul 31, 1983
Bruce Benedict	ATL	Aug 25, 1981	Bobby Brown	SD	Aug 6, 1983
Glenn Hubbard	ATL	Aug 31, 1981	Tim Raines	MON	Aug 7, 1983
George Foster	CIN	Sep 3, 1981	Leon Durham	CHI	Aug 11, 1983
Darrell Porter	STL	Sep 17, 1981	George Foster	NY	Aug 14, 1983
Lonnie Smith	STL	Apr 10, 1982	Mike Schmidt	PHI	Aug 15, 1983
Jeffrey Leonard	SF	Apr 25, 1982	George Foster	NY	Aug 20, 1983
Tony Pena	PIT	Apr 27, 1982	Al Oliver	MON	Aug 28, 1983
Dan Driessen	CIN	May 1, 1982	Mel Hall	CHI	Aug 29, 1983
Mike Easler	PIT	May 4, 1982	Ozzie Virgil	PHI	Sep 2, 1983
Terry Puhl	HOU	May 22, 1982	Mike Easler	PIT	Sep 3, 1983
Jack Clark	SF	May 29, 1982	Al Oliver	MON	Sep 5, 1983
Chili Davis	SF	Jun 19, 1982	Mike Marshall	LA	Sep 7, 1983
George Hendrick	STL	Jun 29, 1982	Gary Carter	MON	Sep 10, 1983
Dusty Baker	LA	Jun 30, 1982	Nick Esasky	CIN	Sep 14, 1983
Willie McGee	STL	Jul 20, 1982	Richie Hebner	PIT	Sep 15, 1983
Chris Chambliss	ATL	Aug 1, 1982	Marvell Wynne	PIT	Sep 16, 1983
Tim Wallach	MON	Aug 5, 1982	Jose Cruz	HOU	Sep 20, 1983
Bill Robinson	PHI	Aug 14, 1982	Mike Easler	PIT	Sep 23, 1983
John Milner	PIT	Aug 15, 1982	Doug Frobel	PIT	Apr 5, 1984
Garry Maddox	PHI	Aug 22, 1982	Nick Esasky	CIN	Apr 10, 1984
Ron Hodges	NY	Sep 8, 1982	Champ Summers	SD	Apr 10, 1984
Bruce Benedict	ATL	Sep 9, 1982	Gary Carter	MON	Apr 17, 1984
Scott Sanderson	MON	Sep 11, 1982	Ron Cey	CHI	May 8, 1984
Richie Hebner	PIT	Sep 14, 1982	Joaquin Andujar	STL	May 15, 1984
Bill Madlock	PIT	Sep 14, 1982	Steve Carlton	PHI	May 16, 1984
Tim Wallach	MON	Sep 18, 1982	Tony Pena	PIT	May 18, 1984
Rick Monday	LA	Oct 1, 1982	Bob Brenly	SF	Jun 6, 1984
Bo Diaz	PHI	Apr 13, 1983	Mike Marshall	LA	Jun 13, 1984
Greg Brock	LA	May 18, 1983	Brad Komminsk	ATL	Jun 19, 1984
Jack Clark	SF	May 18, 1983	Steve Yeager	LA	Jun 21, 1984
Dave Concepcion	CIN	May 20, 1983	Chili Davis	SF	Jun 27, 1984
Ryne Sandberg	CHI	May 31, 1983	Darrell Porter	STL	Jul 18, 1984
Chris Chambliss	ATL	Jun 2, 1983	Benny Distefano	PIT	Jul 24, 1984
Jody Davis	CHI	Jun 12, 1983	Garry Templeton	SD	Jul 29, 1984
Glenn Hubbard	ATL	Jun 20, 1983	Keith Moreland	CHI	Aug 5, 1984
Tim Raines	MON	Jun 22, 1983	Jeffrey Leonard	SF	Aug 5, 1984
Jody Davis	CHI	Jun 26, 1983	Dale Berra	PIT	Aug 8, 1984
Pedro Guerrero	LA	Jun 28, 1983	Dave Parker	CIN	Aug 9, 1984
Steve Garvey	SD	Jul 3, 1983	Jose Cruz	HOU	Aug 22, 1984
Darrell Porter	STL	Jul 4, 1983	Kelvin Chapman	NY	Aug 26, 1984
Tim Flannery	CHI	Jul 11, 1983	Lonnie Smith	STL	Aug 31, 1984

Grand Slam Home Runs, NL (*cont.*)

Player	Team	Date	Player	Team	Date
Craig Reynolds	HOU	Sep 6, 1984	R. J. Reynolds	PIT	Apr 19, 1986
Jody Davis	CHI	Sep 14, 1984	Dave Parker	CIN	Apr 23, 1986
Tony Pena	PIT	Sep 19, 1984	Jody Davis	CHI	Apr 27, 1986
Carmelo Martinez	SD	Apr 15, 1985	Terry Puhl	HOU	May 4, 1986
Terry Pendleton	STL	Apr 21, 1985	Steve Sax	LA	May 7, 1986
Darryl Strawberry	NY	Apr 28, 1985	Hubie Brooks	MON	May 18, 1986
Nick Esasky	CIN	May 4, 1985	George Foster	NY	May 27, 1986
Gary Carter	NY	May 7, 1985	Terry Harper	ATL	May 27, 1986
Tony Perez	CIN	May 13, 1985	Jim Morrison	PIT	Jun 1, 1986
Brian Dayett	CHI	May 22, 1985	Ted Simmons	ATL	Jun 3, 1986
Bill Almon	PIT	May 25, 1985	Tim Raines	MON	Jun 8, 1986
Jim Pankovits	HOU	May 29, 1985	Tim Teufel	NY	Jun 10, 1986
Kurt Bevacqua	SD	Jun 7, 1985	Phil Garner	HOU	Jun 14, 1986
Terry Pendleton	STL	Jun 9, 1985	Juan Samuel	PHI	Jun 29, 1986
Von Hayes	PHI	Jun 11, 1985	Kevin Bass	HOU	Jul 7, 1986
Leon Durham	CHI	Jun 11, 1985	Gary Carter	NY	Jul 11, 1986
Mark Bailey	HOU	Jun 11, 1985	Dave Parker	CIN	Jul 24, 1986
George Foster	NY	Jun 20, 1985	Von Hayes	PHI	Jul 29, 1986
Jerry Royster	SD	Jun 21, 1985	Greg Brock	LA	Aug 1, 1986
Kurt Bevacqua	SD	Jun 23, 1985	Enos Cabell	LA	Aug 2, 1986
Tim Wallach	MON	Jul 6, 1985	Billy Hatcher	HOU	Aug 5, 1986
Darryl Strawberry	NY	Jul 20, 1985	Bob Forsch	STL	Aug 10, 1986
John Russell	PHI	Jul 22, 1985	Candy Maldonado	SF	Aug 13, 1986
Greg Brock	LA	Jul 24, 1985	Ken Griffey	ATL	Aug 14, 1986
Mike Marshall	LA	Jul 26, 1985	Eric Davis	CIN	Aug 27, 1986
Chris Brown	SF	Aug 3, 1985	Bob Horner	ATL	Sep 6, 1986
Ron Cey	CHI	Aug 14, 1985	Robby Thompson	SF	Sep 12, 1986
Dave Concepcion	CIN	Aug 17, 1985	Dan Gladden	SF	Sep 22, 1986
Mark Bailey	HOU	Aug 20, 1985	Kevin McReynolds	SD	Oct 4, 1986
Mike Marshall	LA	Aug 21, 1985	Darryl Strawberry	NY	Oct 5, 1986
Pedro Guerrero	LA	Aug 23, 1985	Candy Maldonado	SF	Oct 5, 1986
Mariano Duncan	LA	Aug 23, 1985	Robby Thompson	SF	Apr 13, 1987
Cesar Cedeno	STL	Sep 6, 1985	Kurt Stillwell	CIN	Apr 17, 1987
Dave Parker	CIN	Sep 7, 1985	Tommy Herr	STL	Apr 18, 1987
Howard Johnson	NY	Sep 10, 1985	Andre Dawson	CHI	Apr 22, 1987
Greg Brock	LA	Sep 10, 1985	Lance Parrish	PHI	Apr 26, 1987
Hubie Brooks	MON	Sep 12, 1985	Eric Davis	CIN	May 1, 1987
Don Robinson	PIT	Sep 12, 1985	Tim Raines	MON	May 2, 1987
Bill Almon	PIT	Sep 16, 1985	Graig Nettles	ATL	May 2, 1987
Hubie Brooks	MON	Sep 19, 1985	Dion James	ATL	May 2, 1987
Dave Parker	CIN	Sep 19, 1985	Eric Davis	CIN	May 3, 1987
Andre Dawson	MON	Sep 21, 1985	Chris Speier	SF	May 5, 1987
Gary Carter	NY	Sep 25, 1985		SF	May 9, 1987
Glenn Wilson	PHI	Sep 27, 1985	Mitch Webster	MON	May 13, 1987
Wayne Krenchicki	CIN	Oct 4, 1985	Tom Pagnozzi	STL	May 17, 1987
Alan Ashby	HOU	Oct 5, 1985	Jack Clark	STL	May 24, 1987
Craig Reynolds	HOU	Apr 12, 1986	Eric Davis	CIN	May 30, 1987

Grand Slam Home Runs, NL (*cont.*)

Player	Team	Date	Player	Team	Date
Andre Dawson	CHI	Jun 1, 1987	Hubie Brooks	MON	Sep 13, 1988
Brian Dayett	CHI	Jun 3, 1987	Benito Santiago	SD	Sep 21, 1988
Billy Hatcher	HOU	Jun 3, 1987	Rafael Palmeiro	CHI	Oct 1, 1988
Keith Moreland	CHI	Jun 3, 1987	Matt Williams	SF	Apr 9, 1989
Alan Ashby	HOU	Jun 10, 1987	Eddie Murray	LA	Apr 10, 1989
Tim Teufel	NY	Jun 12, 1987	Carmelo Martinez	SD	Apr 27, 1989
Mike Fitzgerald	MON	Jun 17, 1987	Chris James	PHI	Apr 29, 1989
Bo Diaz	CIN	Jul 7, 1987	Jeff Hamilton	LA	May 19, 1989
Jim Sundberg	CHI	Jul 8, 1987	Will Clark	SF	May 28, 1989
Dale Murphy	ATL	Jul 9, 1987	Mike Scioscia	LA	Jun 4, 1989
Mitch Webster	MON	Jul 31, 1987	Louie Meadows	HOU	Jun 4, 1989
Howard Johnson	NY	Aug 1, 1987	Paul O'Neill	CIN	Jun 7, 1989
Mike Marshall	LA	Aug 3, 1987	Bill Doran	HOU	Jun 11, 1989
Bob Brenly	SF	Aug 12, 1987	Todd Benzinger	CIN	Jun 27, 1989
Juan Samuel	PHI	Aug 12, 1987	Chris James	SD	Jul 18, 1989
Vance Law	MON	Aug 15, 1987	Dwight Smith	CHI	Jul 31, 1989
Jody Davis	CHI	Aug 16, 1987	Mike Scioscia	LA	Aug 8, 1989
Barry Lyons	NY	Aug 20, 1987	Matt Williams	SF	Aug 11, 1989
Andy Van Slyke	PIT	Aug 29, 1987	Todd Benzinger	CIN	Aug 18, 1989
Gary Carter	NY	Aug 30, 1987	Kevin Bass	HOU	Aug 20, 1989
Terry McGriff	CIN	Sep 15, 1987	Ernest Riles	SF	Aug 20, 1989
Len Dykstra	NY	Sep 16, 1987	Andres Galarraga	MON	Aug 27, 1989
Keith Hernandez	NY	Sep 19, 1987	Rafael Ramirez	HOU	Aug 29, 1989
Darnell Coles	PIT	Sep 20, 1987	Kevin McReynolds	NY	Aug 30, 1989
Nick Esasky	CIN	Sep 20, 1987	Benito Santiago	SD	Sep 3, 1989
Howard Johnson	NY	Sep 21, 1987	Jack Clark	SD	Sep 4, 1989
Hubie Brooks	MON	Sep 26, 1987	Tim Wallach	MON	Sep 5, 1989
Candy Maldonado	SF	Sep 27, 1987	Garry Templeton	SD	Sep 11, 1989
Terry Puhl	HOU	Sep 28, 1987	Craig Biggio	HOU	Sep 14, 1989
Dave Martinez	CHI	Apr 8, 1988	Shawon Dunston	CHI	Sep 15, 1989
Kevin Bass	HOU	Apr 10, 1988	John Kruk	PHI	Sep 17, 1989
John Kruk	SD	Apr 12, 1988	Kevin Bass	HOU	Sep 20, 1989
Mike Marshall	LA	Apr 23, 1988	Mike Fitzgerald	MON	Sep 21, 1989
Keith Hernandez	NY	Apr 26, 1988	Hubie Brooks	MON	Sep 23, 1989
Chris Speier	SF	May 20, 1988	Lloyd McClendon	CHI	Apr 17, 1990
Rafael Ramirez	HOU	May 29, 1988	Pedro Guerrero	STL	Apr 21, 1990
Matt Williams	SF	Jun 4, 1988	Joe Carter	SD	Apr 23, 1990
Nick Esasky	CIN	Jun 14, 1988	Carmelo Martinez	PHI	Apr 27, 1990
Kevin McReynolds	NY	Jun 21, 1988	Andres Thomas	ATL	May 2, 1990
Franklin Stubbs	LA	Jul 6, 1988	Ricky Jordan	PHI	May 6, 1990
Buddy Bell	HOU	Jul 14, 1988	Terry Kennedy	SF	May 15, 1990
Chris James	PHI	Jul 16, 1988	Garry Templeton	SD	May 18, 1990
Mike Fitzgerald	MON	Jul 26, 1988	Bobby Bonilla	PIT	May 18, 1990
Bill Doran	HOU	Aug 2, 1988	Kal Daniels	LA	May 19, 1990
Kevin McReynolds	NY	Aug 11, 1988	Kevin McReynolds	NY	May 21, 1990
Marvell Wynne	SD	Sep 11, 1988	Barry Bonds	PIT	May 22, 1990
Damon Berryhill	CHI	Sep 13, 1988	Mike Marshall	NY	May 22, 1990

Grand Slam Home Runs, NL (cont.)

Player	Team	Date	Player	Team	Date
Shawon Dunston	CHI	Jun 8, 1990	Darryl Strawberry	LA	Aug 21, 1991
Greg Olson	ATL	Jun 12, 1990	Darrin Jackson	SD	Aug 25, 1991
Howard Johnson	NY	Jun 13, 1990	Jeff Blauser	ATL	Aug 26, 1991
Tim Wallach	MON	Jul 15, 1990	Charlie Hayes	PHI	Aug 28, 1991
Eric Davis	CIN	Jul 16, 1990	Chico Walker	CHI	Aug 28, 1991
Matt Williams	SF	Jul 17, 1990	Ryne Sandberg	CHI	Sep 2, 1991
Andres Galarraga	MON	Jul 18, 1990	Sid Bream	ATL	Sep 15, 1991
Jeff King	PIT	Jul 18, 1990	Curtis Wilkerson	PIT	Sep 19, 1991
Gary Redus	PIT	Jul 22, 1990	Daryl Boston	NY	Sep 24, 1991
Dickie Thon	PHI	Jul 23, 1990	John Kruk	PHI	Sep 25, 1991
Mackey Sasser	NY	Jul 29, 1990	Jay Bell	PIT	Sep 30, 1991
Joe Carter	SD	Aug 4, 1990	Joe Oliver	CIN	Oct 1, 1991
Ernest Riles	SF	Aug 19, 1990	Fred McGriff	SD	Apr 10, 1992
Bobby Bonilla	PIT	Aug 23, 1990	Kirk Gibson	PIT	Apr 20, 1992
Chris Gwynn	LA	Aug 29, 1990	Gary Scott	CHI	Apr 20, 1992
Darryl Strawberry	NY	Aug 30, 1990	Barry Bonds	PIT	May 16, 1992
Kal Daniels	LA	Sep 4, 1990	Felix Jose	STL	May 17, 1992
	LA	Sep 14, 1990	Bill Doran	CIN	May 19, 1992
Benito Santiago	SD	Sep 19, 1990	Todd Benzinger	LA	May 27, 1992
Dave Justice	ATL	Sep 25, 1990	Bobby Bonilla	NY	Jun 1, 1992
Tim Raines	MON	Oct 1, 1990	Eddie Murray	NY	Jun 2, 1992
Andre Dawson	CHI	Apr 19, 1991	Gary Sheffield	SD	Jun 18, 1992
Mike LaValliere	PIT	Apr 20, 1991	Glenn Braggs	CIN	Jun 26, 1992
Andre Dawson	CHI	Apr 21, 1991	Kal Daniels	CHI	Jul 5, 1992
Kal Daniels	LA	Apr 24, 1991	Eric Anthony	HOU	Jul 27, 1992
Marquis Grissom	MON	Apr 28, 1991	Darren Daulton	PHI	Jul 28, 1992
Ricky Jordan	PHI	May 8, 1991	Dave Hollins	PHI	Jul 29, 1992
Hubie Brooks	NY	May 14, 1991	Wes Chamberlain	PHI	Aug 1, 1992
Sid Bream	ATL	May 17, 1991	Terry Pendleton	ATL	Aug 8, 1992
Lenny Harris	LA	Jun 10, 1991	Lonnie Smith	ATL	Aug 14, 1992
Howard Johnson	NY	Jun 18, 1991	Gary Sheffield	SD	Aug 14, 1992
Kevin McReynolds	NY	Jun 25, 1991	Andres Galarraga	STL	Aug 15, 1992
Jeff Reed	CIN	Jun 25, 1991	Eric Anthony	HOU	Aug 31, 1992
Orlando Merced	PIT	Jul 4, 1991	Todd Benzinger	LA	Sep 4, 1992
Will Clark	SF	Jul 14, 1991	Eddie Murray	NY	Sep 4, 1992
Darren Daulton	PHI	Jul 15, 1991	Jerald Clark	SD	Sep 7, 1992
Dave Hollins	PHI	Jul 19, 1991	Ryne Sandberg	CHI	Sep 9, 1992
Gary Redus	PIT	Jul 23, 1991	Jeff King	PIT	Sep 9, 1992
Ken Caminiti	HOU	Jul 29, 1991	Ray Lankford	STL	Sep 13, 1992
Tim Teufel	SD	Aug 2, 1991	Darren Daulton	PHI	Sep 21, 1992
Dale Murphy	PHI	Aug 6, 1991	Tom Marsh	PHI	Sep 23, 1992
Fred McGriff	SD	Aug 13, 1991	Moises Alou	MON	Sep 23, 1992
	SD	Aug 14, 1991	Lloyd McClendon	PIT	Sep 26, 1992
Will Clark	SF	Aug 20, 1991	Greg Litton	SF	Oct 4, 1992

Two Grand Slams in One Game

Player	Team	Date
Tony Lazzeri	NY A	May 24, 1936
Jim Tabor	BOS A	Jul 4, 1939
Rudy York	BOS A	Jul 27, 1946
Jim Gentile	BAL A	May 9, 1961
Tony Cloninger	ATL N	Jul 3, 1966
Jim Northrup	DET A	Jun 24, 1968
Frank Robinson	BAL A	Jun 26, 1970

Most Grand Slams, Career

Player	Total
Lou Gehrig	23
Willie McCovey	18
Jimmie Foxx	17
Eddie Murray	17
Ted Williams	17
Hank Aaron	16
Dave Kingman	16
Babe Ruth	16
Gil Hodges	14
Joe DiMaggio	13
George Foster	13
Ralph Kiner	13
Ernie Banks	12
Don Baylor	12
Rogers Hornsby	12
Joe Rudi	12
Rudy York	12
Johnny Bench	11
Gary Carter	11
Hank Greenberg	11
Reggie Jackson	11
Harmon Killebrew	11
Lee May	11
Willie Stargell	11
Joe Adcock	10
Jeff Burroughs	10
Darrell Evans	10
John Milner	10
Roy Sievers	10
Al Simmons	10
Vern Stephens	10
Vic Wertz	10
Dave Winfield	10

Grand Slam In Two Consecutive Games, AL

Player	Team	Date
Babe Ruth	NY	Sep 27, 1927
	NY	Sep 29, 1927
	NY	Aug 6, 1929
	NY	Aug 7, 1929
Bill Dickey	NY	Aug 3, 1937
	NY	Aug 4, 1937
Jimmie Foxx	BOS	May 20, 1940
	BOS	May 21, 1940
Jim Busby	CLE	Jul 5, 1956
	CLE	Jul 6, 1956
Brooks Robinson	BAL	May 6, 1962
	BAL	May 9, 1962
Willie Aikens	CAL	Jun 13, 1979
	CAL	Jun 14, 1979
Greg Luzinski	CHI	Jun 8, 1984
	CHI	Jun 9, 1984
Rob Deer	MIL	Aug 19, 1987
	MIL	Aug 20, 1987

Grand Slam In Two Consecutive Games, NL

Player	Team	Date
Jimmy Bannon	BOS	Aug 6, 1894
	BOS	Aug 7, 1894
Jimmy Sheckard	BKN	Sep 23, 1901
	BKN	Sep 24, 1901
Phil Garner	PIT	Sep 14, 1978
	PIT	Sep 15, 1978
Fred McGriff	SD	Aug 13, 1991
	SD	Aug 14, 1991

Grand Slam in First Major League Game

Player	Team	Date
Bill Duggleby	PHI N	Apr 21, 1898
Bobby Bonds	SF N	Jun 25, 1968

Most Grand Slams, Season, AL

Player	Team	Year	Total
Don Mattingly	NY	1987	6
Jim Gentile	BAL	1961	5
Babe Ruth	BOS	1919	4
Lou Gehrig	NY	1934	4
Rudy York	DET	1938	4
Tommy Henrich	NY	1948	4

Most Grand Slams, Season, AL (cont.)

Player	Team	Year	Total
Al Rosen	CLE	1951	4
Ray Boone	CLE	1953	
	DET	1953	4
Jim Northrup	DET	1968	4
Tris Speaker	CLE	1923	3
Lou Gehrig	NY	1927	3
Babe Ruth	NY	1929	3
Lou Gehrig	NY	1931	3
Jimmie Foxx	PHI	1932	3
	PHI	1934	3
Joe DiMaggio	NY	1937	3
Jimmie Foxx	BOS	1938	3
Bob Johnson	PHI	1938	3
Jimmie Foxx	BOS	1940	3
Don Lenhardt	BOS	1952	
	DET	1952	3
Gus Zernial	PHI	1952	3
Ted Williams	BOS	1955	3
Vic Wertz	BOS	1960	3
Bob Allison	MIN	1961	3
Dick Stuart	BOS	1964	3
Pete Ward	CHI	1964	3
Willie Horton	DET	1969	3
Carl Yastrzemski	BOS	1969	3
Rico Petrocelli	BOS	1972	3
Jeff Burroughs	TEX	1973	3
Gene Tenace	OAK	1974	3
Rod Carew	MIN	1976	3
Reggie Jackson	BAL	1976	3
Joe Rudi	CAL	1978	3
	CAL	1979	3
Andre Thornton	CLE	1979	3
Larry Parrish	TEX	1982	3
Dave Kingman	OAK	1984	3
Kent Hrbek	MIN	1985	3
Eddie Murray	BAL	1985	3
Danny Tartabull	KC	1988	3
Alvin Davis	SEA	1990	3
Ken Griffey, Jr.	SEA	1991	3
Kirby Puckett	MIN	1992	3

Most Grand Slams, Season, NL

Player	Team	Year	Total
Ernie Banks	CHI	1955	5
Wildfire Schulte	CHI	1911	4
Vince DiMaggio	PHI	1945	4

Most Grand Slams, Season, NL (cont.)

Player	Team	Year	Total
Ralph Kiner	PIT	1949	4
Sid Gordon	BOS	1950	4
George Kelly	NY	1921	3
Jim Bottomley	STL	1925	3
Cy Williams	PHI	1926	3
Chuck Klein	PHI	1932	3
Sid Gordon	NY	1948	3
Ralph Kiner	PIT	1951	3
Wes Westrum	NY	1951	3
Del Crandall	MIL	1955	3
Gene Freese	PHI	1959	3
Hank Aaron	MIL	1962	3
Willie McCovey	SF	1967	3
Lee May	CIN	1970	3
John Milner	NY	1976	3
Keith Hernandez	STL	1977	3
Ray Knight	CIN	1980	3
Eric Davis	CIN	1987	3
Kal Daniels	LA	1990	3

Most Pinch-Hit Home Runs, Career

Player	Total
Cliff Johnson	20
Jerry Lynch	18
Gates Brown	16
Smoky Burgess	16
Willie McCovey	16
George Crowe	14
Joe Adcock	12
Bob Cerv	12
Jose Morales	12
Graig Nettles	12
Jay Johnstone	11
Fred Whitfield	11
Cy Williams	11
Jim Dwyer	10
Mike Lum	10
Wally Post	10
Champ Summers	10
Gus Zernial	10
Norm Cash	9
Bobby Hofman	9
Dale Long	9
Candy Maldonado	9
Carl Sawatski	9
Bill Skowron	9
Vic Wertz	9

Most Pinch-Hit Home Runs, Career (*cont.*)

Player	Total	Player	Total
Bob Allison	8	Joe Lefebvre	6
Brant Alyea	8	Danny Litwhiler	6
Benny Ayala	8	Ernie Lombardi	6
Ed Bailey	8	Lloyd McClendon	6
Thad Bosley	8	Sam Mele	6
Mark Carreon	8	Geno Petralli	6
Johnny Frederick	8	Merv Rettenmund	6
Oscar Gamble	8	Hank Sauer	6
Johnny Grubb	8	Art Shamsky	6
Frank Howard	8	Dick Stuart	6
Lee Lacy	8	Ron Swoboda	6
Charlie Maxwell	8	Tim Teufel	6
Johnny Mize	8	Andre Thornton	6
Bobby Murcer	8	Bob Thurman	6
Bill Nicholson	8	Denny Walling	6
Ken Phelps	8	John Wockenfuss	6
Roy Sievers	8		
Willie Stargell	8		
Rusty Staub	8		
Johnny Blanchard	7		
Mike Easler	7		
Tito Francona	7		
Clarence Gaston	7		
Jerry Hairston	7		
Jim Ray Hart	7		
Richie Hebner	7		
Reggie Jackson	7		
Harmon Killebrew	7		
Mickey Mantle	7		
Hal McRae	7		
Lefty O'Doul	7		
Rip Repulski	7		
Bob Skinner	7		
Duke Snider	7		
Earl Torgeson	7		
Claudell Washington	7		
Ted Williams	7		
Jesse Barfield	6		
Dave Bergman	6		
Randy Bush	6		
Walker Cooper	6		
Gavvy Cravath	6		
Tommy Gregg	6		
Jim Hickman	6		
Rex Hudler	6		
Rick Joseph	6		
Andy Kosco	6		
Ron Kittle	6		
Ed Kranepool	6		

Pinch-Hit Home Runs by Same Player in Consecutive At-Bats, AL

Player	Team	Date
Ray Caldwell	NY	Jun 10, 1915
	NY	Jun 11, 1915
Joe Cronin	BOS	Jun 17, 1943
	BOS	Jun 17, 1943
Charlie Keller	NY	Sep 12, 1948
	NY	Sep 14, 1948
Del Wilber	BOS	May 6, 1953
	BOS	May 10, 1953
Ted Williams	BOS	Sep 17, 1957
	BOS	Sep 20, 1957
Johnny Blanchard	NY	Jul 21, 1961
	NY	Jul 22, 1961
Chuck Schilling	BOS	Apr 30, 1965
	BOS	May 1, 1965
Ray Barker	NY	Jun 20, 1965
	NY	Jun 22, 1965
Curt Motton	BAL	May 15, 1968
	BAL	May 17, 1968
Gates Brown	DET	Aug 9, 1968
	DET	Aug 11, 1968
Gary Alexander	CLE	Jul 5, 1980
	CLE	Jul 6, 1980
Daryl Sconiers	CAL	Apr 30, 1983
	CAL	May 7, 1983
Alejandro Sanchez	DET	Jul 20, 1985
	DET	Jul 23, 1985
Randy Bush	MIN	Jun 20, 1986
	MIN	Jun 23, 1986

Pinch-Hit Home Runs by Same Player in Consecutive At-Bats, NL

Player	Team	Date	Player	Team	Date
Lee Lacy	LA	May 2, 1978	Clyde Mashore	MON	May 27, 1973
	LA	May 6, 1978		MON	May 28, 1973
	LA	May 17, 1978	Hal Breeden	MON	Jul 13, 1973
Del Unser	PHI	Jun 30, 1979		MON	Jul 13, 1973
	PHI	Jul 5, 1979	Carmen Fanzone	CHI	Jul 31, 1974
	PHI	Jul 10, 1979		CHI	Sep 10, 1974
Cy Williams	PHI	Jun 2, 1928	Jerry Martin	PHI	May 18, 1978
	PHI	Jun 6, 1928		PHI	May 26, 1978
Lefty O'Doul	PHI	Sep 9, 1930	Candy Maldonado	SF	Apr 25, 1986
	PHI	Sep 13, 1930		SF	Apr 27, 1986
Rip Repulski	PHI	Aug 22, 1958	Rick Lancellotti	SF	Sep 21, 1986
	PHI	Aug 24, 1958		SF	Sep 23, 1986
Gene Freese	PHI	Apr 18, 1959	Darrin Jackson	CHI	Aug 14, 1988
	PHI	Apr 23, 1959		CHI	Aug 16, 1988
Dale Long	CHI	Aug 13, 1959	Luis Salazar	SD	Aug 12, 1989
	CHI	Aug 14, 1959		SD	Aug 16, 1989
Jerry Lynch	CIN	Apr 23, 1961	Ernest Riles	SF	Aug 19, 1990
	CIN	Apr 26, 1961		SF	Aug 23, 1990
Ed Charles	NY	Jun 1, 1968	Jeff Grotewold	PHI	July 7, 1992
	NY	Jun 2, 1968		PHI	July 8, 1992
Jose Pagan	PIT	Aug 6, 1969	Todd Benzinger	LA	Sep 2, 1992
	PIT	Aug 12, 1969		LA	Sep 4, 1992

Pinch-Hit Grand Slams, AL

Player	Team	Date	Opp.	Opp. Pitcher
Marty Kavanagh	CLE	Sep 24, 1916	BOS	Dutch Leonard
Joe Connolly	CLE	Jun 6, 1923	BOS	George Murray
Frank Ellerbe	CLE	Sep 11, 1924	STL	Dave Danforth
Al Simmons	PHI	May 30, 1930	WAS	Garland Braxton
Dib Williams	PHI	Jul 13, 1931	WAS	Bobby Burke
Jimmie Foxx	PHI	Sep 21, 1931	DET	Tommy Bridges
Bob Johnson	PHI	May 2, 1934	BOS	Gordon Rhodes
Cliff Bolton	WAS	Sep 10, 1934	CHI	Hugo Klaerner
Rudy York	DET	May 14, 1939	STL	Lefty Mills
Taffy Wright	CHI	Jul 3, 1940	DET	Lynn Nelson
George Selkirk	NY	May 28, 1941	WAS	Sid Hudson
Al Unser	DET	May 31, 1944	NY	Monk Dubiel
Gene Moore	STL	Jun 11, 1944	CLE	Joe Heving
Zeb Eaton	DET	Jul 15, 1945	NY	Hank Borowy
Early Wynn	WAS	Sep 15, 1946	DET	Johnny Gorsica
Jack Wallaesa	CHI	May 4, 1947	PHI	Russ Christopher
Clyde Vollmer	BOS	Aug 27, 1950	CLE	Al Benton
Johnny Hopp	NY	Sep 17, 1950	STL	Al Widmar
Charlie Maxwell	BOS	Aug 2, 1951	STL	Satchel Paige
Steve Souchock	DET	Jul 26, 1952	NY	Bobby Hogue
Don Kolloway	DET	Sep 3, 1952	CLE	Lou Brissie

Pinch-Hit Grand Slams, AL *(cont.)*

Player	Team	Date	Opp.	Opp. Pitcher
Johnny Mize	NY	Sep 7, 1952	WAS	Walt Masterson
Dick Kryhoski	STL	Apr 25, 1953	CHI	Harry Dorish
Tommy Byrne	CHI	May 16, 1953	NY	Ewell Blackwell
Yogi Berra	NY	Jun 7, 1953	STL	Satchel Paige
Mickey Mantle	NY	Jul 6, 1953	PHI	Frank Fanovich
Gus Zernial	PHI	Aug 9, 1953	DET	Ray Herbert
Bill Skowron	NY	Aug 17, 1954	PHI	Al Sima
Hank Bauer	NY	Jul 12, 1956	CLE	Don Mossi
Walt Dropo	CHI	May 2, 1957	WAS	Chuck Stobbs
Bill Skowron	NY	Jul 14, 1957	CHI	Jim Wilson
Vic Wertz	BOS	Aug 14, 1959	NY	Ryne Duren
Rip Repulski	BOS	May 10, 1960	CHI	Don Ferrarese
Vic Wertz	BOS	Aug 25, 1960	CLE	Don Newcombe
Marv Throneberry	KC	Sep 24, 1960	DET	Bob Bruce
Bob Cerv	NY	May 28, 1961	CHI	Early Wynn
Roy Sievers	CHI	Jun 21, 1961	CLE	Johnny Antonelli
Julio Becquer	MIN	Jul 4, 1961	CHI	Warren Hacker
Jim Gentile	BAL	Jul 7, 1961	KC	Ed Rakow
Sherm Lollar	CHI	Jul 9, 1961	CLE	Frank Funk
Johnny Blanchard	NY	Jul 21, 1961	BOS	Mike Fornieles
Gene Green	WAS	Aug 12, 1961	NY	Luis Arroyo
Yogi Berra	NY	Jun 23, 1962	DET	Phil Regan
George Alusik	KC	Jul 17, 1963	BOS	Hal Kolstad
Fred Whitfield	CLE	May 16, 1965	WAS	Steve Ridzik
Bob Chance	WAS	Apr 17, 1966	DET	Julio Navarro
Rich Reese	MIN	Aug 3, 1969	BAL	Dave McNally
	MIN	Jun 7, 1970	WAS	Dick Bosman
Rick Renick	MIN	Jun 30, 1970	KC	Bob Johnson
Reggie Jackson	OAK	Sep 5, 1970	KC	Tom Burgmeier
Bobby Murcer	NY	Jul 25, 1971	MIL	Lew Krausse
Don Mincher	WAS	Aug 31, 1971	NY	Roger Hambright
Harmon Killebrew	MIN	Sep 3, 1971	OAK	Mudcat Grant
Rich Reese	MIN	Jul 9, 1972	NY	Lindy McDaniel
Buddy Bradford	CHI	Oct 2, 1972	MIN	Dave LaRoche
Danny Walton	MIN	Apr 17, 1973	CAL	Steve Barber
Kurt Bevacqua	KC	Jul 9, 1973	MIL	Jerry Bell
Joe Lahoud	MIL	Aug 22, 1973	CAL	Aurelio Monteagudo
Darrell Porter	MIL	Sep 9, 1974	BAL	Bob Reynolds
Tony Oliva	MIN	Jun 29, 1975	TEX	Mike Bacsik
Leroy Stanton	CAL	Jul 25, 1976	TEX	Steve Foucault
Rod Carew	MIN	Sep 9, 1976	TEX	Steve Hargan
Don Money	MIL	Jul 3, 1977	SEA	Bill Laxton
Merv Rettenmund	CAL	May 3, 1978	CLE	Dennis Kinney
Joe Rudi	CAL	Jun 27, 1978	KC	Steve Mingori
Mike Cubbage	MIN	Aug 8, 1978	SEA	Mike Parrott
Jay Johnstone	NY	Apr 14, 1979	CHI	Lerrin LaGrow
Pat Kelly	BAL	Jul 23, 1979	OAK	Dave Heaverlo

Pinch-Hit Grand Slams, AL (cont.)

Player	Team	Date	Opp.	Opp. Pitcher
Wayne Gross	OAK	Sep 14, 1979	CHI	Ed Farmer
Pat Kelly	BAL	Sep 10, 1980	DET	Dave Rozema
George Brett	KC	Sep 28, 1980	MIN	Pete Redfern
Bobby Murcer	NY	Apr 9, 1981	TEX	Steve Comer
Jesse Barfield	TOR	Apr 24, 1982	BOS	Tom Burgmeier
Jeff Burroughs	OAK	May 18, 1982	DET	Elias Sosa
Benny Ayala	BAL	May 29, 1982	TOR	Jerry Garvin
Dan Ford	BAL	Jun 14, 1982	MIL	Jamie Easterly
Terry Crowley	BAL	Aug 8, 1982	KC	Mike Armstrong
John Wockenfuss	DET	Jul 3, 1983	BAL	Dan Morogiello
John Lowenstein	BAL	Sep 10, 1983	NY	Goose Gossage
Alan Bannister	CLE	Sep 21, 1983	MIL	Rick Waits
Ken Singleton	BAL	Sep 1, 1984	SEA	Ed Vande Berg
Jerry Narron	CAL	May 15, 1985	TOR	Bill Caudill
Don Baylor	NY	Jul 11, 1985	TEX	Chris Welsh
Joe DeSa	CHI	Sep 13, 1985	SEA	Dave Tobik
Johnny Grubb	DET	Jul 23, 1986	MIN	Frank Pastore
Rich Gedman	BOS	Aug 10, 1986	DET	Guillermo Hernandez
Larry Herndon	DET	Aug 16, 1986	BOS	Joe Sambito
Mike Stanley	TEX	Jun 27, 1987	MIN	Jeff Reardon
Casey Parsons	CLE	Aug 6, 1987	TOR	Mark Eichhorn
Mark Ryal	CAL	Sep 10, 1987	TEX	Dale Mohorcic
Pat Sheridan	DET	May 6, 1988	SEA	Mike Jackson
Jose Cruz	NY	Jul 16, 1988	CHI	Melido Perez
Jim Dwyer	MIN	Sep 15, 1988	CHI	Donn Pall
Pete O'Brien	TEX	Sep 18, 1988	CAL	Bryan Harvey
Fred Lynn	DET	Sep 25, 1988	BAL	Tom Niedenfuer
Carmen Castillo	MIN	Apr 11, 1989	DET	Guillermo Hernandez
Phil Bradley	BAL	Jul 13, 1990	MIN	John Candelaria
Sam Horn	BAL	Sep 14, 1990	TOR	Duane Ward
Joe Orsulak	BAL	Jun 16, 1991	TOR	Duane Ward
Dwight Evans	BAL	Jul 26, 1991	OAK	Gene Nelson
Mickey Tettleton	DET	Aug 11, 1991	NY	Lee Guetterman

Pinch-Hit Grand Slams, NL

Player	Team	Date	Opp.	Opp. Pitcher
Mike O'Neill	STL	Jun 3, 1902	BOS	Togie Pittinger
Pat Moran	BOS	Aug 12, 1903	CHI	Jocko Menefee
Beals Becker	NY	Sep 30, 1910	BOS	Cliff Curtis
Cy Williams	PHI	Apr 15, 1926	BOS	Larry Benton
Chick Tolson	CHI	May 1, 1927	PIT	Ray Kremer
Wattie Holm	STL	Jun 2, 1928	PHI	Les Sweetland
Jack Cummings	NY	Jul 13, 1928	STL	Bill Sherdel
Les Bell	BOS	May 26, 1929	NY	Carl Hubbell
Pat Crawford	NY	May 26, 1929	BOS	Socks Seibold
Ethan Allen	NY	Jun 30, 1931	CHI	Pat Malone

Pinch-Hit Grand Slams, NL (cont.)

Player	Team	Date	Opp.	Opp. Pitcher
Rogers Hornsby	CHI	Sep 13, 1931	BOS	Bruce Cunningham
Hack Wilson	BKN	May 14, 1933	PHI	Ad Liska
Harvey Hendrick	CHI	Jul 23, 1933	PHI	Phil Collins
Wally Berger	BOS	Oct 1, 1933	PHI	Reggie Grabowski
Lefty O'Doul	NY	Jun 17, 1934	PIT	Heinie Meine
Joe Moore	NY	Jul 5, 1934	BKN	Ray Benge
Ernie Lombardi	CIN	Jul 31, 1934	PIT	Ralph Birkofer
Sammy Byrd	CIN	May 23, 1936	PIT	Cy Blanton
Ripper Collins	STL	Sep 19, 1936	CHI	Curt Davis
Jimmy Ripple	NY	Apr 30, 1937	BKN	Max Butcher
Harl Maggert	BOS	Apr 30, 1938	PHI	Claude Passeau
Don Padgett	STL	Jul 27, 1939	NY	Manny Salvo
Ken O'Dea	NY	Aug 4, 1941	BKN	Hugh Casey
Bob Scheffing	CHI	Sep 20, 1941	STL	Howie Krist
Dom Dallessandro	CHI	Jun 21, 1942	NY	Bill McGee
Schoolboy Rowe	PHI	May 2, 1943	BOS	Al Javery
Jim Russell	PIT	Aug 20, 1944	BKN	Art Herring
Jimmie Foxx	PHI	May 18, 1945	STL	Ken Burkhart
Vince DiMaggio	PHI	Jun 2, 1945	PIT	Al Gerheauser
Butch Nieman	BOS	Jul 6, 1945	PIT	Xavier Rescigno
Frank Secory	CHI	Jun 6, 1946	NY	Dave Koslo
Ron Northey	STL	Sep 3, 1947	CHI	Doyle Lade
Cliff Aberson	CHI	Sep 9, 1947	BKN	Vic Lombardi
Ron Northey	STL	May 30, 1948	PIT	Elmer Singleton
Ralph Kiner	PIT	Sep 11, 1948	CHI	Hank Borowy
Pete Milne	NY	Apr 27, 1949	BKN	Pat McGlothin
Sibby Sisti	BOS	Jun 30, 1950	NY	Dave Koslo
Jack Phillips	PIT	Jul 8, 1950	STL	Harry Brecheen
Ron Northey	CHI	Sep 18, 1950	BKN	Dan Bankhead
Phil Cavarretta	CHI	Jul 29, 1951	PHI	Robin Roberts
Andy Seminick	CIN	Jul 20, 1952	PHI	Curt Simmons
Bobby Hofman	NY	Jun 25, 1953	STL	Hal White
Bill Serena	CHI	Aug 14, 1953	MIL	Dave Jolly
Whitey Lockman	NY	Sep 11, 1954	CIN	Howie Judson
Joe Cunningham	STL	Jul 30, 1957	NY	Ruben Gomez
Pete Whisenant	CIN	Aug 27, 1958	LA	Fred Kipp
Gene Freese	PHI	Apr 18, 1959	CIN	Mike Cuellar
Earl Averill	CHI	May 12, 1959	MIL	Lew Burdette
Leon Wagner	SF	May 26, 1959	LA	Art Fowler
Gene Freese	PHI	Jul 2, 1959	CIN	Jim Brosnan
George Crowe	STL	Aug 13, 1959	LA	Roger Craig
Willie McCovey	SF	Jun 12, 1960	MIL	Carl Willey
Ed Bailey	SF	Jun 26, 1962	CIN	Joey Jay
Carl Sawatski	STL	Sep 9, 1962	CIN	Jim Brosnan
Ed Bailey	SF	Apr 10, 1963	HOU	Don McMahon
Roy Sievers	PHI	May 26, 1963	CIN	Bill Henry
Gordy Coleman	CIN	Sep 11, 1963	MIL	Ron Piche

Pinch-Hit Grand Slams, NL (cont.)

Player	Team	Date	Opp.	Opp. Pitcher
Willie McCovey	SF	Sep 10, 1965	CHI	Ted Abernathy
Jim Davenport	SF	Jul 8, 1966	CIN	Ted Davidson
Hawk Taylor	NY	Aug 17, 1966	PIT	Bob Veale
Don Pavletich	CIN	Jun 11, 1967	PIT	Roy Face
Jack Hiatt	SF	Jul 31, 1967	HOU	Dan Schneider
Rick Joseph	PHI	Sep 16, 1967	LA	Ron Perranoski
Al Ferrara	SD	May 2, 1969	CIN	George Culver
Jerry May	PIT	Jun 8, 1969	ATL	Paul Doyle
Vic Davalillo	STL	Jul 2, 1969	NY	Ron Taylor
Bob Bailey	MON	May 18, 1970	NY	Cal Koonce
Jim Hutto	PHI	Jul 17, 1970	LA	Jim Brewer
Tom Haller	LA	Jul 22, 1970	MON	Claude Raymond
Carl Taylor	STL	Aug 11, 1970	SD	Ron Herbel
Hal McRae	CIN	Jun 1, 1972	HOU	Jerry Reuss
Clarence Gaston	SD	Jun 14, 1972	CHI	Ferguson Jenkins
Luis Melendez	STL	Jun 24, 1972	NY	Ray Sadecki
Willie Stargell	PIT	Jul 7, 1973	STL	Diego Segui
Hal King	CIN	Jul 9, 1973	MON	Pat Jarvis
Ed Goodson	SF	Aug 1, 1973	SD	Clay Kirby
Milt May	HOU	May 22, 1974	SD	Vicente Romo
Dave Parker	PIT	Sep 8, 1974	MON	Tom Walker
Bill Madlock	CHI	Sep 28, 1974	LA	Don Sutton
Ken McMullen	LA	Apr 24, 1975	SD	Dave Tomlin
Willie McCovey	SD	May 30, 1975	NY	Bob Apodaca
Cliff Johnson	HOU	Jun 15, 1975	STL	Mike Garman
Ted Simmons	STL	Jun 23, 1975	NY	Jon Matlack
Champ Summers	CHI	Aug 23, 1975	HOU	Jim York
Pete LaCock	CHI	Sep 3, 1975	STL	Bob Gibson
Tim Hosley	CHI	Sep 14, 1975	PHI	Randy Lerch
Randy Elliott	SF	May 13, 1977	CIN	Fred Norman
Biff Pocoroba	ATL	May 17, 1977	MON	Bill Atkinson
Steve Henderson	NY	Apr 9, 1978	MON	Darold Knowles
Davey Johnson	PHI	Apr 30, 1978	SD	Bob Shirley
Mike Ivie	SF	May 28, 1978	LA	Don Sutton
Davey Johnson	PHI	Jun 3, 1978	LA	Terry Forster
Dave Rader	CHI	Jun 26, 1978	NY	Dale Murray
Jack Clark	SF	Jun 27, 1978	SD	Dennis Kinney
Mike Ivie	SF	Jun 30, 1978	ATL	Dave Campbell
Bake McBride	PHI	Jul 8, 1978	MON	Rudy May
Wayne Garrett	STL	Aug 31, 1978	CIN	Doug Bair
Roger Freed	STL	May 1, 1979	HOU	Joe Sambito
Mike Vail	CHI	Jun 30, 1979	NY	Dale Murray
John Milner	PIT	Aug 5, 1979	PHI	Tug McGraw
Bill Robinson	PHI	Aug 14, 1982	MON	Ray Burris
John Milner	PIT	Aug 15, 1982	STL	Steve Mura
Kurt Bevacqua	SD	Jul 14, 1983	PIT	Rod Scurry
Ozzie Virgil	PHI	Sep 2, 1983	SF	Gary Lavelle

Pinch-Hit Grand Slams, NL (cont.)

Player	Team	Date	Opp.	Opp. Pitcher
Mike Easler	PIT	Sep 3, 1983	ATL	Steve Bedrosian
Richie Hebner	PIT	Sep 15, 1983	CHI	Lee Smith
Champ Summers	SD	Apr 10, 1984	STL	Bob Forsch
Steve Yeager	LA	Jun 21, 1984	CIN	Bob Owchinko
Chili Davis	SF	Jun 27, 1984	CIN	Charlie Puleo
Brian Dayett	CHI	May 22, 1985	CIN	Tom Browning
Tony Perez	CIN	May 13, 1985	PHI	Dave Rucker
Cesar Cedeno	STL	Sep 6, 1985	ATL	Gene Garber
Hubie Brooks	MON	Sep 19, 1985	PIT	Lee Tunnell
Wayne Krenchicki	CIN	Oct 4, 1985	LA	Alejandro Pena
Craig Reynolds	HOU	Apr 12, 1986	ATL	Rick Mahler
Ted Simmons	ATL	Jun 3, 1986	PIT	Cecilio Guante
Tim Teufel	NY	Jun 10, 1986	PHI	Tom Hume
Dave Parker	CIN	Jul 24, 1986	MON	Bob McClure
Graig Nettles	ATL	May 2, 1987	HOU	Aurelio Lopez
Jim Sundberg	CHI	Jul 8, 1987	SD	Lance McCullers
Candy Maldonado	SF	Sep 27, 1987	ATL	Chuck Cary
Kevin Bass	HOU	Apr 10, 1988	CIN	Pat Perry
Mike Fitzgerald	MON	Jul 26, 1988	CHI	Jeff Pico
Dwight Smith	CHI	Jul 31, 1989	PHI	Greg Harris
Ernest Riles	SF	Aug 19, 1990	NY	Dwight Gooden
Andre Dawson	CHI	Apr 19, 1991	PIT	Stan Belinda
Curtis Wilkerson	PIT	Sep 19, 1991	STL	Lee Smith
Todd Benzinger	LA	Sep 4, 1992	PIT	Bob Patterson
Greg Litton	SF	Oct 4, 1992	CIN	Scott Ruskin

Pinch-Hit Grand Slams in Both Leagues

Player	Team	Date	Opp.	Opp. Pitcher
Jimmie Foxx	PHI A	Sep 21, 1931	DET	Tommy Bridges
	PHI N	May 13, 1945	STL	Ken Burkhart
Roy Sievers	CHI A	Jun 21, 1961	CLE	Johnny Antonelli
	PHI N	May 26, 1963	CIN	Bill Henry
Kurt Bevacqua	KC A	Jul 3, 1973	MIL	Jerry Bell
	SD N	Jul 14, 1983	PIT	Rod Scurry

Most Pinch-Hit Grand Slams, Career

Player	Team	Date	Total	Opp.	Opp. Pitcher
Ron Northey	STL N	Sep 3, 1947		CHI	Doyle Lade
	STL N	May 30, 1948		PIT	Elmer Singleton
	CHI N	Sep 18, 1950	3	BKN	Dan Bankhead
Willie McCovey	SF N	Jun 12, 1960		MIL	Carl Willey
	SF N	Sep 10, 1965		CHI	Ted Abernathy
	SD N	May 30, 1975	3	NY	Bob Apodaca
Rich Reese	MIN A	Aug 3, 1969		BAL	Dave McNally
	MIN A	Jun 7, 1970		WAS	Dick Bosman
	MIN A	Jul 2, 1972	3	NY	Lindy McDaniel

Most Pinch-Hit Grand Slams, Career (*cont.*)

Player	Team	Date	Total	Opp.	Opp. Pitcher
Yogi Berra	NY A	Jun 7, 1953		STL	Satchel Paige
	NY A	Jun 23, 1962	2	DET	Phil Regan
Bill Skowron	NY A	Aug 17, 1954		PHI	Al Sima
	NY A	Jul 14, 1957	2	CHI	Jim Wilson
Gene Freese	PHI N	Apr 18, 1959		CIN	Mike Cuellar
	PHI N	Jul 2, 1959	2	CIN	Jim Brosnan
Vic Wertz	BOS A	Aug 14, 1959		NY	Ryne Duren
	BOS A	Aug 26, 1960	2	CLE	Don Newcombe
Ed Bailey	SF N	Jun 26, 1962		CIN	Joey Jay
	SF N	Apr 10, 1963	2	HOU	Don McMahon
Reggie Jackson	OAK A	Sep 5, 1970		KC	Tom Burgmeier
	BAL A	Aug 11, 1976	2	CHI	Terry Forster
Bobby Murcer	NY A	Jul 25, 1971		MIL	Lew Krausse
	NY A	Apr 9, 1981	2	TEX	Steve Comer
Kurt Bevacqua	KC A	Jul 9, 1973		MIL	Jerry Bell
	SD N	Jul 14, 1983	2	PIT	Rod Scurry
Dave Parker	PIT N	Sep 9, 1974		MON	Tom Walker
	CIN N	Jul 24, 1986	2	MON	Bob McClure
Ted Simmons	STL N	Jun 23, 1975		NY	Jon Matlack
	ATL N	Jun 3, 1986	2	PIT	Cecilio Guante
Champ Summers	CHI N	Aug 23, 1975		HOU	Jim York
	SD N	Apr 10, 1984	2	STL	Bob Forsch
Terry Crowley	BAL A	Sep 9, 1977		CLE	Larry Andersen
	BAL A	Aug 8, 1982	2	KC	Mike Armstrong
Davey Johnson	PHI N	Apr 30, 1978		SD	Bob Shirley
	PHI N	Jun 3, 1978	2	LA	Terry Forster
Mike Ivie	SF N	May 28, 1978		LA	Don Sutton
	SF N	Jun 30, 1978	2	ATL	Dave Campbell
Pat Kelly	BAL A	Jul 23, 1979		OAK	Dave Heaverlo
	BAL A	Sep 10, 1980	2	DET	Dave Rozema
John Milner	PIT N	Aug 5, 1979		PHI	Tug McGraw
	PIT N	Aug 15, 1982	2	STL	Steve Mura

Pinch-Hit Home Run in First At-Bat in Majors, AL

Player	Team	Date	Inn.
Ace Parker	PHI	Apr 30, 1937	9
John Kennedy	WAS	Sep 5, 1962	6
Gates Brown	DET	Jun 19, 1963	5
Bill Roman	DET	Sep 30, 1964	7
Brant Alyea	WAS	Sep 12, 1965	6
Joe Keough	OAK	Aug 7, 1968	8
Al Woods	TOR	Apr 7, 1977	5

Pinch-Hit Home Run in First At-Bat in Majors, NL

Player	Team	Date	Inn.
Eddie Morgan	STL	Apr 14, 1936	7
Les Layton	NY	May 21, 1948	9

Pinch-Hit Home Run in First At-Bat in Majors, NL (cont.)

Player	Team	Date	Inn.
Ted Tappe	CIN	Sep 14, 1950	8
Chuck Tanner	MIL	Apr 12, 1955	8

Most Home Runs, Season, AL

Player	Team	Year	HR
Roger Maris	NY	1961	61
Babe Ruth	NY	1927	60
	NY	1921	59
Jimmie Foxx	PHI	1932	58
Hank Greenberg	DET	1938	58
Babe Ruth	NY	1920	54
	NY	1928	54
Mickey Mantle	NY	1961	54
	NY	1956	52
Cecil Fielder	DET	1990	51
Jimmie Foxx	BOS	1938	50
Babe Ruth	NY	1930	49
Lou Gehrig	NY	1934	49
	NY	1936	49
Harmon Killebrew	MIN	1964	49
Frank Robinson	BAL	1966	49
Harmon Killebrew	MIN	1969	49
Mark McGwire	OAK	1987	49
Jimmie Foxx	PHI	1933	48
Harmon Killebrew	MIN	1962	48
Frank Howard	WAS	1969	48
Babe Ruth	NY	1926	47
Lou Gehrig	NY	1927	47
Reggie Jackson	OAK	1969	47
George Bell	TOR	1987	47
Babe Ruth	NY	1924	46
	NY	1929	46
Lou Gehrig	NY	1931	46
Babe Ruth	NY	1931	46
Joe DiMaggio	NY	1937	46
Jim Gentile	BAL	1961	46
Harmon Killebrew	MIN	1961	46
Jim Rice	BOS	1978	46
Rocky Colavito	DET	1961	45
Harmon Killebrew	MIN	1963	45
Gorman Thomas	MIL	1979	45
Jimmie Foxx	PHI	1934	44
Hank Greenberg	DET	1946	44
Harmon Killebrew	MIN	1967	44
Carl Yastrzemski	BOS	1967	44
Frank Howard	WAS	1968	44

Most Home Runs, Season, AL (*cont.*)

Player	Team	Year	HR
Frank Howard	WAS	1970	44
Jose Canseco	OAK	1991	44
Cecil Fielder	DET	1991	44
Ted Williams	BOS	1949	43
Al Rosen	CLE	1953	43
Tony Armas	BOS	1983	43
Juan Gonzalez	TEX	1992	43
Hal Trosky	CLE	1936	42
Gus Zernial	PHI	1953	42
Roy Sievers	WAS	1957	42
Mickey Mantle	NY	1958	42
Rocky Colavito	CLE	1959	42
Harmon Killebrew	WAS	1959	42
Dick Stuart	BOS	1963	42
Jose Canseco	OAK	1988	42
Mark McGwire	OAK	1992	42
Babe Ruth	NY	1923	41
Lou Gehrig	NY	1930	41
Babe Ruth	NY	1932	41
Jimmie Foxx	BOS	1936	41
Hank Greenberg	DET	1940	41
Rocky Colavito	CLE	1958	41
Norm Cash	DET	1961	41
Harmon Killebrew	MIN	1970	41
Reggie Jackson	NY	1980	41
Ben Oglivie	MIL	1980	41
Hank Greenberg	DET	1937	40
Mickey Mantle	NY	1960	40
Rico Petrocelli	BOS	1969	40
Carl Yastrzemski	BOS	1969	40
	BOS	1970	40
Darrell Evans	DET	1985	40
Jesse Barfield	TOR	1986	40
Ken Williams	STL	1922	39
Joe DiMaggio	NY	1948	39
Vern Stephens	BOS	1949	39
Roy Sievers	WAS	1958	39
Roger Maris	NY	1960	39
Norm Cash	DET	1962	39
Boog Powell	BAL	1964	39
Harmon Killebrew	MIN	1966	39
Jim Rice	BOS	1977	39
	BOS	1979	39
Fred Lynn	BOS	1979	39
Reggie Jackson	CAL	1982	39
Gorman Thomas	MIL	1982	39
Jim Rice	BOS	1983	39

Most Home Runs, Season, AL (*cont.*)

Player	Team	Year	HR
Mark McGwire	OAK	1990	39
Ted Williams	BOS	1946	38
Ted Williams	BOS	1957	38
Bob Cerv	KC	1958	38
Jim Lemon	WAS	1960	38
Gorman Thomas	MIL	1980	38
Tilly Walker	PHI	1922	37
Jimmie Foxx	PHI	1930	37
Goose Goslin	WAS	1930	37
	STL	1930	37
Lou Gehrig	NY	1937	37
Ted Williams	BOS	1941	37
Al Rosen	CLE	1950	37
Mickey Mantle	NY	1955	37
Rocky Colavito	DET	1962	37
Leon Wagner	LA	1962	37
Boog Powell	BAL	1969	37
Dick Allen	CHI	1972	37
Bobby Bonds	CAL	1977	37
Graig Nettles	NY	1977	37
Dave Winfield	NY	1982	37
Carlton Fisk	CHI	1985	37
Jose Canseco	OAK	1990	37
Al Simmons	PHI	1930	36
Jimmie Foxx	PHI	1935	36
Hank Greenberg	DET	1935	36
Jimmie Foxx	BOS	1937	36
	BOS	1940	36
Ted Williams	BOS	1942	36
Frank Howard	WAS	1967	36
Willie Horton	DET	1968	36
Tony Conigliaro	BOS	1970	36
Reggie Jackson	OAK	1975	36
George Scott	MIL	1975	36
Don Baylor	CAL	1979	36
Tony Armas	BOS	1983	36
Steve Balboni	KC	1985	36
Fred McGriff	TOR	1989	36
Babe Ruth	NY	1922	35
Lou Gehrig	NY	1929	35
Al Simmons	PHI	1932	35
Hal Trosky	CLE	1934	35
Rudy York	DET	1937	35
Jimmie Foxx	BOS	1939	35
Jackie Jensen	BOS	1958	35
Rocky Colavito	DET	1960	35
Bob Allison	MIN	1963	35

Most Home Runs, Season, AL (cont.)

Player	Team	Year	HR
Mickey Mantle	NY	1964	35
Ken Harrelson	BOS	1968	35
Boog Powell	BAL	1970	35
Ken Singleton	BAL	1979	35
Tony Armas	OAK	1980	35
Ron Kittle	CHI	1983	35
Dave Kingman	OAK	1984	35
Don Mattingly	NY	1985	35
Dave Kingman	OAK	1986	35
Joe Carter	CLE	1989	35
Fred McGriff	TOR	1990	35
Cecil Fielder	DET	1992	35

Most Home Runs, Season, NL

Player	Team	Year	HR
Hack Wilson	CHI	1930	56
Ralph Kiner	PIT	1949	54
Willie Mays	SF	1965	52
George Foster	CIN	1977	52
Ralph Kiner	PIT	1947	51
Johnny Mize	NY	1947	51
Willie Mays	NY	1955	51
Ted Kluszewski	CIN	1954	49
Willie Mays	SF	1962	49
Andre Dawson	CHI	1987	49
Willie Stargell	PIT	1971	48
Dave Kingman	CHI	1979	48
Mike Schmidt	PHI	1980	48
Ralph Kiner	PIT	1950	47
Eddie Mathews	MIL	1953	47
Ted Kluszewski	CIN	1955	47
Ernie Banks	CHI	1958	47
Willie Mays	SF	1964	47
Hank Aaron	ATL	1971	47
Kevin Mitchell	SF	1989	47
Eddie Mathews	MIL	1959	46
Orlando Cepeda	SF	1961	46
Ernie Banks	CHI	1959	45
Hank Aaron	MIL	1962	45
Willie McCovey	SF	1969	45
Johnny Bench	CIN	1970	45
Mike Schmidt	PHI	1979	45
Ernie Banks	CHI	1955	44
Hank Aaron	MIL	1957	44
	MIL	1963	44
Willie McCovey	SF	1963	44

Most Home Runs, Season, NL *(cont.)*

Player	Team	Year	HR
Hank Aaron	ATL	1966	44
	ATL	1969	44
Willie Stargell	PIT	1973	44
Dale Murphy	ATL	1987	44
Chuck Klein	PHI	1929	43
Johnny Mize	STL	1940	43
Duke Snider	BKN	1956	43
Ernie Banks	CHI	1957	43
Davey Johnson	ATL	1973	43
Rogers Hornsby	STL	1922	42
Mel Ott	NY	1929	42
Ralph Kiner	PIT	1951	42
Duke Snider	BKN	1953	42
Gil Hodges	BKN	1954	42
Duke Snider	BKN	1955	42
Billy Williams	CHI	1970	42
Cy Williams	PHI	1923	41
Roy Campanella	BKN	1953	41
Willie Mays	NY	1954	41
Hank Sauer	CHI	1954	41
Eddie Mathews	MIL	1955	41
Ernie Banks	CHI	1960	41
Darrell Evans	ATL	1973	41
Jeff Burroughs	ATL	1977	41
Chuck Klein	PHI	1930	40
Ralph Kiner	PIT	1948	40
Johnny Mize	NY	1948	40
Gil Hodges	BKN	1951	40
Ted Kluszewski	CIN	1953	40
Eddie Mathews	MIL	1954	40
Duke Snider	BKN	1954	40
Wally Post	CIN	1955	40
Duke Snider	BKN	1957	40
Hank Aaron	MIL	1960	40
Willie Mays	SF	1961	40
Dick Allen	PHI	1966	40
Tony Perez	CIN	1970	40
Johnny Bench	CIN	1972	40
Hank Aaron	ATL	1973	40
George Foster	CIN	1978	40
Mike Schmidt	PHI	1983	40
Ryne Sandberg	CHI	1990	40
Rogers Hornsby	STL	1925	39
Hack Wilson	CHI	1929	39
Stan Musial	STL	1948	39
Hank Aaron	MIL	1959	39
Eddie Mathews	MIL	1960	39

Most Home Runs, Season, NL (*cont.*)

Player	Team	Year	HR
Frank Robinson	CIN	1962	39
Willie McCovey	SF	1965	39
Hank Aaron	ATL	1967	39
Willie McCovey	SF	1970	39
Lee May	CIN	1971	39
Bobby Bonds	SF	1973	39
Greg Luzinski	PHI	1977	39
Darryl Strawberry	NY	1987	39
	NY	1988	39
Wally Berger	BOS	1930	38
Chuck Klein	PHI	1932	38
Mel Ott	NY	1932	38
Joe Adcock	MIL	1956	38
Willie Mays	SF	1963	38
Lee May	CIN	1969	38
Hank Aaron	ATL	1970	38
Nate Colbert	SD	1970	38
	SD	1972	38
Mike Schmidt	PHI	1975	38
	PHI	1976	38
	PHI	1977	38
Howard Johnson	NY	1991	38
Gabby Hartnett	CHI	1930	37
Ralph Kiner	PIT	1952	37
Hank Sauer	CHI	1952	37
Eddie Mathews	MIL	1956	37
Frank Robinson	CIN	1961	37
Ernie Banks	CHI	1962	37
Willie Mays	SF	1966	37
Jimmy Wynn	HOU	1967	37
Tony Perez	CIN	1969	37
Billy Williams	CHI	1972	37
Dave Kingman	NY	1976	37
	NY	1982	37
Dale Murphy	ATL	1985	37
Mike Schmidt	PHI	1986	37
Eric Davis	CIN	1987	37
Darryl Strawberry	NY	1990	37
Mel Ott	NY	1938	36
Willard Marshall	NY	1947	36
Stan Musial	STL	1949	36
Andy Pafko	CHI	1950	36
Willie Mays	NY	1956	36
Wally Post	CIN	1956	36
Frank Robinson	CIN	1959	36
Willie McCovey	SF	1966	36
Joe Torre	ATL	1966	36

Most Home Runs, Season, NL (*cont.*)

Player	Team	Year	HR
Willie McCovey	SF	1968	36
Mike Schmidt	PHI	1974	36
Dave Kingman	NY	1975	36
Dale Murphy	ATL	1982	36
	ATL	1983	36
	ATL	1984	36
Mike Schmidt	PHI	1984	36
Howard Johnson	NY	1987	36
	NY	1989	36
Babe Herman	BKN	1930	35
Ripper Collins	STL	1934	35
Mel Ott	NY	1934	35
Walker Cooper	NY	1947	35
Hank Sauer	CIN	1948	35
Ralph Kiner	PIT/CHI	1953	35
Stan Musial	STL	1954	35
Ted Kluszewski	CIN	1956	35
Willie Mays	NY	1957	35
Frank Thomas	PIT	1958	35
Joe Adcock	MIL	1961	35
Dick Stuart	PIT	1961	35
Orlando Cepeda	SF	1962	35
Greg Luzinski	PHI	1978	35
Bob Horner	ATL	1980	35
Mike Schmidt	PHI	1982	35
	PHI	1987	35
Jack Clark	STL	1987	35
Will Clark	SF	1987	35
Kevin Mitchell	SF	1990	35
Fred McGriff	SD	1992	35

Most Home Runs, Career

Player	HR	Best	Year	50+	40+	30+	Led Lg
Hank Aaron	755	47	1971		8	15	4
Babe Ruth	714	60	1927	4	11	13	12
Willie Mays	660	52	1965	2	6	11	4
Frank Robinson	586	49	1966		1	11	1
Harmon Killebrew	573	49	1964, 69		8	10	6
Reggie Jackson	563	47	1969		2	7	4
Mike Schmidt	548	48	1980		3	13	8
Mickey Mantle	536	54	1961	2	4	9	4
Jimmie Foxx	534	58	1932	2	5	12	4
Ted Williams	521	43	1949		1	8	4
Willie McCovey	521	45	1969		2	7	3
Ernie Banks	512	47	1958		5	7	2
Eddie Mathews	512	47	1953		4	10	2

Most Home Runs, Career (*cont.*)

Player	HR	Best	Year	50+	40+	30+	Led Lg
Mel Ott	511	42	1929		1	8	6
Lou Gehrig	493	49	1934, 36		5	10	3
Stan Musial	475	39	1948			6	
Willie Stargell	475	48	1971		2	6	2
Carl Yastrzemski	452	44	1967		3	3	1
Dave Kingman	442	48	1979		1	7	2
Dave Winfield	432	37	1982			3	
Billy Williams	426	42	1970		1	5	
Darrell Evans	414	41	1973		2	4	1
Eddie Murray	414	33	1983			5	1
Duke Snider	407	43	1956		5	6	1
Andre Dawson	399	49	1987		1	2	1
Al Kaline	399	29	1962, 66				
Dale Murphy	398	44	1987		1	6	2
Graig Nettles	390	37	1977			2	1
Johnny Bench	389	45	1970		2	4	2
Dwight Evans	385	34	1987			3	1
Frank Howard	382	48	1969		3	5	2
Jim Rice	382	46	1978		1	4	3
Orlando Cepeda	379	46	1961		1	5	1
Tony Perez	379	40	1970		1	2	
Norm Cash	377	41	1961		1	5	
Carlton Fisk	375	37	1985			1	
Rocky Colavito	374	45	1961		3	7	1
Gil Hodges	370	42	1954		2	6	
Ralph Kiner	369	54	1949	2	5	7	7
Joe DiMaggio	361	46	1937		1	7	2
Johnny Mize	359	51	1947	1	3	3	4
Yogi Berra	358	30	1952, 56			2	
Lee May	354	39	1971			3	
Dick Allen	351	40	1966		1	6	2
George Foster	348	52	1977	1	2	3	2
Ron Santo	342	33	1965			4	
Jack Clark	340	35	1987			1	
Dave Parker	339	34	1985			3	
Boog Powell	339	39	1964			4	
Don Baylor	338	36	1979			3	
Joe Adcock	336	38	1956			2	
Bobby Bonds	332	39	1973			6	
Hank Greenberg	331	58	1938	1	4	6	4
Willie Horton	325	36	1968			1	
Gary Carter	324	32	1985			2	
Roy Sievers	318	42	1957		1	2	1
Ron Cey	316	30	1977			1	
Lance Parrish	316	33	1984			2	
Reggie Smith	314	32	1977			2	
Greg Luzinski	307	39	1977			4	

Most Home Runs, Career (*cont.*)

Player	HR	Best	Year	50+	40+	30+	Led Lg
Al Simmons	307	36	1930			3	
Fred Lynn	306	39	1979			1	
Rogers Hornsby	301	42	1922		1	3	2
Chuck Klein	300	43	1929		2	4	4

Teammates with 400 or More Home Runs, Career

Player	Team	Career Total	Player	Team	Career Total
Hank Aaron	MIL-ATL N	755	Willie McCovey		521
Eddie Mathews		512	Jimmie Foxx	BOS A	534
Babe Ruth	NY A	714	Ted Williams		521
Lou Gehrig		493	Ernie Banks	CHI N	512
Willie Mays	SF N	660	Billy Williams		426

Club Leaders, Home Runs, Season, AL

Player	Team	HR	Year
Roger Maris	NY Yankees	61	1961
Jimmie Foxx	PHI-KC-OAK Athletics	58	1932
Hank Greenberg	DET Tigers	58	1938
Jimmie Foxx	BOS Red Sox	50	1938
Harmon Killebrew	WAS Senators-MIN Twins	49	1964
Frank Robinson	STL Browns-BAL Orioles	49	1966
Frank Howard	WAS Senators-TEX Rangers	48	1969
George Bell	TOR Blue Jays	47	1987
Gorman Thomas	SEA Pilots-MIL Brewers	45	1979
Al Rosen	CLE Indians	43	1953
Reggie Jackson	LA-CAL Angels	39	1982
Dick Allen	CHI White Sox	37	1972
Carlton Fisk	CHI White Sox	37	1985
Steve Balboni	KC Royals	36	1985
Gorman Thomas	SEA Mariners	32	1985

Club Leaders, Home Runs, Season, NL

Player	Team	HR	Year
Hack Wilson	CHI Cubs	56	1930
Ralph Kiner	PIT Pirates	54	1949
Willie Mays	NY-SF Giants	52	1965
George Foster	CIN Reds	52	1977
Mike Schmidt	PHI Phillies	48	1980
Eddie Mathews	BOS-MIL-ATL Braves	47	1953
Hank Aaron	BOS-MIL-ATL Braves	47	1971
Johnny Mize	STL Cardinals	43	1940
Duke Snider	BKN-LA Dodgers	43	1956
Darryl Strawberry	NY Mets	39	1987, 1988
Nate Colbert	SD Padres	38	1970, 1972

Club Leaders, Home Runs, Season, NL (*cont.*)

Player	Team	HR	Year
Jimmy Wynn	HOU Astros	37	1967
Andre Dawson	MON Expos	32	1983

Best Home Run Ratio, Career (Min. 1,000 G Played)

Player	HR	AB	Ratio
Babe Ruth	714	8399	11.76
Ralph Kiner	369	5205	14.11
Harmon Killebrew	573	8147	14.22
Ted Williams	521	7706	14.79
Dave Kingman	442	6677	15.11
Mickey Mantle	536	8102	15.12
Jimmie Foxx	534	8134	15.23
Mike Schmidt	548	8352	15.24
Hank Greenberg	331	5193	15.69
Willie McCovey	521	8197	15.73
Darryl Strawberry	285	4564	16.01
Lou Gehrig	493	8001	16.23
Hank Aaron	755	12364	16.38
Rob Deer	205	3365	16.41
Willie Mays	660	10881	16.49
Hank Sauer	288	4796	16.65
Eddie Mathews	512	8537	16.67
Willie Stargell	475	7927	16.69
Frank Howard	382	6488	16.98
Frank Robinson	583	10006	17.16
Steve Balboni	181	3115	17.21
Bob Horner	218	3777	17.33
Roy Campanella	242	4205	17.38
Rocky Colavito	374	6503	17.39
Gus Zernial	237	4131	17.43
Reggie Jackson	563	9864	17.52
Gorman Thomas	268	4677	17.45
Dick Stuart	228	3997	17.53
Duke Snider	407	7161	17.59
Norm Cash	377	6705	17.79
Johnny Mize	359	6443	17.95
Dick Allen	351	6332	18.04
Ernie Banks	512	9421	18.40
Mel Ott	511	9456	18.50
Roger Maris	275	5101	18.55
Joe DiMaggio	361	6821	18.89
Gil Hodges	370	7030	19.00
Wally Post	210	4007	19.08
Al Rosen	192	3725	19.40
Hack Wilson	244	4760	19.51
Joe Adcock	336	6606	19.66

Best Home Run Ratio, Career (Min. 1,000 G Played) (*cont.*)

Player	HR	AB	Ratio
Bob Allison	256	5032	19.66
Johnny Bench	389	7658	19.69
Boog Powell	339	6681	19.71
Jesse Barfield	241	4759	19.75
Nate Colbert	173	3422	19.78
Dale Murphy	398	7918	19.89
Charlie Keller	189	3790	20.05
Roy Sievers	318	6387	20.08
Jack Clark	340	6897	20.13
Cliff Johnson	196	3945	20.13
George Foster	348	7023	20.18
Don Mincher	200	4026	20.19
Tony Armas	251	5164	20.57
Andre Thornton	253	5291	20.91
Orlando Cepeda	379	7927	20.92
Leon Wagner	211	4426	20.98
Jim Lemon	164	3445	21.00
Yogi Berra	358	7555	21.10
Don Demeter	163	3443	21.12
Howard Johnson	204	4309	20.12
Larry Doby	253	5348	21.14
Bobby Bonds	332	7043	21.21
Ted Kluszewski	279	5929	21.25
Rudy York	277	5891	21.27
Wally Berger	242	5163	21.33
Lance Parrish	316	6743	21.33
John Mayberry	255	5447	21.36
Kent Hrbek	258	5526	21.42
Joe Carter	242	5201	21.49
Lee May	354	7609	21.49
Jim Rice	382	8225	21.53
Chuck Klein	300	6486	21.62
Darrell Evans	414	8973	21.67
Gene Tenace	201	4390	21.84
Charlie Maxwell	148	3245	21.93
Billy Williams	426	9350	21.95
Frank Thomas	286	6285	21.98

Most Home Runs by Position, Career, AL

Player	Pos.	HR	Player	Pos.	HR
Lou Gehrig	1B	493	Charlie Gehringer	2B	183
Jimmie Foxx	1B	473			
Norm Cash	1B	375	Graig Nettles	3B	319
			Brooks Robinson	3B	267
Joe Gordon	2B	246	Sal Bando	3B	232
Bobby Doerr	2B	223			

Player	Pos.	HR	Player	Pos.	HR
Cal Ripken	SS	265	Carlton Fisk	C	350
Vern Stephens	SS	213	Yogi Berra	C	313
Joe Cronin	SS	152	Lance Parrish	C	263
Babe Ruth	OF	686	Wes Ferrell	P	36
Ted Williams	OF	521	Red Ruffing	P	35
Mickey Mantle	OF	496	Earl Wilson	P	35

Most Home Runs by Position, Career, NL

Player	Pos.	HR	Player	Pos.	HR
Willie McCovey	1B	439	Hank Aaron	OF	661
Gil Hodges	1B	355	Willie Mays	OF	643
Orlando Cepeda	1B	334	Mel Ott	OF	475
Rogers Hornsby	2B	263	Johnny Bench	C	326
Joe Morgan	2B	260*	Gary Carter	C	298
Ryne Sandberg	2B	226	Roy Campanella	C	242
Mike Schmidt	3B	509	Warren Spahn	P	35
Eddie Mathews	3B	482	Don Drysdale	P	29
Ron Santo	3B	334	Bob Gibson	P	24
Ernie Banks	SS	293			
Pee Wee Reese	SS	124			
Leo Cardenas	SS	117			

* Morgan hit 6 in the AL for a career record of 266, the most home runs by a second baseman in major league history.

Most Home Runs by Position, Season, AL

Player	Team	Year	Pos.	HR
Hank Greenberg	DET	1938	1B	58
Joe Gordon	CLE	1948	2B	32
Al Rosen	CLE	1953	3B	43
Rico Petrocelli	BOS	1969	SS	40
Roger Maris	NY	1961	OF	61
Carlton Fisk	CHI	1985	C	33
Wes Ferrell	CLE	1931	P	9

Most Home Runs by Position, Season, NL

Player	Team	Year	Pos.	HR
Johnny Mize	NY	1947	1B	51
Rogers Hornsby	STL	1922	2B	42
Davey Johnson	ATL	1973	2B	42
Mike Schmidt	PHI	1980	3B	48
Ernie Banks	CHI	1958	SS	47
Hack Wilson	CHI	1930	OF	56
Roy Campanella	BKN	1953	C	40
Don Newcombe	BKN	1955	P	7
Don Drysdale	LA	1958	P	7
	LA	1965	P	7

Home Run in First At-Bat in Majors, AL

Player	Team	Date
Earl Averill	CLE	Apr 16, 1929
Ace Parker	PHI	Apr 30, 1937
Bill LeFebvre	BOS	Jun 10, 1938
Hack Miller	DET	Apr 23, 1944
Eddie Pellagrini	BOS	Apr 22, 1946
George Vico	DET	Apr 20, 1948
Bob Nieman	STL	Sep 14, 1951
John Kennedy	WAS	Sep 5, 1962
Buster Narum	BAL	May 3, 1963
Gates Brown	DET	Jun 19, 1963
Bert Campaneris	KC	Jul 23, 1964
Bill Roman	DET	Sep 30, 1964
Brant Alyea	WAS	Sep 12, 1965
John Miller	NY	Sep 11, 1966
Rick Renick	MIN	Jul 11, 1968
Joe Keough	OAK	Aug 7, 1968
Gene Lamont	DET	Sep 2, 1970
Don Rose	CAL	May 24, 1972
Reggie Sanders	DET	Sep 1, 1974
Dave McKay	MIN	Aug 22, 1975
Al Woods	TOR	Apr 7, 1977
Dave Machemer	CAL	Jun 21, 1978
Gary Gaetti	MIN	Sep 20, 1981
Andre David	MIN	Jun 29, 1984
Terry Steinbach	OAK	Sep 12, 1986
Jay Bell	CLE	Sep 29, 1986
Junior Felix	TOR	May 4, 1989

Home Run in First At-Bat in Majors, NL

Player	Team	Date
Bill Duggleby	PHI	Apr 21, 1898
Johnny Bates	BOS	Apr 12, 1906
Clise Dudley	BKN	Apr 27, 1929
Gordon Slade	BKN	May 24, 1930
Eddie Morgan	STL	Apr 14, 1936
Ernie Koy	BKN	Apr 19, 1938
Emmett Mueller	PHI	Apr 19, 1938
Clyde Vollmer	CIN	May 31, 1942

Home Run in First At-Bat in Majors, NL (cont.)

Player	Team	Date
Buddy Kerr	NY	Sep 8, 1943
Whitey Lockman	NY	Jul 5, 1945
Dan Bankhead	BKN	Aug 26, 1947
Les Layton	NY	May 21, 1948
Ed Sanicki	PHI	Sep 14, 1949
Ted Tappe	CIN	Sep 14, 1950
Hoyt Wilhelm	NY	Apr 23, 1952
Wally Moon	STL	Apr 13, 1954
Chuck Tanner	MIL	Apr 12, 1955
Bill White	NY	May 7, 1956
Frank Ernaga	CHI	May 24, 1957
Don Leppert	PIT	Jun 18, 1961
Cuno Barragan	CHI	Sep 1, 1961
Benny Ayala	NY	Aug 27, 1974
Jose Sosa	HOU	Jul 30, 1975
Johnnie LeMaster	SF	Sep 2, 1975
Mike Fitzgerald	NY	Sep 13, 1983
Will Clark	SF	Apr 8, 1986
Jose Offerman	LA	Aug 19, 1990
Dave Eiland	SD	Apr 10, 1992
Jim Bullinger	CHI	Jun 8, 1992

Home Run on First Pitch in Majors, AL

Player	Team	Date
George Vico	DET	Apr 20, 1948
Bert Campaneris	KC	Jul 23, 1964
Brant Alyea	WAS	Sep 12, 1965
Don Rose	CAL	May 24, 1972
Jay Bell	CLE	Sep 29, 1986
Junior Felix	TOR	May 4, 1989

Home Run on First Pitch in Majors, NL

Player	Team	Date
Clise Dudley	BKN	Apr 27, 1929
Eddie Morgan	STL	Apr 14, 1936
Clyde Vollmer	CIN	May 31, 1942
Chuck Tanner	MIL	Apr 12, 1955
Jim Bullinger	CHI	Jun 8, 1992

Two Home Runs in One Inning, AL

Player	Team	Date	Inn.
Ken Williams	STL	Aug 7, 1922	6
Bill Regan	BOS	Jun 16, 1928	4
Joe DiMaggio	NY	Jun 24, 1936	5

Two Home Runs in One Inning, AL (cont.)

Player	Team	Date	Inn.
Al Kaline	DET	Apr 17, 1955	6
Jim Lemon	WAS	Sep 5, 1959	3
Joe Pepitone	NY	May 23, 1962	8
Rick Reichardt	CAL	Apr 30, 1966	8
Cliff Johnson	NY	Jun 30, 1977	8
Ellis Burks	BOS	Aug 27, 1990	4

Two Home Runs in One Inning, NL

Player	Team	Date	Inn.
Charley Jones	BOS	June 10, 1880	8
Bobby Lowe	BOS	May 30, 1894	3
Jake Stenzel	PIT	Jun 6, 1894	3
Hack Wilson	NY	Jul 1, 1925	3
Hank Leiber	NY	Aug 24, 1935	2
Andy Seminick	PHI	Jun 2, 1949	8
Sid Gordon	NY	Jul 31, 1949	2
Willie McCovey	SF	Apr 12, 1973	4
John Boccabella	MON	Jul 6, 1973	6
Lee May	HOU	Apr 29, 1974	6
Willie McCovey	SF	Jun 27, 1977	6
Andre Dawson	MON	Jul 30, 1978	3
Ray Knight	CIN	May 13, 1980	5
Von Hayes	PHI	Jun 11, 1985	1
Andre Dawson	MON	Sep 24, 1985	5
Dale Murphy	ATL	Jul 27, 1989	6

Two Home Runs in One Game Most Often

Player	G	Player	G
Babe Ruth	72	Stan Musial	37
Willie Mays	63	Ted Williams	37
Hank Aaron	62	Willie Stargell	36
Jimmie Foxx	55	Joe DiMaggio	35
Frank Robinson	54	Hank Greenberg	35
Eddie Mathews	49	Lee May	35
Mel Ott	49	Jim Rice	35
Harmon Killebrew	46	Andre Dawson	34
Mickey Mantle	46	Duke Snider	34
Willie McCovey	44	Dick Allen	32
Mike Schmidt	44	Rocky Colavito	32
Lou Gehrig	43	Gus Zernial	32
Dave Kingman	43	Dale Murphy	31
Ernie Banks	42	Hank Sauer	31
Reggie Jackson	42	Billy Williams	31
Ralph Kiner	40	Gil Hodges	30

Two Home Runs in One Game Most Often (cont.)

Player	G	Player	G
Willie Horton	30	Joe Carter	26
Johnny Mize	30	Bob Horner	26
Joe Adcock	28	Frank Howard	26
Chuck Klein	28	Ron Santo	26
Gary Carter	28	Norm Cash	25
Dave Winfield	28	Roger Maris	25
Graig Nettles	27	Eddie Murray	25
Roy Sievers	27	Darryl Strawberry	25
Hack Wilson	27	Hal Trosky	25
Carl Yastrzemski	27		

Three Home Runs in One Game, AL

Player	Team	Date	H/A	Cons.
Ken Williams	STL	Apr 22, 1922	Home	No
Joe Hauser	PHI	Aug 2, 1924	Away	No
Ty Cobb	DET	May 5, 1925	Away	No
Mickey Cochrane	PHI	May 21, 1925	Away	No
Goose Goslin	WAS	Jun 19, 1925	Away	No
Tony Lazzeri	NY	Jun 8, 1927	Home	No
Lou Gehrig	NY	Jun 23, 1927	Away	No
	NY	May 4, 1929	Away	No
Babe Ruth	NY	May 21, 1930	Away	No
Lou Gehrig	NY	May 22, 1930	Away	No
Carl Reynolds	CHI	Jul 2, 1930	Away	Yes
Goose Goslin	STL	Aug 19, 1930	Away	Yes
Earl Averill	CLE	Sep 17, 1930	Home	Yes
Goose Goslin	STL	Jun 23, 1932	Home	Yes
Ben Chapman	NY	Jul 9, 1932	Home	Yes
Jimmie Foxx	PHI	Jul 10, 1932	Away	Yes
Al Simmons	PHI	Jul 15, 1932	Home	Yes
Jimmie Foxx	PHI	Jun 8, 1933	Home	Yes
Hal Trosky	CLE	May 30, 1934	Home	Yes
Ed Coleman	PHI	Aug 17, 1934	Home	Yes
Pinky Higgins	PHI	Jun 27, 1935	Home	Yes
Moose Solters	STL	Jul 7, 1935	Away	Yes
Tony Lazzeri	NY	May 24, 1936	Away	No
Joe DiMaggio	NY	Jun 13, 1937	Away	Yes
Hal Trosky	CLE	Jul 5, 1937	Away	No
Merv Connors	CHI	Sep 17, 1938	Home	Yes
Ken Keltner	CLE	May 25, 1939	Away	Yes
Jim Tabor	BOS	Jul 4, 1939	Away	No
Bill Dickey	NY	Jul 26, 1939	Home	Yes
Pinky Higgins	DET	May 20, 1940	Home	Yes
Charlie Keller	NY	Jul 28, 1940	Away	No
Rudy York	DET	Sep 1, 1941	Home	No
Pat Seerey	CLE	Jul 13, 1945	Away	No

Three Home Runs in One Game, AL (*cont.*)

Player	Team	Date	H/A	Cons.
Ted Williams	BOS	Jul 14, 1946	Home	No
Sam Chapman	PHI	Aug 15, 1946	Away	No
Joe DiMaggio	NY	May 23, 1948	Away	Yes
Pat Mullin	DET	Jun 26, 1949	Away	No
Bobby Doerr	BOS	Jun 8, 1950	Home	No
Larry Doby	CLE	Aug 2, 1950	Home	Yes
Joe DiMaggio	NY	Sep 10, 1950	Away	No
Johnny Mize	NY	Sep 15, 1950	Away	Yes
Gus Zernial	CHI	Oct 1, 1950	Home	No
Bobby Avila	CLE	Jun 20, 1951	Away	No
Clyde Vollmer	BOS	Jul 26, 1951	Home	No
Al Rosen	CLE	Apr 29, 1952	Away	No
Bill Glynn	CLE	Jul 5, 1954	Away	Yes
Al Kaline	DET	Apr 17, 1955	Home	No
Mickey Mantle	NY	May 13, 1955	Home	No
Norm Zauchin	BOS	May 27, 1955	Home	No
Jim Lemon	WAS	Aug 31, 1956	Home	Yes
Ted Williams	BOS	May 8, 1957	Away	No
	BOS	Jun 13, 1957	Away	No
Hector Lopez	KC	Jun 26, 1958	Home	No
Preston Ward	KC	Sep 9, 1958	Home	Yes
Charlie Maxwell	DET	May 3, 1959	Home	Yes
Bob Cerv	KC	Aug 20, 1959	Home	No
Willie Kirkland	CLE	Jul 9, 1961	Home	Yes
Rocky Colavito	DET	Aug 27, 1961	Away	No
Lee Thomas	LA	Sep 5, 1961	Away	No
Rocky Colavito	DET	Jul 5, 1962	Away	Yes
Steve Boros	DET	Aug 6, 1962	Away	No
Don Leppert	WAS	Apr 11, 1963	Home	Yes
Bob Allison	MIN	May 17, 1963	Away	Yes
Boog Powell	BAL	Aug 10, 1963	Away	Yes
Harmon Killebrew	MIN	Sep 21, 1963	Away	No
Jim King	WAS	Jun 8, 1964	Home	No
Boog Powell	BAL	Jun 27, 1964	Away	No
Manny Jimenez	KC	Jul 4, 1964	Away	Yes
Tom Tresh	NY	Jun 6, 1965	Home	Yes
Boog Powell	BAL	Aug 15, 1966	Away	No
Tom McCraw	CHI	May 24, 1967	Away	No
Curt Blefary	BAL	Jun 6, 1967	Away	No
Ken Harrelson	BOS	Jun 14, 1968	Away	Yes
Mike Epstein	WAS	May 16, 1969	Away	No
Joe Lahoud	BOS	Jun 11, 1969	Away	No
Bill Melton	CHI	Jun 24, 1969	Away	Yes
Reggie Jackson	OAK	Jul 2, 1969	Home	No
Paul Blair	BAL	Apr 29, 1970	Away	No
Tony Horton	CLE	May 24, 1970	Home	No
Willie Horton	DET	Jun 9, 1970	Home	No

Three Home Runs in One Game, AL (cont.)

Player	Team	Date	H/A	Cons.
Bobby Murcer	NY	Jun 24, 1970	Home	Yes
Bill Freehan	DET	Aug 9, 1971	Away	No
George Hendrick	CLE	Jun 19, 1973	Home	Yes
Tony Oliva	MIN	Jul 3, 1973	Away	No
Leroy Stanton	CAL	Jul 10, 1973	Away	No
Bobby Murcer	NY	Jul 13, 1973	Home	No
Bobby Grich	BAL	Jun 18, 1974	Home	Yes
Fred Lynn	BOS	Jun 18, 1975	Away	No
John Mayberry	KC	Jul 1, 1975	Away	No
Don Baylor	BAL	Jul 2, 1975	Away	Yes
Tony Solaita	KC	Sep 7, 1975	Away	Yes
Carl Yastrzemski	BOS	May 19, 1976	Away	No
Willie Horton	TEX	May 15, 1977	Away	No
John Mayberry	KC	Jun 1, 1977	Away	Yes
Cliff Johnson	NY	Jun 30, 1977	Away	Yes
Jim Rice	BOS	Aug 29, 1977	Home	Yes
Al Oliver	TEX	May 23, 1979	Home	No
Ben Oglivie	MIL	Jul 8, 1979	Home	No
Claudell Washington	CHI	Jul 14, 1979	Home	No
George Brett	KC	Jul 22, 1979	Away	No
Cecil Cooper	MIL	Jul 27, 1979	Home	No
Eddie Murray	BAL	Aug 29, 1979	Away	Yes
Carney Lansford	CAL	Sep 1, 1979	Away	Yes
Otto Velez	TOR	May 4, 1980	Home	No
Freddie Patek	CAL	Jun 20, 1980	Away	No
Al Oliver	TEX	Aug 17, 1980	Away	No
Eddie Murray	BAL	Sep 14, 1980	Away	No
Jeff Burroughs	SEA	Aug 14, 1981	Away	No
Paul Molitor	MIL	May 12, 1982	Away	No
Larry Herndon	DET	May 18, 1982	Home	Yes
Ben Oglivie	MIL	Jun 20, 1982	Away	No
Harold Baines	CHI	Jul 7, 1982	Home	No
Doug DeCinces	CAL	Aug 3, 1982	Home	No
	CAL	Aug 8, 1982	Away	No
George Brett	KC	Apr 20, 1983	Away	No
Ben Oglivie	MIL	May 14, 1983	Home	No
Dan Ford	BAL	Jul 20, 1983	Away	No
Jim Rice	BOS	Aug 29, 1983	Away	No
Dave Kingman	OAK	Apr 16, 1984	Away	Yes
Harold Baines	CHI	Sep 17, 1984	Away	No
Gorman Thomas	SEA	Apr 11, 1985	Home	No
Larry Parrish	TEX	Apr 19, 1985	Home	Yes
Eddie Murray	BAL	Aug 26, 1985	Away	No
Lee Lacy	BAL	Jun 8, 1986	Away	No
Juan Beniquez	BAL	Jun 12, 1986	Home	Yes
Joe Carter	CLE	Aug 29, 1986	Away	No
Jim Presley	SEA	Sep 1, 1986	Home	No

Three Home Runs in One Game, AL (cont.)

Player	Team	Date	H/A	Cons.
Reggie Jackson	CAL	Sep 18, 1986	Home	No
Cory Snyder	CLE	May 21, 1987	Home	No
Joe Carter	CLE	May 28, 1987	Away	No
Mark McGwire	OAK	Jun 27, 1987	Away	No
Bill Madlock	DET	Jun 28, 1987	Home	No
Brook Jacoby	CLE	July 3, 1987	Home	Yes
Dale Sveum	MIL	July 17, 1987	Home	No
Mickey Brantley	SEA	Sep 14, 1987	Home	No
Ernie Whitt	TOR	Sep 14, 1987	Home	No
Wally Joyner	CAL	Oct 3, 1987	Home	No
George Bell	TOR	Apr 4, 1988	Away	No
Jose Canseco	OAK	Jul 3, 1988	Away	No
Joe Carter	CLE	Jun 24, 1989	Away	Yes
	CLE	Jul 19, 1989	Away	No
Cecil Fielder	DET	May 6, 1990	Away	Yes
	DET	Jun 6, 1990	Away	Yes
Randy Milligan	BAL	Jun 9, 1990	Home	Yes
Bo Jackson	KC	Jul 17, 1990	Away	Yes
Tom Brunansky	BOS	Sep 29, 1990	Home	Yes
Dave Winfield	CAL	Apr 13, 1991	Away	Yes
Harold Baines	OAK	May 7, 1991	Home	No
Danny Tartabull	KC	Jul 6, 1991	Home	No
Jack Clark	BOS	Jul 31, 1991	Home	No
Dave Henderson	OAK	Aug 3, 1991	Home	Yes
Juan Gonzalez	TEX	Jun 7, 1992	Home	No
Albert Belle	CLE	Sep 6, 1992	Away	No

Three Home Runs in One Game, NL

Player	Team	Date	H/A	Cons.
Ned Williamson	CHI	May 30, 1884	Home	No
Cap Anson	CHI	Aug 6, 1884	Home	Yes
Jack Manning	PHI	Oct 9, 1884	Away	Yes
Dan Brouthers	DET	Sep 10, 1886	Away	No
Roger Connor	NY	May 9, 1888	Away	No
Frank Shugart	STL	May 10, 1894	Away	No
Bill Joyce	WAS	Aug 20, 1894	Home	Yes
Tom McCreery	LOU	Jul 12, 1897	Away	No
Jake Beckley	CIN	Sep 26, 1897	Away	No
Butch Henline	PHI	Sep 15, 1922	Home	No
Cy Williams	PHI	May 11, 1923	Home	No
George Kelly	NY	Sep 17, 1923	Away	Yes
	NY	Jun 14, 1924	Home	No
Jack Fournier	BKN	Jul 13, 1926	Away	No
Les Bell	BOS	Jun 2, 1928	Home	No
George Harper	STL	Sep 20, 1928	Away	Yes
Hack Wilson	CHI	Jul 26, 1930	Away	No

Three Home Runs in One Game, NL (*cont.*)

Player	Team	Date	H/A	Cons.
Mel Ott	NY	Aug 31, 1930	Home	Yes
Rogers Hornsby	CHI	Apr 24, 1931	Away	Yes
George Watkins	STL	Jun 24, 1931	Away	Yes
Bill Terry	NY	Aug 13, 1932	Home	No
Babe Herman	CHI	Jul 20, 1933	Home	No
Hal Lee	BOS	Jul 6, 1934	Away	No
Babe Ruth	BOS	May 25, 1935	Away	No
Johnny Moore	PHI	Jul 22, 1936	Home	Yes
Alex Kampouris	CIN	May 9, 1937	Away	No
Johnny Mize	STL	Jul 13, 1938	Home	Yes
	STL	Jul 20, 1938	Home	No
Hank Leiber	CHI	Jul 4, 1939	Home	Yes
Johnny Mize	STL	May 13, 1940	Away	No
	STL	Sep 8, 1940	Home	Yes
Jim Tobin	BOS	May 13, 1942	Home	Yes
Clyde McCullough	CHI	Jul 26, 1942	Away	Yes
Bill Nicholson	CHI	Jul 23, 1944	Away	Yes
Johnny Mize	NY	Apr 24, 1947	Away	Yes
Willard Marshall	NY	Jul 18, 1947	Home	Yes
Ralph Kiner	PIT	Aug 16, 1947	Home	Yes
	PIT	Sep 11, 1947	Home	Yes
	PIT	Jul 5, 1948	Home	No
Gene Hermanski	BKN	Aug 5, 1948	Home	Yes
Andy Seminick	PHI	Jun 2, 1949	Home	No
Walker Cooper	CIN	Jul 6, 1949	Home	No
Bob Elliott	BOS	Sep 24, 1949	Away	Yes
Duke Snider	BKN	May 30, 1950	Home	Yes
Wes Westrum	NY	Jun 24, 1950	Home	No
Andy Pafko	CHI	Aug 2, 1950	Away	Yes
Roy Campanella	BKN	Aug 26, 1950	Away	Yes
Hank Sauer	CHI	Aug 28, 1950	Home	Yes
Tommy Brown	BKN	Sep 18, 1950	Home	Yes
Ralph Kiner	PIT	Jul 18, 1951	Away	No
Del Wilber	PHI	Aug 27, 1951	Home	Yes
Don Mueller	NY	Sep 1, 1951	Home	No
Hank Sauer	CHI	Jun 11, 1952	Home	No
Eddie Mathews	BOS	Sep 27, 1952	Away	Yes
Dusty Rhodes	NY	Aug 26, 1953	Home	Yes
Jim Pendleton	MIL	Aug 30, 1953	Away	No
Stan Musial	STL	May 2, 1954	Home	No
Hank Thompson	NY	Jun 3, 1954	Away	Yes
Dusty Rhodes	NY	Jul 28, 1954	Home	Yes
Duke Snider	BKN	Jun 1, 1955	Home	No
Gus Bell	CIN	Jul 21, 1955	Away	Yes
Del Ennis	PHI	Jul 23, 1955	Home	No
Smoky Burgess	CIN	Jul 29, 1955	Home	No
Ernie Banks	CHI	Aug 4, 1955	Home	No

Three Home Runs in One Game, NL (*cont.*)

Player	Team	Date	H/A	Cons.
Gus Bell	CIN	May 29, 1956	Away	Yes
Ed Bailey	CIN	Jun 24, 1956	Away	No
Ted Kluszewski	CIN	Jul 1, 1956	Away	No
Bob Thurman	CIN	Aug 18, 1956	Home	Yes
Ernie Banks	CHI	Sep 14, 1957	Home	Yes
Roman Mejias	PIT	May 4, 1958	Away	No
Walt Moryn	CHI	May 30, 1958	Home	No
Frank Thomas	PIT	Aug 16, 1958	Away	Yes
Lee Walls	CHI	Aug 24, 1958	Away	No
Don Demeter	LA	Apr 21, 1959	Home	No
Hank Aaron	MIL	Jun 21, 1959	Away	No
Frank Robinson	CIN	Aug 22, 1959	Home	Yes
Dick Stuart	PIT	Jun 30, 1960	Home	No
Willie Mays	SF	Jun 29, 1961	Away	No
Bill White	STL	Jul 5, 1961	Away	Yes
Don Demeter	PHI	Sep 12, 1961	Away	No
Ernie Banks	CHI	May 29, 1962	Home	Yes
Stan Musial	STL	Jul 8, 1962	Away	Yes
Willie Mays	SF	Jun 2, 1963	Away	No
Ernie Banks	CHI	Jun 9, 1963	Home	No
Willie McCovey	SF	Sep 22, 1963	Home	Yes
	SF	Apr 22, 1964	Away	Yes
Johnny Callison	PHI	Sep 27, 1964	Home	Yes
	PHI	Jun 6, 1965	Away	No
Willie Stargell	PIT	Jun 24, 1965	Away	No
Jim Hickman	NY	Sep 3, 1965	Away	Yes
Gene Oliver	ATL	Jul 30, 1966	Home	No
Art Shamsky	CIN	Aug 12, 1966	Home	Yes
Willie McCovey	SF	Sep 17, 1966	Home	No
Roberto Clemente	PIT	May 15, 1967	Away	No
Adolfo Phillips	CHI	Jun 11, 1967	Home	Yes
Jimmy Wynn	HOU	Jun 15, 1967	Home	Yes
Willie Stargell	PIT	May 22, 1968	Away	No
Billy Williams	CHI	Sep 10, 1968	Home	No
Dick Allen	PHI	Sep 29, 1968	Away	Yes
Bob Tillman	ATL	Jul 30, 1969	Away	No
Roberto Clemente	PIT	Aug 13, 1969	Away	Yes
Rico Carty	ATL	May 31, 1970	Home	No
Mike Lum	ATL	Jul 3, 1970	Home	No
Johnny Bench	CIN	Jul 26, 1970	Home	Yes
Orlando Cepeda	ATL	Jul 26, 1970	Away	Yes
Willie Stargell	PIT	Apr 10, 1971	Away	No
	PIT	Apr 21, 1971	Home	Yes
Deron Johnson	PHI	Jul 11, 1971	Home	Yes
Rick Monday	CHI	May 16, 1972	Away	Yes
Nate Colbert	SD	Aug 1, 1972	Away	No
Johnny Bench	CIN	May 9, 1973	Away	No

Three Home Runs in One Game, NL (*cont.*)

Player	Team	Date	H/A	Cons.
Lee May	HOU	Jun 21, 1973	Away	No
George Mitterwald	CHI	Apr 17, 1974	Home	No
Jimmy Wynn	LA	May 11, 1974	Away	No
Davey Lopes	LA	Aug 20, 1974	Away	No
Reggie Smith	STL	May 22, 1976	Away	No
Dave Kingman	NY	Jun 4, 1976	Away	No
Bill Robinson	PIT	Jun 5, 1976	Home	No
Gary Matthews	SF	Sep 25, 1976	Home	No
Gary Carter	MON	Apr 20, 1977	Home	Yes
Larry Parrish	MON	May 29, 1977	Away	Yes
George Foster	CIN	Jul 14, 1977	Home	Yes
Pete Rose	CIN	Apr 29, 1978	Away	No
Dave Kingman	CHI	May 14, 1978	Away	No
Larry Parrish	MON	Jul 30, 1978	Away	Yes
Dave Kingman	CHI	May 17, 1979	Home	No
Dale Murphy	ATL	May 18, 1979	Home	No
Mike Schmidt	PHI	Jul 7, 1979	Home	Yes
Dave Kingman	CHI	Jul 28, 1979	Away	Yes
Larry Parrish	MON	Apr 25, 1980	Away	No
Johnny Bench	CIN	May 29, 1980	Home	No
Claudell Washington	NY	Jun 22, 1980	Away	Yes
Darrell Evans	SF	Jun 15, 1983	Home	No
Darryl Strawberry	NY	Aug 5, 1985	Away	Yes
Gary Carter	NY	Sep 3, 1985	Away	Yes
Andre Dawson	MON	Sep 24, 1985	Away	No
Ken Griffey	ATL	Jul 22, 1986	Away	No
Eric Davis	CIN	Sep 10, 1986	Away	No
	CIN	May 3, 1987	Away	Yes
Tim Wallach	MON	May 4, 1987	Away	No
Mike Schmidt	PHI	Jun 14, 1987	Away	Yes
Andre Dawson	CHI	Aug 1, 1987	Home	No
Glenn Davis	HOU	Sep 10, 1987	Away	Yes
Darnell Coles	PIT	Sep 30, 1987	Home	No
Von Hayes	PHI	Aug 29, 1989	Away	No
Kevin Mitchell	SF	May 25, 1990	Away	Yes
Jeff Treadway	ATL	May 26, 1990	Away	No
Glenn Davis	HOU	Jun 1, 1990	Away	Yes
Barry Larkin	CIN	Jun 28, 1991	Home	Yes
Jeff Blauser	ATL	Jul 12, 1992	Away	No

Four Home Runs in One Game, AL

Player	Team	Date	H/A	Cons.	Inns.
Lou Gehrig	NY	Jun 3, 1932	Away	No	9
Pat Seerey	CHI	Jul 18, 1948	Away	No	11
Rocky Colavito	CLE	Jun 10, 1959	Away	No	9

Four Home Runs in One Game, NL

Player	Team	Date	H/A	Cons.	Inns.
Bobby Lowe	BOS	May 30, 1894	Home	No	9
Ed Delahanty	PHI	Jul 13, 1896	Away	Yes	9
Chuck Klein	PHI	Jul 10, 1936	Away	No	10
Gil Hodges	BKN	Aug 31, 1950	Home	No	9
Joe Adcock	MIL	Jul 31, 1954	Away	Yes	9
Willie Mays	SF	Apr 30, 1961	Away	No	9
Mike Schmidt	PHI	Apr 17, 1976	Away	No	10
Bob Horner	ATL	Jul 6, 1986	Home	No	9

Most Home Runs in a Doubleheader, AL

Player	Team	Date	HR
Earl Averill	CLE	Sep 17, 1930	4
Jimmie Foxx	PHI	Jul 2, 1933	4
Jim Tabor	BOS	Jul 4, 1939	4
Gus Zernial	CHI	Oct 1, 1950	4
Charlie Maxwell	DET	May 3, 1959	4
Roger Maris	NY	Jul 25, 1961	4
Rocky Colavito	DET	Aug 27, 1961	4
Harmon Killebrew	MIN	Sep 21, 1963	4
Bobby Murcer	NY	Jun 24, 1970	4
Graig Nettles	NY	Apr 14, 1974	4
Otto Velez	TOR	May 4, 1980	4
Al Oliver	TEX	Aug 17, 1980	4

Most Home Runs in a Doubleheader, NL

Player	Team	Date	HR
Stan Musial	STL	May 2, 1954	5
Nate Colbert	SD	Aug 1, 1972	5
Bill Nicholson	CHI	Jul 23, 1944	4
Ralph Kiner	PIT	Sep 11, 1947	4
Wally Post	CIN	Apr 29, 1956	4
Bobby Thomson	MIL	May 30, 1956	4
Leo Cardenas	CIN	Jun 5, 1966	4
Adolfo Phillips	CHI	Jun 11, 1967	4
Lee May	CIN	Jul 15, 1969	4
Rusty Staub	MON	Aug 1, 1970	4
Jason Thompson	PIT	Jun 26, 1984	4

Home Runs in Most Consecutive Games

Player	Team	Dates	G	HR
Don Mattingly	NY A	Jul 8–18, 1987	8	10
Dale Long	PIT N	May 19–28, 1956	8	8
Ken Williams	STL A	Jul 28–Aug 2, 1922	6	6
George Kelly	NY N	Jul 11–16, 1924	6	7
Lou Gehrig	NY A	Aug 28–Sep 1, 1931	6	6

Home Runs in Most Consecutive Games (*cont.*)

Player	Team	Dates	G	HR
Walker Cooper	NY N	Jun 22–28, 1947	6	7
Willie Mays	NY N	Sep 14–20, 1956	6	7
Roy Sievers	WAS A	Jul 29–Aug 3, 1957	6	6
Roger Maris	NY A	Aug 11–16, 1961	6	7
Frank Howard	WAS A	May 12–18, 1968	6	10
Reggie Jackson	BAL A	Jul 18–23, 1976	6	6
Graig Nettles	SD N	Aug 11–21, 1984	6	7

Most Leadoff Home Runs, Career

Player	Total	Player	Total
Rickey Henderson	55	Don Buford	15
Bobby Bonds	35	Bert Campaneris	14
Paul Molitor	33	Frank Crosetti	14
Eddie Yost	28	Juan Samuel	14
Davey Lopes	26	Terry Puhl	13
Brian Downing	25	Bill Bruton	12
Lou Whitaker	23	Al Bumbry	12
Lou Brock	22	Oddibe McDowell	12
Jimmy Ryan	22	Joe Morgan	12
Felipe Alou	20	Al Smith	12
Barry Bonds	20	Tom Brown	11
Eddie Joost	19	Ralph Garr	11
Dick McAuliffe	19	Mickey Rivers	11
Hank Bauer	18	Earle Combs	10
Pete Rose	17	Johnny Frederick	10
Tommy Harper	16	Harry Hooper	10
Rick Monday	16	Don Money	10
Devon White	16	Wally Moses	10

Most Leadoff Home Runs, Season

Player	Team	Year	Total
Bobby Bonds	SF N	1973	11
Rickey Henderson	NY A	1986	9
Barry Bonds	PIT N	1988	8
Rickey Henderson	NY A	1985	7
Brian Downing	CAL A	1987	7
Eddie Joost	PHI A	1948	6
Eddie Yost	DET A	1959	6
Tommy Harper	MIL A	1970	6
Bert Campaneris	OAK A	1970	6
Brian Downing	CAL A	1982	6
Paul Molitor	MIL A	1991	6
Devon White	TOR A	1991	6

Leadoff Home Runs in Two Consecutive Games, AL

Player	Team	Date	Opp.
Harry Hooper	BOS	May 30, 1913	WAS
	BOS	May 30, 1913	WAS
Sherry Robertson	WAS	Sep 17, 1946	CLE
	WAS	Sep 18, 1946	CLE
Hank Bauer	NY	Aug 6, 1957	WAS
	NY	Aug 7, 1957	WAS
Tony Kubek	NY	Sep 6, 1964	KC
	NY	Sep 7, 1964	MIN
Dick McAuliffe	DET	Apr 28, 1969	WAS
	DET	Apr 29, 1969	WAS
Al Bumbry	BAL	Aug 4, 1982	BOS
	BAL	Aug 5, 1982	KC
Lou Whitaker	DET	May 6, 1983	CAL
	DET	May 7, 1983	CAL
Damaso Garcia	TOR	Jun 1, 1983	DET
	TOR	Jun 2, 1983	DET
Oddibe McDowell	TEX	Jul 27, 1985	NY
	TEX	Jul 28, 1985	NY
Kirby Puckett	MIN	May 2, 1986	DET
	MIN	May 3, 1986	DET
Rickey Henderson	OAK	May 5, 1990	BOS
	OAK	May 6, 1990	BOS

Leadoff Home Runs in Two Consecutive Games, NL

Player	Team	Date	Opp.
John Crooks	STL	May 10, 1892	PHI
	STL	May 11, 1892	BAL
Sam Mertes	CHI	Jun 8, 1900	BOS
	CHI	Jun 9, 1900	BOS
Jesse Burkett	STL	May 22, 1901	BKN
	STL	May 23, 1901	PHI
Carl Furillo	BKN	Jul 12, 1951	CHI
	BKN	Jul 13, 1951	CHI
Whitey Lockman	NY	Jul 18, 1953	CHI
	NY	Jul 19, 1953	MIL
Denis Menke	MIL	Jul 26, 1964	CIN
	MIL	Jul 27, 1964	CIN
Felipe Alou	MIL	Jul 26, 1965	HOU
	MIL	Jul 27, 1965	HOU
	ATL	Aug 9, 1966	LA
	ATL	Aug 10, 1966	LA
Bobby Bonds	SF	Jun 5, 1973	PIT
	SF	Jun 6, 1973	PIT
Pete Rose	CIN	Jul 25, 1976	ATL
	CIN	Jul 26, 1976	SF
Gary Redus	CIN	Jul 1, 1983	ATL
	CIN	Jul 2, 1983	ATL

Leadoff Home Runs in Two Consecutive Games, NL (*cont.*)

Player	Team	Date	Opp.
Eddie Milner	CIN	Jun 24, 1984	SD
	CIN	Jun 25, 1984	SF
Dan Gladden	SF	Oct 1, 1985	CIN
	SF	Oct 2, 1985	HOU

No Home Runs, Season, AL since 1920 (500 or more at-bats)

Player	Team	Year	G	AB
Joe Gedeon	STL	1920	153	606
Bucky Harris	WAS	1921	154	584
Stuffy McInnis	BOS	1921	152	584
Ernie Johnson	CHI	1922	145	603
Bill Wambsganss	CLE	1922	143	538
	BOS	1924	155	631
Muddy Ruel	WAS	1924	149	501
Willie Kamm	CHI	1927	148	580
Johnny Mostil	CHI	1928	133	503
Tom Oliver	BOS	1930	154	646
	BOS	1931	148	586
Hal Rhyne	BOS	1931	147	565
Billy Rogell	DET	1933	155	587
Bill Knickerbocker	CLE	1935	132	540
Rollie Hemsley	STL	1935	144	504
Cecil Travis	WAS	1935	138	534
Doc Cramer	BOS	1936	154	643
	BOS	1937	153	560
	BOS	1938	148	658
	BOS	1939	137	589
Luke Appling	CHI	1939	148	516
	CHI	1940	150	566
Doc Cramer	DET	1942	151	630
Irv Hall	PHI	1943	151	544
George Myatt	WAS	1944	140	568
Irv Hall	PHI	1944	143	559
Gil Torres	WAS	1944	134	524
George Kell	PHI	1944	139	514
Skeeter Webb	CHI	1944	139	513
Irv Hall	PHI	1945	151	616
Gil Torres	WAS	1945	147	562
Johnny Pesky	BOS	1947	155	638
Barney McCosky	PHI	1948	135	515
Dave Philley	CHI	1949	146	598
Billy Goodman	BOS	1951	141	547
Nellie Fox	CHI	1952	142	648
Billy Goodman	BOS	1955	149	599
Nellie Fox	CHI	1958	155	623
Mark Belanger	BAL	1971	150	500
Rod Carew	MIN	1972	142	535

No Home Runs, Season, AL since 1920 (500 or more at-bats) (cont.)

Player	Team	Year	G	AB
Freddie Patek	KC	1972	135	501
Duane Kuiper	CLE	1976	135	506
Jerry Remy	CAL	1976	113	502
Duane Kuiper	CLE	1978	149	547
Miguel Dilone	CLE	1980	132	528
Jerry Remy	BOS	1982	155	636
	BOS	1983	146	592
Jack Perconte	SEA	1984	155	612
Kirby Puckett	MIN	1984	128	557
Ozzie Guillen	CHI	1988	156	566
Jim Gantner	MIL	1988	155	539
Scott Fletcher	TEX	1988	140	515
Harold Reynolds	SEA	1989	153	613
Alvaro Espinoza	NY	1989	146	503
Lance Johnson	CHI	1991	159	588
Luis Polonia	CAL	1992	149	577

No Home Runs, Season, NL since 1920 (500 or more at-bats)

Player	Team	Year	G	AB
Milt Stock	STL	1920	155	639
Dave Bancroft	PHI/NY	1920	150	613
Heinie Groh	CIN	1920	145	550
Rabbit Maranville	PIT	1922	155	672
Goldie Rapp	PHI	1922	119	502
Babe Pinelli	CIN	1924	144	510
Sparky Adams	CHI	1926	154	624
	CHI	1927	146	647
	PIT	1928	135	539
Dave Bancroft	BKN	1928	149	515
Rabbit Maranville	BOS	1929	145	560
Tommy Thevenow	PHI	1930	156	573
Sparky Adams	STL	1930	137	570
Freddie Maguire	BOS	1930	146	516
Rabbit Maranville	BOS	1931	145	562
Dick Bartell	PHI	1931	135	554
Wally Gilbert	BKN	1931	145	552
Rabbit Maranville	BOS	1932	149	571
Billy Herman	CHI	1933	153	619
Billy Urbanski	BOS	1933	144	566
Joe Moore	NY	1933	132	524
Harry Rice	CIN	1933	143	510
Lloyd Waner	PIT	1933	121	500
Dick Bartell	PHI	1934	146	604
Lloyd Waner	PIT	1935	122	537
George Scharein	PHI	1937	146	511
Danny Murtaugh	PHI	1942	144	506

No Home Runs, Season, NL since 1920 (500 or more at-bats) (cont.)

Player	Team	Year	G	AB
Whitey Wietelmann	BOS	1943	153	534
Eddie Stanky	CHI	1943	142	510
Steve Mesner	CIN	1943	137	504
Emil Verban	STL	1945	155	597
Red Schoendienst	STL	1946	142	606
Emil Verban	PHI	1947	155	540
Stan Rojek	PIT	1949	144	557
Johnny Temple	CIN	1954	146	505
	CIN	1955	150	588
Don Blasingame	STL	1956	150	587
Richie Ashburn	PHI	1957	156	626
Johnny Temple	CIN	1957	145	557
Richie Ashburn	CHI	1960	151	547
Maury Wills	LA	1960	148	516
	LA	1963	134	527
	LA	1965	158	650
Hal Lanier	SF	1965	159	622
Don Kessinger	CHI	1967	149	580
Hal Lanier	SF	1967	151	525
Sonny Jackson	HOU	1967	129	520
Maury Wills	PIT	1968	153	627
Matty Alou	PIT	1968	146	558
Larry Bowa	PHI	1970	145	547
Maury Wills	LA	1970	132	520
Larry Bowa	PHI	1971	159	650
Roger Metzger	HOU	1971	150	562
Enzo Hernandez	SD	1971	143	549
Bud Harrelson	NY	1971	142	547
Don Kessinger	CHI	1973	160	577
Roger Metzger	HOU	1974	143	572
Enzo Hernandez	SD	1974	147	512
Don Kessinger	CHI	1975	154	601
Larry Bowa	PHI	1976	156	624
Frank Taveras	PIT	1976	144	519
Dave Cash	MON	1977	153	650
Frank Taveras	PIT	1978	157	654
Doug Flynn	NY	1978	156	532
Ozzie Smith	SD	1979	156	587
Craig Reynolds	HOU	1979	146	555
Larry Bowa	PHI	1979	147	539
Ozzie Smith	SD	1980	158	609
Rodney Scott	MON	1980	154	567
Frank Taveras	NY	1980	141	562
Manny Trillo	PHI	1982	149	549
Alan Wiggins	SD	1983	144	503
Marvell Wynne	PIT	1984	154	653

No Home Runs, Season, NL since 1920 (500 or more at-bats) (cont.)

Player	Team	Year	G	AB
Vince Coleman	STL	1986	154	600
Ozzie Smith	STL	1986	153	514
	STL	1987	158	600
Gerald Young	HOU	1988	149	576
	HOU	1989	146	533
Alfredo Griffin	LA	1989	136	506
Ozzie Smith	STL	1992	132	518

Switch-Hit Home Runs in One Game, AL

Player	Team	Date	Player	Team	Date
Wally Schang	PHI	Sep 8, 1916	Mike Young	BAL	Aug 13, 1985
Johnny Lucadello	STL	Sep 16, 1940	Eddie Murray	BAL	Aug 26, 1985
Mickey Mantle	NY	May 13, 1955	Nelson Simmons	DET	Sep 16, 1985
	NY	Aug 15, 1955	Roy Smalley	MIN	May 30, 1986
	NY	May 18, 1956	Tony Bernazard	CLE	Jul 1, 1986
	NY	Jul 1, 1956	Ruben Sierra	TEX	Sep 13, 1986
	NY	Jun 12, 1957	Eddie Murray	BAL	May 8, 1987
	NY	Jul 28, 1958		BAL	May 9, 1987
	NY	Sep 15, 1959	Devon White	CAL	Jun 23, 1987
	NY	Apr 26, 1961	Dale Sveum	MIL	Jul 17, 1987
	NY	May 6, 1962		MIL	Jun 12, 1988
Tom Tresh	NY	Sep 1, 1963	Mickey Tettleton	BAL	Jun 13, 1988
	NY	Jul 13, 1964	Chili Davis	CAL	Jul 30, 1988
Mickey Mantle	NY	Aug 12, 1964	Ruben Sierra	TEX	Jun 8, 1989
Tom Tresh	NY	Jun 6, 1965	Chili Davis	CAL	Jul 1, 1989
Reggie Smith	BOS	Aug 20, 1967	Devon White	CAL	Jun 29, 1990
	BOS	Aug 11, 1968	Roberto Alomar	TOR	May 11, 1991
Don Buford	BAL	Apr 9, 1970	Devon White	TOR	Jun 1, 1992
Roy White	NY	May 7, 1970			
Reggie Smith	BOS	Jul 2, 1972			
	BOS	Apr 16, 1973			

Switch-Hit Home Runs in One Game, NL

Player	Team	Date
Roy White	NY	Aug 13, 1973
	NY	Apr 23, 1975
Ken Henderson	CHI	Aug 29, 1975
Eddie Murray	BAL	Aug 3, 1977
Roy White	NY	Jun 13, 1978
Larry Milbourne	SEA	Jul 15, 1978
Willie Wilson	KC	Jun 15, 1979
Eddie Murray	BAL	Aug 29, 1979
U. L. Washington	KC	Sep 21, 1979
Eddie Murray	BAL	Aug 16, 1981
	BAL	Apr 24, 1982
Ted Simmons	MIL	May 2, 1982
Eddie Murray	BAL	Aug 26, 1982
Roy Smalley	NY	Sep 5, 1982
Donnie Scott	SEA	Apr 29, 1985

Below is the "Switch-Hit Home Runs in One Game, NL" table continued:

Player	Team	Date
Augie Galan	CHI	Jun 25, 1937
Jim Russell	BOS	Jun 7, 1948
	BKN	Jul 26, 1950
Red Schoendienst	STL	Jul 8, 1951
Maury Wills	LA	May 30, 1962
Ellis Burton	CHI	Aug 1, 1963
	CHI	Sep 7, 1964
Jim Lefebvre	LA	May 7, 1966
Wes Parker	LA	Jun 5, 1966
Pete Rose	CIN	Aug 30, 1966
	CIN	Aug 2, 1967
Ted Simmons	STL	Apr 17, 1975
Reggie Smith	STL	May 4, 1975
	STL	May 22, 1976

Switch-Hit Home Runs in One Game, NL
(cont.)

Player	Team	Date
Lee Mazzilli	NY	Sep 3, 1978
Ted Simmons	STL	Jun 11, 1979
Alan Ashby	HOU	Sep 27, 1982
Chili Davis	SF	Jun 5, 1983
Mark Bailey	HOU	Sep 16, 1984
Chili Davis	SF	Jun 27, 1987
Bobby Bonilla	PIT	Jul 3, 1987
Kevin Bass	HOU	Aug 3, 1987
	HOU	Sep 2, 1987
Chili Davis	SF	Sep 15, 1987
Bobby Bonilla	PIT	Apr 6, 1988
Tim Raines	MON	Jul 16, 1988
Steve Jeltz	PHI	Jun 8, 1989
Kevin Bass	HOU	Aug 20, 1989
Eddie Murray	LA	Apr 18, 1990
	LA	Jun 9, 1990
Bret Barberie	MON	Aug 2, 1991

Player	Team	Date
Howard Johnson	NY	Aug 31, 1991
Kevin Bass	SF	Aug 2, 1992

Most Extra-Inning Home Runs, Career

Player	Total
Willie Mays	22
Jack Clark	18
Babe Ruth	16
Frank Robinson	15
Jimmie Foxx	14
Mickey Mantle	14
Hank Aaron	13
Ted Williams	13
Harmon Killebrew	11
Stan Musial	11
Willie Stargell	11

Twenty Home Runs With 50 Stolen Bases, Season

Player	Team	Year	G	SB	HR
Lou Brock	STL N	1967	159	52	21
Cesar Cedeno	HOU N	1972	139	55	22
Cesar Cedeno	HOU N	1973	139	56	25
Joe Morgan	CIN N	1973	157	67	26
Cesar Cedeno	HOU N	1974	160	57	26
Joe Morgan	CIN N	1974	149	58	22
	CIN N	1976	141	60	27
Rickey Henderson	NY A	1985	143	80	24
Ryne Sandberg	CHI N	1985	153	54	26
Eric Davis	CIN N	1986	132	80	27
Rickey Henderson	NY A	1986	153	87	28
Eric Davis	CIN N	1987	129	50	37
Barry Bonds	PIT N	1990	151	52	33
Rickey Henderson	OAK A	1990	136	65	28
Brady Anderson	BAL A	1992	159	53	21

Thirty Home Runs with 30 Stolen Bases, Season, AL

Player	Team	Year	G	SB	HR
Ken Williams	STL	1922	153	37	39
Tommy Harper	MIL	1970	154	38	31
Bobby Bonds	NY	1975	145	30	32
	CAL	1977	158	41	37
	CHI, TEX	1978	156	43	31
Joe Carter	CLE	1987	149	31	32
Jose Canseco	OAK	1988	158	40	42

Thirty Home Runs with 30 Stolen Bases, Season, NL

Player	Team	Year	G	SB	HR
Willie Mays	NY	1956	152	40	36
	NY	1957	152	38	35
Hank Aaron	MIL	1963	161	31	44
Bobby Bonds	SF	1969	158	45	32
	SF	1973	160	43	39
Dale Murphy	ATL	1983	162	30	36
Eric Davis	CIN	1987	129	50	37
Darryl Strawberry	NY	1987	154	36	39
Howard Johnson	NY	1987	157	32	36
	NY	1989	153	41	36
Barry Bonds	PIT	1990	151	52	33
Ron Gant	ATL	1990	152	33	32
	ATL	1991	154	34	32
Howard Johnson	NY	1991	156	30	38
Barry Bonds	PIT	1992	140	39	34

Forty Home Runs with 40 Stolen Bases, Season

Player	Team	Year	G	SB	HR
Jose Canseco	OAK A	1988	158	40	42

Forty Home Runs with 200 Hits, Season, AL

Player	Team	Year	HR	H
Babe Ruth	NY	1921	59	204
Jimmie Foxx	PHI	1932	58	213
Lou Gehrig	NY	1934	49	210
	NY	1936	49	205
Jimmie Foxx	PHI	1933	48	204
Lou Gehrig	NY	1927	47	218
	NY	1931	46	211
Babe Ruth	NY	1924	46	200
Joe DiMaggio	NY	1937	46	215
Jim Rice	BOS	1978	46	213
Al Rosen	CLE	1953	43	201
Hal Trosky	CLE	1936	42	216
Lou Gehrig	NY	1930	41	220
Babe Ruth	NY	1923	41	205
Hank Greenberg	DET	1937	40	200

Forty Home Runs with 200 Hits, Season, NL

Player	Team	Year	HR	H
Hank Aaron	MIL	1963	44	201
Chuck Klein	PHI	1929	43	219
Rogers Hornsby	STL	1922	42	250
Billy Williams	CHI	1970	42	205

Forty Home Runs with 200 Hits, Season, NL (*cont.*)

Player	Team	Year	HR	H
Chuck Klein	PHI	1930	40	250
Rogers Hornsby	CHI	1929	40	229

Fifty Home Runs with 150 RBIs, Season

Player	Team	Year	HR	RBI
Babe Ruth	NY A	1921	59	171
	NY A	1927	60	164
Hack Wilson	CHI N	1930	56	190
Jimmie Foxx	PHI A	1932	58	169
	BOS A	1938	50	175

Most Home Runs in Final Season

Player	Team	Year	G	AB	HR
Dave Kingman	OAK A	1986	144	561	35
Ted Williams	BOS A	1960	113	310	29
Hank Greenberg	PIT N	1947	125	405	25
Roy Cullenbine	DET A	1947	142	464	24
Jack Graham	STL A	1949	137	500	24
Joe Gordon	CLE A	1950	119	368	19
Ralph Kiner	CLE A	1955	113	321	18
Joe Adcock	CAL A	1966	83	231	18
Mickey Mantle	NY A	1968	144	435	18
Doug Rader	SD N	1977	148	483	18
	TOR A				
Reggie Smith	SF N	1982	106	349	18
Tony Horton	CLE A	1970	115	413	17
Bill Madlock	LA N				
	DET A	1987	108	387	17
Gorman Thomas	SEA A				
	MIL A	1986	101	315	16
Doug DeCinces	CAL A				
	STL N	1987	137	462	16
Monte Irvin	CHI N	1956	111	339	15
Al Rosen	CLE A	1956	121	416	15
Ted Kluszewski	LA A	1961	107	263	15
Cliff Johnson	TOR A	1986	107	336	15
Reggie Jackson	OAK A	1987	115	336	15

Brothers with Most Home Runs, Career

Player	HR	Player	HR
Hank Aaron	755	Joe DiMaggio	361
Tommie Aaron	13	Vince DiMaggio	125
Total	768	Dom DiMaggio	87
		Total	573

Brothers with Most Home Runs Career, (*cont.*)

Player	HR	Player	HR
Ken Boyer	282	Tony Conigliaro	166
Clete Boyer	162	Billy Conigliaro	40
Total	444	Total	206
Lee May	354	Bill Dickey	202
Carlos May	90	George Dickey	4
Total	444	Total	206
Eddie Murray	414	Jose Cruz	165
Rich Murray	4	Hector Cruz	39
Total	418	Total	204
Graig Nettles	390	Charlie Keller	189
Jim Nettles	16	Hal Keller	1
Total	406	Total	190
Dick Allen	351	Walker Cooper	173
Hank Allen	6	Mort Cooper	6
Ron Allen	1	Total	179
Total	358	Carney Lansford	151
Bob Johnson	288	Joe Lansford	1
Roy Johnson	58	Total	152
Total	346	Paul Waner	112
George Brett	298	Lloyd Waner	28
Ken Brett	10	Total	140
Total	308	Gary Roenicke	121
Hank Sauer	288	Ron Roenicke	17
Ed Sauer	5	Total	138
Total	293	Roger Connor	136
Cal Ripken	273	Joe Connor	1
Billy Ripken	13	Total	137
Total	286	Zack Wheat	132
Felipe Alou	206	Mack Wheat	4
Jesus Alou	32	Total	136
Matty Alou	31	Gee Walker	124
Total	269	Hub Walker	5
Sal Bando	242	Total	129
Chris Bando	27	Ed Delahanty	100
Total	286	Jim Delahanty	18
Joe Torre	252	Frank Delahanty	5
Frank Torre	13	Joe Delahanty	4
Total	265	Total	127
Bob Meusel	156	Frank Bolling	106
Irish Meusel	106	Milt Bolling	19
Total	262	Total	125

Brothers with Most Home Runs Career, (*cont.*)

Player	HR	Player	HR
Gene Freese	115	Dixie Walker	105
George Freese	3	Harry Walker	10
Total	118	Total	115

Home Runs by Brothers in One Game

Player	Team	Date	Inn.	Opp.	Opp. Pitcher
Lloyd Waner	PIT N	Sep 4, 1927	5	CIN	Dolf Luque
Paul Waner	PIT N	Sep 4, 1927	5	CIN	Dolf Luque
	PIT N	Jun 9, 1929	5	BKN	Doug McWeeny
Lloyd Waner	PIT N	Jun 9, 1929	7	BKN	Doug McWeeny
Rick Ferrell	BOS A	Jul 19, 1933	4	CLE	Wes Ferrell
Wes Ferrell	CLE A	Jul 19, 1933	4	BOS	Hank Johnson
Tony Cuccinello	BKN N	Jul 5, 1935	8	NY	Leon Chagnon
Al Cuccinello	NY N	Jul 5, 1935	9	BKN	Johnny Babich
Lloyd Waner	PIT N	Sep 15, 1938	5	NY	Cliff Melton
Paul Waner	PIT N	Sep 15, 1938	5	NY	Cliff Melton
Dom DiMaggio	BOS A	Jun 30, 1950	6	NY	Joe Ostrowski
Joe DiMaggio	NY A	Jun 30, 1950	8	BOS	Walt Masterson
Felipe Alou	SF N	May 15, 1961	1	CHI	Dick Ellsworth
Matty Alou	SF N	May 15, 1961	8	CHI	Joe Schaffernoth
Hank Aaron	MIL N	Jun 12, 1962	2	LA	Phil Ortega
Tommie Aaron	MIL N	Jun 12, 1962	8	LA	Ed Roebuck
	MIL N	Jul 12, 1962	9	STL	Larry Jackson
Hank Aaron	MIL N	Jul 12, 1962	9	STL	Lindy McDaniel
Tommie Aaron	MIL N	Aug 14, 1962	6	CIN	Johnny Klippstein
Hank Aaron	MIL N	Aug 14, 1962	7	CIN	Ted Wills
Jesus Alou	SF N	Aug 12, 1965	6	PIT	Bob Friend
Matty Alou	SF N	Aug 12, 1965	8	PIT	Don Schwall
Billy Conigliaro	BOS A	Jul 4, 1970	4	CLE	Steve Dunning
Tony Conigliaro	BOS A	Jul 4, 1970	7	CLE	Fred Lasher
Billy Conigliaro	BOS A	Sep 19, 1970	4	WAS	Jim Hannan
Tony Conigliaro	BOS A	Sep 19, 1970	7	WAS	Joe Grzenda
Graig Nettles	NY A	Sep 14, 1974	1	DET	Mickey Lolich
Jim Nettles	DET A	Sep 14, 1974	2	NY	Pat Dobson
Jose Cruz	HOU N	May 4, 1981	1	CHI	Mike Krukow
Hector Cruz	CHI N	May 4, 1981	6	HOU	Joaquin Andujar
Billy Ripken	BAL A	Sep 15, 1990	5	TOR	David Wells
Cal Ripken	BAL A	Sep 15, 1990	5	TOR	David Wells

Home Runs by Father and Son in One Game

Player	Team	Date	Inn.	Opp.	Opp. Pitcher
Ken Griffey, Sr.	SEA A	Sep 14, 1990	1	CAL	Kirk McCaskill
Ken Griffey, Jr.	SEA A	Sep 14, 1990	1	CAL	Kirk McCaskill

Most Extra-Base Hits, Game, AL

Player	Team	Date	2B	3B	HR	Total
Lou Boudreau	CLE	Jul 14, 1946	4	0	1	5
Pop Dillon	DET	Apr 25, 1901	4	0	0	4
Mike Donlin	BAL	Jun 24, 1901	2	2	0	4
Snake Wiltse	PHI	Jun 24, 1901	2	2	0	4
John Heidrick	STL	Aug 7, 1902	2	2	0	4
Bill Bradley	CLE	Sep 24, 1903	2	1	1	4
Fielder Jones	CHI	May 18, 1906	2	1	1	4
Hal Chase	NY	Aug 30, 1906	0	3	1	4
Nap Lajoie	CLE	Aug 7, 1911	3	0	1	4
Frank Baker	PHI	Sep 26, 1911	2	0	2	4
Babe Ruth	BOS	May 9, 1918	3	1	0	4
Patsy Gharrity	WAS	Jun 23, 1919	2	2	0	4
Harry Hooper	BOS	Sep 15, 1919	2	2	0	4
Ty Cobb	DET	May 8, 1921	2	1	1	4
Sam Rice	WAS	Jul 24, 1921	3	1	0	4
George Sisler	STL	Aug 13, 1921	2	1	1	4
Ty Cobb	DET	May 7, 1922	3	0	1	4
Larry Gardner	CLE	Aug 1, 1922	3	0	1	4
Babe Ruth	NY	Sep 11, 1922	2	0	2	4
George Burns	CLE	Jun 19, 1924	3	0	1	4
	CLE	Jul 21, 1924	2	0	2	4
Joe Hauser	PHI	Aug 2, 1924	1	0	3	4
Harry Hooper	CHI	Sep 28, 1924	2	2	0	4
Ty Cobb	DET	May 5, 1925	1	0	3	4
Earl Sheely	CHI	May 21, 1926	3	0	1	4
Heinie Manush	DET	Jul 21, 1926	1	2	1	4
Lou Gehrig	NY	Sep 19, 1926	3	0	1	4
Ben Paschal	NY	Jun 13, 1927	1	1	2	4
Babe Ruth	NY	Jul 9, 1927	2	0	2	4
Lou Gehrig	NY	Jun 12, 1928	0	2	2	4
Eddie Morgan	CLE	Jun 16, 1928	3	1	0	4
Heinie Manush	STL	May 24, 1929	2	0	2	4
Lew Fonseca	CLE	May 29, 1929	0	2	2	4
Mickey Cochrane	PHI	Jul 4, 1929	3	0	1	4
Joe Cronin	WAS	Sep 2, 1929	2	1	1	4
Al Simmons	PHI	Apr 19, 1930	2	0	2	4
Lou Gehrig	NY	Jul 29, 1930	1	1	2	4
Joe Vosmik	CLE	Apr 18, 1931	3	1	0	4
Earl Averill	CLE	May 23, 1931	3	0	1	4
Bob Fothergill	DET	Jul 28, 1931	2	1	1	4
Lou Gehrig	NY	Jun 3, 1932	0	0	4	4
Jimmie Foxx	PHI	Jul 10, 1932	1	0	3	4
Al Simmons	PHI	Jul 15, 1932	1	0	3	4
Heinie Manush	WAS	Jul 23, 1932	2	2	0	4
Jimmie Foxx	PHI	Apr 24, 1933	1	0	3	4
	PHI	Jul 2, 1933	1	1	2	4
Sammy West	STL	Aug 5, 1933	1	2	1	4

Most Extra-Base Hits, Game, AL (cont.)

Player	Team	Date	2B	3B	HR	Total
Lou Gehrig	NY	May 10, 1934	2	0	2	4
Earl Averill	CLE	Aug 16, 1934	3	1	0	4
Bill Werber	BOS	July 17, 1935	4	0	0	4
Tony Lazzeri	NY	May 24, 1936	1	0	3	4
Red Rolfe	NY	Jun 11, 1936	3	1	0	4
Joe DiMaggio	NY	Jun 24, 1936	2	0	2	4
Frankie Hayes	PHI	Jul 25, 1936	4	0	0	4
Gee Walker	DET	Aug 8, 1936	3	0	1	4
Joe DiMaggio	NY	Jul 9, 1937	1	1	2	4
Mike Kreevich	CHI	Sep 4, 1937	4	0	0	4
Merv Connors	CHI	Sep 17, 1937	1	0	3	4
Joe Gordon	NY	Sep 4, 1938	2	0	2	4
Jimmie Foxx	BOS	Sep 7, 1938	2	0	2	4
Marv Owen	CHI	Apr 23, 1939	4	0	0	4
Chet Laabs	STL	Jul 16, 1941	1	1	2	4
Joe DiMaggio	NY	Jul 20, 1941	3	0	1	4
Johnny Lindell	NY	Aug 17, 1944	4	0	0	4
Pat Seerey	CLE	Jul 13, 1945	0	1	3	4
Lou Boudreau	CLE	July 14, 1946	4	0	0	4
Rudy York	BOS	Jul 27, 1946	2	0	2	4
Lou Boudreau	CLE	Apr 26, 1948	2	2	0	4
Joe DiMaggio	NY	May 20, 1948	1	1	2	4
Pat Seerey	CLE	Jul 18, 1948	0	0	4	4
George Vico	DET	Aug 14, 1948	2	1	1	4
Al Zarilla	BOS	Jun 7, 1950	4	0	0	4
Hoot Evers	DET	Sep 7, 1950	1	2	1	4
Joe DiMaggio	NY	Sep 10, 1950	1	0	3	4
Bobby Avila	CLE	Jun 20, 1951	1	0	3	4
Mickey Vernon	WAS	May 22, 1954	3	0	1	4
Vic Wertz	CLE	Sep 26, 1956	4	0	0	4
Rocky Colavito	CLE	Jun 10, 1959	0	0	4	4
Gino Cimoli	KC	Apr 17, 1962	2	2	0	4
Charlie Lau	BAL	Jul 13, 1962	4	0	0	4
Bill Bruton	DET	May 19, 1963	4	0	0	4
Carl Yastrzemski	BOS	May 14, 1965	1	1	2	4
Ed Stroud	WAS	Jul 4, 1968	2	2	0	4
Don Baylor	BAL	Apr 6, 1973	3	0	1	4
Orlando Cepeda	BOS	Aug 8, 1973	4	0	0	4
Jim Mason	NY	Jul 8, 1974	4	0	0	4
Hal McRae	KC	Aug 27, 1974	3	0	1	4
Dave Duncan	BAL	Jun 30, 1975	4	0	0	4
Fred Lynn	BOS	Jun 18, 1975	0	1	3	4
Roy Howell	TOR	Sep 10, 1977	2	0	2	4
Jack Brohamer	CHI	Sep 25, 1977	2	1	1	4
George Brett	KC	May 28, 1979	1	1	2	4
Dan Ford	CAL	Aug 10, 1979	2	1	1	4
Freddie Patek	CAL	Jun 20, 1980	2	0	2	4

Most Extra-Base Hits, Game, AL (*cont.*)

Player	Team	Date	2B	3B	HR	Total
Rick Miller	BOS	May 11, 1981	4	0	0	4
Johnny Grubb	DET	Aug 8, 1982	2	1	1	4
Cal Ripken	BAL	Sep 3, 1983	2	0	2	4
Kirk Gibson	DET	Sep 3, 1985	2	0	2	4
Damaso Garcia	TOR	Jun 27, 1986	4	0	0	4
Joe Carter	CLE	Sep 6, 1986	2	0	2	4
Lonnie Smith	KC	Sep 18, 1986	3	1	0	4
Kevin Seitzer	KC	Aug 2, 1987	1	1	2	4
Kirby Puckett	MIN	Aug 30, 1987	2	0	2	4
Jesse Barfield	TOR	Sep 26, 1987	3	1	0	4
Kirby Puckett	MIN	May 13, 1989	4	0	0	4
Wade Boggs	BOS	Jul 25, 1989	3	1	0	4
Dave Winfield	CAL	Apr 13, 1991	1	0	3	4
Harold Baines	OAK	May 7, 1991	1	0	3	4
Robin Ventura	CHI	Jul 19, 1991	2	0	2	4

Most Extra-Base Hits, Game, NL

Player	Team	Date	2B	3B	HR	Total
George Gore	CHI	Jul 9, 1885	3	2	0	5
Larry Twitchell	CLE	Aug 15, 1889	1	3	1	5
Joe Adcock	MIL	Jul 31, 1954	1	0	4	5
Willie Stargell	PIT	Aug 1, 1970	3	0	2	5
Steve Garvey	LA	Aug 28, 1977	3	0	2	5
George Hall	PHI	Jun 14, 1876	0	3	1	4
Wes Fisler	PHI	Jun 15, 1876	3	0	1	4
John O'Rourke	BOS	Sep 15, 1880	4	0	0	4
Cap Anson	CHI	Jul 3, 1883	4	0	0	4
Abner Dalrymple	CHI	Jul 3, 1883	4	0	0	4
Fred Pfeffer	CHI	Sep 6, 1883	4	0	0	4
Tom Burns	CHI	Sep 6, 1883	3	0	1	4
Ned Williamson	CHI	May 30, 1884	1	0	3	4
George Gore	CHI	Jun 6, 1885	1	3	0	4
Sam Wise	BOS	Jun 30, 1885	2	2	0	4
Hardy Richardson	DET	Sep 9, 1886	1	3	0	4
Dan Brouthers	DET	Sep 10, 1886	1	0	3	4
Jack Rowe	DET	Sep 13, 1886	2	2	0	4
Sam Thompson	DET	May 13, 1887	0	3	1	4
Sam Wise	BOS	May 21, 1887	2	2	0	4
George Myers	IND	Apr 20, 1888	3	0	1	4
Jimmy Ryan	CHI	Jul 28, 1888	1	2	1	4
Jim O'Rourke	NY	Jun 26, 1889	3	0	1	4
George Davis	CLE	Apr 25, 1891	0	3	1	4
Jimmy Ryan	CHI	May 16, 1891	3	1	0	4
Monte Ward	BKN	Aug 22, 1892	2	1	1	4
Tommy McCarthy	BOS	Oct 7, 1892	1	1	2	4
Tommy Tucker	BOS	Jul 22, 1893	4	0	0	4
Bobby Lowe	BOS	May 30, 1894	0	0	4	4

Most Extra-Base Hits, Game, NL (*cont.*)

Player	Team	Date	2B	3B	HR	Total
Elmer Smith	PIT	Aug 1, 1894	3	1	0	4
Frank Bonner	BAL	Aug 4, 1894	4	0	0	4
George Treadway	BKN	Aug 20, 1894	2	1	1	4
Joe Kelley	BAL	Sep 3, 1894	4	0	0	4
George Decker	CHI	Sep 16, 1894	1	1	2	4
Hugh Duffy	BOS	Sep 18, 1894	1	3	0	4
Jake Stenzel	PIT	May 14, 1896	3	1	0	4
Ed Delahanty	PHI	Jul 13, 1896	0	0	4	4
Jimmy Sheckard	BKN	Oct 15, 1898	3	0	1	4
Ed Delahanty	PHI	May 13, 1899	4	0	0	4
Bill Joyce	NY	May 18, 1899	0	4	0	4
Buck Freeman	WAS	Jul 5, 1899	2	1	1	4
Ginger Beaumont	PIT	Aug 9, 1899	1	3	0	4
Tom Daly	BKN	Jun 26, 1901	3	1	0	4
Honus Wagner	PIT	Aug 22, 1910	3	0	1	4
Mike Mitchell	CIN	Aug 19, 1911	2	1	1	4
Sherry Magee	PHI	Jun 17, 1914	4	0	0	4
Gavvy Cravath	PHI	Aug 8, 1915	4	0	0	4
	PHI	Jun 23, 1919	4	0	0	4
George Burns	NY	Sep 17, 1920	2	1	1	4
Billy Southworth	BOS	Aug 4, 1921	3	0	1	4
Ross Youngs	NY	Apr 29, 1922	2	1	1	4
Jimmy O'Connell	NY	Jun 1, 1923	3	0	1	4
Hack Miller	CHI	Sep 16, 1923	3	1	0	4
George Kelly	NY	Sep 17, 1923	1	0	3	4
Kiki Cuyler	PIT	Aug 9, 1924	3	1	0	4
Rogers Hornsby	STL	Aug 26, 1924	3	0	1	4
Les Bell	STL	Apr 18, 1925	2	0	2	4
Hack Wilson	NY	Jul 1, 1925	2	0	2	4
Russ Wrightstone	PHI	Jun 11, 1926	2	1	1	4
Paul Waner	PIT	Sep 11, 1926	1	1	2	4
Les Bell	STL	Sep 22, 1926	1	3	0	4
	STL	Jun 13, 1927	1	0	3	4
Fred Lindstrom	NY	May 26, 1928	2	0	2	4
Les Bell	BOS	Jun 2, 1928	0	1	3	4
Babe Herman	BKN	Jun 5, 1929	2	2	0	4
Travis Jackson	NY	Jun 15, 1929	1	1	2	4
Mel Ott	NY	Jun 19, 1929	2	0	2	4
Pinky Whitney	PHI	Jul 30, 1929	1	2	1	4
Chick Hafey	STL	Sep 9, 1929	3	0	1	4
Hod Ford	CIN	May 5, 1930	3	1	0	4
Denny Sothern	PHI	Jun 6, 1930	4	0	0	4
Lefty O'Doul	PHI	Jun 27, 1930	2	2	0	4
Mel Ott	NY	Aug 1, 1930	1	0	3	4
Bill Terry	NY	Sep 13, 1931	2	2	0	4
Ripper Collins	STL	Apr 15, 1932	3	0	1	4
Paul Waner	PIT	May 20, 1932	4	0	0	4

Most Extra-Base Hits, Game, NL (cont.)

Player	Team	Date	2B	3B	HR	Total
Lefty O'Doul	BKN	Aug 4, 1932	1	0	3	4
Dick Bartell	PHI	Apr 25, 1933	4	0	0	4
Pepper Martin	STL	May 5, 1933	2	1	1	4
Johnny Frederick	BKN	Aug 16, 1933	3	1	0	4
Kiki Cuyler	CHI	Jul 4, 1934	3	1	0	4
Ernie Lombardi	CIN	May 8, 1935	4	0	0	4
Joe Medwick	STL	May 30, 1935	3	1	0	4
George Watkins	PHI	Jun 30, 1935	3	1	0	4
Sam Leslie	BKN	Aug 4, 1935	3	0	1	4
Wally Berger	BOS	Aug 11, 1935	2	1	1	4
Hank Leiber	NY	Aug 18, 1935	2	1	1	4
Terry Moore	STL	Aug 28, 1935	3	0	1	4
Billy Herman	CHI	Apr 14, 1936	3	0	1	4
Chuck Klein	PHI	Jul 10, 1936	0	0	4	4
Joe Medwick	STL	May 12, 1937	2	0	2	4
	STL	Aug 4, 1937	4	0	0	4
Johnny Cooney	BKN	Aug 21, 1937	3	1	0	4
Johnny Rizzo	PIT	May 30, 1937	2	0	2	4
Johnny Mize	STL	Jul 3, 1939	1	1	2	4
Bill Werber	CIN	Jun 13, 1940	4	0	0	4
Pete Reiser	BKN	Jun 2, 1942	3	0	1	4
Phil Weintraub	NY	Apr 30, 1944	2	1	1	4
Red Schoendienst	STL	Jun 6, 1948	3	0	1	4
Jim Russell	BOS	Jun 7, 1948	2	0	2	4
Willie Jones	PHI	Apr 20, 1949	4	0	0	4
Lucky Lohrke	NY	May 4, 1949	3	0	1	4
Gil Hodges	BKN	Jun 25, 1949	1	1	2	4
Walker Cooper	CIN	Jul 6, 1949	0	1	3	4
Wes Westrum	NY	Jun 24, 1950	0	1	3	4
Ralph Kiner	PIT	Jun 25, 1950	0	1	3	4
Hank Sauer	CHI	Jun 25, 1950	2	0	2	4
Gil Hodges	BKN	Aug 31, 1950	0	0	4	4
Gus Bell	PIT	Apr 22, 1951	3	0	1	4
Jim Greengrass	CIN	Apr 13, 1954	4	0	0	4
Frank Thomas	PIT	May 2, 1954	3	0	1	4
Duke Snider	BKN	Jun 1, 1954	1	0	3	4
Jackie Robinson	BKN	Jun 17, 1954	2	0	2	4
Gil Hodges	BKN	Aug 8, 1954	1	2	1	4
Bob Thurman	CIN	Aug 18, 1956	1	0	3	4
Willie Mays	SF	May 13, 1958	0	2	2	4
	SF	Apr 30, 1961	0	0	4	4
Hank Aaron	MIL	May 3, 1962	1	1	2	4
Ernie Banks	CHI	May 29, 1962	1	0	3	4
Joe Christopher	NY	Aug 15, 1964	1	2	1	4
Rico Carty	MIL	Aug 24, 1964	3	0	1	4
Wes Covington	PHI	Aug 24, 1964	3	0	1	4
Willie Stargell	PIT	Jun 24, 1965	1	0	3	4

Most Extra-Base Hits, Game, NL (*cont.*)

Player	Team	Date	2B	3B	HR	Total
Felipe Alou	ATL	Apr 26, 1966	2	0	2	4
Bill White	PHI	Jul 31, 1966	3	0	1	4
Willie Stargell	PIT	May 22, 1968	1	0	3	4
Billy Williams	CHI	Apr 9, 1969	4	0	0	4
Hal McRae	CIN	Jul 27, 1971	3	0	1	4
Hal Breeden	MON	Sep 2, 1973	0	2	2	4
Willie Stargell	PIT	Sep 17, 1973	2	1	1	4
Davey Lopes	LA	Aug 20, 1974	1	0	3	4
Mike Schmidt	PHI	Apr 17, 1976	0	0	4	4
Dane Iorg	STL	Aug 11, 1980	3	0	1	4
Bo Diaz	PHI	Apr 24, 1982	2	0	2	4
Bob Horner	ATL	Jul 7, 1985	2	1	1	4
Rafael Ramirez	ATL	May 21, 1986	4	0	0	4
Bob Horner	ATL	Jul 6, 1986	0	0	4	4
Mark Wasinger	SF	May 9, 1987	3	0	1	4
Kevin Bass	HOU	Jun 27 1987	2	1	1	4
Tim Teufel	NY	Jul 5, 1987	2	0	2	4
Tim Raines	MON	Aug 16, 1987	2	1	1	4
Darryl Strawberry	NY	Aug 16, 1987	2	1	1	4
Chris Speier	SF	Jul 9, 1988	2	1	1	4
Mark Grace	CHI	Jul 5, 1989	3	0	1	4
Gregg Jefferies	NY	Sep 7, 1989	2	0	2	4
Bobby Bonilla	PIT	May 20, 1990	2	0	2	4
Billy Hatcher	CIN	Aug 21, 1990	4	0	0	4
Paul O'Neill	CIN	May 11, 1991	2	0	2	4
	CIN	Sep 13, 1991	3	0	1	4

Most Extra-Base Hits, Game, Other Leagues

Player	Team	Date	2B	3B	HR	Total
George Strief	PHI AA	Jun 25, 1885	1	4	0	5
Tom Brown	COL AA	Jul 4, 1883	2	0	2	4
Joe Battin	PIT AA	Jul 12, 1883	3	1	0	4
Lon Knight	PHI AA	Jul 30, 1883	2	1	1	4
Long John Reilly	CIN AA	Sep 12, 1883	1	1	2	4
Tom Brown	COL AA	Jul 4, 1884	2	0	2	4
Dave Orr	NY AA	Jun 12, 1885	2	1	1	4
Henry Larkin	PHI AA	Jun 16, 1885	2	1	1	4
Harry Stovey	PHI AA	Jul 16, 1885	3	1	0	4
Henry Larkin	PHI AA	Jul 29, 1885	4	0	0	4
Jocko Milligan	PHI AA	May 2, 1886	4	0	0	4
Guy Hecker	LOU AA	Aug 15, 1886	1	0	3	4
Bob Caruthers	STL AA	Aug 16, 1886	1	1	2	4
John Kerins	LOU AA	Aug 31, 1886	0	2	2	4
Tip O'Neill	STL AA	Apr 30, 1887	1	1	2	4
Oyster Burns	BAL AA	Jun 30, 1887	3	0	1	4
Mickey Hughes	BKN AA	Apr 20, 1888	2	2	0	4

Most Extra-Base Hits, Game, Other Leagues (*cont.*)

Player	Team	Date	2B	3B	HR	Total
Darby O'Brien	BKN AA	Aug 20, 1889	2	2	0	4
Farmer Weaver	LOU AA	Aug 12, 1890	1	2	1	4
Fred Dunlap	STL U	May 22, 1884	3	1	0	4
Jack McGeachy	BKN P	Jul 6, 1890	3	1	0	4

Most Extra-Base Hits in a Doubleheader, AL

Player	Team	Date	2B	3B	HR	Total	Inns.
John Stone	DET	May 30, 1933	4	0	2	6	
Jimmie Foxx	PHI	Jul 2, 1933	1	1	4	6	19
Hank Majeski	PHI	Aug 27, 1948	6	0	0	6	
Hal McRae	KC	Aug 27, 1974	5	0	1	6	
Al Oliver	TEX	Aug 17, 1980	1	1	4	6	

Most Extra-Base Hits in a Doubleheader, NL

Player	Team	Date	2B	3B	HR	Total	Inns.
Chick Hafey	STL	Jul 28, 1928	4	0	2	6	21
Mel Ott	NY	Jun 19, 1929	4	0	2	6	20
Joe Medwick	STL	May 30, 1935	5	1	0	6	
Red Schoendienst	STL	Jun 6, 1948	5	0	1	6	
Dusty Rhodes	NY	Aug 29, 1954	2	2	2	6	20

Most Extra-Base Hits in Two Consecutive Games, AL

Player	Team	Date	2B	3B	HR	Total
Earl Sheely	CHI	May 20, 1926				
	CHI	May 21, 1926	6	0	1	7

Most Extra-Base Hits in Two Consecutive Games, NL

Player	Team	Date	2B	3B	HR	Total
Ed Delahanty	PHI	Jul 13, 1896				
	PHI	Jul 14, 1896	2	1	4	7
Red Schoendienst	STL	Jun 5, 1948				
	STL	Jun 6, 1948	6	0	1	7
Joe Adcock	MIL	Jul 30, 1954				
	MIL	Jul 31, 1954	2	0	5	7

Most Consecutive Games with Extra-Base Hit

Player	Team	Date	G	2B	3B	HR
Paul Waner	PIT N	Jun 3, 1927				
	PIT N	Jun 19, 1927	14	12	4	4
Jesse Barfield	TOR A	Aug 17, 1985				
	TOR A	Aug 27, 1985	11	8	3	1

Most Consecutive Games with Extra-Base Hit (*cont.*)

Player	Team	Date	G	2B	3B	HR
Don Mattingly	NY A	Jul 7, 1987				
	NY A	Jul 19, 1987	10	4	0	10
Babe Ruth	NY A	Aug 28, 1921				
	NY A	Sep 5, 1921	9	7	1	3

Most Doubles, Game, AL

Player	Team	Date	2B
Pop Dillon	DET	Apr 25, 1901	4
Bill Werber	BOS	Jul 17, 1935	4
Frankie Hayes	PHI	Jul 25, 1936	4
Mike Kreevich	CHI	Sep 4, 1937	4
Marv Owen	CHI	Apr 23, 1939	4
Johnny Lindell	NY	Aug 17, 1944	4
Lou Boudreau	CLE	Jul 14, 1946	4
Al Zarilla	BOS	Jun 8, 1950	4
Vic Wertz	CLE	Sep 26, 1956	4
Charlie Lau	BAL	Jul 13, 1962	4
Bill Bruton	DET	May 19, 1963	4
Orlando Cepeda	BOS	Aug 8, 1973	4
Jim Mason	NY	Jul 8, 1974	4
Dave Duncan	BAL	Jun 30, 1975	4
Rick Miller	BOS	May 11, 1981	4
Damaso Garcia	TOR	Jun 27, 1986	4
Kirby Puckett	MIN	May 13, 1989	4

Most Doubles, Game, NL

Player	Team	Date	2B
John O'Rourke	BOS	Sep 15, 1880	4
Abner Dalrymple	CHI	Jul 3, 1883	4
Cap Anson	CHI	Jul 3, 1883	4
Tommy Tucker	BOS	Jul 22, 1893	4
Frank Bonner	BAL	Aug 4, 1894	4
Joe Kelley	BAL	Sep 3, 1894	4
Ed Delahanty	PHI	May 13, 1899	4
Gavvy Cravath	PHI	Aug 8, 1915	4
	PHI	Jun 23, 1919	4
Denny Sothern	PHI	Jun 6, 1930	4
Paul Waner	PIT	May 20, 1932	4
Dick Bartell	PHI	Apr 25, 1933	4
Ernie Lombardi	CIN	May 8, 1935	4
Joe Medwick	STL	Aug 4, 1937	4
Bill Werber	CIN	May 13, 1940	4
Willie Jones	PHI	Apr 20, 1949	4
Jim Greengrass	CIN	Apr 13, 1954	4

Most Doubles, Game, NL (cont.)

Player	Team	Date	2B
Billy Williams	CHI	Apr 9, 1969	4
Rafael Ramirez	ATL	May 21, 1986	4
Billy Hatcher	CIN	Aug 21, 1990	4

Most Doubles, Game, Other Leagues

Player	Team	Date	2B
Henry Larkin	PHI AA	Jul 29, 1885	4
Jocko Milligan	PHI AA	May 2, 1886	4

Two Doubles in One Inning, AL

Player	Team	Date
Pop Dillon	DET	Apr 25, 1901
Smoky Joe Wood	BOS	Jul 4, 1913
Hal Janvrin	BOS	Jun 9, 1914
Shano Collins	CHI	Aug 8, 1916
Larry Gardner	BOS	Apr 29, 1917
Happy Felsch	CHI	Sep 4, 1917
Riggs Stephenson	CLE	Jul 7, 1923
Bob Shawkey	NY	Jul 12, 1923
Grover Hartley	BOS	May 28, 1927
Jimmie Foxx	PHI	Aug 16, 1928
Bing Miller	PHI	Apr 19, 1929
Carl Reynolds	CHI	Jul 28, 1931
Earle Combs	NY	Jul 3, 1932
Lyn Lary	NY	Jul 3, 1932
Ted Lyons	CHI	Jul 28, 1935
Joe Cronin	BOS	Aug 3, 1939
	BOS	Jul 13, 1941
Hal Peck	CLE	Aug 12, 1948
Nellie Fox	CHI	Apr 17, 1957
Chuck Cottier	WAS	May 11, 1962
Floyd Robinson	CHI	Sep 24, 1963
Mark Belanger	BAL	Aug 18, 1969
Reggie Jackson	NY	Jun 4, 1977
Dave McKay	TOR	Jun 26, 1978
Otto Velez	TOR	Jun 26, 1978
Ken Landreaux	MIN	Jul 3, 1979
Rick Miller	BOS	May 11, 1981
Duane Kuiper	CLE	Aug 30, 1982
Bobby Jones	TEX	Jul 3, 1983
Pete Incaviglia	TEX	May 11, 1986
Don Mattingly	NY	Apr 11, 1987
Phil Bradley	BAL	Aug 30, 1989
Jody Reed	BOS	Sep 8, 1991
Paul Molitor	MIL	Sep 20, 1992

Two Doubles in One Inning, NL

Player	Team	Date
Fred Goldsmith	CHI	Sep 6, 1883
Tom Burns	CHI	Sep 6, 1883
Tommy Tucker	BOS	Jul 22, 1893
Hugh Duffy	BOS	Jul 10, 1894
Joe Kelley	BAL	Sep 3, 1894
George Davis	NY	Jun 27, 1896
Hugh Duffy	BOS	Sep 27, 1896
Herman Long	BOS	Sep 27, 1897
Jimmy Collins	BOS	Sep 27, 1897
Ed Delahanty	PHI	May 13, 1899
Frank Bowerman	PIT	Aug 9, 1899
Bobby Byrne	PIT	Aug 23, 1913
Gavvy Cravath	PHI	Aug 8, 1915
Edd Roush	CIN	Aug 23, 1919
Curt Walker	PHI	Aug 16, 1922
Sparky Adams	CHI	Aug 24, 1927
Chick Hafey	STL	Jul 6, 1929
Jake Flowers	BKN	Apr 21, 1930
Ernie Orsatti	STL	Jul 20, 1932
George Kelly	BKN	Jul 26, 1932
Pinky Whitney	PHI	Aug 1, 1932
Leo Durocher	STL	Aug 5, 1936
Buck Jordan	BOS	Aug 25, 1936
Tony Cuccinello	BOS	Aug 25, 1936
Gene Moore	BOS	Aug 25, 1936
Gib Brack	PHI	Jul 30, 1938
Hank Borowy	CHI	May 5, 1946
Hal Jeffcoat	CHI	May 2, 1948
Bill Howerton	STL	Jul 6, 1950
Bob Thorpe	BOS	Jun 5, 1952
Alvin Dark	NY	Sep 14, 1952
Steve Bilko	STL	May 29, 1953
Jim Gilliam	BKN	May 19, 1957
Rocky Nelson	PIT	Aug 6, 1959

Two Doubles in One Inning, NL (*cont.*)

Player	Team	Date	Player	Team	Date
Harvey Kuenn	SF	Jul 24, 1964	Pete Rose	CIN	Jul 7, 1973
Rico Carty	MIL	May 20, 1965	Jimmy Wynn	LA	Jun 3, 1975
Gene Clines	PIT	May 9, 1971	Mike Ivie	SD	May 30, 1977
Cesar Cedeno	HOU	Apr 9, 1973	Rick Schu	PHI	Oct 3, 1985

Most Triples, Game, AL

Player	Team	Date	3B	Inns.
Elmer Flick	CLE	Jul 6, 1902	3	
Bill Bradley	CLE	Jul 28, 1903	3	
Patsy Dougherty	BOS	Sep 5, 1903	3	
Billy Lush	DET	Sep 26, 1903	3	
Nap Lajoie	CLE	Jul 13, 1904	3	
Hal Chase	NY	Aug 30, 1906	3	10
Joe Jackson	CLE	Jun 30, 1912	3	
Gus Williams	STL	Apr 24, 1913	3	
Joe Judge	WAS	Aug 9, 1921	3	19
Baby Doll Jacobson	STL	Sep 9, 1922	3	
Jackie Tavener	DET	Sep 12, 1925	3	13
Earle Combs	NY	Sep 22, 1927	3	
Charlie Gehringer	DET	Aug 5, 1929	3	
Joe Kuhel	WAS	May 13, 1937	3	
Joe DiMaggio	NY	Aug 27, 1938	3	
Ben Chapman	CLE	Jul 3, 1939	3	
Bert Campaneris	KC	Aug 29, 1967	3	10
Al Bumbry	BAL	Sep 22, 1973	3	
Ken Landreaux	MIN	Jul 3, 1980	3	

Most Triples, Game, NL

Player	Team	Date	3B	Inns.
Bill Joyce	NY	May 18, 1897	4	
George Hall	PHI	Jun 14, 1876	3	
Ezra Sutton	PHI	Jun 14, 1876	3	
Buck Ewing	NY	Jun 9, 1883	3	
King Kelly	CHI	Sep 29, 1885	3	
Hardy Richardson	DET	Sep 9, 1886	3	
Sam Thompson	DET	May 13, 1887	3	
Marty Sullivan	CHI	May 17, 1887	3	
Larry Twitchell	CLE	Aug 15, 1889	3	
Long John Reilly	CIN	Jun 14, 1890	3	
Bid McPhee	CIN	Jun 28, 1890	3	
George Davis	CLE	Apr 25, 1891	3	
Billy Hamilton	PHI	Jul 14, 1891	3	
Harry Stovey	BAL	Jul 21, 1892	3	
Jouett Meekin	NY	Jul 4, 1894	3	
George Davis	NY	Jul 14, 1894	3	
Bill Hassamaer	WAS	Jul 25, 1894	3	

Most Triples, Game, NL (*cont.*)

Player	Team	Date	3B	Inns.
Hugh Duffy	BOS	Sep 18, 1894	3	
Frank Shugart	LOU	Jul 30, 1895	3	
Bill Dahlen	CHI	May 3, 1896	3	
Jake Beckley	CIN	May 19, 1898	3	
Bill Dahlen	CHI	Jun 6, 1898	3	
Elmer Flick	PHI	Jun 20, 1898	3	
Ginger Beaumont	PIT	Aug 9, 1899	3	
Harry Wolverton	PHI	Jul 13, 1900	3	
Jimmy Sheckard	BKN	Apr 18, 1901	3	
Mike Donlin	CIN	Sep 22, 1903	3	
Miller Huggins	CIN	Oct 8, 1904	3	
Dave Brain	STL	May 29, 1905	3	
	STL	Aug 8, 1905	3	10
Pat Moran	BOS	Aug 10, 1905	3	
Owen Wilson	PIT	Jul 24, 1911	3	
Ross Youngs	NY	May 11, 1920	3	
Ray Powell	BOS	Sep 27, 1921	3	
Charlie Hollocher	CHI	Aug 13, 1922	3	
Jim Bottomley	STL	May 15, 1923	3	
Les Bell	STL	Sep 22, 1926	3	
Jim Bottomley	STL	Jun 21, 1927	3	
Lance Richbourg	BOS	Jul 31, 1929	3	
Carlos Bernier	PIT	May 2, 1953	3	
Danny O'Connell	MIL	Jun 13, 1956	3	
Roberto Clemente	PIT	Sep 8, 1958	3	
Willie Mays	SF	Sep 15, 1960	3	11
Ernie Banks	CHI	Jun 11, 1966	3	
Doug Flynn	NY	Aug 5, 1980	3	
Craig Reynolds	HOU	May 16, 1981	3	
Shawon Dunston	CHI	Jul 28, 1990	3	
Herm Winningham	CIN	Aug 15, 1990	3	12

Most Triples, Game, Other Leagues

Player	Team	Date	3B
George Strief	PHI AA	Jun 25, 1885	4
Dave Rowe	STL U	Jun 24, 1884	3
Charley Jones	CIN AA	Jul 20, 1884	3
Harry Stovey	PHI AA	Aug 18, 1884	3
Sadie Houck	PHI AA	Aug 27, 1884	3
Oyster Burns	BAL AA	Jun 13, 1887	3
Billy Hamilton	KC AA	Jun 28, 1889	3
Sid Farrar	PHI P	Aug 28, 1890	3
Tom Brown	BOS AA	May 7, 1891	3
Jack Lewis	PIT F	May 7, 1914	3
Fred Smith	BUF F	Apr 27, 1915	3
Al Shaw	KC F	Jul 4, 1915	3

Two Triples in One Inning

Player	Team	Date	Inn.
Joe Hornung	BOS N	May 6, 1882	8
Harry Wheeler	CIN AA	Jun 28, 1882	11
Harry Stovey	PHI AA	Aug 18, 1884	8
Heinie Peitz	STL N	Jul 2, 1895	1
Frank Shugart	LOU N	Jul 30, 1895	5
Buck Freeman	BOS N	Jul 25, 1900	1
Bill Dahlen	BKN N	Aug 30, 1900	8
Curt Walker	CIN N	Jul 22, 1926	2
Al Zarilla	STL A	Jul 13, 1946	4
Gil Coan	WAS A	Apr 21, 1951	6

Home Run and Double in One Inning, AL

Player	Team	Date
Roy Hartzell	NY	Jul 12, 1911
George Sisler	STL	Jun 3, 1919
Earl Averill	CLE	Jul 29, 1930
Ben Chapman	CLE	Aug 30, 1939
Rudy York	DET	Aug 19, 1945
Vern Stephens	BOS	Jul 26, 1949
Bobby Knoop	CAL	Apr 30, 1966
Aurelio Rodriguez	DET	Aug 20, 1972
Tom Grieve	TEX	Apr 23, 1976
Frank White	KC	Apr 19, 1977
Ron Hassey	CLE	Sep 30, 1980
Gorman Thomas	MIL	Sep 19, 1982
Graig Nettles	NY	Jun 30, 1983
Gorman Thomas	CLE	Sep 3, 1983
Dave Kingman	OAK	Aug 27, 1984
Carlos Quintana	BOS	Jul 30, 1991
Harold Baines	OAK	Jun 22, 1992

Home Run and Double in One Inning, NL

Player	Team	Date
Adonis Terry	CHI	May 19, 1895
Wildfire Schulte	CHI	Aug 15, 1911
Fred Merkle	NY	May 13, 1911
Cliff Heathcote	STL	Jun 21, 1918
Cotton Tierney	PIT	Jun 25, 1923
Pie Traynor	PIT	Jul 3, 1926
Johnny Frederick	BKN	Jun 26, 1931
Johnny Vergez	NY	Jun 7, 1934
Joe Medwick	STL	Jun 20, 1934
Bill Werber	CIN	May 1, 1940
Joe Gallagher	BKN	Aug 24, 1940
Ralph Kiner	PIT	May 20, 1948
Andy Seminick	PHI	Jul 26, 1949
Stan Musial	STL	Sep 14, 1952
Ernie Banks	CHI	Sep 5, 1964
Cliff Johnson	HOU	May 31, 1976
Lenny Randle	CHI	May 2, 1980
Rick Rhoden	PIT	May 15, 1982
Darrell Evans	SF	May 13, 1983

Twenty Doubles, 20 Triples, and 20 Home Runs, Season, AL

Player	Team	Year	G	2B	3B	HR	BA
Jeff Heath	CLE	1941	151	32	20	24	.340
George Brett	KC	1979	154	42	20	23	.329

Twenty Doubles, 20 Triples, and 20 Home Runs, Season, NL

Player	Team	Year	G	2B	3B	HR	BA
Wildfire Schulte	CHI	1911	154	30	21	21	.300
Jim Bottomley	STL	1928	149	42	20	31	.325
Willie Mays	NY	1957	152	26	20	35	.333

Most Total Bases, Game, AL

Player	Team	Date	1B	2B	3B	HR	TB	Inns.
Ty Cobb	DET	May 5, 1925	2	1	0	3	16	
Lou Gehrig	NY	Jun 3, 1932	0	0	0	4	16	
Jimmie Foxx	PHI	Jul 10, 1932	2	1	0	3	16	18
Pat Seerey	CHI	Jul 18, 1948	0	0	0	4	16	11
Rocky Colavito	CLE	Jun 10, 1959	0	0	0	4	16	
Fred Lynn	BOS	Jun 18, 1975	1	0	1	3	16	
Tony Lazzeri	NY	May 24, 1936	0	0	1	3	15	
Pat Seerey	CLE	Jul 13, 1945	0	0	1	3	15	
Bobby Avila	CLE	Jun 20, 1951	1	1	0	3	15	
Dave Winfield	CAL	Apr 13, 1991	1	1	0	3	15	

Most Total Bases, Game, NL

Player	Team	Date	1B	2B	3B	HR	TB	Inns.
Joe Adcock	MIL	Jul 31, 1954	0	1	0	4	18	
Bobby Lowe	BOS	May 30, 1894	1	0	0	4	17	
Ed Delahanty	PHI	Jul 13, 1896	1	0	0	4	17	
Gil Hodges	BKN	Aug 31, 1950	1	0	0	4	17	
Mike Schmidt	PHI	Apr 17, 1976	1	0	0	4	17	10
Larry Twitchell	CLE	Aug 15, 1889	1	1	3	1	16	
Chuck Klein	PHI	Jul 10, 1936	0	0	0	4	16	10
Willie Mays	SF	Apr 30, 1961	0	0	0	4	16	
Bob Horner	ATL	Jul 6, 1986	0	0	0	4	16	
Dan Brouthers	DET	Sep 10, 1886	1	1	0	3	15	
George Kelly	NY	Sep 17, 1923	1	1	0	3	15	
Les Bell	BOS	Jun 2, 1928	0	0	1	3	15	
Walker Cooper	CIN	Jul 6, 1949	3	0	0	3	15	
Wes Westrum	NY	Jun 24, 1950	0	0	1	3	15	
Willie Mays	SF	May 13, 1958	1	0	2	2	15	
Willie Stargell	PIT	May 22, 1968	1	1	0	3	15	
Davey Lopes	LA	Aug 20, 1974	1	1	0	3	15	

Most Total Bases, Season, AL

Player	Team	Year	TB
Babe Ruth	NY	1921	457
Lou Gehrig	NY	1927	447
Jimmie Foxx	PHI	1932	438
Lou Gehrig	NY	1930	419
Joe DiMaggio	NY	1937	418
Babe Ruth	NY	1927	417
Lou Gehrig	NY	1931	410
	NY	1934	409
Jim Rice	BOS	1978	406

Most Total Bases, Season, AL (cont.)

Player	Team	Year	TB
Hal Trosky	CLE	1936	405
Jimmie Foxx	PHI	1933	403
Lou Gehrig	NY	1936	403

Most Total Bases, Season, NL

Player	Team	Year	TB
Rogers Hornsby	STL	1922	450
Chuck Klein	PHI	1930	445
Stan Musial	STL	1948	429
Hack Wilson	CHI	1930	423
Chuck Klein	PHI	1932	420
Babe Herman	BKN	1930	416
Rogers Hornsby	CHI	1929	409
Joe Medwick	STL	1937	406
Chuck Klein	PHI	1929	405
Hank Aaron	MIL	1959	400

Most Times Walked, Game, AL

Player	Team	Date	BB
Jimmie Foxx	BOS	Jun 16, 1938	6
Andre Thornton	CLE	May 2, 1984	6
Sammy Strang	CHI	Apr 27, 1902	5
Kid Elberfeld	DET	Aug 1, 1902	5
Charlie Hemphill	NY	Aug 3, 1911	5
Tris Speaker	BOS	Oct 1, 1912	5
Roger Peckinpaugh	NY	Jun 2, 1919	5
Whitey Witt	NY	Jul 2, 1924	5
Ira Flagstead	BOS	May 8, 1925	5
Max Bishop	PHI	Apr 29, 1929	5
	PHI	May 21, 1930	5
Earl Averill	CLE	Aug 29, 1932	5
Jo-Jo White	DET	Apr 18, 1935	5
Lou Gehrig	NY	Aug 27, 1935	5
Ben Chapman	NY	May 24, 1936	5
Billy Rogell	DET	Aug 8, 1938	5
Charlie Keller	NY	Aug 17, 1939	5
Herschel Martin	NY	Sep 1, 1944	5
Russ Derry	NY	Sep 6, 1945	5
Ted Williams	BOS	May 23, 1951	5
Larry Doby	CLE	Sep 19, 1951	5
	CLE	Jul 1, 1952	5
Danny Walton	MIL	May 22, 1970	5
Carl Yastrzemski	BOS	May 25, 1971	5
Tony Muser	CHI	Jul 3, 1973	5

Most Times Walked, Game, AL (*cont.*)

Player	Team	Date	BB
Billy North	OAK	Sep 17, 1973	5
Sal Bando	MIL	May 29, 1977	5
Jim Norris	CLE	Jul 8, 1977	5
Roy Smalley	MIN	May 7, 1978	5
Rickey Henderson	OAK	Apr 8, 1982	5
Jose Canseco	OAK	Aug 4, 1992	5

Most Times Walked, Game, NL

Player	Team	Date	BB
Walt Wilmot	CHI	Aug 22, 1891	6
Fred Carroll	PIT	Jul 4, 1889	5
	PIT	Jul 27, 1889	5
Pop Smith	BOS	Apr 17, 1890	5
Jimmy Ryan	CHI	May 28, 1892	5
Piggy Ward	CIN	Jun 18, 1893	5
Elmer Flick	PHI	Oct 15, 1898	5
Kip Selbach	CIN	Jun 11, 1899	5
Sam Mertes	NY	Aug 12, 1903	5
Fred Tenney	BOS	Aug 16, 1907	5
Heinie Groh	NY	May 26, 1922	5
Hughie Critz	CIN	May 28, 1926	5
Mel Ott	NY	Oct 5, 1929	5
Gus Suhr	PIT	Apr 29, 1930	5
Paul Waner	PIT	Sep 22, 1931	5
Mel Ott	NY	Sep 1, 1933	5
	NY	Jun 7, 1943	5
	NY	Apr 30, 1944	5
Max West	PIT	Apr 25, 1948	5
Gene Hermanski	BKN	Sep 22, 1949	5
Solly Hemus	STL	Sep 15, 1951	5
Andy Seminick	PHI	Sep 30, 1951	5
Richie Ashburn	PHI	Jul 16, 1954	5
Hank Aaron	MIL	Sep 3, 1960	5
Joe Morgan	HOU	Jun 2, 1966	5
Dick Allen	PHI	Aug 16, 1968	5
Hank Aaron	ATL	Jul 11, 1972	5
Ellie Hendricks	CHI	Sep 16, 1972	5
Tim Foli	MON	Sep 7, 1973	5
Ted Sizemore	STL	Aug 12, 1974	5
Joe Ferguson	HOU	Jun 24, 1978	5
Johnny Bench	CIN	Jul 22, 1979	5
Rodney Scott	MON	Apr 12, 1980	5
Dale Murphy	ATL	Apr 22, 1983	5
Greg Brock	LA	May 17, 1983	5
Dale Murphy	ATL	May 23, 1987	5
Brett Butler	SF	Apr 12, 1990	5

Most Times Walked, Game, NL (cont.)

Player	Team	Date	BB
Andre Dawson	CHI	May 22, 1990	5
Von Hayes	PHI	Jun 6, 1990	5
Vince Coleman	NY	Aug 10, 1992	5

Most Times Walked, Game, Other Leagues

Player	Team	Date	BB
Henry Larkin	PHI AA	May 2, 1887	5
Hugh Nichol	CIN AA	Aug 27, 1887	5
Joe Visner	PIT P	Aug 7, 1890	5

Walked Twice in One Inning, AL

Player	Team	Date	Inn.
Donie Bush	DET	Aug 27, 1909	4
Walt Kuhn	CHI	Sep 22, 1914	7
Burt Shotton	STL	Jun 17, 1915	5
Hugh High	NY	Jun 8, 1917	1
Joe Judge	WAS	Jul 27, 1920	2
George Orme	BOS	Sep 7, 1920	7
Tris Speaker	CLE	May 8, 1922	5
Steve O'Neill	CLE	Jul 7, 1923	6
Roy Elsh	CHI	Apr 27, 1925	8
Jackie Tavener	DET	Jun 17, 1925	6
Earl Sheely	CHI	Jul 17, 1924	7
Ira Flagstead	BOS	May 8, 1925	5
Fred Haney	DET	Jun 17, 1925	6
George Sisler	STL	Sep 12, 1925	4
Harry Heilmann	DET	May 16, 1928	8
Joe Cronin	WAS	May 6, 1929	5
Jimmy Dykes	PHI	Jul 31, 1929	5
Joe Cronin	WAS	Jun 25, 1930	2
Max Bishop	PHI	May 25, 1931	2
Charlie Jamieson	CLE	Jun 29, 1931	5
Willis Hudlin	CLE	Jul 6, 1931	6
Earle Combs	NY	Sep 7, 1931	6
	NY	Sep 5, 1932	1
Gowell Claset	PHI	Jun 3, 1933	3
George Selkirk	NY	Jun 24, 1935	5
Jake Powell	NY	Aug 24, 1936	4
George Selkirk	NY	Aug 28, 1936	2
	NY	Aug 4, 1938	5
Bob Johnson	PHI	May 1, 1938	3
Lou Finney	PHI	Aug 29, 1939	1
Skeeter Webb	CHI	Jul 20, 1940	5
George Selkirk	NY	Aug 22, 1940	2
Skeeter Webb	CHI	Sep 3, 1940	1
Jim McDonald	NY	May 2, 1954	5

Walked Twice in One Inning, AL (*cont.*)

Player	Team	Date	Inn.
Luis Aparicio	CHI	Apr 22, 1959	7
Nellie Fox	CHI	Apr 22, 1959	7
Pete Runnels	BOS	Aug 15,1959	3
Zoilo Versalles	MIN	Apr 16, 1961	1
Lenny Green	MIN	Apr 16, 1961	1
Carroll Hardy	BOS	May 4, 1962	5
Elston Howard	NY	Jul 26, 1964	2
Bob Tillman	BOS	Jun 25, 1965	5
Merv Rettenmund	BAL	Jun 22, 1970	7
Ed Herrmann	CHI	Sep 5, 1971	7
Bert Campaneris	OAK	Jun 18, 1975	7
Alex Cole	CLE	Oct 2, 1990	1
Jerry Browne	CLE	Oct 2, 1990	1

Walked Twice in One Inning, NL

Player	Team	Date	Inn.
Walt Wilmot	CHI	Aug 22, 1891	6
Elmer Smith	PIT	Apr 22, 1892	1
Piggy Ward	CIN	Jun 18, 1893	1
Joe Kelley	BAL	Apr 24, 1894	9
Heinie Reitz	BAL	Apr 24, 1894	9
Hugh Duffy	BOS	Jun 18, 1894	1
Ed Abbaticchio	PIT	Sep 25, 1907	2
Honus Wagner	PIT	Sep 3, 1909	1
	PIT	Sep 3, 1917	5
Jesse Barnes	BOS	Oct 2, 1917	2
Dave Bancroft	NY	Apr 15, 1922	1
Ross Youngs	NY	May 31, 1926	9
Heinie Sand	PHI	Apr 19, 1928	6
Hank DeBerry	BKN	Apr 21, 1930	2
Eddie Stanky	NY	Jun 22, 1950	5
	NY	Aug 30, 1950	6
Pee Wee Reese	BKN	May 21, 1952	6
Enos Slaughter	STL	Sep 14, 1952	5
Jackie Robinson	BKN	Apr 24, 1953	6
Gil Hodges	BKN	Aug 30, 1953	6
Bruce Edwards	CHI	Apr 17, 1954	5
Clem Labine	BKN	Aug 8, 1954	8
Steve Boros	CHI	May 30, 1963	4
Dick Bertell	CHI	May 30, 1963	4
Ed Bailey	CHI	Aug 5, 1965	9
Wayne Garrett	NY	May 11, 1969	1
Larry Hisle	PHI	May 3, 1970	5
Denny Doyle	PHI	May 5, 1970	1
Joe Foy	NY	May 9, 1970	5
Willie Mays	SF	Jun 22, 1970	4

Walked Twice in One Inning, NL (*cont.*)

Player	Team	Date	Inn.
Johnny Edwards	HOU	Jul 22, 1970	4
Ron Santo	CHI	Jun 25, 1971	7
Greg Luzinski	PHI	Jun 15, 1972	7
Richie Hebner	PIT	Aug 27, 1974	3
Frank Taveras	PIT	Jun 29, 1976	1
Chris Sabo	CIN	May 20, 1992	7
Otis Nixon	ATL	Sep 9, 1992	1

Most Times Walked in a Doubleheader, AL

Player	Team	Date	BB
Max Bishop	PHI	May 21, 1930	8
	BOS	Jul 8, 1934	8
Jimmie Foxx	BOS	Sep 16, 1938	6

Most Times Walked in a Doubleheader, NL

Player	Team	Date	BB
Walt Wilmot	CHI	Aug 22, 1891	6
Mel Ott	NY	Oct 5, 1929	6
Johnny Mize	STL	Aug 26, 1939	6
Mel Ott	NY	Apr 30, 1944	6
Clay Dalrymple	PHI	Jul 4, 1967	6
Cleon Jones	NY	Jun 25, 1971	6
Jack Clark	STL	Jul 8, 1987	6

Struck Out Twice in One Inning, AL

Player	Team	Date	Inn.
Billy Purtell	CHI	May 10, 1910	6
Del Gainor	DET	Aug 15, 1913	9
Bob Groom	STL	Aug 29, 1916	7
Joe Judge	WAS	Jul 27, 1920	2
Elmer Miller	BOS	Sep 7, 1922	7
Lefty Gomez	NY	Jul 24, 1932	7
Frankie Crosetti	NY	Sep 9, 1932	7
Babe Ruth	NY	Jul 31, 1934	1
Gee Walker	DET	Jul 16, 1937	6
Mickey Mantle	NY	May 24, 1951	6
Rudy May	CAL	Jun 12, 1965	6
Boog Powell	BAL	Jul 19, 1966	5
Chuck Manuel	MIN	Jun 30, 1969	9
Deron Johnson	OAK	Sep 23, 1973	5
Bo Jackson	KC	Apr 8, 1987	4
Randy Milligan	BAL	Apr 21, 1992	4

Struck Out Twice in One Inning, NL

Player	Team	Date	Inn.
Walt Wilmot	CHI	Aug 12, 1891	6
Edd Roush	CIN	Jul 22, 1916	6
Joe Oeschger	PHI	Aug 26, 1917	3
Lynn Brenton	CIN	Oct 2, 1920	7
Tony Kaufmann	CHI	Aug 25, 1922	2
Van Lingle Mungo	BKN	May 16, 1932	4
Pep Young	PIT	Jul 3, 1937	7
Jackie Robinson	BKN	Aug 30, 1953	3
Duke Snider	BKN	Aug 14, 1954	6
Ed Roebuck	BKN	Sep 4, 1957	8
Chris Krug	CHI	Aug 8, 1965	9
Curt Flood	STL	Apr 17, 1966	7
Billy O'Dell	PIT	Jun 9, 1967	5
Duffy Dyer	NY	May 9, 1969	5
Amos Otis	NY	May 14, 1969	8
Jose Arcia	SD	Aug 16, 1970	1
John Bateman	MON	Aug 29, 1971	2
Bob Gibson	STL	Aug 2, 1972	4
Larry McWilliams	ATL	Apr 22, 1979	4
Greg Harris	SD	May 31, 1992	2

Most Times Struck Out, Game, AL

Player	Team	Date	SO	Inns.
Carl Weilman	STL	Jul 25,1913	6	15
Rick Reichardt	CAL	May 31, 1966	6	17
Billy Cowan	CAL	Jul 9, 1971	6	20
Cecil Cooper	BOS	Jun 14, 1974	6	15
Sam Horn	BAL	Jul 17, 1991	6	15
Donie Bush	DET	May 1, 1910	5	10
Cy Morgan	PHI	Sep 18, 1911	5	12
Lefty Williams	CHI	May 15, 1918	5	18
Scott Perry	PHI	Apr 25, 1919	5	11
Ossie Bluege	WAS	Jun 17, 1923	5	11
Lefty Grove	PHI	Jun 10, 1933	5	
Johnny Broaca	NY	Jun 25, 1934	5	
Chet Laabs	DET	Oct 2, 1938	5	
Larry Doby	CLE	Apr 25, 1948	5	
Jim Landis	CHI	Jul 28, 1957	5	
Bill Skowron	NY	Jun 7, 1964	5	15
Bob Allison	MIN	Sep 2, 1965	5	
George Scott	BOS	Apr 15, 1966	5	12
Sandy Valdespino	MIN	Aug 9, 1967	5	20
Reggie Jackson	OAK	Sep 27, 1968	5	
Ray Jarvis	BOS	Apr 20, 1969	5	
Rick Monday	OAK	Apr 29, 1970	5	
Frank Howard	WAS	Sep 19, 1970	5	

Most Times Struck Out, Game, AL (*cont.*)

Player	Team	Date	SO	Inns.
Tony Conigliaro	CAL	Jul 9, 1971	5	20
Don Buford	BAL	Aug 26, 1971	5	
Bobby Darwin	MIN	May 12, 1972	5	22
Roy Smalley	MIN	Aug 28, 1976	5	17
Rick Manning	CLE	May 15, 1977	5	
Gorman Thomas	MIL	Jul 13, 1979	5	17
Kevin Bell	CHI	Apr 26, 1980	5	12
Dave Stegman	CHI	May 4, 1984	5	25
Bo Jackson	KC	Apr 18, 1987	5	
Rob Deer	MIL	Aug 8, 1987	5	
Jeffrey Leonard	MIL	Aug 24, 1988	5	14
Joey Meyer	MIL	Sep 20, 1988	5	
Phil Bradley	BAL	Sep 7, 1989	5	
Sammy Sosa	CHI	May 5, 1990	5	
Cecil Fielder	DET	Aug 2, 1990	5	14
Bernie Williams	NY	Aug 21, 1991	5	
Dean Palmer	TEX	Sep 23, 1991	5	11
Phil Plantier	BOS	Oct 1, 1991	5	

Most Times Struck Out, Game, NL

Player	Team	Date	SO	Inns.
Don Hoak	CHI	May 2, 1956	6	17
Oscar Walker	BUF	Jun 20, 1879	5	
Harry Stovey	BOS	Jun 30, 1891	5	10
Pete Dowling	LOU	Aug 15, 1899	5	
Benny Kauff	NY	May 23, 1918	5	14
Les Bell	STL	May 12, 1927	5	11
Pep Young	PIT	Sep 29, 1935	5	
Steve Bilko	STL	May 28, 1953	5	10
Ron Kline	PIT	Sep 22, 1958	5	14
Bob Sadowski	MIL	Apr 20, 1964	5	
Dick Allen	PHI	Jun 28, 1964	5	
Deron Johnson	CIN	Aug 29, 1964	5	11
	CIN	Sep 30, 1964	5	16
Adolfo Phillips	CHI	Aug 10, 1966	5	10
Ron Swoboda	NY	Jun 22, 1969	5	
Steve Whitaker	SF	Apr 14, 1970	5	
Dick Allen	STL	May 24, 1970	5	10
Larry Hisle	PHI	May 28, 1970	5	11
Bill Russell	LA	Jun 9, 1971	5	
Pepe Mangual	MON	Aug 11, 1975	5	
Frank Taveras	NY	May 1, 1979	5	
Dave Kingman	NY	May 28, 1982	5	
Eric Davis	CIN	Apr 25, 1987	5	10
Jack Clark	SD	Jun 11, 1989	5	12
Darren Daulton	PHI	Apr 16, 1991	5	13

Most Times Struck Out, Game, NL (cont.)

Player	Team	Date	SO	Inns.
Darryl Strawberry	LA	May 1, 1991	5	
Delino DeShields	MON	Sep 17, 1991	5	

Most Hits, Game, AL

Player	Team	Date	H	AB	2B	3B	HR	Inns.
Johnny Burnett	CLE	Jul 10, 1932	9	11	2	0	0	18
Rocky Colavito	DET	Jun 24, 1962	7	10	0	1	0	22
Cesar Gutierrez	DET	Jun 21, 1970	7	7	1	0	0	12
Mike Donlin	BAL	Jun 24, 1901	6	6	2	2	0	
Doc Nance	DET	Jul 13, 1901	6	6	1	0	0	
Ervin Harvey	CLE	Apr 25, 1902	6	6	0	0	0	
Danny Murphy	PHI	Jul 8, 1902	6	6	0	0	1	
Jimmy Williams	BAL	Aug 25, 1902	6	6	1	1	0	
Bobby Veach	DET	Sep 17, 1920	6	6	1	1	1	12
George Sisler	STL	Aug 9, 1921	6	9	0	1	0	19
Frank Brower	CLE	Aug 7, 1923	6	6	1	0	0	
George Burns	CLE	Jun 19, 1924	6	6	3	1	0	
Ty Cobb	DET	May 5, 1925	6	6	1	0	3	
Jimmie Foxx	PHI	May 30, 1930	6	7	2	1	0	
Doc Cramer	PHI	Jun 20, 1932	6	6	0	0	0	
Jimmie Foxx	PHI	Jul 10, 1932	6	9	1	0	3	18
Sammy West	STL	Apr 13, 1933	6	6	1	0	0	11
Myril Hoag	NY	Jun 6, 1934	6	6	0	0	0	
Bob Johnson	PHI	Jun 16, 1934	6	6	1	0	2	11
Doc Cramer	PHI	Jul 13, 1935	6	6	1	0	0	
Bruce Campbell	CLE	Jul 2, 1936	6	6	1	0	0	
Rip Radcliff	CHI	Jul 18, 1936	6	7	2	0	0	
Hank Steinbacher	CHI	Jun 22, 1938	6	6	1	0	0	
George Myatt	WAS	May 1, 1944	6	6	1	0	0	
Stan Spence	WAS	Jun 1, 1944	6	6	0	0	1	
George Kell	DET	Sep 20, 1946	6	7	1	0	0	
Jim Fridley	CLE	Apr 29, 1952	6	6	0	0	0	
Jimmy Piersall	BOS	Jun 10, 1953	6	6	1	0	0	
Joe DeMaestri	KC	Jul 8, 1955	6	6	0	0	0	11
Pete Runnels	BOS	Aug 30, 1960	6	7	1	0	0	15
Floyd Robinson	CHI	Jul 22, 1962	6	6	0	0	0	
Bob Oliver	KC	May 4, 1969	6	6	1	0	1	
Jim Northrup	DET	Aug 28, 1969	6	6	0	0	2	13
John Briggs	MIL	Aug 4, 1973	6	6	2	0	0	
Jorge Orta	CLE	Jun 15, 1980	6	6	1	0	0	
Jerry Remy	BOS	Sep 3, 1981	6	10	0	0	0	20
Kevin Seitzer	KC	Aug 2, 1987	6	6	1	0	2	
Kirby Puckett	MIN	Aug 30, 1987	6	6	2	0	2	
	MIN	May 23, 1991	6	7	0	1	0	11
Carlos Baerga	CLE	Apr 11, 1992	6	9	0	0	0	19

Most Hits, Game, NL

Player	Team	Date	H	AB	2B	3B	HR	Inns.
Wilbert Robinson	BAL	Jun 10, 1892	7	7	1	0	0	
Rennie Stennett	PIT	Sep 16, 1975	7	7	2	1	0	
Davy Force	PHI	Jun 27, 1876	6	6	1	0	0	
Cal McVey	CHI	Jul 22, 1876	6	7	1	0	0	
	CHI	Jul 25, 1876	6	7	1	0	0	
Ross Barnes	CHI	Jul 27, 1876	6	6	1	1	0	
Paul Hines	PRO	Aug 26, 1879	6	6	0	0	0	10
George Gore	CHI	May 7, 1880	6	6	0	0	0	
Buttercup Dickerson	WOR	Jun 16, 1881	6	6	0	1	0	
Sam Wise	BOS	Jun 20, 1883	6	7	1	1	0	
Dan Brouthers	BUF	Jul 19, 1883	6	6	2	0	0	
Danny Richardson	NY	Jun 11, 1887	6	7	0	0	0	
King Kelly	BOS	Aug 27, 1887	6	7	1	0	1	
Jerry Denny	IND	May 4, 1889	6	6	1	0	1	
Larry Twitchell	CLE	Aug 15, 1889	6	6	1	3	1	
Jack Glasscock	NY	Sep 27, 1890	6	6	0	0	0	
Bobby Lowe	BOS	Jun 11, 1891	6	6	1	0	1	
Henry Larkin	WAS	Jun 7, 1892	6	7	0	1	0	
Jack Boyle	PHI	Jul 6, 1893	6	6	1	0	0	11
Duff Cooley	STL	Sep 30, 1893	6	6	1	0	0	
Ed Delahanty	PHI	Jun 16, 1894	6	6	1	0	0	
Steve Brodie	BAL	Jul 9, 1894	6	6	2	1	0	
Chief Zimmer	CLE	Jul 11, 1894	6	6	2	0	0	10
Sam Thompson	PHI	Aug 17, 1894	6	7	1	1	1	
Roger Connor	STL	Jun 1, 1895	6	6	2	1	0	
George Davis	NY	Aug 15, 1895	6	6	2	1	0	
Jake Stenzel	PIT	May 14, 1896	6	6	0	0	0	
Fred Tenney	BOS	May 31, 1897	6	8	1	0	0	
Dick Harley	STL	Jun 24, 1897	6	6	1	0	0	12
Barry McCormick	CHI	Jun 29, 1897	6	8	0	1	1	
Tommy Tucker	WAS	Jul 15, 1897	6	6	1	0	0	
Willie Keeler	BAL	Sep 3, 1897	6	6	0	1	0	
Jack Doyle	BAL	Sep 3, 1897	6	6	2	0	0	
Chick Stahl	BOS	May 31, 1899	6	6	0	0	0	
Ginger Beaumont	PIT	Jul 22, 1899	6	6	0	0	0	
Kip Selbach	NY	Jun 9, 1901	6	7	2	0	0	
George Cutshaw	BKN	Aug 9, 1915	6	6	0	0	0	
Carson Bigbee	PIT	Aug 22, 1917	6	11	0	0	0	22
Dave Bancroft	NY	Jun 28, 1920	6	6	0	0	0	
Johnny Gooch	PIT	Jul 7, 1922	6	8	1	0	0	18
Max Carey	PIT	Jul 7, 1922	6	6	1	0	0	18
Jack Fournier	BKN	Jun 29, 1923	6	6	2	0	1	
Kiki Cuyler	PIT	Aug 9, 1924	6	6	3	1	0	
Frankie Frisch	NY	Sep 10, 1924	6	7	0	0	1	
Jim Bottomley	STL	Sep 16, 1924	6	6	1	0	2	
Paul Waner	PIT	Aug 26, 1926	6	6	2	1	0	
Lloyd Waner	PIT	Jun 15, 1929	6	8	1	1	0	14

Most Hits, Game, NL (cont.)

Player	Team	Date	H	AB	2B	3B	HR	Inns.
Hank DeBerry	BKN	Jun 23, 1929	6	7	0	0	0	14
Wally Gilbert	BKN	May 30, 1931	6	7	1	0	0	
Jim Bottomley	STL	Aug 5, 1931	6	6	1	0	0	
Tony Cuccinello	CIN	Aug 13, 1931	6	6	2	1	0	
Terry Moore	STL	Sep 5, 1935	6	6	1	0	0	
Ernie Lombardi	CIN	May 9, 1937	6	6	1	0	0	
Frank Demaree	CHI	Jul 5, 1937	6	7	3	0	0	14
Cookie Lavagetto	BKN	Sep 23, 1939	6	6	1	1	0	
Walker Cooper	CIN	Jul 6, 1949	6	7	0	0	3	
Johnny Hopp	PIT	May 14, 1950	6	6	0	0	2	
Connie Ryan	PHI	Apr 16, 1953	6	6	2	0	0	
Dick Groat	PIT	May 13, 1960	6	6	3	0	0	
Jesus Alou	SF	Jul 10, 1964	6	6	0	0	1	
Joe Morgan	HOU	Jul 8, 1965	6	6	0	1	2	12
Felix Millan	ATL	Jul 6, 1970	6	6	1	1	0	
Don Kessinger	CHI	Jul 17, 1971	6	6	1	0	0	10
Willie Davis	LA	May 24, 1973	6	9	0	0	0	19
Bill Madlock	CHI	Jul 26, 1975	6	6	0	1	0	10
Jose Cardenal	CHI	May 2, 1976	6	7	1	0	1	14
Gene Richards	SD	Jul 26, 1977	6	7	1	0	0	15
Joe Lefebvre	SD	Sep 13, 1982	6	8	1	0	1	16
Wally Backman	PIT	Apr 27, 1990	6	6	1	0	0	

Most Hits, Game, Other Leagues

Player	Team	Date	H	AB	2B	3B	HR
Denny Mack	LOU AA	May 26, 1882	6	6	0	0	0
Hick Carpenter	CIN AA	Sep 12, 1883	6	7	0	0	0
Long John Reilly	CIN AA	Sep 12, 1883	6	7	1	1	1
Oscar Walker	BKN AA	May 31, 1884	6	6	1	1	0
Lon Knight	PHI AA	Jul 30, 1884	6	6	0	1	0
Dave Orr	NY AA	Jun 12, 1885	6	6	2	1	1
Henry Larkin	PHI AA	Jun 16, 1885	6	6	2	1	1
George Pinckney	BKN AA	Jun 25, 1885	6	6	0	0	0
Arlie Latham	STL AA	Apr 24, 1886	6	6	0	1	0
Guy Hecker	LOU AA	Aug 15, 1886	6	7	0	0	3
Denny Lyons	PHI AA	Apr 26, 1887	6	6	2	1	0
Pete Hotaling	CLE AA	Jun 6, 1888	6	7	0	1	0
Jim McTamany	KC AA	Jun 15, 1888	6	6	0	0	1
Darby O'Brien	BKN AA	Aug 8, 1889	6	6	3	0	0
Farmer Weaver	LOU AA	Aug 12, 1890	6	6	1	2	1
Frank Scheibeck	TOL AA	Sep 27, 1890	6	6	1	1	0
Ed Delahanty	CLE P	Jun 2, 1890	6	6	1	1	0
Bill Shindle	PHI P	Aug 26, 1890	6	6	2	1	0

Most Games with Five or More Hits, Career

Player	G	Player	G
Ty Cobb	14	Fred Clarke	9
Ed Delahanty	11	Willie Keeler	9
Cap Anson	10	Roberto Clemente	8
Pete Rose	10	Stan Musial	8
Max Carey	9	Lefty O'Doul	8

Two Hits in One Inning Twice in One Game

Player	Team	Date	Inn.	Inn.
Max Carey	PIT N	Jun 22, 1925	1	8
Johnny Hodapp	CLE A	Jul 29, 1928	2	6
Sherm Lollar	CHI A	Apr 23, 1955	2	6
Rennie Stennett	PIT N	Sep 16, 1975	1	5

.300 Batting Average in Final Season (Min. 100 G)

Player	Team	Year	G	AB	H	BA
Joe Jackson	CHI A	1920	146	470	218	.382
Dave Orr	BKN P	1890	107	464	173	.373
Happy Felsch	CHI A	1920	142	556	188	.338
Henry Moore	WAS U	1884	111	461	155	.336
Buck Weaver	CHI A	1920	151	630	210	.333
Bill Lange	CHI N	1899	107	416	135	.325
Chicken Hawks	PHI N	1925	105	320	103	.322
Sam Dungan	WAS A	1901	138	559	179	.320
Bill Keister	PHI N	1903	100	400	128	.320
Ted Williams	BOS A	1960	113	310	98	.316
Tex Vache	BOS A	1925	110	252	79	.313
Buzz Arlett	PHI N	1931	121	418	131	.313
Joe Knight	CIN N	1890	127	481	150	.312
Johnny Hodapp	BOS A	1933	115	413	129	.312
Roberto Clemente	PIT N	1972	102	378	118	.312
Sam Wise	WAS N	1893	122	521	162	.311
Irv Waldron	MIL A	1901				
	WAS A	1901	141	598	186	.311
Vin Campbell	NWK F	1915	127	525	163	.310
Jack Tobin	BOS A	1927	111	374	116	.310
George Sisler	BOS N	1930	116	431	133	.309
Steve Evans	BKN F	1915				
	BAL F	1915	151	556	171	.308
Tony Cuccinello	CHI A	1945	118	402	124	.308
Curt Walker	CIN N	1930	134	472	145	.307
Richie Ashburn	NY N	1962	135	389	119	.306
Lou Brock	STL N	1979	120	405	123	.304
Ray Chapman	CLE A	1920	111	435	132	.303
Del Pratt	DET A	1924	121	429	130	.303

.300 Batting Average in Final Season (Min. 100 G) (*cont.*)

Player	Team	Year	G	AB	H	BA
Perry Werden	LOU N	1897	131	506	153	.302
Johnny Dickshot	CHI A	1945	130	486	147	.302
Rene Monteagudo	PHI N	1945	114	193	58	.301
Mickey Rivers	TEX A	1984	102	313	94	.300

Most Combined Hits and Walks, Season, AL

Player	Team	Year	H	BB	Total
Babe Ruth	NY	1923	205	170	375
Ted Williams	BOS	1949	194	162	356
Babe Ruth	NY	1921	204	144	348
Ted Williams	BOS	1947	181	162	343
Babe Ruth	NY	1924	200	142	342
Wade Boggs	BOS	1988	214	125	339
	BOS	1985	240	96	336
Lou Gehrig	NY	1936	205	130	335
Ted Williams	BOS	1946	176	156	332
	BOS	1942	186	145	331
Babe Ruth	NY	1927	192	138	330
Ted Williams	BOS	1941	185	145	330
Jimmie Foxx	PHI	1932	213	116	329
Babe Ruth	NY	1926	184	144	328
Lou Gehrig	NY	1931	211	117	328
	NY	1927	218	109	327
Babe Ruth	NY	1931	199	128	327
Lou Gehrig	NY	1937	200	127	327
Ty Cobb	DET	1915	208	118	326
Babe Ruth	NY	1930	186	136	322
Lou Gehrig	NY	1930	220	101	321
Babe Ruth	NY	1920	172	148	320
Lou Gehrig	NY	1934	210	109	319
Mickey Mantle	NY	1957	173	146	319
Norm Cash	DET	1961	193	124	317
Lou Gehrig	NY	1932	208	108	316
Jimmie Foxx	BOS	1938	197	119	316
Frank Thomas	CHI	1991	178	138	316
Ted Williams	BOS	1948	186	126	314
Carl Yastrzemski	BOS	1970	186	128	314
Charlie Gehringer	DET	1934	214	99	313
Ted Williams	BOS	1951	169	144	313
Wade Boggs	BOS	1986	207	105	312
	BOS	1989	205	107	312
Tris Speaker	CLE	1920	214	97	311
	CLE	1923	218	93	311
Buddy Myer	WAS	1935	215	96	311
Charlie Gehringer	DET	1936	227	83	310
Eddie Yost	WAS	1950	169	141	310

Most Combined Hits and Walks, Season, AL (cont.)

Player	Team	Year	H	BB	Total
Babe Ruth	NY	1928	173	135	308
Lou Gehrig	NY	1935	176	132	308
Rod Carew	MIN	1977	239	69	308
Frank Thomas	CHI	1992	185	122	307
Lu Blue	CHI	1931	179	127	306
Lou Gehrig	NY	1928	210	95	305
Wade Boggs	BOS	1987	200	105	305
Tris Speaker	BOS	1912	222	82	304
George Sisler	STL	1920	257	46	303
Jimmie Foxx	BOS	1936	198	105	303
Charlie Jamieson	CLE	1923	222	80	302
Hank Greenberg	DET	1937	200	102	302
Wade Boggs	BOS	1983	210	92	302
Jimmie Foxx	PHI	1933	204	96	300
Mickey Mantle	NY	1956	188	112	300

Most Combined Hits and Walks, Season, NL

Player	Team	Year	H	BB	Total
Billy Hamilton	PHI	1894	223	126	346
Lefty O'Doul	PHI	1929	254	76	330
Rogers Hornsby	STL	1924	227	89	316
	CHI	1929	229	87	316
	STL	1922	250	65	315
Woody English	CHI	1930	214	100	314
Stan Musial	STL	1949	207	107	314
Hack Wilson	CHI	1930	208	105	313
Richie Ashburn	PHI	1958	215	97	312
Bill Terry	NY	1930	254	57	311
Jesse Burkett	CLE	1895	235	74	309
Stan Musial	STL	1948	230	79	309
Arky Vaughan	PIT	1936	190	118	308
Babe Herman	BKN	1930	241	66	307
Joe Kelley	BAL	1894	199	107	306
Pete Rose	CIN	1969	218	88	306
Stan Musial	STL	1953	200	105	305
Chuck Klein	PHI	1930	250	54	304
Stan Musial	STL	1951	205	98	303
Pete Rose	PHI	1979	208	95	303
Hugh Duffy	BOS	1894	236	66	302
Eddie Stanky	NY	1950	158	144	302
Billy Hamilton	BOS	1896	191	110	301
Stan Musial	STL	1946	228	73	301
Ralph Kiner	PIT	1951	164	137	301
Pete Rose	CIN	1976	215	86	301
Paul Waner	PIT	1928	223	77	300
Kiki Cuyler	CHI	1930	228	72	300

Most Combined Hits and Walks, Season, NL (cont.)

Player	Team	Year	H	BB	Total
Richie Ashburn	PHI	1954	175	125	300
Tony Gwynn	SD	1987	218	82	300

Easiest to Double Up, Career (Min 1,000 G)

Player	AB	DP	Ratio
Ernie Lombardi	5260	261	20.1
Walt Dropo	4124	166	24.8
George Scott	7433	287	25.9
Jim Rice	8225	311	26.4
Jerry Adair	4019	149	27.0
Sammy White	3502	129	27.1
Rico Carty	5606	206	27.2
Hal Lanier	3703	135	27.4
Joe Torre	7874	284	27.7
Danny Cater	4451	160	27.8
Julio Franco	5416	194	27.9
Lou Piniella	5867	209	28.1
Earl Battey	3586	127	28.2
Jackie Jensen	5236	185	28.3
Tony Pena	5550	196	28.3
Bill Jurges	5564	195	28.5
Sid Gordon	4992	174	28.7
Bill Skowron	5547	192	28.9
Ken Singleton	7189	248	29.0
Sherm Lollar	5351	184	29.1
Walker Cooper	4702	160	29.4
Gary Ward	4479	152	29.4
Roy Campanella	4205	143	29.4
Joe Adcock	6606	223	29.6
Frank Howard	6488	219	29.6
Bill Tuttle	4268	143	29.8
Rich Dauer	3829	128	29.9
Mickey Owen	3649	122	29.9

Grounded Into Most Double Plays, Career

Player	DP	Player	DP
Hank Aaron	328	Al Kaline	271
Carl Yastrzemski	323	Frank Robinson	269
Jim Rice	315	Tony Perez	268
Rusty Staub	297	Dave Concepcion	266
Brooks Robinson	297	Ernie Lombardi	261
Dave Winfield	292	Ron Santo	256
George Scott	287	Buddy Bell	255
Ted Simmons	287	Al Oliver	254
Joe Torre	284	Willie Mays	254
Roberto Clemente	275	Steve Garvey	251

Hardest to Double Up, Career (Min. 1,000 G)

Player	AB	DP	Ratio
Don Buford	4553	33	138.0
Brett Butler	6169	47	131.3
Mickey Rivers	5621	44	127.9
Vince Coleman	4042	32	126.3
Don Blasingame	5296	43	123.2
Omar Moreno	4992	45	110.9
Rob Deer	3365	31	108.5
Joe Moore	5053	48	105.3
Will Clark	3778	37	102.1
Gary Redus	3258	32	101.8
Richie Ashburn	8365	83	100.8
Cesar Tovar	5569	58	96.0
George Case	4494	48	93.6
Vic Davalillo	4017	43	93.4
Craig Reynolds	4466	49	91.1
Stan Hack	7100	78	91.0
Bill Nicholson	5534	61	90.7
Lou Brock	10332	114	90.6
Bud Harrelson	4744	53	89.5
Wally Moses	5188	58	89.4
Joe Morgan	9277	105	88.4
Arky Vaughan	6125	70	87.5
Whitey Lockman	5940	68	87.4
Rick Monday	6136	71	86.4
Mitch Webster	3107	36	86.3
Willie Wilson	7489	88	85.1
Del Unser	5215	62	84.1
Dave Collins	4907	59	83.2
Bill Bruton	6066	73	83.1
Terry Puhl	4855	59	83.0
Darryl Strawberry	4564	55	83.0
Maury Wills	7588	92	82.5
Augie Galan	5937	72	82.5
Sandy Alomar	4760	58	82.1
Bert Campaneris	8684	106	81.9
Mel Ott	6669	82	81.3
Don Gutteridge	4202	52	80.8
Alfredo Griffin	6685	83	80.5
Dick McAuliffe	6185	77	80.3

Grounded into Most Double Plays, Game, AL

Player	Team	Date	DP	Opp.
Goose Goslin	DET	Apr 28, 1934	4	CLE
Mike Kreevich	CHI	Aug 4, 1939	4	WAS
Riggs Stephenson	CLE	Sep 30, 1924	3	CHI
Sammy Hale	PHI	May 12, 1927	3	DET

Grounded into Most Double Plays, Game, AL (cont.)

Player	Team	Date	DP	Opp.
Zeke Bonura	CHI	May 11, 1934	3	WAS
Earl Averill	CLE	Jul 8, 1939	3	STL
Eddie Robinson	NY	May 30, 1955	3	NY
Jerry Terrell	MIN	Apr 11, 1977	3	SEA
Jose Morales	MIN	May 17, 1980	3	MIL
Jim Presley	SEA	Apr 27, 1985	3	CAL
Rich Gedman	BOS	Apr 23, 1986	3	DET
Matt Nokes	NY	May 3, 1992	3	MIN

Grounded into Most Double Plays, Game, NL

Player	Team	Date	DP	Opp.
Joe Torre	NY	Jul 21, 1975	4	HOU
Hal Irelan	PHI	Sep 5, 1914	3	BOS
Walt Cruise	BOS	Sep 18, 1921	3	CIN
Burleigh Grimes	BKN	Sep 22, 1925	3	CIN
Adam Comorosky	CIN	Jul 22, 1934	3	NY
Babe Herman	CIN	Jun 26, 1936	3	PHI
Bill Brubaker	PIT	Sep 19, 1936	3	CIN
Johnny Hudson	BKN	Aug 25, 1938	3	CHI
Zeke Bonura	NY	Jul 8, 1939	3	BKN
Roy Hughes	PHI	Sep 5, 1939	3	NY
Billy Herman	CHI	Aug 17, 1940	3	PIT
Ralph Kiner	PIT	Sep 4, 1946	3	CIN
Monte Irvin	NY	Jul 30, 1953	3	MIL
Randy Jackson	CHI	Aug 15, 1953	3	MIL
Joe Adcock	MIL	Jul 20, 1955	3	PIT
Richie Ashburn	PHI	Jun 28, 1959	3	SF
Jesus Alou	SF	Jul 17, 1966	3	PIT
Tommie Agee	NY	May 29, 1970	3	HOU
Roberto Clemente	PIT	May 23, 1972	3	STL

Most Hits in Two Consecutive Games, AL

Player	Team	Date	H
Johnny Burnett	CLE	Jul 9, 1932	2
	CLE	Jul 10, 1932	9
Total			11
Johnny Burnett	CLE	Jul 10, 1932	9
	CLE	Jul 11, 1932	1
Total			10
Kirby Puckett	MIN	Aug 29, 1987	4
	MIN	Aug 30, 1987	6
Total			10
Joe Cronin	WAS	Jun 19, 1933	5
	WAS	Jun 21, 1933	4
Total			9

Most Hits in Two Consecutive Games, AL (*cont.*)

Player	Team	Date	H
Walt Dropo	DET	Jul 14, 1952	5
	DET	Jul 15, 1952	4
Total			9
Don Baylor	BAL	Aug 13, 1973	4
	BAL	Aug 14, 1973	5
Total			9
Mickey Hatcher	MIN	Apr 27, 1985	5
	MIN	Apr 28, 1985	4
Total			9
Kirby Puckett	MIN	May 22, 1991	3
	MIN	May 23, 1991	6
Total			9

Most Hits in Two Consecutive Games, NL

Player	Team	Date	H
Cal McVey	CHI	Jul 22, 1876	6
	CHI	Jul 15, 1876	6
Total			12
Willie Keeler	BAL	Sep 3, 1897	6
	BAL	Sep 4, 1897	5
Total			11
Roberto Clemente	PIT	Aug 22, 1970	5
	PIT	Aug 23, 1970	5
Total			10
Rennie Stennett	PIT	Sep 16, 1975	7
	PIT	Sep 17, 1975	3
Total			10
Willie Keeler	BAL	Sep 4, 1897	5
	BAL	Sep 6, 1897	4
Total			9
Stan Musial	STL	May 19, 1948	5
	STL	May 20, 1948	4
Total			9
Andres Galarraga	MON	Jul 1, 1988	4
	MON	Jul 2, 1988	5
Total			9
Darnell Coles	CIN	Jul 25, 1992	4
	CIN	Jul 26, 1992	5
Total			9

Most Hits in Three Consecutive Games, AL

Player	Team	Date	H
Joe Cronin	WAS	Jun 19, 1933	5
	WAS	Jun 21, 1933	4
	WAS	Jun 22, 1933	4
Total			13
Walt Dropo	DET	Jul 14, 1952	5
	DET	Jul 15, 1952	4
	DET	Jul 15, 1952	4
Total			13
Kevin Seitzer	KC	Aug 2, 1987	6
	KC	Aug 3, 1987	2
	KC	Aug 4, 1987	4
Total			12

Most Hits in Three Consecutive Games, NL

Player	Team	Date	H
Cal McVey	CHI	Jul 20, 1876	3
	CHI	Jul 22, 1876	6
	CHI	Jul 25, 1876	6
Total			15
Willie Keeler	BAL	Sep 3, 1897	6
	BAL	Sep 4, 1897	5
	BAL	Sep 6, 1897	4
Total			15
Willie Keeler	BKN	Jun 19, 1901	4
	BKN	Jun 20, 1901	3
	BKN	Jun 21, 1901	5
Total			12
Milt Stock	BKN	Jun 30, 1925	4
	BKN	Jul 1, 1925	4
	BKN	Jul 2, 1925	4
Total			12
Stan Musial	STL	Aug 11, 1946	4
	STL	Aug 11, 1946	4
	STL	Aug 12, 1946	4
Total			12
Rennie Stennett	PIT	Sep 16, 1975	7
	PIT	Sep 17, 1975	3
	PIT	Sep 18, 1975	2
Total			12

Most Hits in Four Consecutive Games, AL

Player	Team	Date	H
Joe Cronin	WAS	Jun 18, 1933	2
	WAS	Jun 19, 1933	5

Most Hits in Four Consecutive Games, AL (*cont.*)

Player	Team	Date	H
	WAS	Jun 21, 1933	4
	WAS	Jun 22, 1933	4
Total			15
Joe Cronin	WAS	Jun 19, 1933	5
	WAS	Jun 21, 1933	4
	WAS	Jun 22, 1933	4
	WAS	Jun 23, 1933	2
Total			15
Buddy Lewis	WAS	Jul 25, 1937	5
	WAS	Jul 25, 1937	3
	WAS	Jul 27, 1937	3
	WAS	Jul 28, 1937	4
Total			15
Walt Dropo	DET	Jul 14, 1952	5
	DET	Jul 15, 1952	4
	DET	Jul 15, 1952	4
	DET	Jul 16, 1952	2
Total			15

Most Hits in Four Consecutive Games, NL

Player	Team	Date	H
Cal McVey	CHI	Jul 22, 1876	6
	CHI	Jul 25, 1876	6
	CHI	Jul 27, 1876	3
	CHI	Jul 28, 1876	2
Total			17
Willie Keeler	BAL	Sep 2, 1897	2
	BAL	Sep 3, 1897	6
	BAL	Sep 4, 1897	5
	BAL	Sep 6, 1897	4
Total			17
Milt Stock	BKN	Jun 30, 1925	4
	BKN	Jul 1, 1925	4
	BKN	Jul 2, 1925	4
	BKN	Jul 3, 1925	4
Total			16

Batting Champion with Two Different Clubs

Player	Team	Year	BA
Jesse Burkett	CLE N	1895	.409
	CLE N	1896	.410
	STL N	1901	.382
Ed Delahanty	PHI N	1899	.408
	WAS A	1902	.376

Batting Champion with Two Different Clubs (*cont.*)

Player	Team	Year	BA
Nap Lajoie	PHI A	1901	.422
	CLE A	1903	.355
	CLE A	1904	.381
Rogers Hornsby	STL N	1920	.370
	STL N	1921	.397
	STL N	1922	.401
	STL N	1923	.384
	STL N	1924	.424
	STL N	1925	.403
	BOS N	1928	.387
Lefty O'Doul	PHI N	1929	.398
	BKN N	1932	.368
Ernie Lombardi	CIN N	1938	.342
	BOS N	1942	.330
Bill Madlock	CHI N	1975	.354
	CHI N	1976	.339
	PIT N	1981	.341
	PIT N	1983	.323

Batting Champion in Three Different Decades

Player	Team	Year	BA
George Brett	KC A	1976	.333
	KC A	1980	.390
	KC A	1990	.329

Hardest to Strike Out, Career (Min. 1,000 G)

Player	Yrs.	AB	SO	Ratio
Joe Sewell	14	7132	114	62.6
Lloyd Waner	18	7772	173	44.9
Nellie Fox	19	9232	216	42.7
Tommy Holmes	11	4992	122	40.9
Tris Speaker	16	7899	220	35.9
Stuffy McInnis	15	6667	189	35.3
Andy High	13	4400	130	33.8
Sam Rice	20	9269	215	33.7
Frankie Frisch	19	9112	272	33.5
Dale Mitchell	11	3984	119	33.5
Johnny Cooney	20	3372	107	31.5
Frank McCormick	15	5723	189	30.3

Easiest to Strike Out, Career (Min. 1,000 G)

Player	Yrs.	AB	SO	Ratio
Rob Deer	9	3365	1210	2.78
Gorman Thomas	13	4677	1339	3.49
Dave Kingman	16	6677	1816	3.68

Easiest to Strike Out, Career (Min. 1,000 G)

Player	Yrs.	AB	SO	Ratio
Reggie Jackson	21	9864	2597	3.80
Bobby Bonds	14	7043	1757	4.01
Dick Allen	15	6332	1556	4.06
Rick Monday	19	6136	1513	4.06
Donn Clendenon	12	4648	1140	4.08
Darryl Strawberry	9	4564	1119	4.08
Willie Stargell	21	7927	1936	4.09
Dick Stuart	10	3997	957	4.18
Tommie Agee	12	3912	918	4.26
Woodie Held	14	4019	944	4.26
Juan Samuel	10	5146	1208	4.26
Tony Armas	14	5164	1201	4.30
Bobby Knoop	9	3622	833	4.35
Greg Luzinski	15	6505	1495	4.35
Gene Tenace	15	4390	998	4.40
Mike Schmidt	18	8352	1883	4.44
Frank Howard	16	6488	1460	4.44
Larry Hisle	14	4205	941	4.47
Deron Johnson	16	5940	1318	4.51
Dwayne Murphy	12	4347	953	4.56
Dale Murphy	17	7918	1733	4.57
Vince DiMaggio	10	3849	837	4.60
Jimmy Wynn	15	6653	1427	4.66
Lance Parrish	16	6743	1442	4.68
Mickey Mantle	18	8102	1710	4.74
Jack Clark	18	6847	1441	4.75
Jim Hickman	13	3974	832	4.78
Harmon Killebrew	22	8147	1699	4.80
Lee May	18	7609	1570	4.85
Bob Allison	13	5032	1033	4.87
Jeff Burroughs	16	5536	1135	4.88
Doug Rader	11	5186	1057	4.90
Wally Post	15	4007	813	4.93
Steve Yeager	15	3584	726	4.94
George Foster	18	7023	1419	4.95

Triple Crown Winners, AL

Player	Team	Year	HR	RBI	BA
Nap Lajoie	PHI	1901	14	125	.422
Ty Cobb	DET	1909	9	115	.377
Jimmie Foxx	PHI	1933	48	163	.356
Lou Gehrig	NY	1934	49	165	.363
Ted Williams	BOS	1942	36	137	.356
	BOS	1947	32	114	.343
Mickey Mantle	NY	1956	52	130	.353
Frank Robinson	BAL	1966	49	122	.316
Carl Yastrzemski	BOS	1967	44	121	.326

Triple Crown Winners, NL

Player	Team	Year	HR	RBI	BA
Paul Hines	PRO	1878	4	50	.358
Hugh Duffy	BOS	1894	18	145	.438
Heinie Zimmerman	CHI	1912	14	103	.372
Rogers Hornsby	STL	1922	42	152	.401
	STL	1925	39	143	.403
Chuck Klein	PHI	1933	28	120	.368
Joe Medwick	STL	1937	31	154	.374

Players Who Just Missed Triple Crowns, AL

Player	Team	Year	HR	RBI	BA	2nd
Ty Cobb	DET	1907	5	119	.350	HR
	DET	1911	8	127	.420	HR
Babe Ruth	NY	1923	41	130	.393	BA
	NY	1924	46	121	.378	RBI
	NY	1926	47	145	.372	BA
Jimmie Foxx	PHI	1932	58	169	.364	BA
	BOS	1938	50	175	.349	HR
Ted Williams	BOS	1949	43	159	.343	BA
Al Rosen	CLE	1953	43	145	.336	BA

Players Who Just Missed Triple Crowns, NL

Player	Team	Year	HR	RBI	BA	2nd
Cy Seymour	CIN	1905	8	121	.377	HR
Honus Wagner	PIT	1908	10	109	.354	HR
Gavvy Cravath	PHI	1913	19	128	.341	BA
Rogers Hornsby	STL	1921	21	126	.397	HR
Stan Musial	STL	1948	39	131	.376	HR

Two Legs of Triple Crown, AL

Player	Team	Year	HR	RBI	BA
Buck Freeman	BOS	1903	13	104	
Nap Lajoie	CLE	1904		102	.381
Harry Davis	PHI	1905	8	83	
	PHI	1906	12	96	
Ty Cobb	DET	1907		119	.350
	DET	1908		108	.324
	DET	1911		127	.420
Frank Baker	PHI	1912	10	130	
	PHI	1913	12	117	
Sam Crawford	DET	1914	8	104	
Babe Ruth	BOS	1919	29	112	
	NY	1920	54	137	
	NY	1921	59	171	
Ken Williams	STL	1922	39	155	
Babe Ruth	NY	1923	41	131	

Two Legs of Triple Crown, AL (cont.)

Player	Team	Year	HR	RBI	BA
Babe Ruth	NY	1924	46		.378
Bob Meusel	NY	1925	33	138	
Babe Ruth	NY	1926	47	145	
	NY	1928	54	142	
Lou Gehrig	NY	1931	46	184	
Jimmie Foxx	PHI	1932	58	169	
Hank Greenberg	DET	1935	36	170	
Jimmie Foxx	BOS	1938		175	.349
Hank Greenberg	DET	1940	41	150	
Ted Williams	BOS	1941	37		.406
Rudy York	DET	1943	34	118	
Hank Greenberg	DET	1946	44	127	
Joe DiMaggio	NY	1948	39	155	
Ted Williams	BOS	1949	43	159	
Gus Zernial	CHI	1951			
	PHI	1951	33	129	
Al Rosen	CLE	1953	43	145	
Larry Doby	CLE	1954	32	126	
Roy Sievers	WAS	1957	42	114	
Roger Maris	NY	1961	61	142	
Harmon Killebrew	MIN	1962	48	126	
	MIN	1969	49	140	
Frank Howard	WAS	1970	44	126	
Dick Allen	CHI	1972	37	113	
Reggie Jackson	OAK	1973	32	117	
George Scott	MIL	1975	36	109	
Jim Rice	BOS	1978	46	139	
Eddie Murray	BAL	1981	22	78	
Jim Rice	BOS	1983	39	126	
Tony Armas	BOS	1984	43	123	
Jose Canseco	OAK	1988	42	124	
Cecil Fielder	DET	1990	51	132	
	DET	1991	44	133	

Two Legs of Triple Crown, NL

Player	Team	Year	HR	RBI	BA
Deacon White	BOS	1877		49	.387
Cap Anson	CHI	1881		82	.399
Sam Thompson	DET	1887		166	.372
Cap Anson	CHI	1888		84	.344
Dan Brouthers	BKN	1892		124	.335
Ed Delahanty	PHI	1893	19	146	
Sam Thompson	PHI	1895	18	165	
Ed Delahanty	PHI	1899		137	.408
Cy Seymour	CIN	1905		121	.377
Honus Wagner	PIT	1908		109	.354

Two Legs of Triple Crown, NL *(cont.)*

Player	Team	Year	HR	RBI	BA
Honus Wagner	PIT	1909		100	.339
Sherry Magee	PHI	1910		123	.331
Wildfire Schulte	CHI	1911	21	107	
Gavvy Cravath	PHI	1913	19	128	
	PHI	1915	24	115	
Rogers Hornsby	STL	1920		94	.370
	STL	1921		126	.397
Paul Waner	PIT	1927		131	.380
Jim Bottomley	STL	1928	31	136	
Hack Wilson	CHI	1930	56	190	
Chuck Klein	PHI	1931	31	121	
Mel Ott	NY	1934	35	135	
Wally Berger	BOS	1935	34	130	
Johnny Mize	STL	1939	28		.349
	STL	1940	43	137	
Dolf Camilli	BKN	1941	34	120	
Bill Nicholson	CHI	1943	29	128	
	CHI	1944	33	122	
Johnny Mize	NY	1947	51	138	
Stan Musial	STL	1948		131	.376
Ralph Kiner	PIT	1949	54	127	
Hank Sauer	CHI	1952	37	121	
Ted Kluszewski	CIN	1954	49	141	
Hank Aaron	MIL	1957	44	132	
Ernie Banks	CHI	1958	47	129	
Orlando Cepeda	SF	1961	46	142	
Tommy Davis	LA	1962		153	.346
Hank Aaron	MIL	1963	44	130	
	ATL	1966	44	127	
Willie McCovey	SF	1968	36	105	
	SF	1969	45	126	
Johnny Bench	CIN	1970	45	148	
Joe Torre	STL	1971		137	.363
Johnny Bench	CIN	1972	40	125	
Willie Stargell	PIT	1973	44	119	
George Foster	CIN	1977	52	149	
	CIN	1978	40	120	
Mike Schmidt	PHI	1980	48	121	
	PHI	1981	31	91	
Al Oliver	MON	1982		109	.331
Mike Schmidt	PHI	1983	36	106	
	PHI	1986	37	119	
Andre Dawson	CHI	1987	49	137	
Kevin Mitchell	SF	1989	47	125	
Howard Johnson	NY	1991	38	117	

Two Legs of Triple Crown, Other Leagues

Player	Team	Year	HR	RBI	BA
Fred Dunlap	STL U	1884	13		.412
Tip O'Neill	STL AA	1887	14		.435
John Reilly	CIN AA	1888	13	103	
Harry Stovey	PHI AA	1889	19	119	
Duke Farrell	BOS AA	1891	12	110	

Cycle Hitters, AL

Player	Team	Date
Earl Averill	CLE	Aug 17, 1933
Frank Baker	PHI	Jul 3, 1911
Lyman Bostock	MIN	Jul 24, 1976
Bill Bradley	CLE	Sep 24, 1903
George Brett	KC	May 28, 1979
	KC	Jul 25, 1990
Jack Brohamer	CHI	Sep 24, 1977
Rod Carew	MIN	May 20, 1970
Roy Carlyle	BOS	Jul 21, 1925
Sam Chapman	PHI	May 5, 1939
Lu Clinton	BOS	Jul 13, 1962
Otis Clymer	WAS	Oct 2, 1908
Mickey Cochrane	PHI	Jul 22, 1932
	PHI	Aug 2, 1933
Doc Cramer	PHI	Jun 10, 1934
Joe Cronin	WAS	Sep 2, 1929
	BOS	Aug 2, 1940
Mike Cubbage	MIN	Jul 27, 1978
Leon Culberson	BOS	Jul 3, 1943
Bert Daniels	NY	Jul 25, 1912
Harry Davis	PHI	Jul 10, 1901
Joe DiMaggio	NY	Jul 9, 1937
	NY	May 20, 1948
Larry Doby	CLE	May 4, 1952
Bobby Doerr	BOS	May 17, 1944
	BOS	May 13, 1947
Patsy Dougherty	BOS	Jul 29, 1903
Dwight Evans	BOS	Jun 28, 1984
Hoot Evers	DET	Sep 7, 1950
Carlton Fisk	CHI	May 16, 1984
Dan Ford	CAL	Aug 10, 1979
Bob Fothergill	DET	Sep 26, 1926
Jimmie Foxx	PHI	Aug 14, 1933
Buck Freeman	BOS	Jun 21, 1903
Jim Fregosi	LA	Jul 28, 1964
	CAL	May 20, 1968
Rich Gedman	BOS	Sep 18, 1985

Cycle Hitters, AL (*cont.*)

Player	Team	Date
Lou Gehrig	NY	Jun 25, 1934
	NY	Aug 1, 1937
Charlie Gehringer	DET	May 27, 1939
Joe Gordon	NY	Sep 8, 1940
Goose Goslin	WAS	Aug 28, 1924
Mike Greenwell	BOS	Sep 14, 1988
Kelly Gruber	TOR	Apr 16, 1989
Odell Hale	CLE	Jul 12, 1938
Mike Hegan	MIL	Sep 3, 1976
Pinky Higgins	PHI	Aug 6, 1933
Larry Hisle	MIN	Jun 4, 1976
Tony Horton	CLE	Jul 2, 1970
Baby Doll Jacobson	STL	Apr 17, 1924
Bob Johnson	BOS	Jul 6, 1944
George Kell	DET	Jun 2, 1950
Jim King	WAS	May 26, 1964
Nap Lajoie	PHI	Jul 30, 1901
Tony Lazzeri	NY	Jun 3, 1932
Fred Lynn	BOS	May 13, 1980
Mickey Mantle	NY	Jul 23, 1957
John Mayberry	KC	Aug 5, 1977
Oddibe McDowell	TEX	Jul 23, 1985
George McQuinn	STL	Jul 19, 1941
Oscar Melillo	STL	May 23, 1929
Bob Meusel	NY	May 7, 1921
	NY	Jul 3, 1922
	NY	Jul 26, 1928
Paul Molitor	MIL	May 15, 1991
Charlie Moore	MIL	Oct 1, 1980
Bobby Murcer	NY	Aug 29, 1972
Danny Murphy	PHI	Aug 25, 1910
Freddie Patek	KC	Jul 9, 1971
Tony Phillips	OAK	May 16, 1986
Kirby Puckett	MIN	Aug 1, 1986
Cal Ripken	BAL	May 6, 1984
Brooks Robinson	BAL	Jul 15, 1960
Buddy Rosar	NY	Jul 19, 1940
Ray Schalk	CHI	Jun 27, 1922
George Sisler	STL	Aug 8, 1920
	STL	Aug 13, 1921
Moose Solters	BOS	Aug 19, 1934
Tris Speaker	BOS	Jun 9, 1912
Andre Thornton	CLE	Apr 22, 1978
Cesar Tovar	MIN	Sep 19, 1972
Elmer Valo	PHI	Aug 2, 1950
Bobby Veach	DET	Sep 17, 1920
Mickey Vernon	WAS	May 19, 1946

Cycle Hitters, AL (*cont.*)

Player	Team	Date
Gee Walker	DET	Apr 20, 1937
Gary Ward	MIN	Sep 18, 1980
Bob Watson	BOS	Sep 15, 1979
Vic Wertz	DET	Sep 14, 1947
Frank White	KC	Sep 26, 1979
	KC	Aug 3, 1982
Ted Williams	BOS	Jul 21, 1946
Dave Winfield	CAL	Jun 24, 1991
Carl Yastrzemski	BOS	May 14, 1965
Robin Yount	MIL	Jun 12, 1988

Cycle Hitters, NL

Player	Team	Date
Tommie Agee	NY	Jul 6, 1970
Dave Bancroft	NY	Jun 1, 1921
Johnny Bates	BOS	Apr 26, 1907
Gus Bell	PIT	Jun 4, 1951
Jim Bottomley	STL	Jul 15, 1927
Ken Boyer	STL	Sep 14, 1961
	STL	Jun 16, 1964
Lou Brock	STL	May 27, 1975
George Burns	NY	Sep 17, 1920
Oyster Burns	BKN	Aug 1, 1890
Johnny Callison	PHI	Jun 27, 1963
Max Carey	PIT	Jun 20, 1925
Fred Carroll	PIT	May 2, 1887
Ed Cartwright	WAS	Sep 30, 1895
Andujar Cedeno	HOU	Aug 25, 1992
Cesar Cedeno	HOU	Aug 2, 1972
	HOU	Aug 9, 1976
Frank Chance	CHI	Jun 14, 1904
Fred Clarke	PIT	Jul 23, 1901
	PIT	May 7, 1903
Bill Collins	BOS	Oct 6, 1910
Duff Cooley	BOS	Jun 20, 1904
Harry Craft	CIN	Jun 8, 1940
Lave Cross	PHI	Apr 24, 1894
Kiki Cuyler	PIT	Jun 4, 1925
Harry Danning	NY	Jun 15, 1940
Andre Dawson	CHI	Apr 29, 1987
Eric Davis	CIN	Jun 2, 1989
George Decker	CHI	Sep 16, 1894
Ivan DeJesus	CHI	Apr 22, 1980
Tommy Dowd	STL	Aug 16, 1895
Fred Dunlap	STL	May 24, 1886
Mike Easler	PIT	Jun 12, 1980

Cycle Hitters, NL (cont.)

Player	Team	Date
Bob Elliott	PIT	Jul 15, 1945
Curry Foley	BUF	May 25, 1882
Tim Foli	MON	Apr 22, 1976
Jack Glasscock	IND	Aug 8, 1889
Heinie Groh	CIN	Jul 5, 1915
Chick Hafey	STL	Aug 21, 1930
Albert Hall	ATL	Sep 23, 1987
Jim Ray Hart	SF	Jul 8, 1970
Bill Hassamaer	WAS	Jun 13, 1894
Cliff Heathcote	STL	Jun 13, 1918
Babe Herman	BKN	May 18, 1931
	BKN	Jul 24, 1931
	CHI	Sep 30, 1933
Keith Hernandez	NY	Jul 4, 1985
Jim Hickman	NY	Aug 7, 1963
Gil Hodges	BKN	Jun 25, 1949
Randy Hundley	CHI	Aug 11, 1966
Jimmy Johnston	BKN	May 25, 1922
Bill Joyce	WAS	May 30, 1896
Ralph Kiner	PIT	Jun 25, 1950
Dave Kingman	SF	Apr 16, 1972
Chuck Klein	PHI	Jul 1, 1931
	PHI	May 26, 1933
Ray Lankford	STL	Sep 15, 1991
Jeffrey Leonard	SF	Jun 27, 1985
Sam Leslie	NY	May 24, 1936
Freddie Lindstrom	NY	May 8, 1930
Herman Long	BOS	May 9, 1896
Candy Maldonado	SF	May 4, 1987
Pepper Martin	STL	May 5, 1933
Willie McGee	STL	Jun 23, 1984
Mox McQuery	DET	Sep 28, 1885
Kevin McReynolds	NY	Aug 1, 1989
Joe Medwick	STL	Jun 29, 1935
Sam Mertes	NY	Oct 4, 1904
Chief Meyers	NY	Jun 10, 1912
Mike Mitchell	CIN	Aug 19, 1911
Johnny Mize	STL	Jul 13, 1940
Don Mueller	NY	Jul 11, 1954
Stan Musial	STL	Jul 24, 1949
Jim O'Rourke	BUF	Jun 16, 1884
Mel Ott	NY	May 16, 1929
Wes Parker	LA	May 7, 1970
Tom Parrott	CIN	Sep 28, 1894
Mike Phillips	NY	Jun 25, 1976
Long John Reilly	CIN	Aug 6, 1890
Dave Robertson	PIT	Aug 30, 1921

Cycle Hitters, NL (*cont.*)

Player	Team	Date
Frank Robinson	CIN	May 2, 1959
Jackie Robinson	BKN	Aug 29, 1948
Jack Rowe	DET	Aug 21, 1886
Jimmy Ryan	CHI	Jul 28, 1888
	CHI	Jul 1, 1891
Bill Salkeld	PIT	Aug 4, 1945
Wildfire Schulte	CHI	Jul 20, 1911
Roy Smalley	CHI	Jun 28, 1950
Chris Speier	MON	Jul 20, 1978
	SF	Jul 9, 1988
Willie Stargell	PIT	Jul 22, 1964
Bill Terry	NY	May 29, 1928
Robby Thompson	SF	Apr 22, 1991
Sam Thompson	PHI	Aug 17, 1894
Mike Tiernan	NY	Aug 25, 1888
Joe Torre	STL	Jun 27, 1973
Pie Traynor	PIT	Jul 7, 1923
Larry Twitchell	CLE	Aug 15, 1889
Arky Vaughan	PIT	Jun 24, 1933
	PIT	Jul 19, 1939
Honus Wagner	PIT	Aug 22, 1912
Dixie Walker	BKN	Sep 2, 1944
Lee Walls	CHI	Jul 2, 1957
Bob Watson	HOU	Jun 24, 1977
Wally Westlake	PIT	Jul 30, 1948
	PIT	Jun 14, 1949
Bill White	STL	Aug 14, 1960
Billy Williams	CHI	Jul 17, 1966
Cy Williams	PHI	Aug 5, 1927
Hack Wilson	CHI	Jun 23, 1930
Owen Wilson	PIT	Jul 3, 1910
George Wood	DET	Jun 13, 1885
Ross Youngs	NY	Apr 29, 1922
Richie Zisk	PIT	Jun 9, 1974

Cycle Hitters, Other Leagues

Player	Team	Date
Sam Barkley	KC AA	Jun 13, 1888
Pete Browning	LOU AA	Aug 8, 1886
	LOU AA	Jun 7, 1889
Roger Connor	NY P	Jul 21, 1890
Abner Dalrymple	MIL AA	Sep 12, 1891
Jumbo Davis	BKN AA	Jul 18, 1890
Lon Knight	PHI AA	Jul 30, 1883
Henry Larkin	PHI AA	Jun 16, 1885
Ed Lennox	PIT F	May 6, 1914
Chippy McGarr	PHI AA	Sep 23, 1886

Cycle Hitters, Other Leagues (*cont.*)

Player	Team	Date
Bid McPhee	CIN AA	Aug 26, 1887
Tip O'Neill	STL AA	Apr 30, 1887
	STL AA	May 7, 1887
Dave Orr	NY AA	Jun 12, 1885
	NY AA	Aug 10, 1887
Long John Reilly	CIN AA	Sep 12, 1883
	CIN AA	Sep 19, 1883
Harry Stovey	PHI AA	May 15, 1888
Bill Van Dyke	TOL AA	Jul 5, 1890
Farmer Weaver	LOU AA	Aug 12, 1890

The Worst Hitters (Min. 2,500 AB)

Player	G	AB	H	BA
Bill Bergen	947	3028	516	.170
Billy Sullivan	1146	3657	777	.212
Dave Duncan	929	2885	617	.214
Bobby Wine	1164	3172	682	.215
Dal Maxvill	1423	3443	748	.217
George McBride	1658	5526	1203	.218
Mal Kittridge	1215	4030	882	.219
Lee Tannehill	1089	3778	833	.220
Lou Criger	1012	3202	709	.221
Rob Deer	1002	3365	746	.222
Johnnie LeMaster	1039	3191	709	.222
Ed Brinkman	1818	5970	1337	.224
George Strickland	971	2824	633	.224
Gorman Thomas	1435	4677	1051	.225
Buck Martinez	1049	2743	618	.225
Charley O'Leary	954	3230	731	.226
Dick Schofield (Ducky)	1321	3083	699	.227
Mark Belanger	2016	5784	1316	.228
Jim Hegan	1666	4772	1087	.228
Hal Lanier	1196	3703	843	.228
Steve Yeager	1269	3584	816	.228
Steve Balboni	958	3115	711	.228
Dick Schofield	1203	3818	875	.229
Rabbit Warstler	1206	4088	935	.229
John Bateman	1017	3330	765	.230
Mickey Doolan	1727	5976	1376	.230
Roger Metzger	1219	4201	972	.231
Bob Swift	1001	2750	635	.231
Eddie Ainsmith	1068	3048	707	.232
Rick Dempsey	1766	4692	1093	.233
Larry Brown	1129	3449	803	.233
Wayne Gross	1106	3125	727	.233
Clay Dalrymple	1079	3042	710	.233

The Worst Hitters (Min. 2,500 AB) (cont.)

Player	G	AB	H	BA
Monte Cross	1681	5817	1364	.234
Ron Hansen	1384	4311	1007	.234
Oscar Stanage	1094	3503	819	.234
Andy Etchebarren	948	2618	615	.235
Mike Pagliarulo	1044	3290	774	.235
Don Zimmer	1095	3283	773	.235

The .400 Hitters, AL

Player	Team	Year	G	AB	H	2B	3B	HR	R	RBI	BA
Nap Lajoie	PHI	1901	131	543	229	48	14	14	146	125	.422
Ty Cobb	DET	1911	146	591	248	47	24	8	147	144	.420
George Sisler	STL	1922	142	586	246	52	18	8	134	105	.420
Ty Cobb	DET	1912	140	553	227	30	23	7	119	90	.410
Joe Jackson	CLE	1911	147	571	233	43	19	7	126	83	.408
George Sisler	STL	1920	154	631	257	49	18	19	136	122	.407
Ted Williams	BOS	1941	143	456	185	33	3	37	135	120	.406
Harry Heilmann	DET	1923	144	524	211	44	11	18	121	115	.403
Ty Cobb	DET	1922	137	526	211	42	16	4	99	99	.401

The .400 Hitters, NL

Player	Team	Year	G	AB	H	2B	3B	HR	R	RBI	BA
Hugh Duffy	BOS	1894	124	539	236	50	13	18	160	145	.438
Willie Keeler	BAL	1897	129	564	239	27	19	1	153	74	.424
Rogers Hornsby	STL	1924	143	536	227	43	14	25	121	94	.424
Jesse Burkett	CLE	1896	133	586	240	27	16	6	160	72	.410
Ed Delahanty	PHI	1899	146	581	238	55	9	9	135	137	.410
Jesse Burkett	CLE	1895	131	550	225	22	13	5	153	83	.409
Sam Thompson	PHI	1894	102	458	185	29	27	13	115	141	.404
Rogers Hornsby	STL	1925	138	504	203	41	10	39	123	143	.403
Jesse Burkett	STL	1899	138	567	228	17	10	7	115	71	.402
Rogers Hornsby	STL	1922	154	623	250	46	14	42	141	152	.401
Bill Terry	NY	1930	154	633	254	39	15	23	139	129	.401
Ed Delahanty	PHI	1894	114	497	199	36	16	4	149	131	.400

The .400 Hitters, Other Leagues

Player	Team	Year	G	AB	H	2B	3B	HR	R	BA
Tip O'Neill	STL AA	1887	124	517	225	52	19	14	167	.435
Fred Dunlap	STL U	1884	101	449	185	39	8	13	160	.412
Pete Browning	LOU AA	1887	134	547	220	36	18	4	137	.402
Harry Stovey	PHI AA	1884	104	448	179	25	25	11	126	.400

.400 Average and 20 Home Runs, Season

Player	Team	Year	BA	HR
Rogers Hornsby	STL N	1922	.401	42
	STL N	1924	.424	25

.400 Average and 20 Home Runs, Season

Player	Team	Year	BA	HR
	STL N	1925	.403	39
Bill Terry	NY N	1930	.401	23
Ted Williams	BOS A	1941	.406	37

Most Hits, Season

Player	Team	Year	H
George Sisler	STL A	1920	257
Bill Terry	NY N	1930	254
Lefty O'Doul	PHI N	1929	254
Al Simmons	PHI A	1925	253
Rogers Hornsby	STL N	1922	250
Chuck Klein	PHI N	1930	250
Ty Cobb	DET A	1911	248
George Sisler	STL A	1922	246
Babe Herman	BKN N	1930	241
Heinie Manush	STL A	1928	241
Jesse Burkett	CLE N	1896	240
Wade Boggs	BOS A	1985	240

Highest Batting Average, Career

Player	BA	Player	BA
Ty Cobb	.367	Pete Browning	.341
Rogers Hornsby	.358	Bill Terry	.341
Joe Jackson	.356	George Sisler	.340
Ed Delahanty	.346	Lou Gehrig	.340
Ted Williams	.344	Jesse Burkett	.339
Billy Hamilton	.344	Nap Lajoie	.338
Tris Speaker	.344	Wade Boggs	.338
Willie Keeler	.343	Riggs Stephenson	.336
Dan Brouthers	.342	Al Simmons	.334
Babe Ruth	.342	Paul Waner	.333
Harry Heilmann	.342	Eddie Collins	.333

The 3,000 Hit Club

Player	Yrs.	G	AB	H	BA
Pete Rose	24	3562	14053	4256	.303
Ty Cobb	24	3033	11429	4191	.367
Hank Aaron	23	3298	12364	3771	.305
Stan Musial	22	3026	10972	3630	.331
Tris Speaker	22	2790	10196	3515	.345
Carl Yastrzemski	23	3308	11988	3419	.285
Honus Wagner	21	2789	10441	3418	.327
Eddie Collins	25	2826	9949	3311	.333
Willie Mays	22	2992	10881	3283	.302
Nap Lajoie	21	2479	9592	3244	.338

The 3,000 Hit Club (*cont.*)

Player	Yrs.	G	AB	H	BA
Paul Waner	20	2549	9459	3152	.333
Rod Carew	19	2469	9315	3053	.328
George Brett	20	2562	9789	3005	.307
Lou Brock	19	2616	10332	3023	.292
Al Kaline	22	2834	10116	3007	.297
Robin Yount	19	2729	10554	3025	.287
Cap Anson	22	2276	9108	3000	.329
Roberto Clemente	18	2433	9454	3000	.317

The 3000th Hit

Player	Team	Date	Age	Yrs.	H	Opp.	Opp. Pitcher
Cap Anson	CHI N	1897	45	22			
Honus Wagner	PIT N	1914	40	18			
Nap Lajoie	CLE A	1914	39	20			
Ty Cobb	DET A	Aug 19, 1921	34	17	1B	BOS	Elmer Myers
Tris Speaker	CLE A	May 17, 1925	37	18	1B	WAS	Tom Zachary
Eddie Collins	CHI A	Jun 3, 1925	38	18	1B	DET	Rip Collins
Paul Waner	BOS N	Jun 19, 1942	39	17	1B	PIT	Rip Sewell
Stan Musial	STL N	May 13, 1958	37	16	2B	CHI	Moe Drabowsky
Hank Aaron	ATL N	May 17, 1970	36	17	1B	CIN	Wayne Simpson
Willie Mays	SF N	Jul 18, 1970	39	19	1B	MON	Mike Wegener
Roberto Clemente	PIT N	Sep 30, 1972	38	18	2B	NY	Jon Matlack
Al Kaline	DET A	Sep 24, 1974	39	21	2B	BAL	Dave McNally
Pete Rose	CIN N	May 5, 1978	37	16	1B	MON	Steve Rogers
Lou Brock	STL N	Aug 13, 1979	37	18	1B	CHI	Dennis Lamp
Carl Yastrzemski	BOS A	Sep 12, 1979	40	19	1B	NY	Jim Beattie
Rod Carew	CAL A	Aug 4, 1985	39	19	1B	MIN	Frank Viola
Robin Yount	MIL A	Sep 9, 1992	36	19	1B	CLE	Jose Mesa
George Brett	KC A	Sep 30, 1992	39	20	1B	CAL	Tim Fortugno

Four Hundred Home Runs and 3,000 Hits

Player	HR	H
Hank Aaron	755	3771
Willie Mays	660	3283
Stan Musial	475	3630
Carl Yastrzemski	452	3419

Most Seasons with 200 Hits

Player	Total	Best
Pete Rose	10	230
Ty Cobb	9	248
Lou Gehrig	8	220
Willie Keeler	8	239

Most Seasons with 200 Hits (*cont.*)

Player	Total	Best
Paul Waner	8	237
Wade Boggs	7	240
Charlie Gehringer	7	227
Rogers Hornsby	7	250
Jesse Burkett	6	240
Steve Garvey	6	210
Stan Musial	6	230
Sam Rice	6	227
Al Simmons	6	253
George Sisler	6	257
Bill Terry	6	254
Chuck Klein	5	250
Nap Lajoie	5	229

Most Seasons with 200 Hits (cont.)

Player	Total	Best
Kirby Puckett	5	234
Lou Brock	4	206
Rod Carew	4	239
Roberto Clemente	4	211
Tony Gwynn	4	218
Harry Heilmann	4	237
Joe Jackson	4	233
Heinie Manush	4	241
Joe Medwick	4	237
Vada Pinson	4	208
Jim Rice	4	213
Tris Speaker	4	222
Jack Tobin	4	236
Lloyd Waner	4	234
Hank Aaron	3	223
Richie Ashburn	3	215

Most Seasons with 200 Hits (cont.)

Player	Total	Best
Cecil Cooper	3	219
Doc Cramer	3	214
Kiki Cuyler	3	228
Ed Delahanty	3	238
Frankie Frisch	3	223
Ralph Garr	3	219
Hank Greenberg	3	203
Billy Herman	3	227
Don Mattingly	3	238
Lefty O'Doul	3	254
Johnny Pesky	3	208
Babe Ruth	3	205
Sam Thompson	3	222
Zack Wheat	3	221
Billy Williams	3	205

More Walks than Hits, Season, AL

Player	Team	Year	BB	H	BA
Max Bishop	PHI	1926	116	106	.265
	PHI	1927	105	103	.277
	PHI	1929	128	110	.232
	PHI	1930	128	111	.252
	PHI	1932	110	104	.254
Roy Cullenbine	DET	1947	137	104	.224
Eddie Joost	PHI	1947	114	111	.206
	PHI	1949	149	138	.263
Ted Williams	BOS	1954	136	133	.345
Eddie Yost	WAS	1956	151	119	.231
Mickey Mantle	NY	1962	122	121	.321
	NY	1968	106	103	.237
Gene Tenace	OAK	1974	110	102	.211

More Walks than Hits, Season, NL

Player	Team	Year	BB	H	BA
Eddie Stanky	BKN	1945	148	143	.258
	BKN	1946	137	132	.273
Hank Greenberg	PIT	1947	104	100	.249
Eddie Stanky	NY	1951	127	127	.247
Jimmy Wynn	HOU	1969	148	133	.269
	LA	1975	110	102	.248
Gene Tenace	SD	1977	125	102	.233
Jack Clark	STL	1987	136	120	.286
	SD	1989	132	110	.242

Batting Champion by Widest Margin, AL

Player	Team	Year	BA	Diff.
Nap Lajoie	PHI	1901	.422	
Mike Donlin	BOS	1901	.347	.075
Rod Carew	MIN	1977	.388	
Lyman Bostock	MIN	1977	.336	.052
Rod Carew	MIN	1974	.364	
Jorge Orta	CHI	1974	.316	.048
Ted Williams	BOS	1941	.406	
Cecil Travis	WAS	1941	.359	.047
Rod Carew	MIN	1973	.350	
George Scott	MIL	1973	.306	.044

Batting Champion by Widest Margin, NL

Player	Team	Year	BA	Diff.
Cap Anson	CHI	1881	.399	
Marty Powell	DET	1881	.338	.061
Rogers Hornsby	STL	1924	.424	
Zack Wheat	BKN	1924	.375	.049
Rogers Hornsby	STL	1922	.401	
Ray Grimes	CHI	1922	.354	.047
Harry Walker	PHI	1947		
	STL	1947	.363	
Bob Elliott	BOS	1947	.317	.046
Rogers Hornsby	STL	1921	.397	
Edd Roush	CIN	1921	.352	.045
Stan Musial	STL	1948	.376	
Richie Ashburn	PHI	1948	.333	.043
Rico Carty	ATL	1970	.366	
Joe Torre	STL	1970	.325	.041

No-Hit Spoilers—The Only Hit Most Often

Player	Team	Date	H	Opp.	Opp. Pitcher
Cesar Tovar	MIN A	Apr 30, 1967	1	WAS	Barry Moore
	MIN A	May 15, 1969	1	BAL	Dave McNally
	MIN A	Aug 10, 1969	1	BAL	Mike Cuellar
	MIN A	Aug 13, 1970	1	WAS	Dick Bosman
	TEX A	May 31, 1975	1	NY	Catfish Hunter
Eddie Milner	CIN N	Apr 28, 1982	1	CHI	Dickie Noles
	CIN N	Jun 11, 1982	1	LA	Jerry Reuss
	CIN N	Aug 24, 1983	1	CHI	Chuck Rainey
	CIN N	Jun 14, 1984	1	ATL	Len Barker
				ATL	Donnie Moore
	CIN N	Aug 2, 1986	1	LA	Alejandro Pena

No-Hit Spoilers—The Only Hit Most Often (*cont.*)

Player	Team	Date	H	Opp.	Opp. Pitcher
				LA	Tom Niedenfuer
Don Blasingame	CIN N	Jul 13, 1962	1	CHI	Cal Koonce
	WAS A	Aug 6, 1963	1	NY	Stan Williams
	WAS A	Aug 20, 1963	1	KC	Moe Drabowsky
	WAS A	Sep 25, 1965	1	MIN	Mudcat Grant
Patsy Dougherty	BOS A	May 2, 1904	1	PHI	Rube Waddell
	CHI A	Sep 24, 1904	1	NY	Joe Lake
	CHI A	Aug 28, 1909	1	WAS	Dolly Gray
	CHI A	Jul 29, 1910	1	DET	Ed Summers
Sherry Magee	PHI N	Sep 8, 1906	1	BOS	Irv Young
	PHI N	Jun 13, 1908	2	CHI	Three Finger Brown
	PHI N	May 6, 1910	1	CHI	Orval Overall
	BOS N	Sep 29, 1915	1	PHI	Grover Alexander
Ed Konetchy	STL N	Jun 22, 1913	1	CHI	George Pearce
	BOS N	Sep 28, 1916	1	NY	Ferdie Schupp
	BOS N	Sep 30, 1916	1	NY	Rube Benton
	BOS N	Aug 21, 1917	1	STL	Marv Goodwin
Billy Williams	CHI N	Sep 24, 1961	2	MIL	Warren Spahn
	CHI N	Jul 5, 1966	3	PIT	Woodie Fryman
	CHI N	Sep 5, 1969	4	PIT	Steve Blass
	CHI N	Jul 25, 1970	2	ATL	Phil Niekro
Zoilo Versalles	MIN A	Sep 10, 1962	1	LA	Dean Chance
	MIN A	Sep 2, 1964	1	BAL	Milt Pappas
	MIN A	Sep 6, 1964	1	BOS	Bill Monbouquette
	LA N	May 28, 1968	1	CIN	Jim Maloney
Al Bumbry	BAL A	Jun 10, 1975	1	OAK	Jim Perry
	BAL A	May 24, 1976	1	CLE	Dennis Eckersley
				CLE	Stan Thomas
	BAL A	Aug 16, 1983	1	TEX	John Butcher
	BAL A	Sep 15, 1984	2	MIL	Bob Gibson
Jake Stahl	WAS A	Jul 8, 1904	1	PHI	Eddie Plank
	WAS A	May 21, 1905	1	CHI	Frank Smith
	WAS A	Aug 31, 1905	1	CHI	Frank Smith
Honus Wagner	PIT N	Sep 12, 1905	2	STL	Jack Taylor
	PIT N	May 27, 1911	1	CIN	Art Fromme
	PIT N	Oct 2, 1914	1	CIN	Phil Douglas
Buck Weaver	CHI A	Jul 6, 1912	1	DET	Jean Dubuc
	CHI A	Jul 6, 1913	1	CLE	Willie Mitchell
	CHI A	May 5, 1917	1	STL	Ernie Koob
Harry Hooper	BOS A	Jul 14, 1913	1	CHI	Reb Russell
	BOS A	Apr 4, 1915	1	PHI	Herb Pennock
	BOS A	Sep 9, 1915	1	WAS	Walter Johnson
Terry Turner	CLE A	Jun 20, 1909	1	CHI	Ed Walsh
	CLE A	Jun 2, 1914	1	STL	Wiley Taylor
	CLE A	Jul 27, 1915	1	WAS	Bert Gallia
Fred Pfeffer	CHI N	May 11, 1886	1	BOS	Bill Stemmeyer
	CHI N	Aug 6, 1887	1	PHI	Charlie Buffinton

No-Hit Spoilers—The Only Hit Most Often (*cont.*)

Player	Team	Date	H	Opp.	Opp. Pitcher
	CHI N	Aug 9, 1887	1	PHI	Charlie Buffinton
Freddy Parent	BOS A	Sep 11, 1905	1	WAS	Cy Falkenberg
	BOS A	May 1, 1906	1	NY	Bill Hogg
	BOS A	Aug 7, 1908	2	CLE	Addie Joss
Possum Whitted	PHI N	Sep 9, 1915	1	STL	Red Ames
	PIT N	Aug 28, 1919	1	STL	Ferdie Schupp
	PIT N	Jun 30, 1920	1	CHI	Hippo Vaughn
Billy Southworth	PIT N	Jul 25, 1918	1	BKN	Burleigh Grimes
	PIT N	Sep 16, 1920	1	NY	Art Nehf
	STL N	Jun 27, 1926	1	CHI	Sheriff Blake
Fred Snodgrass	NY N	Apr 21, 1911	1	PHI	Earl Moore
	NY N	Sep 1, 1915	1	CIN	Fred Toney
	BOS N	Jul 7, 1916	1	CHI	Gene Packard
Harlond Clift	STL A	Jun 12, 1938	1	PHI	Bud Thomas
	STL A	May 29, 1941	1	CHI	Bill Dietrich
	STL A	Sep 2, 1942	1	NY	Hank Borowy
Bob Johnson	PHI A	Jun 8, 1937	1	DET	Eldon Auker
	PHI A	Jun 30, 1937	1	NY	Lefty Gomez
	BOS A	Aug 30, 1945	1	NY	Bill Bevens
Bob Elliott	PIT N	Aug 8, 1941	1	CHI	Paul Erickson
	PIT N	Sep 12, 1943	1	CIN	Elmer Riddle
	BOS N	May 15, 1951	1	CIN	Ewell Blackwell
Del Ennis	PHI N	Jun 8, 1946	1	STL	Red Barrett
	PHI N	Apr 22, 1947	1	BKN	Hal Gregg
	PHI N	Apr 29, 1956	1	NY	Ray Monzant
Jim Northrup	DET A	Apr 24, 1968	1	CLE	Steve Hargan
	DET A	May 6, 1968	1	BAL	Dave Leonhard
	DET A	Apr 12, 1969	1	NY	Mel Stottlemyre
Tony Perez	CIN N	Sep 5, 1969	1	ATL	Phil Niekro
	CIN N	Sep 17, 1971	1	HOU	Don Wilson
	CIN N	Sep 4, 1974	1	HOU	Don Wilson
				HOU	Mike Cosgrove
Phil Cavarretta	CHI N	Sep 6, 1937	1	CIN	Lee Grissom
	CHI N	Sep 19, 1949	1	BKN	Rex Barney
	CHI N	Sep 2, 1950	1	CIN	Ewell Blackwell
Enos Slaughter	STL N	Sep 25, 1940	2	CIN	Junior Thompson
	STL N	Jul 18, 1947	1	BKN	Ralph Branca
	NY A	Sep 9, 1954	1	BAL	Joe Coleman
Denis Menke	MIL N	Apr 19, 1965	1	CIN	Jim Maloney
	STL N	May 4, 1966	2	PHI	Chris Short
	HOU N	Jul 6, 1969	1	SD	Dick Kelley
Tommy Holmes	BOS N	Jun 13, 1942	1	CHI	Bill Fleming
	BOS N	Aug 25, 1942	3	PIT	Rip Sewell
	BOS N	Aug 28, 1943	2	NY	Van Lingle Mungo
Lou Brock	STL N	May 24, 1967	1	ATL	Denny Lemaster
	STL N	Apr 27, 1973	2	SF	Jim Barr
	STL N	May 18, 1975	2	SF	Jim Barr

No-Hit Spoilers—The Only Hit Most Often (*cont.*)

Player	Team	Date	H	Opp.	Opp. Pitcher
John Stearns	NY N	May 3, 1975	1	MON	Woodie Fryman
	NY N	Jun 10, 1977	2	HOU	Joaquin Andujar
	NY N	Aug 12, 1978	1	STL	John Denny
				STL	Roy Thomas
Ralph Kiner	PIT N	Jun 24, 1949	2	BKN	Rex Barney
	PIT N	Jun 23, 1951	1	BKN	Don Newcombe
	PIT N	Aug 5, 1951	1	PHI	Bubba Church
Jimmy Wynn	HOU N	May 18, 1964	1	PHI	Jim Bunning
	HOU N	Jun 19, 1971	1	LA	Don Sutton
	LA N	Jun 13, 1975	2	PHI	Jim Lonborg
Duane Kuiper	CLE A	Jul 2, 1977	1	KC	Andy Hassler
	CLE A	May 5, 1978	1	CAL	Nolan Ryan
	CLE A	Sep 24, 1978	2	NY	Ron Guidry
John Mayberry	TOR A	Jul 7, 1979	1	TEX	Doc Medich
				TEX	Jim Kern
	TOR A	Jun 6, 1980	1	MIN	Geoff Zahn
	TOR A	Sep 26, 1980	1	BOS	Dennis Eckersley
Ken Griffey	CIN N	May 12, 1977	1	STL	John D'Acquisto
				STL	Buddy Schultz
				STL	Al Hrabosky
	CIN N	Aug 27, 1981	1	MON	Ray Burris
				MON	Jeff Reardon
	NY A	Oct 2, 1983	1	BAL	Mike Boddicker
				BAL	Sammy Stewart
Von Hayes	PHI N	Jun 1, 1983	1	LA	Bob Welch
	PHI N	May 11, 1985	1	NY	Sid Fernandez
				NY	Roger McDowell
	PHI N	May 24, 1986	2	LA	Fernando Valenzuela
Tony Gwynn	SD N	Apr 26, 1985	1	LA	Orel Hershiser
	SD N	Jun 8, 1988	1	CIN	Tom Browning
	SD N	Aug 29, 1988	1	NY	David Cone
Harold Reynolds	SEA A	Sep 13, 1987	1	CHI	Floyd Bannister
	SEA A	Jun 3, 1989	1	TEX	Nolan Ryan
	SEA A	Aug 15, 1989	1	TEX	Charlie Hough
Rickey Henderson	OAK A	Jul 8, 1979	1	NY	Luis Tiant
	OAK A	Jul 13, 1979	1	BOS	Steve Renko
	NY A	May 26, 1989	1	OAK	Todd Burns
				OAK	Rick Honeycutt
				OAK	Eric Plunk
Kevin Seitzer	KC A	Oct 5, 1986	1	OAK	Curt Young
	KC A	May 4, 1989	1	CLE	John Farrell
				CLE	Doug Jones
	KC A	Sep 22, 1989	2	SEA	Bill Swift
				SEA	Mike Jackson
				SEA	Mike Schooler
Tim Raines	MON N	Jul 12, 1986	2	CIN	John Denny
				CIN	Ron Robinson

No-Hit Spoilers—The Only Hit Most Often (*cont.*)

Player	Team	Date	H	Opp.	Opp. Pitcher
	MON N	Sep 26, 1986	1	PHI	Marvin Freeman
				PHI	Kent Tekulve
	MON N	Apr 22, 1990	2	NY	Sid Fernandez
Dan Pasqua	NY A	May 5, 1987	2	CHI	Bill Long
	CHI A	Sep 24, 1991	1	MIN	Scott Erickson
	CHI A	Aug 26, 1992	1	TOR	Todd Stottlemyre
Kenny Williams	CHI A	Jun 6, 1987	1	OAK	Curt Young
	CHI A	May 19, 1988	2	CLE	Greg Swindell
	MON N	Sep 10, 1991	1	NY	Pete Schourek

Batted .300 after Age 40

Player	Team	Birth Date	Age	Year	G	AB	H	2B	3B	HR	BA
Ty Cobb	PHI A	Dec 16, 1886	40	1927	134	490	175	32	7	5	.357
Sam Rice	WAS A	Feb 20, 1890	40	1930	147	593	207	35	13	1	.349
Stan Musial	STL N	Nov 21, 1920	41	1962	135	433	143	18	1	19	.330
Pete Rose	PHI N	Apr 14, 1941	40	1981	107	431	140	18	5	0	.325
Ty Cobb	PHI A	Dec 16, 1886	41	1928	95	353	114	27	4	1	.323
Sam Rice	WAS A	Feb 20, 1890	42	1932	106	288	93	16	7	1	.323
Johnny Cooney	BOS N	Mar 18, 1901	40	1941	123	442	141	25	2	0	.319
Ted Williams	BOS A	Aug 30, 1918	41	1960	113	310	98	15	0	29	.316
Luke Appling	CHI A	Apr 2, 1907	41	1948	139	497	156	16	2	0	.314
Sam Rice	WAS A	Feb 20, 1890	41	1931	120	413	128	21	8	0	.310
Luke Appling	CHI A	Apr 2, 1907	40	1947	139	503	154	29	0	8	.306
Lou Brock	STL N	Jun 18, 1939	40	1979	120	405	123	15	4	5	.304
Luke Appling	CHI A	Apr 2, 1907	42	1949	142	492	148	21	5	5	.301

Most Runs, Season, AL

Player	Team	Year	R
Babe Ruth	NY	1921	177
Lou Gehrig	NY	1936	167
Babe Ruth	NY	1928	163
Lou Gehrig	NY	1931	163
Babe Ruth	NY	1920	158
	NY	1927	158
	NY	1923	151
Jimmie Foxx	PHI	1932	151
Joe DiMaggio	NY	1937	151

Most Runs, Season, NL

Player	Team	Year	R
Billy Hamilton	PHI	1894	196
	PHI	1895	166
Joe Kelley	BAL	1894	165
Willie Keeler	BAL	1894	165
	BAL	1895	162

Most Runs, Season, NL (cont.)

Player	Team	Year	R
Hugh Duffy	BOS	1894	160
Jesse Burkett	CLE	1896	160
Hughie Jennings	BAL	1895	159
Bobby Lowe	BOS	1894	158
Chuck Klein	PHI	1930	158

Most Runs, Career

Player	R	Player	R
Ty Cobb	2245	Paul Waner	1626
Babe Ruth	2174	Al Kaline	1622
Hank Aaron	2174	Fred Clarke	1621
Pete Rose	2165	Roger Connor	1620
Willie Mays	2062	Lou Brock	1610
Stan Musial	1949	Ed Delahanty	1601
Lou Gehrig	1888	Jake Beckley	1600
Tris Speaker	1881	Bill Dahlen	1590
Mel Ott	1859	Rogers Hornsby	1579
Frank Robinson	1829	Robin Yount	1570
Eddie Collins	1818	Hugh Duffy	1551
Carl Yastrzemski	1816	Reggie Jackson	1551
Ted Williams	1798	Dave Winfield	1551
Charlie Gehringer	1774	Max Carey	1545
Jimmie Foxx	1751	George Davis	1544
Honus Wagner	1735	Frankie Frisch	1532
Willie Keeler	1727	Dan Brouthers	1523
Cap Anson	1719	Tom Brown	1521
Jesse Burkett	1718	Sam Rice	1515
Billy Hamilton	1692	George Brett	1514
Bid McPhee	1684	Eddie Mathews	1509
Mickey Mantle	1677	Al Simmons	1507
Joe Morgan	1650	Mike Schmidt	1506
Jimmy Ryan	1643	Nap Lajoie	1503
George Van Haltren	1639		

Most Runs, Game, AL

Player	Team	Date	R
Johnny Pesky	BOS	May 8, 1946	6
Spike Owen	BOS	Aug 21, 1986	6
Mike Donlin	BAL	Jun 24, 1901	5
Herm McFarland	BAL	Aug 25, 1902	5
Harry Bay	CLE	Sep 2, 1902	5
Bill Bradley	CLE	Sep 2, 1902	5
Dave Fultz	PHI	Aug 8, 1902	5
Fielder Jones	CHI	May 3, 1904	5

Most Runs, Game, AL (cont.)

Player	Team	Date	R
Jiggs Donahue	CHI	Jun 27, 1904	5
Bill Bradley	CLE	Jul 13, 1904	5
Dave Altizer	WAS	Jul 2, 1906	5
Bob Ganley	WAS	Jul 7, 1907	5
Germany Schaefer	DET	Jul 17, 1908	5
Rollie Zeider	CHI	Oct 8, 1911	5
Jimmy Walsh	PHI	Sep 23, 1913	5
Harry Hooper	BOS	Jun 24, 1915	5
Ty Cobb	DET	Jul 30, 1917	5
Tris Speaker	CLE	Aug 11, 1919	5
George Sisler	STL	Jun 30, 1921	5
Earl Sheely	CHI	Sep 9, 1921	5
Bill Wambsganss	CLE	Sep 10, 1921	5
Charlie Jamieson	CLE	Sep 15, 1921	5
George Sisler	STL	Apr 19, 1922	5
Babe Ruth	NY	Aug 20, 1922	5
Lu Blue	DET	Aug 22, 1922	5
Sam Rice	WAS	Aug 24, 1923	5
Ty Cobb	DET	Sep 21, 1923	5
Johnny Mostil	CHI	Jun 30, 1924	5
Ira Flagstead	BOS	May 8, 1925	5
Babe Ruth	NY	Apr 20, 1926	5
Ben Paschal	NY	Jun 13, 1927	5
Ira Flagstead	BOS	Aug 29, 1927	5
Lou Gehrig	NY	Jun 12, 1928	5
Al Simmons	PHI	Jun 21, 1929	5
Carl Reynolds	CHI	May 11, 1930	5
Tony Lazzeri	NY	May 21, 1930	5
Al Simmons	PHI	Jun 23, 1930	5
Earle Combs	NY	Sep 29, 1930	5
Oscar Melillo	STL	Jun 22, 1931	5
Eddie Morgan	CLE	Aug 28, 1931	5
Jimmie Foxx	PHI	May 5, 1932	5
Bob Johnson	PHI	Aug 25, 1933	5
Ray Pepper	STL	May 29, 1934	5
Bill Werber	BOS	Jul 6, 1934	5
Jimmie Foxx	PHI	May 4, 1935	5
John Stone	WAS	Jun 16, 1935	5
Lou Gehrig	NY	May 3, 1936	5
Roy Hughes	CLE	Jul 2, 1936	5
Earl Averill	CLE	Jul 24, 1936	5
Lou Gehrig	NY	Jul 28, 1930	5
Fabian Gafke	BOS	Jul 14, 1937	5
Mel Almada	WAS	Jul 25, 1937	5
Jeff Heath	CLE	Aug 20, 1938	5
Dixie Walker	DET	Apr 30, 1939	5
Jimmie Foxx	BOS	Jun 9, 1939	5

Most Runs, Game, AL (cont.)

Player	Team	Date	R
Jim Tabor	BOS	Jul 4, 1939	5
Hank Greenberg	DET	Jul 30, 1939	5
Ben Chapman	CLE	Sep 19, 1939	5
Dom DiMaggio	BOS	Sep 27, 1940	5
Roy Cullenbine	STL	Jul 31, 1941	5
Rudy York	DET	May 24, 1942	5
Bobby Doerr	BOS	Jul 6, 1944	5
Catfish Metkovich	BOS	Sep 30, 1944	5
Gene Woodling	NY	May 8, 1949	5
Dom DiMaggio	BOS	Apr 30, 1950	5
Walt Dropo	BOS	Jun 7, 1950	5
Hoot Evers	DET	Jul 8, 1951	5
Hank Bauer	NY	Aug 12, 1953	5
Eddie Yost	WAS	Sep 7, 1953	5
Chico Carrasquel	CHI	Apr 23, 1955	5
Minnie Minoso	CHI	Apr 23, 1955	5
Frank Bolling	DET	May 18, 1959	5
Rocky Colavito	CLE	Jun 10, 1959	5
Norm Siebern	KC	May 5, 1962	5
Carl Yastrzemski	BOS	Jun 16, 1963	5
Tommie Agee	CHI	Apr 21, 1966	5
Walt Williams	CHI	May 31, 1970	5
Al Kaline	DET	Jun 28, 1971	5
Bobby Murcer	NY	Jun 3, 1972	5
Tony Solaita	KC	Jun 18, 1975	5
Tom Poquette	KC	Jun 15, 1976	5
Rod Carew	MIN	Jun 26, 1977	5
Dave Edwards	MIN	Aug 8, 1978	5
Mike Hargrove	CLE	Jul 31, 1983	5
Tim Teufel	MIN	Sep 16, 1983	5
Lou Whitaker	DET	Jun 10, 1984	5
Joe Carter	CLE	Sep 6, 1986	5
Pete O'Brien	TEX	May 29, 1987	5
Mark McGwire	OAK	Jun 27, 1987	5
Don Mattingly	NY	Apr 30, 1988	5
Luis Polonia	OAK	Sep 9, 1988	5

Most Runs, Game, NL

Player	Team	Date	R
Jim Whitney	BOS	Jun 9, 1883	6
Cap Anson	CHI	Aug 24, 1886	6
Mike Tiernan	NY	Jun 15, 1887	6
King Kelly	BOS	Aug 27, 1887	6
Ezra Sutton	BOS	Aug 27, 1887	6
Jimmy Ryan	CHI	Jul 25, 1894	6

Most Runs, Game, NL (*cont.*)

Player	Team	Date	R
Bobby Lowe	BOS	May 3, 1895	6
Ginger Beaumont	PIT	Jul 22, 1899	6
Mel Ott	NY	Aug 4, 1934	6
	NY	Apr 30, 1944	6
Frank Torre	MIL	Sep 2, 1957	6
George Van Haltren	NY	Jun 9, 1901	5
Piano Legs Hickman	NY	Jun 9, 1901	5
Willie Keeler	BKN	Jun 21, 1901	5
Tom Daly	BKN	Sep 23, 1901	5
Willie Keeler	BKN	Apr 24, 1902	5
Ginger Beaumont	PIT	Jul 16, 1903	5
Cy Seymour	CIN	Jul 23, 1904	5
Miller Huggins	CIN	Aug 5, 1905	5
Honus Wagner	PIT	Apr 20, 1907	5
Cy Seymour	NY	Aug 11, 1909	5
Jimmy Sheckard	CHI	Jun 11, 1911	5
John Titus	PHI	Jun 4, 1912	5
Miller Huggins	STL	Aug 5, 1912	5
Lee Magee	STL	Apr 20, 1913	5
Bob Bescher	CIN	May 15, 1913	5
Max Carey	PIT	Jul 25, 1913	5
	PIT	Sep 3, 1914	5
Ross Youngs	NY	Apr 29, 1922	5
Jimmy Johnston	BKN	Jun 10, 1922	5
Cotton Tierney	PIT	Aug 8, 1922	5
Reb Russell	PIT	Aug 8, 1922	5
Cliff Heathcote	CHI	Aug 25, 1922	5
Reb Russell	PIT	Jul 7, 1923	5
Eddie Moore	PIT	Sep 25, 1923	5
Jim Bottomley	STL	Sep 14, 1924	5
Rogers Hornsby	STL	Apr 18, 1925	5
Kiki Cuyler	PIT	May 12, 1925	5
	PIT	Jun 20, 1925	5
Taylor Douthit	STL	Sep 16, 1926	5
Hack Wilson	CHI	Aug 24, 1927	5
Chuck Dressen	CIN	Jul 4, 1928	5
Johnny Frederick	BKN	May 18, 1929	5
Fred Lindstrom	NY	Aug 24, 1929	5
George Watkins	STL	May 7, 1930	5
Denny Sothern	PHI	Jun 6, 1930	5
Hack Wilson	CHI	Jun 23, 1930	5
Curt Walker	CIN	Jul 5, 1930	5
George Grantham	PIT	Jul 23, 1930	5
Woody English	CHI	Aug 19, 1930	5
Rabbit Maranville	BOS	Jun 10, 1931	5
Ripper Collins	STL	Jul 6, 1934	5
Lou Chiozza	PHI	Apr 19, 1935	5

Most Runs, Game, NL (*cont.*)

Player	Team	Date	R
Lloyd Waner	PIT	May 15, 1935	5
Chuck Klein	CHI	Aug 21, 1935	5
Frank Demaree	CHI	Jul 5, 1937	5
Frank McCormick	CIN	Jun 8, 1940	5
Arky Vaughan	PIT	Jun 27, 1941	5
Joe Medwick	NY	Apr 30, 1944	5
Phil Weintraub	NY	Apr 30, 1944	5
	NY	Jun 12, 1944	5
Phil Cavarretta	CHI	Jul 3, 1945	5
Don Johnson	CHI	Jul 3, 1945	5
Stan Hack	CHI	Jul 3, 1945	5
Pete Coscarart	PIT	Jul 15, 1945	5
Stan Musial	STL	May 19, 1948	5
Wally Westlake	PIT	Jun 5, 1948	5
Pee Wee Reese	BKN	May 21, 1949	5
Bruce Edwards	BKN	Jun 30, 1949	5
Walker Cooper	CIN	Jul 6, 1949	5
Wes Westrum	NY	Jun 24, 1950	5
Gil Hodges	BKN	Aug 31, 1950	5
Bob Elliott	BOS	Jul 20, 1951	5
Solly Hemus	STL	May 20, 1953	5
Jim Pendleton	MIL	Aug 30, 1953	5
Wally Moon	STL	May 12, 1954	5
Willie Mays	NY	May 25, 1954	5
Alvin Dark	NY	Jun 3, 1954	5
Joe Adcock	MIL	Jul 31, 1954	5
Wally Post	CIN	Jul 14, 1955	5
Vada Pinson	CIN	Jul 9, 1961	5
Don Demeter	PHI	Sep 12, 1961	5
Frank Robinson	CIN	Jul 8, 1962	5
Willie Mays	SF	Apr 24, 1964	5
Rico Carty	MIL	Aug 24, 1964	5
Willie Mays	SF	Sep 19, 1964	5
Billy Grabarkewitz	LA	May 26, 1970	5
Billy Williams	CHI	May 31, 1970	5
Willie Stargell	PIT	Aug 1, 1970	5
Lou Brock	STL	Aug 21, 1971	5
Ron Hunt	MON	Jun 8, 1973	5
Bill Madlock	CHI	Apr 17, 1974	5
Rennie Stennett	PIT	Sep 16, 1975	5
George Foster	CIN	Apr 25, 1977	5
Garry Templeton	STL	Apr 27, 1977	5
Larry Parrish	MON	May 29, 1977	5
Joe Morgan	CIN	May 30, 1977	5
Steve Garvey	LA	Aug 28, 1977	5
Lenny Randle	NY	May 18, 1978	5
Dave Cash	MON	May 27, 1978	5

Most Runs, Game, NL (cont.)

Player	Team	Date	R
Lee Mazzilli	NY	Aug 15, 1979	5
Eric Davis	CIN	Sep 10, 1986	5
Jody Davis	CHI	Jun 3, 1987	5
Tim Raines	MON	Aug 13, 1987	5
Darryl Strawberry	NY	Aug 16, 1987	5
Dave Collins	CIN	Oct 2, 1987	5
Kal Daniels	CIN	Sep 6, 1988	5
Lonnie Smith	ATL	May 6, 1989	5
John Kruk	PHI	Aug 10, 1989	5
Bobby Bonilla	PIT	May 20, 1990	5
Mariano Duncan	PHI	May 3, 1992	5

Most Runs, Game, Other Leagues

Player	Team	Date	R
Guy Hecker	LOU AA	Aug 15, 1886	7
Long John Reilly	CIN AA	Sep 12, 1883	6
Monk Cline	KC AA	Sep 30, 1888	6

Most RBIs, Season, AL

Player	Team	Year	RBI
Lou Gehrig	NY	1931	184
Hank Greenberg	DET	1937	183
Lou Gehrig	NY	1927	175
Jimmie Foxx	BOS	1938	175
Lou Gehrig	NY	1930	174
Babe Ruth	NY	1921	171
Hank Greenberg	DET	1935	170
Jimmie Foxx	PHI	1932	169
Joe DiMaggio	NY	1937	167
Al Simmons	PHI	1930	165
Lou Gehrig	NY	1934	165
Babe Ruth	NY	1927	164
	NY	1931	163
Jimmie Foxx	PHI	1933	163
Hal Trosky	CLE	1936	162
Lou Gehrig	NY	1937	159
Ted Williams	BOS	1949	159
Vern Stephens	BOS	1949	159
Al Simmons	PHI	1929	157
Jimmie Foxx	PHI	1930	156
Ken Williams	STL	1922	155
Joe DiMaggio	NY	1948	155
Babe Ruth	NY	1929	154
	NY	1930	153

Most RBIs, Season, AL (cont.)

Player	Team	Year	RBI
Lou Gehrig	NY	1936	152
	NY	1932	151
Al Simmons	PHI	1932	151
Hank Greenberg	DET	1940	150

Most RBIs, Season, NL

Player	Team	Year	RBI
Hack Wilson	CHI	1930	190
Chuck Klein	PHI	1930	170
Sam Thompson	DET	1887	166
	PHI	1895	165
Hack Wilson	CHI	1929	159
Joe Medwick	STL	1937	154
Tommy Davis	LA	1962	153
Rogers Hornsby	STL	1922	152
Mel Ott	NY	1929	151

Most RBIs, Career

Player	RBI	Player	RBI
Hank Aaron	2297	Ernie Banks	1636
Babe Ruth	2211	Goose Goslin	1609
Lou Gehrig	1990	Nap Lajoie	1599
Ty Cobb	1961	Mike Schmidt	1595
Stan Musial	1951	Rogers Hornsby	1584
Jimmie Foxx	1921	Harmon Killebrew	1584
Willie Mays	1903	Al Kaline	1583
Mel Ott	1861	Jake Beckley	1575
Carl Yastrzemski	1844	Eddie Murray	1562
Ted Williams	1839	Tris Speaker	1559
Al Simmons	1827	Willie McCovey	1555
Frank Robinson	1812	Harry Heilmann	1551
Honus Wagner	1732	Willie Stargell	1540
Cap Anson	1715	Joe DiMaggio	1537
Dave Winfield	1710	Sam Crawford	1525
Reggie Jackson	1702	George Brett	1520
Tony Perez	1652	Mickey Mantle	1509

Most Runs Produced, Season, AL

Player	Team	Year	R	RBI	HR	RP
Lou Gehrig	NY	1931	163	184	46	301
Babe Ruth	NY	1921	177	171	59	289
Ty Cobb	DET	1911	147	144	8	283
Al Simmons	PHI	1930	152	165	36	281
Hank Greenberg	DET	1937	137	183	40	280

Most Runs Produced, Season, AL (cont.)

Player	Team	Year	R	RBI	HR	RP
Lou Gehrig	NY	1927	149	175	47	277
	NY	1930	143	174	41	276
Joe DiMaggio	NY	1937	151	167	46	272
Lou Gehrig	NY	1936	167	152	49	270
Babe Ruth	NY	1931	149	163	46	266
Ted Williams	BOS	1949	150	159	43	266
Jimmie Foxx	BOS	1938	139	175	50	264
Babe Ruth	NY	1927	158	164	60	262
Jimmie Foxx	PHI	1932	151	169	58	262
Al Simmons	PHI	1932	144	151	35	260
Lou Gehrig	NY	1937	138	159	37	260
Nap Lajoie	PHI	1901	145	125	14	256
Lou Gehrig	NY	1932	138	151	34	255
Hank Greenberg	DET	1935	121	170	36	255
Lou Gehrig	NY	1928	139	142	27	254
Babe Ruth	NY	1930	150	153	49	254
	NY	1928	163	142	54	251
Earl Averill	CLE	1931	140	143	32	251
Charlie Gehringer	DET	1934	134	127	11	250

Most Runs Produced, Season, NL

Player	Team	Year	R	RBI	HR	RP
Chuck Klein	PHI	1930	158	170	40	288
Hugh Duffy	BOS	1894	160	145	18	287
Hughie Jennings	BAL	1895	159	125	4	280
Hack Wilson	CHI	1930	146	190	56	280
Billy Hamilton	PHI	1894	196	87	4	279
Sam Thompson	PHI	1895	131	165	18	278
Ed Delahanty	PHI	1894	149	131	4	276
Kiki Cuyler	CHI	1930	155	134	13	276
Sam Thompson	DET	1887	118	166	11	273
Ed Delahanty	PHI	1893	145	146	19	272
Joe Kelley	BAL	1894	167	111	6	272
	BAL	1895	148	134	10	272
Rogers Hornsby	CHI	1929	156	149	40	265
Ed Delahanty	PHI	1899	135	137	9	263
Hugh Duffy	BOS	1893	147	118	6	259
Dan Brouthers	BAL	1894	137	128	9	256
Bobby Lowe	BOS	1894	158	115	17	256
Hack Wilson	CHI	1929	135	159	39	255
Cap Anson	CHI	1886	117	147	10	254
Willie Keeler	BAL	1894	165	94	5	254
Rogers Hornsby	STL	1922	141	152	42	251
Chuck Klein	PHI	1932	152	137	38	251

Most Runs Produced, Career

Player	R	RBI	HR	RP
Ty Cobb	2244	1959	118	4085
Hank Aaron	2174	2297	755	3716
Babe Ruth	2174	2204	714	3664
Stan Musial	1949	1951	475	3425
Lou Gehrig	1888	1990	493	3385
Honus Wagner	1735	1732	101	3366
Cap Anson	1719	1715	96	3338
Tris Speaker	1881	1562	117	3326
Pete Rose	2165	1314	160	3319
Willie Mays	2062	1903	660	3305
Mel Ott	1859	1860	511	3208
Carl Yastrzemski	1816	1844	452	3208
Jimmie Foxx	1751	1921	534	3138
Ted Williams	1798	1839	521	3116
Jake Beckley	1600	1575	88	3087
Eddie Collins	1818	1299	47	3070
Frank Robinson	1829	1812	586	3055
Al Simmons	1507	1827	307	3027
Nap Lajoie	1503	1599	83	3019
Charlie Gehringer	1774	1427	184	3017
Ed Delahanty	1601	1464	100	2965
George Davis	1544	1435	74	2905
Rogers Hornsby	1584	1579	301	2862
Goose Goslin	1483	1609	248	2844
Dave Winfield	1551	1710	432	2826
Paul Waner	1626	1309	112	2823
Sam Crawford	1393	1525	97	2821
Al Kaline	1622	1583	399	2806
Hugh Duffy	1551	1299	103	2747
Bill Dahlen	1590	1233	84	2739
George Brett	1514	1520	298	2736
Robin Yount	1570	1355	233	2692
Reggie Jackson	1551	1702	563	2690
Frankie Frisch	1532	1244	105	2671
Harry Heilmann	1291	1551	183	2659
Mickey Mantle	1677	1509	536	2650
Lave Cross	1333	1345	47	2631
Jimmy Ryan	1643	1093	118	2618
Roger Connor	1620	1125	136	2609
Jesse Burkett	1718	952	75	2595
George Van Haltren	1639	1014	69	2584
Fred Clarke	1621	1015	67	2569
Joe DiMaggio	1390	1537	361	2566
Sam Rice	1515	1078	34	2559
Mike Schmidt	1506	1595	548	2553
Joe Kelley	1424	1193	65	2552
Tony Perez	1272	1652	379	2545
Joe Morgan	1650	1133	268	2515

One Hundred or More RBIs with Fewer than 15 Home Runs (Since 1946)

Player	Team	Year	HR	RBI
George Kell	DET A	1950	8	101
Tommy Herr	STL N	1985	8	110
Dixie Walker	BKN N	1946	9	116
Hoot Evers	DET A	1948	10	103
Enos Slaughter	STL N	1950	10	101
Wes Parker	LA N	1970	10	111
Willie Montanez	PHI N	1975		
	SF N	1975	10	101
Enos Slaughter	STL N	1952	11	101
Floyd Robinson	CHI A	1962	11	109
Keith Hernandez	STL N	1979	11	105
Willie McGee	STL N	1987	11	105
Hank Majeski	PHI A	1948	12	120
Ray Jablonski	STL N	1954	12	104
Minnie Minoso	CHI A	1957	12	103
Thurman Munson	NY A	1975	12	102
Ted Simmons	MIL A	1983	13	108
Hubie Brooks	MON N	1985	13	100
Rod Carew	MIN A	1977	14	100
Keith Moreland	CHI N	1985	14	106
Glenn Wilson	PHI N	1985	14	102

Most RBIs in One Inning, AL

Player	Team	Date	RBI	Inn.
Bob Johnson	PHI	Aug 29, 1937	6	1
Tom McBride	BOS	Aug 4, 1945	6	4
Joe Astroth	PHI	Sep 23, 1950	6	6
Gil McDougald	NY	May 3, 1951	6	9
Sam Mele	CHI	Jun 10, 1952	6	4
Jim Lemon	WAS	Sep 5, 1959	6	3
Carlos Quintana	BOS	Jul 30, 1991	6	3
Ty Cobb	DET	Aug 27, 1909	5	4
Ray Bates	PHI	May 14, 1917	5	7
Chick Gandil	CHI	Jul 3, 1919	5	4
Al Simmons	PHI	May 22, 1929	5	5
Joe DiMaggio	NY	Jun 24, 1936	5	5
Mike Cubbage	MIN	Aug 7, 1977	5	4
Don Mattingly	NY	Apr 11, 1987	5	7
Harold Baines	OAK	Jun 22, 1992	5	3

Most RBIs in One Inning, NL

Player	Team	Date	RBI	Inn.
Fred Merkle	NY	May 13, 1911	6	1
Jim Ray Hart	SF	Jul 8, 1970	6	5
Andre Dawson	MON	Sep 24, 1985	6	5

Most RBIs in One Inning, NL (cont.)

Player	Team	Date	RBI	Inn.
Dale Murphy	ATL	Jul 27, 1989	6	6
Chick Hafey	STL	May 7, 1930	5	5
Billy Williams	CHI	May 1, 1964	5	1
Felix Millan	ATL	Sep 20, 1972	5	2
John Boccabella	MON	Jul 6, 1973	5	6
Dusty Baker	LA	Sep 13, 1977	5	2
Ray Knight	CIN	May 13, 1980	5	5
Jack Clark	SF	Aug 18, 1982	5	5
Von Hayes	PHI	Jun 11, 1985	5	1

Most RBIs in One Inning, Other Leagues

Player	Team	Date	RBI	Inn.
Ed Cartwright	STL AA	Sep 23, 1890	7	3

Most RBIs, Game, AL

Player	Team	Date	RBI
Tony Lazzeri	NY	May 24, 1936	11
Rudy York	BOS	Jul 27, 1946	10
Norm Zauchin	BOS	May 27, 1955	10
Reggie Jackson	OAK	Jun 14, 1969	10
Fred Lynn	BOS	Jun 18, 1975	10
Jimmie Foxx	PHI	Aug 14, 1933	9
Jim Tabor	BOS	Jul 4, 1939	9
Jackie Jensen	BOS	Aug 2, 1956	9
Jim Gentile	BAL	May 9, 1961	9
Roy Howell	TOR	Sep 10, 1977	9
Eddie Murray	BAL	Aug 26, 1985	9
Chris James	CLE	May 4, 1991	9
Danny Tartabull	NY	Sep 9, 1992	9
Roy Hartzell	NY	Jul 12, 1911	8
Joe Jackson	CHI	Aug 4, 1920	8
Babe Ruth	NY	Apr 20, 1926	8
Harry Heilmann	DET	Jul 26, 1928	8
Lou Gehrig	NY	May 22, 1930	8
Carl Reynolds	CHI	Jul 2, 1930	8
Earl Averill	CLE	Jul 12, 1930	8
Jimmie Foxx	PHI	Jul 10, 1932	8
Lou Gehrig	NY	Sep 9, 1932	8
George Selkirk	NY	Aug 10, 1935	8
Bob Johnson	PHI	Jun 12, 1938	8
George Selkirk	NY	Aug 12, 1938	8
Jimmie Foxx	BOS	Sep 7, 1938	8
Joe DiMaggio	NY	Aug 28, 1939	8
	NY	Aug 13, 1940	8
Pat Seerey	CLE	Jul 13, 1945	8

Most RBIs, Game, AL (cont.)

Player	Team	Date	RBI
Ted Williams	BOS	Jul 14, 1946	8
Bobby Doerr	BOS	Jun 8, 1950	8
Bill Glynn	CLE	Jul 5, 1954	8
Yogi Berra	NY	Jul 3, 1957	8
Lee Thomas	LA	Sep 5, 1961	8
Leon Wagner	LA	Sep 28, 1961	8
Elston Howard	NY	Aug 19, 1962	8
Tom McCraw	CHI	May 27, 1967	8
Jim Northrup	DET	Jun 24, 1968	8
Mike Epstein	WAS	Jun 19, 1970	8
Frank Robinson	BAL	Jun 26, 1970	8
Jim Northrup	DET	Jul 11, 1973	8
Jim Spencer	CHI	May 14, 1977	8
Glenn Adams	MIN	Jun 26, 1977	8
Jim Spencer	CHI	Jul 2, 1977	8
Don Baylor	CAL	Aug 25, 1979	8
Dave Kingman	OAK	Apr 16, 1984	8
Alvin Davis	SEA	May 9, 1986	8
Randy Bush	MIN	May 20, 1989	8

Most RBIs, Game, NL

Player	Team	Date	RBI
Jim Bottomley	STL	Sep 16, 1924	12
Wilbert Robinson	BAL	Jun 10, 1892	11
Phil Weintraub	NY	Apr 30, 1944	11
Walker Cooper	CIN	Jul 6, 1949	10
Harry Staley	BOS	Jun 1, 1893	9
Heinie Zimmerman	CHI	Jun 11, 1911	9
Johnny Rizzo	PIT	May 30, 1939	9
Gil Hodges	BKN	Aug 31, 1950	9
Smoky Burgess	CIN	Jul 29, 1955	9
Tony Cloninger	ATL	Jul 3, 1966	9
Harry Stovey	BAL	Jul 21, 1892	8
Kitty Bransfield	PHI	Jul 11, 1910	8
Gavvy Cravath	PHI	Aug 18, 1915	8
Dave Robertson	PIT	Aug 19, 1921	8
George Kelly	NY	Jun 14, 1923	8
Travis Jackson	NY	Aug 4, 1923	8
Rogers Hornsby	CHI	Apr 24, 1931	8
Chick Hafey	STL	Aug 23, 1931	8
Babe Herman	CHI	Apr 20, 1933	8
Mel Ott	NY	May 11, 1936	8
Alex Kampouris	CIN	May 9, 1937	8
Augie Bergamo	STL	Jul 4, 1945	8
Gil Hodges	BKN	Jun 12, 1949	8
Ralph Kiner	PIT	Jun 25, 1950	8

Most RBIs, Game, NL (cont.)

Player	Team	Date	RBI
Hank Thompson	NY	Jun 3, 1954	8
Gus Bell	CIN	Sep 21, 1955	8
Joe Adcock	MIL	Jul 19, 1956	8
Lee Walls	CHI	Apr 24, 1958	8
Willie Jones	PHI	Aug 20, 1958	8
Willie Mays	SF	Apr 30, 1961	8
Orlando Cepeda	SF	Jul 4, 1961	8
Ed Bailey	CHI	Jul 22, 1965	8
Ron Santo	CHI	Sep 6, 1970	8
Nate Colbert	SD	Aug 1, 1972	8
George Mitterwald	CHI	Apr 17, 1974	8
Ron Cey	LA	Jul 31, 1974	8
Mike Schmidt	PHI	Apr 17, 1976	8
Dave Kingman	NY	Jun 4, 1976	8
Ken Reitz	STL	Jun 28, 1977	8
Dave Kingman	CHI	May 14, 1978	8
Barry Foote	CHI	Apr 22, 1980	8
Chris Speier	MON	Sep 22, 1982	8
Andre Dawson	MON	Sep 24, 1985	8
Dave Parker	CIN	Sep 15, 1987	8
Tim Wallach	MON	May 13, 1990	8

Most RBIs in a Doubleheader, AL

Player	Team	Date	RBI
Earl Averill	CLE	Sep 17, 1930	11
Jim Tabor	BOS	Jul 4, 1939	11
Boog Powell	BAL	Jul 6, 1966	11
Pete Fox	DET	Jun 30, 1935	10

Most RBIs in a Doubleheader, NL

Player	Team	Date	RBI
Nate Colbert	SD	Aug 1, 1972	13
Phil Weintraub	NY	Apr 30, 1944	11
Enos Slaughter	STL	Jun 29, 1947	10

More RBIs than Games Played, Season, AL

Player	Team	Year	RBI	G	Diff.
Lou Gehrig	NY	1931	184	155	29
Hank Greenberg	DET	1937	183	154	29
Al Simmons	PHI	1930	165	138	27
Jimmie Foxx	BOS	1938	175	149	26
Lou Gehrig	NY	1927	175	155	20
	NY	1930	174	154	20
Babe Ruth	NY	1921	171	152	19
	NY	1929	154	135	19

More RBIs than Games Played, Season, AL

Player	Team	Year	RBI	G	Diff.
	NY	1931	153	145	18
Hank Greenberg	DET	1935	170	152	18
Joe DiMaggio	NY	1937	167	151	16
Jimmie Foxx	PHI	1932	169	154	15
Al Simmons	PHI	1929	157	143	14
Jimmie Foxx	PHI	1933	163	149	14
Babe Ruth	NY	1927	164	151	13
Lou Gehrig	NY	1934	165	154	11
Hal Trosky	CLE	1936	162	151	11
Babe Ruth	NY	1930	153	145	8
Walt Dropo	BOS	1950	144	136	8
Joe DiMaggio	NY	1939	126	120	6
Babe Ruth	NY	1932	137	133	4
Vern Stephens	BOS	1949	159	155	4
Ted Williams	BOS	1949	159	155	4
Ken Williams	STL	1925	105	102	3
Jimmie Foxx	PHI	1930	156	153	3
Ken Williams	STL	1922	155	153	2
Al Simmons	PHI	1927	108	106	2
Lou Gehrig	NY	1937	159	157	2
Hank Greenberg	DET	1940	150	148	2
Joe DiMaggio	NY	1948	155	153	2
	NY	1940	133	132	1
George Brett	KC	1980	118	117	1

More RBIs than Games Played, Season, NL

Player	Team	Year	RBI	G	Diff.
Hack Wilson	CHI	1930	190	155	35
Chuck Klein	PHI	1930	170	156	14
Hack Wilson	CHI	1929	159	150	9
Rogers Hornsby	STL	1925	143	138	5
Mel Ott	NY	1929	151	150	1

Most Stolen Bases, Season, AL

Player	Team	Year	SB
Rickey Henderson	OAK	1982	130
	OAK	1983	108
	OAK	1980	100
Ty Cobb	DET	1915	96
Rickey Henderson	NY	1988	93
Clyde Milan	WAS	1912	88
Rickey Henderson	NY	1986	87
Ty Cobb	DET	1911	83
Willie Wilson	KC	1979	83
Eddie Collins	PHI	1910	81
Rickey Henderson	NY	1985	80

Most Stolen Bases, Season, AL (cont.)

Player	Team	Year	SB
Willie Wilson	KC	1980	79
Ron LeFlore	DET	1979	78
Rudy Law	CHI	1983	77
Rickey Henderson	NY	1989	
	OAK	1989	77
Ty Cobb	DET	1909	76
Clyde Milan	WAS	1913	75
Billy North	OAK	1976	75
Fritz Maisel	NY	1914	74
Tommy Harper	SEA	1969	73
Mickey Rivers	CAL	1975	70
Ty Cobb	DET	1916	68
Ron LeFlore	DET	1978	68
Eddie Collins	PHI	1909	67
Rickey Henderson	OAK	1984	66
Kenny Lofton	CLE	1992	66
Ty Cobb	DET	1910	65
Rickey Henderson	OAK	1990	65
Eddie Collins	PHI	1912	63
Sam Rice	WAS	1920	63
Danny Moeller	WAS	1913	62
Bert Campaneris	OAK	1968	62
	OAK	1969	62
Ty Cobb	DET	1912	61
Ben Chapman	NY	1931	61
George Case	WAS	1943	61
Miguel Dilone	CLE	1980	61
Dave Collins	TOR	1984	60
Harold Reynolds	SEA	1987	60

Most Stolen Bases, Season, NL

Player	Team	Year	SB
Lou Brock	STL	1974	118
Vince Coleman	STL	1985	110
	STL	1987	109
	STL	1986	107
Maury Wills	LA	1962	104
Ron LeFlore	MON	1980	97
Omar Moreno	PIT	1980	96
Maury Wills	LA	1965	94
Tim Raines	MON	1983	90
Bob Bescher	CIN	1911	81
Vince Coleman	STL	1988	81
Eric Davis	CIN	1986	80
Dave Collins	CIN	1980	79

Most Stolen Bases, Season, NL (cont.)

Player	Team	Year	SB
Tim Raines	MON	1982	78
Marquis Grissom	MON	1992	78
Jimmy Sheckard	BAL	1899	77
Davey Lopes	LA	1975	77
Omar Moreno	PIT	1979	77
Vince Coleman	STL	1990	77
Marquis Grissom	MON	1991	76
Tim Raines	MON	1984	75
Lou Brock	STL	1966	74
John McGraw	BAL	1899	73
Juan Samuel	PHI	1984	72
Otis Nixon	ATL	1991	72
Omar Moreno	PIT	1978	71
Bob Bescher	CIN	1910	70
Lou Brock	STL	1973	70
Frank Taveras	PIT	1977	70
Alan Wiggins	SD	1984	70
Tim Raines	MON	1985	70
	MON	1986	70
Lonnie Smith	STL	1982	68
Frank Chance	CHI	1903	67
Jimmy Sheckard	BKN	1903	67
Bob Bescher	CIN	1912	67
Joe Morgan	CIN	1973	67
	CIN	1975	67
Alan Wiggins	SD	1983	66
Gerald Young	HOU	1988	65
Vince Coleman	STL	1989	65
Lou Brock	STL	1971	64
Eric Yelding	HOU	1990	64
Max Carey	PIT	1916	63
Lou Brock	STL	1965	63
	STL	1972	63
Davey Lopes	LA	1976	63
Rodney Scott	MON	1980	63
George Burns	NY	1914	62
Lou Brock	STL	1968	62
Honus Wagner	PIT	1907	61
Josh Devore	NY	1911	61
Max Carey	PIT	1913	61
Cesar Cedeno	HOU	1977	61
Gene Richards	SD	1980	61
Joe Morgan	CIN	1976	60
Omar Moreno	PIT	1982	60

Most Stolen Bases, Career

Player	SB	Player	SB
Rickey Henderson	1042	Clyde Milan	495
Lou Brock	938	Omar Moreno	487
Ty Cobb	892	Bobby Bonds	461
Eddie Collins	743	Jimmy Sheckard	460
Max Carey	738	Ron LeFlore	455
Tim Raines	730	Sherry Magee	441
Honus Wagner	703	Brett Butler	437
Joe Morgan	689	Steve Sax	437
Willie Wilson	660	Tris Speaker	433
Bert Campaneris	649	Bob Bescher	428
Vince Coleman	610	Frankie Frisch	419
Maury Wills	586	Paul Molitor	412
Davey Lopes	557	Tommy Harper	408
Cesar Cedeno	550	Frank Chance	405
Ozzie Smith	542	Donie Bush	403
Luis Aparicio	506		

Most Stolen Bases, Game, AL

Player	Team	Date	SB
Eddie Collins	PHI	Sep 11, 1912	6
	PHI	Sep 22, 1912	6
Clyde Milan	WAS	Jun 14, 1912	5
Johnny Neun	DET	Jul 9, 1927	5
Amos Otis	KC	Sep 7, 1971	5
Bert Campaneris	OAK	May 24, 1976	5
Rickey Henderson	OAK	Jul 29, 1989	5
Alex Cole	CLE	Aug 1, 1990	5
	CLE	May 3, 1992	5
Dave Fultz	PHI	Aug 8, 1902	4
Topsy Hartsel	PHI	Aug 29, 1902	4
Dave Fultz	PHI	Sep 4, 1902	4
George Davis	CHI	Jun 14, 1905	4
Nixey Callahan	CHI	Sep 16, 1905	4
Germany Schaefer	DET	Oct 6, 1906	4
Ty Cobb	DET	Oct 2, 1907	4
Otis Clymer	WAS	May 29, 1909	4
Ty Cobb	DET	Jul 22, 1909	4
	DET	Jul 12, 1911	4
Birdie Cree	NY	Sep 28, 1911	4
Hal Chase	NY	Sep 28, 1911	4
Eddie Collins	PHI	May 18, 1912	4
Rollie Zeider	CHI	Jun 21, 1912	4
Guy Zinn	NY	Aug 15, 1912	4
Fritz Maisel	NY	Apr 17, 1914	4
Charlie Mullen	NY	Aug 16, 1914	4
Fritz Maisel	NY	Apr 17, 1915	4

Most Stolen Bases, Game, AL (cont.)

Player	Team	Date	SB
Charlie Pick	PHI	May 17, 1916	4
Frank Gilhooley	NY	Jun 28, 1916	4
Ray Chapman	CLE	May 14, 1917	4
Frank Baker	NY	May 17, 1917	4
Ty Cobb	DET	Sep 24, 1917	4
George Sisler	STL	Jun 23, 1918	4
Ray Chapman	CLE	Sep 16, 1919	4
Braggo Roth	WAS	Jun 12, 1920	4
George Sisler	STL	Oct 11, 1922	4
Ty Cobb	DET	Aug 10, 1924	4
Willie Kamm	CLE	May 29, 1931	4
Oris Hockett	CLE	Aug 6, 1945	4
Tommy Harper	SEA	Jun 18, 1969	4
Amos Otis	KC	May 1, 1975	4
Larry Hisle	MIL	Jun 3, 1976	4
Rickey Henderson	OAK	Jul 27, 1980	4
	OAK	Sep 21, 1980	4
	OAK	Sep 27, 1980	4
	OAK	May 30, 1982	4
	OAK	Jun 13, 1982	4
	OAK	Aug 27, 1982	4
Julio Cruz	SEA	May 24, 1983	4
Rickey Henderson	OAK	Jul 3, 1983	4
	OAK	Aug 19, 1983	4
Damaso Garcia	TOR	Apr 25, 1984	4
Rickey Henderson	OAK	Jul 2, 1984	4
Dave Collins	TOR	Aug 5, 1984	4
Rickey Henderson	NY	Jun 26, 1985	4
	NY	May 3, 1987	4
	NY	Apr 11, 1988	4
	NY	May 7, 1988	4
Harold Reynolds	SEA	Jun 10, 1988	4
Rickey Henderson	NY	Aug 11, 1988	4
Roberto Kelly	NY	May 15, 1989	4
Devon White	CAL	Sep 9, 1989	4
Rickey Henderson	OAK	Sep 20, 1989	4
Henry Cotto	SEA	Jun 23, 1990	4
Roberto Alomar	TOR	Jun 8, 1991	4
Rickey Henderson	OAK	Jun 15, 1991	4
	OAK	Oct 5, 1991	4
Kenny Lofton	CLE	Apr 12, 1992	4
Luis Polonia	CAL	Jun 10, 1992	4
John Jaha	MIL	Sep 12, 1992	4

Most Stolen Bases, Game, NL

Player	Team	Date	SB
Otis Nixon	ATL	Jun 16, 1991	6
Dan McGann	NY	May 27, 1904	5
Davey Lopes	LA	Aug 24, 1974	5
Lonnie Smith	STL	Sep 4, 1982	5
Alan Wiggins	SD	May 17, 1984	5
Tony Gwynn	SD	Sep 20, 1986	5
Jimmy Ryan	CHI	Aug 8, 1900	4
John Heidrick	STL	Aug 25, 1900	4
Honus Wagner	PIT	Sep 20, 1900	4
	PIT	Aug 13, 1902	4
Dan McGann	NY	May 7, 1903	4
Honus Wagner	PIT	May 21, 1904	4
Joe Tinker	CHI	Aug 4, 1904	4
Sherry Magee	PHI	Jul 12, 1906	4
	PHI	Aug 3, 1906	4
Johnny Evers	CHI	Jun 16, 1907	4
Honus Wagner	PIT	Sep 22, 1907	4
Fred Clarke	PIT	Sep 25, 1907	4
Honus Wagner	PIT	Sep 15, 1908	4
Larry Doyle	NY	Sep 18, 1911	4
Dick Hoblitzell	CIN	Sep 27, 1911	4
Josh Devore	NY	Jun 20, 1912	4
Max Carey	PIT	Jul 25, 1913	4
	PIT	Apr 19, 1922	4
Howard Freigau	STL	Jun 3, 1924	4
Johnny Barrett	PIT	Aug 1, 1944	4
Wally Moon	STL	May 24, 1954	4
Willie Mays	NY	May 6, 1956	4
Maury Wills	LA	Sep 7, 1962	4
Lou Brock	STL	Aug 29, 1966	4
Davey Lopes	LA	Aug 4, 1974	4
Lou Brock	STL	Sep 1, 1974	4
Davey Lopes	LA	Jun 24, 1975	4
Ken Griffey	CIN	May 30, 1976	4
Garry Maddox	PHI	May 29, 1978	4
Davey Lopes	LA	Jun 18, 1978	4
Rudy Law	LA	May 12, 1980	4
Omar Moreno	PIT	Jun 2, 1980	4
Gene Richards	SD	Jul 13, 1980	4
Ron LeFlore	MON	Aug 8, 1980	4
Rodney Scott	MON	Aug 22, 1980	4
Tim Raines	MON	Apr 21, 1981	4
	MON	May 8, 1981	4
	MON	Oct 2, 1983	4
Gary Redus	CIN	Apr 28, 1984	4
	CIN	Jun 3, 1984	4
Tim Raines	MON	Sep 18, 1984	4

Most Stolen Bases, Game, NL (*cont.*)

Player	Team	Date	SB
Eddie Milner	CIN	Sep 26, 1985	4
Vince Coleman	STL	Sep 28, 1985	4
	STL	Jun 30, 1986	4
Eric Davis	CIN	Jul 24, 1986	4
Vince Coleman	STL	Aug 4, 1986	4
	STL	Aug 10, 1986	4
	STL	Apr 9, 1987	4
	STL	Jun 10, 1987	4
Gerald Young	HOU	Sep 14, 1987	4
Kevin Bass	HOU	May 7, 1989	4
Gerald Young	HOU	May 28, 1989	4
Jerome Walton	CHI	Jun 18, 1989	4
Tim Raines	MON	Sep 21, 1989	4
Eric Yelding	HOU	May 23, 1990	4
Vince Coleman	STL	Jun 3, 1990	4
	STL	Jul 24, 1990	4
Ced Landrum	CHI	Oct 5, 1991	4
Vince Coleman	NY	Jun 26, 1992	4
Marquis Grissom	MON	Jul 21, 1992	4

Stole 2nd, 3rd, and Home in One Game, AL

Player	Team	Date
Dave Fultz	PHI	Sep 4, 1902
Wild Bill Donovan	DET	May 7, 1906
Bill Coughlin	DET	Jun 6, 1906
Ty Cobb	DET	Sep 2, 1907
	DET	Jul 23, 1909
	DET	Jul 12, 1911
	DET	Jul 4, 1912
Joe Jackson	CLE	Aug 11, 1912
Eddie Collins	PHI	Sep 22, 1912
Eddie Ainsmith	WAS	Jun 26, 1913
Fritz Maisel	NY	Apr 17, 1915
Red Faber	CHI	Jul 14, 1915
Danny Moeller	WAS	Jul 19, 1915
Ty Cobb	DET	Jun 18, 1917
Buck Weaver	CHI	Sep 6, 1919
Braggo Roth	WAS	May 31, 1920
Ty Cobb	DET	Aug 10, 1924
Bob Meusel	NY	May 16, 1927
Jackie Tavener	DET	Jul 10, 1927
	DET	Jul 25, 1928
Don Kolloway	CHI	Jun 28, 1941
Rod Carew	MIN	May 18, 1969
Dave Nelson	TEX	Aug 30, 1974

Stole 2nd, 3rd, and Home in One Game, AL (cont.)

Player	Team	Date
Paul Molitor	MIL	Jul 26, 1987
Devon White	CAL	Sep 9, 1989

Stole 2nd, 3rd, and Home in One Game, NL

Player	Team	Date
Honus Wagner	PIT	Jun 15, 1902
	PIT	Sep 25, 1907
Buck Herzog	NY	Sep 9, 1908
Hans Lobert	CIN	Sep 27, 1908
Honus Wagner	PIT	May 2, 1909
Bill O'Hara	NY	Aug 8, 1909
Dode Paskert	CIN	May 23, 1910
Wilbur Good	CHI	Aug 18, 1915
Jimmy Johnston	BKN	Sep 22, 1916
Greasy Neale	CIN	Aug 15, 1919
Max Carey	PIT	Aug 18, 1923
	PIT	Aug 26, 1925
Harvey Hendrick	BKN	Jun 12, 1928
Jackie Robinson	BKN	Apr 23, 1954
Pete Rose	PHI	May 11, 1980
Dusty Baker	SF	Jun 27, 1984

Most Steals of Home, Career

Player	Total	Player	Total
Ty Cobb	54	Ben Chapman	14
Max Carey	33	Fritz Maisel	14
George Burns	27	Vic Saier	14
Sherry Magee	23	Honus Wagner	14
Wildfire Schulte	22	Heinie Zimmerman	13
Johnny Evers	21	Harry Hooper	11
Frankie Frisch	19	Fred Merkle	11
Jackie Robinson	19	George Moriarty	11
George Sisler	19	Braggo Roth	11
Jimmy Sheckard	18	Shano Collins	10
Rod Carew	17	Buck Herzog	10
Eddie Collins	17	Jimmy Johnston	10
Larry Doyle	17	Sam Rice	10
Joe Tinker	17	Babe Ruth	10
Lou Gehrig	15	Bill Werber	10
Tris Speaker	15	Ross Youngs	10

Most Times Caught Stealing, Game, AL

Player	Team	Date	Total	Opp.
Tris Speaker	BOS	Jul 22, 1912	3	NY
Larry Chappell	CHI	Aug 20, 1913	3	BOS

Most Times Caught Stealing, Game, AL (cont.)

Player	Team	Date	Total	Opp.
Eddie Murphy	PHI	Jun 20, 1914	3	STL
Fritz Maisel	NY	Apr 26, 1916	3	PHI
Larry Gardner	BOS	Jun 27, 1916	3	PHI
Lee Magee	NY	Jun 29, 1916	3	PHI
Rickey Henderson	OAK	Jul 27, 1982	3	CAL

Most Times Caught Stealing, Game, NL

Player	Team	Date	Total	Inns.	Opp.
Robby Thompson	SF	Jun 27, 1986	4	12	CIN
Rabbit Maranville	BOS	Jun 6, 1913	3		CHI
Miller Huggins	STL	Jul 14, 1914	3		BOS
Bill McKechnie	NY	May 30, 1916	3		PHI
Jack Smith	STL	Jun 1, 1916	3		CIN
Tommy Long	STL	Apr 14, 1917	3		CIN
Fred Toney	CIN	Jun 24, 1917	3		STL
Hy Myers	BKN	Aug 25, 1917	3		STL
Rodney Scott	MON	Apr 15, 1979	3		CHI

Most Pinch Hits, Season, AL

Player	Team	Year	Total
Dave Philley	BAL	1961	24
Smoky Burgess	CHI	1966	21
Ed Coleman	STL	1936	20
Smoky Burgess	CHI	1965	20
Bob Fothergill	DET	1929	19
Johnny Mize	NY	1953	19
Bob Hale	CLE	1960	19
Joe Cronin	BOS	1943	18
Julio Becquer	WAS	1957	18
Gates Brown	DET	1968	18
Jerry Hairston	CHI	1984	18
Sammy Hale	DET	1920	17
Bob Boyd	BAL	1960	17
Vic Wertz	DET	1962	17
Pete Ward	CHI	1969	17
Jerry Hairston	CHI	1983	17
Bill Rumler	STL	1917	16
Enos Slaughter	NY	1955	
	KC	1955	16
Dick Williams	BOS	1963	16
Gomer Hodge	CLE	1971	16
Winston Llenas	CAL	1973	16
Gates Brown	DET	1974	16
Rick Miller	BOS	1983	16

Most Pinch Hits, Season, AL (cont.)

Player	Team	Year	Total
Eddie Robinson	NY	1954	15
Ron Northey	CHI	1956	15
Gus Zernial	DET	1958	15
Bob Johnson	BAL	1964	15
Tito Francona	OAK	1970	
	MIL	1970	15
Hal McRae	KC	1986	15

Most Pinch Hits, Season, NL

Player	Team	Year	Total
Jose Morales	MON	1976	25
Vic Davalillo	STL	1970	24
Rusty Staub	NY	1983	24
Sam Leslie	NY	1932	22
Peanuts Lowrey	STL	1953	22
Red Schoendienst	STL	1962	22
Wallace Johnson	MON	1988	22
Merv Rettenmund	SD	1977	21
Doc Miller	PHI	1913	20
Frenchy Bordagaray	STL	1938	20
Joe Frazier	STL	1954	20
Ken Boswell	HOU	1976	20
Jerry Turner	SD	1978	20
Thad Bosley	CHI	1985	20
Chris Chambliss	ATL	1986	20
Jerry Lynch	CIN	1960	19
	CIN	1961	19
Jose Pagan	PIT	1969	19
Greg Gross	PHI	1982	19
Rene Monteagudo	PHI	1945	18
Dave Philley	PHI	1958	18
Rusty Staub	NY	1982	18
Ken Oberkfell	SF	1989	18
Tommy Gregg	ATL	1990	18
Jim Bolger	CHI	1957	17
George Crowe	STL	1959	17
Bob Will	CHI	1962	17
Merritt Ranew	CHI	1963	17
Carl Taylor	PIT	1969	17
Ramon Webster	SD	1970	17
Ed Kranepool	NY	1974	17
Tony Taylor	PHI	1974	17
Mike Lum	ATL	1979	17
Kurt Bevacqua	SD	1980	
	PIT		17
Jesus Figueroa	CHI	1980	17

Most Pinch Hits, Season, NL (*cont.*)

Player	Team	Year	Total
Steve Braun	STL	1984	17
Candy Maldonado	SF	1986	17
Wallace Johnson	MON	1987	17
Lee Mazzilli	NY	1987	17
Mitch Webster	LA	1992	17
Sid Gautreaux	BKN	1936	16
Mike Rogodzinski	PHI	1973	16
Jesus Alou	HOU	1978	16
Charlie Spikes	ATL	1979	16
Duane Walker	CIN	1983	16
Lee Mazzilli	PIT	1985	16
Milt Thompson	STL	1992	16
Babe Twombly	CHI	1921	15
Red Lucas	CIN	1931	15
Harry McCurdy	PHI	1933	15
Schoolboy Rowe	PHI	1943	15
Frankie Baumholz	CHI	1955	15
Bob Skinner	STL	1965	15
Chuck Hiller	NY	1966	15
Jose Morales	MON	1975	15
Champ Summers	CHI	1975	15
Biff Pocoroba	ATL	1980	15
Mike Jorgensen	NY	1982	15
Steve Braun	STL	1983	15
Greg Gross	PHI	1987	15
Joel Youngblood	SF	1988	15

Most Pinch Hits, Career

Player	Total	Player	Total
Manny Mota	150	Jay Johnstone	92
Smoky Burgess	145	Ed Kranepool	90
Greg Gross	143	Elmer Valo	90
Jose Morales	123	Dave Collins	85
Jerry Lynch	116	Jesus Alou	82
Red Lucas	114	Kurt Bevacqua	82
Steve Braun	113	Thad Bosley	82
Terry Crowley	108	Tim McCarver	82
Denny Walling	108	Tito Francona	81
Gates Brown	107	Dalton Jones	81
Mike Lum	103	Tommy Hutton	79
Jim Dwyer	100	Wallace Johnson	78
Rusty Staub	100	Enos Slaughter	77
Larry Biittner	95	George Crowe	76
Vic Davalillo	95	Bob Fothergill	76
Jerry Hairston	94	Lee Mazzilli	76
Dave Philley	93	Harry Spilman	76
Joel Youngblood	93		

.300 Batting Average as a Pinch Hitter, Career

Player	PH	PHAB	BA
Tommy Davis	63	197	.320
Frenchy Bordagaray	54	173	.312
Frankie Baumholtz	47	153	.307
Red Schoendienst	56	185	.303
Bob Fothergill	76	253	.300

Most Consecutive Pinch Hits

Player	Team	Year	Total
Dave Philley	PHI N	1958	
	PHI N	1959	9
Rusty Staub	NY N	1983	8
Peanuts Lowrey	STL N	1952	7
Bill Stein	TEX A	1981	7
Randy Bush	MIN A	1991	7
Bobby Adams	CHI N	1958	6
Bob Johnson	BAL A	1964	6
Mike Vail	CHI N	1978	6
Joe Schultz	STL N	1922	5
Rogers Hornsby	STL N	1933	5
Max Macon	BKN N	1942	5
Johnny Mize	NY A	1953	5
Bob Hale	CLE A	1960	5
Vic Wertz	DET A	1962	5
Andre Rodgers	PIT N	1965	5
Charley Smith	NY A	1968	5
Richie Scheinblum	KC A	1972	5
Rowland Office	ATL N	1975	5
Rafael Ramirez	HOU N	1991	5

Longest Hitting Streaks, AL

Player	Team	Year	G
Joe DiMaggio	NY	1941	56
George Sisler	STL	1922	41
Ty Cobb	DET	1911	40
	DET	1912	34
Paul Molitor	MIL	1987	39
Ty Cobb	DET	1917	35
George Sisler	STL	1925	34
George McQuinn	STL	1938	34
Dom DiMaggio	BOS	1949	34
Hal Chase	NY	1907	33
Heinie Manush	WAS	1933	33
Nap Lajoie	CLE	1906	31
Sam Rice	WAS	1924	31
Ken Landreaux	MIN	1980	31
Tris Speaker	BOS	1912	30

Longest Hitting Streaks, AL (*cont.*)

Player	Team	Year	G
Goose Goslin	DET	1934	30
Ron LeFlore	DET	1976	30
George Brett	KC	1980	30
Bill Bradley	CLE	1902	29
Roger Peckinpaugh	NY	1919	29
Sam Rice	WAS	1920	29
Bill Lamar	PHI	1925	29
Dale Alexander	DET	1930	29
Earle Combs	NY	1931	29
Pete Fox	DET	1935	29
Mel Almada	STL	1938	29
Joe Gordon	NY	1942	29
Joe Jackson	CLE	1911	28
Ken Williams	STL	1922	28
Bing Miller	PHI	1929	28
Sam Rice	WAS	1930	28
Hal Trosky	CLE	1936	28
Wade Boggs	BOS	1985	28
Socks Seybold	PHI	1901	27
Hal Chase	NY	1907	27
Heinie Manush	STL	1930	
	WAS	1930	27
Al Simmons	PHI	1931	27
Luke Appling	CHI	1936	27
Gee Walker	DET	1937	27
Bruce Campbell	CLE	1938	27
Bob Dillinger	STL	1948	27
Dom DiMaggio	BOS	1951	27
Ron LeFlore	DET	1978	27
Harry Bay	CLE	1902	26
Buck Freeman	BOS	1902	26
Hobe Ferris	STL	1908	26
Babe Ruth	NY	1921	26
Heinie Manush	WAS	1933	26
Bob Johnson	PHI	1938	26
Guy Curtright	CHI	1943	26
Johnny Pesky	BOS	1947	26
Kid Gleason	DET	1901	25
Ty Cobb	DET	1906	25
George Sisler	STL	1920	25
Goose Goslin	WAS	1928	25
Catfish Metkovich	BOS	1944	25
Rod Carew	CAL	1982	25
Wade Boggs	BOS	1987	25
Brian Harper	MIN	1990	25
Lance Johnson	CHI	1992	25
Jimmie Foxx	PHI	1929	24

Longest Hitting Streaks, AL (cont.)

Player	Team	Year	G
Cecil Travis	WAS	1941	24
Chico Carrasquel	CHI	1950	24
Ferris Fain	PHI	1952	24
Lenny Green	MIN	1961	24
Dave May	MIL	1973	24
Mickey Rivers	TEX	1980	24
Carney Lansford	OAK	1984	24
Sam Crawford	DET	1909	23
Harry Heilmann	DET	1921	23
George Burns	BOS	1922	23
Del Pratt	BOS	1922	23
Charlie Jamieson	CLE	1923	23
Tris Speaker	CLE	1923	23
Al Simmons	PHI	1925	23
John Stone	DET	1931	23
Joe DiMaggio	NY	1940	23
Ted Williams	BOS	1941	23
Dale Mitchell	CLE	1951	23
Minnie Minoso	CHI	1955	23
Ray Fosse	CLE	1970	23
Mike Hargrove	CLE	1980	23
Kent Hrbek	MIN	1982	23
Tris Speaker	BOS	1913	22
Eddie Collins	CHI	1920	22
Al Simmons	PHI	1925	22
Johnny Hodapp	CLE	1929	22
Red Kress	STL	1930	22
Joe Cronin	WAS	1932	22
Heinie Manush	WAS	1932	22
Doc Cramer	PHI	1932	22
Joe DiMaggio	NY	1937	22
Mickey Vernon	WAS	1946	22
Dale Mitchell	CLE	1947	22
Sam Mele	CHI	1953	22
Al Smith	CLE	1956	22
Hector Lopez	KC	1957	22
Vic Power	KC	1958	22
Harvey Kuenn	DET	1959	22
Johnny Romano	CLE	1961	22
Al Kaline	DET	1961	22
Sandy Alomar	CAL	1970	22
Denny Doyle	BOS	1975	22
Jim Sundberg	TEX	1978	22
Cecil Cooper	MIL	1980	22
Eddie Murray	BAL	1984	22
Julio Franco	CLE	1988	22
George Bell	TOR	1989	22

Longest Hitting Streaks, AL (*cont.*)

Player	Team	Year	G
Brian McRae	KC	1991	22
Shane Mack	MIN	1992	22
Nap Lajoie	CLE	1904	21
Eddie Foster	WAS	1918	21
Jack Tobin	STL	1922	21
Wally Pipp	NY	1923	21
Harry Heilmann	DET	1923	21
Ty Cobb	DET	1926	21
	PHI	1927	21
Charlie Gehringer	DET	1927	21
Buddy Myer	WAS	1935	21
Beau Bell	STL	1936	21
Odell Hale	CLE	1936	21
Joe Vosmik	STL	1937	21
Joe DiMaggio	NY	1937	21
Taffy Wright	WAS	1938	21
Dick Wakefield	DET	1943	21
Johnny Berardino	STL	1946	21
Dale Mitchell	CLE	1948	21
Larry Doby	CLE	1951	21
Dale Mitchell	CLE	1953	21
Roy Sievers	CHI	1960	21
Sandy Alomar	CAL	1970	21
Doug DeCinces	BAL	1978	21
John Grubb	TEX	1979	21
Dan Meyer	SEA	1979	21
Richie Zisk	SEA	1982	21
Damaso Garcia	TOR	1983	21
Lloyd Moseby	TOR	1983	21
Joe Carter	CLE	1986	21
Julio Franco	CLE	1988	21
Mike Greenwell	BOS	1989	21
Joe Orsulak	BAL	1991	21
Kid Gleason	DET	1901	20
Sam Crawford	DET	1903	20
Tris Speaker	BOS	1912	20
	BOS	1912	20
Eddie Collins	CHI	1916	20
Wally Schang	PHI	1916	20
Johnny Watwood	CHI	1930	20
Joe Cronin	WAS	1930	20
Smead Jolley	BOS	1932	20
Jack Burns	STL	1932	20
Earl Averill	CLE	1936	20
Roy Weatherly	CLE	1936	20
Joe Vosmik	CLE	1936	20
Doc Cramer	BOS	1936	20

Longest Hitting Streaks, AL (cont.)

Player	Team	Year	G
Harlond Clift	STL	1937	20
Charlie Gehringer	DET	1937	20
Rip Radcliff	CHI	1937	20
Wally Moses	PHI	1938	20
George Case	WAS	1939	20
Eric McNair	CHI	1939	20
Buddy Hassett	NY	1942	20
Jackie Jensen	WAS	1952	20
Mickey Vernon	WAS	1953	20
Al Rosen	CLE	1953	20
Dave Philley	PHI	1953	20
Bob Nieman	BAL	1956	20
Hal Smith	KC	1958	20
Vic Power	KC	1958	20
	CLE	1960	20
Jerry Lumpe	KC	1962	20
Ed Bressoud	BOS	1964	20
Ken Berry	CHI	1967	20
Ted Uhlaender	MIN	1969	20
Fred Lynn	BOS	1975	20
Mickey Rivers	NY	1976	20
Fred Lynn	BOS	1979	20
Bobby Grich	CAL	1979	20
Buddy Bell	TEX	1980	20
Mickey Rivers	TEX	1980	20
Damaso Garcia	TOR	1982	20
Mike Easler	BOS	1984	20
Alan Trammell	DET	1984	20
Dave Winfield	NY	1984	20
Don Mattingly	NY	1985	20
Lee Lacy	BAL	1985	20
Wade Boggs	BOS	1986	20
Chuck Knoblauch	MIN	1991	20

Longest Hitting Streaks, NL

Player	Team	Year	G
Willie Keeler	BAL	1897	44
Pete Rose	CIN	1978	44
Bill Dahlen	CHI	1894	42
Tommy Holmes	BOS	1945	37
Billy Hamilton	PHI	1894	36
Fred Clarke	LOU	1895	35
Benito Santiago	SD	1987	34
George Davis	NY	1893	33
Rogers Hornsby	STL	1922	32
Ed Delahanty	PHI	1899	31

Longest Hitting Streaks, NL (*cont.*)

Player	Team	Year	G
Willie Davis	LA	1969	31
Rico Carty	ATL	1970	31
Elmer Smith	CIN	1898	30
Stan Musial	STL	1950	30
Jerome Walton	CHI	1989	30
Zack Wheat	BKN	1916	29
Harry Walker	STL	1943	29
Ken Boyer	STL	1959	29
Rowland Office	ATL	1976	29
Bill Dahlen	CHI	1894	28
Joe Medwick	STL	1935	28
Red Schoendienst	STL	1954	28
Ron Santo	CHI	1966	28
Jimmy Williams	PIT	1899	27
Piano Legs Hickman	NY	1900	27
Edd Roush	CIN	1920	27
	CIN	1924	27
Hack Wilson	CHI	1929	27
Joe Medwick	BKN	1942	27
Duke Snider	BKN	1953	27
Vada Pinson	CIN	1965	27
Glenn Beckert	CHI	1968	27
Hugh Duffy	BOS	1894	26
George Decker	CHI	1896	26
Willie Keeler	BAL	1896	26
Jimmy Williams	PIT	1899	26
Willie Keeler	BKN	1902	26
Bill Sweeney	BOS	1911	26
Zack Wheat	BKN	1918	26
Chuck Klein	PHI	1930	26
	PHI	1930	26
Gabby Hartnett	CHI	1937	26
Danny O'Connell	PIT	1953	26
Lou Brock	STL	1971	26
Glenn Beckert	CHI	1973	26
Jack Clark	SF	1978	26
Charlie Grimm	PIT	1923	25
Clyde Barnhart	PIT	1925	25
Hack Wilson	CHI	1926	25
Rube Bressler	CIN	1927	25
Harvey Hendrick	BKN	1929	25
Freddie Lindstrom	PIT	1933	25
Buzz Boyle	BKN	1934	25
Hank Aaron	MIL	1956	25
	MIL	1962	25
Pete Rose	CIN	1967	25
Willie Davis	LA	1971	25
Tony Gwynn	SD	1983	25

Longest Hitting Streaks, NL (cont.)

Player	Team	Year	G
Steve Sax	LA	1986	25
Cy Seymour	CIN	1903	24
Mike Donlin	NY	1908	24
Zack Wheat	BKN	1924	24
Hughie Critz	CIN	1928	24
Pie Traynor	PIT	1929	24
Fred Lindstrom	NY	1930	24
Pepper Martin	STL	1935	24
Gabby Hartnett	CHI	1937	24
Stan Hack	CHI	1945	24
Stan Musial	STL	1952	24
Don Mueller	NY	1955	24
Wally Moon	STL	1957	24
Willie McCovey	SF	1963	24
Tommy Harper	CIN	1966	24
Maury Wills	PIT	1968	24
Willie Montanez	PHI	1974	24
Hubie Brooks	NY	1984	24
John Shelby	LA	1988	24
Gene DeMontreville	BOS	1901	23
Honus Wagner	PIT	1901	23
Heinie Zimmerman	CHI	1912	23
Hy Myers	BKN	1915	23
Heinie Groh	CIN	1917	23
Carson Bigbee	PIT	1921	23
Goldie Rapp	PHI	1921	23
Cy Williams	PHI	1923	23
Clyde Barnhart	PIT	1927	23
Paul Waner	PIT	1927	23
Joe Moore	NY	1934	23
Lloyd Waner	PIT	1935	23
Pepper Martin	STL	1935	23
Richie Ashburn	PHI	1948	23
Alvin Dark	BOS	1948	23
Danny Murtaugh	PIT	1948	23
Red Schoendienst	MIL	1957	23
Vada Pinson	CIN	1965	23
Cleon Jones	NY	1970	23
Al Oliver	PIT	1974	23
Mike Vail	NY	1975	23
Pete Rose	PHI	1979	23
Jose Oquendo	STL	1989	23
Len Dykstra	PHI	1990	23
Brett Butler	LA	1991	23
Jake Daubert	CIN	1922	22
Kiki Cuyler	PIT	1926	22
Paul Waner	PIT	1927	22
Taylor Douthit	STL	1930	22

Longest Hitting Streaks, NL (*cont.*)

Player	Team	Year	G
Hack Wilson	CHI	1930	22
Chuck Klein	PHI	1931	22
Lloyd Waner	PIT	1932	22
Chick Fullis	PHI	1933	22
Johnny Mize	STL	1936	22
Lloyd Waner	PIT	1938	22
Harry Walker	STL	1943	22
Stan Musial	STL	1943	22
Whitey Kurowski	STL	1943	22
Babe Young	NY	1947	22
Earl Torgeson	BOS	1950	22
Duke Snider	BKN	1950	22
Pee Wee Reese	BKN	1951	22
Alvin Dark	NY	1952	22
Hank Aaron	MIL	1959	22
Willie McCovey	SF	1959	22
Pete Rose	CIN	1968	22
Felipe Alou	ATL	1968	22
Vada Pinson	STL	1969	22
Joe Torre	STL	1971	22
Hank Aaron	ATL	1971	22
Ralph Garr	ATL	1971	22
Dave Parker	PIT	1977	22
	PIT	1977	22
Cesar Cedeno	HOU	1977	22
Willie McGee	STL	1990	22
Jay Bell	PIT	1992	22
Sam Thompson	DET	1887	21
Cy Seymour	CIN	1905	21
Cotton Tierney	PIT	1922	21
Les Bell	STL	1926	21
Pie Traynor	PIT	1930	21
Paul Waner	PIT	1930	21
Lloyd Waner	PIT	1930	21
Ernie Orsatti	STL	1932	21
Joe Medwick	STL	1932	21
Mel Ott	NY	1937	21
Chuck Klein	PIT	1939	21
Enos Slaughter	STL	1940	21
Danny Litwhiler	PHI	1940	21
Lou Klein	STL	1943	21
Jackie Robinson	BKN	1947	21
Don Mueller	NY	1954	21
Willie Mays	NY	1954	21
	NY	1957	21
Glenn Beckert	CHI	1966	21
Gene Alley	PIT	1969	21
Lee May	HOU	1973	21

Longest Hitting Streaks, NL (*cont.*)

Player	Team	Year	G
Al Oliver	PIT	1974	21
Steve Garvey	LA	1978	21
Warren Cromartie	MON	1979	21
Dickie Thon	HOU	1982	21
Pete Rose	PHI	1982	21
Bobby Brown	SD	1983	21
Barry Larkin	CIN	1988	21
Ed Konetchy	STL	1910	20
Jimmy Johnston	BKN	1921	20
Reb Russell	PIT	1922	20
Zack Wheat	BKN	1923	20
Chuck Klein	PHI	1929	20
Joe Moore	NY	1932	20
Johnny Frederick	BKN	1933	20
Billy Herman	CHI	1934	20
Paul Waner	PIT	1939	20
Terry Moore	STL	1942	20
Al Libke	CIN	1945	20
Tommy Holmes	BOS	1946	20
	BOS	1949	20
Richie Ashburn	PHI	1951	20
Andy Pafko	MIL	1953	20
Richie Ashburn	PHI	1953	20
Stan Musial	STL	1957	20
Wally Moon	STL	1957	20
Joe Adcock	MIL	1959	20
Pancho Herrera	PHI	1960	20
Tommy Davis	LA	1960	20
Willie Mays	SF	1964	20
Tommy Davis	LA	1964	20
Bill White	STL	1964	20
Roberto Clemente	PIT	1965	20
Maury Wills	LA	1965	20
Rusty Staub	HOU	1967	20
Lou Brock	STL	1967	20
Tony Perez	CIN	1968	20
Tommie Agee	NY	1970	20
Pete Rose	CIN	1977	20
	CIN	1977	20
Rennie Stennett	PIT	1977	20
Steve Garvey	LA	1978	20
Garry Maddox	PHI	1978	20
Bob Horner	ATL	1979	20
Rafael Palmeiro	CHI	1988	20
Otis Nixon	ATL	1991	20

Most Consecutive Games Played

Player	G	Player	G
Lou Gehrig	2130	Sandy Alomar	648
Cal Ripken	1735	Eddie Brown	618
Everett Scott	1307	Roy McMillan	598
Steve Garvey	1207	George Pinckney	577
Billy Williams	1117	Steve Brodie	574
Joe Sewell	1103	Aaron Ward	565
Stan Musial	895	Candy LaChance	540
Eddie Yost	829	Buck Freeman	535
Gus Suhr	822	Fred Luderus	533
Nellie Fox	798	Clyde Milan	512
Pete Rose	745	Charlie Gehringer	511
Dale Murphy	740	Vada Pinson	508
Richie Ashburn	730	Joe Carter	507
Ernie Banks	717	Tony Cuccinello	504
Pete Rose	678	Charlie Gehringer	504
Earl Averill	673	Omar Moreno	503
Frank McCormick	652		

Fewest Games Missed (10-Year Period)

Player	First	Last	G	G Mis	Pct.
Cal Ripken	1983	1992	1617	0	100.0
Lou Gehrig	1929	1938	1543	0	100.0
Pete Rose	1973	1982	1562	4	99.7
Billy Williams	1962	1971	1614	10	99.4
Cap Anson	1883	1892	1258	11	99.1
Nellie Fox	1952	1961	1544	15	99.0
Stan Musial	1946	1955	1533	17	98.9
John Morrill	1878	1887	957	13	98.7
Dale Murphy	1980	1989	1537	20	98.7
Ron Santo	1961	1970	1595	23	98.6
Richie Ashburn	1949	1958	1524	22	98.6
Roger Connor	1880	1889	1083	17	98.5
George Van Haltren	1891	1900	1389	22	98.4
George Burns	1914	1923	1487	25	98.3
Willie Mays	1954	1963	1536	26	98.3
Jim O'Rourke	1876	1885	819	14	98.3
Jimmie Foxx	1929	1938	1495	30	98.0
Brooks Robinson	1960	1969	1578	33	98.0
Sam Crawford	1906	1915	1507	33	97.9
Hugh Duffy	1889	1898	1350	30	97.8
Paul Hines	1877	1886	896	21	97.7
Hank Aaron	1955	1964	1534	37	97.6
Mel Ott	1929	1938	1498	38	97.5

RBI in Most Consecutive Games, AL

Player	Team	Last Date	G	RBI
Taffy Wright	CHI	May 20, 1941	13	22
Joe Cronin	BOS	Jul 9, 1939	12	19
Ted Williams	BOS	Sep 13, 1942	12	18
Al Simmons	PHI	May 12, 1931	11	20
Babe Ruth	NY	Jul 2, 1931	11	18
Ted Williams	BOS	Jun 10, 1950	11	21
Frank White	KC	Jun 11, 1983	11	13
Larry Parrish	TEX	Jun 20, 1984	11	18
Kirby Puckett	MIN	Sep 25, 1988	11	15
Lou Gehrig	NY	Jun 17, 1930	10	27
	NY	Sep 1, 1931	10	27
	NY	May 22, 1934	10	22
Rick Monday	OAK	Apr 30, 1969	10	18
Graig Nettles	NY	Apr 24, 1974	10	18
Jeff Burroughs	TEX	May 23, 1974	10	20
Willie Horton	DET	May 1, 1976	10	17
Butch Hobson	BOS	Apr 23, 1978	10	18
Reggie Jackson	NY	May 14, 1978	10	20
Greg Luzinski	CHI	Aug 7, 1984	10	14
Fred Lynn	CAL	Sep 8, 1984	10	18
Wally Joyner	CAL	Jul 13, 1986	10	14

RBI in Most Consecutive Games, NL

Player	Team	Last Date	G	RBI
Ray Grimes	CHI	Jul 23, 1922	17	27
Paul Waner	PIT	Jun 16, 1927	12	20
Mel Ott	NY	Jun 20, 1929	11	27
Andy Van Slyke	PIT	Jun 20, 1988	11	16
George Kelly	NY	Jun 27, 1921	10	14
Mel Ott	NY	Jun 9, 1928	10	12
Pinky Whitney	PHI	Jun 27, 1931	10	11
Bill White	STL	Aug 30, 1961	10	15
Richie Zisk	PIT	May 18, 1974	10	21
Joe Morgan	CIN	Jun 13, 1976	10	17
Matt Williams	SF	Sep 7, 1991	10	11

Most Consecutive Hits, AL

Player	Team	Year	H
Pinky Higgins	BOS	1938	12
Walt Dropo	DET	1952	12
Tris Speaker	CLE	1920	11
Johnny Pesky	BOS	1946	11
George Sisler	STL	1921	10
Harry Heilmann	DET	1922	10
Harry McCurdy	CHI	1926	10

Most Consecutive Hits, AL (cont.)

Player	Team	Year	H
Ken Singleton	BAL	1981	10
Doc Johnston	CLE	1919	9
Ty Cobb	DET	1925	9
Sam Rice	WAS	1925	9
Hal Trosky	CLE	1936	9
Ted Williams	BOS	1939	9
Joe Tipton	CLE	1945	9
Tony Oliva	MIN	1967	9
Rick Monday	OAK	1970	9
Mickey Hatcher	MIN	1985	9
Nap Lajoie	CLE	1910	8
George Sisler	STL	1922	8
	STL	1927	8
Buddy Myer	WAS	1929	8
Oscar Melillo	STL	1931	8
Sammy West	STL	1933	8
Johnny Groth	DET	1950	8
Hank Bauer	NY	1952	8
Jim Fregosi	CAL	1966	8
Amos Otis	KC	1970	8
Rico Carty	TEX	1973	8
Don Baylor	CAL	1978	8
Dan Ford	CAL	1979	8
George Brett	KC	1980	8
Jorge Orta	CLE	1980	8
George Vukovich	CLE	1983	8
Bobby Grich	CAL	1984	8
Rance Mulliniks	TOR	1984	8
Rickey Henderson	NY	1985	8
Oddibe McDowell	TEX	1985	8
Pat Tabler	CLE	1987	8
Darnell Coles	SEA	1988	8
Dwight Evans	BOS	1988	8
Harold Reynolds	SEA	1988	8
Dan Gladden	MIN	1989	8
Scott Fletcher	CHI	1990	8

Most Consecutive Hits, NL

Player	Team	Year	H
Ed Delahanty	PHI	1897	10
Jake Gettman	WAS	1897	10
Ed Konetchy	BKN	1919	10
Kiki Cuyler	PIT	1925	10
Chick Hafey	STL	1929	10
Joe Medwick	STL	1936	10
Buddy Hassett	BOS	1940	10

Most Consecutive Hits, NL (*cont.*)

Player	Team	Year	H
Woody Williams	CIN	1943	10
Bip Roberts	CIN	1992	10
George Van Haltren	BAL	1892	9
Joe Kelley	BAL	1894	9
Rogers Hornsby	STL	1924	9
Taylor Douthit	STL	1926	9
Babe Herman	BKN	1926	9
Bill Jurges	NY	1941	9
Terry Moore	STL	1947	9
Felipe Alou	SF	1962	9
Willie Stargell	PIT	1966	9
Rennie Stennett	PIT	1975	9
Ron Cey	LA	1977	9
Roger Connor	STL	1895	8
Sammy Strang	CHI	1900	8
Jack Fournier	BKN	1923	8
Jimmy Johnston	BKN	1923	8
Glenn Wright	PIT	1924	8
Chick Hafey	STL	1928	8
Lefty O'Doul	NY	1928	8
Kiki Cuyler	CIN	1936	8
Augie Galan	BKN	1944	8
Wayne Terwilliger	CHI	1949	8
Johnny Hopp	PIT	1950	8
Dick Sisler	PHI	1950	8
Eddie Waitkus	PHI	1950	8
Sid Gordon	BOS	1952	8
Lee Walls	CHI	1958	8
Curt Flood	STL	1964	8
Julio Gotay	HOU	1967	8
Jerry Grote	NY	1970	8
Billy Williams	CHI	1972	8
Jeff Burroughs	ATL	1978	8
Bobby Murcer	CHI	1978	8
Pete Rose	PHI	1979	8
Dave Winfield	SD	1979	8
Art Howe	HOU	1980	8
Andre Dawson	MON	1983	8
Steve Nicosia	SF	1984	8
Marvell Wynne	PIT	1984	8
Keith Hernandez	NY	1985	8
Andre Dawson	CHI	1989	8
Felix Jose	STL	1991	8
Ryne Sandberg	CHI	1992	8

Most Consecutive Times Struck Out, AL

Player	Team	Year	SO
Jim Hannan	WAS	1968	13
Dean Chance	CAL	1965	11c
Joe Grzenda	WAS	1970	10c
Bill Melton	CHI	1970	10
Dick Drago	KC	1970	9c
Vida Blue	OAK	1972	9
Steve Balboni	KC	1984	9c
Reggie Jackson	OAK	1987	9c
Bo Jackson	KC	1988	9c
Pedro Ramos	CLE	1963	8
Ray Culp	BOS	1971	8c
Dave Lemonds	CHI	1972	8c
Jim Fuller	BAL	1973	8c
Gorman Thomas	MIL	1975	8c
Jay Buhner	SEA	1990	8

c = Consecutive Plate Appearances

Most Consecutive Times Struck Out, NL

Player	Team	Year	SO
Bill Hands	CHI	1968	14
Juan Eichelberger	SD	1980	14
Jose DeJesus	PHI	1991	14
Sandy Koufax	BKN	1955	12c
Tommie Sisk	PIT	1966	10c
Adolfo Phillips	PHI	1966	9c
Gary Gentry	NY	1969	9c
Wayne Twitchell	PHI	1973	9c
Eric Davis	CIN	1987	9c
Jerry Koosman	NY	1969	8c
Richie Hebner	PIT	1971	8c
Ruppert Jones	SD	1982	8
Bruce Ruffin	PHI	1991	8c

c = Consecutive Plate Appearances

Home Runs in Most Consecutive At-Bats, AL

Player	Team	Date	HR	Total
Lou Gehrig	NY	Jun 3, 1932	4	4
Jimmie Foxx	PHI	Jun 7, 1933	1	
	PHI	Jun 8, 1933	3	4
Hank Greenberg	DET	Jul 26, 1938	2	
	DET	Jul 27, 1938	2	4
Ted Williams	BOS	Sep 17, 1957	1	
	BOS	Sep 20, 1957	1	

Home Runs in Most Consecutive At-Bats, AL (*cont.*)

Player	Team	Date	HR	Total
	BOS	Sep 21, 1957	1	
	BOS	Sep 22, 1957	1	4
Charlie Maxwell	DET	May 3, 1959	1	
	DET	May 3, 1959	3	4
Rocky Colavito	CLE	Jun 10, 1959	4	4
Willie Kirkland	CLE	Jul 9, 1961	3	
	CLE	Jul 13, 1961	1	4
Johnny Blanchard	NY	Jul 21, 1961	1	
	NY	Jul 22, 1961	1	
	NY	Jul 26, 1961	2	4
Mickey Mantle	NY	Jul 4, 1962	2	
	NY	Jul 6, 1962	2	4
Bobby Murcer	NY	Jun 24, 1970	1	
	NY	Jun 24, 1970	3	4
Mike Epstein	OAK	Jun 15, 1971	2	
	OAK	Jun 16, 1971	2	4
Don Baylor	BAL	Jul 1, 1975	1	
	BAL	Jul 2, 1975	3	4
Larry Herndon	DET	May 16, 1982	1	
	DET	May 18, 1982	3	4
Bo Jackson	KC	July 17, 1990	3	4
	KC	Aug 26, 1990	1	

Home Runs in Most Consecutive At-Bats, NL

Player	Team	Date	HR	Total
Bobby Lowe	BOS	May 30, 1894	4	4
Bill Nicholson	CHI	Jul 22, 1944	1	
	CHI	Jul 23, 1944	3	4
Ralph Kiner	PIT	Aug 15, 1947	1	
	PIT	Aug 16, 1947	3	4
	PIT	Sep 11, 1949	2	
	PIT	Sep 13, 1949	2	4
Stan Musial	STL	Jul 7, 1962	1	
	STL	Jul 8, 1962	3	4
Art Shamsky	CIN	Aug 12, 1966	3	
	CIN	Aug 14, 1966	1	4
Deron Johnson	PHI	Jul 10, 1971	1	
	PHI	Jul 11, 1971	3	4
Mike Schmidt	PHI	Apr 17, 1976	4	4
	PHI	Jul 6, 1979	1	
	PHI	Jul 7, 1979	3	4

Batting Accomplishments in AL and NL

Player	Team	Accomplishment
Frank Robinson	CIN N 1961	Most Valuable Player
	BAL A 1966	

Batting Accomplishments in AL and NL (*cont.*)

Player	Team	Accomplishment
Sam Crawford	CIN N 1901	Home Run Champion
	DET A 1908	
Buck Freeman	WAS N 1899	Home Run Champion
	BOS A 1903	
Ed Delahanty	PHI N 1899	Batting Champion
	WAS A 1902	
Bob Watson	HOU N 1977	Hit for Cycle
	BOS A 1979	

INDIVIDUAL
PITCHING
RECORDS

●

Most Shutouts, Career

Player	ShO
Walter Johnson	110
Grover Alexander	90
Christy Mathewson	80
Cy Young	76
Eddie Plank	69
Warren Spahn	63
Nolan Ryan	61
Tom Seaver	61
Bert Blyleven	60
Don Sutton	58
Ed Walsh	57
Three Finger Brown	57
Pud Galvin	57
Bob Gibson	56
Steve Carlton	55
Jim Palmer	53
Gaylord Perry	53
Juan Marichal	52
Rube Waddell	50
Vic Willis	50
Don Drysdale	49
Luis Tiant	49
Ferguson Jenkins	49
Early Wynn	49
Red Ruffing	48
Kid Nichols	48
Babe Adams	47
Jack Powell	47
Tommy John	46
Addie Joss	46
Doc White	46
Bob Feller	46
Whitey Ford	45
Phil Niekro	45
Robin Roberts	45
Milt Pappas	43
Catfish Hunter	42
Bucky Walters	42
Mickey Lolich	41
Hippo Vaughn	41
Chief Bender	41
Sandy Koufax	40
Claude Osteen	40
Jim Bunning	40
Mel Stottlemyre	40
Larry French	40
Ed Reulbach	40
Mickey Welch	40
Tim Keefe	40
Sam Leever	39
Eppa Rixey	39
Jerry Reuss	38
Nap Rucker	38
Billy Pierce	38
Stan Coveleski	38
Steve Rogers	37
Vida Blue	37
Larry Jackson	37
John Clarkson	37
Camilo Pascual	36
Allie Reynolds	36
Bill Doak	36
Bob Friend	36
Curt Simmons	36
Mike Cuellar	36
Eddie Cicotte	36
Sad Sam Jones	36
Carl Hubbell	36
Wilbur Cooper	36
Tommy Bond	36
Will White	36
Virgil Trucks	35
Jack Coombs	35
Joe Bush	35
Herb Pennock	35
Jack Chesbro	35
Wild Bill Donovan	35
Lefty Grove	35
Burleigh Grimes	35
George Mullin	35
Old Hoss Radbourn	35

Most Shutout Losses, Career

Player	ShO L
Walter Johnson	65
Nolan Ryan	63
Phil Niekro	49
Cy Young	48
Claude Osteen	47
Bob Friend	45
Ferguson Jenkins	45
Early Wynn	45
Robin Roberts	44
Jim McCormick	43

Most Shutout Losses, Career (*cont.*)

Player	ShO L	Player	ShO L
Pud Galvin	42	Bobo Newsom	37
Gaylord Perry	42	Hippo Vaughn	37
Jack Powell	42	Vic Willis	37
Jim Bunning	41	Paul Derringer	36
Mickey Lolich	41	Don Drysdale	36
Steve Carlton	39	Burleigh Grimes	36
Grover Alexander	38	Rudy May	36
Red Ames	38	Nap Rucker	36
Fritz Peterson	38	Tom Seaver	36
Stan Bahnsen	37	Jim Kaat	35

Most Shutouts, Season, AL

Player	Team	Year	ShO
Jack Coombs	PHI	1910	13
Ed Walsh	CHI	1908	12
Walter Johnson	WAS	1913	12
Dean Chance	LA	1964	11
Cy Young	BOS	1904	10
Ed Walsh	CHI	1906	10
Smoky Joe Wood	BOS	1912	10
Walter Johnson	WAS	1914	10
Bob Feller	CLE	1946	10
Bob Lemon	CLE	1948	10
Jim Palmer	BAL	1975	10
Addie Joss	CLE	1906	9
	CLE	1908	9
Walter Johnson	WAS	1914	9
Babe Ruth	BOS	1916	9
Stan Coveleski	CLE	1917	9
Bob Porterfield	WAS	1953	9
Luis Tiant	CLE	1968	9
Denny McLain	DET	1969	9
Nolan Ryan	CAL	1972	9
Bert Blyleven	MIN	1973	9
Ron Guidry	NY	1978	9
Rube Waddell	PHI	1904	8
Ed Killian	DET	1905	8
Rube Waddell	PHI	1906	8
Eddie Plank	PHI	1907	8
Ed Walsh	CHI	1909	8
Russ Ford	NY	1910	8
Walter Johnson	WAS	1910	8
	WAS	1912	8
Reb Russell	CHI	1913	8
Walter Johnson	WAS	1915	8
Joe Bush	PHI	1916	8
Walter Johnson	WAS	1917	8

Most Shutouts, Season, AL (*cont.*)

Player	Team	Year	ShO
Jim Bagby	CLE	1917	8
Walter Johnson	WAS	1918	8
Carl Mays	BOS	1918	8
Hal Newhouser	DET	1945	8
Steve Barber	BAL	1961	8
Camilo Pascual	MIN	1961	8
Whitey Ford	NY	1964	8
Vida Blue	OAK	1971	8
Wilbur Wood	CHI	1972	8
Roger Clemens	BOS	1988	8

Most Shutouts, Season, NL

Player	Team	Year	ShO
George Bradley	STL	1876	16
Grover Alexander	PHI	1916	16
Bob Gibson	STL	1968	13
Tommy Bond	BOS	1879	12
Pud Galvin	BUF	1884	12
Christy Mathewson	NY	1908	12
Grover Alexander	PHI	1915	12
Old Hoss Radbourn	PRO	1884	11
Sandy Koufax	LA	1963	11
John Clarkson	CHI	1885	10
Three Finger Brown	CHI	1906	10
Carl Hubbell	NY	1933	10
Mort Cooper	STL	1942	10
Juan Marichal	SF	1965	10
John Tudor	STL	1985	10
Tommy Bond	BOS	1878	9
Monte Ward	PRO	1880	9
George Derby	DET	1881	9
Cy Young	CLE	1892	9
Joe McGinnity	NY	1904	9
Christy Mathewson	NY	1905	9
	NY	1907	9
Three Finger Brown	CHI	1908	9
Orval Overall	CHI	1909	9
Grover Alexander	PHI	1913	9
	CHI	1919	9
Bill Lee	CHI	1938	9
Don Sutton	LA	1972	9
Al Spalding	CHI	1876	8
Charlie Buffinton	BOS	1884	8
Tim Keefe	NY	1888	8
John Clarkson	BOS	1889	8
Jack Chesbro	PIT	1902	8

Most Shutouts, Season, NL (cont.)

Player	Team	Year	ShO
Christy Mathewson	NY	1902	8
Jack Taylor	CHI	1902	8
Christy Mathewson	NY	1905	8
Lefty Leifield	PIT	1906	8
Three Finger Brown	CHI	1909	8
Christy Mathewson	NY	1909	8
Jeff Tesreau	NY	1914	8
	NY	1915	8
Al Mamaux	PIT	1915	8
Grover Alexander	PHI	1917	8
Lefty Tyler	CHI	1918	8
Babe Adams	PIT	1920	8
Sandy Koufax	LA	1965	8
Don Drysdale	LA	1968	8
Juan Marichal	SF	1969	8
Steve Carlton	PHI	1972	8
Dwight Gooden	NY	1985	8
Orel Hershiser	LA	1988	8
Tim Belcher	LA	1989	8

Most Shutouts, Season, Other Leagues

Player	Team	Year	ShO
Ed Morris	PIT AA	1886	12
Dave Foutz	STL AA	1886	11
Dave Davenport	STL F	1915	10
Cy Falkenberg	IND F	1914	9
Will White	CIN AA	1882	8
Tony Mullane	TOL AA	1884	8

Most Shutout Losses, Season, AL

Player	Team	Year	ShO L	W	L
Walter Johnson	WAS	1909	10	13	25
Casey Patten	WAS	1904	9	15	23
Patsy Flaherty	CHI	1903	8	11	25
Harry Howell	STL	1905	8	15	22
Joe Harris	BOS	1906	8	3	21
Fred Glade	STL	1906	8	16	15
Ed Walsh	CHI	1907	8	24	18
Tom Murphy	CAL	1971	8	6	17
Nolan Ryan	CAL	1976	8	17	18

Most Shutout Losses, Season, NL

Player	Team	Year	ShO L	W	L
Jim Devlin	LOU	1876	14	30	35
Dupee Shaw	PRO	1885	11	23	26

Most Shutout Losses, Season, NL (cont.)

Player	Team	Year	ShO L	W	L
Bugs Raymond	STL	1908	11	14	25
Jim McCormick	CLE	1880	10	45	28
	CLE	1879	9	20	40
Irv Young	BOS	1906	9	16	25
Roger Craig	NY	1963	9	5	22
Ferguson Jenkins	CHI	1968	9	20	15
Tommy Bond	BOS	1880	8	26	29
Will White	CIN	1880	8	18	42
Jim McCormick	CLE	1882	8	35	29
Vive Lindaman	BOS	1906	8	12	23
Jim Pastorius	BKN	1908	8	4	20
George McQuillan	PHI	1908	8	23	17
Erv Kantlehner	PIT	1915	8	6	12
Bob Bruce	HOU	1965	8	9	18
Ray Sadecki	SF	1968	8	12	18

Shutout in First Start in Majors, AL

Player	Team	Date	Score	Inns.	Opp.
Bill Cristall	CLE	Sep 2, 1901	4–0		BOS
Addie Joss	CLE	Apr 26, 1902	3–0		STL
Jack Coombs	PHI	Jul 5, 1906	3–0		WAS
Slow Joe Doyle	NY	Aug 25, 1906	2–0		CLE
Rube Kroh	BOS	Sep 30, 1906	2–0		STL
Tex Neuer	NY	Aug 28, 1907	1–0		BOS
Pete Wilson	NY	Sep 15, 1908	1–0		BOS
King Brady	BOS	Oct 5, 1908	4–0		NY
Jim Scott	CHI	Apr 25, 1909	1–0		STL
Larry Pape	BOS	Jul 6, 1909	2–0		WAS
Sailor Stroud	DET	Apr 29, 1910	5–0		STL
Fred Blanding	CLE	Sep 15, 1910	3–0		WAS
Lefty Russell	PHI	Oct 1, 1910	3–0		BOS
Buck O'Brien	BOS	Sep 9, 1911	2–0		PHI
Elmer Brown	STL	Sep 16, 1911	6–0		WAS
Stan Coveleski	PHI	Sep 12, 1912	3–0		DET
Jack Bentley	WAS	Oct 1, 1913	1–0	8	PHI
Adam Johnson	BOS	Apr 13, 1914	5–0		WAS
George Dumont	WAS	Sep 14, 1915	3–0		CLE
Elmer Myers	PHI	Oct 6, 1915	4–0		WAS
Claude Thomas	WAS	Sep 18, 1916	1–0		PHI
Bob Clark	CLE	Aug 15, 1920	5–0		DET
Ray Benge	CLE	Sep 26, 1925	6–0		PHI
Bob Weiland	CHI	Sep 30, 1928	1–0		PHI
Schoolboy Rowe	DET	Apr 15, 1933	3–0		CHI
Russ Van Atta	NY	Apr 25, 1933	16–0		WAS
Johnny Marcum	PHI	Sep 7, 1933	6–0		CLE
George Hockette	BOS	Sep 17, 1934	3–0		STL

Shutout in First Start in Majors, AL (cont.)

Player	Team	Date	Score	Inns.	Opp.
Vito Tamulis	NY	Sep 25, 1934	5–0		PHI
Henry Coppola	WAS	Jun 6, 1935	3–0		PHI
George Gill	DET	May 13, 1937	4–0		BOS
Boo Ferriss	BOS	Apr 29, 1945	2–0		PHI
Bill McCahan	PHI	Sep 15, 1946	2–0	7	CLE
Fred Sanford	STL	Sep 15, 1946	1–0		NY
Sandy Consuegra	WAS	Jun 10, 1950	6–0	5	CHI
Mike Fornieles	WAS	Sep 2, 1952	5–0		PHI
Raul Sanchez	WAS	Sep 5, 1952	2–0		BOS
Bobo Holloman	STL	May 6, 1953	6–0		PHI
Ben Flowers	BOS	Aug 5, 1953	5–0		STL
Wally Burnette	KC	Jul 15, 1956	8–0		WAS
Charlie Beamon	BAL	Sep 26, 1956	1–0		NY
Lew Krausse	KC	Jun 16, 1961	4–0		LA
Dave McNally	BAL	Sep 26, 1962	3–0		KC
Dave Morehead	BOS	Apr 13, 1963	3–0		WAS
Luis Tiant	CLE	Jul 19, 1964	3–0		NY
Don Loun	WAS	Sep 23, 1964	1–0		BOS
Tom Phoebus	BAL	Sep 15, 1966	2–0		CAL
Billy Rohr	BOS	Apr 14, 1967	3–0		NY
Mike Norris	OAK	Apr 10, 1975	9–0		CHI
Ben McDonald	BAL	Jul 21, 1990	2–0		CHI

Shutout in First Start in Majors, NL

Player	Team	Date	Score	Inns.	Opp.
Al Spalding	CHI	Apr 25, 1876	4–0		LOU
Monte Ward	PRO	Jul 20, 1878	3–0		IND
John Hibbard	CHI	Jul 31, 1884	4–0		DET
John Henry	CLE	Aug 13, 1884	1–0		DET
Bill Stemmeyer	BOS	Oct 3, 1885	18–0	6	BUF
Frank Dwyer	CHI	Sep 20, 1888	11–0		WAS
John Scheible	CLE	Sep 8, 1893	7–0		WAS
Roger Bresnahan	WAS	Aug 27, 1897	3–0		STL
Jim Hughes	BAL	Apr 18, 1898	9–0		WAS
Bill Phyle	CHI	Sep 17, 1898	9–0		WAS
Alex Hardy	CHI	Sep 4, 1902	1–0		BKN
Red Ames	NY	Sep 14, 1903	5–0	5	STL
Lefty Leifield	PIT	Sep 3, 1905	1–0	6	CHI
Vive Lindaman	BOS	Apr 14, 1906	1–0		BKN
Nick Maddox	PIT	Sep 13, 1907	4–0		STL
Bob Spade	CIN	Sep 22, 1907	1–0		NY
Tom Tuckey	BOS	Aug 11, 1908	2–0		STL
Cliff Curtis	BOS	Sep 2, 1909	1–0		PIT
King Cole	CHI	Oct 6, 1909	8–0		STL
Eddie Stack	PHI	Jun 7, 1910	1–0		CHI
Wilbur Cooper	PIT	Sep 6, 1912	8–0		STL

Shutout in First Start in Majors, NL (cont.)

Player	Team	Date	Score	Inns.	Opp.
Al Demaree	NY	Sep 26, 1912	4–0		BOS
Erv Kantlehner	PIT	Apr 17, 1914	2–0		STL
Pete Schneider	CIN	Jun 28, 1914	1–0		PIT
Carmen Hill	PIT	Sep 17, 1915	5–0		NY
Harry Shriver	BKN	May 1, 1922	2–0		PHI
Earl Caldwell	PHI	Sep 8, 1928	4–0		BOS
Van Lingle Mungo	BKN	Sep 7, 1931	2–0		BOS
Ray Starr	STL	Sep 15, 1932	3–0		BKN
Hal Smith	PIT	Sep 22, 1932	7–0		CHI
Bill Lee	CHI	May 7, 1934	2–0		PHI
Hal Kelleher	PHI	Sep 17, 1935	1–0		CIN
Tot Pressnell	BKN	Apr 21, 1938	9–0		PHI
Don Newcombe	BKN	May 22, 1949	3–0		CIN
Bill MacDonald	PIT	May 23, 1950	6–0		PHI
Paul LaPalme	PIT	Jun 5, 1951	8–0		BOS
Niles Jordan	PHI	Aug 26, 1951	2–0		CIN
Jackie Collum	STL	Sep 21, 1951	6–0		CHI
Stu Miller	STL	Aug 12, 1952	1–0		CHI
Al Worthington	NY	Jul 6, 1953	6–0		PIT
Karl Spooner	BKN	Sep 22, 1954	3–0		NY
Von McDaniel	STL	Jun 21, 1957	2–0		BKN
Carl Willey	MIL	Jun 23, 1958	7–0		SF
Juan Marichal	SF	Jul 19, 1960	2–0		PHI
Nick Willhite	LA	Jun 16, 1963	2–0		CHI
Grover Powell	NY	Aug 20, 1963	4–0		PHI
Dick Rusteck	NY	Jun 10, 1966	5–0		CIN
Jim Cosman	STL	Oct 2, 1966	2–0		CHI
Wayne Simpson	CIN	Apr 9, 1970	3–0		LA
Ed Acosta	SD	Aug 24, 1971	2–0		PHI
Dave Downs	PHI	Sep 2, 1972	3–0		ATL
Eric Rasmussen	STL	Jul 21, 1975	4–0		SD
Charlie Leibrandt	CIN	Apr 13, 1980	5–0		ATL
Marty Bystrom	PHI	Sep 10, 1980	5–0		NY
Fernando Valenzuela	LA	Apr 9, 1981	2–0		HOU
Jimmy Jones	SD	Sep 21, 1986	5–0		HOU
Jeff Pico	CHI	May 31, 1988	4–0		CIN
Mike Remlinger	SF	Jun 15, 1991	4–0		PIT
Pedro Astacio	LA	Jul 3, 1992	2–0		PHI

Shutout in First Two Major League Starts, AL

Player	Team	Date	Score	Opp.
Slow Joe Doyle	NY	Aug 25, 1906	2–0	CLE
	NY	Aug 30, 1906	5–0	WAS
Johnny Marcum	PHI	Sep 7, 1933	6–0	CLE
	PHI	Sep 11, 1933	8–0	CHI
Boo Ferriss	BOS	Apr 29, 1945	2–0	PHI

Shutout in First Two Major League Starts, AL (*cont.*)

Player	Team	Date	Score	Opp.
	BOS	May 6, 1945	5–0	NY
Tom Phoebus	BAL	Sep 15, 1966	2–0	CAL
	BAL	Sep 20, 1966	4–0	KC

Shutout in First Two Major League Starts, NL

Player	Team	Date	Score	Opp.
Al Spalding	CHI	Apr 25, 1876	4–0	LOU
	CHI	Apr 27, 1876	10–0	LOU
Jim Hughes	BAL	Apr 18, 1898	9–0	WAS
	BAL	Apr 22, 1898	8–0	BOS
Al Worthington	NY	Jul 6, 1953	6–0	PHI
	NY	Jul 11, 1953	6–0	BKN
Karl Spooner	BKN	Sep 22, 1954	3–0	NY
	BKN	Sep 26, 1954	1–0	PIT

Shutout with Most Hits Allowed, AL

Player	Team	Date	Score	H	Inns.	Opp.
Walter Johnson	WAS	Jul 3, 1913	1–0	15	15	BOS
Milt Gaston	WAS	Jul 10, 1928	9–0	14		CLE
Mudcat Grant	MIN	Jul 15, 1964	6–0	13		WAS
Bob Shawkey	NY	Jul 13, 1920	14–0	12		CLE
Duster Mails	CLE	Jul 10, 1921	10–0	12		PHI
Stan Bahnsen	CHI	Jun 21, 1973	2–0	12		OAK
Harry Howell	STL	Jun 23, 1906	9–0	11		CLE
Jack Chesbro	NY	Aug 19, 1908	8–0	11		DET
Reb Russell	CHI	May 24, 1917	1–0	11	12	WAS
Jim Bagby	CLE	Aug 6, 1918	1–0	11	10	WAS
Waite Hoyt	NY	Jul 1, 1924	7–0	11		PHI
Earl Whitehill	DET	Jul 5, 1924	3–0	11		STL
Herb Pennock	NY	Jun 6, 1933	4–0	11		BOS
Ed Lopat	NY	Jul 17, 1948	4–0	11		STL
Bob Kuzava	NY	Aug 17, 1953	9–0	11		PHI
Robin Roberts	BAL	Jul 17, 1964	5–0	11		DET
Jim Kaat	MIN	Apr 11, 1971	6–0	11		CHI
Marty Pattin	MIL	Jun 26, 1971	5–0	11		MIN
Gaylord Perry	TEX	Jul 28, 1977	3–0	11		TOR
Rick Lysander	MIN	Aug 1, 1983	7–0	11		OAK

Shutout with Most Hits Allowed, NL

Player	Team	Date	Score	H	Opp.
Larry Cheney	CHI	Sep 14, 1913	7–0	14	NY
Scott Stratton	LOU	Sep 19, 1893	3–0	13	NY
Ned Garvin	CHI	Sep 22, 1899	3–0	13	BOS
Bill Lee	CHI	Sep 17, 1938	4–0	13	NY
Nixey Callahan	CHI	Apr 30, 1899	4–0	12	STL

Shutout with Most Hits Allowed, NL (cont.)

Player	Team	Date	Score	H	Opp.
Pol Perritt	NY	Sep 14, 1917	5–0	12	BOS
Rube Benton	NY	Aug 28, 1920	4–0	12	CIN
Leon Cadore	BKN	Sep 4, 1920	10–0	12	BOS
George Smith	PHI	Aug 12, 1921	4–0	12	BOS
Hal Schumacher	NY	Jul 19, 1934	4–0	12	CIN
Fritz Ostermueller	PIT	May 17, 1947	4–0	12	BKN
Bob Friend	PIT	Sep 24, 1959	6–0	12	STL
Jouett Meekin	NY	Jun 17, 1897	5–0	11	CLE
Bill Damman	CIN	May 6, 1899	11–0	11	STL
Charlie Case	PIT	Aug 1, 1904	4–0	11	CHI
Babe Adams	PIT	Aug 9, 1910	10–0	11	BOS
Three Finger Brown	CHI	Aug 15, 1910	14–0	11	BKN
Christy Mathewson	NY	Aug 11, 1911	6–0	11	PHI
Dan Griner	STL	Jun 24, 1913	1–0	11	CHI
Fred Baczewski	CIN	Jun 10, 1954	6–0	11	PIT
Bob Purkey	CIN	Aug 15, 1960	4–0	11	MIL
Billy O'Dell	SF	Jul 30, 1963	5–0	11	PHI

No-Hitters, AL (9 innings or more)

Player	Team	Date	Score	BB	SO	E	Opp.	Opp. Pitcher
Nixey Callahan	CHI	Sep 20, 1902	3–0	2	2	1	DET	Wish Egan
Cy Young	BOS	May 5, 1904	3–0	0	8	0	PHI	Rube Waddell
Jesse Tannehill	BOS	Aug 17, 1904	6–0	1	4	0	CHI	Ed Walsh
Weldon Henley	PHI	Jul 22, 1905	6–0	3	5	1	STL	Barney Pelty
Frank Smith	CHI	Sep 6, 1905	15–0	3	8	0	DET	Jimmy Wiggs
Bill Dinneen	BOS	Sep 27, 1905	2–0	2	6	0	CHI	Frank Owen
Cy Young	BOS	Jun 30, 1908	8–0	1	2	0	NY	Rube Manning
Bob Rhoads	CLE	Sep 18, 1908	2–1	2	2	2	BOS	Frank Arellanes
Frank Smith	CHI	Sep 20, 1908	1–0	1	2	1	PHI	Eddie Plank
Addie Joss	CLE	Oct 2, 1908	1–0	0	3	0	CHI	Ed Walsh
	CLE	Apr 20, 1910	1–0	2	2	1	CHI	Doc White
Chief Bender	PHI	May 12, 1910	4–0	1	4	0	CLE	Fred Link
Smoky Joe Wood	BOS	Jul 29, 1911	5–0	2	12	1	STL	Joe Lake
Ed Walsh	CHI	Aug 27, 1911	5–0	1	8	0	BOS	Ray Collins
George Mullin	DET	Jul 4, 1912	7–0	5	5	1	STL	Willie Adams
Earl Hamilton	STL	Aug 30, 1912	5–1	2	3	2	DET	Jean Dubuc
Joe Benz	CHI	May 31, 1914	6–1	2	6	3	CLE	Abe Bowman
Rube Foster	BOS	Jun 21, 1916	2–0	3	3	0	NY	Bob Shawkey
Joe Bush	PHI	Aug 26, 1916	5–0	1	7	0	CLE	Stan Coveleski
Dutch Leonard	BOS	Aug 30, 1916	4–0	2	5	0	STL	Carl Weilman
Eddie Cicotte	CHI	Apr 14, 1917	11–0	3	5	1	STL	Earl Hamilton
George Mogridge	NY	Apr 24, 1917	2–1	3	3	3	BOS	Dutch Leonard
Ernie Koob	STL	May 5, 1917	1–0	5	2	2	CHI	Eddie Cicotte
Bob Groom	STL	May 6, 1917	3–0	3	4	0	CHI	Joe Benz
Dutch Leonard	BOS	Jun 3, 1918	5–0	1	4	0	DET	Hooks Dauss
Ray Caldwell	CLE	Sep 10, 1919	3–0	1	5	1	NY	Carl Mays

No-Hitters, AL (9 innings or more) (*cont.*)

Player	Team	Date	Score	BB	SO	E	Opp.	Opp. Pitcher
Walter Johnson	WAS	Jul 1, 1920	1–0	0	10	1	BOS	Harry Harper
Charlie Robertson	CHI	Apr 30, 1922	2–0	0	6	0	DET	Herman Pillette
Sad Sam Jones	NY	Sep 4, 1923	2–0	1	0	1	PHI	Bob Hasty
Howard Ehmke	BOS	Sep 7, 1923	4–0	1	1	1	PHI	Slim Harriss
Ted Lyons	CHI	Aug 21, 1926	6–0	1	2	1	BOS	Slim Harriss
Wes Ferrell	CLE	Apr 29, 1931	9–0	3	8	3	STL	Sam Gray
Bobby Burke	WAS	Aug 8, 1931	5–0	5	8	0	BOS	Wilcy Moore
Vern Kennedy	CHI	Aug 31, 1935	5–0	4	5	0	CLE	Willis Hudlin
Bill Dietrich	CHI	Jun 1, 1937	8–0	2	5	1	STL	Chief Hogsett
Monte Pearson	NY	Aug 27, 1938	13–0	2	7	0	CLE	John Humphries
Bob Feller	CLE	Apr 16, 1940	1–0	5	8	1	CHI	Eddie Smith
Dick Fowler	PHI	Sep 9, 1945	1–0	4	6	0	STL	Ox Miller
Bob Feller	CLE	Apr 30, 1946	1–0	5	11	2	NY	Bill Bevens
Don Black	CLE	Jul 10, 1947	3–0	6	5	0	PHI	Bill McCahan
Bill McCahan	PHI	Sep 3, 1947	3–0	0	2	1	WAS	Ray Scarborough
Bob Lemon	CLE	Jun 30, 1948	2–0	3	4	0	DET	Art Houtteman
Bob Feller	CLE	Jul 1, 1951	2–1	3	5	2	DET	Bob Cain
Allie Reynolds	NY	Jul 12, 1951	1–0	3	4	1	CLE	Bob Feller
	NY	Sep 28, 1951	8–0	4	9	1	BOS	Mel Parnell
Virgil Trucks	DET	May 15, 1952	1–0	1	7	3	WAS	Bob Porterfield
	DET	Aug 25, 1952	1–0	1	8	2	NY	Bill Miller
Bobo Holloman	STL	May 6, 1953	6–0	5	3	1	PHI	Morrie Martin
Mel Parnell	BOS	Jul 14, 1956	4–0	2	4	0	CHI	Jim McDonald
Don Larsen	NY	Oct 8, 1956	2–0	0	7	0	BKN	Sal Maglie
Bob Keegan	CHI	Aug 20, 1957	6–0	2	1	0	WAS	Chuck Stobbs
Jim Bunning	DET	Jul 20, 1958	3–0	2	12	0	BOS	Frank Sullivan
Hoyt Wilhelm	BAL	Sep 20, 1958	1–0	2	8	0	NY	Don Larsen
Bo Belinsky	LA	May 1, 1962	2–0	5	9	1	BAL	Steve Barber
Earl Wilson	BOS	Jun 26, 1962	2–0	4	5	0	LA	Bo Belinsky
Bill Monbouquette	BOS	Aug 1, 1962	1–0	1	7	0	CHI	Early Wynn
Jack Kralick	MIN	Aug 26, 1962	1–0	1	3	0	KC	Bill Fischer
Dave Morehead	BOS	Sep 16, 1965	2–0	1	8	0	CLE	Luis Tiant
Sonny Siebert	CLE	Jun 10, 1966	2–0	1	7	1	WAS	Phil Ortega
Dean Chance	MIN	Aug 25, 1967	2–1	5	9	1	CLE	Sonny Siebert
Joe Horlen	CHI	Sep 10, 1967	6–0	0	4	1	DET	Joe Sparma
Tom Phoebus	BAL	Apr 27, 1968	6–0	3	9	0	BOS	Gary Waslewski
Catfish Hunter	OAK	May 8, 1968	4–0	0	11	0	MIN	Dave Boswell
Jim Palmer	BAL	Aug 13, 1969	8–0	6	8	2	OAK	Chuck Dobson
Clyde Wright	CAL	Jul 3, 1970	4–0	3	1	0	OAK	Chuck Dobson
Vida Blue	OAK	Sep 21, 1970	6–0	1	9	0	MIN	Jim Perry
Steve Busby	KC	Apr 27, 1973	3–0	6	4	0	DET	Jim Perry
Nolan Ryan	CAL	May 15, 1973	3–0	3	12	0	KC	Bruce Dal Canton
	CAL	Jul 15, 1973	6–0	4	17	0	DET	Jim Perry
Jim Bibby	TEX	Jul 30, 1973	8–0	6	13	0	OAK	Vida Blue
Steve Busby	KC	Jun 19, 1974	2–0	1	3	0	MIL	Clyde Wright
Dick Bosman	CLE	Jul 19, 1974	4–0	0	4	1	OAK	Dave Hamilton
Nolan Ryan	CAL	Sep 28, 1974	4–0	8	15	0	MIN	Joe Decker

No-Hitters, AL (9 innings or more) (*cont.*)

Player	Team	Date	Score	BB	SO	E	Opp.	Opp. Pitcher
	CAL	Jun 1, 1975	1–0	4	9	1	BAL	Ross Grimsley
Jim Colborn	KC	May 14, 1977	6–0	1	6	0	TEX	Tommy Boggs
Dennis Eckersley	CLE	May 30, 1977	1–0	1	12	0	CAL	Frank Tanana
Bert Blyleven	TEX	Sep 22, 1977	6–0	1	7	0	CAL	Paul Hartzell
Len Barker	CLE	May 15, 1981	3–0	0	11	0	TOR	Luis Leal
Dave Righetti	NY	Jul 4, 1983	4–0	4	9	0	BOS	John Tudor
Mike Warren	OAK	Sep 29, 1983	3–0	3	5	0	CHI	Britt Burns
Jack Morris	DET	Apr 7, 1984	4–0	6	8	0	CHI	Floyd Bannister
Mike Witt	CAL	Sep 30, 1984	1–0	0	10	0	TEX	Charlie Hough
Joe Cowley	CHI	Sep 19, 1986	7–1	7	8	0	CAL	Kirk McCaskill
Juan Nieves	MIL	Apr 15, 1987	7–0	5	7	0	BAL	Mike Flanagan
Randy Johnson	SEA	Jun 2, 1990	2–0	6	8	1	DET	Jeff Robinson
Nolan Ryan	TEX	Jun 11, 1990	5–0	2	14	0	OAK	Scott Sanderson
Dave Stewart	OAK	Jun 29, 1990	5–0	3	12	0	TOR	John Cerutti
Dave Stieb	TOR	Sep 2, 1990	3–0	4	9	0	CLE	Bud Black
Nolan Ryan	TEX	May 1, 1991	3–0	2	16	0	TOR	Jimmy Key
Wilson Alvarez	CHI	Aug 11, 1991	7–0	5	7	1	BAL	Dave Johnson
Bret Saberhagen	KC	Aug 26, 1991	7–0	2	5	1	CHI	Charlie Hough

No-Hitters, NL (9 innings or more)

Player	Team	Date	Score	BB	SO	E	Opp.	Opp. Pitcher
George Bradley	STL	Jul 15, 1876	2–0	1	3	3	HAR	Tommy Bond
Lee Richmond	WOR	Jun 12, 1880	1–0	0	5	0	CLE	Jim McCormick
Monte Ward	PRO	Jun 17, 1880	5–0	0	7	0	BUF	Pud Galvin
Larry Corcoran	CHI	Aug 19, 1880	6–0	2	4	2	BOS	Tommy Bond
Pud Galvin	BUF	Aug 20, 1880	1–0	0	2	6	WOR	Fred Corey
Larry Corcoran	CHI	Sep 20, 1882	5–0	1	3	4	WOR	Frank Mountain
Old Hoss Radbourn	PRO	Jul 25, 1883	8–0	0	6	1	CLE	One Arm Daily
One Arm Daily	CLE	Sep 13, 1883	1–0	3	2	2	PHI	John Coleman
Larry Corcoran	CHI	Jun 27, 1884	6–0	1	6	6	PRO	Charlie Sweeney
Pud Galvin	BUF	Aug 4, 1884	18–0	0	7	2	DET	Frank Meinke
John Clarkson	CHI	Jul 27, 1885	4–0	0	4	5	PRO	Old Hoss Radbourn
Charlie Ferguson	PHI	Aug 29, 1885	1–0	2	8	6	PRO	Dupee Shaw
Tom Lovett	BKN	Jun 22, 1891	4–0	3	4	0	NY	Amos Rusie
Amos Rusie	NY	Jul 31, 1891	6–0	8	4	2	BKN	Adonis Terry
Jack Stivetts	BOS	Aug 6, 1892	11–0	5	6	3	BKN	Ed Stein
Ben Sanders	LOU	Aug 22, 1892	6–2	3	0	4	BAL	Sadie McMahon
Bumpus Jones	CIN	Oct 15, 1892	7–1	3	1	0	PIT	Mark Baldwin
Bill Hawke	BAL	Aug 16, 1893	5–0	2	6	0	WAS	George Stephens
Cy Young	CLE	Sep 18, 1897	6–0	1	3	3	CIN	Billy Rhines
Ted Breitenstein	CIN	Apr 22, 1898	11–0	1	2	1	PIT	Charlie Hastings
Jim Hughes	BAL	Apr 22, 1898	8–0	2	3	0	BOS	Ted Lewis
Red Donahue	PHI	Jul 8, 1898	5–0	2	1	0	BOS	Vic Willis
Walter Thornton	CHI	Aug 21, 1898	2–0	3	3	0	BKN	Brickyard Kennedy
Deacon Phillippe	LOU	May 25, 1899	7–0	2	1	0	NY	Ed Doheny
Vic Willis	BOS	Aug 7, 1899	7–1	4	5	3	WAS	Bill Dinneen

No-Hitters, NL (9 innings or more) (cont.)

Player	Team	Date	Score	BB	SO	E	Opp.	Opp. Pitcher
Noodles Hahn	CIN	Jul 12, 1900	4–0	2	8	1	PHI	Bill Bernhard
Christy Mathewson	NY	Jul 15, 1901	5–0	4	4	1	STL	Willie Sudhoff
Chick Fraser	PHI	Sep 18, 1903	10–0	5	4	4	CHI	Peaches Graham
Christy Mathewson	NY	Jun 13, 1905	1–0	0	2	2	CHI	Three Finger Brown
Johnny Lush	PHI	May 1, 1906	1–0	3	11	1	BKN	Mal Eason
Mal Eason	BKN	Jul 20, 1906	2–0	3	5	1	STL	Gus Thompson
Big Jeff Pfeffer	BOS	May 8, 1907	6–0	1	3	1	CIN	Del Mason
Nick Maddox	PIT	Sep 20, 1907	2–1	3	5	2	BKN	Elmer Stricklett
Hooks Wiltse	NY	Jul 4, 1908	1–0	0	6	0	PHI	George McQuillan (10 innings)
Nap Rucker	BKN	Sep 5, 1908	6–0	0	14	3	BOS	Patsy Flaherty
Jeff Tesreau	NY	Sep 6, 1912	3–0	2	2	2	PHI	Eppa Rixey
George Davis	BOS	Sep 9, 1914	7–0	5	4	2	PHI	Ben Tincup
Rube Marquard	NY	Apr 15, 1915	2–0	2	2	1	BKN	Nap Rucker
Jimmy Lavender	CHI	Aug 31, 1915	2–0	1	8	1	NY	Rube Schauer
Tom Hughes	BOS	Jun 16, 1916	2–0	2	3	0	PIT	Erv Kantlehner
Fred Toney	CIN	May 2, 1917	1–0	2	3	0	CHI	Hippo Vaughn (10 innings)
Hod Eller	CIN	May 11, 1919	6–0	3	8	0	STL	Jakie May
Jesse Barnes	NY	May 7, 1922	6–0	1	5	0	PHI	Lee Meadows
Jesse Haines	STL	Jul 17, 1924	5–0	3	5	2	BOS	Tim McNamara
Dazzy Vance	BKN	Sep 13, 1925	10–1	1	9	3	PHI	Clarence Mitchell
Carl Hubbell	NY	May 8, 1929	11–0	1	4	3	PIT	Jesse Petty
Paul Dean	STL	Sep 21, 1934	3–0	1	6	0	BKN	Ray Benge
Johnny Vander Meer	CIN	Jun 11, 1938	3–0	3	4	0	BOS	Danny MacFayden
	CIN	Jun 15, 1938	6–0	8	7	0	BKN	Max Butcher
Tex Carleton	BKN	May 30, 1940	3–0	2	4	3	CIN	Jim Turner
Lon Warneke	STL	Aug 30, 1941	2–0	1	2	2	CIN	Elmer Riddle
Jim Tobin	BOS	Apr 27, 1944	2–0	2	6	0	BKN	Fritz Ostermueller
Clyde Shoun	CIN	May 15, 1944	1–0	1	1	0	BOS	Jim Tobin
Ed Head	BKN	Apr 23, 1946	5–0	3	2	1	BOS	Mort Cooper
Ewell Blackwell	CIN	Jun 18, 1947	6–0	4	3	0	BOS	Ed Wright
Rex Barney	BKN	Sep 9, 1948	2–0	3	4	2	NY	Monte Kennedy
Vern Bickford	BOS	Aug 11, 1950	7–0	4	3	0	BKN	Carl Erskine
Cliff Chambers	PIT	May 6, 1951	3–0	8	4	0	BOS	George Estock
Carl Erskine	BKN	Jun 19, 1952	5–0	1	1	0	CHI	Warren Hacker
Jim Wilson	MIL	Jun 12, 1954	2–0	2	6	0	PHI	Robin Roberts
Sam Jones	CHI	May 12, 1955	4–0	7	6	0	PIT	Nellie King
Carl Erskine	BKN	May 12, 1956	3–0	2	3	0	NY	Al Worthington
Sal Maglie	BKN	Sep 25, 1956	5–0	2	3	0	PHI	Jack Meyer
Don Cardwell	CHI	May 15, 1960	4–0	1	7	0	STL	Lindy McDaniel
Lew Burdette	MIL	Aug 18, 1960	1–0	0	3	0	PHI	Gene Conley
Warren Spahn	MIL	Sep 16, 1960	4–0	2	15	0	PHI	John Buzhardt
	MIL	Apr 28, 1961	1–0	2	9	0	SF	Sam Jones
Sandy Koufax	LA	Jun 30, 1962	5–0	5	13	0	NY	Bob Miller
	LA	May 11, 1963	8–0	2	4	0	SF	Juan Marichal
Don Nottebart	HOU	May 17, 1963	4–1	3	8	1	PHI	Jack Hamilton

No-Hitters, NL (9 innings or more) (cont.)

Player	Team	Date	Score	BB	SO	E	Opp.	Opp. Pitcher
Juan Marichal	SF	Jun 15, 1963	1–0	2	5	0	HOU	Dick Drott
Ken Johnson	HOU	Apr 23, 1964	0–1	2	9	2	CIN	Joe Nuxhall
Sandy Koufax	LA	Jun 4, 1964	3–0	1	10	0	PHI	Chris Short
Jim Bunning	PHI	Jun 21, 1964	6–0	0	10	0	NY	Tracy Stallard
Jim Maloney	CIN	Aug 19, 1965	1–0	10	12	1	CHI	Larry Jackson (10 innings)
Sandy Koufax	LA	Sep 9, 1965	1–0	0	14	0	CHI	Bob Hendley
Don Wilson	HOU	Jun 18, 1967	2–0	3	15	0	ATL	Phil Niekro
George Culver	CIN	Jul 29, 1968	6–1	5	4	3	PHI	Chris Short
Gaylord Perry	SF	Sep 17, 1968	1–0	2	9	1	STL	Bob Gibson
Ray Washburn	STL	Sep 18, 1968	2–0	5	8	0	SF	Bobby Bolin
Bill Stoneman	MON	Apr 17, 1969	7–0	5	8	0	PHI	Jerry Johnson
Jim Maloney	CIN	Apr 30, 1969	10–0	5	13	0	HOU	Wade Blasingame
Don Wilson	HOU	May 1, 1969	4–0	6	15	1	CIN	Jim Merritt
Ken Holtzman	CHI	Aug 19, 1969	3–0	3	0	0	ATL	Phil Niekro
Bob Moose	PIT	Sep 20, 1969	4–0	3	6	0	NY	Gary Gentry
Dock Ellis	PIT	Jun 12, 1970	2–0	8	6	0	SD	Dave Roberts
Bill Singer	LA	Jul 20, 1970	5–0	0	10	2	PHI	Woodie Fryman
Ken Holtzman	CHI	Jun 3, 1971	1–0	4	6	0	CIN	Gary Nolan
Rick Wise	PHI	Jun 23, 1971	4–0	1	3	0	CIN	Ross Grimsley
Bob Gibson	STL	Aug 14, 1971	11–0	3	10	0	PIT	Bob Johnson
Burt Hooton	CHI	Apr 16, 1972	4–0	7	7	0	PHI	Dick Selma
Milt Pappas	CHI	Sep 2, 1972	8–0	1	6	0	SD	Mike Caldwell
Bill Stoneman	MON	Oct 2, 1972	7–0	7	9	1	NY	Jim McAndrew
Phil Niekro	ATL	Aug 5, 1973	9–0	3	4	2	SD	Steve Arlin
Ed Halicki	SF	Aug 24, 1975	6–0	2	10	1	NY	Craig Swan
Larry Dierker	HOU	Jul 9, 1976	6–0	4	8	0	MON	Don Stanhouse
John Candelaria	PIT	Aug 9, 1976	2–0	1	7	2	LA	Doug Rau
John Montefusco	SF	Sep 29, 1976	9–0	1	4	0	ATL	Jamie Easterly
Bob Forsch	STL	Apr 16, 1978	5–0	2	3	1	PHI	Randy Lerch
Tom Seaver	CIN	Jun 16, 1978	4–0	3	3	1	STL	John Denny
Ken Forsch	HOU	Apr 7, 1979	6–0	2	5	0	ATL	Larry McWilliams
Jerry Reuss	LA	Jun 27, 1980	8–0	0	2	1	SF	Vida Blue
Charlie Lea	MON	May 10, 1981	4–0	4	8	0	SF	Ed Whitson
Nolan Ryan	HOU	Sep 26, 1981	5–0	3	11	0	LA	Ted Power
Bob Forsch	STL	Sep 26, 1983	3–0	0	6	1	MON	Steve Rogers
Mike Scott	HOU	Sep 25, 1986	2–0	2	13	0	SF	Juan Berenguer
Tom Browning	CIN	Sep 16, 1988	1–0	0	7	0	LA	Tim Belcher
Fernando Valenzuela	LA	Jun 29, 1990	6–0	3	7	1	STL	Jose DeLeon
Terry Mulholland	PHI	Aug 15, 1990	6–0	0	8	1	SF	Don Robinson
Tommy Greene	PHI	May 23, 1991	2–0	7	10	0	MON	Oil Can Boyd
Dennis Martinez	MON	Jul 28, 1991	2–0	0	5	0	LA	Mike Morgan
Kevin Gross	LA	Aug 17, 1992	2–0	2	6	0	SF	Francisco Oliveras

No-Hitters, Other Leagues

Player	Team	Date	Score	Opp.
Tony Mullane	LOU AA	Sep 11, 1882	2–0	CIN
Guy Hecker	LOU AA	Sep 19, 1882	3–1	PIT
Al Atkinson	PHI AA	May 24, 1884	10–1	PIT
Ed Morris	COL AA	May 29, 1884	5–0	PIT
Frank Mountain	COL AA	Jun 5, 1884	12–0	WAS
Sam Kimber	BKN AA	Oct 4, 1884	0–0	TOL
			(10 innings)	
Al Atkinson	PHI AA	May 1, 1886	3–2	NY
Adonis Terry	BKN AA	Jul 24, 1886	1–0	STL
Matt Kilroy	BAL AA	Oct 6, 1886	6–0	PIT
Adonis Terry	BKN AA	May 27, 1888	4–0	LOU
Henry Porter	KC AA	Jun 6, 1888	4–0	BAL
Ed Seward	PHI AA	Jul 26, 1888	12–2	CIN
Gus Weyhing	PHI AA	Jul 31, 1888	4–0	KC
Cannonball Titcomb	ROC AA	Sep 15, 1890	7–0	SYR
Ted Breitenstein	STL AA	Oct 4, 1891	8–0	LOU
Dick Burns	CIN U	Aug 26, 1884	3–1	KC
Ed Cushman	MIL U	Sep 28, 1884	5–0	WAS
Ed Lafitte	BKN F	Sep 19, 1914	6–2	KC
Frank Allen	PIT F	Apr 24, 1915	2–0	STL
Claude Hendrix	CHI F	May 15, 1915	10–0	PIT
Alex Main	KC F	Aug 16, 1915	3–0	BUF
Dave Davenport	STL F	Sep 7, 1915	3–0	CHI

No Hits Allowed, Less Than Nine Innings

Player	Team	Date	Inns.	Score	Opp.
Larry McKeon	IND AA	May 6, 1884	6	0–0	CIN
Charlie Gagus	WAS U	Aug 21, 1884	8	12–1	WIL
Charlie Getzien	DET N	Oct 1, 1884	6	1–0	PHI
Charlie Sweeney/	STL U	Oct 5, 1884	2	0–1	STP
Henry Boyle	(combined 5 innings)		3		
Dupee Shaw	PRO N	Oct 7, 1885	5	4–0	BUF
George Van Haltren	CHI N	Jun 21, 1888	6	1–0	PIT
Cannonball Crane	NY N	Sep 27, 1888	7	3–0	WAS
Matt Kilroy	BAL AA	Jul 29, 1889	7	0–0	STL
Silver King	CHI P	Jun 21, 1890	8	0–1	BKN
George Nichol	STL AA	Sep 23, 1890	7	21–2	PHI
Hank Gastright	COL AA	Oct 12, 1890	8	6–0	TOL
Jack Stivetts	BOS N	Oct 15, 1892	5	4–0	WAS
Icebox Chamberlain	CIN N	Sep 23, 1893	7	6–0	BOS
Ed Stein	BKN N	Jun 2, 1894	6	1–0	CHI
Red Ames	NY N	Sep 14, 1903	5	5–0	STL
Rube Waddell	PHI A	Aug 15, 1905	5	2–0	STL
Jake Weimer	CIN N	Aug 24, 1906	7	1–0	BKN
Jimmy Dygert/	PHI A	Aug 29, 1906	3	4–3	CHI
Rube Waddell	(combined 5 innings)		2		

No Hits Allowed, Less Than Nine Innings (*cont.*)

Player	Team	Date	Inns.	Score	Opp.
Stoney McGlynn	STL N	Sep 24, 1906	7	1–1	BKN
Lefty Leifield	PIT N	Sep 26, 1906	6	8–0	PHI
Ed Walsh	CHI A	May 26, 1907	5	8–1	NY
Ed Karger	STL N	Aug 11, 1907	7P	4–0	BOS
Howie Camnitz	PIT N	Aug 23, 1907	5	1–0	NY
Rube Vickers	PHI A	Oct 5, 1907	5P	4–0	WAS
Johnny Lush	STL N	Aug 6, 1908	6	2–0	BKN
King Cole	CHI N	Jul 31, 1910	7	4–0	STL
Jay Cashion	WAS A	Aug 20, 1912	6	2–0	CLE
Walter Johnson	WAS A	Aug 25, 1924	7	2–0	STL
Fred Frankhouse	BKN N	Aug 27, 1937	8	5–0	CIN
John Whitehead	STL A	Aug 5, 1940	6	4–0	DET
Jim Tobin	BOS N	Jun 22, 1944	5	7–0	PHI
Mike McCormick	SF N	Jun 12, 1959	5	3–0	PHI
Sam Jones	SF N	Sep 26, 1959	7	4–0	STL
Dean Chance	MIN A	Aug 6, 1967	5P	2–0	BOS
David Palmer	MON N	Apr 21, 1984	5P	4–0	STL
Pascual Perez	MON N	Sep 24, 1988	5	1–0	PHI
Andy Hawkins	NY A	Jul 1, 1990	8*	0–4	CHI
Melido Perez	CHI A	Jul 12, 1990	6	8–0	NY
Matt Young	BOS A	Apr 12, 1992	8*	1–2	CLF

P = Perfect Innings
* = 9 Inning Game

No-Hitters Broken Up in Extra Innings

Player	Team	Date	Score	Opp.	Result
Earl Moore	CLE A	May 9, 1901	2–4	CHI	Hit in 10th, lost in 10th
Bob Wicker	NY N	Jun 11, 1904	1–0	CHI	Hit in 10th, won in 12th
Harry McIntire	BKN N	Aug 1, 1906	0–1	PIT	Hit in 11th, lost in 13th
Red Ames	NY N	Apr 15, 1909	0–3	BKN	Hit in 10th, lost in 13th
Tom Hughes	NY A	Aug 30, 1910	0–5	CLE	Hit in 10th, lost in 11th
Jim Scott	CHI A	May 14, 1914	0–1	WAS	Hit in 10th, lost in 10th
Hippo Vaughn	CHI N	May 2, 1917	0–1	CIN	Hit in 10th, lost in 10th
Bobo Newsom	STL A	Sep 18, 1934	1–2	BOS	Hit in 10th, lost in 10th
John Klippstein	CIN N	May 26, 1956	1–2	MIL	Hit in 10th, lost in 11th
Hersh Freeman	(Klippstein pitched 7 innings, Freeman 2 innings, and				
Joe Black	Black 2.1 innings)				

No-Hitters Broken Up in Extra Innings (*cont.*)

Player	Team	Date	Score	Opp.	Result
Harvey Haddix	PIT N	May 26, 1959	0–1	MIL	Hit in 13th, lost in 13th
Jim Maloney	CIN N	Jun 14, 1965	0–1	NY	Hit in 11th, lost in 11th
Mark Gardner	MON N	Jul 26, 1991	0–1	LA	Hit in 10th, lost in 10th

Combined No-Hitters

Player	Team	Date	Score	IP	BB	E	Opp.	Opp. Pitcher
Babe Ruth	BOS	Jun 23, 1917	4–0	0	1	0	WAS	Doc Ayers
Ernie Shore				9	0	0		
Steve Barber	BAL A	Apr 30, 1967	1–2	8.2	10	2	DET	Earl Wilson
Stu Miller				.1	0	0		
Vida Blue	OAK A	Sep 28, 1975	6–0	5	2	1	CAL	Gary Ross
Glenn Abbott				1	0	0		
Paul Lindblad				1	0	0		
Rollie Fingers				2	0	0		
Blue Moon Odom	CHI A	Jul 28, 1976	2–1	5	9	0	OAK	Paul Lindblad
Francisco Barrios				4	2	0		
Mark Langston	CAL A	Apr 11, 1990	1–0	7	4	1	SEA	Gary Eave
Mike Witt				2	0	0		
Bob Milacki	BAL A	Jul 13, 1991	2–0	6	3	0	OAK	Eric Show
Mike Flanagan				1	1	0		
Mark Williamson				1	0	0		
Gregg Olson				1	0	0		
Kent Mercker	ATL N	Sep 11, 1991	1–0	6	2	0	SD	Greg Harris
Mark Wohlers				2	0	0		
Alejandro Pena				1	0	1		

Most No-Hitters, Career

Player	Team	Date	Score	Opp.
Nolan Ryan	CAL A	May 15, 1973	3–0	KC
	CAL A	Jul 15, 1973	6–0	DET
	CAL A	Sep 28, 1974	4–0	DET
	CAL A	Jun 1, 1975	1–0	BAL
	HOU N	Sep 26, 1981	5–0	LA
	TEX A	Jun 11, 1990	5–0	OAK
	TEX A	May 1, 1991	3–0	TOR
Sandy Koufax	LA N	Jun 30, 1962	5–0	NY
	LA N	May 11, 1963	8–0	SF
	LA N	Jun 4, 1964	3–0	PHI
	LA N	Sep 9, 1965	1–0	CHI
Larry Corcoran	CHI N	Aug 19, 1880	6–0	BOS
	CHI N	Sep 20, 1882	5–0	WOR
	CHI N	Jun 27, 1884	6–0	PRO
Cy Young	CLE N	Sep 18, 1897	6–0	CIN

Most No-Hitters, Career (*cont.*)

Player	Team	Date	Score	Opp.
	BOS A	May 5, 1904	3–0	PHI
	BOS A	Jun 30, 1908	8–0	NY
Bob Feller	CLE A	Apr 16, 1940	1–0	CHI
	CLE A	Apr 30, 1946	1–0	NY
	CLE A	Jul 1, 1951	2–1	DET
Ted Breitenstein	STL AA	Oct 4, 1891	8–0	LOU
	CIN N	Apr 22, 1898	11–0	PIT
Jim Maloney	CIN N	Aug 19, 1965	1–0	CHI
	CIN N	Apr 30, 1969	10–0	HOU
Christy Mathewson	NY N	Jul 15, 1901	5–0	STL
	NY N	Jun 13, 1905	1–0	CHI
Addie Joss	CLE A	Oct 2, 1908	1–0	CHI
	CLE A	Apr 20, 1910	1–0	CHI
Johnny Vander Meer	CIN N	Jun 11, 1938	3–0	BOS
	CIN N	Jun 15, 1938	6–0	BKN
Allie Reynolds	NY A	Jul 12, 1951	1–0	CLE
	NY A	Sep 28, 1951	8–0	BOS
Virgil Trucks	DET A	May 15, 1952	1–0	WAS
	DET A	Aug 25, 1952	1–0	NY
Jim Bunning	DET A	Jul 20, 1958	3–0	BOS
	PHI N	Jun 21, 1964	6–0	NY
Warren Spahn	MIL N	Sep 16, 1960	4–0	PHI
	MIL N	Apr 28, 1961	1–0	SF
Ken Holtzman	CHI N	Aug 19, 1969	3–0	ATL
	CHI N	Jun 3, 1971	1–0	CIN
Bill Stoneman	MON N	Apr 17, 1969	7–0	PHI
	MON N	Oct 2, 1972	7–0	NY
Steve Busby	KC A	Apr 27, 1973	3–0	DET
	KC A	Jun 19, 1974	2–0	MIL
Frank Smith	CHI A	Sep 6, 1905	15–0	DET
	CHI A	Sep 20, 1908	1–0	PHI
Dutch Leonard	BOS A	Aug 30, 1916	4–0	STL
	BOS A	Jun 3, 1918	5–0	DET
Carl Erskine	BKN N	Jun 19, 1952	5–0	CHI
	BKN N	May 12, 1956	3–0	NY
Don Wilson	HOU N	Jun 18, 1967	2–0	ATL
	HOU N	May 1, 1969	4–0	CIN
Al Atkinson	PHI AA	May 24, 1884	10–1	PIT
	PHI AA	May 1, 1886	3–2	NY
Adonis Terry	BKN AA	Jul 24, 1886	1–0	STL
	BKN AA	May 27, 1888	4–0	LOU
Pud Galvin	BUF N	Aug 20, 1880	1–0	WOR
	BUF N	Aug 4, 1884	18–0	DET
Bob Forsch	STL N	Apr 16, 1978	5–0	PHI
	STL N	Sep 26, 1983	3–0	MON

Perfect Games (9 innings or more)

Player	Team	Date	Score	SO	Opp.	Opp. Pitcher
Lee Richmond	WOR N	Jun 12, 1880	1–0	5	CLE	Jim McCormick
Monte Ward	PRO N	Jun 17, 1880	5–0	7	BUF	Pud Galvin
Cy Young	BOS A	May 5, 1904	3–0	8	PHI	Rube Waddell
Addie Joss	CLE A	Oct 2, 1908	1–0	3	CHI	Ed Walsh
Charlie Robertson	CHI A	Apr 30, 1922	2–0	6	DET	Herman Pillette
Don Larsen	NY A	Oct 8, 1956	2–0	7	BKN	Sal Maglie
Jim Bunning	PHI N	Jun 21, 1964	6–0	10	NY	Tracy Stallard
Sandy Koufax	LA N	Sep 9, 1965	1–0	14	CHI	Bob Hendley
Catfish Hunter	OAK A	May 8, 1968	4–0	11	MIN	Dave Boswell
Len Barker	CLE A	May 15, 1981	3–0	11	TOR	Luis Leal
Mike Witt	CAL A	Sep 30, 1984	1–0	10	TEX	Charlie Hough
Tom Browning	CIN N	Sep 16, 1988	1–0	10	LA	Tim Belcher
Dennis Martinez	MON N	Jul 28, 1991	2–0	5	LA	Mike Morgan

No-Hitters Broken Up by Home Runs, AL

Player	Team	Date	Opp.	Opp. Batter
Tommy Bridges	DET	May 24, 1933	WAS	Joe Kuhel
Jimmie DeShong	NY	Jul 28, 1934	PHI	Jimmie Foxx
Lefty Gomez	NY	Jun 30, 1937	PHI	Bob Johnson
Marius Russo	NY	Jun 26, 1941	STL	Glenn McQuillen
Steve Sundra	STL	Aug 11, 1943	NY	Charlie Keller
Connie Marrero	WAS	Apr 26, 1951	PHI	Barney McCosky
Bob Lemon	CLE	May 29, 1951	DET	Vic Wertz
Vic Raschi	NY	Jul 13, 1952	DET	Joe Ginsberg
Hal Brown	BAL	Jun 1, 1960	NY	Mickey Mantle
Dick Donovan	WAS	Sep 24, 1961	MIN	Joe Altobelli
Bill Monbouquette	BOS	Sep 9, 1964	MIN	Zoilo Versalles
Gary Peters	CHI	May 14, 1967	CAL	Bill Skowron
Rich Hand	CLE	Aug 28, 1970	CAL	Roger Repoz
Mike Kekich	NY	Jul 18, 1971	CHI	Mike Andrews
Dick Drago	KC	Jul 30, 1971	BAL	Frank Robinson
Jim Colborn	MIL	May 9, 1973	TEX	Jeff Burroughs
Jim Kaat	MIN	Jul 1, 1973	CAL	Frank Robinson
Bert Blyleven	MIN	Jul 4, 1974	TEX	Toby Harrah
Joe Coleman	DET	May 6, 1975	MIL	George Scott
Vida Blue	OAK	Aug 28, 1976	DET	Mickey Stanley
Chris Knapp	CAL	Sep 3, 1978	TOR	Willie Horton
Steve Stone	BAL	Jul 30, 1979	MIL	Charlie Moore
Dennis Eckersley	BOS	Sep 26, 1980	TOR	John Mayberry
Richard Dotson	CHI	May 18, 1983	BAL	Dan Ford
Tim Conroy	OAK	Jun 23, 1984	TEX	Alan Bannister
Frank Tanana	DET	Aug 2, 1985	MIL	Ben Oglivie
Danny Darwin	MIL	Aug 19, 1985	MIN	Roy Smalley
Kirk McCaskill	CAL	Jun 25, 1986	TEX	Steve Buechele
Curt Young	OAK	Jun 9, 1987	CHI	Kenny Williams
Jeff Robinson	DET	May 25, 1988	MIL	Greg Brock

No-Hitters Broken Up by Home Runs, AL (cont.)

Player	Team	Date	Opp.	Opp. Batter
Ted Higuera	MIL	Jun 15, 1988	SEA	Steve Balboni
Willie Fraser	CAL	Aug 10, 1988	SEA	Alvin Davis
Brian Holman	SEA	Apr 20, 1990	OAK	Ken Phelps
Jack McDowell	CHI	Jul 14, 1991	MIL	Paul Molitor
Scott Erickson	MIN	Sep 24, 1991	CHI	Dan Pasqua

No-Hitters Broken Up by Home Runs, NL

Player	Team	Date	Opp.	Opp. Batter
Charlie Buffinton	PHI	Aug 9, 1887	CHI	Fred Pfeffer
Jesse Barnes	NY	Jul 4, 1919	PHI	Gavvy Cravath
Whit Wyatt	BKN	May 20, 1942	NY	Johnny Mize
Carl Hubbell	NY	Jun 5, 1943	PIT	Elbie Fletcher
Charley Schanz	PHI	May 2, 1944	NY	Joe Medwick
Johnny Beazley	STL	Aug 3, 1946	PHI	Frank McCormick
Kirby Higbe	BKN	Sep 9, 1946	NY	Ernie Lombardi
Carl Erskine	BKN	Sep 12, 1950	CIN	Ted Kluszewski
Robin Roberts	PHI	May 13, 1954	CIN	Bobby Adams
Lew Burdette	MIL	May 22, 1954	BKN	Gil Hodges
Billy Loes	BKN	Sep 10, 1954	MIL	Joe Adcock
Warren Hacker	CHI	May 21, 1955	MIL	George Crowe
Sam Jones	SF	Apr 16, 1960	CHI	Walt Moryn
Dick Ellsworth	CHI	May 15, 1965	LA	Al Ferrara
Sandy Koufax	LA	Jun 20, 1965	NY	Jim Hickman
Bob Shaw	SF	Jun 25, 1965	PHI	Wes Covington
Phil Niekro	ATL	Sep 5, 1969	CIN	Tony Perez
Luke Walker	PIT	Jul 18, 1971	LA	Joe Ferguson
Clay Kirby	SD	Sep 18, 1971	SF	Willie McCovey
Don Sutton	LA	Apr 15, 1975	CIN	Johnny Bench
Silvio Martinez	STL	May 30, 1978	NY	Steve Henderson
Steve Rogers	MON	Jun 8, 1978	LA	Reggie Smith
Rick Mahler	ATL	Sep 5, 1982	MON	Al Oliver
Mario Soto	CIN	May 12, 1984	STL	George Hendrick
Alejandro Pena	LA	Aug 2, 1986	CIN	Eddie Milner
Bruce Hurst	SD	Apr 10, 1989	ATL	Lonnie Smith
Danny Jackson	PIT	Jul 25, 1992	ATL	Dave Justice
Jim Bullinger	CHI	Aug 30, 1992	SF	Kirt Manwaring
Curt Schilling	PHI	Sep 9, 1992	NY	Bobby Bonilla

Most Complete 1–0 Wins, Career

Player	Total	Player	Total
Walter Johnson	38	Dean Chance	13
Grover Alexander	17	Ed Walsh	13
Eddie Plank	15	Doc White	13
Bert Blyleven	15	Cy Young	13
Christy Mathewson	14	Steve Carlton	12
Three Finger Brown	13	Stan Coveleski	12

Most Complete 1–0 Wins, Career (con't)

Player	Total
Gaylord Perry	12
Ferguson Jenkins	11
Kid Nichols	11
Nap Rucker	11
Nolan Ryan	11
Joe Bush	10
Paul Derringer	10
Bill Doak	10
Addie Joss	10
Sandy Koufax	10
Dick Rudolph	10
Warren Spahn	10
Lefty Tyler	10
Hippo Vaughn	10

Most 1–0 Losses, Career

Player	Total
Walter Johnson	26
Jim Bunning	15
Ferguson Jenkins	13
Lee Meadows	13
Jack Powell	13
Eddie Cicotte	12
Eddie Plank	12
Wilbur Cooper	11
Christy Mathewson	11
Doc White	11
Three Finger Brown	10
Bob Gibson	10
Larry Jackson	10
Ken Raffensberger	10
Nap Rucker	10

Worst Won-Lost Record, Season (12 or more losses)

Player	Team	Year	W	L	Pct.	ERA
Terry Felton	MIN A	1982	0	13	.000	4.99
Steve Gerkin	PHI A	1945	0	12	.000	3.62
Russ Miller	PHI N	1928	0	12	.000	5.42
Jack Nabors	PHI A	1916	1	20	.048	3.47
Frank Bates	STL N	1899				
	CLE N	1899	1	18	.053	6.90
Art Hagan	PHI N	1883				
	BUF N	1883	1	16	.059	5.27
Tom Sheehan	PHI A	1916	1	16	.059	3.69
Mike Parrott	SEA A	1980	1	16	.059	7.28
Howie Judson	CHI A	1949	1	14	.067	4.54
Kyle Abbott	PHI N	1992	1	14	.067	5.13
Fred Corey	WOR N	1882	1	13	.071	3.56
Jim McElroy	PHI N	1884				
	WIL U	1884	1	13	.071	5.12
Tony Madigan	WAS N	1886	1	13	.071	5.06
Guy Morton	CLE A	1914	1	13	.071	3.02
Roy Moore	PHI A	1920	1	13	.071	4.68
Pascual Perez	ATL N	1985	1	13	.071	6.14
Steve Hargan	CLE A	1971	1	13	.071	6.21
Troy Herriage	KC A	1956	1	13	.071	6.64
George Gill	DET A	1939				
	STL A	1939	1	13	.071	7.21
Zane Smith	ATL N	1989				
	MON N	1989	1	13	.071	3.49
Walt Leverenz	STL A	1914	1	12	.077	3.80
Carl Scheib	PHI A	1951	1	12	.077	4.47

Worst Won-Lost Record, Season (12 or more losses) (*cont.*)

Player	Team	Year	W	L	Pct.	ERA
Bob Miller	NY N	1962	1	12	.077	4.89
Tricky Nichols	BAL AA	1882	1	12	.077	5.02
Wally Hebert	STL A	1932	1	12	.077	6.48
Jim Walkup	STL A	1938	1	12	.077	6.80

Best Won-Lost Record, Season, AL (20 or more wins)

Player	Team	Year	W	L	Pct.
Ron Guidry	NY	1978	25	3	.893
Lefty Grove	PHI	1931	31	4	.886
Smoky Joe Wood	BOS	1912	34	5	.872
Wild Bill Donovan	DET	1907	25	4	.862
Whitey Ford	NY	1961	25	4	.862
Roger Clemens	BOS	1986	24	4	.857
Lefty Grove	PHI	1930	28	5	.848
Lefty Gomez	NY	1934	26	5	.839
Denny McLain	DET	1968	31	6	.838
Walter Johnson	WAS	1913	36	7	.837
Spud Chandler	NY	1943	20	4	.833
Chief Bender	PHI	1910	23	5	.821
Bob Welch	OAK	1990	27	6	.818
Russ Ford	NY	1910	26	6	.813
Eddie Plank	PHI	1912	26	6	.813
General Crowder	STL	1928	21	5	.808
Bobo Newsom	DET	1940	21	5	.808
Ernie Bonham	NY	1942	21	5	.808
Dave McNally	BAL	1971	21	5	.808
Catfish Hunter	OAK	1973	21	5	.808
Eddie Cicotte	CHI	1919	29	7	.806
Boo Ferriss	BOS	1946	25	6	.806
Stan Coveleski	WAS	1925	20	5	.800

Best Won-Lost Record, Season, NL (20 or more wins)

Player	Team	Year	W	L	Pct.
Preacher Roe	BKN	1951	22	3	.880
Fred Goldsmith	CHI	1880	21	3	.875
David Cone	NY	1988	20	3	.870
Dwight Gooden	NY	1985	24	4	.857
Old Hoss Radbourn	PRO	1884	60	12	.833
King Cole	CHI	1910	20	4	.833
Sandy Koufax	LA	1963	25	5	.833
Jim Hughes	BKN	1899	28	6	.824
Jack Chesbro	PIT	1902	28	6	.824
Dazzy Vance	BKN	1924	28	6	.824
Bob Purkey	CIN	1962	23	5	.821
Joe McGinnity	NY	1904	35	8	.814

Best Won-Lost Record, Season, NL (20 or more wins) *(cont.)*

Player	Team	Year	W	L	Pct.
Three Finger Brown	CHI	1906	26	6	.813
Carl Hubbell	NY	1936	26	6	.813
Bill Hoffer	BAL	1895	30	7	.811
Dizzy Dean	STL	1934	30	7	.811
Larry Jansen	NY	1947	21	5	.808
Howie Camnitz	PIT	1909	25	6	.806
Christy Mathewson	NY	1909	25	6	.806
Juan Marichal	SF	1966	25	6	.806
Mickey Welch	NY	1885	44	11	.800
Jocko Flynn	CHI	1886	24	6	.800
Sam Leever	PIT	1905	20	5	.800
Robin Roberts	PHI	1952	28	7	.800
Don Newcombe	BKN	1955	20	5	.800
John Candelaria	PIT	1977	20	5	.800

Twenty Wins One Year, 20 Losses the Next, AL

Player	Team	Year	W	L
George Mullin	DET	1906	21	18
	DET	1907	20	20
Al Orth	NY	1906	27	17
	NY	1907	14	21
Russ Ford	NY	1911	22	11
	NY	1912	13	21
Walter Johnson	WAS	1915	27	13
	WAS	1916	25	20
Hooks Dauss	DET	1919	21	9
	DET	1920	13	21
Bobo Newsom	DET	1940	21	5
	DET	1941	12	20
Alex Kellner	PHI	1949	20	12
	PHI	1950	8	20
Mel Stottlemyre	NY	1965	20	9
	NY	1966	12	20
Luis Tiant	CLE	1968	21	9
	CLE	1969	9	20
Stan Bahnsen	CHI	1972	21	16
	CHI	1973	18	21
Wilbur Wood	CHI	1972	24	17
	CHI	1973	24	20
	CHI	1974	20	19
	CHI	1975	16	20

Twenty Wins One Year, 20 Losses the Next, NL since 1900

Player	Team	Year	W	L
Togie Pittinger	BOS	1902	27	16
	BOS	1903	19	23

Twenty Wins One Year, 20 Losses the Next, NL since 1900 (*cont.*)

Player	Team	Year	W	L
Oscar Jones	BKN	1903	20	16
	BKN	1904	17	25
Jack Taylor	STL	1904	21	19
	STL	1905	15	21
Irv Young	BOS	1905	20	21
	BOS	1906	16	25
Nap Rucker	BKN	1911	22	18
	BKN	1912	18	21
Howie Camnitz	PIT	1912	22	12
	PIT			
	PHI	1913	9	20
Rube Marquard	NY	1913	23	10
	NY	1914	12	22
Eppa Rixey	PHI	1916	22	10
	PHI	1917	16	21
Joe Oeschger	BOS	1921	20	14
	BOS	1922	6	21
Murry Dickson	PIT	1951	20	16
	PIT	1952	14	21
Larry Jackson	CHI	1964	24	11
	CHI	1965	14	21
Steve Carlton	PHI	1972	27	10
	PHI	1973	13	20
Jerry Koosman	NY	1976	21	10
	NY	1977	8	20

Twenty Wins One Year, 20 Losses the Next, Two Leagues

Player	Team	Year	W	L
Joe McGinnity	BKN N	1900	29	9
	BAL A	1901	26	20
	BAL A			
	NY N	1902	21	18
	NY N	1903	31	20

Twenty Wins One Year, 20 Losses the Next, Other Leagues since 1900

Player	Team	Year	W	L
Jack Quinn	BAL F	1914	26	14
	BAL F	1915	9	22

Twenty Wins with Last-Place Team, AL

Player	Team	Year	W	L	Team W	Team L
Scott Perry	PHI	1918	21	19	52	76
Howard Ehmke	BOS	1923	20	17	61	91
Sloppy Thurston	CHI	1924	20	14	66	87
Ned Garver	STL	1951	20	12	52	102
Nolan Ryan	CAL	1974	22	16	68	94

Twenty Wins with Last-Place Team, NL

Player	Team	Year	W	L	W	L
Lee Richmond	WOR	1881	25	26	32	50
Mark Baldwin	PIT	1891	22	28	55	80
Sadie McMahon	BAL	1892	20	25	46	101
Noodles Hahn	CIN	1901	22	19	52	87
Steve Carlton	PHI	1972	27	10	59	97
Phil Niekro	ATL	1979	21	20	66	94

Highest Percentage of Team's Wins, AL

Player	Team	Year	W	L	Team W	Team L	Pct.
Ed Walsh	CHI	1908	40	15	88	64	45.5
Jack Chesbro	NY	1904	41	12	92	59	44.6
Cy Young	BOS	1901	33	10	79	57	41.8
Joe Bush	PHI	1916	15	22	36	117	41.7
Cy Young	BOS	1902	32	11	77	60	41.6
Eddie Rommel	PHI	1922	27	13	65	89	41.5
Scott Perry	PHI	1918	21	19	52	76	40.4
Red Faber	CHI	1921	25	15	62	92	40.3
Walter Johnson	WAS	1913	36	7	90	64	40.0

Highest Percentage of Team's Wins, NL since 1900

Player	Team	Year	W	L	Team W	Team L	Pct.
Steve Carlton	PHI	1972	27	10	59	97	45.8
Noodles Hahn	CIN	1901	22	19	52	87	42.3

Twenty Wins and 20 Losses in Same Year, AL

Player	Team	Year	W	L
Joe McGinnity	BAL	1901	26	20
Bill Dinneen	BOS	1902	21	21
George Mullin	DET	1905	21	20
	DET	1907	20	20
Jim Scott	CHI	1913	20	20
Walter Johnson	WAS	1916	25	20
Wilbur Wood	CHI	1973	24	20

Twenty Wins and 20 Losses, Season, NL since 1900

Player	Team	Year	W	L
Joe McGinnity	NY	1903	31	20
Irv Young	BOS	1906	20	21
Phil Niekro	ATL	1979	21	20

Thirty-Game Winners, AL

Player	Team	Year	W	L	Pct.	ERA	IP	BB	SO	ShO
Jack Chesbro	NY	1904	41	12	.774	1.82	455	88	239	6
Ed Walsh	CHI	1908	40	15	.727	1.42	464	56	269	12
Walter Johnson	WAS	1913	36	7	.837	1.09	346	38	243	12
Smoky Joe Wood	BOS	1912	34	5	.872	1.91	344	82	258	10
Cy Young	BOS	1901	33	10	.767	1.62	371	37	158	5
	BOS	1902	32	11	.744	2.15	385	53	160	3
Walter Johnson	WAS	1912	32	12	.727	1.39	368	76	303	8
Lefty Grove	PHI	1931	31	4	.886	2.06	289	62	175	3
Denny McLain	DET	1968	31	6	.838	1.96	336	63	280	6
Jack Coombs	PHI	1910	31	9	.769	1.30	353	115	224	13
Jim Bagby	CLE	1920	31	12	.721	2.89	340	79	73	3

Thirty-Game Winners, NL since 1900

Player	Team	Year	W	L	Pct.	ERA	IP	BB	SO	ShO
Christy Mathewson	NY	1908	37	11	.771	1.43	391	42	259	12
Joe McGinnity	NY	1904	35	8	.814	1.61	408	86	144	9
Christy Mathewson	NY	1904	33	12	.733	2.03	368	78	212	4
Grover Alexander	PHI	1916	33	12	.733	1.55	389	50	167	16
Christy Mathewson	NY	1905	31	8	.795	1.27	339	64	206	9
Grover Alexander	PHI	1915	31	10	.756	1.22	376	64	241	12
Joe McGinnity	NY	1903	31	20	.608	2.43	434	109	171	3
Dizzy Dean	STL	1934	30	7	.811	2.66	312	75	195	7
Grover Alexander	PHI	1917	30	13	.698	1.86	388	58	201	8
Christy Mathewson	NY	1903	30	13	.698	2.26	366	100	267	3

Most 20-Win Seasons

Player	Total	Player	Total
Cy Young	15	Clark Griffith	7
Christy Mathewson	13	Ferguson Jenkins	7
Warren Spahn	13	Tim Keefe	7
Walter Johnson	12	Bob Lemon	7
Kid Nichols	11	Gus Weyhing	7
Pud Galvin	10	Three Finger Brown	6
Grover Alexander	9	Steve Carlton	6
Old Hoss Radbourn	9	Bob Caruthers	6
Mickey Welch	9	Bob Feller	6
John Clarkson	8	Wes Ferrell	6
Lefty Grove	8	Juan Marichal	6
Jim McCormick	8	Deacon Phillippe	6
Joe McGinnity	8	Robin Roberts	6
Tony Mullane	8	Jack Stivetts	6
Jim Palmer	8	Jesse Tannehill	6
Eddie Plank	8	Tommy Bond	5
Amos Rusie	8	Jack Chesbro	5
Vic Willis	8	Larry Corcoran	5
Charlie Buffinton	7	Stan Coveleski	5

Most 20-Win Seasons (*cont.*)

Player	Total	Player	Total
Bob Gibson	5	George Mullin	5
Burleigh Grimes	5	Gaylord Perry	5
Carl Hubbell	5	Tom Seaver	5
Catfish Hunter	5	Hippo Vaughn	5
Silver King	5	Will White	5
Carl Mays	5	Jim Whitney	5
Sadie McMahon	5	Early Wynn	5

Undefeated Seasons (5 or more wins)

Player	Team	Year	W
Tom Zachary	NY A	1929	12
Dennis Lamp	TOR A	1985	11
Howie Krist	STL N	1941	10
Joe Pate	PHI A	1926	9
Ken Holtzman	CHI N	1967	9
Frank DiPino	STL N	1989	9
Ted Wilks	STL N	1946	8
Grant Jackson	BAL A	1973	8
Piano Legs Hickman	BOS N	1899	7
Duster Mails	CLE A	1920	7
Wes Stock	BAL A	1963	7
Mike Wallace	PHI N	1974	
	NY A	1974	7
Ed Rodriguez	MIL A	1975	7
Tom Burgmeier	BOS A	1982	7
Tom Filer	TOR A	1985	7
Roy Thomas	SEA A	1985	7
Tim Burke	MON N	1987	7
Pascual Perez	MON N	1987	7
Pete Smith	ATL N	1992	7
Earl Hamilton	PIT N	1918	6
Allyn Stout	STL N	1931	6
Max Lanier	STL N	1946	6
Freddie Martin	STL N	1949	6
Luis Aloma	CHI A	1951	6
Sandy Consuegra	WAS A	1952	6
Moe Drabowsky	BAL A	1966	6
Bob Veale	PIT N	1971	6
Fred Beene	NY A	1973	6
Tom Gorman	NY N	1984	6
Rob Murphy	CIN N	1986	6
Andy McGaffigan	MON N	1988	6
Jack Taylor	CHI N	1898	5
Archie McKain	DET A	1940	5
Bill Connelly	NY N	1952	5
Wes Stock	BAL A	1961	5

Undefeated Seasons (5 or more wins) *(cont.)*

Player	Team	Year	W
Joe Nuxhall	CIN N	1962	
	LA A	1962	5
Bill Stafford	NY A	1964	5
Fred Gladding	DET A	1966	5
Ramon Hernandez	PIT N	1972	5
Marty Bystrom	PHI N	1980	5
Odell Jones	MIL A	1988	5
Jay Tibbs	BAL A	1989	5

Most Wins, Career

Player	W	L	Player	W	L
Cy Young	511	315	Bob Gibson	251	174
Walter Johnson	416	279	Vic Willis	248	204
Christy Mathewson	373	188	Joe McGinnity	247	144
Grover Alexander	373	208	Jack Quinn	247	217
Warren Spahn	363	245	Amos Rusie	246	174
Kid Nichols	361	208	Jack Powell	245	256
Pud Galvin	361	308	Juan Marichal	243	142
Tim Keefe	342	225	Clark Griffith	240	144
Steve Carlton	329	244	Herb Pennock	240	162
Eddie Plank	327	193	Three Finger Brown	239	129
John Clarkson	326	177	Jack Morris	237	168
Don Sutton	324	256	Waite Hoyt	237	182
Nolan Ryan	319	287	Whitey Ford	236	106
Phil Niekro	318	274	Frank Tanana	233	219
Gaylord Perry	314	265	Charlie Buffinton	232	151
Old Hoss Radbourn	311	194	Will White	229	166
Tom Seaver	311	205	Luis Tiant	229	172
Mickey Welch	309	209	Sad Sam Jones	229	217
Lefty Grove	300	141	George Mullin	228	196
Early Wynn	300	244	Catfish Hunter	224	166
Tommy John	288	231	Jim Bunning	224	184
Bert Blyleven	287	250	Mel Harder	223	186
Robin Roberts	286	245	Paul Derringer	223	212
Tony Mullane	285	220	Hooks Dauss	222	182
Ferguson Jenkins	284	226	Jerry Koosman	222	209
Jim Kaat	283	237	Joe Niekro	221	204
Red Ruffing	273	225	Jerry Reuss	220	191
Burleigh Grimes	270	212	Earl Whitehill	218	185
Jim Palmer	268	152	Bob Caruthers	218	97
Bob Feller	266	162	Freddie Fitzsimmons	217	146
Eppa Rixey	266	251	Mickey Lolich	217	191
Jim McCormick	265	213	Wilbur Cooper	216	178
Gus Weyhing	264	235	Stan Coveleski	215	142
Ted Lyons	260	230	Jim Perry	215	174
Red Faber	254	213	Rick Reuschel	214	191
Carl Hubbell	253	154			

Most Wins, Career (cont.)

Player	W	L	Player	W	L
Billy Pierce	211	169	Lee Meadows	188	180
Bobo Newsom	211	222	Rick Wise	188	181
Chief Bender	210	127	Urban Shocker	187	117
Jesse Haines	210	158	Brickyard Kennedy	187	159
Vida Blue	209	161	Wild Bill Donovan	186	139
Milt Pappas	209	164	Tom Zachary	186	191
Don Drysdale	209	166	Mike Cuellar	185	130
Carl Mays	208	126	Mike Torrez	185	160
Eddie Cicotte	208	149	Dave McNally	184	119
Bob Lemon	207	128	Art Nehf	184	120
Hal Newhouser	207	150	Bill Hutchinson	184	163
Silver King	207	152	Red Ames	183	167
Jack Stivetts	204	131	Allie Reynolds	182	107
Lew Burdette	203	144	Dennis Eckersley	181	145
Al Orth	202	188	Ed Reulbach	181	105
Charlie Hough	202	191	Hippo Vaughn	178	137
Charlie Root	201	160	Larry Corcoran	177	90
Rube Marquard	201	177	John Candelaria	177	119
George Uhle	200	166	Virgil Trucks	177	135
Bob Welch	199	129	Guy Bush	176	136
Jack Chesbro	199	131	Frank Dwyer	176	152
Bucky Walters	198	160	Chick Fraser	176	213
Jesse Tannehill	197	116	Sadie McMahon	175	127
Dazzy Vance	197	140	Guy Hecker	175	146
Larry French	197	171	Dave Steib	174	132
Bob Friend	197	230	Ken Holtzman	174	150
Bob Shawkey	196	150	Camilio Pascual	174	170
Claude Osteen	196	195	Slim Salee	173	143
Ed Walsh	195	126	Murry Dickson	172	181
Sam Leever	194	101	Ed Rommel	171	119
Tommy Bridges	194	138	Ed Morris	171	123
Babe Adams	194	140	Ron Guidry	170	91
Doyle Alexander	194	174	Bill Doak	170	157
Joe Bush	194	183	Dizzy Trout	170	161
Larry Jackson	194	183	Bill Dinneen	170	176
Tommy Bond	193	115	Bill Lee (Big Bill)	169	157
Lon Warneke	193	121	Bob Forsch	168	136
Wes Ferrell	193	128	General Crowder	167	115
Dennis Martinez	193	156	Mike Flanagan	167	143
Dolph Luque	193	179	Red Donahue	167	173
Curt Simmons	193	182	Pink Hawley	167	178
Rube Waddell	191	145	Ed Lopat	166	112
Jim Whitney	191	204	Bob Buhl	166	132
Doc White	190	157	Bobby Mathews	166	138
Emil "Dutch" Leonard	190	182	Paul Splittorff	166	143
Lefty Gomez	189	102	Howard Ehmke	166	166
Deacon Phillippe	189	107	Sandy Koufax	165	87

Most Wins, Career (cont.)

Player	W	L	Player	W	L
Monte Ward	165	100	Dennis Leonard	144	106
Bill Sherdel	165	146	Ray Kremer	143	85
Mel Stottlemyre	164	139	Rip Sewell	143	97
Wilbur Wood	164	156	Bruce Hurst	143	110
Ted Breitenstein	164	169	Harry Gumbert	143	113
Frank Viola	163	137	Claude Hendrix	143	117
Nig Cuppy	162	98	Scott Sanderson	143	121
Frank Killen	162	131	Hoyt Wilhelm	143	122
Vern Law	162	147	Dwight Gooden	142	66
Claude Passeau	162	150	Johnny Allen	142	75
Earl Moore	161	153	Mike Garcia	142	97
Bump Hadley	161	165	Matt Kilroy	142	133
Addie Joss	160	97	Joe Coleman	142	135
Jack Coombs	159	110	Bert Cunningham	142	167
Schoolboy Rowe	158	101	Fernando Valenzuela	141	118
Jeff Pfeffer	158	112	Lindy McDaniel	141	119
Hal Schumacher	158	120	Sam McDowell	141	134
Curt Davis	158	131	Woodie Fryman	141	155
Steve Rogers	158	152	Sonny Siebert	140	114
Willis Hudlin	158	156	Jim Clancy	140	167
Icebox Chamberlain	157	120	Hooks Wiltse	139	90
Red Lucas	157	135	Frank Smith	139	111
Jim Lonborg	157	137	Hubert "Dutch" Leonard	139	112
Rube Benton	156	145	Johnny Sain	139	116
Rick Sutcliffe	155	125	Larry Dierker	139	123
Rube Walberg	155	141	Red Ehret	139	167
Mark Baldwin	154	165	Scott McGregor	138	108
Jouett Meekin	153	133	Dock Ellis	138	119
Jesse Barnes	153	149	Dutch Ruether	137	95
Roger Clemens	152	72	Jack Sanford	137	101
Rudy May	152	156	Fred Toney	137	102
Rick Rhoden	151	125	Joe Dobson	137	103
Burt Hooton	151	136	Harry Staley	137	119
Jack Taylor (John W.)	151	139	George Bradley	137	127
Dizzy Dean	150	83	Mike Caldwell	137	130
Don Newcombe	149	90	Harvey Haddix	136	113
Johnny Podres	148	116	Joe Nuxhall	135	117
Dave Foutz	147	66	Ray Sadecki	135	131
Firpo Marberry	147	89	Jim Maloney	134	84
Dave Stewart	146	106	Pat Malone	134	92
Ron Reed	146	140	Gerry Staley	134	111
Stan Bahnsen	146	149	Pete Donohue	134	118
Bob Knepper	146	155	Mike McCormick	134	128
Jack Billingham	145	113	Nap Rucker	134	134
Mudcat Grant	145	119	Floyd Bannister	134	143
Bill Gullickson	145	122	Steve Renko	134	146
Charlie Getzein	145	139	Howie Camnitz	133	106

Most Wins, Career (*cont.*)

Player	W	L	Player	W	L
Ray Caldwell	133	120	Mel Parnell	123	75
George Mogridge	133	130	Ad Gumbert	123	102
Fritz Peterson	133	131	Al Downing	123	107
Vic Raschi	132	66	John Denny	123	108
Harry Brecheen	132	92	Steve Gromek	123	108
Mike Moore	132	142	Danny Darwin	123	124
Danny MacFayden	132	159	Dick Ruthven	123	127
Denny McLain	131	91	Carl Erskine	122	78
Juan Pizarro	131	105	Larry Jansen	122	89
Charlie Leibrandt	131	109	Dick Donovan	122	99
Mike Boddicker	131	111	Ray Culp	122	101
Howie Pollet	131	116	Dick Rudolph	122	108
Cy Falkenberg	131	121	Pat Dobson	122	129
Harry Howell	131	146	Steve Barber	121	106
Win Mercer	131	164	Earl Wilson	121	109
Long Tom Hughes	131	174	Gary Bell	121	117
Andy Messersmith	130	99	Tully Sparks	121	138
Eldon Auker	130	101	Ed Brandt	121	146
Noodles Hahn	129	93	Bob Veale	120	95
Nellie Briles	129	112	Van Lingle Mungo	120	115
Bob Purkey	129	115	Jack Taylor (Brewery Jack)	120	117
Ned Garver	129	157	Sal Maglie	119	62
Mort Cooper	128	75	Jeff Tesreau	119	72
Dean Chance	128	115	Bill Lee (Spaceman)	119	90
Mark Langston	128	115	Bobby Shantz	119	99
Frank Lary	128	116	Milt Wilcox	119	113
Frank Kitson	128	118	Johnny Vander Meer	119	121
Preacher Roe	127	84	Bob Groom	119	150
Jim Bagby, Sr.	127	87	Ken Raffensberger	119	154
George Earnshaw	127	93	Kirby Higbe	118	101
Joaquin Andujar	127	118	Bill Singer	118	127
Lefty Tyler	127	119	Jimmy Ring	118	149
Larry Benton	127	128	John Tudor	117	72
Bob Rush	127	152	Ron Darling	117	89
Larry Gura	126	97	Goose Gossage	117	102
Johnny Antonelli	126	110	Thornton Lee	117	124
Ed Whitson	126	123	Tommy Thomas	117	128
Dan Petry	125	104	Pedro Ramos	117	160
Bob Ewing	125	118	Smoky Joe Wood	116	57
Jon Matlack	125	126	Bill Bernhard	116	82
Clarence Mitchell	125	139	Orel Hershiser	116	82
Lefty Leifield	124	96	Jimmy Key	116	89
Ross Grimsley	124	99	Larry Cheney	116	100
Gary Peters	124	103	Togie Pittinger	116	114
Doc Medich	124	105	Joel Horlen	116	117
Mike Scott	124	108	Kid Carsey	116	138
Mike Krukow	124	117	Earl Hamilton	116	147

Most Wins, Career (*cont.*)

Player	W	L	Player	W	L
Bruce Kison	115	88	J. R. Richard	107	71
Bob Stanley	115	97	Steve Stone	107	93
Dummy Taylor	115	106	Ralph Terry	107	99
Dick Ellsworth	115	137	Jim Scott	107	113
Billy Rhines	114	103	Chuck Stobbs	107	130
Marty Pattin	114	109	Bob Harmon	107	133
Bill Monboquette	114	112	Orval Overall	106	71
Ken Forsch	114	113	Bryn Smith	106	90
Mike Witt	114	114	Whit Wyatt	106	95
Fritz Ostermueller	114	115	Fred Frankhouse	106	97
Rollie Fingers	114	118	Dick Farrell	106	111
Sherry Smith	114	118	Bob Smith	106	139
Hal Carlson	114	120	Flint Rhem	105	97
Toad Ramsey	114	124	Billy O'Dell	105	100
Ron Kline	114	144	Stu Miller	105	103
Tom Browning	113	80	Reggie Cleveland	105	106
Bret Saberhagen	113	83	Bud Black	105	110
Tony Cloninger	113	97	Jim Tobin	105	112
Bob Ojeda	113	97	Casey Patten	105	127
Dave Goltz	113	109	Mark Gubicza	104	92
Fred Goldsmith	112	67	Don Wilson	104	92
Sam Gray	112	115	Roy Face	104	95
Syl Johnson	112	117	Fred Norman	104	103
Watty Clark	111	97	Ray Herbert	104	107
Jim Bibby	111	101	George Blaeholder	104	125
Geoff Zahn	111	109	Sid Hudson	104	152
Bill Hands	111	110	Ernie Bonham	103	72
Richard Dotson	111	113	Steve Blass	103	76
Shane Rawley	111	118	Johnny Morrison	103	80
Walt Terrell	111	124	Jim Rooker	103	109
Gary Nolan	110	70	Jim Scott	103	109
Ed Stein	110	78	Dave Roberts	103	125
Jack Lynch	110	105	Willie Sudhoff	103	136
Spud Chandler	109	43	Doc Crandall	102	62
Don Gullett	109	50	Ellis Kinder	102	71
Storm Davis	109	84	George Pipgras	102	73
Jim Hearn	109	89	Ed Killian	102	78
Stan Williams	109	94	Jumbo McGinnis	102	78
Don Robinson	109	106	Bill Hallahan	102	94
Denny Galehouse	109	118	Ed Willett	102	99
Hank Borowy	108	82	Sam Jones (Toothpick)	102	101
Rip Collins	108	82	Don Cardwell	102	138
Max Lanier	108	82	Don Mossi	101	80
Bob Shaw	108	98	Bob Turley	101	85
Dick Drago	108	117	Eric Show	101	89
Bill Dietrich	108	128	Duke Esper	101	100
Ray Burris	108	134	Jim Barr	101	112

Most Wins, Career (cont.)

Player	W	L
Alex Kellner	101	112
Johnny Klippstein	101	118
Ray Benge	101	130
Si Johnson	101	165
Monte Pearson	100	61
Tex Carleton	100	76
Moose Haas	100	83
George Suggs	100	90
Mario Soto	100	92
Dave Giusti	100	93
Dick Tidrow	100	94
Lefty Stewart	100	98
Clyde Wright	100	111
Randy Jones	100	123
Rick Honeycutt	100	135
Stump Weidman	100	156

Most Losses, Career

Player	L
Cy Young	315
Pud Galvin	308
Nolan Ryan	287
Walter Johnson	279
Phil Niekro	274
Gaylord Perry	265
Jack Powell	256
Don Sutton	256
Bert Blyleven	250
Eppa Rixey	251
Robin Roberts	245
Warren Spahn	245

The 300-Win Club

Player	W	L	ERA	ShO	SO
Cy Young	511	315	2.63	76	2796
Walter Johnson	416	279	2.17	110	3508
Christy Mathewson	373	188	2.13	80	2502
Grover Alexander	373	208	2.56	90	2199
Warren Spahn	363	245	3.09	63	2583
Kid Nichols	361	208	2.94	48	1877
Pud Galvin	361	308	2.87	57	1799
Tim Keefe	342	225	2.62	40	2527
Steve Carlton	329	244	3.22	55	4136
Eddie Plank	327	193	2.34	69	2246
John Clarkson	326	177	2.81	37	1978
Don Sutton	324	256	3.26	58	3574
Nolan Ryan	319	287	3.17	61	5668
Phil Niekro	318	274	3.35	45	3342
Gaylord Perry	314	265	3.10	53	3534
Old Hoss Radbourn	311	194	2.67	35	1830
Tom Seaver	311	205	2.86	61	3640
Mickey Welch	308	209	2.71	40	1850
Lefty Grove	300	141	3.06	35	2266
Early Wynn	300	244	3.54	49	2334

Most Wins by Age, Season, AL

Player	Team	Year	Age	W
Bob Feller	CLE	1936	17	5
	CLE	1937	18	9
Wally Bunker	BAL	1964	19	19
Bob Feller	CLE	1939	20	24

Most Wins by Age, Season, AL (cont.)

Player	Team	Year	Age	W
	CLE	1940	21	27
Smoky Joe Wood	BOS	1912	22	34
Hal Newhouser	DET	1944	23	29
Walter Johnson	WAS	1912	24	32
	WAS	1913	25	36
Ed Walsh	CHI	1908	26	40
Walter Johnson	WAS	1915	27	27
George Uhle	CLE	1926	27	27
George Mullin	DET	1909	28	29
Walter Johnson	WAS	1916	29	25
Jack Chesbro	NY	1904	30	41
Lefty Grove	PHI	1931	31	31
Jim Bagby	CLE	1920	32	31
Eddie Cicotte	CHI	1917	33	28
Cy Young	BOS	1901	34	33
	BOS	1902	35	32
	BOS	1903	36	28
	BOS	1904	37	26
	BOS	1905	38	18
Early Wynn	CHI	1959	39	22
Cy Young	BOS	1907	40	21
	BOS	1908	41	21
	CLE	1909	42	19
Jack Quinn	PHI	1927	43	15
	PHI	1928	44	18
Phil Niekro	NY	1984	45	16
	NY	1985	46	16
	CLE	1986	47	11
	CLE	1987	48	7

Most Wins by Age, Season, NL Since 1900

Player	Team	Year	Age	W
Mike McCormick	NY	1957	18	3
Dwight Gooden	NY	1984	19	17
	NY	1985	20	24
Rube Marquard	NY	1911	21	24
Christy Mathewson	NY	1903	22	30
	NY	1904	23	33
	NY	1905	24	31
Robin Roberts	PHI	1952	25	28
Vic Willis	BOS	1902	26	27
Dick Rudolph	BOS	1914	26	27
Christy Mathewson	NY	1908	27	37
Grover Alexander	PHI	1915	28	31
	PHI	1916	29	33
	PHI	1917	30	30
Three Finger Brown	CHI	1908	31	29

Most Wins by Age, Season, NL Since 1900 (*cont.*)

Player	Team	Year	Age	W
Joe McGinnity	NY	1903	32	31
	NY	1904	33	35
Burleigh Grimes	PIT	1928	34	25
Joe McGinnity	NY	1906	35	27
Grover Alexander	CHI	1923	36	22
Steve Carlton	PHI	1982	37	23
Warren Spahn	MIL	1959	38	21
	MIL	1960	39	21
Grover Alexander	STL	1927	40	21
Warren Spahn	MIL	1961	40	21
Phil Niekro	ATL	1979	40	21
Warren Spahn	MIL	1962	41	18
	MIL	1963	42	23
Phil Niekro	ATL	1982	43	17
	ATL	1983	44	11
Dolph Luque	NY	1935	45	1
Hoyt Wilhelm	ATL	1969	46	2
	ATL	1970		
	CHI	1970	47	6
Jack Quinn	BKN	1932	48	3

Most Strikeouts, Season, AL

Player	Team	Year	SO
Nolan Ryan	CAL	1973	383
	CAL	1974	367
Rube Waddell	PHI	1904	349
Bob Feller	CLE	1946	348
Nolan Ryan	CAL	1977	341
	CAL	1972	329
	CAL	1976	327
Sam McDowell	CLE	1965	325
Walter Johnson	WAS	1910	313
Mickey Lolich	DET	1971	308
Sam McDowell	CLE	1970	304
Walter Johnson	WAS	1912	303
Rube Waddell	PHI	1903	302
Vida Blue	OAK	1971	301
Nolan Ryan	TEX	1989	301
Roger Clemens	BOS	1988	291
Rube Waddell	PHI	1905	287
Sam McDowell	CLE	1968	283
Denny McLain	DET	1968	280
Sam McDowell	CLE	1969	279
Hal Newhouser	DET	1946	275
Mickey Lolich	DET	1969	271
Ed Walsh	CHI	1908	269

Most Strikeouts, Season, AL (*cont.*)

Player	Team	Year	SO
Frank Tanana	CAL	1975	269
Luis Tiant	CLE	1968	264
Herb Score	CLE	1956	263
Mark Langston	SEA	1987	262
Bob Feller	CLE	1940	261
Frank Tanana	CAL	1976	261
Bob Feller	CLE	1941	260
Nolan Ryan	CAL	1978	260
Ed Walsh	CHI	1910	258
Smoky Joe Wood	BOS	1912	258
Bert Blyleven	MIN	1973	258
Roger Clemens	BOS	1987	256
Ed Walsh	CHI	1911	255
	CHI	1912	254
Mickey Lolich	DET	1972	250
Bert Blyleven	MIN	1974	249
Ron Guidry	NY	1978	248
Bob Feller	CLE	1939	246
Jim Lonborg	BOS	1967	246
Herb Score	CLE	1955	245
Mark Langston	SEA	1986	245
Dennis Leonard	KC	1977	244
Walter Johnson	WAS	1913	243
Bill Singer	CAL	1973	241
Roger Clemens	BOS	1991	241
Randy Johnson	SEA	1992	241
Bob Feller	CLE	1938	240
Ted Higuera	MIL	1987	240
Jack Chesbro	NY	1904	239
Gaylord Perry	CLE	1973	238
Roger Clemens	BOS	1986	238
Sam McDowell	CLE	1967	236
Joe Coleman	DET	1971	236
Mark Langston	SEA	1988	235
Dean Chance	MIN	1968	234
Gaylord Perry	CLE	1972	234
Bert Blyleven	MIN	1975	233
Gaylord Perry	CLE		
	TEX	1975	233
Rube Waddell	PHI	1907	232
	PHI	1908	232
Nolan Ryan	TEX	1990	232
Smoky Joe Wood	BOS	1911	231
Mickey Lolich	DET	1970	230
Roger Clemens	BOS	1989	230
Walter Johnson	WAS	1916	228
Bert Blyleven	MIN	1972	228

Most Strikeouts, Season, AL (*cont.*)

Player	Team	Year	SO
Randy Johnson	SEA	1991	228
Bobo Newsom	STL	1938	226
Mickey Lolich	DET	1965	226
Walter Johnson	WAS	1914	225
Sam McDowell	CLE	1966	225
Ferguson Jenkins	TEX	1974	225
Jack Coombs	PHI	1910	224
Bert Blyleven	MIN	1971	224
Nolan Ryan	CAL	1979	223
Jack Morris	DET	1986	223
Charlie Hough	TEX	1987	223
Joe Coleman	DET	1972	222
Camilo Pascual	MIN	1961	221
Bobby Witt	TEX	1990	221
Dean Chance	MIN	1967	220
Luis Tiant	CLE	1967	219
Bert Blyleven	TEX	1976	219
Melido Perez	NY	1992	218
Al Downing	NY	1964	217
Gaylord Perry	CLE	1974	216
Gary Peters	CHI	1967	215
Bert Blyleven	MIN	1986	215
Mickey Lolich	DET	1973	214
Camilo Pascual	MIN	1964	213
Hal Newhouser	DET	1945	212
Jim Kaat	MIN	1967	211
Andy Messersmith	CAL	1969	211
Erik Hanson	SEA	1990	211
Rube Waddell	PHI	1902	210
Eddie Plank	PHI	1905	210
Cy Young	BOS	1905	210
Bob Turley	NY	1955	210
Wilbur Wood	CHI	1971	210
Russ Ford	NY	1910	209
Lefty Grove	PHI	1930	209
Whitey Ford	NY	1961	209
Tom Bradley	CHI	1972	209
Floyd Bannister	SEA	1982	209
Roger Clemens	BOS	1990	209
Mike Witt	CAL	1986	208
Jack Morris	DET	1987	208
Roger Clemens	BOS	1992	208
Walter Johnson	WAS	1911	207
Dean Chance	LA	1964	207
Ted Higuera	MIL	1986	207
Ed Walsh	CHI	1907	206
Camilo Pascual	MIN	1962	206

Most Strikeouts, Season, AL (cont.)

Player	Team	Year	SO
Bob Johnson	KC	1970	206
Tom Bradley	CHI	1971	206
Luis Tiant	BOS	1973	206
Bert Blyleven	CLE		
	MIN	1985	206
Gary Peters	CHI	1964	205
Jim Kaat	MIN	1966	205
Frank Tanana	CAL	1977	205
Dave Stewart	OAK	1987	205
Dave Boswell	MIN	1967	204
Walter Johnson	WAS	1915	203
Nolan Ryan	TEX	1991	203
Jack Powell	NY	1904	202
Camilo Pascual	MIN	1963	202
Dave McNally	BAL	1968	202
Joe Coleman	DET	1973	202
Mickey Lolich	DET	1974	202
Mark Langston	SEA	1984	202
Kirk McCaskill	CAL	1986	202
Eddie Plank	PHI	1904	201
Jim Bunning	DET	1959	201
	DET	1960	201
Ron Guidry	NY	1979	201
Cy Young	BOS	1904	200
Earl Wilson	BOS		
	DET	1966	200
Dennis Eckersley	CLE	1976	200

Most Strikeouts, Season, NL since 1900

Player	Team	Year	SO
Sandy Koufax	LA	1965	382
	LA	1966	317
J. R. Richard	HOU	1979	313
Steve Carlton	PHI	1972	310
Sandy Koufax	LA	1963	306
Mike Scott	HOU	1986	306
J. R. Richard	HOU	1978	303
Tom Seaver	NY	1971	289
Steve Carlton	PHI	1980	286
	PHI	1982	286
Tom Seaver	NY	1970	283
Bob Veale	PIT	1965	276
Dwight Gooden	NY	1984	276
Steve Carlton	PHI	1983	275
Bob Gibson	STL	1970	274
Ferguson Jenkins	CHI	1970	274

Most Strikeouts, Season, NL since 1900 (*cont.*)

Player	Team	Year	SO
Mario Soto	CIN	1982	274
Ferguson Jenkins	CHI	1969	273
Bob Gibson	STL	1965	270
Nolan Ryan	HOU	1987	270
Sandy Koufax	LA	1961	269
Bob Gibson	STL	1969	269
Jim Bunning	PHI	1965	268
Bob Gibson	STL	1968	268
Dwight Gooden	NY	1985	268
Christy Mathewson	NY	1903	267
Jim Maloney	CIN	1963	265
Ferguson Jenkins	CHI	1971	263
Dazzy Vance	BKN	1924	262
Phil Niekro	ATL	1977	262
Ferguson Jenkins	CHI	1968	260
Christy Mathewson	NY	1908	259
Jim Bunning	PHI	1967	253
	PHI	1966	252
Don Drysdale	LA	1963	251
Bill Stoneman	MON	1971	251
Tom Seaver	NY	1973	251
Bob Veale	PIT	1964	250
Tom Seaver	NY	1972	249
Juan Marichal	SF	1963	248
Phil Niekro	ATL	1978	248
Bill Singer	LA	1969	247
Don Drysdale	LA	1960	246
Bob Gibson	STL	1964	245
Nolan Ryan	HOU	1982	245
Jim Maloney	CIN	1965	244
Tom Seaver	NY	1975	243
Don Drysdale	LA	1959	242
Mario Soto	CIN	1983	242
Fernando Valenzuela	LA	1986	242
Grover Alexander	PHI	1915	241
David Cone	NY	1991	241
Juan Marichal	SF	1965	240
Steve Carlton	PHI	1974	240
Fernando Valenzuela	LA	1984	240
Noodles Hahn	CIN	1901	239
Van Lingle Mungo	BKN	1936	238
Rube Marquard	NY	1911	237
Don Drysdale	LA	1964	237
Chris Short	PHI	1965	237
Ferguson Jenkins	CHI	1967	236
Don Wilson	HOU	1969	235
Tom Seaver	NY	1976	235

Most Strikeouts, Season, NL since 1900 (cont.)

Player	Team	Year	SO
Gaylord Perry	SF	1969	233
Mike Scott	HOU	1987	233
David Cone	NY	1990	233
Don Drysdale	LA	1962	232
Larry Dierker	HOU	1969	232
Clay Kirby	SD	1971	231
Gaylord Perry	SF	1967	230
Bob Veale	PIT	1966	229
Nolan Ryan	HOU	1988	228
Grover Alexander	PHI	1911	227
Bill Singer	LA	1968	227
Wild Bill Donovan	BKN	1901	226
Tom Seaver	CIN	1978	226
Long Tom Hughes	CHI	1901	225
Vic Willis	BOS	1902	225
Sam Jones	STL	1958	225
Bob Gibson	STL	1966	225
Sandy Koufax	LA	1964	223
Steve Carlton	PHI	1973	223
Dwight Gooden	NY	1990	223
Ramon Martinez	LA	1990	223
Juan Marichal	SF	1966	222
Christy Mathewson	NY	1901	221
Dazzy Vance	BKN	1925	221
Andy Messersmith	LA	1974	221
Jim Bunning	PHI	1964	219
Juan Marichal	SF	1967	218
Don Sutton	LA	1969	217
Sandy Koufax	LA	1962	216
Jim Maloney	CIN	1966	216
John Montefusco	SF	1975	215
John Smoltz	ATL	1992	215
Grover Alexander	PHI	1914	214
Jim Maloney	CIN	1964	214
Gaylord Perry	SF	1970	214
J. R. Richard	HOU	1976	214
	HOU	1977	214
Mario Soto	CIN	1985	214
David Cone	NY	1992	214
Bob Veale	PIT	1969	213
Andy Messersmith	LA	1975	213
Steve Carlton	PHI	1979	213
David Cone	NY	1988	213
Christy Mathewson	NY	1904	212
Tony Cloninger	MIL	1965	211
Don Drysdale	LA	1965	210
Steve Carlton	STL	1969	210

Most Strikeouts, Season, NL since 1900 (*cont.*)

Player	Team	Year	SO
Sam Jones	SF	1959	209
Don Sutton	LA	1966	209
Nolan Ryan	HOU	1985	209
Bob Gibson	STL	1962	208
Tom Seaver	NY	1969	208
Bob Gibson	STL	1972	208
Phil Niekro	ATL	1979	208
Fernando Valenzuela	LA	1985	208
Jose DeLeon	STL	1988	208
Don Sutton	LA	1972	207
Christy Mathewson	NY	1905	206
Juan Marichal	SF	1964	206
Gary Nolan	CIN	1967	206
Ray Sadecki	SF	1968	206
Steve Rogers	MON	1977	206
Orval Overall	CHI	1909	205
Stan Williams	LA	1961	205
Tom Seaver	NY	1968	205
Juan Marichal	SF	1969	205
Jon Matlack	NY	1973	205
Bob Gibson	STL	1963	204
Dick Farrell	HOU	1962	203
Mike Cuellar	HOU	1967	203
Johnny Vander Meer	CIN	1941	202
Chris Short	PHI	1968	202
Ken Holtzman	CHI	1970	202
Floyd Youmans	MON	1986	202
Nap Rucker	BKN	1909	201
Grover Alexander	PHI	1917	201
Gaylord Perry	SF	1966	201
Don Sutton	LA	1970	201
Tom Seaver	NY	1974	201
Jose DeLeon	STL	1989	201
Dazzy Vance	BKN	1928	200
Tom Griffin	HOU	1969	200
Don Sutton	LA	1973	200
Jerry Koosman	NY	1976	200
Nolan Ryan	HOU	1980	200
Sid Fernandez	NY	1986	200
Dwight Gooden	NY	1986	200
Tim Belcher	LA	1989	200

Most Strikeouts, Season before 1900

Player	Team	Year	SO
Matt Kilroy	BAL AA	1886	513
Toad Ramsey	LOU AA	1886	499

Most Strikeouts, Season before 1900 (*cont.*)

Player	Team	Year	SO
One Arm Daily	CHI U		
	PIT U		
	WAS U	1884	483
Dupee Shaw	DET N		
	BOS U	1884	451
Old Hoss Radbourn	PRO N	1884	441
Charlie Buffinton	BOS N	1884	417
Guy Hecker	LOU AA	1884	385
Bill Sweeney	BAL U	1884	374
Pud Galvin	BUF N	1884	369
Mark Baldwin	COL AA	1889	368
Tim Keefe	NY AA	1883	361
Charlie Sweeney	PRO N		
	STL U	1884	360
Toad Ramsey	LOU AA	1887	355
Hardie Henderson	BAL AA	1884	346
Jim Whitney	BOS N	1883	345
Mickey Welch	NY N	1884	345
Amos Rusie	NY N	1890	341
Jim McCormick	CLE N		
	CIN U	1884	343
Amos Rusie	NY N	1891	337
Tony Mullane	TOL AA	1884	334
Tim Keefe	NY N	1888	333
Ed Morris	PIT AA	1886	326
Tim Keefe	NY N	1884	323
Lady Baldwin	DET N	1886	323
Bill Hutchinson	CHI N	1892	316
Old Hoss Radbourn	PRO N	1883	315
John Clarkson	CHI N	1886	313
	CHI N	1884	308
Larry McKeon	IND AA	1884	308
Ed Morris	COL AA	1884	302

Most Strikeouts, Season, Other Leagues, since 1900

Player	Team	Year	SO
Cy Falkenberg	IND F	1914	236
Dave Davenport	STL F	1915	229
Earl Mosely	IND F	1914	205

Four Strikeouts in One Inning, AL

Player	Team	Date	Inn.	Opp.	Opp. Batters
Walter Johnson	WAS	Apr 15, 1911	5	BOS	Ray Collins
	WAS			BOS	Larry Gardner
	WAS			BOS	Harry Hooper

Four Strikeouts in One Inning, AL (cont.)

Player	Team	Date	Inn.	Opp.	Opp. Batters
	WAS			BOS	Duffy Lewis
Guy Morton	CLE	Jun 11, 1916	6	PHI	Whitey Witt
	CLE			PHI	Charlie Pick
	CLE			PHI	Nap Lajoie
	CLE			PHI	Stuffy McInnis
Ryne Duren	LA	May 18, 1961	7	CHI	Minnie Minoso
	LA			CHI	Roy Sievers
	LA			CHI	J. C. Martin
	LA			CHI	Sammy Esposito
Lee Stange	CLE	Sep 2, 1964	7	WAS	Don Lock
	CLE			WAS	Willie Kirkland
	CLE			WAS	Mike Brumley
	CLE			WAS	Don Zimmer
Mike Cuellar	BAL	May 29, 1970	4	CAL	Alex Johnson
	BAL			CAL	Ken McMullen
	BAL			CAL	Tommie Reynolds
	BAL			CAL	Jim Spencer
Mike Paxton	CLE	Jul 21, 1978	5	SEA	Bruce Bochte
	CLE			SEA	Tom Paciorek
	CLE			SEA	Dan Meyer
	CLE			SEA	Bill Stein
Bobby Witt	TEX	Aug 2, 1987	2	BAL	Ray Knight
	TEX			BAL	Terry Kennedy
	TEX			BAL	Mike Young
	TEX			BAL	Ken Gerhart
Charlie Hough	TEX	Jul 4, 1988	1	NY	Claudell Washington
	TEX			NY	Jack Clark
	TEX			NY	Dave Winfield
	TEX			NY	Mike Pagliarulo
Matt Young	SEA	Sep 9, 1990	1	BOS	Jody Reed
	SEA			BOS	Carlos Quintana
	SEA			BOS	Wade Boggs
	SEA			BOS	Mike Greenwell

Four Strikeouts in One Inning, NL

Player	Team	Date	Inn.	Opp.	Opp. Batters
Cannonball Crane	NY	Oct 4, 1888	5	CHI	Fred Pfeffer
	NY			CHI	Ned Williamson
	NY			CHI	Tom Burns
	NY			CHI	John Tener
Hooks Wiltse	NY	May 15, 1906	5	CIN	Jim Delahanty
	NY			CIN	Tommy Corcoran
	NY			CIN	Admiral Schlei

Four Strikeouts in One Inning, NL (*cont.*)

Player	Team	Date	Inn.	Opp.	Opp. Batters
	NY			CIN	Chick Fraser
Jim Davis	CHI	May 27, 1956	6	STL	Hal Smith
	CHI			STL	Jackie Brandt
	CHI			STL	Lindy McDaniel
	CHI			STL	Don Blasingame
Joe Nuxhall	CIN	Aug 11, 1959	6	MIL	Eddie Mathews
	CIN			MIL	Joe Adcock
	CIN			MIL	Del Crandall
	CIN			MIL	Johnny Logan
Pete Richert	LA	Apr 12, 1962	3	CIN	Frank Robinson
	LA			CIN	Gordy Coleman
	LA			CIN	Wally Post
	LA			CIN	Johnny Edwards
Don Drysdale	LA	Apr 17, 1965	2	PHI	Wes Covington
	LA			PHI	Tony Gonzalez
	LA			PHI	Dick Stuart
	LA			PHI	Clay Dalrymple
Bob Gibson	STL	Jun 7, 1966	4	PIT	Jerry Lynch
	STL			PIT	Jim Pagliaroni
	STL			PIT	Bill Mazeroski
	STL			PIT	Don Cardwell
Bill Bonham	CHI	Jul 31, 1974	2	MON	Mike Torrez
	CHI			MON	Ron Hunt
	CHI			MON	Tim Foli
	CHI			MON	Willie Davis
Phil Niekro	ATL	Jul 29, 1977	6	PIT	Dave Parker
	ATL			PIT	Bill Robinson
	ATL			PIT	Rennie Stennett
	ATL			PIT	Omar Moreno
Mario Soto	CIN	May 17, 1984	3	CHI	Tom Veryzer
	CIN			CHI	Dick Ruthven
	CIN			CHI	Bob Dernier
	CIN			CHI	Ryne Sandberg
Mike Scott	HOU	Sep 3, 1986	5	CHI	Chris Speier
	HOU			CHI	Chico Walker
	HOU			CHI	Dave Martinez
	HOU			CHI	Ryne Sandberg
Paul Assenmacher	ATL	Aug 22, 1989	5	STL	Terry Pendleton
	ATL			STL	Milt Thompson
	ATL			STL	Tony Pena
	ATL			STL	Ted Power
Tim Birtsas	CIN	Jun 4, 1990	7	SF	Greg Litton
	CIN			SF	Will Clark
	CIN			SF	Matt Williams
	CIN			SF	Gary Carter

Perfect Innings, AL (3 strikeouts on 9 pitches)

Player	Team	Date	Inn.	Opp.
Rube Waddell	PHI	Jul 1, 1902	3	BAL
Sloppy Thurston	CHI	Aug 22, 1923	12	PHI
Lefty Grove	PHI	Aug 23, 1928	2	CLE
	PHI	Sep 27, 1928	7	CHI
Jim Bunning	DET	Aug 2, 1959	9	BOS
Al Downing	NY	Aug 11, 1967	2	CLE
Nolan Ryan	CAL	Jul 9, 1972	2	BOS
Ron Guidry	NY	Aug 7, 1984	9	CHI

Perfect Innings, NL (3 strikeouts on 9 pitches)

Player	Team	Date	Inn.	Opp.
Pat Ragan	BKN	Oct 5, 1914	8	BOS
Hod Eller	CIN	Aug 21, 1917	9	NY
Joe Oeschger	BOS	Sep 8, 1921	4	PHI
Dazzy Vance	BKN	Sep 14, 1924	3	CHI
Sandy Koufax	LA	Jun 30, 1962	1	NY
	LA	Apr 18, 1964	3	CIN
Bob Bruce	HOU	Apr 19, 1964	8	STL
Nolan Ryan	NY	Apr 19, 1968	3	LA
Bob Gibson	STL	May 12, 1969	7	LA
Lynn McGlothen	STL	Aug 19, 1975	2	CIN
Bruce Sutter	CHI	Sep 8, 1977	9	STL
Jeff Robinson	PIT	Sep 7, 1987	8	CHI
Andy Ashby	PHI	Jun 15, 1991	4	CIN
David Cone	NY	Aug 30, 1991	5	CIN
Pete Harnisch	HOU	Sep 6, 1991	7	PHI
Trevor Wilson	SF	Jun 7, 1992	9	HOU

Most Strikeouts, Career

Player	SO	Best	Year	300+	200+	Led Lg.
Nolan Ryan	5668	383	1973	6	15	11
Steve Carlton	4136	310	1972	1	8	5
Bert Blyleven	3701	258	1973		8	1
Tom Seaver	3640	289	1971		10	5
Don Sutton	3574	217	1969		5	
Gaylord Perry	3534	238	1973		8	
Walter Johnson	3508	313	1910	2	7	12
Phil Niekro	3342	262	1977		3	1
Ferguson Jenkins	3192	274	1970		6	1
Bob Gibson	3117	274	1970		9	1
Jim Bunning	3433	268	1965		6	3
Mickey Lolich	2832	308	1971	1	7	1
Cy Young	2796	210	1905		2	2
Frank Tanana	2657	269	1975		3	1
Warren Spahn	2583	191	1950			4
Bob Feller	2581	348	1946	1	5	7
Jerry Koosman	2556	200	1976		1	

Most Strikeouts, Career (cont.)

Player	SO	Best	Year	300+	200+	Led Lg.
Tim Keefe	2527	361	1883	3	6	2
Christy Mathewson	2502	267	1903		5	5
Don Drysdale	2486	251	1963		6	3
Jim Kaat	2461	211	1967		2	
Sam McDowell	2453	325	1965	2	6	5
Luis Tiant	2416	264	1968		3	
Sandy Koufax	2396	382	1965	3	6	4
Robin Roberts	2357	198	1953			2
Early Wynn	2334	184	1957			2
Rube Waddell	2316	349	1904	2	5	7
Juan Marichal	2303	248	1963		6	
Jack Morris	2275	232	1983		3	1
Lefty Grove	2266	209	1930		1	7
Eddie Plank	2246	210	1905		2	
Tommy John	2245	138	1966,70			
Jim Palmer	2212	199	1970			
Grover Alexander	2199	241	1915		4	5
Vida Blue	2175	301	1971	1	1	
Charlie Hough	2171	223	1987		1	
Camilo Pascual	2167	221	1961		4	3
Dennis Eckersley	2118	200	1976		1	
Bobo Newsom	2082	226	1938		1	1
Dazzy Vance	2045	262	1924		3	7
Rick Reuschel	2015	168	1973			
Catfish Hunter	2012	196	1967			

Most Strikeouts in Nine-Inning Game, AL

Player	Team	Date	SO	Opp.
Roger Clemens	BOS	Apr 29, 1986	20	SEA
Nolan Ryan	CAL	Aug 12, 1974	19	BOS
Bob Feller	CLE	Oct 2, 1938	18	DET
Nolan Ryan	CAL	Sep 10, 1976	18	CHI
Ron Guidry	NY	Jun 17, 1978	18	CAL
Randy Johnson	SEA	Sep 27, 1992	18	TEX
Bob Feller	CLE	Sep 13, 1936	17	PHI
Bill Monbouquette	BOS	May 12, 1961	17	WAS
Nolan Ryan	CAL	Sep 30, 1972	17	MIN
	CAL	Jul 15, 1973	17	DET
Frank Tanana	CAL	Jun 21, 1975	17	TEX
Rube Waddell	STL	Jul 29, 1908	16	PHI
Bob Feller	CLE	Aug 25, 1937	16	BOS
Jack Harshman	CHI	Jul 25, 1954	16	BOS
Herb Score	CLE	May 1, 1955	16	BOS
Luis Tiant	CLE	Aug 22, 1967	16	CAL
Sam McDowell	CLE	May 1, 1968	16	OAK
Luis Tiant	CLE	Sep 9, 1968	16	MIN

Most Strikeouts in Nine-Inning Game, AL (cont.)

Player	Team	Date	SO	Opp.
Mickey Lolich	DET	May 23, 1969	16	CAL
	DET	Jun 9, 1969	16	SEA
Nolan Ryan	CAL	Jul 1, 1972	16	OAK
	CAL	Jul 9, 1972	16	BOS
Rudy May	CAL	Aug 10, 1972	16	MIN
Nolan Ryan	CAL	Jun 9, 1979	16	DET
Mike Witt	CAL	Jul 23, 1984	16	SEA
Jose Rijo	OAK	Apr 19, 1986	16	SEA
Nolan Ryan	TEX	Apr 26, 1990	16	CHI
	TEX	May 1, 1991	16	TOR
Rube Waddell	PHI	Jun 16, 1902	15	DET
Fred Glade	STL	Jul 15, 1904	15	WAS
Ed Walsh	CHI	Oct 2, 1908	15	CLE
	CHI	Aug 11, 1910	15	BOS
Smoky Joe Wood	BOS	Jul 29, 1911	15	STL
Jack Coombs	PHI	May 18, 1912	15	CHI
Jim Scott	CHI	Jun 22, 1913	15	STL
Eddie Cicotte	CHI	Aug 26, 1914	15	NY
Bob Shawkey	NY	Sep 27, 1919	15	PHI
Lefty Grove	PHI	Aug 23, 1928	15	CLE
Bob Feller	CLE	Aug 23, 1936	15	STL
Herb Score	CLE	May 19, 1956	15	WAS
Paul Foytack	DET	Jul 28, 1956	15	WAS
Camilo Pascual	WAS	Apr 18, 1960	15	BOS
	MIN	Jul 19, 1961	15	LA
Dean Chance	LA	Jun 2, 1963	15	BOS
Sonny Siebert	CLE	Jun 17, 1965	15	WAS
Pedro Ramos	CLE	Jul 31, 1963	15	LA
Jorge Rubio	CAL	Oct 2, 1966	15	CLE
Sam McDowell	CLE	Jul 12, 1968	15	OAK
	CLE	May 6, 1970	15	CHI
	CLE	Jul 6, 1970	15	WAS
Nolan Ryan	CAL	Sep 12, 1972	15	TEX
Mickey Lolich	DET	Oct 3, 1972	15	BOS
Joe Decker	MIN	Jun 26, 1973	15	CHI
Nolan Ryan	CAL	Apr 30, 1974	15	BOS
	CAL	Sep 28, 1974	15	MIN
Frank Tanana	CAL	Jun 30, 1975	15	MIN
Nolan Ryan	CAL	Jun 19, 1976	15	BOS
	CAL	May 6, 1977	15	BOS
	CAL	Apr 24, 1978	15	SEA
Jerry Koosman	MIN	Jun 23, 1980	15	KC
Roger Clemens	BOS	Aug 21, 1984	15	KC
Mark Langston	SEA	Jul 25, 1986	15	CLE
Bert Blyleven	MIN	Aug 1, 1986	15	OAK
Greg Swindell	CLE	May 10, 1987	15	KC
Roger Clemens	BOS	Jul 9, 1988	15	CHI

Most Strikeouts in Nine-Inning Game, AL (cont.)

Player	Team	Date	SO	Opp.
Nolan Ryan	TEX	Apr 12, 1989	15	MIL
Chuck Finley	CAL	Jun 24, 1989	15	BAL
Nolan Ryan	TEX	Aug 17, 1990	15	CHI
Randy Johnson	SEA	Aug 16, 1992	15	CAL

Most Strikeouts in Extra-Inning Game, AL

Player	Team	Date	SO	Inns.	Opp.
Tom Cheney	WAS	Sep 12, 1962	21	16	BOS
Luis Tiant	CLE	Jul 3, 1968	19	10	MIN
Nolan Ryan	CAL	Jun 14, 1974	19	12	BOS
	CAL	Aug 20, 1974	19	11	DET
	CAL	Jun 8, 1977	19	10	TOR
Jack Coombs	PHI	Sep 1, 1906	18	24	BOS
Rube Waddell	PHI	Sep 5, 1905	17	13	BOS
	STL	Sep 20, 1908	17	10	WAS
Vida Blue	OAK	Jul 9, 1971	17	11	CAL
Nolan Ryan	CAL	Aug 18, 1975	17	17	DET
Rube Waddell	PHI	Jul 9, 1902	16	17	BOS
	PHI	Apr 21, 1904	16	12	NY
	PHI	Oct 18, 1905	16	12	STL
Walter Johnson	WAS	Jul 25, 1913	16	11	STL
Nolan Ryan	CAL	Sep 27, 1973	16	11	MIN
Walter Johnson	WAS	Jul 25, 1913	16	11	STL
Rube Waddell	PHI	Aug 19, 1904	15	11	CLE
	PHI	May 29, 1907	15	12	BOS
Mickey McDermott	BOS	Jul 28, 1951	15	16	CLE
Sam McDowell	CLE	Jun 5, 1965	15	10	DET
Frank Tanana	CAL	Sep 6, 1976	15	10	OAK

Most Strikeouts in Nine-Inning Game, NL

Player	Team	Date	SO	Opp.
Charlie Sweeney	PRO	Jun 7, 1884	19	BOS
Steve Carlton	STL	Sep 15, 1969	19	NY
Tom Seaver	NY	Apr 22, 1970	19	SD
David Cone	NY	Oct 6, 1991	19	PHI
Sandy Koufax	LA	Aug 31, 1959	18	SF
	LA	Apr 24, 1962	18	CHI
Don Wilson	HOU	Jul 14, 1968	18	CIN
Bill Gullickson	MON	Sep 10, 1980	18	CHI
Ramon Martinez	LA	Jun 4, 1990	18	ATL
Charlie Buffinton	BOS	Sep 2, 1884	17	CLE
Dizzy Dean	STL	Jul 30, 1933	17	CHI
Art Mahaffey	PHI	Apr 23, 1961	17	CHI
Jim Whitney	BOS	Jun 14, 1883	16	CHI
Charlie Buffinton	BOS	Jul 30, 1885	16	DET
John Clarkson	CHI	Aug 18, 1886	16	KC

Most Strikeouts in Nine-Inning Game, NL (*cont.*)

Player	Team	Date	SO	Opp.
Frank Gilmore	WAS	Sep 28, 1886	16	STL
Noodles Hahn	CIN	May 22, 1901	16	BOS
Christy Mathewson	NY	Oct 3, 1904	16	STL
Nap Rucker	BKN	Jul 24, 1909	16	PIT
Sandy Koufax	LA	Jun 22, 1959	16	PHI
	LA	May 26, 1962	16	PHI
Jim Maloney	CIN	May 21, 1963	16	MIL
Bob Veale	PIT	Jun 1, 1965	16	PHI
Steve Carlton	STL	Sep 20, 1967	16	PHI
Don Wilson	HOU	Sep 10, 1968	16	CIN
Steve Carlton	STL	May 21, 1970	16	PHI
Bob Gibson	STL	May 23, 1970	16	PHI
Nolan Ryan	NY	May 29, 1971	16	SD
Tom Seaver	NY	May 29, 1973	16	SF
Steve Carlton	PHI	Jun 9, 1982	16	CHI
Dwight Gooden	NY	Sep 12, 1984	16	PIT
	NY	Sep 17, 1984	16	PHI
	NY	Aug 20, 1985	16	SF
Nolan Ryan	HOU	Sep 9, 1987	16	SF
Sid Fernandez	NY	Jul 14, 1989	16	ATL
Dazzy Vance	BKN	May 2, 1922	15	NY
	BKN	Aug 1, 1924	15	STL
	BKN	Sep 26, 1926	15	CHI
	BKN	Jun 17, 1927	15	CHI
Danny MacFayden	BOS	Sep 28, 1935	15	NY
Van Lingle Mungo	BKN	Sep 29, 1935	15	PHI
Karl Spooner	BKN	Sep 26, 1953	15	NY
Dick Drott	CHI	May 26, 1957	15	MIL
Sandy Koufax	LA	May 6, 1958	15	PHI
	LA	May 6, 1960	15	PHI
Warren Spahn	MIL	Sep 16, 1960	15	PHI
Bob Veale	PIT	Sep 22, 1964	15	MIL
Don Wilson	HOU	Jun 25, 1966	15	STL
Gaylord Perry	SF	Jul 22, 1966	15	PHI
Gary Nolan	CIN	Jun 7, 1967	15	SF
Don Wilson	HOU	Jun 18, 1967	15	ATL
Woodie Fryman	PIT	Sep 1, 1967	15	PHI
Bob Gibson	STL	Aug 24, 1968	15	PIT
Mike Wegener	MON	Sep 10, 1969	15	NY
Nolan Ryan	NY	Apr 18, 1970	15	PHI
Bob Gibson	STL	Apr 26, 1970	15	CIN
Tom Seaver	NY	May 15, 1970	15	PHI
J. R. Richard	HOU	Sep 5, 1971	15	SF
Burt Hooton	CHI	Sep 15, 1971	15	NY
Fred Norman	SD	Sep 15, 1972	15	CIN
Tom Seaver	NY	Sep 20, 1972	15	PIT
J. R. Richard	HOU	Aug 3, 1979	15	ATL

Most Strikeouts in Nine-Inning Game, NL (*cont.*)

Player	Team	Date	SO	Opp.
	HOU	Sep 16, 1979	15	CIN
Mario Soto	CIN	Aug 17, 1982	15	NY
Fernando Valenzuela	LA	May 23, 1984	15	PHI
Rick Sutcliffe	CHI	Sep 3, 1984	15	PHI
Floyd Youmans	MON	Sep 27, 1986	15	PHI
Dwight Gooden	NY	May 11, 1990	15	LA
Mike Scott	HOU	Jun 8, 1990	15	CIN
John Smoltz	ATL	May 24, 1992	15	MON

Most Strikeouts in Nine-Inning Game, Other Leagues

Player	Team	Date	SO	Opp.
One Arm Daily	CHI U	Jul 7, 1884	19	BOS
Dupee Shaw	BOS U	Jul 19, 1884	18	STL
Henry Porter	MIL U	Oct 3, 1884	18	BOS
Guy Hecker	LOU AA	Aug 26, 1884	17	COL
Toad Ramsey	LOU AA	Aug 7, 1886	17	NY
	LOU AA	Jun 21, 1887	17	CLE
Jack Lynch	NY AA	Aug 12, 1884	16	RIC
Larry McKeon	IND AA	Oct 1, 1884	16	RIC
Ed Cushman	MIL U	Oct 4, 1884	16	BOS
Bobby Mathews	PHI AA	Oct 13, 1884	16	CLE
Toad Ramsey	LOU AA	Jul 29, 1886	16	BAL
Matt Kilroy	BAL AA	Aug 24, 1886	16	PHI
Toad Ramsey	LOU AA	Jun 30, 1887	16	STL

Most Strikeouts in Extra-Inning Game, NL

Player	Team	Date	SO	Inns.	Opp.
Jim Whitney	BOS	Jun 14, 1884	18	15	PRO
Warren Spahn	BOS	Jun 14, 1952	18	15	CHI
Jim Maloney	CIN	Jun 14, 1965	18	11	NY
Chris Short	PHI	Oct 2, 1965	18	15	NY
Jack Pfiester	CHI	May 30, 1906	17	15	STL
Dazzy Vance	BKN	Jul 20, 1925	17	10	STL
Bob Veale	PIT	Sep 30, 1964	16	12	CIN
Sandy Koufax	LA	Jul 27, 1966	16	11	PHI
Tom Seaver	NY	May 1, 1974	16	12	LA
Long Tom Hughes	CHI	Aug 26, 1901	15	14	CIN
Kid Nichols	STL	Aug 11, 1904	15	17	BKN
Grover Alexander	CHI	Aug 12, 1919	15	14	PHI
Dazzy Vance	BKN	May 2, 1923	15	10	NY
Sandy Koufax	LA	May 28, 1958	15	13	CIN
	LA	May 28, 1960	15	13	CIN
	LA	Sep 20, 1961	15	13	CHI
Jerry Koosman	NY	May 28, 1969	15	10	SD
Clay Kirby	SD	Sep 24, 1971	15	15	HOU

Most Walks, Season

Player	Team	BB	Player	Team	BB
Amos Rusie	NY N 1893	218	Tony Mullane	CIN N 1893	
Cy Seymour	NY N 1898	213		BAL N 1893	189
Bob Feller	CLE A 1938	208	Kid Gleason	STL N 1893	187
Nolan Ryan	CAL A 1977	204	Sam Jones	CHI N 1955	185
	CAL A 1974	202	Nolan Ryan	CAL A 1976	183
Amos Rusie	NY N 1894	200	Bob Turley	BAL A 1954	181
Bob Feller	CLE A 1941	194	Willie McGill	CHI N 1893	181
Bobo Newsom	STL A 1938	192	Bob Harmon	STL N 1911	181
Ted Breitenstein	STL N 1894	191			

Most Walks in One Game, AL

Player	Team	Date	BB	Inns.	Opp.
Bruno Haas	PHI	Jun 23, 1915	16		NY
Tommy Byrne	NY	Aug 22, 1951	16	13	WAS
Boardwalk Brown	NY	Jul 12, 1915	15		DET
Skipper Friday	WAS	Jun 17, 1923	14		CHI
George Turbeville	PHI	Aug 24, 1935	13	15	CLE
Tommy Byrne	NY	Jun 8, 1949	13	11	DET
Dick Weik	WAS	Sep 1, 1949	13		CHI
Jack Townsend	WAS	Aug 1, 1902	12		DET
John Wyckoff	PHI	Sep 24, 1913	12		BOS
Cap Crowell	PHI	Sep 8, 1915	12		BOS
Bud Davis	PHI	Sep 20, 1915	12		CLE
Carl Ray	PHI	May 9, 1916	12		DET
Sam Gibson	DET	Jul 13, 1927	12		WAS
Tommy Bridges	DET	Aug 25, 1930	12		STL
Bobby Burke	WAS	May 3, 1932	12		NY
Fritz Ostermueller	BOS	Jul 30, 1935	12		WAS
Bobo Newsom	WAS	Aug 27, 1935	12		STL
Vallie Eaves	CHI	Apr 22, 1940	12		DET
Bill Kennedy	STL	Jun 21, 1948	12		PHI
Sid Hudson	WAS	Aug 7, 1948	12		DET
Bob Turley	BAL	Jul 25, 1954	12		PHI
Jack Fisher	BAL	Aug 30, 1961	12		LA
Gus Dorner	CLE	May 25, 1903	11		PHI
John Deering	NY	Sep 7, 1903	11	10	BOS
Doc Newton	NY	Sep 8, 1905	11		STL
Dolly Gray	WAS	Aug 28, 1909	11		CHI
George Curry	STL	Jul 16, 1911	11		PHI
Henry Courtney	WAS	Sep 13, 1919	11		DET
Bobby Burke	WAS	May 3, 1932	11		NY
Sugar Cain	PHI	Jul 22, 1933	11		STL
Lefty Gomez	NY	Aug 1, 1941	11		STL
Bob Feller	CLE	Aug 7, 1941	11	13	DET
Ken Chase	BOS	Jun 13, 1943	11		WAS
Marino Pieretti	WAS	Apr 28, 1945	11	13	NY

Most Walks in One Game, AL (cont.)

Player	Team	Date	BB	Inns.	Opp.
Mickey McDermott	BOS	May 20, 1948	11		CLE
Bill McCahan	PHI	Jul 10, 1948	11		BOS
Camilo Pascual	WAS	May 19, 1956	11		CLE
Mel Stottlemyre	NY	May 21, 1970	11		WAS
Rudy May	CAL	Sep 17, 1973	11	12	OAK
Rick Jones	SEA	Jun 18, 1977	11		TEX
Bill Reidy	MIL	Sep 18, 1901	10		WAS
Ike Butler	BAL	Jul 1, 1902	10		PHI
Elmer Myers	PHI	May 11, 1916	10		DET
Hub Pruett	STL	May 27, 1923	10		CLE
Dixie Davis	STL	Apr 28, 1925	10	10	DET
Dick Coffman	STL	Apr 23, 1930	10		DET
Lefty Gomez	NY	Sep 10, 1932	10		DET
Bob Feller	CLE	Aug 6, 1937	10		NY
	CLE	Aug 5, 1937	10		NY
Joe Krakauskas	WAS	Apr 25, 1939	10		BOS
Jack Wilson	BOS	Jun 9, 1939	10		STL
Vern Kennedy	DET	Sep 7, 1939	10		CHI
Ken Chase	WAS	Apr 30, 1941	10		CHI
Russ Christopher	PHI	Jul 23, 1942	10		STL
Spud Chandler	NY	Sep 2, 1942	10		STL
Pinky Woods	BOS	Jul 30, 1944	10		CLE
Emmett O'Neill	BOS	Jul 14, 1945	10		DET
Bob Feller	CLE	May 13, 1947	10		PHI
Phil Marchildon	PHI	Jun 24, 1948	10		STL
Tommy Byrne	NY	Jul 18, 1948	10		DET
Dick Weik	WAS	Sep 8, 1948	10		PHI
Chuck Stobbs	BOS	Aug 17, 1949	10		PHI
Ted Gray	DET	Jun 29, 1949	10		CLE
Dick Weik	WAS	Aug 9, 1949	10		PHI
Bob Kuzava	CHI	Sep 20, 1949	10		NY
Dick Weik	WAS	May 25, 1950	10		CLE
Bob Lemon	CLE	Jun 11, 1950	10		PHI
Ray Scarborough	CHI	Jun 16, 1950	10		NY
Gene Bearden	CLE	Jun 17, 1950	10		PHI
Chuck Stobbs	BOS	Sep 10, 1950	10		PHI
Herb Score	CLE	Jun 14, 1955	10		DET
Art Ditmar	KC	Aug 21, 1955	10		CLE
George Brunet	CAL	Jul 6, 1966	10		DET
Steve Barber	BAL	Apr 30, 1967	10		DET
Nolan Ryan	CAL	Apr 5, 1974	10		CHI
	CAL	Jun 14, 1974	10	13	BOS
Andy Hassler	CAL	Sep 4, 1974	10		OAK
Charlie Hough	TEX	Aug 27, 1990	10		CAL
Bobby Witt	TEX	Sep 1, 1990	10		OAK
Randy Johnson	SEA	Jul 17, 1991	10		MIL
	SEA	May 1, 1992	10		BAL
Bobby Witt	TEX	Aug 15, 1992	10		DET

Most Walks in One Game, NL

Player	Team	Date	BB	Inns.	Opp.
Bill George	NY	May 30, 1887	16		CHI
George Van Haltren	CHI	Jun 27, 1887	16		BOS
Cannonball Crane	WAS	Sep 1, 1886	14		CHI
Piano Legs Hickman	BOS	Aug 16, 1899	14		LOU
Henry Mathewson	NY	Oct 5, 1906	14		BOS
Bill George	NY	May 17, 1887	13		IND
John Kirby	IND	Jun 9, 1887	13		DET
Bill George	NY	Jun 15, 1887	13		IND
Jesse Burkett	NY	Sep 23, 1890	13		PIT
Cy Seymour	NY	May 24, 1899	13	10	CIN
Mal Eason	BOS	Sep 3, 1902	13		PIT
Pete Schneider	CIN	Jul 6, 1918	13		PHI
Bud Podbielan	CIN	May 18, 1953	13	11	BKN
Henry Gruber	CLE	Sep 9, 1889	12		NY
Crazy Schmit	PIT	Jun 12, 1890	12		CHI
George Nicol	PIT	Jun 13, 1894	12		PHI
Wiley Piatt	BOS	Jun 10, 1903	12		CHI
	BOS	Aug 14, 1903	12		CHI
Fred Mitchell	PHI	Aug 27, 1903	12		BKN
Red Causey	BOS	Sep 8, 1919	12		PIT
Bob Smith	BOS	Sep 28, 1928	12	15	STL
Johnny Vander Meer	CIN	Apr 21, 1948	12		STL
Curt Simmons	PHI	Sep 6, 1948	12	7	NY
Al Bauers	STL	May 1, 1886	11		DET
Larry Corcoran	IND	May 11, 1887	11		CHI
Cannonball Crane	NY	Jun 25, 1889	11		CHI
Charlie Gray	PIT	May 24, 1890	11		PHI
Kid Nichols	BOS	Jul 9, 1890	11		PIT
Tony Mullane	CIN	Aug 11, 1890	11		CLE
Ed Beatin	CLE	Aug 21, 1890	11		BOS
Duke Esper	PHI	Sep 24, 1890	11		CHI
John Thornton	PHI	Apr 22, 1892	11		BKN
Amos Rusie	NY	Sep 23, 1893	11	11	STL
Willie McGill	CHI	Apr 22, 1894	11		CIN
Tom Smith	PHI	Jun 26, 1895	11		BOS
Cy Seymour	NY	Oct 13, 1899	11		WAS
	NY	Jun 7, 1900	11		STL
Barney McFadden	CIN	Jun 4, 1901	11		BKN
Harry McIntire	BKN	Aug 9, 1906	11		CHI
Sandy Burk	BKN	Sep 23, 1910	11		STL
Harry Coveleski	CIN	Sep 28, 1910	11		NY
Larry Cheney	CHI	Sep 29, 1914	11		BOS
Van Lingle Mungo	BKN	Jun 5, 1932	11		PHI
Johnny Vander Meer	CIN	Jun 15, 1937	11		BKN
Hal Gregg	BKN	Jun 15, 1944	11		NY
Max Lanier	NY	Jul 12, 1952	11		STL
Al Worthington	NY	Sep 10, 1953	11		STL

Most Walks in One Game, NL (cont.)

Player	Team	Date	BB	Inns.	Opp.
Sammy Ellis	CIN	Apr 24, 1962	11		NY
J. R. Richard	HOU	May 4, 1975	11		SF
Bill George	NY	Jun 7, 1887	10		PHI
Ed Daily	PHI	Jun 11, 1887	10		BOS
Al Krumm	PIT	May 19, 1889	10		NY
Dan Casey	PHI	Jun 11, 1889	10		WAS
Hank O'Day	NY	Aug 20, 1889	10		WAS
Cy Young	CLE	Apr 22, 1891	10		CIN
Tom Parrott	CIN	Sep 16, 1894	10		BAL
Henry Lampe	PHI	Jul 12, 1895	10		STL
Wiley Piatt	PHI	Jun 19, 1898	10		NY
Kid Carsey	CLE	Jun 2, 1899	10		BKN
Ed Doheny	NY	Aug 27, 1899	10		CHI
Jack Fifield	WAS	Sep 4, 1899	10		PHI
Cy Seymour	NY	Sep 28, 1899	10		PHI
Jack Townsend	PHI	Jul 12, 1901	10		BKN
Bob Ewing	CIN	Apr 18, 1902	10		CHI
Togie Pittinger	BOS	May 8, 1903	10		BKN
Johnny Lush	PHI	Apr 16, 1906	10		NY
Jim Pastorius	BKN	Aug 3, 1909	10		PIT
Harry Coveleski	CIN	May 4, 1910	10		STL
Orval Overall	CHI	May 30, 1910	10		PIT
Bill Foxen	PHI	Jul 20, 1910	10		STL
King Cole	CHI	Sep 9, 1910	10		STL
Sandy Burk	BKN	Sep 15, 1910	10		CIN
Jack Rowan	CIN	Sep 26, 1910	10		NY
Art Fromme	CIN	Sep 27, 1910	10		NY
Marty O'Toole	PIT	Aug 30, 1911	10		BOS
Dana Fillingim	BOS	Jun 4, 1922	10		NY
Bill Hallahan	STL	Jul 31, 1929	10		BKN
	STL	May 1, 1932	10		CHI
Charley Schanz	PHI	Aug 25, 1944	10		BOS
Mel Bosser	CIN	May 14, 1945	10		PHI
Ralph Branca	BKN	Sep 1, 1945	10		NY
Clint Hartung	NY	Aug 17, 1947	10		PHI
Ralph Hamner	CHI	Sep 22, 1947	10		STL
Paul Erickson	PHI	Jun 5, 1948	10		CHI
Ewell Blackwell	CIN	Jul 6, 1950	10		STL
Johnny Lindell	PIT	Apr 15, 1953	10		BKN
Jim Maloney	CIN	Aug 19, 1965	10	10	CHI
Clay Kirby	SD	Jul 15, 1969	10		SF
Ernie McAnally	MON	Sep 23, 1971	10		PHI
J. R. Richard	HOU	Jul 6, 1976	10	10	NY
Mike Torrez	NY	Jul 21, 1983	10		CIN
Mike Dunne	PIT	Jun 11, 1988	10		PHI

Most Games with Ten or More Strikeouts, Career

Player	G	Player	G
Nolan Ryan	215	David Cone	33
Sandy Koufax	98	Dazzy Vance	33
Steve Carlton	83	Jim Maloney	32
Sam McDowell	74	Luis Tiant	32
Bob Gibson	72	Sid Fernandez	30
Tom Seaver	70	Don Sutton	30
Rube Waddell	70	Frank Tanana	30
Bob Feller	54	Christy Mathewson	29
Walter Johnson	53	Fernando Valenzuela	29
Bert Blyleven	51	Vida Blue	28
Roger Clemens	51	Toad Ramsey	28
Mickey Lolich	50	Don Drysdale	27
Jim Bunning	49	Mario Soto	27
Ferguson Jenkins	46	Lefty Grove	26
Dwight Gooden	45	Bill Singer	26
Gaylord Perry	41	Randy Johnson	25
Mark Langston	41	Jerry Koosman	25
Camilo Pascual	39	Juan Marichal	25
J. R. Richard	39		

Most Strikeouts per Nine Innings, Career (Min 1,500 IP)

Player	W	L	IP	SO	Ratio
Nolan Ryan	319	287	5321	5668	9.59
Sandy Koufax	165	87	2324	2396	9.28
Sam McDowell	141	134	2492	2453	8.86
J. R. Richard	107	71	1606	1493	8.37
Roger Clemens	152	72	2031	1873	8.30
Bob Veale	120	95	1926	1703	7.96
Dwight Gooden	142	66	1920	1686	7.90
Mark Langston	128	115	2073	1805	7.84
Jim Maloney	134	84	1849	1605	7.81
Jose DeLeon	75	113	1697	1422	7.54
Sam Jones	102	101	1643	1376	7.54
Mario Soto	100	92	1730	1449	7.54
Goose Gossage	117	102	1714	1433	7.52
Bob Gibson	251	174	3885	3117	7.22
Steve Carlton	329	244	5217	4136	7.14
Rube Waddell	191	145	2961	2316	7.04
Mickey Lolich	217	191	3640	2832	7.00
Rollie Fingers	114	118	1701	1299	6.87
Tom Seaver	311	205	4782	3640	6.85
Jim Bunning	224	184	3760	2855	6.83

Most Strikeouts per Nine Innings, Career (Min 1,500 IP) *(cont.)*

Player	W	L	IP	SO	Ratio
Fernando Valenzuela	141	118	2356	1762	6.73
Juan Pizarro	131	105	2034	1522	6.73
Bobby Bolin	88	75	1576	1175	6.71
Bert Blyleven	287	250	4970	3701	6.70
Ray Culp	122	101	1897	1411	6.69
Ron Guidry	170	91	2392	1778	6.69
Camilo Pascual	174	170	2930	2167	6.66
Stan Williams	109	94	1764	1305	6.66
Bob Turley	101	85	1713	1265	6.65
Don Wilson	104	92	1748	1283	6.60
Tug McGraw	96	92	1516	1109	6.58
Denny Lemaster	90	105	1788	1305	6.57
Andy Messersmith	130	99	2230	1625	6.56
Don Drysdale	209	166	3432	2486	6.52
Al Downing	123	107	2268	1639	6.50

Most Consecutive Wins, AL

Player	Team	Year	W
Walter Johnson	WAS	1912	16
Smoky Joe Wood	BOS	1912	16
Lefty Grove	PHI	1931	16
Schoolboy Rowe	DET	1934	16
General Crowder	WAS	1932	15
Johnny Allen	CLE	1937	15
Dave McNally	BAL	1969	15
Gaylord Perry	CLE	1974	15
Jack Chesbro	NY	1904	14
Walter Johnson	WAS	1913	14
Chief Bender	PHI	1914	14
Lefty Grove	PHI	1928	14
Whitey Ford	NY	1961	14
Steve Stone	BAL	1980	14
Roger Clemens	BOS	1986	14
Walter Johnson	WAS	1924	13
Stan Coveleski	WAS	1925	13
Wes Ferrell	CLE	1930	13
Bobo Newsom	DET	1940	13
Ellis Kinder	BOS	1949	13
Dave McNally	BAL	1971	13
Catfish Hunter	OAK	1973	13
Ron Guidry	NY	1978	13
LaMarr Hoyt	CHI	1983	13
Cy Young	BOS	1901	12
Russ Ford	NY	1910	12
Dutch Leonard	BOS	1914	12

Most Consecutive Wins, AL (*cont.*)

Player	Team	Year	W
Tom Zachary	NY	1929	12
George Earnshaw	PHI	1931	12
Johnny Allen	CLE	1938	12
Atley Donald	NY	1939	12
Boo Ferriss	BOS	1946	12
Luis Arroyo	NY	1961	12
Whitey Ford	NY	1963	12
Dave McNally	BAL	1968	12
Pat Dobson	BAL	1971	12
Ron Guidry	NY	1985	12
Bobby Witt	TEX	1990	12
Scott Erickson	MIN	1991	12
Bill Bernhard	CLE	1902	11
Rube Waddell	PHI	1905	11
Ed Walsh	CHI	1906	11
George Mullin	DET	1909	11
Jean Dubuc	DET	1912	11
Joe Boehling	WAS	1913	11
Bob Shawkey	NY	1920	11
General Crowder	STL	1928	11
Earl Whitehill	DET	1930	11
Firpo Marberry	WAS	1930	11
Lefty Gomez	NY	1932	11
Bump Hadley	NY	1936	11
Johnny Rigney	CHI	1937	11
Steve Sundra	NY	1939	11
Tex Hughson	BOS	1942	11
Bobby Shantz	PHI	1952	11
Vic Raschi	NY	1952	11
Gary Peters	CHI	1963	11
Roger Moret	BOS	1973	11
Jim Palmer	BAL	1973	11
Bob Stanley	BOS	1978	11
Ron Guidry	NY	1979	11
Rich Gale	KC	1980	11
Dennis Lamp	TOR	1985	11
Cy Young	BOS	1902	10
Rube Waddell	PHI	1903	10
	PHI	1905	10
	PHI	1906	10
Addie Joss	CLE	1907	10
Harry Krause	PHI	1909	10
Walter Johnson	WAS	1911	10
	WAS	1913	10
Cy Falkenberg	CLE	1913	10
Bob Shawkey	NY	1919	10
Ted Blankenship	CHI	1925	10

Most Consecutive Wins, AL (*cont.*)

Player	Team	Year	W
Johnny Allen	NY	1932	10
Tony Freitas	PHI	1932	10
Lefty Gomez	NY	1934	10
Vern Kennedy	CHI	1934	10
Monte Pearson	NY	1938	10
Hal Newhouser	DET	1940	10
Boo Ferriss	BOS	1946	10
Bob Lemon	CLE	1947	10
Allie Reynolds	NY	1954	10
Ike Delock	BOS	1958	10
Ken McBride	LA	1962	10
Dick Radatz	BOS	1963	10
Whitey Ford	NY	1964	10
Vida Blue	OAK	1971	10
Jim Palmer	BAL	1973	10
Fritz Peterson	CLE	1975	10
Dennis Martinez	BAL	1979	10
Storm Davis	OAK	1988	10
Bert Blyleven	CAL	1989	10
Juan Guzman	TOR	1991	10
Chris Bosio	MIL	1992	10
Cal Eldred	MIL	1992	10

Most Consecutive Wins, NL

Player	Team	Year	W
Tim Keefe	NY	1888	19
Rube Marquard	NY	1912	19
Old Hoss Radbourn	PRO	1884	18
Mickey Welch	NY	1885	17
Pat Luby	CHI	1890	17
Roy Face	PIT	1959	17
Jim McCormick	CHI	1886	16
Carl Hubbell	NY	1936	16
Ewell Blackwell	CIN	1947	16
Jack Sanford	SF	1962	16
Dazzy Vance	BKN	1924	15
Bob Gibson	STL	1968	15
Steve Carlton	PHI	1972	15
Jim McCormick	CHI	1885	14
Jocko Flynn	CHI	1886	14
Joe McGinnity	NY	1904	14
Ed Reulbach	CHI	1909	14
Rick Sutcliffe	CHI	1984	14
Dwight Gooden	NY	1985	14
Larry Corcoran	CHI	1880	13
Charlie Buffinton	BOS	1884	13

Most Consecutive Wins, NL (*cont.*)

Player	Team	Year	W
Cy Young	CLE	1892	13
Frank Killen	PIT	1893	13
Frank Dwyer	CIN	1896	13
Fred Klobedanz	BOS	1897	13
Ted Lewis	BOS	1898	13
Christy Mathewson	NY	1909	13
Deacon Phillippe	PIT	1910	13
Burleigh Grimes	NY	1927	13
Brooks Lawrence	CIN	1956	13
Phil Regan	LA	1966	13
Dock Ellis	PIT	1971	13
Tom Glavine	ATL	1992	13
John Clarkson	CHI	1885	12
Charlie Ferguson	PHI	1886	12
Jack Chesbro	PIT	1902	12
Hooks Wiltse	NY	1904	12
Ed Reulbach	CHI	1906	12
Dick Rudolph	BOS	1914	12
Burt Hooton	LA	1975	12
Tom Lovett	BKN	1890	11
Christy Mathewson	NY	1905	11
Vic Willis	PIT	1909	11
Grover Alexander	PHI	1913	11
	CHI	1920	11
Guy Bush	CHI	1929	11
Hal Schumacher	NY	1935	11
Elmer Riddle	CIN	1941	11
Ted Wilks	STL	1944	11
Sal Maglie	NY	1950	11
Johnny Antonelli	NY	1954	11
Warren Spahn	MIL	1954	11
Sandy Koufax	LA	1964	11
	LA	1965	11
Bob Gibson	STL	1972	11
Andy Hawkins	SD	1985	11
LaMarr Hoyt	SD	1985	11
Dennis Martinez	MON	1989	11
Tommy Bond	HAR	1876	10
Al Spalding	CHI	1876	10
Pud Galvin	BUF	1879	10
Larry Corcoran	CHI	1882	10
Old Hoss Radbourn	PRO	1883	10
Joe McGinnity	BKN	1900	10
Sam Leever	PIT	1903	10
Orval Overall	CIN	1905	10
Tully Sparks	PHI	1907	10
Three Finger Brown	CHI	1907	10

Most Consecutive Wins, NL (cont.)

Player	Team	Year	W
Vic Willis	PIT	1909	10
Grover Alexander	PHI	1913	10
Dick Rudolph	BOS	1916	10
Slim Sallee	NY	1917	10
Burleigh Grimes	BKN	1918	10
Jesse Barnes	NY	1919	10
Dazzy Vance	BKN	1923	10
Bill Doak	BKN	1924	10
Burleigh Grimes	PIT	1929	10
Clarence Mitchell	NY	1930	10
Dizzy Dean	STL	1934	10
Johnny Vander Meer	CIN	1938	10
Paul Derringer	CIN	1939	10
Howie Krist	STL	1941	10
Larry French	BKN	1942	10
Whit Wyatt	BKN	1943	10
Max Lanier	STL	1944	10
Preacher Roe	BKN	1951	10
	BKN	1951	10
Eddie Yuhas	STL	1952	10
Preacher Roe	BKN	1953	10
Don Newcombe	BKN	1955	10
Willard Schmidt	STL	1957	10
Warren Spahn	MIL	1961	10
Juan Marichal	SF	1968	10
Ron Kline	PIT	1968	10
Juan Marichal	SF	1969	10
Tom Seaver	NY	1969	10
Clay Carroll	CIN	1969	10
Bob Gibson	STL	1970	10
Wayne Simpson	CIN	1970	10
Butch Metzger	SD	1976	10
Terry Leach	NY	1987	10
Juan Agosto	HOU	1988	10
Andy Benes	SD	1991	10

Most Consecutive Losses, AL

Player	Team	Year	L
Jack Nabors	PHI	1916	19
Mike Parrott	SEA	1980	16
Bob Groom	WAS	1909	15
Joe Harris	BOS	1906	14
Paul Calvert	WAS	1949	14
Howie Judson	CHI	1949	14
Matt Keough	OAK	1979	14
Guy Morton	CLE	1914	13

Most Consecutive Losses, AL (*cont.*)

Player	Team	Year	L
Roy Moore	PHI	1920	13
Dutch Henry	CHI	1930	13
Lum Harris	PHI	1943	13
Terry Felton	MIN	1982	13
Red Ruffing	BOS	1929	12
Milt Gaston	BOS	1931	12
Walt Masterson	WAS	1940	12
Steve Gerkin	PHI	1945	12
Bobo Newsom	PHI	1945	12
Charlie Bishop	PHI	1953	12
Bill Piercy	BOS	1923	11
Eddie Smith	PHI	1937	11
Roger Wolff	WAS	1944	11
Early Wynn	WAS	1944	11
Troy Herriage	KC	1956	11
Chuck Stobbs	WAS	1957	11
Andy Hassler	CAL	1975	11
Chris Bosio	MIL	1988	11
Russ Van Atta	STL	1935	10
Jim Walkup	STL	1938	10
Bennie Daniels	WAS	1962	10
Mickey Lolich	DET	1967	10
Jerry Garvin	TOR	1977	10
Danny Darwin	MIL	1985	10
Jay Tibbs	BAL	1988	10

Most Consecutive Losses, NL

Player	Team	Year	L
Cliff Curtis	BOS	1910	18
Roger Craig	NY	1963	18
Dory Dean	CIN	1876	16
Sam Weaver	MIL	1878	16
Jim Hughey	CLE	1899	16
Craig Anderson	NY	1962	16
Frank Gilmoe	WAS	1887	14
Frank Bates	CLE	1899	14
Jim Pastorius	BKN	1908	14
Buster Brown	BOS	1911	14
Anthony Young	NY	1992	14
Sam Moffett	CLE	1884	13
Burleigh Grimes	PIT	1917	13
Joe Oeschger	BOS	1922	13
Ben Cantwell	BOS	1935	13
Dutch McCall	CHI	1948	13
Blondie Purcell	CIN	1880	12
John Coleman	PHI	1883	12

Most Consecutive Losses, NL (cont.)

Player	Team	Year	L
Henry Thielman	CIN	1902	12
Mal Eason	BKN	1905	12
Rube Marquard	NY	1914	12
Pete Schneider	CIN	1914	12
Russ Miller	PHI	1928	12
Si Johnson	CIN	1933	12
Max Butcher	PHI		
	PIT	1939	12
Hugh Mulcahy	PHI	1940	12
Bob Miller	NY	1962	12
Ken Reynolds	PHI	1972	12
Pete Conway	BUF	1885	11
Jersey Bakely	CLE	1889	11
Guy Hecker	PIT	1890	11
Irv Young	BOS	1907	11
George Ferguson	BOS	1909	11
Jim Yeargin	BOS	1924	11
Charley Schanz	PHI	1945	11
Dick Drott	HOU	1963	11
Gary Ross	SD	1969	11
Barry Lersch	PHI	1971	11
Jose DeLeon	PIT	1985	11
Rick Honeycutt	LA	1987	11
Kyle Abbott	PHI	1992	11
Charlie Ferguson	PHI	1884	10
Red Donahue	STL	1897	10
John McFetridge	PHI	1903	10
Stoney McGlynn	STL	1907	10
Fred Beebe	STL	1909	10
Joe Oeschger	BOS	1923	10
Ed Holley	PHI	1934	10
Manny Salvo	BOS	1941	10
Dick Barrett	PHI	1945	10
Bud Podbielan	CIN	1953	10
Dave Roberts	SD	1970	10
Billy Champion	PHI	1972	10
Steve Arlin	SD	1972	10
Steve Renko	MON	1973	10
Gary Lucas	SD	1982	10

Most Consecutive Strikeouts, AL

Player	Team	Date	SO	Opp.
Nolan Ryan	CAL	Jul 9, 1972	8	BOS
	CAL	Jul 15, 1973	8	DET
Ron Davis	NY	May 4, 1981	8	OAK
Roger Clemens	BOS	Apr 29, 1986	8	SEA
Ryne Duren	LA	Jun 9, 1961	7	BOS

Most Consecutive Strikeouts, AL (cont.)

Player	Team	Date	SO	Opp.
Denny McLain	DET	Jun 15, 1965	7	BOS
Pete Richert	WAS	Apr 24, 1966	7	DET
Phil Ortega	WAS	May 29, 1966	7	BOS
Jim Merritt	MIN	Jul 21, 1966	7	WAS
John Hiller	DET	Oct 1, 1970	7	CLE
Sammy Stewart	BAL	Sep 1, 1978	7	CLE
Mark Langston	SEA	Jun 15, 1984	7	BOS
Joe Cowley	CHI	May 28, 1986	7	TEX
Nolan Ryan	TEX	Jul 7, 1991	7	CAL
Roger Clemens	BOS	Sep 7, 1992	7	TEX
Randy Johnson	SEA	Sep 27, 1992	7	TEX

Most Consecutive Strikeouts, NL

Player	Team	Date	SO	Opp.
Tom Seaver	NY	Apr 22, 1970	10	SD
Mickey Welch	NY	Aug 28, 1884	9	PIT
Charlie Buffinton	BOS	Sep 2, 1884	8	CLE
Max Surkont	MIL	May 25, 1953	8	CIN
Johnny Podres	LA	Jul 2, 1962	8	PHI
Jim Maloney	CIN	May 21, 1963	8	MIL
Don Wilson	HOU	Jul 14, 1968	8	CIN
Jim Deshaies	HOU	Sep 23, 1986	8	LA
John Clarkson	CHI	Sep 30, 1884	7	NY
Hooks Wiltse	NY	May 15, 1906	7	CIN
Dazzy Vance	BKN	Aug 1, 1924	7	CHI
Van Lingle Mungo	BKN	Jun 25, 1936	7	CIN
Juan Marichal	SF	Sep 6, 1964	7	PHI
Steve Renko	MON	Oct 3, 1972	7	NY
Al Downing	LA	Jul 14, 1973	7	CHI
Jamie Moyer	CHI	Jul 3, 1987	7	SF
Sid Fernandez	NY	Jul 20, 1990	7	ATL

Most Consecutive Strikeouts, Other Leagues

Player	Team	Date	SO	Opp.
Ed Cushman	NY AA	Sep 16, 1885	8	PIT
Jack Stivetts	STL AA	May 3, 1890	7	LOU

Most Relief Wins, Career

Player	W	Player	W
Hoyt Wilhelm	124	Sparky Lyle	99
Lindy McDaniel	119	Roy Face	96
Goose Gossage	108	Gene Garber	94
Rollie Fingers	107	Kent Tekulve	94

Most Relief Wins, Career (cont.)

Player	W	Player	W
Mike Marshall	92	Johnny Klippstein	59
Don McMahon	90	Elias Sosa	59
Tug McGraw	89	John Franco	58
Clay Carroll	88	Aurelio Lopez	58
Bob Stanley	85	Phil Regan	58
Bill Campbell	80	Ted Abernathy	57
Gary Lavelle	80	Bob Locker	57
Tom Burgmeier	79	Roger McDowell	57
Stu Miller	79	Mace Brown	56
Ron Perranoski	79	Greg Minton	56
Johnny Murphy	73	Dan Quisenberry	56
John Hiller	72	Gerry Staley	56
Mark Clear	71	Dave Giusti	55
Dick Hall	71	Tippy Martinez	55
Guillermo Hernandez	70	Ron Kline	54
Pedro Borbon	69	Jack Quinn	54
Jeff Reardon	68	Ron Reed	54
Bruce Sutter	68	Al Worthington	54
Lee Smith	65	Doug Bair	53
Al Hrabosky	64	Firpo Marberry	53
Jim Brewer	62	Dale Murray	53
Clem Labine	63	Dave Smith	53
Darold Knowles	63	Dick Radatz	52
Jesse Orosco	63	Ed Roebuck	52
Dick Farrell	62	Sammy Stewart	52
Eddie Fisher	62	Hugh Casey	51
Grant Jackson	62	Mike Henneman	51
Dave LaRoche	62	Jim Konstanty	51
Paul Lindblad	62	Eddie Rommel	51
Frank Linzy	62	Jim Kern	50
Joe Heving	60	Dick Tidrow	50
Steve Bedrosian	59		

Most Relief Wins, Season, AL

Player	Team	Year	W
John Hiller	DET	1974	17
Bill Campbell	MIN	1976	17
Dick Radatz	BOS	1964	16
Tom Johnson	MIN	1977	16
Luis Arroyo	NY	1961	15
Dick Radatz	BOS	1963	15
Eddie Fisher	CHI	1965	15
Joe Page	NY	1947	14
Stu Miller	BAL	1965	14
Ron Davis	NY	1979	14
Mark Clear	BOS	1982	14
Jim Slaton	MIL	1983	14

Most Relief Wins, Season, AL *(cont.)*

Player	Team	Year	W
Mark Eichhorn	TOR	1986	14
Wilcy Moore	NY	1927	13
Joe Page	NY	1949	13
Gerry Staley	CHI	1960	13
Rollie Fingers	OAK	1976	13
Bill Campbell	BOS	1977	13
Sparky Lyle	NY	1977	13
Bob Stanley	BOS	1978	13
Aurelio Lopez	DET	1980	13
Goose Gossage	NY	1983	13
Johnny Murphy	NY	1937	12
	NY	1943	12
Hoyt Wilhelm	CHI	1964	12
Wilbur Wood	CHI	1968	12
Lindy McDaniel	NY	1973	12
Sid Monge	CLE	1979	12
Danny Darwin	TEX	1980	12
Dan Quisenberry	KC	1980	12
Bill Caudill	SEA	1982	12
Dan Spillner	CLE	1982	12
Bob Stanley	BOS	1982	12
Dave Righetti	NY	1985	12
Jeff Musselman	TOR	1987	12
Jack Russell	WAS	1933	11
Clint Brown	CHI	1939	11
Joe Heving	BOS	1939	11
Ike Delock	BOS	1956	11
Dick Hall	BAL	1965	11
Moe Drabowsky	KC	1969	11
Rollie Fingers	OAK	1972	11
John Hiller	DET	1976	11
Mark Clear	CAL	1979	11
	CAL	1980	11
Dennis Lamp	TOR	1985	11
Mike Henneman	DET	1987	11
	DET	1989	11
Lee Guetterman	NY	1990	11
Barry Jones	CHI	1990	11

Most Relief Wins, Season, NL

Player	Team	Year	W
Roy Face	PIT	1959	18
Jim Konstanty	PHI	1950	16
Ron Perranoski	LA	1963	16
Mace Brown	PIT	1938	15
Hoyt Wilhelm	NY	1952	15

Most Relief Wins, Season, NL (*cont.*)

Player	Team	Year	W
Mike Marshall	LA	1974	15
Dale Murray	MON	1975	15
Joe Black	BKN	1952	14
Hersh Freeman	CIN	1956	14
Stu Miller	SF	1961	14
Phil Regan	LA	1966	14
Frank Linzy	SF	1969	14
Mike Marshall	MON	1972	14
	MON	1973	14
Roger McDowell	NY	1986	14
Clyde Shoun	CIN	1943	13
Clyde King	BKN	1951	13
Lindy McDaniel	STL	1959	13
Larry Sherry	LA	1960	13
Lindy McDaniel	CHI	1963	13
Al Hrabosky	STL	1975	13
Gary Lavelle	SF	1978	13
Ron Reed	PHI	1979	13
Jesse Orosco	NY	1983	13
Ben Cantwell	BOS	1932	12
Joe Beggs	CIN	1940	12
Frank Smith	CIN	1952	12
Hoyt Wilhelm	NY	1954	12
Lindy McDaniel	STL	1960	12
Jack Baldschun	PHI	1962	12
Ron Kline	PIT	1968	12
Phil Regan	LA	1968	
	CHI	1968	12
	CHI	1969	12
Jerry Johnson	SF	1971	12
Charlie Hough	LA	1976	12
Kent Tekulve	PIT	1982	12
John Franco	CIN	1985	12
Jeff Parrett	MON	1988	12
	PHI	1989	12
Mitch Williams	PHI	1991	12
Ace Adams	NY	1945	11
Hugh Casey	BKN	1946	11
Eddie Yuhas	STL	1952	11
Dave Jolly	MIL	1954	11
Roy Face	PIT	1956	11
Jack Baldschun	PHI	1963	11
Al McBean	PIT	1963	11
Hal Woodeshick	HOU	1963	11
Clay Carroll	CIN	1969	11
Tug McGraw	NY	1971	11
Cecil Upshaw	ATL	1971	11

Most Relief Wins, Season, NL (cont.)

Player	Team	Year	W
Pedro Borbon	CIN	1973	11
Rawly Eastwick	CIN	1976	11
Butch Metzger	SD	1976	11
Goose Gossage	PIT	1977	11
Doug Bair	CIN	1979	11
Dick Tidrow	CHI	1979	11
Rollie Fingers	SD	1980	11
Bill Dawley	HOU	1984	11
Charley Kerfeld	HOU	1986	11
Kent Tekulve	PHI	1986	11
Scott Garrelts	SF	1987	11
Don Robinson	PIT		
	SF	1987	11
Jeff Robinson	PIT	1988	11
Danny Darwin	HOU	1989	11
Bill Sampen	MON	1990	11
Doug Jones	HOU	1992	11

Most Relief Losses, Career

Player	L	Player	L
Gene Garber	108	Don McMahon	66
Hoyt Wilhelm	103	Bill Campbell	65
Rollie Fingers	101	Greg Minton	62
Mike Marshall	98	Bob Stanley	61
Kent Tekulve	90	John Hiller	58
Lindy McDaniel	88	Frank Linzy	57
Roy Face	82	Jesse Orosco	56
Goose Gossage	80	Guillermo Hernandez	55
Sparky Lyle	76	Tom Burgmeier	53
Gary Lavelle	75	Steve Bedrosian	54
Ron Perranoski	74	Ron Davis	53
Darold Knowles	71	Jim Kern	52
Jeff Reardon	71	Dave LaRoche	52
Bruce Sutter	71	Dick Farrell	51
Tug McGraw	69	Claude Raymond	51
Lee Smith	69	Dale Murray	50
Clay Carroll	68	Al Worthington	50
Stu Miller	67		

Most Relief Losses, Season, AL

Player	Team	Year	L
Darold Knowles	WAS	1970	14
John Hiller	DET	1974	14
Mike Marshall	MIN	1979	14
Wilbur Wood	CHI	1970	13

Most Relief Losses, Season, AL (cont.)

Player	Team	Year	L
Ken Sanders	MIL	1971	12
Jim Willoughby	BOS	1976	12
Mike Marshall	MIN	1978	12
Frank Funk	CLE	1961	11
Dick Radatz	BOS	1965	11
Wilbur Wood	CHI	1968	11
	CHI	1969	11
Rollie Fingers	OAK	1976	11
Goose Gossage	NY	1978	11
Dave Heaverlo	OAK	1979	11
Dave LaRoche	CAL	1979	11
Mark Clear	CAL	1979	11
Jim Kern	TEX	1980	11
Ron Davis	MIN	1984	11
Clint Brown	CHI	1939	10
Al Benton	DET	1940	10
Johnny Murphy	NY	1942	10
Hoyt Wilhelm	BAL	1962	10
Ken Sanders	BOS/KC	1966	10
Stu Miller	BAL	1967	10
Ron Perranoski	MIN	1969	10
Lindy McDaniel	NY	1971	10
Tom Murphy	MIL	1974	10
Jim Kern	CLE	1977	10
	CLE	1977	10
Tom Buskey	TOR	1979	10
Sid Monge	CLE	1979	10
Dan Spillner	CLE	1982	10
Bob Stanley	BOS	1983	10
	BOS	1984	10
Guillermo Hernandez	DET	1985	10
Keith Atherton	OAK/MIN	1986	10
Doug Jones	CLE	1989	10
Duane Ward	TOR	1989	10

Most Relief Losses, Season, NL

Player	Team	Year	L
Gene Garber	ATL	1979	16
Rollie Fingers	SD	1978	13
Skip Lockwood	NY	1978	13
Roy Face	PIT	1956	12
	PIT	1961	12
Mike Marshall	LA	1974	12
	LA	1975	12
Gene Garber	PHI	1975	12
Charlie Hough	LA	1977	12

Most Relief Losses, Season, NL (cont.)

Player	Team	Year	L
Kent Tekulve	PIT	1980	12
Ken Howell	LA	1986	12
Nels Potter	BOS	1949	11
Frank Linzy	SF	1966	11
Mike Marshall	MON	1973	11
Greg Minton	SF	1983	11
Mark Davis	SF	1985	11
Joe Boever	ATL	1989	11
Harry Gumbert	CIN	1947	10
Jim Konstanty	PHI	1951	10
Clem Labine	LA	1959	10
Dan McGinn	MON	1969	10
Gary Lavelle	SF	1978	10
Bruce Sutter	CHI	1978	10
Dale Murray	NY/MON	1978	10
Neil Allen	NY	1980	10
Dick Tidrow	CHI	1981	10
Tom Hume	CIN	1980	10
Gene Garber	ATL	1982	10
Gary Lucas	SD	1982	10
Steve Bedrosian	ATL	1983	10
Lee Smith	CHI	1983	10
Bruce Sutter	STL	1983	10
Al Holland	PHI	1984	10
Kent Tekulve	PHI	1985	10
Todd Worrell	STL	1986	10
Gene Garber	ATL	1987	10
Lance McCullers	SD	1987	10
Lee Smith	CHI	1987	10
Mark Davis	SD	1988	10

Most Saves, Career

Player	SV	Player	SV
Jeff Reardon	357	Dave Smith	216
Lee Smith	355	Bobby Thigpen	200
Rollie Fingers	341	Roy Face	193
Goose Gossage	308	Mike Marshall	188
Bruce Sutter	300	Steve Bedrosian	184
Dave Righetti	251	Kent Tekulve	184
Dan Quisenberry	244	Tug McGraw	180
Dennis Eckersley	239	Ron Perranoski	179
Sparky Lyle	238	Lindy McDaniel	172
Hoyt Wilhelm	227	Doug Jones	164
John Franco	226	Stu Miller	154
Tom Henke	220	Jay Howell	153
Gene Garber	218	Don McMahon	153

Most Saves, Career (*cont.*)

Player	SV	Player	SV
Greg Minton	150	Rick Aguilera	122
Roger McDowell	149	Jesse Orosco	122
Ted Abernathy	148	Dick Radatz	122
Guillermo Hernandez	147	Tippy Martinez	115
Dave Giusti	145	Jeff Montgomery	115
Clay Carroll	143	Jeff Russell	113
Darold Knowles	143	Frank Linzy	111
Mitch Williams	143	Al Worthington	110
Gary Lavelle	136	Fred Gladding	109
Dan Plesac	133	Wayne Granger	108
Jim Brewer	132	Ron Kline	108
Bob Stanley	132	Johnny Murphy	107
Randy Myers	131	Bill Caudill	106
Gregg Olson	131	Mike Hennemann	104
Ron Davis	130	Steve Farr	103
Todd Worrell	129	Ron Reed	103
Terry Forster	127	John Wyatt	103
Bill Campbell	126	Tom Burgmeier	102
Bryan Harvey	126	Tim Burke	102
Dave LaRoche	126	Ellis Kinder	102
John Hiller	125	Firpo Marberry	101
Jack Aker	123	Craig Lefferts	100

Most Saves, Season, AL

Player	Team	Year	SV
Bobby Thigpen	CHI	1990	57
Dennis Eckersley	OAK	1992	51
	OAK	1990	48
Dave Righetti	NY	1986	46
Bryan Harvey	CAL	1991	46
Dan Quisenberry	KC	1983	45
Dennis Eckersley	OAK	1988	45
Dan Quisenberry	KC	1984	44
Doug Jones	CLE	1990	43
Dennis Eckersley	OAK	1991	43
Jeff Reardon	MIN	1988	42
Rick Aguilera	MIN	1991	42
	MIN	1992	41
Jeff Reardon	BOS	1991	40
Jeff Montgomery	KC	1992	39
John Hiller	DET	1973	38
Jeff Russell	TEX	1989	38
Dan Quisenberry	KC	1985	37
Doug Jones	CLE	1988	37
Gregg Olson	BAL	1990	37

Most Saves, Season, AL (cont.)

Player	Team	Year	SV
Bill Caudill	OAK	1984	36
Dave Righetti	NY	1990	36
Gregg Olson	BAL	1992	36
Sparky Lyle	NY	1972	35
Dan Quisenberry	KC	1982	35
Ron Perranoski	MIN	1970	34
Don Aase	BAL	1986	34
Tom Henke	TOR	1987	34
Bobby Thigpen	CHI	1988	34
	CHI	1989	34
Tom Henke	TOR	1992	34
Goose Gossage	NY	1980	33
Dan Quisenberry	KC	1980	33
Bob Stanley	BOS	1983	33
Dennis Eckersley	OAK	1989	33
Dan Plesac	MIL	1989	33
Mike Schooler	SEA	1989	33
Jeff Montgomery	KC	1991	33
Jack Aker	KC	1966	32
Mike Marshall	MIN	1979	32
Guillermo Hernandez	DET	1984	32
Bob James	CHI	1985	32
Doug Jones	CLE	1989	32
Rick Aguilera	MIN	1990	32
Tom Henke	TOR	1990	32
	TOR	1991	32
Ron Perranoski	MIN	1969	31
Ken Sanders	MIL	1971	31
Bill Campbell	BOS	1977	31
Dave Righetti	NY	1984	31
Guillermo Hernandez	DET	1985	31
Donnie Moore	CAL	1985	31
Jeff Reardon	MIN	1987	31
Dave Righetti	NY	1987	31
Jeff Reardon	MIN	1989	31
Gregg Olson	BAL	1991	31
Ed Farmer	CHI	1980	30
Goose Gossage	NY	1982	30
Ron Davis	MIN	1983	30
Dan Plesac	MIL	1988	30
Mike Schooler	SEA	1990	30
Jeff Russell	TEX	1991	30
Bobby Thigpen	CHI	1991	30
Steve Farr	NY	1992	30
Jeff Russell	TEX	1992	30
	OAK		

Most Saves, Season, NL

Player	Team	Year	SV
Lee Smith	STL	1991	47
Bruce Sutter	STL	1984	45
Mark Davis	SD	1989	44
Lee Smith	STL	1992	43
Jeff Reardon	MON	1985	41
Steve Bedrosian	PHI	1987	40
John Franco	CIN	1988	39
Randy Myers	SD	1992	38
Clay Carroll	CIN	1972	37
Rollie Fingers	SD	1978	37
Bruce Sutter	CHI	1979	37
John Wetteland	MON	1992	37
Bruce Sutter	STL	1982	36
Todd Worrell	STL	1986	36
Lee Smith	CHI	1987	36
Mitch Williams	CHI	1989	36
Doug Jones	HOU	1992	36
Wayne Granger	CIN	1970	35
Rollie Fingers	SD	1977	35
Jeff Reardon	MON	1986	35
Jim Gott	PIT	1988	34
Lee Smith	CHI	1984	33
	CHI	1985	33
Dave Smith	HOU	1986	33
Todd Worrell	STL	1987	33
John Franco	NY	1990	33
	CIN	1987	32
Todd Worrell	STL	1988	32
John Franco	CIN	1989	32
Ted Abernathy	CHI	1965	31
Mike Marshall	MON	1973	31
Bruce Sutter	CHI	1977	31
Kent Tekulve	PIT	1978	31
	PIT	1979	31
Jesse Orosco	NY	1984	31
Lee Smith	CHI	1986	31
Randy Myers	CIN	1990	31
Rob Dibble	CIN	1991	31
Dave Giusti	PIT	1971	30
Gene Garber	ATL	1982	30
Greg Minton	SF	1982	30
John Franco	NY	1991	30
Mitch Williams	PHI	1991	30

Most Wins Plus Saves, Season

Player	Team	Year	G	IP	SO	W	L	SV	W&S	ERA
Bobby Thigpen	CHI A	1990	77	89	70	4	6	57	61	1.83
Dennis Eckersley	OAK A	1992	69	80	93	7	1	51	58	1.91

Most Wins Plus Saves, Season (*cont.*)

Player	Team	Year	G	IP	SO	W	L	SV	W&S	ERA
Dave Righetti	NY A	1986	74	107	83	8	8	46	54	2.45
Lee Smith	STL N	1991	67	73	67	6	3	47	53	2.34
Dennis Eckersley	OAK A	1990	63	73	73	4	2	48	52	0.61
Dan Quisenberry	KC A	1983	69	139	48	5	3	45	50	1.94
	KC A	1984	72	129	41	6	3	44	50	2.64
Bruce Sutter	STL N	1984	71	123	77	5	7	45	50	1.54
Dennis Eckersley	OAK A	1988	60	73	70	4	2	45	49	2.35
John Hiller	DET A	1973	65	125	124	10	5	38	48	1.44
Mark Davis	SD N	1989	70	93	92	4	3	44	48	1.85
Doug Jones	CLE A	1990	66	84	55	5	5	43	48	2.56
Dennis Eckersley	OAK A	1991	67	76	87	5	4	43	48	2.96
Bryan Harvey	CAL A	1991	67	79	101	2	4	46	48	1.60
Doug Jones	HOU N	1992	80	112	93	11	8	36	47	1.85
Lee Smith	STL N	1992	70	75	60	4	9	43	47	3.12
Rick Aguilera	MIN A	1991	63	69	61	4	5	42	46	2.35
Dick Radatz	BOS A	1964	79	157	181	16	9	29	45	2.29
Mike Marshall	MON N	1973	92	179	124	14	11	31	45	2.66
Dan Quisenberry	KC A	1980	75	128	37	12	7	33	45	3.11
Bruce Sutter	STL N	1982	70	102	61	9	8	36	45	2.90
Bill Caudill	OAK A	1984	68	96	89	9	7	36	45	2.71
Dan Quisenberry	KC A	1985	84	129	54	8	9	37	45	2.37
Todd Worrell	STL N	1986	74	104	73	9	10	36	45	2.08
Steve Bedrosian	PHI N	1987	65	89	74	5	3	40	45	2.83
John Franco	CIN N	1988	70	86	46	6	6	39	45	1.57
Luis Arroyo	NY A	1961	65	119	87	15	5	29	44	2.19
Sparky Lyle	NY A	1972	59	108	75	9	5	35	44	1.92
Bill Campbell	BOS A	1977	69	140	114	13	9	31	44	2.96
Dan Quisenberry	KC A	1982	72	137	46	9	7	35	44	2.57
Jeff Reardon	MIN A	1988	63	73	56	2	4	42	44	2.47
Jeff Russell	TEX A	1989	71	73	77	6	4	38	44	1.98
Clay Carroll	CIN N	1972	65	96	51	6	4	37	43	2.25
Rollie Fingers	SD N	1977	78	132	113	8	9	35	43	3.00
	SD N	1978	67	107	72	6	13	37	43	2.52
Bruce Sutter	CHI N	1979	62	101	110	6	6	37	43	2.23
Jeff Reardon	MON N	1985	63	88	67	2	8	41	43	3.18
Gregg Olson	BAL A	1990	64	74	74	6	5	37	43	2.42
Rick Aguilera	MIN A	1992	64	67	52	2	6	41	43	2.84
Jim Kern	TEX A	1979	71	143	136	13	5	29	42	1.57
Mike Marshall	MIN A	1979	90	143	81	10	15	32	42	2.64
Lee Smith	CHI N	1984	69	101	86	9	7	33	42	3.65
Jeff Reardon	MON N	1986	62	89	67	7	9	35	42	3.94
Mitch Williams	PHI N	1991	69	88	84	12	5	30	42	2.34
Wayne Granger	CIN N	1970	67	85	38	6	5	35	41	2.65
Ron Perranoski	MIN A	1970	67	111	55	7	8	34	41	2.43
Kent Tekulve	PIT N	1979	74	134	75	10	8	31	41	2.75
Bob Stanley	BOS A	1983	64	145	65	8	10	33	41	2.85
Guillermo Hernandez	DET A	1984	80	140	112	9	3	32	41	1.92

Most Wins Plus Saves, Season (*cont.*)

Player	Team	Year	G	IP	SO	W	L	SV	W&S	ERA
Jesse Orosco	NY N	1984	60	87	85	10	6	31	41	2.59
Dave Righetti	NY A	1985	74	107	92	12	7	29	41	2.78
Jeff Reardon	BOS A	1991	57	59	44	1	4	40	41	3.03
Randy Myers	SD N	1992	66	80	66	3	6	38	41	4.29
John Wetteland	MON N	1992	67	83	99	4	4	37	41	2.92
Todd Worrell	STL N	1987	75	95	92	8	6	33	41	2.66
Dick Radatz	BOS A	1963	66	125	162	15	6	25	40	1.97
Jack Aker	KC A	1966	66	113	68	8	4	32	40	1.99
Ron Perranoski	MIN A	1969	75	120	62	9	10	31	40	2.11
Greg Minton	SF N	1982	78	123	58	10	4	30	40	1.83
Bob James	CHI A	1985	69	110	88	8	7	32	40	2.13
Lee Smith	CHI N	1985	65	98	112	7	4	33	40	3.04
Don Aase	BAL A	1986	66	82	67	6	7	34	40	2.98
Lee Smith	CHI N	1986	66	90	93	9	9	31	40	3.09
John Franco	CIN N	1987	68	82	61	8	5	32	40	2.52
Lee Smith	CHI N	1987	62	84	96	4	10	36	40	3.12
Jim Gott	PIT N	1988	67	77	76	6	6	34	40	3.49
Doug Jones	CLE A	1988	51	83	72	3	4	37	40	2.27
Mitch Williams	CHI N	1989	76	82	67	4	4	36	40	2.64
Jeff Montgomery	KC A	1992	65	83	69	1	6	39	40	2.18

Two Complete Game Wins in One Day, AL

Player	Team	Date	Score	H	SO	BB	Opp.
Frank Owen	CHI	Jul 1, 1905	3–2	4	2	3	STL
	CHI	Jul 1, 1905	3–0	3	0	0	STL
George Mullin	DET	Sep 22, 1906	5–3	11	4	1	WAS
	DET	Sep 22, 1906	4–3	9	5	2	WAS
Ed Summers	DET	Sep 25, 1908	7–2	6	1	3	PHI
	DET	Sep 25, 1908	1–0	2	6	0	PHI
Ed Walsh	CHI	Sep 29, 1908	5–1	3	10	0	BOS
	CHI	Sep 29, 1908	2–0	4	5	1	BOS
Ray Collins	BOS	Sep 22, 1914	5–3	12	3	1	DET
	BOS	Sep 22, 1914	5–0	4	0	1	DET
Dave Davenport	STL	Jul 29, 1916	3–1	4	4	3	NY
	STL	Jul 29, 1916	3–2	7	7	3	NY
Carl Mays	BOS	Aug 30, 1918	12–0	9	2	0	PHI
	BOS	Aug 30, 1918	4–1	4	3	2	PHI
Urban Shocker	STL	Sep 6, 1924	6–2	9	1	1	CHI
	STL	Sep 6, 1924	6–2	5	0	4	CHI
Dutch Levsen	CLE	Aug 28, 1926	6–1	4	0	1	BOS
	CLE	Aug 28, 1926	5–1	4	0	2	BOS

Two Complete Game Wins in One Day, NL since 1900

Player	Team	Date	Score	H	SO	BB	Opp.
Joe McGinnity	NY	Aug 1, 1903	4–1	6	5	1	BOS
	NY	Aug 1, 1903	5–2	6	3	1	BOS
	NY	Aug 8, 1903	6–1	8	2	0	BKN
	NY	Aug 8, 1903	4–3	5	5	4	BKN
	NY	Aug 31, 1903	4–1	5	4	3	PHI
	NY	Aug 31, 1903	9–2	6	9	1	PHI
Doc Scanlan	BKN	Oct 3, 1905	4–0	3	8	2	STL
	BKN	Oct 3, 1905	3–2	9	5	0	STL
Ed Reulbach	CHI	Sep 26, 1908	5–0	5	6	1	BKN
	CHI	Sep 26, 1908	3–0	3	4	4	BKN
Pol Perritt	NY	Sep 9, 1916	3–1	4	3	2	PHI
	NY	Sep 9, 1916	3–0	4	0	3	PHI
Al Demaree	PHI	Sep 20, 1916	7–0	9	4	2	PIT
	PHI	Sep 20, 1916	3–2	12	3	0	PIT
Grover Alexander	PHI	Sep 23, 1916	7–3	12	3	0	CIN
	PHI	Sep 23, 1916	4–0	8	4	1	CIN
Fred Toney	CIN	Jul 1, 1917	4–1	3	3	1	PIT
	CIN	Jul 1, 1917	5–1	3	1	1	PIT
Grover Alexander	PHI	Sep 3, 1917	5–0	4	5	1	BKN
	PHI	Sep 3, 1917	9–3	9	2	0	BKN
Bill Doak	STL	Sep 18, 1917	2–0	2	1	1	BKN
	STL	Sep 18, 1917	12–4	12	4	2	BKN
Mule Watson	BOS	Aug 13, 1921	4–3	9	2	2	PHI
	BOS	Aug 13, 1921	8–0	2	5	0	PHI
Johnny Stuart	STL	Jul 10, 1923	11–1	3	0	2	BOS
	STL	Jul 10, 1923	6–3	10	0	2	BOS
Hi Bell	STL	Jul 19, 1924	6–1	4	2	1	BOS
	STL	Jul 19, 1924	2–1	9	1	1	BOS

Two Complete Game Wins in One Day, NL before 1900

Player	Team	Date	Score	Inns.	Opp.
Candy Cummings	HAR	Sep 9, 1876	14–4		CIN
	HAR	Sep 9, 1876	8–4		CIN
Monte Ward	PRO	Aug 9, 1878	12–6		IND
	PRO	Aug 9, 1878	8–5		IND
Pud Galvin	BUF	Jul 12, 1879	4–3		TRO
	BUF	Jul 12, 1879	5–4	12	TRO
Mickey Welch	TRO	Jul 4, 1881	8–0		BUF
	TRO	Jul 4, 1881	12–3		BUF
Pud Galvin	BUF	Jul 4, 1882	9–5		WOR
	BUF	Jul 4, 1882	18–8		WOR
Old Hoss Radbourn	PRO	May 30, 1884	12–9		CHI
	PRO	May 30, 1884	9–2		CHI
Dupee Shaw	PRO	Oct 7, 1885	4–0	5	BUF
	PRO	Oct 7, 1885	6–1	5	BUF
	PRO	Oct 10, 1885	3–0	6	BUF
	PRO	Oct 10, 1885	7–3	5	BUF

Two Complete Game Wins in One Day, NL before 1900 (*cont.*)

Player	Team	Date	Score	Inns.	Opp.
Charlie Ferguson	PHI	Oct 9, 1886	5–1		DET
	PHI	Oct 9, 1886	6–1	6	DET
Jim Whitney	WAS	Aug 20, 1887	3–1		BOS
	WAS	Aug 20, 1887	4–3		BOS
John Clarkson	BOS	Sep 12, 1889	3–2		CLE
	BOS	Sep 12, 1889	5–0		CLE
Bill Hutchison	CHI	May 30, 1890	6–4		BKN
	CHI	May 30, 1890	11–7		BKN
Cy Young	CLE	Oct 4, 1890	5–1		PHI
	CLE	Oct 4, 1890	7–3		PHI
Mark Baldwin	PIT	Sep 12, 1891	13–3		BKN
	PIT	Sep 12, 1891	8–4		BKN
Amos Rusie	NY	Sep 26, 1891	10–4		BOS
	NY	Sep 26, 1891	13–5	6	BOS
Mark Baldwin	PIT	May 30, 1892	11–1		BAL
	PIT	May 30, 1892	4–3		BAL
Amos Rusie	NY	Oct 4, 1892	6–4		WAS
	NY	Oct 4, 1892	9–5		WAS
Cy Seymour	NY	Jun 3, 1897	6–1		LOU
	NY	Jun 3, 1897	10–6	7	LOU

Two Complete Game Wins in One Day, Other Leagues

Player	Team	Date	Score	Inns.	Opp.
Tim Keefe	NY AA	Jul 4, 1883	9–1		COL
	NY AA	Jul 4, 1883	3–0		COL
Guy Hecker	LOU AA	Jul 4, 1884	5–4		BKN
	LOU AA	Jul 4, 1884	8–2		BKN
Matt Kilroy	BAL AA	Jul 26, 1887	8–0	7	COL
	BAL AA	Jul 26, 1887	9–1		COL
	BAL AA	Oct 1, 1887	5–2		PHI
	BAL AA	Oct 1, 1887	8–1	7	PHI
Tony Mullane	CIN AA	Sep 20, 1888	1–0		PHI
	CIN AA	Sep 20, 1888	2–1		PHI
Henry Gruber	CLE P	Jul 26, 1890	6–1		NY
	CLE P	Jul 26, 1890	8–7		NY
Bert Cunningham	BUF P	Aug 20, 1890	6–2		CHI
	BUF P	Aug 20, 1890	7–0		CHI
Cannonball Crane	NY P	Sep 27, 1890	9–8		BUF
	NY P	Sep 27, 1890	8–3		BUF

Best Control Pitchers, Career (Min., 1,500 IP)

Player	IP	BB	Ratio	Player	IP	BB	Ratio
Deacon Phillippe	2607	363	1.25	Addie Joss	2336	370	1.43
Babe Adams	2995	430	1.29	Cy Young	7356	1217	1.49

Best Control Pitchers, Career (Min., 1,500 IP) (*cont.*)

Player	IP	BB	Ratio	Player	IP	BB	Ratio
Jesse Tannehill	2770	478	1.55	Bret Saberhagen	1758	358	1.83
Christy Mathewson	4782	846	1.59	Slim Sallee	2819	572	1.83
Red Lucas	2542	455	1.61	Lew Burdette	3068	628	1.84
Nick Altrock	1515	272	1.62	Curt Davis	2325	479	1.85
Grover Alexander	5189	953	1.65	Ed Walsh	2964	617	1.87
Ernie Bonham	1551	287	1.67	Paul Derringer	3646	761	1.88
Noodles Hahn	2012	379	1.70	Ken Raffensberger	2152	449	1.88
Fritz Peterson	2218	426	1.73	Three Finger Brown	3172	673	1.91
Robin Roberts	4689	902	1.73	Sherry Smith	2053	440	1.93
Al Orth	3355	661	1.77	Bill Swift	1638	351	1.93
Dick Rudolph	2049	402	1.77	Jack Quinn	3935	859	1.96
Jesse Barnes	2570	515	1.80	Watty Clark	1747	383	1.97
Pete Donohue	2112	422	1.80	Doc White	3059	670	1.97
Carl Hubbell	3589	724	1.82	Ferguson Jenkins	4500	997	1.99
Juan Marichal	3509	709	1.82	Sam Leever	2661	587	1.99

Lowest ERA, Season, AL

Player	Team	Year	ERA
Dutch Leonard	BOS	1914	1.01
Walter Johnson	WAS	1913	1.09
Addie Joss	CLE	1908	1.16
Cy Young	BOS	1908	1.26
Ed Walsh	CHI	1910	1.27
Walter Johnson	WAS	1918	1.27
Jack Coombs	PHI	1910	1.30
Walter Johnson	WAS	1910	1.35
	WAS	1912	1.39
Ed Walsh	CHI	1909	1.41
	CHI	1908	1.42
Rube Waddell	PHI	1905	1.48
Smoky Joe Wood	BOS	1915	1.49
Walter Johnson	WAS	1919	1.49
Doc White	CHI	1906	1.52
Eddie Cicotte	CHI	1917	1.53
Barney Pelty	STL	1906	1.59
Addie Joss	CLE	1904	1.59
Ed Walsh	CHI	1907	1.60
Luis Tiant	CLE	1968	1.60
Cy Young	BOS	1901	1.62
Rube Waddell	PHI	1904	1.62
Spud Chandler	NY	1943	1.64
Russell Ford	NY	1910	1.65
Dean Chance	LA	1964	1.65
Chief Bender	PHI	1909	1.66
Otto Hess	CLE	1904	1.67

Lowest ERA, Season, AL (*cont.*)

Player	Team	Year	ERA
Smoky Joe Wood	BOS	1910	1.68
Eddie Plank	PHI	1909	1.70
Addie Joss	CLE	1909	1.71
	CLE	1906	1.72
Doc White	CHI	1909	1.72
Walter Johnson	WAS	1914	1.72
Carl Mays	BOS	1917	1.74
Ron Guidry	NY	1978	1.74

Lowest ERA, Season, NL since 1900

Player	Team	Year	ERA
Three Finger Brown	CHI	1906	1.04
Bob Gibson	STL	1968	1.12
Christy Mathewson	NY	1909	1.14
Jack Pfiester	CHI	1907	1.15
Carl Lundgren	CHI	1907	1.17
Grover Alexander	PHI	1915	1.22
Christy Mathewson	NY	1905	1.27
Three Finger Brown	CHI	1909	1.31
Jack Taylor	CHI	1902	1.33
Three Finger Brown	CHI	1907	1.39
Ed Reulbach	CHI	1905	1.42
Orval Overall	CHI	1909	1.42
Christy Mathewson	NY	1908	1.43
Three Finger Brown	CHI	1908	1.47
George McQuillan	PHI	1908	1.53
Dwight Gooden	NY	1985	1.53
Grover Alexander	PHI	1916	1.55
Jack Pfiester	CHI	1906	1.56
Howie Camnitz	PIT	1908	1.56
Rube Marquard	BKN	1916	1.58
George McQuillan	PHI	1910	1.60
Joe McGinnity	NY	1904	1.61
Howie Camnitz	PIT	1909	1.62
Ed Reulbach	CHI	1906	1.65
Sam Leever	PIT	1907	1.66
Carl Hubbell	NY	1933	1.66
Ed Reulbach	CHI	1907	1.69
Nolan Ryan	HOU	1981	1.69
Orval Overall	CHI	1907	1.70
Bill Doak	STL	1914	1.72
Grover Alexander	CHI	1919	1.72
Vic Willis	PIT	1906	1.73
Sandy Koufax	LA	1966	1.73
Hippo Vaughn	CHI	1918	1.74
Sandy Koufax	LA	1964	1.74

Most Innings Pitched, Game, AL

Player	Team	Date	IP	H	R	SO	BB	Score	Opp.
Jack Coombs	PHI	Sep 1, 1906	24	15	1	18	6	4–1	BOS
Joe Harris	BOS	Sep 1, 1906	24	16	4	14	2	1–4	PHI
Ted Lyons	CHI	May 24, 1929	21	24	6	4	2	5–6	DET
Rube Waddell	PHI	Jul 4, 1905	20	15	2	11	4	4–2	BOS
Cy Young	BOS	Jul 4, 1905	20	13	4	9	0	2–4	PHI
George Uhle	DET	May 24, 1929	20	17	5	4	3	6–5	CHI
Les Mueller	DET	Jul 21, 1945	19.2	13	1	6	5	1–1	PHI
Eddie Plank	PHI	Sep 27, 1912	19	12	5	10	6	4–5	WAS
Stan Coveleski	CLE	May 24, 1918	19	12	2	4	6	3–2	NY
Dixie Davis	STL	Aug 9, 1921	19	13	6	8	5	8–6	WAS
Ed Summers	DET	Jul 16, 1909	18	7	0	10	1	0–0	WAS
Walter Johnson	WAS	May 15, 1918	18	10	0	9	1	1–0	CHI
Lefty Williams	CHI	May 15, 1918	18	8	1	3	2	0–1	WAS

Most Innings Pitched, Game, NL

Player	Team	Date	IP	H	R	SO	BB	Score	Opp.
Leon Cadore	BKN	May 1, 1920	26	15	1	7	5	1–1	BOS
Joe Oeschger	BOS	May 1, 1920	26	9	1	7	4	1–1	BKN
Bob Smith	BOS	May 17, 1927	22	20	4	5	9	3–4	CHI
Rube Marquard	NY	May 17, 1914	21	15	1	2	2	3–1	PIT
Babe Adams	PIT	May 17, 1914	21	12	3	6	0	1–3	NY
Lefty Tyler	CHI	Jul 17, 1918	21	13	1	8	1	2–1	PHI
Art Nehf	BOS	Aug 1, 1918	21	12	2	8	5	0–2	PIT
Ad Gumbert	CHI	Jun 30, 1892	20	12	7	2	3	7–7	CIN
Tony Mullane	CIN	Jun 30, 1892	20	14	7	5	3	7–7	CHI
Ed Reulbach	CHI	Aug 24, 1905	20	13	1	7	4	2–1	PHI
Tully Sparks	PHI	Aug 24, 1905	20	19	2	6	1	1–2	CHI
Milt Watson	PHI	Jul 17, 1918	20	19	2	5	4	1–2	CHI
Joe Oeschger	PHI	Apr 30, 1919	20	22	9	2	5	9–9	BKN
Burleigh Grimes	BKN	Apr 30, 1919	20	15	9	7	7	9–9	PHI
Jack Taylor	CHI	Jun 22, 1902	19	14	2	6	1	3–2	PIT
Otto Hess	BOS	Jul 31, 1912	19	14	7	3	8	6–7	PIT
Dana Fillingim	BOS	May 3, 1920	19	12	1	4	4	2–1	BKN
Deacon Phillippe	PIT	Jun 22, 1902	18.2	14	3	6	3	2–3	CHI
Zip Zabel	CHI	Jun 17, 1915	18.1	15	2	6	1	4–3	BKN
Jeff Pfeffer	BKN	Jun 17, 1915	18.1	15	4	6	8	3–4	CHI
Sherry Smith	BKN	May 3, 1920	18.1	13	2	3	5	1–2	BOS
Monte Ward	PRO	Aug 17, 1882	18	9	0	4	1	1–0	DET
Wild Bill Donovan	BKN	Aug 17, 1902	18	14	7	13	7	7–7	STL
Ed Reulbach	CHI	Jun 24, 1905	18	14	1	6	6	2–1	STL
Jack Taylor	STL	Jun 24, 1905	18	11	2	7	4	1–2	CHI
Jeff Pfeffer	BKN	Jun 1, 1919	18	23	10	6	3	9–10	PHI
Guy Bush	CHI	May 14, 1927	18	11	2	5	8	7–2	BOS
Carl Hubbell	NY	Jul 2, 1933	18	6	0	12	0	1–0	STL
Vern Law	PIT	Jul 19, 1955	18	9	2	12	3	4–3	MIL

Triple-Crown Pitchers, AL (most wins, lowest ERA, most strikeouts)

Player	Team	Year	W	L	SO	ERA
Cy Young	BOS	1901	33	10	158	1.62
Rube Waddell	PHI	1905	26	11	287	1.48
Walter Johnson	WAS	1913	36	7	303	1.09
	WAS	1918	23	13	162	1.27
	WAS	1924	23	7	158	2.72
Lefty Grove	PHI	1930	28	5	209	2.54
	PHI	1931	31	4	175	2.06
Lefty Gomez	NY	1934	26	5	158	2.33
	NY	1937	21	11	194	2.33
Hal Newhouser	DET	1945	25	9	212	1.81

Triple-Crown Pitchers, NL (most wins, lowest ERA, most strikeouts)

Player	Team	Year	W	L	SO	ERA
Tommy Bond	BOS	1877	40	17	170	2.11
Old Hoss Radbourn	PRO	1884	60	12	441	1.38
Tim Keefe	NY	1888	35	12	333	1.74
John Clarkson	BOS	1889	49	19	284	2.73
Amos Rusie	NY	1894	36	13	195	2.78
Christy Mathewson	NY	1905	31	8	206	1.27
	NY	1908	37	11	259	1.43
Grover Alexander	PHI	1915	31	10	241	1.22
	PHI	1916	33	12	167	1.55
	PHI	1917	30	13	201	1.86
Hippo Vaughn	CHI	1918	22	10	148	1.74
Grover Alexander	CHI	1920	27	14	173	1.91
Dazzy Vance	BKN	1924	28	6	262	2.16
Bucky Walters	CIN	1939	27	11	137	2.29
Sandy Koufax	LA	1963	25	5	306	1.88
	LA	1965	26	8	382	2.04
	LA	1966	27	9	317	1.73
Steve Carlton	PHI	1972	27	10	310	1.97
Dwight Gooden	NY	1985	24	4	268	1.53

Fewest Base Runners per Nine Innings, Career (Min. 1,500 IP)

Player	W	L	IP	H	BB	BR/9
Addie Joss	160	97	2336	1895	370	8.73
Ed Walsh	195	126	2964	2346	617	9.00
Christy Mathewson	373	188	4782	4216	838	9.51
Walter Johnson	416	279	5923	4921	1355	9.54
Three Finger Brown	239	129	3172	2708	673	9.59
Babe Adams	194	140	2995	2841	430	9.83
Juan Marichal	243	142	3509	3153	709	9.91
Rube Waddell	191	145	2961	2460	803	9.92
Deacon Phillippe	189	107	2607	2518	363	9.95
Sandy Koufax	165	87	2324	1754	817	9.96

Fewest Base Runners per Nine Innings, Career (Min. 1,500 IP) (*cont.*)

Player	W	L	IP	H	BB	BR/9
Roger Clemens	152	72	2031	1703	552	9.99
Chief Bender	210	127	3017	2645	712	10.01
Eddie Plank	327	193	4505	3956	1072	10.04
Tom Seaver	311	205	4782	3971	1390	10.09
Grover Alexander	373	208	5189	4868	953	10.10
Hoyt Wilhelm	143	122	2254	1757	778	10.12
Cy Young	511	315	7356	7092	1217	10.17
Hooks Wiltse	139	90	2112	1892	498	10.18
Catfish Hunter	224	166	3448	2958	954	10.21
Sam Leever	194	101	2661	2449	587	10.27
Ferguson Jenkins	284	226	4500	4142	997	10.28
Don Sutton	324	256	5280	4692	1343	10.29
Ed Reulbach	181	105	2633	2117	892	10.29
Andy Messersmith	130	99	2230	1719	831	10.29
Barney Pelty	92	117	1918	1663	532	10.30
Jeff Tesreau	119	72	1679	1350	572	10.30
Gary Nolan	110	70	1675	1505	413	10.31
Don Drysdale	209	166	3432	3084	855	10.33
Old Hoss Radbourn	311	194	4535	4335	875	10.34
Ernie Bonham	103	72	1551	1501	287	10.38
Dennis Eckersley	181	145	2971	2747	679	10.38
Eddie Cicotte	208	149	3224	2897	827	10.40
Rollie Fingers	114	118	1701	1474	492	10.40
Dick Rudolph	122	108	2049	1971	402	10.42
Orval Overall	106	71	1532	1230	551	10.46
Denny McLain	131	91	1886	1646	548	10.47
Frank Smith	139	111	2273	1975	676	10.49
Dwight Gooden	142	66	1920	1664	575	10.50
Carl Hubbell	253	154	3589	3463	724	10.50
Robin Roberts	286	245	4689	4582	902	10.53
Slim Sallee	173	143	2819	2726	572	10.53
Jesse Tannehill	197	116	2770	2787	477	10.57
Orel Hershiser	116	82	1805	1587	539	10.60
Jim Bunning	224	184	3760	3433	1000	10.61
Jack Taylor	151	139	2617	2502	582	10.61
John Candelaria	177	119	2507	2374	583	10.62
Gaylord Perry	314	265	5351	4938	1379	10.62
Jim Palmer	268	152	3948	3349	1311	10.62
Bret Saberhagen	113	83	1687	1635	358	10.63
Joe McGinnity	247	144	3459	3276	812	10.64
Ron Guidry	170	91	2392	2198	633	10.65
Luis Tiant	229	172	3486	3075	1104	10.67
Ralph Terry	107	99	1849	1748	446	10.68
Mario Soto	100	92	1730	1395	657	10.68
Bob Gibson	251	174	3885	3279	1336	10.69
Fred Toney	137	102	2206	2037	583	10.69
Harry Brecheen	132	92	1908	1731	536	10.69

Fewest Base Runners per Nine Innings, Career (Min. 1,500 IP) (cont.)

Player	W	L	IP	H	BB	BR/9
Fritz Peterson	133	131	2218	2217	426	10.72
Joe Horlen	116	117	2001	1829	554	10.72
Jim Scott	107	113	1872	1624	609	10.74
Eddie Fisher	85	70	1538	1398	438	10.74
Warren Spahn	363	245	5244	4830	1434	10.75
Jimmy Key	116	81	1696	1624	404	10.76
Mike Cuellar	185	130	2808	2538	822	10.77
Bert Blyleven	287	250	4970	4632	1322	10.78
Ken Johnson	91	106	1737	1670	413	10.79
Hippo Vaughn	178	137	2730	2461	817	10.81
Don Newcombe	149	90	2155	2102	490	10.83
Howie Camnitz	133	106	2085	1852	656	10.83
Carl Mays	208	126	3020	2912	734	10.87
John Clarkson	326	177	4536	4295	1191	10.88
Sonny Siebert	140	114	2153	1919	692	10.91
Dean Chance	128	115	2148	1864	739	10.91
Don Wilson	104	92	1748	1479	640	10.91
Dizzy Dean	150	83	1966	1927	458	10.92
Don Mossi	101	80	1548	1493	385	10.92
Dave McNally	184	119	2729	2488	826	10.93
Ron Reed	146	140	2476	2374	633	10.93
Whitey Ford	236	106	3170	2766	1086	10.94
Mort Cooper	128	75	1841	1666	571	10.94
Larry Dierker	139	123	2334	2130	711	10.96
Mel Stottlemyre	164	139	2662	2435	809	10.97

Most Complete Games, Season, AL

Player	Team	Year	CG
Jack Chesbro	NY	1904	48
George Mullin	DET	1904	42
Ed Walsh	CHI	1908	42
Cy Young	BOS	1902	41
	BOS	1904	40
Joe McGinnity	BAL	1901	39
Bill Dinneen	BOS	1902	39
Eddie Plank	PHI	1903	39
Rube Waddell	PHI	1904	39
Cy Young	BOS	1901	38
Jack Powell	NY	1904	38
Walter Johnson	WAS	1910	38
Bill Dinneen	BOS	1904	37
Casey Patten	WAS	1904	37
Eddie Plank	PHI	1904	37
Ed Walsh	CHI	1907	37
Frank Smith	CHI	1909	37
Al Orth	WAS	1902	36
Jack Powell	STL	1902	36

Most Complete Games, Season, AL (*cont.*)

Player	Team	Year	CG
Al Orth	NY	1906	36
Walter Johnson	WAS	1911	36
	WAS	1916	36
Bob Feller	CLE	1946	36
Chick Fraser	PHI	1901	35
Roscoe Miller	DET	1901	35
Bill Bernhard	CLE	1904	35
Harry Howell	STL	1905	35
George Mullin	DET	1905	35
Eddie Plank	PHI	1905	35
George Mullin	DET	1906	35
	DET	1907	35
Jack Coombs	PHI	1910	35
Smoky Joe Wood	BOS	1912	35
Walter Johnson	WAS	1915	35
Babe Ruth	BOS	1917	35
Bill Carrick	WAS	1901	34
Wild Bill Donovan	DET	1903	34
Rube Waddell	PHI	1903	34
Cy Young	BOS	1903	34
Frank Owen	CHI	1904	34
Addie Joss	CLE	1907	34
Walter Johnson	WAS	1911	34
	WAS	1912	34
Red Donahue	STL	1902	33
Casey Patten	WAS	1902	33
Eddie Plank	PHI	1902	33
Jack Chesbro	NY	1903	33
Jack Powell	STL	1903	33
Ed Killian	DET	1905	33
Otto Hess	CLE	1906	33
Eddie Plank	PHI	1907	33
Cy Young	BOS	1907	33
Walter Johnson	WAS	1914	33
Dizzy Trout	DET	1944	33
Bill Dinneen	BOS	1903	32
Addie Joss	CLE	1903	32
Casey Patten	WAS	1903	32
Ed Killian	DET	1904	32
Frank Owen	CHI	1905	32
Cy Young	BOS	1905	32
Red Faber	CHI	1921	32
George Uhle	CLE	1926	32
Ted Lewis	BOS	1901	31
Eddie Plank	PHI	1901	31
Snake Wiltse	PHI	1902	
	BAL	1902	31

Most Complete Games, Season, AL (*cont.*)

Player	Team	Year	CG
George Mullin	DET	1903	31
Nick Altrock	CHI	1904	31
Barney Pelty	STL	1904	31
Jack Townsend	WAS	1904	31
Nick Altrock	CHI	1905	31
Addie Joss	CLE	1905	31
Bob Rhoads	CLE	1906	31
Ray Caldwell	NY	1915	31
Elmer Myers	PHI	1916	31
Urban Shocker	STL	1921	31
Red Faber	CHI	1922	31
Wes Ferrell	BOS	1935	31
Bobo Newsom	STL	1938	31
Bob Feller	CLE	1940	31
Roy Patterson	CHI	1901	30
Chief Bender	PHI	1903	30
Al Orth	WAS	1903	30
Willie Sudhoff	STL	1903	30
Red Donahue	CLE	1904	30
Wild Bill Donovan	DET	1904	30
Fred Glade	STL	1904	30
Cy Falkenberg	WAS	1906	30
Cy Young	BOS	1908	30
	CLE	1909	30
Walter Johnson	WAS	1913	30
	WAS	1917	30
Scott Perry	PHI	1918	30
Ted Lyons	CHI	1927	30
Thornton Lee	CHI	1941	30
Bob Feller	CLE	1946	30
Catfish Hunter	NY	1975	30

Most Complete Games, Season, NL since 1900

Player	Team	Year	CG
Vic Willis	BOS	1902	45
Joe McGinnity	NY	1903	44
Noodles Hahn	CIN	1901	41
Irv Young	BOS	1905	41
Jack Taylor	STL	1904	39
Vic Willis	BOS	1904	39
Oscar Jones	BKN	1904	38
Joe McGinnity	NY	1904	38
Grover Alexander	PHI	1916	38
Dummy Taylor	NY	1901	37
Christy Mathewson	NY	1903	37
Irv Young	BOS	1906	37

Most Complete Games, Season, NL since 1900 (*cont.*)

Player	Team	Year	CG
Wild Bill Donovan	BKN	1901	36
Christy Mathewson	NY	1901	36
Togie Pittinger	BOS	1902	36
Vic Willis	BOS	1905	36
Grover Alexander	PHI	1915	36
Togie Pittinger	BOS	1903	35
Christy Mathewson	NY	1904	35
Kid Nichols	STL	1904	35
Grover Alexander	PHI	1917	35
Pink Hawley	NY	1900	34
Red Donahue	PHI	1901	34
Noodles Hahn	CIN	1902	34
Doc White	PHI	1902	34
Noodles Hahn	CIN	1903	34
Jack Taylor	STL	1905	34
Christy Mathewson	NY	1908	34
Bill Dinneen	BOS	1900	33
Jack Powell	STL	1901	33
Vic Willis	BOS	1901	33
Jack Taylor	CHI	1902	33
	CHI	1903	33
Noodles Hahn	CIN	1904	33
Togie Pittinger	BOS	1904	33
Christy Mathewson	NY	1905	33
Big Jeff Pfeffer	BOS	1906	33
Kaiser Wilhelm	BKN	1908	33
Grover Alexander	CHI	1920	33
Burleigh Grimes	BKN	1923	33
Robin Roberts	PHI	1953	33
Nixey Callahan	CHI	1900	32
Bill Carrick	NY	1900	32
Cy Young	STL	1900	32
Long Tom Hughes	CHI	1901	32
Patsy Flaherty	PIT	1904	32
Chick Fraser	PHI	1904	32
Joe McGinnity	NY	1906	32
Jack Taylor	STL	1906	
	CHI	1906	32
Vic Willis	PIT	1906	32
Bob Ewing	CIN	1907	32
George McQuillan	PHI	1908	32
Three Finger Brown	CHI	1909	32
Grover Alexander	PHI	1914	32
Bill Dinneen	BOS	1901	31
Jack Chesbro	PIT	1902	31
Oscar Jones	BKN	1903	31
Deacon Phillippe	PIT	1903	31

Most Complete Games, Season, NL since 1900 (*cont.*)

Player	Team	Year	CG
Jake Weimer	CHI	1904	31
	CIN	1906	31
Christy Mathewson	NY	1907	31
Hooks Wiltse	NY	1908	31
Grover Alexander	PHI	1911	31
Dick Rudolph	BOS	1914	31
Fred Toney	CIN	1917	31
Bucky Walters	CIN	1939	31
Al Orth	PHI	1901	30
Deacon Phillippe	PIT	1901	30
Jack Taylor	CHI	1901	30
Wild Bill Donovan	BKN	1902	30
Christy Mathewson	NY	1902	30
Ned Garvin	BKN	1903	30
Sam Leever	PIT	1903	30
Bob Ewing	CIN	1905	30
Gus Dorner	BOS	1906	30
Nap Rucker	BKN	1908	30
Bill James	BOS	1914	30
Dick Rudolph	BOS	1915	30
Jeff Pfeffer	BKN	1916	30
Burleigh Grimes	BKN	1921	30
	BKN	1924	30
Robin Roberts	PHI	1952	30
Juan Marichal	SF	1968	30
Ferguson Jenkins	CHI	1971	30
Steve Carlton	PHI	1972	30

Most Innings Pitched, Season, AL

Player	Team	Year	IP
Ed Walsh	CHI	1908	464
Jack Chesbro	NY	1904	455
Ed Walsh	CHI	1907	422
	CHI	1912	393
Jack Powell	NY	1904	390
Cy Young	BOS	1902	385
Rube Waddell	PHI	1904	383
Joe McGinnity	BAL	1901	382
George Mullin	DET	1904	382
Cy Young	BOS	1904	380
Wilbur Wood	CHI	1972	377
Mickey Lolich	DET	1971	376
Walter Johnson	WAS	1910	373
	WAS	1914	372
Cy Young	BOS	1901	371
Bill Dinneen	BOS	1902	371
Walter Johnson	WAS	1916	371

Most Innings Pitched, Season, AL (cont.)

Player	Team	Year	IP
Bob Feller	CLE	1946	371
Ed Walsh	CHI	1910	370
	CHI	1911	369
Walter Johnson	WAS	1912	368
Eddie Plank	PHI	1904	365
Frank Smith	CHI	1909	365
Wilbur Wood	CHI	1973	359
Casey Patten	WAS	1904	358
George Uhle	CLE	1923	358
George Mullin	DET	1907	357
Jack Coombs	PHI	1910	353
Red Faber	CHI	1922	353
Dizzy Trout	DET	1944	352
George Mullin	DET	1905	348
Urban Shocker	STL	1922	348
Eddie Plank	PHI	1904	347
Walter Johnson	WAS	1913	346
Eddie Plank	PHI	1907	344
Smoky Joe Wood	BOS	1912	344
Gaylord Perry	CLE	1973	344
Cy Young	BOS	1907	343
Bob Feller	CLE	1941	343
Gaylord Perry	CLE	1972	343
Cy Young	BOS	1903	342
Eddie Cicotte	CHI	1917	342
Otto Hess	CLE	1906	340
Al Orth	NY	1906	339
Addie Joss	CLE	1907	339
Jack Coombs	PHI	1911	337
Walter Johnson	WAS	1915	337
Eddie Plank	PHI	1902	336
Bill Dinneen	BOS	1904	336
Denny McLain	DET	1968	336
Frank Owen	CHI	1905	334
Wilbur Wood	CHI	1971	334
Nolan Ryan	CAL	1974	333
Roscoe Miller	DET	1901	332
Ed Killian	DET	1904	332
Scott Perry	PHI	1918	332
Chick Fraser	PHI	1901	331
Red Faber	CHI	1921	331
George Mullin	DET	1906	330
Bobo Newsom	STL	1938	330
Rube Waddell	PHI	1905	329
Jack Powell	STL	1902	328
Walter Johnson	WAS	1917	328
Ferguson Jenkins	TEX	1974	328

Most Innings Pitched, Season, AL (*cont.*)

Player	Team	Year	IP
Urban Shocker	STL	1921	327
General Crowder	WAS	1932	327
Mickey Lolich	DET	1972	327
Babe Ruth	BOS	1917	326
Nolan Ryan	CAL	1973	326
Jack Chesbro	NY	1903	325
	NY	1906	325
Addie Joss	CLE	1908	325
Walter Johnson	WAS	1918	325
Denny McLain	DET	1969	325
Bert Blyleven	MIN	1973	325

Most Innings Pitched, Season, NL since 1900

Player	Team	Year	IP
Joe McGinnity	NY	1903	434
Vic Willis	BOS	1902	410
Joe McGinnity	NY	1904	408
Christy Mathewson	NY	1908	391
Togie Pittinger	BOS	1902	389
Grover Alexander	PHI	1916	389
	PHI	1917	388
Irv Young	BOS	1905	378
Oscar Jones	BKN	1904	377
Grover Alexander	PHI	1915	376
Noodles Hahn	CIN	1901	375
Christy Mathewson	NY	1904	368
Grover Alexander	PHI	1911	367
Christy Mathewson	NY	1903	366
Grover Alexander	CHI	1920	363
George McQuillan	PHI	1908	360
Irv Young	BOS	1906	358
Grover Alexander	PHI	1914	355
Dummy Taylor	NY	1901	353
Togie Pittinger	BOS	1903	352
Jack Taylor	STL	1904	352
Stoney McGlynn	STL	1907	352
Wild Bill Donovan	BKN	1902	351
Vic Willis	BOS	1904	350
Bob Harmon	STL	1911	348
Joe McGinnity	BKN	1900	347
Robin Roberts	PHI	1953	347
Steve Carlton	PHI	1972	346
Three Finger Brown	CHI	1909	343
Bill Carrick	NY	1900	342
Vic Willis	BOS	1905	342
Pete Schneider	CIN	1917	342
Phil Niekro	ATL	1979	342

Most Innings Pitched, Season, NL since 1900 (*cont.*)

Player	Team	Year	IP
Dick Rudolph	BOS	1915	341
Joe McGinnity	NY	1906	340
Fred Toney	CIN	1917	340
Christy Mathewson	NY	1905	339
Jack Powell	STL	1901	338
Togie Pittinger	PHI	1905	337
Robin Roberts	PHI	1954	337
Christy Mathewson	NY	1901	336
Dick Rudolph	BOS	1914	336
Sandy Koufax	LA	1965	336
Togie Pittinger	BOS	1904	335
Phil Niekro	ATL	1978	334
Bob Ewing	CIN	1907	333
Nap Rucker	BKN	1908	333
Kaiser Wilhelm	BKN	1908	332
Bill James	BOS	1914	332
Burleigh Grimes	PIT	1928	331
Hooks Wiltse	NY	1908	330
Robin Roberts	PHI	1952	330
Phil Niekro	ATL	1977	330
Pink Hawley	NY	1900	329
Jeff Pfeffer	BKN	1916	329
Gaylord Perry	SF	1970	329
Wilbur Cooper	PIT	1920	327
	PIT	1921	327
Burleigh Grimes	BKN	1923	327
Kid Nichols	BOS	1901	326
Juan Marichal	SF	1968	326
Jack Taylor	CHI	1902	325
Gaylord Perry	SF	1969	325

Most Grand Slams Allowed, Career

Player	Total	Player	Total
Ned Garver	9	Frank Viola	8
Jim Kaat	9	Early Wynn	8
Milt Pappas	9	Doug Bair	7
Jerry Reuss	9	Larry French	7
Bert Blyleven	8	Jim Hearn	7
Jim Brewer	8	Phil Niekro	7
Roy Face	8	Gaylord Perry	7
Bob Feller	8	Ray Sadecki	7
Johnny Klippstein	8	Jack Sanford	7
Lindy McDaniel	8	Don Sutton	7
Tug McGraw	8	Mike Torrez	7
Nolan Ryan	8	Lon Warneke	7
Frank Tanana	8		

Most Wins Since Age 40

Player	Birth Date	W	L
Phil Niekro	Apr 1, 1939	121	103
Jack Quinn	Jul 5, 1883	109	97
Cy Young	Mar 29, 1867	75	60
Warren Spahn	Apr 23, 1921	75	63
Gaylord Perry	Sep 15, 1938	68	65
Nolan Ryan	Jan 31, 1947	66	57
Hoyt Wilhelm	Jul 26, 1923	54	47
Tommy John	May 22, 1943	51	60
Red Faber	Sep 8, 1888	49	64
Grover Alexander	Feb 26, 1887	46	30
Charlie Hough	Jan 5, 1948	44	63
Don Sutton	Apr 2, 1945	44	38
Jerry Koosman	Dec 23, 1942	42	33
Connie Marrero	Apr 25, 1911	33	30
Dazzy Vance	Mar 4, 1891	33	31
Babe Adams	May 18, 1882	32	27

Pitching Accomplishments in AL and NL

Player	Team	Accomplishment
Gaylord Perry	CLE A 1972	Cy Young Award
	SD N 1978	
Cy Young	CLE N 1897	No-Hitter
	BOS A 1904	
	BOS A 1908	
Jim Bunning	DET A 1958	No-Hitter
	PHI N 1964	
Nolan Ryan	CAL A 1973	No-Hitter
	CAL A 1973	
	CAL A 1974	
	CAL A 1975	
	TEX A 1990	
	TEX A 1991	
	HOU N 1981	
Cy Young		200 or More Wins, Career
Jim Bunning		100 or More Wins, Career
Ferguson Jenkins		100 or More Wins, Career
Gaylord Perry		100 or More Wins, Career
Nolan Ryan		100 or More Wins, Career

Won 20 and Hit .300 in Same Year, AL

Player	Team	Year	W	L	AB	H	HR	RBI	BA
Clark Griffith	CHI	1901	24	7	89	27	2	14	.303
Cy Young	BOS	1903	28	9	137	44	1	14	.321
Ed Killian	DET	1907	25	13	122	39	0	11	.320
Jack Coombs	PHI	1911	28	12	141	45	2	23	.319

Won 20 and Hit .300 in Same Year, AL (cont.)

Player	Team	Year	W	L	AB	H	HR	RBI	BA
Babe Ruth	BOS	1917	24	13	123	40	2	12	.325
Carl Mays	NY	1921	27	9	143	49	2	22	.343
Joe Bush	NY	1922	26	7	95	31	0	12	.311
George Uhle	CLE	1923	26	16	144	52	0	22	.361
Joe Shaute	CLE	1924	20	17	107	34	1	10	.318
Walter Johnson	WAS	1925	20	7	97	42	2	20	.433
Ted Lyons	CHI	1930	22	15	122	36	1	15	.311
Wes Ferrell	CLE	1931	22	12	116	37	9	30	.319
Schoolboy Rowe	DET	1934	24	8	109	33	2	22	.303
Wes Ferrell	BOS	1935	25	14	150	52	7	32	.347
Red Ruffing	NY	1939	21	7	114	35	1	20	.307
Ned Garver	STL	1951	20	12	95	29	1	9	.305
Catfish Hunter	OAK	1971	21	11	103	36	1	12	.350

Won 20 and Hit .300 in Same Year, NL

Player	Team	Year	W	L	AB	H	HR	RBI	BA
Jesse Tannehill	PIT	1900	20	6	110	37	0	17	.336
Brickyard Kennedy	BKN	1900	20	13	123	37	0	15	.301
Claude Hendrix	PIT	1912	24	9	121	39	1	15	.322
Burleigh Grimes	BKN	1920	23	11	111	34	0	16	.306
Wilbur Cooper	PIT	1924	20	14	104	36	0	15	.346
Pete Donohue	CIN	1926	20	14	106	33	0	14	.311
Burleigh Grimes	PIT	1928	25	14	131	42	0	16	.321
Curt Davis	STL	1939	22	16	105	40	1	17	.381
Bucky Walters	CIN	1939	27	11	120	39	1	16	.325
Johnny Sain	BOS	1947	21	12	107	37	0	18	.346
Don Newcombe	BKN	1955	20	5	117	42	7	23	.359
Warren Spahn	MIL	1958	22	11	108	36	2	15	.333
Don Drysdale	LA	1965	23	12	130	39	7	19	.300
Bob Gibson	STL	1970	23	7	109	33	2	19	.303

Most Home Runs, Pitcher, Career

Player	HR	Player	HR
Wes Ferrell	38	Gary Peters	19
Bob Lemon	37	Schoolboy Rowe	18
Red Ruffing	36	Jim Whitney	18
Warren Spahn	35	Cy Young	18
Earl Wilson	35	Jim Tobin	17
Don Drysdale	29	Early Wynn	17
John Clarkson	24	Jim Kaat	16
Bob Gibson	24	Johnny Antonelli	15
Walter Johnson	24	Don Cardwell	15
Jack Stivetts	21	Dick Donovan	15
Milt Pappas	20	Lefty Grove	15
Dizzy Trout	20	Ad Gumbert	15
Jack Harshman	19	Jouett Meekin	15

Most Home Runs, Pitcher, Career (cont.)

Player	HR
Don Newcombe	15
Joe Nuxhall	15
Claude Passeau	15
Pedro Ramos	15
Babe Ruth	15
Hal Schumacher	15
Rick Wise	15
Tommy Byrne	14
Freddie Fitzsimmons	14
Don Larsen	14
Steve Carlton	13
Claude Hendrix	13
Ferguson Jenkins	13
Don Robinson	13
Mickey Welch	13
Lew Burdette	12
Bob Forsch	12
Bill Hutchinson	12
Tim Keefe	12
Blue Moon Odom	12
Al Orth	12
Tom Seaver	12
Sonny Siebert	12
Monte Ward	12
Grover Alexander	11
Larry Christenson	11
Tony Cloninger	11
Curt Davis	11
Pink Hawley	11
Harry Howell	11
Frank Killen	11
Vern Law	11
Charlie Root	11
Bucky Walters	11
Mark Baldwin	10
Henry Boyle	10
Ken Brett	10
Tom Griffin	10
J. R. Richard	10

Three Home Runs in One Game, Pitcher

Player	Team	Date
Guy Hecker	LOU AA	Aug 15, 1886
Jim Tobin	BOS N	May 13, 1942

Two Home Runs in One Game, Pitcher, AL

Player	Team	Date
Ed Summers	DET	Sep 17, 1910
Ed Willett	DET	Jun 30, 1912
Jim Shaw	WAS	May 2, 1919
Garland Buckeye	CLE	Sep 10, 1925
Jess Doyle	DET	Sep 28, 1925
Red Ruffing	NY	Sep 18, 1930
Wes Ferrell	CLE	Aug 31, 1931
Chief Hogsett	DET	Aug 31, 1932
Wes Ferrell	BOS	Jul 13, 1934
	BOS	Aug 22, 1934
	BOS	Jul 31, 1935
Mel Harder	CLE	Jul 31, 1935
Red Ruffing	NY	Jun 17, 1936
Wes Ferrell	BOS	Aug 12, 1936
Eldon Auker	DET	Aug 14, 1937
Jack Wilson	BOS	Jun 16, 1940
Spud Chandler	NY	Jul 26, 1940
Bob Lemon	CLE	Jul 24, 1949
Babe Birrer	DET	Jul 19, 1955
Dixie Howell	CHI	Jun 16, 1957
Billy Hoeft	DET	Jul 14, 1957
Jack Harshman	BAL	Jul 16, 1958
	BAL	Sep 23, 1958
Milt Pappas	BAL	Aug 27, 1961
Dick Donovan	CLE	May 18, 1962
Pedro Ramos	CLE	May 30, 1962
Dick Donovan	CLE	Aug 31, 1962
Pedro Ramos	CLE	Jul 31, 1963
Earl Wilson	BOS	Aug 16, 1965
Jim Rooker	KC	Jul 7, 1969
Sonny Siebert	BOS	Sep 2, 1971

Two Home Runs in One Game, Pitcher, NL

Player	Team	Date
Monte Ward	NY	May 3, 1883
Fred Goldsmith	CHI	May 27, 1884
John Clarkson	CHI	Oct 9, 1884
Harry Staley	BOS	Jun 1, 1893
Scott Stratton	CHI	Jul 27, 1894
Frank Foreman	CIN	Jul 4, 1895
Jack Stivetts	BOS	Jun 12, 1896
Art Nehf	NY	Jul 29, 1924
Tony Kaufmann	CHI	Jul 4, 1925
Jack Knight	PHI	Jun 24, 1926
Phil Collins	PHI	Jul 22, 1930
Hal Schumacher	NY	Apr 24, 1934

Two Home Runs in One Game, Pitcher, NL (cont.)

Player	Team	Date
Bill Lee	CHI	May 7, 1941
Bucky Walters	CIN	May 20, 1945
Dave Koslo	NY	Jul 7, 1949
Ben Wade	BKN	Jul 6, 1952
Don Newcombe	BKN	Apr 14, 1955
	BKN	May 30, 1955
Jim Hearn	NY	Jun 9, 1955
Don Newcombe	BKN	Sep 19, 1956
Lew Burdette	MIL	Aug 13, 1957
	MIL	Jul 10, 1958
Don Drysdale	LA	Aug 23, 1958
Don Cardwell	CHI	Sep 2, 1960
Glen Hobbie	CHI	Jul 2, 1961
Tony Cloninger	ATL	Jun 16, 1966
	ATL	Jul 3, 1966
Rick Wise	PHI	Jun 23, 1971
	PHI	Aug 28, 1971
Ferguson Jenkins	CHI	Sep 1, 1971
Larry Christenson	PHI	Sep 5, 1976
Randy Lerch	PHI	Sep 30, 1978
Walt Terrell	NY	Aug 6, 1983
Jim Gott	SF	May 12, 1985
Derek Lilliquist	ATL	May 1, 1990

Two Home Runs in One Game, Pitcher, Other Leagues

Player	Team	Date
Bob Caruthers	STL AA	Aug 16, 1886
Jack Stivetts	STL AA	Jun 10, 1890
	STL AA	Aug 6, 1891

Two Home Runs in One Game Twice in One Season, Pitcher

Player	Team	Date
Wes Ferrell	BOS A	Jul 13, 1934
	BOS A	Aug 22, 1934
Don Newcombe	BKN N	Apr 14, 1955
	BKN N	May 30, 1955
Jack Harshman	BAL A	Jul 16, 1958
	BAL A	Sep 23, 1958
Dick Donovan	CLE A	May 18, 1962
	CLE A	Aug 31, 1962
Tony Cloninger	ATL N	Jun 16, 1966
	ATL N	Jul 3, 1966
Rick Wise	PHI N	Jun 23, 1971
	PHI N	Aug 28, 1971

Pinch-Hit Grand Slams, Pitcher

Player	Team	Date	Opp.	Opp. Pitcher
Mike O'Neill	STL N	Jun 3, 1902	BOS	Togie Pittinger
Schoolboy Rowe	PHI N	May 2, 1943	BOS	Al Javery
Zeb Eaton	DET A	Jul 15, 1945	NY	Hank Borowy
Early Wynn	WAS A	Sep 15, 1946	DET	Johnny Gorsica
Tommy Byrne	CHI A	May 16, 1953	NY	Ewell Blackwell

Grand Slams, Pitcher, AL

Player	Team	Date	Opp.	Opp. Pitcher
Cy Falkenberg	WAS	Jul 18, 1906	CHI	Frank Owen
Walter Johnson	WAS	Jun 21, 1914	DET	George Boehler
Jim Shaw	WAS	May 5, 1919	PHI	Jing Johnson
Babe Ruth	BOS	May 20, 1919	STL	Dave Davenport
George Uhle	CLE	Apr 28, 1921	DET	Dutch Leonard
Red Ruffing	NY	Apr 14, 1933	BOS	Bob Weiland
Lefty Grove	BOS	Jul 27, 1935	PHI	George Blaeholder
Wes Ferrell	BOS	Aug 12, 1936	PHI	Hod Lisenbee
Lynn Nelson	PHI	Jul 21, 1937	CLE	Ivy Andrews
Monty Stratton	CHI	Jun 10, 1938	BOS	Charlie Wagner
Schoolboy Rowe	DET	Jul 22, 1939	PHI	Nel Potter

Grand Slams, Pitcher, AL

Player	Team	Date	Opp.	Opp. Pitcher
Spud Chandler	NY	Jul 26, 1940	CHI	Pete Appleton
Zeb Eaton	DET	Jul 15, 1945	NY	Hank Borowy
Early Wynn	WAS	Sep 15, 1946	DET	Johnny Gorsica
Carl Scheib	PHI	May 8, 1948	CHI	Bob Gillespie
Dizzy Trout	DET	Jul 28, 1949	WAS	Al Gettel
	DET	Jun 23, 1950	NY	Tommy Bryne
Saul Rogovin	DET	Jul 23, 1950	NY	Ed Lopat
Ellis Kinder	BOS	Aug 6, 1950	CHI	Billy Pierce
Tommy Byrne	STL	Sep 18, 1951	WAS	Sid Hudson
Bob Porterfield	WAS	May 5, 1953	DET	Bill Wright
Tommy Byrne	CHI	May 16, 1953	NY	Ewell Blackwell
Don Larsen	NY	Apr 22, 1956	BOS	Frank Sullivan
Bob Grim	KC	Apr 15, 1959	CHI	Barry Latman
Camilo Pascual	WAS	Aug 4, 1960	NY	Bob Turley
Pedro Ramos	CLE	May 30, 1962	BAL	Chuck Estrada
Orlando Pena	KC	May 31, 1963	WAS	Don Rudolph
Camilo Pascual	MIN	Apr 27, 1965	CLE	Stan Williams
Mel Stottlemyre	NY	Jul 20, 1965	BOS	Bill Monbouquette
Earl Wilson	DET	Aug 13, 1966	BOS	Dan Osinski
John O'Donoghue	CLE	Jun 1, 1967	DET	Denny McLain
Gary Peters	CHI	May 5, 1968	NY	Al Downing
Dave McNally	BAL	Aug 26, 1968	OAK	Chuck Dobson
Fred Talbot	SEA	Jul 9, 1969	CAL	Eddie Fisher
Steve Dunning	CLE	May 11, 1971	OAK	Diego Segui

Grand Slams, Pitcher, NL

Player	Team	Date	Opp.	Opp. Pitcher
Mike O'Neill	STL	Jun 3, 1902	BOS	Togie Pittinger
Patsy Flaherty	BOS	May 24, 1907	NY	Hooks Wiltse
Deacon Phillippe	PIT	Jul 22, 1910	BKN	Fred Miller
George Ferguson	BOS	Sep 22, 1910	CIN	Jack Rowan
Lee Meadows	PHI	Apr 28, 1921	BOS	Jack Scott
Mule Watson	NY	Jun 8, 1924	PIT	Johnny Morrison
Jimmy Ring	PHI	May 12, 1925	PIT	Vic Aldridge
Phil Collins	PHI	Jun 23, 1929	BOS	Kent Greenfield
Bill Walker	NY	May 5, 1930	PIT	Larry French
Freddie Fitzsimmons	NY	May 10, 1931	CHI	Pat Malone
Roy Parmelee	NY	Jul 17, 1934	CHI	Lon Warneke
Al Hollingsworth	CIN	May 28, 1936	STL	Lon Warneke
Clay Bryant	CHI	Aug 28, 1937	BOS	Frank Gabler
Curt Davis	STL	Apr 26, 1938	CIN	Al Hollingsworth
Claude Passeau	CHI	May 19, 1941	BKN	Hugh Casey
Schoolboy Rowe	PHI	May 2, 1943	BOS	Al Javery
Ox Miller	CHI	Sep 7, 1947	PIT	Kirby Higbe
Monte Kennedy	NY	Jul 3, 1949	BKN	Morrie Martin
Erv Palica	BKN	Sep 24, 1950	PHI	Bubba Church

Grand Slams, Pitcher, NL (*cont.*)

Player	Team	Date	Opp.	Opp. Pitcher
Lew Burdette	MIL	Jul 10, 1958	LA	Johnny Podres
Bob Purkey	CIN	Aug 1, 1959	CHI	John Buzhardt
Don Drysdale	LA	Aug 9, 1961	MIL	Don Nottebart
Art Mahaffey	PHI	Aug 2, 1962	NY	Craig Anderson
Carl Willey	NY	Jul 15, 1963	HOU	Ken Johnson
Bob Gibson	STL	Sep 29, 1965	SF	Gaylord Perry
Tony Cloninger	ATL	Jul 3, 1966	SF	Bob Priddy
	ATL	Jul 3, 1966	SF	Ray Sadecki
Jack Hamilton	NY	May 20, 1967	STL	Al Jackson
Al McBean	PIT	Jul 28, 1968	STL	Larry Jaster
Mike Corkins	SD	Sep 4, 1970	CIN	Jim Merritt
Rick Wise	PHI	Aug 28, 1971	SF	Don McMahon
Burt Hooton	CHI	Sep 16, 1972	NY	Tom Seaver
Bob Gibson	STL	Jul 26, 1973	NY	John Strohmayer
Rick Wise	STL	Aug 21, 1973	ATL	Roric Harrison
Jim Lonborg	PHI	Jun 24, 1974	MON	Chuck Taylor
Don Stanhouse	MON	Jul 6, 1977	CHI	Bill Bonham
Larry Christenson	PHI	Sep 27, 1977	CHI	Dennis Lamp
Bruce Kison	PIT	Aug 26, 1979	SD	Bob Shirley
Enrique Romo	PIT	Oct 1, 1980	NY	Roy Lee Jackson
Scott Sanderson	MON	Sep 11, 1982	CHI	Randy Martz
Joaquin Andujar	STL	May 15, 1984	ATL	Jeff Dedmon
Steve Carlton	PHI	May 16, 1984	LA	Fernando Valenzuela
Don Robinson	PIT	Sep 12, 1985	CHI	Warren Brusstar
Bob Forsch	STL	Aug 10, 1986	PIT	Mike Bielecki

Most Home Runs, Pitcher, Season

Player	Team	Year	HR
Wes Ferrell	CLE A	1931	9
Jack Stivetts	STL AA	1890	8
Wes Ferrell	BOS A	1935	7
Bob Lemon	CLE A	1949	7
Don Newcombe	BKN N	1955	7
Don Drysdale	LA N	1958	7
	LA N	1965	7
Earl Wilson	BOS A	1966	
	DET A	1966	7
	DET A	1968	7
John Clarkson	CHI N	1887	6
Bill Hutchinson	CHI N	1894	6
Hal Schumacher	NY N	1934	6
Jim Tobin	BOS N	1942	6
Bob Lemon	CLE A	1950	6
Jack Harshman	CHI A	1956	6
	BAL A	1958	6
Earl Wilson	BOS A	1965	6

Most Home Runs, Pitcher, Season *(cont.)*

Player	Team	Year	HR
Ferguson Jenkins	CHI N	1971	6
Sonny Siebert	BOS A	1971	6
Rick Wise	PHI N	1971	6
Pink Hawley	PIT N	1895	5
Art Nehf	NY N	1924	5
Wes Ferrell	BOS A	1936	5
Red Ruffing	NY A	1936	5
Dizzy Trout	DET A	1944	5
Jim Tobin	BOS N	1945	5
Bob Lemon	CLE A	1948	5
	CLE A	1956	5
Don Cardwell	PHI N	1960	
	CHI N	1960	5
Don Drysdale	LA N	1961	5
Earl Wilson	BOS A	1964	5
Bob Gibson	STL N	1965	5
Tony Cloninger	ATL N	1966	5
Blue Moon Odom	OAK A	1969	5
Bob Gibson	STL N	1972	5

Most Hits, Pitcher, Career

Player	H
Cy Young	623
Walter Johnson	542
Red Ruffing	520
George Mullin	397
George Uhle	393
Red Lucas	392
Al Orth	389
Burleigh Grimes	380
Grover Alexander	378
Early Wynn	365
Ted Lyons	364
Warren Spahn	363
Christy Mathewson	362
Steve Carlton	346
Brickyard Kennedy	333
Eddie Plank	331
Wes Ferrell	316
Jack Powell	310
Joe Bush	306

Pitchers Who Stole Home, AL

Player	Team	Date
Win Mercer	WAS	Aug 10, 1901
Frank Owen	CHI	Aug 2, 1904
	CHI	Jun 13, 1905
Wild Bill Donovan	DET	Sep 14, 1905
	DET	May 7, 1906
Frank Owen	CHI	Apr 27, 1908
Ed Walsh	CHI	Jun 13, 1908
	CHI	Jul 2, 1909
Eddie Plank	PHI	Aug 30, 1909
Jack Warhop	NY	Aug 27, 1910
	NY	Jul 12, 1912
Ray Fisher	NY	May 3, 1915
Red Faber	CHI	Jul 14, 1915
Reb Russell	CHI	Aug 7, 1916
Jim Bagby	CLE	May 20, 1917
Babe Ruth	BOS	Aug 24, 1918
Dickie Kerr	CHI	Jul 8, 1921
Red Faber	CHI	Apr 23, 1923
George Mogridge	WAS	Aug 15, 1923
Joe Haynes	CHI	Sep 17, 1944
Fred Hutchinson	DET	Aug 29, 1947
Harry Dorish	STL	Jun 2, 1950

Pitchers Who Stole Home, NL since 1900

Player	Team	Date	Player	Team	Date
Jesse Tannehill	PIT	Sep 20, 1900	Sherry Smith	BKN	Apr 19, 1916
Jock Menefee	CHI	Jul 15, 1902	Tom Seaton	CHI	Jun 23, 1916
Joe McGinnity	NY	Aug 8, 1903	Bob Steele	NY	Jul 26, 1918
Henry Schmidt	BKN	Aug 15, 1903	Hippo Vaughn	CHI	Aug 9, 1919
Joe McGinnity	NY	Apr 29, 1904	Dutch Ruether	CIN	Sep 3, 1919
Jake Weimer	CIN	Jul 28, 1907	Jesse Barnes	NY	Jul 27, 1920
Lefty Leifield	PIT	Jul 27, 1911	Dutch Ruether	BKN	May 4, 1921
Christy Mathewson	NY	Sep 12, 1911	Johnny Vander Meer	CIN	Sep 23, 1943
Red Ames	NY	May 22, 1912	Bucky Walters	CIN	Apr 20, 1946
Rube Benton	CIN	Jun 23, 1912	Don Newcombe	BKN	May 26, 1955
Christy Mathewson	NY	Jun 28, 1912	Curt Simmons	STL	Sep 1, 1963
Slim Sallee	STL	Jul 22, 1913	Pascual Perez	ATL	Sep 7, 1984
Jack Quinn	BOS	Sep 15, 1913	Rick Sutcliffe	CHI	Jul 29, 1988

Easiest Pitcher to Strike Out, Season since 1900

Player	Team	Year	SO	AB	Pct.
Bill Stoneman	MON N	1969	55	73	.753
Dean Chance	CAL A	1965	56	75	.747
	CAL A	1966	54	76	.711
Gary Gentry	NY N	1969	52	74	.703
Jerry Koosman	NY N	1968	62	91	.681
Dean Chance	MIN A	1968	63	93	.677
Jim Nash	OAK A	1968	50	74	.676
Steve Barber	BAL A	1965	43	65	.662
Gary Gentry	NY N	1970	39	59	.661
Jerry Koosman	NY N	1970	46	70	.657
Bill Stoneman	MON N	1971	61	93	.656

Most At-Bats with No Hits, Pitcher, Season since 1900

Player	Team	Year	AB
Bob Buhl	MIL N	1962	
	CHI N	1962	70
Bill Wight	CHI A	1950	61
Ron Herbel	SF N	1964	47
Karl Drews	STL A	1949	46
Ernie Koob	STL A	1916	41
Randy Tate	NY N	1975	41
Ed Rakow	DET A	1964	39
Darryl Kile	HOU N	1991	38
Harry Parker	NY N	1974	36
Steve Stone	SF N	1971	34
Ed Lynch	NY N	1982	33
Ellis Kinder	BOS A	1952	32
Luke Walker	PIT N	1969	32
Bob Miller	MIN A	1969	31

Most At-Bats with No Hits, Pitcher, Season since 1900 (*cont.*)

Player	Team	Year	AB
Don Carman	PHI N	1986	31
Karl Adams	CHI N	1915	30
Rick Wise	PHI N	1966	30

Best-Hitting Pitchers, Season, AL

Player	Team	Year	G	AB	R	H	2B	3B	HR	RBI	BA
Walter Johnson	WAS	1925	36	97	12	42	6	1	2	20	.433
Red Ruffing	BOS	1930									
	NY	1930	58	110	17	40	8	2	4	22	.364
George Uhle	CLE	1923	58	144	23	52	10	3	0	22	.361
Gene Bearden	STL	1952	45	65	6	23	3	0	0	8	.354
Win Mercer	WAS	1901	24	68	13	24	4	1	0	10	.353
Catfish Hunter	OAK	1971	38	103	14	36	1	1	1	12	.350
Wes Ferrell	BOS	1935	75	150	25	52	7	1	7	32	.347
Elam Vangilder	STL	1922	45	93	16	32	10	2	2	11	.344
Carl Mays	NY	1921	51	143	18	49	5	1	2	22	.343
George Uhle	DET	1929	40	108	18	37	1	1	0	17	.343
Chad Kimsey	STL	1930	60	70	14	24	4	1	2	14	.343
George Mullin	DET	1902	35	111	19	38	4	3	0	11	.342
Joe Bush	NY	1924	60	124	13	42	9	3	1	14	.339
Red Ruffing	NY	1935	50	109	13	37	10	0	2	18	.339

Best-Hitting Pitchers, Season, NL since 1900

Player	Team	Year	G	AB	R	H	2B	3B	HR	RBI	BA
Jack Bentley	NY	1923	52	89	9	38	6	2	1	14	.427
Curt Davis	STL	1939	63	105	10	40	5	0	1	17	.381
Don Newcombe	LA	1958									
	CIN	1958	50	72	11	26	1	0	1	9	.361
	BKN	1955	57	117	18	42	9	1	7	18	.359
Erv Brame	PIT	1930	50	116	20	41	5	0	3	22	.353
Dutch Ruether	BKN	1921	49	97	12	34	5	2	2	13	.351
Wilbur Cooper	PIT	1924	38	104	11	36	5	2	0	15	.346
Dolf Luque	CIN	1926	34	78	8	27	5	0	0	8	.346
Johnny Sain	BOS	1947	40	107	13	37	7	0	0	18	.346
Joe Bowman	PIT	1939	70	96	9	33	8	1	0	18	.344
Bill Phillips	CIN	1902	38	114	11	39	1	3	0	11	.342
Doc Crandall	NY	1910	44	73	10	25	2	4	1	13	.342
Jack Scott	BOS	1921	51	88	14	30	5	1	1	12	.341
Jesse Tannehill	PIT	1900	29	94	16	32	7	0	0	15	.340

Best-Hitting Pitchers, Career

Player	AB	R	H	2B	3B	HR	RBI	BA
Babe Ruth	490	75	149	34	11	15	73	.304
George Uhle	1363	172	393	60	21	9	187	.288
Doc Crandall	573	77	163	23	15	8	91	.284
Red Lucas	1388	150	392	60	13	3	183	.282
Wes Ferrell	1128	169	316	55	12	38	202	.280
Al Orth	1400	166	389	54	28	12	165	.278
Ad Gumbert	832	134	230	30	17	15	109	.276
Jack Scott	678	67	186	31	4	5	73	.274
Don Newcombe	878	94	238	33	3	15	108	.271
Sloppy Thurston	648	65	175	38	10	5	79	.270
Red Ruffing	1932	207	520	97	13	36	273	.269
Carl Mays	1085	113	291	32	21	5	110	.268
Nixey Callahan	683	100	181	24	12	1	79	.265
Johnny Marcum	533	56	141	18	1	5	70	.265
George Mullin	1504	162	397	70	23	3	135	.264
Jesse Tannehill	1091	147	288	44	21	5	111	.264
Schoolboy Rowe	909	116	239	36	9	18	153	.263
Fred Hutchinson	649	71	171	23	3	4	83	.263
Brickyard Kennedy	1275	150	333	50	21	1	148	.261
Dutch Ruether	947	81	245	30	11	7	109	.259
Joe Shaute	657	63	170	28	4	1	63	.259

Worst-Hitting Pitchers, Career (Min. 100 AB)

Player	AB	H	BA
Ron Herbel	206	6	.029
Andy McGaffigan	126	6	.048
Ed Klepfer	125	6	.048
Bill Butler	117	6	.051
John Burkett	174	9	.052
Taylor Phillips	113	6	.053
Bill Trotter	109	6	.055
Don Carman	209	12	.057
Don Johnson	155	9	.058
Luke Walker	188	11	.059
Buster Narum	118	7	.059
Ryne Duren	114	7	.061
Marv Breuer	157	10	.064
Rip Hagerman	123	8	.065
Dean Chance	662	44	.066
Joe Engel	104	7	.067
Mark Grant	104	7	.067
Bob Bowman	101	7	.069
Billy McCool	101	7	.069
Ernie Koob	128	9	.070
Mike Kilkenny	114	8	.070
Bill Greif	166	12	.072

Worst-Hitting Pitchers, Career (Min. 100 AB) *(cont.)*

Player	AB	H	BA
Rick Camp	175	13	.074
Clem Labine	227	17	.075
Pete Burnside	132	10	.076
Dick Drago	274	21	.077
Dan Spillner	130	10	.077
Dick Woodson	117	9	.077
Bill Hands	472	37	.078
Wayne Simpson	153	12	.078
Brent Strom	102	8	.078
Lee Stange	305	24	.079
Mike Bielecki	267	21	.079
Ken Howell	114	9	.079
Bruce Ruffin	263	21	.080
Gary Lavelle	111	9	.081
Terry Mulholland	294	24	.082
Karl Drews	254	21	.083
Kent Tekulve	121	10	.083
Wilbur Wood	322	27	.084
Ed Rakow	226	19	.084
Roger Craig	448	38	.085
Hank Aguirre	388	33	.085
Ike Delock	361	31	.086
Bill Stoneman	338	29	.086
Dave Wickersham	324	28	.086
Bob Kuzava	256	22	.086
Greg Harris	105	9	.086
Bob Savage	104	9	.087
Dick Ellsworth	673	59	.088
Hoyt Wilhelm	432	38	.088
Dean Stone	170	15	.088
Bruce Sutter	102	9	.088
Bob Buhl	857	76	.089
George Brunet	418	37	.089
Ted Power	157	14	.089
Pete Broberg	101	9	.089
Jim Deshaies	367	33	.090
Tom Gorman	155	14	.090
Johnny Broaca	254	23	.091
Jim Hannan	209	19	.091
LaMarr Hoyt	110	10	.091
Kent Peterson	110	10	.091
Ron Kline	491	45	.092
Jose DeLeon	413	38	.092
Hal Woodeshick	174	16	.092
Howie Judson	150	14	.093
Bob Keefe	107	10	.093
Wally Bunker	331	31	.094

Worst-Hitting Pitchers, Career (Min. 100 AB) *(cont.)*

Player	AB	H	BA
Tommie Sisk	235	22	.094
Art Decatur	159	15	.094
Steve Bedrosian	149	14	.094
Gary Gentry	285	27	.095
Bob Hendley	243	23	.095
Charles Hudson	210	20	.095
Tom Kelley	116	11	.095
Rollie Sheldon	209	20	.096
Hi Bell	178	17	.096
Ron Perranoski	167	16	.096
Pete Smith	166	16	.096
Bob Johnson	157	15	.096
Jack Lamabe	156	15	.096
Dick Kelley	125	12	.096
Sandy Koufax	776	75	.097
John Montefusco	455	44	.097
George Smith	349	34	.097
Satchel Paige	124	12	.097
Al Benton	512	50	.098
Clay Kirby	478	47	.098
Cannonball Titcomb	224	22	.098
Dave Hillman	163	16	.098
Carl Willey	263	26	.099
Les Tietje	171	17	.099
Craig McMurtry	152	15	.099
Casey Cox	151	15	.099
Rick Matula	111	11	.099

INDIVIDUAL
FIELDING
RECORDS

●

Best Fielding Percentage by Position, Career

Player	Pos.	Pct.	Player	Pos.	Pct.
Wes Parker	1B	.996	Terry Puhl	OF	.993
Steve Garvey	1B	.996	Bill Freehan	C	.993
Don Mattingly	1B	.996	Elston Howard	C	.993
Ryne Sandberg	2B	.990	Jim Sundberg	C	.993
Brooks Robinson	3B	.971	Don Mossi	P	.990
Larry Bowa	SS	.980	Gary Nolan	P	.990
Tony Fernandez	SS	.980			

Fewest Errors by Position, Season, AL (Min. 150 G, excl. Pitchers)

Player	Team	Year	Pos.	G	E	TC
Stuffy McInnis	BOS	1921	1B	152	1	1652
Jerry Adair	BAL	1964	2B	153	5	822
Bobby Grich	BAL	1973	2B	162	5	945
Roberto Alomar	TOR	1992	2B	150	5	668
Don Money	MIL	1974	3B	157	5	472
Cal Ripken	BAL	1990	SS	161	3	1288
Rocky Colavito	CLE	1965	OF	162	0	274
Brian Downing	CAL	1982	OF	158	0	330
Jim Sundberg	TEX	1979	C	150	4	833
Walter Johnson	WAS	1913	P	47	0	103

Fewest Errors by Position, Season, NL (Min. 150 G, excl. Pitchers)

Player	Team	Year	Pos.	G	E	TC
Steve Garvey	SD	1984	1B	159	0	1319
Jose Oquendo	STL	1990	2B	150	3	681
Ken Reitz	STL	1980	3B	150	8	387
Ozzie Smith	STL	1991	SS	150	8	639
Danny Litwhiler	PHI	1942	OF	151	0	317
Curt Flood	STL	1966	OF	159	0	396
Brett Butler	LA	1991	OF	161	0	380
Randy Hundley	CHI	1967	C	152	4	928
Randy Jones	SD	1976	P	40	0	112

Most Errors by Position, Season, AL

Player	Team	Year	Pos.	G	E
Jerry Freeman	WAS	1908	1B	154	41
Kid Gleason	DET	1901	2B	136	64
Sammy Strang	CHI	1902	3B	137	62
John Gochnaur	CLE	1903	SS	128	98
Roy Johnson	DET	1929	OF	146	31
Oscar Stanage	DET	1911	C	141	41
Jack Chesbro	NY	1904	P	55	15
Rube Waddell	PHI	1905	P	46	15
Ed Walsh	CHI	1912	P	62	15

Most Errors by Position, Season, NL since 1900

Player	Team	Year	Pos.	G	E
Jack Doyle	NY	1900	1B	130	41
George Grantham	CHI	1923	2B	150	55
Piano Legs Hickman	NY	1900	3B	118	91
Rudy Hulswitt	PHI	1903	SS	138	81
Cy Seymour	CIN	1903	OF	135	36
Red Dooin	PHI	1909	C	140	40
Doc Newton	CIN	1901	P	33	17

Most Consecutive Errorless Games by Position, AL

Player	Pos.	G	Began	Ended
Mike Hegan	1B	178	1970	1973
Jerry Adair	2B	89	1964	1965
Don Money	3B	88	1973	1974
Cal Ripken	SS	95	1990	1990
Brian Downing	OF	244	1981	1983
Rick Cerone	C	159	1987	1989
Paul Lindblad	P	385	1966	1974

Most Consecutive Errorless Games by Position, NL

Player	Pos.	G	Began	Ended
Steve Garvey	1B	193	1983	1985
Ryne Sandberg	2B	123	1989	1990
Jim Davenport	3B	97	1966	1968
Kevin Elster	SS	88	1988	1989
Doug Dascenzo	OF	242	1988	1991
Johnny Edwards	C	138	1970	1971
Lee Smith	P	484	1982	1991

Most Consecutive Errorless Games by Outfielder, Both Leagues

Player	G	Began	Ended
Don Demeter	266	1962	1965

Unassisted Triple Plays

Player	Team	Date	Pos.	Opp.	Opp. Batter
Neal Ball	CLE A	Jul 19, 1909	SS	BOS	Amby McConnell
Bill Wambsganss	CLE A	Oct 10, 1920	2B	BKN	Clarence Mitchell
George Burns	BOS A	Sept 14, 1923	1B	CLE	Frank Brower
Ernie Padgett	BOS N	Oct 6, 1923	SS	PHI	Walter Holke
Glenn Wright	PIT N	May 7, 1925	SS	STL	Jim Bottomley
Jimmy Cooney	CHI N	May 30, 1927	SS	PIT	Paul Waner
Johnny Neun	DET A	May 31, 1927	1B	CLE	Homer Summa
Ron Hansen	WAS A	Jul 29, 1968	SS	CLE	Joe Azcue
Mickey Morandini	PHI N	Sep 20, 1992	2B	PIT	Jeff King

Most Double Plays, Second Baseman, Season, AL

Player	Team	Year	DP
Gerry Priddy	DET	1950	150
Nellie Fox	CHI	1957	141
Buddy Myer	WAS	1935	138
Jerry Coleman	NY	1950	137
Carlos Baerga	CLE	1992	137
Bobby Richardson	NY	1966	136
Cass Michaels	CHI	1949	135
Bobby Knoop	CAL	1966	135
Bobby Doerr	BOS	1949	134
Harold Reynolds	SEA	1991	133
Bobby Doerr	BOS	1942	132
Gerry Priddy	STL	1948	132
Bobby Grich	BAL	1974	132
Bobby Doerr	BOS	1950	130
Bobby Grich	BAL	1973	130

Most Double Plays, Second Baseman, Season, NL

Player	Team	Year	DP
Bill Mazeroski	PIT	1966	161
	PIT	1961	144
Dave Cash	PHI	1974	141
Bill Mazeroski	PIT	1962	138
Jackie Robinson	BKN	1951	137
Red Schoendienst	STL	1954	137
Jackie Robinson	BKN	1950	133
Bill Mazeroski	PIT	1963	131
	PIT	1967	131
Tommy Helms	CIN	1971	130

Most Double Plays, Shortstop, Season, AL

Player	Team	Year	DP
Rick Burleson	BOS	1980	147
Roy Smalley	MIN	1979	144
Lou Boudreau	CLE	1944	134
Spike Owen	SEA	1986	
	BOS	1986	133
Vern Stephens	BOS	1949	128
Zoilo Versalles	MIN	1962	127
Eddie Joost	PHI	1949	126
Johnny Lipon	DET	1950	126
Leo Cardenas	MIN	1969	126
Alfredo Griffin	TOR	1980	126
Jim Fregosi	CAL	1966	125
Dick Schofield	CAL	1988	125
Alfredo Griffin	TOR	1979	124

Most Double Plays, Shortstop, Season, AL (*cont.*)

Player	Team	Year	DP
Phil Rizzuto	NY	1950	123
Cal Ripken	BAL	1985	123
Lou Boudreau	CLE	1943	122
Cal Ripken	BAL	1984	122
Roy Smalley	MIN	1978	121
Frankie Crosetti	NY	1938	120
Lou Boudreau	CLE	1947	120

Most Double Plays, Shortstop, Season, NL

Player	Team	Year	DP
Bobby Wine	MON	1970	137
Rafael Ramirez	ATL	1982	130
Roy McMillan	CIN	1954	129
Hod Ford	CIN	1928	128
Gene Alley	PIT	1966	128
Dick Groat	PIT	1958	127
	PIT	1962	126
Eddie Miller	CIN	1943	123
	BOS	1940	122

Most Putouts, Outfielder, Game

Player	Team	Date	Pos.	PO	Inns.
Fred Treacey	NY N	Jul 10, 1876	LF	12	16
Harry Bay	CLE A	Jul 19, 1904	CF	12	12
Earl Clark	BOS N	May 10, 1929	CF	12	
Carden Gillenwater	BOS N	Sep 11, 1946	CF	12	17
Tom McBride	WAS A	Jul 2, 1948	LF	12	
Lloyd Merriman	CIN N	Sep 7, 1951	CF	12	18
Lyman Bostock	MIN A	May 25, 1977	CF	12	
Ruppert Jones	SEA A	May 16, 1978	CF	12	16
Rick Manning	MIL A	Jun 11, 1983	CF	12	15
Garry Maddox	PHI N	Jun 10, 1984	CF	12	12
Gary Pettis	CAL A	Jun 4, 1985	CF	12	15
Oddibe McDowell	TEX A	Jul 20, 1985	CF	12	15
Rolando Roomes	CIN N	Jul 28, 1989	RF	12	17
Fred Treacey	NY N	Jul 8, 1876	LF	11	15
Dick Harley	STL N	Jun 30, 1898	LF	11	
Topsy Hartsel	CHI N	Sep 10, 1901	LF	11	
George Burns	NY N	July 17, 1914	LF	11	21
Roy Massey	BOS N	Jul 31, 1918	CF	11	21
Ty Cobb	DET A	Aug 4, 1918	CF	11	18
Burt Shotton	WAS A	Aug 4, 1918	LF	11	18
Hy Myers	BKN N	Apr 30, 1919	CF	11	20
Happy Felsch	CHI A	Jun 23, 1919	CF	11	
Max Carey	PIT N	Jul 25, 1921	CF	11	
Johnny Mostil	CHI A	May 22, 1928	CF	11	

Most Putouts, Outfielder, Game (*cont.*)

Player	Team	Date	Pos.	PO	Inns.
Harry Rice	NY A	Jun 12, 1930	CF	11	
Johnny Hopp	STL N	May 3, 1944	CF	11	
Paul Lehner	PHI A	Jun 25, 1950	LF	11	
Irv Noren	WAS A	Sep 22, 1951	CF	11	
Willie Horton	DET A	Jul 18, 1969	LF	11	
Mickey Stanley	DET A	Jul 13, 1973	CF	11	
Dave Henderson	SEA A	Apr 27, 1982	CF	11	11
Tony Armas	OAK A	Jun 12, 1982	RF	11	

Most Assists, Outfielder, Game

Player	Team	Date	Pos.	A	Inns.
Harry Schafer	BOS N	Sep 26, 1877	RF	4	
Bill Crowley	BUF N	May 24, 1880	CF	4	
	BUF N	Aug 27, 1880	CF	4	
Dusty Miller	CIN N	May 30, 1895	LF	4	11
Ducky Holmes	CHI A	Aug 21, 1903	LF	4	
Fred Clarke	PIT N	Aug 23, 1910	LF	4	
Lee Magee	NY A	Jun 28, 1916	CF	4	
Happy Felsch	CHI A	Aug 14, 1919	CF	4	
Bob Meusel	NY A	Sep 5, 1921	CF	4	
Sam Langford	CLE A	May 1, 1928	CF	4	
Wally Berger	BOS N	Apr 27, 1931	CF	4	

Unassisted Double Plays, Outfielder

Player	Team	Date	Pos.	Opp.
Billy Sunday	PIT N	Sep 11, 1888	CF	WAS
Steve Brodie	BOS N	Jun 29, 1891	CF	NY
Tommy McCarthy	BOS N	Apr 30, 1894	LF	PHI
Fielder Jones	CHI A	Jul 1, 1904	CF	STL
Sam Mertes	NY N	Jul 24, 1905	LF	CIN
George Stone	STL A	Aug 23, 1905	LF	NY
Socks Seybold	PHI A	Aug 15, 1907	RF	CLE
	PHI A	Sep 10, 1907	RF	BOS
Tris Speaker	BOS A	Jun 1, 1909	CF	PHI
	BOS A	Apr 23, 1910	CF	PHI
	BOS A	Apr 21, 1914	CF	PHI
	BOS A	Aug 8, 1914	CF	DET
Elmer Smith	CLE A	Jul 15, 1915	RF	BOS
Bill Hinchman	PIT N	Apr 28, 1916	RF	CIN
Benny Kauff	NY N	Jul 19, 1916	CF	CHI
Tris Speaker	CLE A	Apr 18, 1918	CF	DET
	CLE A	Apr 29, 1918	CF	CHI
Elmer Smith	CLE A	Sep 6, 1920	RF	STL
	NY A	Jul 18, 1923	RF	DET
Sam Rice	WAS A	Jul 21, 1923	RF	CLE
Ty Cobb	DET A	Jul 15, 1924	CF	PHI

Unassisted Double Plays, Outfielder (*cont.*)

Player	Team	Date	Pos.	Opp.
Elmer Smith	CIN N	Jul 13, 1925	RF	BOS
Jack Smith	STL N	Aug 5, 1925	RF	BOS
Ty Tyson	NY N	Aug 2, 1926	CF	STL
Ty Cobb	PHI A	Apr 26, 1927	RF	BOS
Adam Comorosky	PIT N	May 31, 1931	LF	CHI
	PIT N	Jun 13, 1931	LF	NY
Al Simmons	CHI A	Apr 20, 1933	LF	STL
Danny Taylor	BKN N	Jun 20, 1933	CF	STL
Dom DiMaggio	BOS A	Aug 2, 1942	CF	DET
George Case	WAS A	Jun 8, 1944	CF	PHI
Leon Culberson	BOS A	May 25, 1945	CF	STL
Curt Flood	STL N	Jun 19, 1967	CF	HOU
Jose Cardenal	CLE A	Jun 8, 1968	CF	DET
	CLE A	Jul 16, 1968	CF	CAL
Bobby Bonds	SF N	May 31, 1972	RF	NY
Billy North	OAK A	Jul 28, 1974	CF	CHI
Andy Van Slyke	PIT N	Jul 17, 1992	CF	HOU
Brian McRae	KC A	Aug 23, 1992	CF	CHI

Best Double-Play Combinations, Season

Player	Team	Year	DP
Bill Mazeroski	PIT N	1966	161
Gene Alley	PIT N	1966	128
Total			289
Gerry Priddy	DET A	1950	150
Johnny Lipon	DET A	1950	126
Total			276
Bill Mazeroski	PIT N	1962	138
Dick Groat	PIT N	1962	126
Total			264
Bobby Doerr	BOS A	1949	134
Vern Stephens	BOS A	1949	128
Total			262
Bill Mazeroski	PIT N	1961	144
Dick Groat	PIT N	1961	117
Total			261
Jerry Coleman	NY A	1950	137
Phil Rizzuto	NY A	1950	123
Total			260
Bobby Knoop	CAL A	1966	135
Jim Fregosi	CAL A	1966	125
Total			260
Hughie Critz	CIN N	1928	124
Hod Ford	CIN N	1928	128
Total			252

Best Double-Play Combinations, Season (*cont.*)

Player	Team	Year	DP
Johnny Temple	CIN N	1954	117
Roy McMillan	CIN N	1954	129
Total			246
Ray Mack	CLE A	1943	123
Lou Boudreau	CLE A	1943	122
Total			245
Bobby Doerr	BOS A	1950	130
Vern Stephens	BOS A	1950	115
Total			245
Bill Mazeroski	PIT N	1958	118
Dick Groat	PIT N	1958	127
Total			245
Dave Cash	PHI N	1974	141
Larry Bowa	PHI N	1974	104
Total			245
Jackie Robinson	BKN N	1951	137
Pee Wee Reese	BKN N	1951	106
Total			243
Nellie Fox	CHI A	1960	126
Luis Aparicio	CHI A	1960	117
Total			243
Bobby Richardson	NY A	1961	136
Tony Kubek	NY A	1961	107
Total			243
Glenn Hubbard	ATL N	1985	127
Rafael Ramirez	ATL N	1985	115
Total			242
Glenn Hubbard	ATL N	1982	111
Rafael Ramirez	ATL N	1982	130
Total			241
Damaso Garcia	TOR A	1980	112
Alfredo Griffin	TOR A	1980	126
Total			238
Harold Reynolds	SEA A	1991	133
Omar Vizquel	SEA A	1991	105
Total			238
Red Schoendienst	STL N	1954	137
Alex Grammas	STL N	1954	100
Total			237
Dave Stapleton	BOS A	1980	90
Rick Burleson	BOS A	1980	147
Total			237

Best Double-Play Combinations, Season (cont.)

Player	Team	Year	DP
Bernie Allen	MIN A	1962	109
Zoilo Versalles	MIN A	1962	127
Total			236
Bill Mazeroski	PIT N	1967	131
Gene Alley	PIT N	1967	105
Total			236
Rob Wilfong	MIN A	1979	92
Roy Smalley	MIN A	1979	144
Total			236
Joe Gordon	NY A	1942	121
Phil Rizzuto	NY A	1942	114
Total			235
Willie Randolph	NY A	1979	128
Bucky Dent	NY A	1979	107
Total			235
Joe Gordon	NY A	1939	116
Frankie Crosetti	NY A	1939	118
Total			234
Lonny Frey	CIN N	1943	112
Eddie Miller	CIN N	1943	121
Total			233
Don Blasingame	STL N	1957	128
Alvin Dark	STL N	1957	105
Total			233
Bobby Doerr	BOS A	1948	119
Vern Stephens	BOS A	1948	113
Total			232
Bobby Grich	BAL A	1974	132
Mark Belanger	BAL A	1974	100
Total			232
Eddie Stanky	NY N	1951	117
Alvin Dark	NY N	1951	114
Total			231
Tommy Herr	STL N	1985	120
Ozzie Smith	STL N	1985	111
Total			231
Steve Sax	NY A	1989	117
Alvaro Espinoza	NY A	1989	114
Total			231
Joe Gordon	CLE A	1947	110
Lou Boudreau	CLE A	1947	120
Total			230

Best Double-Play Combinations, Season (*cont.*)

Player	Team	Year	DP
Cass Michaels	CHI A	1949	135
Luke Appling	CHI A	1949	95
Total			230
Johnny Temple	CIN N	1955	119
Roy McMillan	CIN N	1955	111
Total			230
Bobby Grich	BAL A	1973	130
Mark Belanger	BAL A	1973	100
Total			230
Eddie Stanky	NY N	1950	128
Alvin Dark	NY N	1950	101
Total			229
Cookie Rojas	KC A	1974	114
Freddie Patek	KC A	1974	115
Total			229
Billy Ripken	BAL A	1988	110
Cal Ripken	BAL A	1988	119
Total			229
Bobby Doerr	BOS A	1938	118
Joe Cronin	BOS A	1938	110
Total			228
Ryne Sandberg	CHI N	1983	126
Larry Bowa	CHI N	1983	102
Total			228
Charlie Gehringer	DET A	1933	111
Billy Rogell	DET A	1933	116
Total			227
Pep Young	PIT N	1938	120
Arky Vaughan	PIT N	1938	107
Total			227
Jackie Robinson	BKN N	1950	133
Pee Wee Reese	BKN N	1950	94
Total			227
Bobby Grich	BAL A	1975	122
Mark Belanger	BAL A	1975	105
Total			227
Jackie Hayes	CHI A	1937	115
Luke Appling	CHI A	1937	111
Total			226
Nellie Fox	CHI A	1958	141
Luis Aparicio	CHI A	1958	85
Total			226

Best Double-Play Combinations, Season (*cont.*)

Player	Team	Year	DP
Marv Breeding	BAL A	1960	116
Ron Hansen	BAL A	1960	110
Total			226
Bill Mazeroski	PIT N	1963	131
Dick Schofield	PIT N	1963	95
Total			226
Bucky Harris	WAS A	1923	120
Roger Peckinpaugh	WAS A	1923	105
Total			225
Ray Mack	CLE A	1940	109
Lou Boudreau	CLE A	1940	116
Total			225
Bobby Doerr	BOS A	1946	129
Johnny Pesky	BOS A	1946	96
Total			225

Most Games Caught, Season

Player	Team	Year	Total
Randy Hundley	CHI N	1968	160
Frankie Hayes	PHI A	1944	155
Ray Mueller	CIN N	1944	155
Jim Sundberg	TEX A	1975	155
Johnny Bench	CIN N	1968	154
Ted Simmons	STL N	1975	154
Carlton Fisk	BOS A	1978	154
Ted Simmons	STL N	1973	153
Gary Carter	MON N	1982	153
Jim Hegan	CLE A	1949	152
Randy Hundley	CHI N	1967	152
Gary Carter	MON N	1978	152
Ray Schalk	CHI A	1920	151
Frankie Hayes	PHI A		
	CLE A	1945	151
Johnny Edwards	HOU N	1969	151
Randy Hundley	CHI N	1969	151
Manny Sanguillen	PIT N	1974	151
Carlton Fisk	BOS A	1977	151
Jim Sundberg	TEX A	1980	151
Benito Santiago	SD N	1991	151
George Gibson	PIT N	1909	150
Mike Tresh	CHI A	1945	150
Buck Rodgers	LA A	1962	150
Jim Sundberg	TEX A	1979	150
Jody Davis	CHI N	1983	150

Most Games Caught, Career

Player	G Cau	Yrs.	BA
Bob Boone	2225	19	.254
Carlton Fisk	2204	23	.270
Gary Carter	2056	19	.262
Jim Sundberg	1927	16	.248
Al Lopez	1918	19	.261
Rick Ferrell	1806	18	.281
Gabby Hartnett	1790	20	.297
Ted Simmons	1771	21	.285
Johnny Bench	1742	17	.267
Ray Schalk	1726	18	.253
Bill Dickey	1712	17	.313
Lance Parrish	1703	16	.253
Yogi Berra	1696	19	.285
Rick Dempsey	1633	24	.233
Jim Hegan	1629	17	.228
Deacon McGuire	1611	26	.278
Tony Pena	1589	13	.267
Bill Freehan	1581	15	.262
Sherm Lollar	1571	18	.264
Luke Sewell	1561	20	.259
Ernie Lombardi	1542	17	.306
Steve O'Neill	1528	17	.263
Darrell Porter	1506	17	.247
Rollie Hemsley	1495	19	.262
Del Crandall	1479	16	.254
Johnny Roseboro	1476	14	.249
Mickey Cochrane	1451	13	.320
Wally Schang	1439	19	.284
Muddy Ruel	1413	19	.275
Mike Scioscia	1395	13	.258
Johnny Edwards	1392	14	.242
Tim McCarver	1387	21	.271
Terry Kennedy	1378	14	.264
Gus Mancuso	1360	14	.265
Jimmie Wilson	1359	18	.284
Bob O'Farrell	1338	21	.273
Jerry Grote	1325	15	.251
Wilbert Robinson	1316	17	.273
Frankie Hayes	1309	14	.259
Alan Ashby	1299	17	.245
Spud Davis	1291	16	.308
Rick Cerone	1284	18	.245
Thurman Munson	1278	11	.288
Del Rice	1249	17	.237
Frank Snyder	1249	16	.265
Butch Wynegar	1247	13	.255
Ernie Whitt	1246	15	.249

Most Games Caught, Career (*cont.*)

Player	G Cau	Yrs.	BA
Chief Zimmer	1239	19	.269
Ivy Wingo	1231	17	.260
Steve Yeager	1230	15	.228
Hank Severeid	1225	15	.289
Walker Cooper	1223	18	.285
Andy Seminick	1213	15	.243
Tom Haller	1199	12	.257
George Gibson	1196	14	.236
Mal Kittridge	1196	16	.219
Red Dooin	1194	15	.240
Roy Campanella	1183	10	.276
Mickey Owen	1175	13	.255
Johnny Kling	1168	13	.271
Smoky Burgess	1139	18	.295
Elston Howard	1138	14	.274
Billy Sullivan	1121	16	.212
Manny Sanguillen	1114	13	.296
Cy Perkins	1111	17	.259
Birdie Tebbetts	1108	14	.270
Phil Masi	1101	14	.264
Earl Battey	1087	13	.270
Mike Heath	1083	14	.252
Oscar Stanage	1074	14	.234
Jack Clements	1073	17	.286
Ed Bailey	1064	14	.256
Jody Davis	1039	10	.245
Milt May	1034	15	.263
Jack Warner	1032	14	.249
Sammy White	1027	11	.262
Randy Hundley	1026	14	.236
Mike Tresh	1019	12	.249
Buck Martinez	1009	17	.225
Bill Killefer	1006	13	.238
Clay Dalrymple	1003	12	.233
Duke Farrell	1003	18	.275

Most No-Hitters Caught, Career

Player	Team	Date	Opp.	No-Hit Pitcher
Bill Carrigan	BOS A	Jul 29, 1911	STL	Smoky Joe Wood
	BOS A	Jun 21, 1916	NY	Rube Foster
	BOS A	Aug 30, 1916	STL	Dutch Leonard
Ray Schalk	CHI A	May 31, 1914	CLE	Joe Benz
	CHI A	Apr 14, 1917	STL	Eddie Cicotte
	CHI A	Apr 30, 1922	DET	Charlie Robertson
Val Picinich	PHI A	Aug 26, 1916	CLE	Joe Bush
	WAS A	Jul 1, 1920	BOS	Walter Johnson

Most No-Hitters Caught, Career (cont.)

Player	Team	Date	Opp.	No-Hit Pitcher
	BOS A	Sep 7, 1923	PHI	Howard Ehmke
Luke Sewell	CLE A	Apr 29, 1931	STL	Wes Ferrell
	CHI A	Aug 31, 1935	STL	Vern Kennedy
	CHI A	Jun 1, 1937	STL	Bill Dietrich
Jim Hegan	CLE A	Jul 10, 1947	PHI	Don Black
	CLE A	Jun 30, 1948	DET	Bob Lemon
	CLE A	Jul 1, 1951	DET	Bob Feller
Yogi Berra	NY A	Jul 12, 1951	CLE	Allie Reynolds
	NY A	Sep 28, 1951	BOS	Allie Reynolds
	NY A	Oct 8, 1956	BKN	Don Larsen
Roy Campanella	BKN N	Jun 19, 1952	CHI	Carl Erskine
	BKN N	May 12, 1956	NY	Carl Erskine
	BKN N	Sep 25, 1956	PHI	Sal Maglie
Del Crandall	MIL N	Jun 12, 1954	PHI	Jim Wilson
	MIL N	Aug 18, 1960	PHI	Lew Burdette
	MIL N	Sep 16, 1960	PHI	Warren Spahn
Jeff Torborg	LA N	Sep 9, 1965	CHI	Sandy Koufax
	LA N	Jul 20, 1970	PHI	Bill Singer
	CAL A	May 15, 1973	KC	Nolan Ryan
Alan Ashby	HOU N	Apr 4, 1979	ATL	Ken Forsch
	HOU N	Sep 26, 1981	LA	Nolan Ryan
	HOU N	Sep 25, 1986	SF	Mike Scott
Herm McFarland	CHI A	Sep 20, 1902	DET	Nixey Callahan
	CHI A	Sep 6, 1905	DET	Frank Smith
Nig Clarke	CLE A	Oct 2, 1908	CHI	Addie Joss
	CLE A	Apr 20, 1910	CHI	Addie Joss
Art Wilson	NY N	Sep 6, 1912	PHI	Jeff Tesreau
	CHI N	May 2, 1917	CIN	Hippo Vaughn
Hank Gowdy	BOS N	Sep 9, 1914	PHI	George Davis
	BOS N	Jun 16, 1916	PIT	Tom Hughes
Rollie Hemsley	STL A	Sep 18, 1934	BOS	Bobo Newsom
	CLE A	Apr 16, 1940	CHI	Bob Feller
Ernie Lombardi	CIN N	Jun 11, 1938	BOS	Johnny Vander Meer
	CIN N	Jun 15, 1938	BKN	Johnny Vander Meer
Walker Cooper	STL N	Aug 30, 1941	CIN	Lon Warneke
	BOS N	Aug 11, 1950	BKN	Vern Bickford
Buddy Rosar	PHI A	Sep 9, 1945	STL	Dick Fowler
	PHI A	Sep 3, 1947	WAS	Bill McCahan
Gus Triandos	BAL A	Sep 20, 1958	NY	Hoyt Wilhelm
	PHI N	Jun 21, 1964	NY	Jim Bunning
Bob Tillman	BOS A	Jun 26, 1962	LA	Earl Wilson
	BOS A	Sep 16, 1965	CLE	Dave Morehead
Jim Pagliaroni	BOS A	Aug 1, 1962	CHI	Bill Monbouquette
	OAK A	May 8, 1968	MIN	Catfish Hunter
Johnny Roseboro	LA N	Jun 30, 1962	NY	Sandy Koufax
	LA N	May 31, 1963	SF	Sandy Koufax
John Bateman	HOU N	May 17, 1963	PHI	Don Nottebart

Most No-Hitters Caught, Career (*cont.*)

Player	Team	Date	Opp.	No-Hit Pitcher
John Bateman	MON N	Apr 17, 1969	PHI	Bill Stoneman
Joe Azcue	CLE A	Jun 10, 1966	WAS	Sonny Siebert
	CAL A	Jul 3, 1970	OAK	Clyde Wright
Johnny Edwards	CIN N	Aug 19, 1965	CHI	Jim Maloney
	STL N	Sep 18, 1968	SF	Ray Washburn
Ted Simmons	STL N	Aug 14, 1971	PIT	Bob Gibson
	STL N	Apr 16, 1978	PHI	Bob Forsch
Tim McCarver	PHI N	Jun 23, 1971	CIN	Rick Wise
	MON N	Oct 2, 1972	NY	Bill Stoneman
Randy Hundley	CHI N	Apr 16, 1972	PHI	Burt Hooton
	CHI N	Sep 2, 1972	SD	Milt Pappas
Fran Healy	KC A	Apr 27, 1973	DET	Steve Busby
	KC A	Jun 19, 1974	MIL	Steve Busby
Darrell Porter	KC A	May 14, 1977	TEX	Jim Colborn
	STL N	Sep 26, 1983	MON	Bob Forsch
Ron Hassey	CLE A	May 15, 1981	TOR	Len Barker
	MON N	Jul 28, 1991	LA	Dennis Martinez
Lance Parrish	DET A	Apr 7, 1984	CHI	Jack Morris
	CAL A	Apr 11, 1990	SEA	Mark Langston
				Mike Witt
Ron Karkovice	CHI A	Sep 19, 1986	CAL	Joe Cowley
	CHI A	Aug 11, 1991	BAL	Wilson Alvarez
Mike Scioscia	LA N	Jun 29, 1990	STL	Fernando Valenzuela
	LA N	Aug 17, 1992	SF	Kevin Gross

Most Putouts in Nine Innings, First Baseman

Player	Team	Date	PO
Tom Jones	STL A	May 11, 1906	22
Hal Chase	NY A	Sep 21, 1906	22
Ernie Banks	CHI N	May 9, 1963	22
Don Mattingly	NY A	Jul 20, 1987	22
Alvin Davis	SEA A	May 28, 1988	22
Cap Anson	CHI N	Aug 19, 1880	21
Harry Stovey	WOR N	Sep 24, 1880	21
Ed Swartwood	PIT AA	Jun 25, 1883	21
Charlie Householder	BKN AA	Jun 9, 1884	21
Billy O'Brien	WAS N	Sep 22, 1888	21
John Anderson	BKN N	Aug 26, 1896	21
Jake Beckley	CIN N	Sep 27, 1898	21
Hal Chase	NY A	Aug 5, 1905	21
Jiggs Donahue	CHI A	May 31, 1908	21
Jake Daubert	BKN N	May 6, 1910	21
Hal Chase	NY A	Jun 23, 1911	21
Vic Saier	CHI N	Sep 7, 1913	21
Stuffy McInnis	BOS A	Jul 19, 1918	21
Harvey Cotter	CHI N	Jul 14, 1924	21
Bill Sweeney	BOS A	June 24, 1931	21

Most Putouts in Nine Innings, First Baseman (*cont.*)

Player	Team	Date	PO
Bill Terry	NY N	Apr 17, 1932	21
Elbie Fletcher	PIT N	Jun 6, 1941	21

Most Assists, First Baseman, Game

Player	Team	Date	A	Inns.
Bob Skinner	PIT N	Jul 22, 1954	8	14
Bob Robertson	PIT N	Jun 21, 1971	8	
Kitty Bransfield	PIT N	May 3, 1904	7	
George Stovall	STL A	Aug 7, 1912	7	
Fred Luderus	PHI N	Aug 22, 1918	7	
Ferris Fain	PHI A	Jun 9, 1949	7	12

Most Putouts, Second Baseman, Game

Player	Team	Date	PO	Inns.
Jake Pitler	PIT N	Aug 22, 1917	15	22
Thorny Hawkes	TRO N	Jul 30, 1879	12	10
Lou Bierbauer	PHI AA	Jun 22, 1888	12	
Billy Gardner	BAL A	May 21, 1957	12	16
Bobby Knoop	CAL A	Aug 30, 1966	12	
Vern Fuller	CLE A	Apr 11, 1969	12	16

Most Assists, Second Baseman, Game

Player	Team	Date	A	Inns.
Lave Cross	PHI N	Aug 5, 1897	15	12
Morrie Rath	CIN N	Aug 26, 1919	13	15
Bobby Avila	CLE A	Jul 1, 1952	13	19
Willie Randolph	NY A	Aug 25, 1976	13	19
Fred Dunlap	CLE N	Jul 24, 1882	12	
Sam Crane	NY AA	Jun 1, 1883	12	
Monte Ward	BKN N	Jun 10, 1892	12	
Danny Richardson	WAS N	Jun 20, 1892	12	
Danny Murphy	PHI A	Oct 6, 1907	12	14
Joe Gedeon	STL A	Aug 19, 1918	12	14
Lee Magee	BKN N	Apr 30, 1919	12	20
Frankie Frisch	NY N	Aug 21, 1923	12	10
Billy Herman	CHI N	Jun 29, 1933	12	12
Hughie Critz	NY N	Jul 3, 1933	12	18
Don Heffner	STL A	May 22, 1938	12	13
Pep Young	PIT N	May 30, 1938	12	17
Don Gutteridge	STL A	Jul 4, 1944	12	14
Gerry Priddy	WAS A	Sep 6, 1946	12	11
Jim Gilliam	BKN N	Jul 21, 1956	12	
Red Schoendienst	MIL N	Aug 17, 1957	12	11
Vern Fuller	CLE A	Apr 11, 1969	12	16

Most Assists, Second Baseman, Game (*cont.*)

Player	Team	Date	A	Inns.
Don Money	MIL A	Jun 24, 1977	12	
Ryne Sandberg	CHI N	Jun 12, 1983	12	
Glenn Hubbard	ATL N	Apr 14, 1985	12	
Juan Samuel	PHI N	Apr 20, 1985	12	
Tony Phillips	OAK A	Jul 6, 1986	12	
Harold Reynolds	SEA A	Aug 27, 1986	12	

Most Putouts, Third Baseman, Game

Player	Team	Date	PO
Willie Kuehne	PIT N	May 24, 1889	10
Pat Dillard	STL N	Jun 18, 1900	9
Art Devlin	NY N	May 23, 1908	8

Most Assists, Third Baseman, Game

Player	Team	Date	A	Inns.
Bobby Byrne	PIT N	Jun 18, 1910	12	11
Jerry Denny	PRO N	Aug 17, 1882	11	18
Deacon White	BUF N	May 16, 1884	11	
Jerry Denny	NY N	May 29, 1890	11	
Frank Baker	NY A	May 24, 1918	11	19
Damon Phillips	BOS N	Aug 29, 1944	11	
Ken McMullen	WAS A	Sep 26, 1966	11	
Mike Ferraro	NY A	Sep 14, 1968	11	
Doug DeCinces	CAL A	May 7, 1983	11	12
Chris Sabo	CIN N	Apr 7, 1988	11	

Most Putouts, Shortstop, Game

Player	Team	Date	PO	Inns.
Monte Cross	PHI N	Jul 7, 1899	14	11
Shorty Fuller	NY N	Aug 20, 1895	11	
Joe Cassidy	WAS A	Aug 30, 1904	11	
Russ Wrightstone	PHI N	Sep 4, 1922	11	16
Hod Ford	CIN N	Sep 18, 1929	11	

Most Assists, Shortstop, Game

Player	Team	Date	PO	Inns.
Rick Burleson	CAL A	Apr 13, 1982	15	20
Herman Long	BOS N	May 6, 1892	14	14
Tommy Corcoran	CIN N	Aug 7, 1903	14	
Heinie Wagner	BOS A	Aug 7, 1907	14	14
Rogers Hornsby	STL N	May 26, 1917	14	15
Rabbit Maranville	PIT N	Jul 26, 1923	14	12
Bud Harrelson	NY N	May 24, 1973	14	19
Arthur Irwin	WOR N	Aug 31, 1880	13	14
Danny Richardson	WAS N	Jun 30, 1892	13	
Otto Krueger	STL N	Aug 17, 1902	13	18
Dave Bancroft	PHI N	Jul 13, 1918	13	21
Ivy Olson	BKN N	Aug 11, 1920	13	
Bobby Reeves	WAS A	Aug 7, 1927	13	

Most Assists, Shortstop, Game (*cont.*)

Player	Team	Date	PO	Inns.
Bill Almon	SD N	May 4, 1977	13	
Germany Smith	BKN AA	Jun 29, 1889	12	
Bill Shindle	PHI P	Sep 26, 1890	12	
Bobby Wallace	STL N	May 4, 1901	12	
Kid Elberfeld	DET A	Sep 2, 1901	12	
Freddy Parent	BOS A	Jul 9, 1902	12	17
Bill Dahlen	NY N	Aug 16, 1906	12	
Art Fletcher	NY N	May 21, 1916	12	
Hod Ford	BOS N	Jun 16, 1921	12	
Eddie Miller	BOS N	Jun 27, 1939	12	23
Lou Boudreau	CLE A	Sep 14, 1939	12	

ROOKIE
RECORDS

●

Two Hundred or More Hits, Rookie, AL

Player	Team	Year	H
Tony Oliva	MIN	1964	217
Dale Alexander	DET	1929	215
Harvey Kuenn	DET	1953	209
Kevin Seitzer	KC	1987	207
Hal Trosky	CLE	1934	206
Joe DiMaggio	NY	1936	206
Johnny Pesky	BOS	1942	205
Earle Combs	NY	1925	203
Roy Johnson	DET	1929	201
Dick Wakefield	DET	1943	200

Two Hundred or More Hits, Rookie, NL

Player	Team	Year	H
Lloyd Waner	PIT	1927	223
Jimmy Williams	PIT	1899	217
Frank McCormick	CIN	1938	209
Johnny Frederick	BKN	1929	206
Billy Herman	CHI	1932	206
Vada Pinson	CIN	1959	205
Dick Allen	PHI	1964	201

Thirty or More Home Runs, Rookie, AL

Player	Team	Year	HR
Mark McGwire	OAK	1987	49
Al Rosen	CLE	1950	37
Hal Trosky	CLE	1934	35
Rudy York	DET	1937	35
Ron Kittle	CHI	1983	35
Walt Dropo	BOS	1950	34
Jimmie Hall	MIN	1963	33
Jose Canseco	OAK	1986	33
Tony Oliva	MIN	1964	32
Ted Williams	BOS	1939	31
Bob Allison	WAS	1959	30
Pete Incaviglia	TEX	1986	30

Thirty or More Home Runs, Rookie, NL

Player	Team	Year	HR
Wally Berger	BOS	1930	38
Frank Robinson	CIN	1956	38
Earl Williams	ATL	1971	33
Jim Ray Hart	SF	1964	31
Willie Montanez	PHI	1971	30

.300 Average in Rookie Year Only, AL

Player	Team	Year	BA
Claude Rossman	CLE	1906	.300
Simon Nicholls	PHI	1907	.302
Bucky Harris	WAS	1920	.300
Tex Vache	BOS	1925	.313
Joe Boley	PHI	1927	.311
Hank Steinbacher	CHI	1938	.331
Charlie Keller	NY	1939	.334
Ralph Hodgin	CHI	1943	.314
Sam Mele	BOS	1947	.302
Walt Dropo	BOS	1950	.322
Jim Finigan	PHI	1954	.302
Manny Jiminez	KC	1962	.301
Willie Smith	LA	1964	.301
Rich Coggins	BAL	1973	.319
Bob Bailor	TOR	1977	.310
Mitchell Page	OAK	1977	.307

.300 Average in Rookie Year Only, NL

Player	Team	Year	BA
Fred Snodgrass	NY	1910	.321
Johnny Gooch	PIT	1922	.329
Bart Griffith	BKN	1922	.308
Dick Cox	BKN	1925	.329
Buzz Arlett	PHI	1931	.319
Les Mallon	PHI	1931	.309
Tuck Stainback	CHI	1934	.306
Les Scarsella	CIN	1936	.313
Johnny Rizzo	PIT	1938	.301
Bama Rowell	BOS	1940	.305
Bernie Carbo	CIN	1970	.310

Most Hits in First Game

Player	Team	Date	H	2B	3B	HR
Fred Clarke	LOU N	Jun 30, 1894	5	1	0	0
Cecil Travis	WAS A	May 16, 1933	5	0	0	0
Ray Jansen	STL A	Sep 30, 1910	4	0	0	0
Casey Stengel	BKN N	Jul 17, 1912	4	0	0	0
Art Shires	CHI A	Aug 20, 1928	4	0	1	0
Russ Van Atta	NY A	Apr 25, 1933	4	0	1	0
Ed Freed	PHI N	Sep 11, 1942	4	2	1	0
Spook Jacobs	PHI A	Apr 13, 1954	4	0	0	0
Willie McCovey	SF N	Jul 30, 1959	4	0	2	0
Mack Jones	MIL N	Jul 13, 1961	4	1	0	0
Ted Cox	BOS A	Sep 18, 1977	4	0	0	0
Kirby Puckett	MIN A	May 8, 1984	4	0	0	0

Most Hits in First Game (*cont.*)

Player	Team	Date	H	2B	3B	HR
Billy Bean	DET A	Apr 25, 1987	4	2	0	0
Delino DeShields	MON N	Apr 9, 1990	4	1	0	0

Most Doubles, Rookie, AL

Player	Team	Year	2B
Fred Lynn	BOS	1975	47
Roy Johnson	DET	1929	45
Hal Trosky	CLE	1934	45
Bob Johnson	PHI	1933	44
Joe DiMaggio	NY	1936	44
Ted Williams	BOS	1939	44
Dale Alexander	DET	1929	43
Earl Averill	CLE	1929	43
Tony Oliva	MIN	1964	43
Carl Lind	CLE	1928	42
Bob Meusel	NY	1920	40

Most Doubles, Rookie, NL

Player	Team	Year	2B
Johnny Frederick	BKN	1929	52
Vada Pinson	CIN	1959	47
Billy Herman	CHI	1932	42
Warren Cromartie	MON	1977	41
Johnny Bench	CIN	1968	40
Chris Sabo	CIN	1988	40
Kiddo Davis	PHI	1932	39
Alvin Dark	BOS	1948	39
Ray Grimes	CHI	1921	38
Gene Moore	BOS	1936	38
Orlando Cepeda	SF	1958	38
Dick Allen	PHI	1964	38

Most Triples, Rookie, AL

Player	Team	Year	3B
Joe Cassidy	WAS	1904	19
Frank Baker	PHI	1909	19
Charlie Gehringer	DET	1926	17
Russ Scarritt	BOS	1929	17
Hobe Ferris	BOS	1901	15
Del Pratt	STL	1912	15
Red Barnes	WAS	1928	15
Dale Alexander	DET	1929	15
Joe DiMaggio	NY	1936	15
Socks Seybold	PHI	1901	14

Most Triples, Rookie, AL (*cont.*)

Player	Team	Year	3B
Tony Lazzeri	NY	1926	14
Doug Taitt	BOS	1928	14
Roy Johnson	DET	1929	14
Joe Vosmik	CLE	1931	14
Barney McCosky	DET	1939	14
Minnie Minoso	CLE	1951	
	CHI	1951	14
Jake Wood	DET	1961	14

Most Triples, Rookie, NL

Player	Team	Year	3B
Jimmy Williams	PIT	1899	27
Tommy Long	STL	1915	25
Paul Waner	PIT	1926	22
Juan Samuel	PHI	1984	19
Harry Lumley	BKN	1904	18
Glenn Wright	PIT	1924	18
Ival Goodman	CIN	1935	18
George Treadway	BAL	1893	17
Kip Selbach	WAS	1894	17
Jim Gilliam	BKN	1953	17

One Hundred or More RBIs, Rookie, AL

Player	Team	Year	RBI
Ted Williams	BOS	1939	145
Walt Dropo	BOS	1950	144
Hal Trosky	CLE	1934	142
Dale Alexander	DET	1929	137
Joe DiMaggio	NY	1936	125
Mark McGwire	OAK	1987	118
Joe Vosmik	CLE	1931	117
Jose Canseco	OAK	1986	117
Al Rosen	CLE	1950	116
Alvin Davis	SEA	1984	116
Tony Lazzeri	NY	1926	114
Smead Jolley	CHI	1930	114
Ken Keltner	CLE	1938	113
Ping Bodie	CHI	1911	112
Zeke Bonura	CHI	1934	110
Luke Easter	CLE	1950	107
Fred Lynn	BOS	1975	105
Rudy York	DET	1937	103
Al Simmons	PHI	1924	102
Jim Rice	BOS	1975	102
Ron Kittle	CHI	1983	100
Wally Joyner	CAL	1986	100

One Hundred or More RBIs, Rookie, NL

Player	Team	Year	RBI
Wally Berger	BOS	1930	119
Jimmy Williams	PIT	1899	116
Ray Jablonski	STL	1953	112
Glenn Wright	PIT	1924	111
Johnny Rizzo	PIT	1938	111
Gus Suhr	PIT	1930	107
Del Bissonette	BKN	1928	106
Pinky Whitney	PHI	1928	103
Bill Brubaker	PIT	1936	102
Jim Greengrass	CIN	1953	102
Babe Young	NY	1940	101

Highest Batting Average, Rookie, AL (Min. 300 AB)

Player	Team	Year	BA
Wade Boggs	BOS	1982	.349
Dale Alexander	DET	1929	.343
Patsy Dougherty	BOS	1902	.342
Earle Combs	NY	1925	.342
Al Bumbry	BAL	1973	.337
Socks Seybold	PHI	1901	.334
Heinie Manush	DET	1923	.334
Charlie Keller	NY	1939	.334
Mickey Cochrane	PHI	1925	.331
Earl Averill	CLE	1929	.331
Hank Steinbacher	CHI	1938	.331
Johnny Pesky	BOS	1942	.331
Fred Lynn	BOS	1975	.331

Highest Batting Average, Rookie, NL (Min. 300 AB)

Player	Team	Year	BA
George Watkins	STL	1930	.373
Bill Everett	CHI	1895	.358
Jimmy Williams	PIT	1899	.355
Lloyd Waner	PIT	1927	.355
Fielder Jones	BKN	1896	.354
Chick Stahl	BOS	1897	.354
Kiki Cuyler	PIT	1924	.354
Ginger Beaumont	PIT	1899	.352
Dan Gladden	SF	1984	.351
Cuckoo Christensen	CIN	1926	.350
Hal Morris	CIN	1990	.340
Paul Waner	PIT	1926	.336

Rookie No-Hitters, AL

Player	Team	Date	Score	Opp.
Charlie Robertson	CHI	Apr 30, 1922	2–0	DET
Vern Kennedy	CHI	Aug 31, 1935	5–0	CLE
Bill McCahan	PHI	Sep 3, 1947	3–0	WAS
Bobo Holloman	STL	May 6, 1953	6–0	PHI
Bo Belinsky	LA	May 5, 1962	2–0	BAL
Vida Blue	OAK	Sep 21, 1970	6–0	MIN
Steve Busby	KC	Apr 27, 1973	3–0	DET
Jim Bibby	TEX	Jul 30, 1973	8–0	OAK
Mike Warren	OAK	Sep 29, 1983	3–0	CHI
Wilson Alvarez	CHI	Aug 11, 1991	7–0	BAL

Rookie No-Hitters, NL

Player	Team	Date	Score	Opp
Lee Richmond	WOR	Jun 12, 1880	1–0	CLE
Larry Corcoran	CHI	Aug 19, 1880	6–0	BOS
Bumpus Jones	CIN	Oct 15, 1892	7–1	PIT
Jim Hughes	BAL	Apr 22, 1898	8–0	BOS
Deacon Phillippe	LOU	May 25, 1899	7–0	NY
Christy Mathewson	NY	Jul 15, 1901	5–0	STL
Nick Maddox	PIT	Sep 20, 1907	2–1	BKN
Jeff Tesreau	NY	Sep 6, 1912	3–0	PHI
Paul Dean	STL	Sep 21, 1934	3–0	BKN
Don Wilson	HOU	Jun 18, 1967	2–0	ATL
Burt Hooton	CHI	Apr 16, 1972	4–0	PHI

Rookie No-Hitters, Other Leagues

Player	Team	Date	Score	Opp.
Tony Mullane	LOU AA	Sep 11, 1882	2–0	CIN
Guy Hecker	LOU AA	Sep 19, 1882	3–1	PIT
Al Atkinson	PHI AA	May 24, 1884	10–1	PIT
Ed Morris	COL AA	May 29, 1884	5–0	PIT
Sam Kimber	BKN AA	Oct 4, 1884	0–0	TOL
Matt Kilroy	BAL AA	Oct 6, 1886	6–0	PIT
Ted Breitenstein	STL AA	Oct 4, 1891	8–0	LOU

Twenty or More Wins, Rookie, AL

Player	Team	Year	W	L
Russ Ford	NY	1910	26	6
Ed Summers	DET	1908	24	12
Vean Gregg	CLE	1911	23	7
Roscoe Miller	DET	1901	23	13
Monte Weaver	WAS	1932	22	10
Wes Ferrell	CLE	1929	21	10
Boo Ferriss	BOS	1945	21	10

Twenty or More Wins, Rookie, AL (cont.)

Player	Team	Year	W	L
Reb Russell	CHI	1913	21	17
Scott Perry	PHI	1918	21	19
Bob Grim	NY	1954	20	6
Gene Bearden	CLE	1948	20	7
Hugh Bedient	BOS	1912	20	9
Alex Kellner	PHI	1949	20	12
Roy Patterson	CHI	1901	20	16

Twenty or More Wins, Rookie, NL since 1900

Player	Team	Year	W	L
Grover Alexander	PHI	1911	28	13
Larry Cheney	CHI	1912	26	10
Jeff Pfeffer	BKN	1914	23	12
George McQuillan	PHI	1908	23	17
Larry Jansen	NY	1947	21	5
Johnny Beazley	STL	1942	21	6
Henry Schmidt	BKN	1903	21	13
Bill Voiselle	NY	1944	21	16
King Cole	CHI	1910	20	4
Jake Weimer	CHI	1903	20	8
Jack Pfiester	CHI	1906	20	8
Cliff Melton	NY	1937	20	9
Harvey Haddix	STL	1953	20	9
Tom Browning	CIN	1985	20	9
Lou Fette	BOS	1937	20	10
Jim Turner	BOS	1937	20	11
Christy Mathewson	NY	1901	20	17
Irv Young	BOS	1905	20	21

ERA Under 2.00, Rookie, AL (Min. 130 IP)

Player	Team	Year	ERA
Harry Krause	PHI	1909	1.39
Bob Lee	LA	1964	1.51
Ed Summers	DET	1908	1.64
Russ Ford	NY	1910	1.65
Frank Lange	CHI	1910	1.65
Otto Hess	CLE	1904	1.67
Bill Burns	WAS	1908	1.69
Mark Eichhorn	TOR	1986	1.72
Rube Bressler	PHI	1914	1.77
Vean Gregg	CLE	1911	1.81
Hippo Vaughn	NY	1910	1.83
Ernie Shore	BOS	1914	1.89
Reb Russell	CHI	1913	1.91

ERA Under 2.00, Rookie, AL (Min. 130 IP) (cont.)

Player	Team	Year	ERA
Scott Perry	PHI	1918	1.98
Doug Corbett	MIN	1980	1.99

ERA Under 2.00, Rookie, NL since 1900 (Min. 130 IP)

Player	Team	Year	ERA
Babe Adams	PIT	1909	1.11
Ed Reulbach	CHI	1905	1.42
George McQuillan	PHI	1908	1.53
Steve Rogers	MON	1973	1.54
Jack Pfiester	CHI	1906	1.56
King Cole	CHI	1910	1.80
Jeff Tesreau	NY	1912	1.96
Carl Lundgren	CHI	1902	1.97
Jeff Pfeffer	BKN	1914	1.97

Three Hundred or More Innings Pitched, Rookie, AL

Player	Team	Year	IP
Roscoe Miller	DET	1901	332
Scott Perry	PHI	1918	332
Reb Russell	CHI	1913	316
Elmer Myers	PHI	1916	315
Roy Patterson	CHI	1901	312
Bill Reidy	MIL	1901	301
Ed Summers	DET	1908	301
Russ Ford	NY	1910	300

Three Hundred or More Innings Pitched, Rookie, NL since 1900

Player	Team	Year	IP
Irv Young	BOS	1905	378
Grover Alexander	PHI	1911	367
George McQuillan	PHI	1908	360
Christy Mathewson	NY	1901	336
Oscar Jones	BKN	1903	324
Ed Scott	CIN	1900	323
Orval Overall	CIN	1905	318
Al Mattern	BOS	1909	316
Jeff Pfeffer	BKN	1914	315
Bill Voiselle	NY	1944	313
Jack Harper	STL	1901	309
Harry McIntire	BKN	1905	309
Long Tom Hughes	CHI	1901	308
Vive Lindaman	BOS	1906	307
Larry Cheney	CHI	1912	303
Jesse Haines	STL	1920	302
Henry Schmidt	BKN	1903	301

Most Strikeouts, Rookie, AL

Player	Team	Year	SO
Herb Score	CLE	1955	245
Russ Ford	NY	1910	209
Bob Johnson	KC	1970	206
Mark Langston	SEA	1984	204
Gary Peters	CHI	1963	189
Elmer Myers	PHI	1916	182
Ken McBride	LA	1961	180
Frank Tanana	CAL	1974	180
Tom Phoebus	BAL	1967	179
Ron Guidry	NY	1977	176
Al Downing	NY	1963	171

Most Strikeouts, Rookie, NL since 1900

Player	Team	Year	SO
Dwight Gooden	NY	1984	276
Grover Alexander	PHI	1911	227
Long Tom Hughes	CHI	1901	225
Christy Mathewson	NY	1901	221
John Montefusco	SF	1975	215
Don Sutton	LA	1966	209
Gary Nolan	CIN	1967	206
Tom Griffin	HOU	1969	200
Sam Jones	CHI	1955	198
Dizzy Dean	STL	1932	191
Jack Sanford	PHI	1957	188
Fernando Valenzuela	LA	1981	180
Jerry Koosman	NY	1968	178
Ray Culp	PHI	1963	176
Orval Overall	CIN	1905	173
Dick Drott	CHI	1957	170
Tom Seaver	NY	1967	170

Most Complete Games, Rookie, AL

Player	Team	Year	CG
Roscoe Miller	DET	1901	35
Elmer Myers	PHI	1916	31
Roy Patterson	CHI	1901	30
Ed Siever	DET	1901	30
Fred Glade	STL	1904	30
Scott Perry	PHI	1918	30
Chief Bender	PHI	1903	29
Russ Ford	NY	1910	29
Earl Moore	CLE	1901	28
Eddie Plank	PHI	1901	28

Most Complete Games, Rookie, AL (cont.)

Player	Team	Year	CG
Bill Reidy	MIL	1901	28
Addie Joss	CLE	1902	28

Most Complete Games, Rookie, NL since 1900

Player	Team	Year	CG
Irv Young	BOS	1905	41
Christy Mathewson	NY	1901	36
Ed Scott	CIN	1900	32
Long Tom Hughes	CHI	1901	32
Orval Overall	CIN	1905	32
Vive Lindaman	BOS	1906	32
George McQuillan	PHI	1908	32
Oscar Jones	BKN	1903	31
Grover Alexander	PHI	1911	31
Henry Schmidt	BKN	1903	29
Harry McIntire	BKN	1905	29

Most Shutouts, Rookie, AL

Player	Team	Year	ShO
Russ Ford	NY	1910	8
Reb Russell	CHI	1913	8
Harry Krause	PHI	1908	7
Fred Glade	STL	1904	6
Gene Bearden	CLE	1948	6
Addie Joss	CLE	1902	5
Ed Summers	DET	1908	5
Hippo Vaughn	NY	1910	5
Vean Gregg	CLE	1911	5
Boo Ferriss	BOS	1945	5
Mike Garcia	CLE	1949	5
Ron Guidry	NY	1977	5
Mike Boddicker	BAL	1983	5

Most Shutouts, Rookie, NL since 1900

Player	Team	Year	ShO
Fernando Valenzuela	LA	1981	8
Irv Young	BOS	1905	7
George McQuillan	PHI	1908	7
Grover Alexander	PHI	1911	7
Jerry Koosman	NY	1968	7
Ewell Blackwell	CIN	1946	6
Harvey Haddix	STL	1953	6
Christy Mathewson	NY	1901	5
Henry Schmidt	BKN	1903	5

Most Shutouts, Rookie, NL since 1900 (*cont.*)

Player	Team	Year	ShO
Ed Reulbach	CHI	1905	5
Dazzy Vance	BKN	1922	5
Paul Dean	STL	1934	5
Lou Fette	BOS	1937	5
Jim Turner	BOS	1937	5
Don Newcombe	BKN	1949	5
Ray Culp	PHI	1963	5
Larry Jaster	STL	1966	5
Gary Nolan	CIN	1967	5

Rookies of the Year Who Later Won MVP or Cy Young Awards

Player	Rookie Year	MVP	Cy Young
Jackie Robinson	1947	1949	
Don Newcombe	1949	1956	1956
Willie Mays	1951	1954	
		1965	
Frank Robinson	1956	1961	
		1966	
Orlando Cepeda	1958	1967	
Willie McCovey	1959	1969	
Pete Rose	1963	1973	
Dick Allen	1964	1972	
Rod Carew	1967	1977	
Tom Seaver	1967		1969
			1973
			1975
Johnny Bench	1968	1970	
		1972	
Thurman Munson	1970	1976	
Vida Blue	1971		1971
Fred Lynn	1975	1975	
Andre Dawson	1977	1987	
Rick Sutcliffe	1979		1984
Fernando Valenzuela	1981		1981
Cal Ripken	1982	1983	
		1991	
Dwight Gooden	1984		1985
Jose Canseco	1986	1988	

Pennant-Winning Rookie Managers, AL

Manager	Team	Year	W	L	Pct.
Clark Griffith	CHI	1901	83	55	.610
Hughie Jennings	DET	1907	92	58	.613
Kid Gleason	CHI	1919	88	52	.629
Bucky Harris	WAS	1924	92	62	.597
Joe Cronin	WAS	1933	99	53	.651

Pennant-Winning Rookie Managers, AL (*cont.*)

Manager	Team	Year	W	L	Pct.
Mickey Cochrane	DET	1934	101	53	.656
Ralph Houk	NY	1961	109	53	.678
Yogi Berra	NY	1964	99	63	.611
Dick Williams	BOS	1967	92	70	.568
Jim Frey	KC	1980	97	65	.599
Tom Kelly	MIN	1987	85	77	.525

Pennant-Winning Rookie Managers, NL

Manager	Team	Year	W	L	Pct.
Frank Chance	CHI	1906	116	36	.763
Pat Moran	PHI	1915	90	62	.592
Gabby Street	STL	1930	92	62	.597
Charlie Grimm	CHI	1932	90	44	.584
Bill Terry	NY	1933	91	61	.599
Gabby Hartnett	CHI	1938	89	63	.586
Eddie Dyer	STL	1946	98	58	.628
Sparky Anderson	CIN	1970	102	60	.630
Tom Lasorda	LA	1977	98	64	.605

TEAM
RECORDS

●

Miscellaneous Records
319

Team Batting Records
346

Team Pitching Records
425

Most Wins, Season, AL

Team	Year	W	L	Pct.	Place
CLE	1954	111	43	.721	1
NY	1927	110	44	.714	1
NY	1961	109	53	.673	1
BAL	1969	109	53	.673	1
BAL	1970	108	54	.667	1
PHI	1931	107	45	.704	1
NY	1932	107	47	.695	1
NY	1939	106	45	.702	1
BOS	1912	105	47	.691	1
PHI	1929	104	46	.693	1
BOS	1946	104	50	.675	1
NY	1963	104	57	.646	1
DET	1984	104	58	.642	1
OAK	1988	104	58	.642	1
NY	1942	103	51	.669	1
NY	1954	103	51	.669	2
DET	1968	103	59	.636	1
NY	1980	103	59	.636	1
OAK	1990	103	59	.636	1
PHI	1910	102	48	.680	1
PHI	1930	102	52	.662	1
NY	1936	102	51	.667	1
NY	1937	102	52	.662	1
MIN	1965	102	60	.630	1
KC	1977	102	60	.630	1
BAL	1979	102	57	.642	1
PHI	1911	101	50	.669	1
BOS	1915	101	50	.669	1
NY	1928	101	53	.656	1
DET	1934	101	53	.656	1
NY	1941	101	53	.656	1
DET	1961	101	61	.623	2
BAL	1971	101	57	.639	1
DET	1915	100	54	.649	2
CHI	1917	100	54	.649	1
NY	1977	100	62	.617	1
NY	1978	100	63	.613	1
BAL	1980	100	62	.617	2

Most Wins, Season, NL

Team	Year	W	L	Pct.	Place
CHI	1906	116	36	.763	1
PIT	1909	110	42	.724	1
CIN	1975	108	54	.667	1
NY	1986	108	54	.667	1
CHI	1907	107	45	.704	1
NY	1904	106	47	.693	1

Most Wins, Season, NL (cont.)

Team	Year	W	L	Pct.	Place
STL	1942	106	48	.688	1
NY	1905	105	48	.686	1
STL	1943	105	49	.682	1
STL	1944	105	49	.682	1
BKN	1953	105	49	.682	1
CHI	1909	104	49	.680	2
CHI	1910	104	50	.675	1
BKN	1942	104	50	.675	2
PIT	1902	103	36	.741	1
NY	1912	103	48	.682	1
SF	1962	103	62	.624	1
BOS	1892	102	48	.680	1
BOS	1898	102	47	.685	1
LA	1962	102	63	.618	2
CIN	1970	102	60	.630	1
LA	1974	102	60	.630	1
CIN	1976	102	60	.630	1
BKN	1899	101	47	.682	1
NY	1913	101	51	.664	1
STL	1931	101	53	.656	1
STL	1967	101	60	.627	1
PHI	1976	101	61	.623	1
PHI	1977	101	61	.623	1
STL	1985	101	61	.623	1
CHI	1935	100	54	.649	1
CIN	1940	100	53	.654	1
BKN	1941	100	54	.649	1
NY	1969	100	62	.617	1
NY	1988	100	60	.625	1

Most Losses, Season, AL

Team	Year	W	L	Pct.	Place
PHI	1916	36	117	.235	8
WAS	1904	38	113	.251	8
BOS	1932	43	111	.279	8
STL	1939	43	111	.279	8
WAS	1909	42	110	.276	8
PHI	1915	47	109	.283	8
TOR	1979	53	109	.327	7
STL	1937	46	108	.299	8
OAK	1979	54	108	.333	7
STL	1910	47	107	.305	8
STL	1911	45	107	.296	8
BOS	1926	46	107	.301	8
TOR	1977	54	107	.335	7
BAL	1988	54	107	.335	7
PHI	1920	48	106	.312	8

Most Losses, Season, AL (cont.)

Team	Year	W	L	Pct.	Place
WAS	1963	56	106	.346	10
CHI	1970	56	106	.346	6
BOS	1906	49	105	.318	8
BOS	1925	47	105	.309	8
PHI	1943	49	105	.318	8
PHI	1946	49	105	.318	8
KC	1964	57	105	.352	10
TEX	1973	57	105	.352	6
CLE	1991	57	105	.352	7
PHI	1919	36	104	.257	8
WAS	1949	50	104	.325	8
DET	1952	50	104	.325	8
SEA	1978	58	104	.350	7
NY	1908	51	103	.331	8
BOS	1927	51	103	.331	8
PHI	1954	51	103	.331	8
KC	1965	59	103	.364	10
SEA	1980	59	103	.364	7
DET	1989	59	103	.364	7
WAS	1907	49	102	.325	8
NY	1912	50	102	.329	8
CLE	1914	51	102	.333	8
BOS	1930	52	102	.338	8
CHI	1932	49	102	.325	7
PHI	1950	52	102	.338	8
STL	1951	52	102	.338	8
KC	1956	52	102	.338	8
CLE	1971	60	102	.370	6
DET	1975	57	102	.358	6
TOR	1978	59	102	.366	7
MIN	1982	60	102	.370	7
SEA	1983	60	102	.370	7
CLE	1985	60	102	.370	7
STL	1912	53	101	.344	7
CHI	1948	51	101	.336	8
STL	1949	53	101	.344	7
WAS	1955	53	101	.344	8
WAS	1962	60	101	.373	10
CLE	1987	61	101	.377	7
PHI	1921	53	100	.346	8
PHI	1936	53	100	.346	8
PHI	1940	54	100	.351	8
STL	1953	54	100	.351	8
BAL	1954	54	100	.351	7
KC	1961	61	100	.379	9
WAS	1961	61	100	.379	9
WAS	1964	62	100	.383	9

Most Losses, Season, AL (cont.)

Team	Year	W	L	Pct.	Place
BOS	1965	62	100	.383	9
TEX	1972	54	100	.351	6

Most Losses, Season, NL

Team	Year	W	L	Pct.	Place
CLE	1899	20	134	.130	12
NY	1962	40	120	.250	10
BOS	1935	38	115	.248	8
PIT	1890	23	113	.169	8
PIT	1952	42	112	.273	8
NY	1965	50	112	.309	10
STL	1898	39	111	.260	12
PHI	1941	43	111	.279	8
NY	1963	51	111	.315	10
MON	1969	52	110	.321	6
SD	1969	52	110	.321	6
PHI	1928	43	109	.283	8
PHI	1942	42	109	.278	8
NY	1964	53	109	.327	10
BOS	1909	45	108	.294	8
PHI	1945	46	108	.299	8
BOS	1911	44	107	.291	8
PHI	1961	47	107	.305	8
MON	1976	55	107	.340	6
PHI	1939	45	106	.298	8
ATL	1988	54	106	.338	6
STL	1908	49	105	.318	8
PHI	1938	45	105	.300	8
BKN	1905	48	104	.316	8
PHI	1923	50	104	.325	8
PIT	1953	50	104	.325	8
PIT	1985	57	104	.354	6
BOS	1905	51	103	.331	7
PIT	1917	51	103	.331	8
PHI	1921	51	103	.331	8
PHI	1927	51	103	.331	8
BOS	1928	50	103	.327	7
PHI	1940	50	103	.327	8
CHI	1962	59	103	.364	9
CHI	1966	59	103	.364	10
STL	1897	29	102	.221	12
BOS	1906	49	102	.325	8
PHI	1930	52	102	.338	8
SD	1973	60	102	.370	6
SD	1974	60	102	.370	6
BAL	1892	46	101	.313	12

Most Losses, Season, NL (cont.)

Team	Year	W	L	Pct.	Place
WAS	1898	51	101	.336	11
STL	1907	52	101	.340	8
BKN	1908	53	101	.344	7
BOS	1912	52	101	.340	8
PIT	1954	53	101	.344	8
NY	1967	61	101	.377	10
ATL	1977	61	101	.377	6
CIN	1982	61	101	.377	6
PHI	1904	52	100	.342	8
BOS	1910	53	100	.346	8
BOS	1922	53	100	.346	8
BOS	1923	54	100	.351	7
BOS	1924	53	100	.346	8
PHI	1936	54	100	.351	8
SD	1971	61	100	.379	6
SF	1985	62	100	.383	6

Most Losses, Season, Other Leagues

Team	Year	W	L	Pct.	Place
LOU AA	1889	27	111	.196	8
BAL F	1915	47	107	.305	8

Most Wins, Season, First Year Expansion Team since 1961

Team	Year	W	L	Pct.	Place
LA A	1961	70	91	.435	8
KC A	1969	69	93	.426	4
HOU N	1962	64	96	.400	8
SEA A	1969	64	98	.395	6
SEA A	1977	64	98	.395	6

Most Losses, Season, First Year Expansion Team since 1961

Team	Year	W	L	Pct.	Place
NY N	1962	40	120	.250	10
MON N	1969	52	110	.321	6
SD N	1969	52	110	.321	6
TOR A	1977	54	107	.335	7
WAS A	1961	61	100	.379	10

Most Consecutive Wins, Season, AL

Team	Year	W	Home	Away
CHI	1906	19	11	8
NY	1947	19	6	13
NY	1953	18	3	15

Most Consecutive Wins, Season, AL (*cont.*)

Team	Year	W	Home	Away
WAS	1912	17	1	16
PHI	1931	17	5	12
NY	1926	16	12	4
KC	1977	16	9	7
NY	1906	15	12	3
PHI	1913	15	13	2
BOS	1946	15	11	4
NY	1960	15	9	6
MIN	1991	15	10	5
DET	1909	14	14	0
STL	1916	14	13	1
DET	1934	14	9	5
NY	1941	14	6	8
CHI	1951	14	3	11
BAL	1973	14	10	4
OAK	1988	14	5	9
TEX	1991	14	7	7
CHI	1908	13	12	1
PHI	1910	13	12	1
DET	1927	13	13	0
PHI	1931	13	13	0
WAS	1933	13	1	12
CLE	1942	13	4	9
BOS	1948	13	12	1
CLE	1951	13	7	6
NY	1954	13	8	5
NY	1961	13	12	1
BAL	1978	13	3	10
MIL	1987	13	6	7

Most Consecutive Wins, Season, NL

Team	Year	W	Home	Away
NY	1916	26	26	0
CHI	1880	21	11	10
CHI	1935	21	18	3
PRO	1884	20	16	4
CHI	1885	18	14	4
BOS	1891	18	16	2
BAL	1894	18	13	5
NY	1904	18	13	5
BOS	1897	17	16	1
NY	1907	17	14	3
NY	1916	17	0	17
PHI	1887	16	5	11
PHI	1890	16	14	2
PHI	1892	16	11	5

Most Consecutive Wins, Season, NL (*cont.*)

Team	Year	W	Home	Away
PIT	1909	16	12	4
NY	1912	16	11	5
NY	1951	16	13	3
DET	1886	15	12	3
PIT	1903	15	11	4
BKN	1924	15	3	12
CHI	1936	15	11	4
NY	1936	15	7	8
BAL	1895	14	13	1
CIN	1899	14	10	4
PIT	1903	14	7	7
CHI	1906	14	14	0
PIT	1909	14	12	2
NY	1913	14	6	8
CHI	1932	14	14	0
STL	1935	14	12	2
SF	1965	14	6	8
CIN	1890	13	13	0
CHI	1892	13	11	2
NY	1905	13	8	5
PIT	1911	13	9	4
PIT	1922	13	2	11
CHI	1928	13	13	0
PIT	1938	13	5	8
BKN	1947	13	2	11
BKN	1953	13	7	6
LA	1962	13	8	5
LA	1965	13	7	6
PHI	1977	13	8	5
ATL	1982	13	8	5
PHI	1991	13	9	4
ATL	1992	13	3	10

Most Consecutive Losses, Season, AL

Team	Year	L	Home	Away
BAL	1988	21	8	13
BOS	1906	20	19	1
PHI	1916	20	1	19
PHI	1943	20	3	17
DET	1975	19	9	10
PHI	1920	18	0	18
WAS	1948	18	8	10
WAS	1959	18	3	15
BOS	1926	17	14	3
BOS	1907	16	9	7
BOS	1927	15	10	5

Most Consecutive Losses, Season, AL (*cont.*)

Team	Year	L	Home	Away
PHI	1937	15	10	5
TEX	1972	15	5	10
STL	1911	14	6	8
BOS	1930	14	3	11
STL	1940	14	0	14
PHI	1945	14	14	0
BAL	1954	14	7	7
WAS	1961	14	11	3
WAS	1970	14	4	10
OAK	1977	14	9	5
MIN	1982	14	6	8
SEA	1992	14	4	10
WAS	1904	13	7	6
NY	1913	13	7	6
DET	1920	13	5	8
CHI	1924	13	2	11
PHI	1935	13	10	3
STL	1936	13	2	11
DET	1953	13	12	1
WAS	1958	13	4	9
KC	1959	13	4	9
MIN	1961	13	0	13
WAS	1962	13	7	6

Most Consecutive Losses, Season, NL

Team	Year	L	Home	Away
CLE	1899	24	3	21
PIT	1890	23	1	22
PHI	1961	23	6	17
LOU	1894	20	0	20
MON	1969	20	12	8
BOS	1906	19	3	16
CIN	1914	19	6	13
CIN	1876	18	9	9
LOU	1894	18	0	18
WAS	1894	17	7	10
NY	1962	17	7	10
ATL	1977	17	8	9
TRO	1882	16	5	11
DET	1884	16	5	11
CLE	1899	16	0	16
BOS	1907	16	5	11
BOS	1911	16	8	8
BKN	1944	16	0	16
BOS	1909	15	0	15
STL	1909	15	11	4

Most Consecutive Losses, Season, NL (*cont.*)

Team	Year	L	Home	Away
BOS	1927	15	0	15
BOS	1935	15	0	15
NY	1963	15	8	7
NY	1982	15	6	9
MIL	1878	14	7	7
WOR	1882	14	2	12
STL	1896	14	5	9
CLE	1899	14	0	14
BOS	1911	14	14	0
STL	1916	14	0	14
BOS	1935	14	4	10
PHI	1936	14	10	4
BKN	1937	14	0	14
CIN	1937	14	10	4
PRO	1885	13	2	11
WAS	1886	13	13	0
NY	1902	13	5	8
BOS	1909	13	13	0
STL	1910	13	5	8
PHI	1919	13	0	13
PHI	1919	13	7	6
CIN	1930	13	1	12
PHI	1942	13	4	9
CHI	1944	13	7	6
NY	1944	13	0	13
CIN	1945	13	2	11
PHI	1955	13	9	4
NY	1962	13	9	4
ATL	1976	13	6	7
CHI	1985	13	4	9

Forfeited Games since 1900

Team	Date	Loser	Site	Inns.	Score
DET A	May 2, 1901	CHI	CHI	9	7–5
NY N	May 13, 1901	BKN	NY	9	7–7
DET A	May 31, 1901	BAL	DET	9	5–5
NY N	Jun 9, 1901	CIN	CIN	9	25–13
CLE A	Jul 23, 1901	WAS	CLE	9	4–4
DET A	Aug 21, 1901	BAL	BAL	4	7–4
PIT N	Jun 16, 1902	BOS	BOS	4	4–0
BOS A	Jun 28, 1902	BAL	BAL	8	9–4
STL A	Jul 17, 1902	BAL	BAL	0	
DET A	Aug 8, 1903	CLE	CLE	11	6–5
STL N	Oct 4, 1904	NY	NY	4	2–1
PIT N	Aug 5, 1905	NY	PIT	9	5–5
WAS A	Aug 22, 1905	DET	DET	11	2–1

Forfeited Games since 1900 (*cont.*)

Team	Date	Loser	Site	Inns.	Score
PIT N	Jun 9, 1906	PHI	PHI	8	7–1
NY A	Jul 2, 1906	PHI	PHI	9	5–1
CHI N	Aug 7, 1906	NY	NY	0	
NY A	Sep 3, 1906	PHI	NY	9	3–3
PHI N	Apr 11, 1907	NY	NY	8	3–0
STL N	Oct 5, 1907	CHI	STL	4	0–2
NY N	Oct 4, 1909	PHI	NY	4	1–1
STL N	Jul 6, 1913	CHI	CHI	3	4–0
PHI A	Jun 26, 1914	WAS	PHI	4	2–0
BKN N	Jul 18, 1916	CHI	CHI	10	4–4
CHI A	Sep 9, 1917	CLE	CHI	10	3–3
CLE A	Jul 20, 1918	PHI	PHI	9	9–1
CHI A	Aug 20, 1920	PHI	PHI	9	5–2
NY A	Jun 13, 1924	DET	DET	9	10–6
CLE A	Apr 26, 1925	CHI	CHI	9	7–2
STL N	Jun 6, 1937	PHI	PHI	4	8–2
BOS A	Aug 15, 1941	WAS	WAS	8	3–6
BOS N	Sep 26, 1942	NY	NY	8	2–5
NY N	Aug 21, 1949	PHI	PHI	9	4–2
PHI N	Jul 18, 1954	STL	STL	4	8–1
NY A	Sep 30, 1971	WAS	WAS	9	5–7
TEX A	Jun 4, 1974	CLE	CLE	9	5–5
TOR A	Sep 15, 1977	BAL	TOR	5	4–0
DET A	Jul 12, 1979	CHI	CHI	0	

Most Lopsided Wins since 1900

Team	Date	Loser	Score	Diff.
BOS A	Jun 8, 1950	STL	29–4	25
CLE A	Jul 7, 1923	BOS	27–3	24
CIN N	Jun 4, 1911	BOS	26–3	23
NY A	May 24, 1936	PHI	25–2	23
CLE A	Aug 12, 1948	STL	26–3	23
CHI A	Apr 23, 1955	KC	29–6	23
CIN N	May 13, 1902	PHI	24–2	22
PHI A	May 18, 1912	DET	24–2	22
STL N	Jul 6, 1929	PHI	28–6	22
CHI N	Jul 3, 1945	BOS	24–2	22
PIT N	Sep 16, 1975	CHI	22–0	22
CAL A	Aug 25, 1979	TOR	24–2	22
DET A	Sep 15, 1901	CLE	21–0	21
NY N	Sep 10, 1924	BOS	22–1	21
NY A	Jun 28, 1939	PHI	23–2	21
NY A	Aug 13, 1939	PHI	21–0	21
CIN N	Jun 8, 1940	BKN	23–2	21
NY A	Aug 12, 1953	WAS	22–1	21
CLE A	Aug 7, 1923	WAS	22–2	20

Most Lopsided Wins since 1900 (*cont.*)

Team	Date	Loser	Score	Diff.
NY A	Sep 28, 1923	BOS	24–4	20
STL N	Sep 16, 1926	PHI	23–3	20
NY A	Jul 4, 1927	WAS	21–1	20
NY A	May 2, 1939	DET	22–2	20
BOS A	Sep 27, 1940	WAS	24–4	20
BOS A	Jun 18, 1953	DET	23–3	20
CIN N	Jun 1, 1957	CHI	22–2	20
MIL A	Aug 28, 1992	TOR	22–2	20
BKN N	Sep 23, 1901	CIN	25–6	19
CHI N	Jun 7, 1906	NY	19–0	19
DET A	Jul 17, 1908	PHI	21–2	19
BOS N	Sep 18, 1915	STL	20–1	19
CIN N	Jul 6, 1949	CHI	23–4	19
BOS A	Apr 30, 1950	PHI	19–0	19
CLE A	May 18, 1955	BOS	19–0	19
CHI N	May 13, 1969	SD	19–0	19
MON N	Jul 30, 1978	ATL	19–0	19
PHI N	Jun 11, 1985	NY	26–7	19
BOS A	Aug 21, 1986	CLE	24–5	19
SF N	Jul 9, 1988	STL	21–2	19
NY A	Jul 14, 1904	CLE	21–3	18
PHI N	Jul 11, 1901	PIT	18–0	18
PHI A	Jul 25, 1921	CLE	21–3	18
DET A	Jun 17, 1925	NY	19–1	18
PIT N	Jun 22, 1925	STL	24–6	18
CLE A	Jul 29, 1928	NY	24–6	18
PHI A	May 1, 1929	BOS	24–6	18
CLE A	May 11, 1930	PHI	25–7	18
PHI N	Aug 10, 1930	CIN	18–0	18
PHI N	Jul 14, 1934	CIN	18–0	18
DET A	Apr 29, 1935	STL	18–0	18
NY N	Apr 30, 1944	BKN	26–8	18
STL N	Jun 10, 1944	CIN	18–0	18
KC A	Apr 25, 1961	MIN	20–2	18
CIN N	Aug 8, 1965	LA	18–0	18
CAL A	Jun 20, 1980	BOS	20–2	18
PHI N	Jun 23, 1986	CHI	19–1	18
MIL A	Apr 16, 1990	BOS	18–0	18

Longest Games, AL

Team	Date	Opp.	Inns.	Score
CHI	May 8, 1984	MIL	25	7–6
PHI	Sep 1, 1906	BOS	24	4–1
DET	Jul 21, 1945	PHI	24	1–1
NY	Jun 24, 1962	DET	22	9–7
WAS	Jun 12, 1967	CHI	22	6–5

Longest Games, AL (*cont.*)

Team	Date	Opp.	Inns.	Score
MIL	May 12, 1972	MIN	22	4–3
DET	May 24, 1929	CHI	21	6–5
OAK	Jun 4, 1971	WAS	21	5–3
CHI	May 26, 1973	CLE	21	6–3
PHI	Jul 4, 1905	BOS	20	4–2
WAS	Aug 9, 1967	MIN	20	9–7
NY	Aug 29, 1967	BOS	20	4–3
BOS	Jul 27, 1969	SEA	20	5–3
OAK	Jul 9, 1971	CAL	20	1–0
WAS	Sep 14, 1971	CLE	20	8–6
SEA	Sep 3, 1981	BOS	20	8–7
CAL	Apr 13, 1982	SEA	20	4–3

Longest Games, NL

Team	Date	Opp.	Inns.	Score
BKN	May 1, 1920	BOS	26	1–1
STL	Sep 11, 1974	NY	25	4–3
HOU	Apr 15, 1968	NY	24	1–0
BKN	Jun 27, 1939	BOS	23	2–2
SF	May 31, 1964	NY	23	8–6
BKN	Aug 22, 1917	PIT	22	6–5
CHI	May 17, 1927	BOS	22	4–3
HOU	Jun 3, 1989	LA	22	5–4
LA	Aug 23, 1989	MON	22	1–0
NY	Jul 17, 1914	PIT	21	3–1
CHI	Jul 17, 1918	PHI	21	2–1
PIT	Aug 1, 1918	BOS	21	2–0
SF	Sep 1, 1967	CIN	21	1–0
HOU	Sep 24, 1971	SD	21	2–1
SD	May 21, 1977	MON	21	11–8
LA	Aug 17, 1982	CHI	21	2–1
CHI	Jun 30, 1892	CIN	20	7–7
CHI	Aug 24, 1905	PHI	20	2–1
BKN	Apr 30, 1919	PHI	20	9–9
STL	Aug 28, 1930	CHI	20	8–7
BKN	Jul 5, 1940	BOS	20	6–2
PHI	May 4, 1973	ATL	20	5–4
PIT	Jul 6, 1980	CHI	20	5–4
HOU	Aug 15, 1980	SD	20	3–1

Career Spent with One Team (15 or more years)

Player	Team	Yrs.	Pos.
Brooks Robinson	BAL A	23	3B
Carl Yastrzemski	BOS A	23	OF-1B
Cap Anson	CHI N	22	1B

Career Spent with One Team (15 or more years) *(cont.)*

Player	Team	Yrs.	Pos.
Al Kaline	DET A	22	OF
Stan Musial	STL N	22	OF-1B
Mel Ott	NY N	22	OF
Fred Clarke	LOU N		
	PIT N	21	OF
Walter Johnson	WAS A	21	P
Ted Lyons	CHI A	21	P
Willie Stargell	PIT N	21	OF-1B
Honus Wagner	LOU N		
	PIT N	21	SS
Luke Appling	CHI A	20	SS
Red Faber	CHI A	20	P
Mel Harder	CLE A	20	P
Ernie Banks	CHI A	19	SS-1B
George Brett	KC A	19	3B-1B
Dave Concepcion	CIN N	19	SS
Charlie Gehringer	DET A	19	2B
Jim Palmer	BAL A	19	P
Ted Williams	BOS A	19	OF
Robin Yount	MIL A	19	SS-OF
Ossie Bluege	WAS A	18	3B
Roberto Clemente	PIT N	18	OF
Bob Feller	CLE A	18	P
Ed Kranepool	NY N	18	1B-OF
Mickey Mantle	NY A	18	OF-1B
Bill Russell	LA N	18	SS
Mike Schmidt	PHI N	18	3B
Frank White	KC A	18	2B
Johnny Bench	CIN N	17	C
Frankie Crosetti	NY A	17	SS
Bill Dickey	NY A	17	C
Jim Gantner	MIL A	17	2B
Lou Gehrig	NY A	17	1B
Bob Gibson	STL N	17	P
Bill Mazeroski	PIT N	17	2B
Pie Traynor	PIT N	17	3B
Tommy Bridges	DET A	16	P
Whitey Ford	NY A	16	P
Stan Hack	CHI N	16	3B
Carl Hubbell	NY N	16	P
Vern Law	PIT N	16	P
Clyde Milan	WAS A	16	OF
Pee Wee Reese	BKN N		
	LA N	16	SS
Jim Rice	BOS A	16	OF
Alan Trammell	DET A	16	SS
Lou Whitaker	DET A	16	2B

Career Spent with One Team (15 or more years) (*cont.*)

Player	Team	Yrs.	Pos.
Hooks Dauss	DET A	15	P
Bill Freehan	DET A	15	C
Carl Furillo	BKN N		
	LA N	15	OF
John Hiller	DET A	15	P
Travis Jackson	NY N	15	SS-3B
Bob Lemon	CLE A	15	P
Tony Oliva	MIN A	15	OF
Paul Splittorff	KC A	15	P
Mickey Stanley	DET A	15	OF
Roy White	NY A	15	OF

Great Players Who Never Played In a World Series

Player	Yrs.
Phil Niekro	24
Gaylord Perry	22
Nap Lajoie	21
Ted Lyons	21
Luke Appling	20
Mel Harder	20
Ernie Banks	19
Rod Carew	19
Ferguson Jenkins	19
Billy Williams	18
Jim Bunning	17
Harry Heilmann	17
George Sisler	15
George Kell	15

Retired Numbers, AL

Player	Team	No.
Earl Weaver	BAL	4
Brooks Robinson	BAL	5
Frank Robinson	BAL	20
Jim Palmer	BAL	22
Eddie Murray	BAL	33
Bobby Doerr	BOS	1
Joe Cronin	BOS	4
Carl Yastrzemski	BOS	8
Ted Williams	BOS	9
Gene Autry	CAL	26
Rod Carew	CAL	29
Nolan Ryan	CAL	30
Nellie Fox	CHI	2

Retired Numbers, AL (*cont.*)

Player	Team	No.
Harold Baines	CHI	3
Luke Appling	CHI	4
Minnie Minoso	CHI	9
Luis Aparicio	CHI	11
Ted Lyons	CHI	16
Billy Pierce	CHI	19
Earl Averill	CLE	3
Lou Boudreau	CLE	5
Mel Harder	CLE	18
Bob Feller	CLE	19
Charlie Gehringer	DET	2
Hank Greenberg	DET	5
Al Kaline	DET	6
Dick Howser	KC	10
Rollie Fingers	MIL	34
Hank Aaron	MIL	44
Harmon Killebrew	MIN	3
Rod Carew	MIN	29
Billy Martin	NY	1
Babe Ruth	NY	3
Lou Gehrig	NY	4
Joe DiMaggio	NY	5
Mickey Mantle	NY	7
Yogi Berra	NY	8
Bill Dickey	NY	8
Roger Maris	NY	9
Phil Rizzuto	NY	10
Thurman Munson	NY	15
Whitey Ford	NY	16
Elston Howard	NY	32
Casey Stengel	NY	37
Catfish Hunter	OAK	27

Retired Numbers, NL

Player	Team	No.	Player	Team	No.
Dale Murphy	ATL	3	Mel Ott	SF	4
Warren Spahn	ATL	21	Carl Hubbell	SF	11
Phil Niekro	ATL	35	Willie Mays	SF	24
Eddie Mathews	ATL	41	Juan Marichal	SF	27
Hank Aaron	ATL	44	Willie McCovey	SF	44
Ernie Banks	CHI	14	Stan Musial	STL	6
Billy Williams	CHI	26	Ken Boyer	STL	14
Fred Hutchinson	CIN	1	Dizzy Dean	STL	17
Johnny Bench	CIN	5	Lou Brock	STL	20
Jose Cruz	HOU	25	Bob Gibson	STL	45
Jim Umbricht	HOU	32	August A. Busch, Jr.	STL	85
Mike Scott	HOU	33			
Don Wilson	HOU	40			
Pee Wee Reese	LA	1			
Duke Snider	LA	4			
Jim Gilliam	LA	19			
Walter Alston	LA	24			
Sandy Koufax	LA	32			
Roy Campanella	LA	39			
Jackie Robinson	LA	42			
Don Drysdale	LA	53			
Gil Hodges	NY	14			
Casey Stengel	NY	37			
Tom Seaver	NY	41			
Mike Schmidt	PHI	20			
Steve Carlton	PHI	32			
Robin Roberts	PHI	36			
Billy Meyer	PIT	1			
Ralph Kiner	PIT	4			
Willie Stargell	PIT	8			
Bill Mazeroski	PIT	9			
Pie Traynor	PIT	20			
Honus Wagner	PIT	33			
Danny Murtaugh	PIT	40			
Steve Garvey	SD	6			
Christy Mathewson	SF				
John McGraw	SF				
Bill Terry	SF	3			

Elected to Hall of Fame in First Year Eligible

Player	Year
Bob Feller	1962
Jackie Robinson	1962
Ted Williams	1966
Stan Musial	1969
Sandy Koufax	1972
Mickey Mantle	1974
Ernie Banks	1977
Willie Mays	1979
Al Kaline	1980
Bob Gibson	1981
Hank Aaron	1982
Frank Robinson	1982
Brooks Robinson	1983
Lou Brock	1985
Willie McCovey	1986
Willie Stargell	1988
Johnny Bench	1989
Carl Yastrzemski	1989
Joe Morgan	1990
Jim Palmer	1990
Rod Carew	1991
Tom Seaver	1992
Reggie Jackson	1993

Most Wins, Manager, Career

Manager	Yrs.	W	L	Pct.
Connie Mack	53	3731	3948	.486
John McGraw	33	2784	1959	.587
Bucky Harris	29	2157	2218	.493
Joe McCarthy	24	2125	1337	.615

Most Wins, Manager, Career (*cont.*)

Manager	Yrs.	W	L	Pct.
Walter Alston	23	2040	1613	.556
Leo Durocher	24	2008	1709	.540
Sparky Anderson	23	1996	1611	.553
Casey Stengel	25	1905	1842	.508
Gene Mauch	25	1902	2037	.483
Bill McKechnie	25	1899	1724	.524
Ralph Houk	20	1619	1531	.514
Fred Clarke	19	1602	1181	.576
Dick Williams	21	1571	1451	.520
Clark Griffith	20	1491	1367	.522
Earl Weaver	17	1480	1060	.583
Miller Huggins	17	1413	1134	.555
Al Lopez	17	1410	1004	.584
Jimmy Dykes	21	1406	1541	.477
Wilbert Robinson	19	1399	1398	.500
Chuck Tanner	18	1352	1381	.495
Tom Lasorda	17	1341	1201	.528
Ned Hanlon	19	1315	1164	.530
Cap Anson	20	1292	945	.578
Charlie Grimm	19	1287	1067	.547
Frank Selee	16	1284	862	.598
Whitey Herzog	18	1281	1125	.532
Billy Martin	16	1253	1013	.553
Bill Rigney	18	1239	1321	.484
Joe Cronin	15	1236	1055	.540
Hughie Jennings	14	1163	984	.542
Lou Boudreau	16	1162	1224	.487
John McNamara	18	1150	1215	.486
Frankie Frisch	16	1138	1078	.514
Tony LaRussa	14	1134	949	.544
Danny Murtaugh	15	1115	950	.540
Billy Southworth	13	1044	704	.597
Red Schoendienst	14	1041	955	.522
Steve O'Neill	14	1040	821	.559
Chuck Dressen	16	1008	973	.509
Harry Wright	18	1000	825	.548

Pennant-Winning Managers in AL and NL

Manager	Team	Year	W	L
Joe McCarthy	CHI N	1929	98	54
	NY A	1932	107	47
	NY A	1936	102	51
	NY A	1937	102	52
	NY A	1938	99	53
	NY A	1939	106	45
	NY A	1941	101	53

Pennant-Winning Managers in AL and NL (*cont.*)

Manager	Team	Year	W	L
	NY A	1942	103	51
	NY A	1943	98	56
Sparky Anderson	CIN N	1970	102	60
	CIN N	1972	95	59
	CIN N	1975	108	54
	CIN N	1976	102	60
	DET A	1984	104	58
Dick Williams	BOS A	1967	92	70
	OAK A	1972	93	62
	OAK A	1973	94	68
	SD N	1984	92	70
Alvin Dark	SF N	1962	103	62
	OAK A	1974	90	72
Yogi Berra	NY A	1964	99	63
	NY N	1973	82	79

Most League Pennants Won, Manager

Manager	Total	Manager	Total
Casey Stengel	10	Sparky Anderson	5
John McGraw	10	Cap Anson	5
Connie Mack	9	Ned Hanlon	5
Joe McCarthy	9	Frank Selee	5
Walter Alston	7		
Miller Huggins	6		

Most Consecutive Years Managing One Club

Manager	Team	First	Last	Yrs.
Connie Mack	PHI A	1901	1950	50
John McGraw	NY N	1902	1932	31
Walter Alston	BKN N			
	LA N	1954	1976	23
Cap Anson	CHI N	1879	1897	19
Fred Clarke	LOU N			
	PIT N	1897	1915	19
Wilbert Robinson	BKN N	1914	1931	18
Joe McCarthy	NY A	1931	1946	16
Tom Lasorda	LA N	1977		16
Earl Weaver	BAL A	1968	1982	15
Hughie Jennings	DET A	1907	1920	14
Sparky Anderson	DET A	1979		14
Joe Cronin	BOS A	1935	1947	13
Jimmy Dykes	CHI A	1934	1946	13

Brother Batteries, AL

Player	Team	Pos.	First	Last
Tommy Thompson	NY	P	1912	1912
Homer Thompson	NY	C		
Milt Gaston	BOS	P	1929	1929
Alex Gaston	BOS	C		
Wes Ferrell	BOS	P	1934	1937
Rick Ferrell	BOS	C		
Wes Ferrell	WAS	P	1937	1937
Rick Ferrell	WAS	C		
Bobby Shantz	PHI	P	1954	1954
Billy Shantz	PHI	C		
Bobby Shantz	KC	P	1955	1955
Billy Shantz	KC	C		
Bobby Shantz	NY	P	1960	1960
Billy Shantz	NY	C		

Brother Batteries, NL

Player	Team	Pos.	First	Last
Will White	BOS	P	1877	1877
Deacon White	BOS	C		
Will White	CIN	P	1878	1879
Deacon White	CIN	C		
Pete Wood	BUF	P	1885	1885
Fred Wood	BUF	C		
John Ewing	NY	P	1891	1891
Buck Ewing	NY	C		
Mike O'Neill	STL	P	1902	1903
Jack O'Neill	STL	C		
Lefty Tyler	BOS	P	1914	1914
Fred Tyler	BOS	C		
Mort Cooper	STL	P	1940	1945
Walker Cooper	STL	C		
Mort Cooper	NY	P	1947	1947
Walker Cooper	NY	C		
Elmer Riddle	CIN	P	1941	1941
Johnny Riddle	CIN	C		
Elmer Riddle	CIN	P	1944	1945
Johnny Riddle	CIN	C		
Elmer Riddle	PIT	P	1948	1948
Johnny Riddle	PIT	C		
Jim Bailey	CIN	P	1959	1959
Ed Bailey	CIN	C		
Larry Sherry	LA	P	1959	1962
Norm Sherry	LA	C		

Brother Batteries, Other Leagues

Player	Team	Pos.	First	Last
Ed Dugan	RIC AA	P	1884	1884
Bill Dugan	RIC AA	C		
Dick Conway	BAL AA	P	1886	1886
Bill Conway	BAL AA	C		
John Ewing	NY P	P	1890	1890
Buck Ewing	NY P	C		

Pitching Brothers, Same Team, AL

Player	Team	First	Last	W	L
Vean Gregg	CLE	1913	1913	20	13
Dave Gregg	CLE			0	0
Ted Blankenship	CHI	1922	1923	17	24
Homer Blankenship	CHI			1	1
Alex Kellner	PHI	1952	1953	23	26
Walt Kellner	PHI			0	0
Gaylord Perry	CLE	1974	1975	27	22
Jim Perry	CLE			18	18
Phil Niekro	NY	1985	1985	16	12
Joe Niekro	NY			2	1

Pitching Brothers, Same Team, NL

Player	Team	First	Last	W	L
Larry Corcoran	CHI	1884	1884	35	23
Mike Corcoran	CHI			0	1
John Clarkson	BOS	1892	1892	8	6
Dad Clarkson	BOS			1	0
Frank Foreman	CIN	1896	1896	15	6
Brownie Foreman	CIN			0	4
Christy Mathewson	NY	1906	1907	46	25
Henry Mathewson	NY			0	1
Howie Camnitz	PIT	1909	1909	25	6
Harry Camnitz	PIT			0	0
Grover Lowdermilk	STL	1911	1911	0	1
Lou Lowdermilk	STL			3	4
Jesse Barnes	NY	1919	1923	76	42
Virgil Barnes	NY			3	4
Johnny Morrison	PIT	1921	1921	9	7
Phil Morrison	PIT			0	0
Dizzy Dean	STL	1934	1937	95	42
Paul Dean	STL			43	28
Eddie O'Brien	PIT	1956	1958	1	0
Johnny O'Brien	PIT			1	3
Lindy McDaniel	STL	1957	1958	18	16
Von McDaniel	STL			7	5
Dennis Bennett	PHI	1964	1964	12	14

Pitching Brothers, Same Team, NL (cont.)

Player	Team	First	Last	W	L
Dave Bennett	PHI			0	0
Phil Niekro	ATL	1973	1974	33	23
Joe Niekro	ATL			5	6
Rick Reuschel	CHI	1975	1976	25	29
Paul Reuschel	CHI			5	5
Mickey Mahler	ATL	1979	1979	5	11
Rick Mahler	ATL			0	0
Ramon Martinez	LA	1992		8	11
Pedro Martinez	LA			0	1

Three or More Brothers in Baseball

Player	First	Last	Player	First	Last
Dick Allen	1963	1977	Dave Edwards	1978	1982
Hank Allen	1965	1973	Marshall Edwards	1981	1983
Ron Allen	1972	1972	Hugh High	1913	1918
Felipe Alou	1958	1974	Charlie High	1919	1920
Matty Alou	1960	1974	Andy High	1922	1934
Jesus Alou	1963	1979	Mike Mansell	1879	1884
Cloyd Boyer	1949	1955	Tom Mansell	1879	1884
Ken Boyer	1955	1969	John Mansell	1882	1882
Clete Boyer	1955	1971	Mike O'Neill	1901	1907
John Clarkson	1882	1894	Jack O'Neill	1902	1906
Dad Clarkson	1891	1896	Steve O'Neill	1911	1928
Walter Clarkson	1904	1908	Jim O'Neill	1920	1923
Amos Cross	1885	1887	John Paciorek	1963	1963
Lave Cross	1887	1907	Tom Paciorek	1970	1987
Frank Cross	1901	1901	Jim Paciorek	1987	1987
Jose Cruz	1970	1988	Eddie Sadowski	1960	1966
Hector Cruz	1973	1982	Ted Sadowski	1960	1962
Tommy Cruz	1973	1977	Bob Sadowski	1963	1966
Ed Delahanty	1888	1903	Joe Sewell	1920	1933
Tom Delahanty	1894	1897	Luke Sewell	1921	1942
Jim Delahanty	1901	1915	Tommy Sewell	1927	1927
Frank Delahanty	1905	1915	Len Sowders	1886	1886
Joe Delahanty	1907	1909	John Sowders	1887	1890
Joe DiMaggio	1936	1951	Bill Sowders	1888	1890
Vince DiMaggio	1937	1946	George Wright	1876	1882
Dom DiMaggio	1940	1953	Sam Wright	1876	1881
Mike Edwards	1977	1980	Harry Wright	1876	1877

Most Wins by Brothers

Player	Yrs.	W	L
Phil Niekro	24	318	274
Joe Niekro	22	221	204
Total	46	539	478

Most Wins by Brothers (*cont.*)

Player	Yrs.	W	L
Gaylord Perry	22	314	265
Jim Perry	17	215	174
Total	39	529	439
John Clarkson	12	326	177
Dad Clarkson	6	39	39
Walter Clarkson	5	18	16
Total	23	383	232
Christy Mathewson	17	373	188
Henry Mathewson	2	0	1
Total	19	373	189
Stan Coveleski	14	215	142
Harry Coveleski	9	81	55
Total	23	296	197
Bob Forsch	16	168	136
Ken Forsch	16	114	113
Total	32	282	249
Gus Weyhing	14	264	235
John Weyhing	2	3	4
Total	16	267	239
Rick Reuschel	19	214	191
Paul Reuschel	5	16	16
Total	24	230	207
Will White	10	229	166
Deacon White	2	0	0
Total	12	229	166
Jesse Barnes	13	153	149
Virgil Barnes	9	61	59
Total	22	214	208
Dizzy Dean	12	150	83
Paul Dean	9	50	34
Total	21	200	117
Jeff Pfeffer	13	158	112
Big Jeff Pfeffer	6	31	40
Total	19	189	152
Larry Corcoran	8	177	90
Mike Corcoran	1	0	1
Total	9	177	91
Camilo Pascual	18	174	170
Carlos Pascual	1	1	1
Total	19	175	171

Most Wins by Brothers (*cont.*)

Player	Yrs.	W	L
Hooks Wiltse	12	139	90
Snake Wiltse	3	30	31
Total	15	169	121
Lindy McDaniel	21	141	119
Von McDaniel	2	7	5
Total	23	148	124
Matt Kilroy	10	142	133
Mike Kilroy	2	0	3
Total	12	142	136
Howie Camnitz	11	133	106
Harry Camnitz	2	1	0
Total	13	134	106
Long Tom Hughes	13	131	174
Ed Hughes	2	3	2
Total	15	134	176
Ad Gumbert	9	123	102
Billy Gumbert	3	7	8
Total	12	130	110
Frank Lary	12	128	116
Al Lary	3	0	1
Total	15	128	117
Pascual Perez	11	67	68
Melido Perez	6	58	62
Total	17	125	130
Jim Hughes	4	83	41
Mickey Hughes	3	39	28
Total	7	122	69
Greg Maddux	7	95	75
Mike Maddux	7	19	18
Total	14	114	93
Rick Mahler	13	96	111
Mickey Mahler	8	14	32
Total	21	110	143
Frank Foreman	11	98	93
Brownie Foreman	2	11	13
Total	13	109	106
Johnny Morrison	10	103	80
Phil Morrison	1	0	0
Total	11	103	80

Most Wins by Brothers (*cont.*)

Player	Yrs.	W	L
George Pipgras	11	102	73
Ed Pipgras	1	0	1
Total	12	102	74
Alex Kellner	12	101	112
Walt Kellner	2	0	0
Total	14	101	112

Best-Hitting Brothers

Player	Yrs.	G	H	2B	3B	HR	RBI	BA
Paul Waner	20	2549	3152	603	190	112	1309	.333
Lloyd Waner	18	1992	2459	281	118	28	598	.316
Total	38	4541	5611	884	308	140	1907	.325
Tony Gwynn	11	1463	1864	275	75	59	591	.327
Chris Gwynn	6	290	124	15	5	11	60	.261
Total	17	1753	1988	290	80	70	651	.322
Ed Delahanty	16	1835	2597	520	183	100	1464	.346
Jim Delahanty	13	1186	1159	191	60	18	489	.283
Frank Delahanty	6	287	223	22	82	5	94	.222
Joe Delahanty	3	269	222	30	15	4	100	.238
Tom Delahanty	3	19	16	5	0	0	6	.239
Total	41	3596	4217	768	340	127	2153	.311
Bob Meusel	11	1407	1693	368	95	156	1067	.309
Irish Meusel	11	1294	1521	250	92	107	820	.310
Total	22	2701	3214	618	187	263	1887	.309
Jim O'Rourke	19	1774	2304	414	132	51	830	.310
John O'Rourke	3	230	279	58	24	11	98	.295
Total	22	2004	2583	472	156	62	928	.308
George Brett	20	2562	3005	634	141	298	1523	.307
Ken Brett	14	385	91	18	1	10	44	.262
Total	34	2947	3096	652	142	308	1567	.305
Dixie Walker	18	1905	2064	376	96	105	1023	.306
Harry Walker	11	807	786	126	37	10	214	.296
Total	19	2712	2850	502	133	115	1237	.303
Hank Aaron	23	3298	3771	624	98	755	2297	.305
Tommie Aaron	7	437	216	42	6	13	94	.229
Total	30	3735	3987	666	104	768	2391	.300
Joe DiMaggio	13	1737	2219	389	131	361	1507	.325
Dom DiMaggio	11	1399	1680	308	57	87	618	.298
Vince DiMaggio	10	1110	959	209	24	125	584	.249
Total	34	4246	4858	906	212	573	2709	.298

Best-Hitting Brothers (*cont.*)

Player	Yrs.	G	H	2B	3B	HR	RBI	BA
Bob Johnson	13	1863	2051	396	95	288	1283	.296
Roy Johnson	10	1153	1292	275	83	58	556	.296
Total	23	3016	3343	671	178	346	1839	.296
Joe Sewell	14	1902	2226	436	68	49	1051	.312
Luke Sewell	20	1630	1393	273	56	20	696	.259
Tommy Sewell	1	1	0	0	0	0	0	.000
Total	35	3533	3619	709	124	69	1747	.292
Lave Cross	21	2275	2644	411	135	47	1345	.292
Amos Cross	3	117	118	16	7	1		.268
Frank Cross	1	1	3	0	0	0	0	.600
Total	25	2393	2765	427	142	48	1345	.291
Gee Walker	15	1783	1991	399	76	124	997	.294
Hub Walker	5	297	205	43	6	5	60	.263
Total	20	2080	2196	442	82	129	1057	.291
Dick Allen	15	1749	1848	320	79	351	1119	.292
Hank Allen	7	389	212	27	9	6	128	.241
Ron Allen	1	7	1	0	0	1	1	.091
Total	23	2145	2061	347	88	358	1248	.285
Felipe Alou	17	2082	2101	359	49	206	852	.286
Matty Alou	15	1667	1777	236	50	31	427	.307
Jesus Alou	15	1380	1216	170	27	32	377	.280
Total	47	5129	5094	765	126	269	1656	.280
Cal Ripken	12	1800	1922	369	34	273	1014	.277
Billy Ripken	6	667	510	92	5	13	168	.244
Total	18	2467	2432	461	39	286	1182	.269
Lee May	18	2071	2031	340	31	354	1244	.267
Carlos May	10	1165	1127	172	23	90	536	.274
Total	28	3236	3158	512	54	444	1780	.269
Ken Boyer	15	2034	2143	318	68	282	1141	.287
Clete Boyer	16	1725	1396	200	33	162	654	.242
Cloyd Boyer	5	113	20	5	1	0	8	.167
Total	36	3872	3559	523	102	444	1803	.266
Tony Conigliaro	8	876	849	139	23	166	516	.264
Billy Conigliaro	5	347	289	56	10	40	128	.256
Total	13	1223	1138	195	33	206	644	.262
Steve O'Neill	17	1586	1259	248	34	13	537	.263
Jack O'Neill	5	303	185	24	5	1	74	.196
Mike O'Neill	5	137	97	14	9	2	41	.255
Jim O'Neill	2	109	94	18	7	1	43	.287
Total	29	2135	1635	304	55	17	695	.254

Fathers and Sons in Baseball

Player	First	Last	Player	First	Last
Bobby Adams	1946	1959	Eddie Collins	1906	1930
Mike Adams	1972	1978	Eddie Collins	1939	1942
Sandy Alomar	1964	1978	Ed Connolly	1929	1932
Roberto Alomar	1988		Ed Connolly	1964	1967
Sandy Alomar	1988		Jimmy Cooney	1890	1892
Felipe Alou	1958	1974	Jimmy Cooney	1917	1928
Moises Alou	1990		Johnny Cooney	1921	1944
Ruben Amaro	1958	1969	Red Corriden	1910	1915
Ruben Amaro	1991		John Corriden	1946	1946
Angel Aragon	1914	1917	Bill Crouch	1910	1910
Jack Aragon	1941	1941	Bill Crouch	1939	1945
Earl Averill	1921	1941	Herm Doscher	1879	1882
Earl Averill	1956	1963	Jack Doscher	1903	1908
Jim Bagby	1912	1923	Jim Eschen	1915	1915
Jim Bagby	1938	1947	Larry Eschen	1942	1942
Clyde Barnhart	1920	1928	Tom Fletcher	1962	1962
Vic Barnhart	1944	1946	Darrin Fletcher	1989	
Charlie Beamon	1956	1958	Tito Francona	1956	1970
Charlie Beamon	1978	1981	Terry Francona	1981	1990
Gus Bell	1950	1964	Len Gabrielson	1939	1939
Buddy Bell	1972	1989	Len Gabrielson	1960	1970
Yogi Berra	1946	1965	Charlie Ganzel	1884	1897
Dale Berra	1978	1987	Babe Ganzel	1927	1928
Charlie Berry	1884	1884	Charlie Gilbert	1940	1947
Charlie Berry	1925	1938	Tookie Gilbert	1950	1953
Joe Berry	1902	1902	Peaches Graham	1902	1912
Joe Berry	1921	1922	Jack Graham	1946	1949
Bobby Bonds	1968	1981	Freddie Green	1959	1964
Barry Bonds	1986		Gary Green	1986	
Ray Boone	1948	1960	Ray Grimes	1920	1926
Bob Boone	1972	1990	Oscar Grimes	1938	1946
Bob Boone	1972	1990	Ken Griffey	1973	1991
Bret Boone	1992		Ken Griffey	1989	
Pedro Borbon	1969	1980	Ross Grimsley	1951	1951
Pedro Borbon	1992		Ross Grimsley	1971	1982
Fred Brickell	1926	1933	Sam Hairston	1951	1951
Fritzie Brickell	1958	1961	John Hairston	1969	1969
Earle Brucker	1937	1943	Jerry Hairston	1973	1989
Earle Brucker	1948	1948	Larry Haney	1966	1978
Dolf Camilli	1933	1945	Chris Haney	1991	
Doug Camilli	1960	1969	Jim Hegan	1941	1960
Al Campanis	1943	1943	Mike Hegan	1964	1977
Jim Campanis	1966	1973	Ken Heintzelman	1937	1952
Camilo Carreon	1959	1966	Tom Heintzelman	1973	1978
Mark Carreon	1987		Wally Hood	1920	1922
Joe Coleman	1942	1955	Wally Hood	1949	1949
Joe Coleman	1965	1979	Bruce Howard	1963	1968

Fathers and Sons in Baseball (*cont.*)

Player	First	Last	Player	First	Last
Dave Howard	1991		Pinky May	1939	1943
Randy Hundley	1964	1977	Milt May	1970	1984
Todd Hundley	1990		Jim McKnight	1960	1962
Julian Javier	1960	1972	Jeff McKnight	1989	
Stan Javier	1984		Hal McRae	1968	1985
John Jeter	1969	1974	Brian McRae	1990	
Shawn Jeter	1992		Frank Meinke	1884	1885
Adam Johnson	1914	1918	Bob Meinke	1910	1910
Adam Johnson	1941	1941	Willie Mills	1901	1901
Ernie Johnson	1912	1925	Art Mills	1927	1928
Don Johnson	1943	1948	Gene Moore	1909	1912
Bob Kennedy	1939	1957	Gene Moore	1931	1945
Terry Kennedy	1978	1991	Guy Morton	1914	1924
Marty Keough	1956	1966	Guy Morton	1954	1954
Matt Keough	1977	1986	Manny Mota	1962	1982
Lew Krausse	1931	1932	Andy Mota	1991	
Lew Krausse	1961	1974	Jose Mota	1991	
Bill Kunkel	1961	1963	Walter Mueller	1922	1926
Jeff Kunkel	1984		Don Mueller	1948	1959
Joe Landrum	1950	1952	Bill Narleski	1929	1930
Bill Landrum	1986		Ray Narleski	1954	1959
Max Lanier	1938	1953	Julio Navarro	1962	1970
Hal Lanier	1964	1973	Jaime Navarro	1989	
Vern Law	1950	1967	Chet Nichols	1926	1932
Vance Law	1980	1991	Chet Nichols	1951	1964
Thornton Lee	1933	1948	Ron Northey	1942	1957
Don Lee	1957	1966	Scott Northey	1969	1969
Dutch Lerchen	1910	1910	Frank Okrie	1920	1920
George Lerchen	1932	1933	Len Okrie	1948	1952
Glenn Liebhardt	1906	1909	Ed Olivares	1960	1961
Glenn Liebhardt	1930	1938	Omar Olivares	1990	
Freddie Lindstrom	1924	1934	Jim O'Rourke	1876	1904
Charlie Lindstrom	1958	1958	Queenie O'Rourke	1908	1908
Jack Lively	1911	1911	Patsy O'Rourke	1908	1908
Bud Lively	1947	1949	Joe O'Rourke	1929	1929
Connie Mack	1886	1896	Tiny Osborne	1922	1925
Earle Mack	1910	1914	Bobo Osborne	1957	1963
Harl Maggert	1907	1912	Steve Partenheimer	1913	1913
Harl Maggert	1938	1938	Stan Partenheimer	1944	1945
Charlie Malay	1905	1905	Herman Pillette	1917	1924
Joe Malay	1933	1935	Duane Pillette	1949	1956
Barney Martin	1953	1953	Mel Queen	1942	1952
Jerry Martin	1974	1984	Mel Queen	1964	1972
Wally Mattick	1912	1918	Walt Ripley	1935	1935
Bobby Mattick	1938	1942	Allen Ripley	1978	1982
Dave May	1967	1978	Ebba St. Claire	1951	1954
Derrick May	1990		Randy St. Claire	1984	

Fathers and Sons in Baseball (*cont.*)

Player	First	Last
Ralph Savidge	1908	1909
Don Savidge	1929	1929
Dick Schofield	1953	1971
Dick Schofield	1983	
Joe Schultz	1912	1925
Joe Schultz	1939	1948
Diego Segui	1962	1977
David Segui	1990	
Earl Sheely	1921	1931
Bud Sheely	1951	1953
Dick Siebert	1932	1945
Paul Siebert	1974	1978
George Sisler	1915	1930
Dick Sisler	1946	1953
Dave Sisler	1956	1962
Bob Skinner	1954	1966
Joel Skinner	1983	
Roy Smalley	1948	1958
Roy Smalley	1975	1987
Ed Sprague	1968	1976
Ed Sprague	1991	
Joe Stephenson	1945	1947
Jerry Stephenson	1963	1970
Ron Stillwell	1961	1962
Kurt Stillwell	1986	
Mel Stottlemyre	1964	1974
Todd Stottlemyre	1988	
Mel Stottlemyre	1990	1990
Billy Sullivan	1899	1916
Billy Sullivan	1931	1947
Haywood Sullivan	1955	1963
Marc Sullivan	1982	1987
George Susce	1929	1944
George Susce	1955	1959
Jose Tartabull	1962	1970
Danny Tartabull	1984	
Ricardo Torres	1920	1922
Gil Torres	1940	1946
Mike Tresh	1939	1949
Tom Tresh	1961	1969
Hal Trosky	1933	1946
Hal Trosky	1958	1958
Dizzy Trout	1939	1957
Steve Trout	1978	1989
Al Unser	1942	1945
Del Unser	1968	1982
Ozzie Virgil	1956	1969

Player	First	Last
Ozzie Virgil	1980	1989
Howard Wakefield	1905	1907
Dick Wakefield	1941	1952
Dixie Walker	1909	1912
Dixie Walker	1931	1949
Harry Walker	1940	1955
Ed Walsh	1904	1917
Ed Walsh	1928	1932
Jo-Jo White	1932	1944
Mike White	1963	1965
Maury Wills	1959	1962
Bump Wills	1977	1982
Bobby Wine	1960	1972
Robbie Wine	1986	1987
Smoky Joe Wood	1908	1922
Joe Wood	1944	1944
Del Young	1909	1915
Del Young	1937	1940

Fathers and Sons with Most Career Home Runs

Player	HR
Bobby Bonds	332
Barry Bonds	176
Total	508
Gus Bell	206
Buddy Bell	201
Total	407
Yogi Berra	358
Dale Berra	49
Total	407
Earl Averill, Sr.	238
Earl Averill, Jr.	44
Total	282
Dolf Camilli	239
Doug Camilli	18
Total	257
Ray Boone	151
Bob Boone	105
Total	256
Ken Griffey	152
Ken Griffey, Jr.	87
Total	239

Fathers and Sons with most Career Home Runs (cont.)

Player	HR
Roy Smalley, Jr.	61
Roy Smalley III	163
Total	224
Hal McRae	191
Brian McRae	14
Total	205
Jose Tartabull	2
Danny Tartabull	177
Total	179
Bob Kennedy	63
Terry Kennedy	113
Total	176
Mike Tresh	2
Tom Tresh	153
Total	155
George Sisler	99
Dick Sisler	55
Total	154
Jim Hegan	92
Mike Hegan	53
Total	145
Tito Francona	125
Terry Francona	16
Total	141
Bob Skinner	103
Joel Skinner	17
Total	120
Ozzie Virgil	14
Ozzie Virgil, Jr.	98
Total	112
Bob Boone	105
Bret Boone	4
Total	109

Two Grand Slams in One Game, AL

Player	Team	Date
Dummy Hoy	CHI	May 1, 1901
Herm McFarland	CHI	May 1, 1901

Two Grand Slams in One Game, AL (cont.)

Player	Team	Date
Danny Murphy	PHI	Jul 8, 1902
Harry Davis	PHI	Jul 8, 1902
Bucky Walters	BOS	May 13, 1934
Eddie Morgan	BOS	May 13, 1934
Tony Lazzeri	NY	May 24, 1936
	NY	May 24, 1936
Jim Tabor	BOS	Jul 4, 1939
	BOS	Jul 4, 1939
Rudy York	BOS	Jul 27, 1946
	BOS	Jul 27, 1946
Ray Boone	DET	Jun 11, 1954
Al Kaline	DET	Jun 11, 1954
Albie Pearson	BAL	Apr 24, 1960
Billy Klaus	BAL	Apr 24, 1960
Vic Wertz	BOS	May 10, 1960
Rip Repulski	BOS	May 10, 1960
Jim Gentile	BAL	May 9, 1961
	BAL	May 9, 1961
Harmon Killebrew	MIN	Jul 18, 1962
Bob Allison	MIN	Jul 18, 1962
Jim Northrup	DET	Jun 24, 1968
	DET	Jun 24, 1968
Frank Robinson	BAL	Jun 26, 1970
	BAL	Jun 26, 1970
Darrell Porter	MIL	Jun 17, 1973
Joe Lahoud	MIL	Jun 17, 1973
Cecil Cooper	MIL	Apr 12, 1980
Don Money	MIL	Apr 12, 1980
Fred Lynn	CAL	Apr 27, 1983
Daryl Sconiers	CAL	Apr 27, 1983
Bill Buckner	BOS	Aug 7, 1984
Tony Armas	BOS	Aug 7, 1984
Brian Downing	CAL	Jul 31, 1986
Bob Boone	CAL	Jul 31, 1986
Larry Sheets	BAL	Aug 6, 1986
Jim Dwyer	BAL	Aug 6, 1986
Ellis Burks	BOS	Jun 10, 1987
Marty Barrett	BOS	Jun 10, 1987
Don Mattingly	NY	Jun 29, 1987
Dave Winfield	NY	Jun 29, 1987
Cory Snyder	CLE	Apr 22, 1988
Joe Carter	CLE	Apr 22, 1988

Two Grand Slams in One Game, NL

Player	Team	Date	Player	Team	Date
Joe Kelley	BKN	Sep 23, 1901	Wes Westrum	NY	Jul 13, 1951
Jimmy Sheckard	BKN	Sep 23, 1901	Davey Williams	NY	Jul 13, 1951
Joe Stanley	BOS	Aug 12, 1903	Bob Thurman	CIN	Jul 29, 1955
Pat Moran	BOS	Aug 12, 1903	Smoky Burgess	CIN	Jul 29, 1955
Ralph Miller	PHI	Apr 28, 1921	Tony Cloninger	ATL	Jul 3, 1966
Lee Meadows	PHI	Apr 28, 1921		ATL	Jul 3, 1966
George Kelly	NY	Sep 5, 1924	Denis Menke	HOU	Jul 30, 1969
Travis Jackson	NY	Sep 5, 1924	Jimmy Wynn	HOU	Jul 30, 1969
George Grantham	PIT	Jun 22, 1925	Willie McCovey	SF	Apr 26, 1970
Pie Traynor	PIT	Jun 22, 1925	Dick Dietz	SF	Apr 26, 1970
Jim Bottomley	STL	Jul 6, 1929	Richie Hebner	PIT	Sep 14, 1982
Chick Hafey	STL	Jul 6, 1929	Bill Madlock	PIT	Sep 14, 1982
Arky Vaughan	PIT	May 1, 1933	Pedro Guerrero	LA	Aug 23, 1985
Earl Grace	PIT	May 1, 1933	Mariano Duncan	LA	Aug 23, 1985
Gene Moore	BOS	Apr 30, 1938	Graig Nettles	ATL	May 2, 1987
Harl Maggert	BOS	Apr 30, 1938	Dion James	ATL	May 2, 1987
Dick Bartell	NY	Jul 4, 1938	Brian Dayett	CHI	Jun 3, 1987
Gus Mancuso	NY	Jul 4, 1938	Keith Moreland	CHI	Jun 3, 1987

Two Grand Slams in One Inning, Team

Player	Team	Date	Inn.	Opp.	Opp. Pitcher
Tom Burns	CHI N	Aug 16, 1890	5	PIT	Bill Phillips
Mal Kittridge	CHI N	Aug 16, 1890	5	PIT	Bill Phillips
Bob Alison	MIN A	Jul 18, 1962	1	CLE	Barry Latman
Harmon Killebrew	MIN A	Jul 18, 1962	1	CLE	Jim Perry
Denis Menke	HOU N	Jul 30, 1969	9	NY	Cal Koonce
Jimmy Wynn	HOU N	Jul 30, 1969	9	NY	Ron Taylor
Cecil Cooper	MIL A	Apr 11, 1980	2	BOS	Mike Torrez
Don Money	MIL A	Apr 11, 1980	2	BOS	Chuck Rainey
Larry Sheets	BAL A	Aug 6, 1986	4	TEX	Bobby Witt
Jim Dwyer	BAL A	Aug 6, 1986	4	TEX	Jeff Russell

Two Pinch-Hit Home Runs in One Inning, Team, AL

Player	Team	Date	Inn.	Opp.
Bob Cerv	NY	Jul 23, 1955	9	KC
Elston Howard	NY	Jul 23, 1955	9	KC
Vic Roznovsky	BAL	Aug 26, 1966	9	BOS
Boog Powell	BAL	Aug 26, 1966	9	BOS
Bob Stinson	SEA	Apr 27, 1979	8	NY
Dan Meyer	SEA	Apr 27, 1979	8	NY
Dave Engle	MIN	May 16, 1983	9	OAK
Mickey Hatcher	MIN	May 16, 1983	9	OAK
Wayne Gross	BAL	Aug 12, 1985	9	CLE
Larry Sheets	BAL	Aug 12, 1985	9	CLE
Oddibe McDowell	TEX	Sep 1, 1986	9	BOS
Darrell Porter	TEX	Sep 1, 1986	9	BOS

Two Pinch-Hit Home Runs in One Inning, Team, NL

Player	Team	Date	Inn.	Opp.
Bobby Hofman	NY	Jun 20, 1954	6	STL
Dusty Rhodes	NY	Jun 20, 1954	6	STL
Hank Sauer	SF	Jun 4, 1958	10	MIL
Bob Schmidt	SF	Jun 4, 1958	10	MIL
Frank Howard	LA	Aug 8, 1963	5	CHI
Bill Skowron	LA	Aug 8, 1963	5	CHI
Willie Crawford	LA	Jul 23, 1975	9	STL
Lee Lacy	LA	Jul 23, 1975	9	STL
Mackey Sasser	NY	May 4, 1991	9	SF
Mark Carreon	NY	May 4, 1991	9	SF

Back-to-Back Pinch-Hit Home Runs, Team

Player	Team	Date	Inn.	Opp.	Opp. Pitcher
Hank Sauer	SF N	Jun 4, 1958	10	MIL	Ernie Johnson
Bob Schmidt	SF N	Jun 4, 1958	10	MIL	Ernie Johnson
Frank Howard	LA N	Aug 8, 1963	5	CHI	Bob Buhl
Bill Skowron	LA N	Aug 8, 1963	5	CHI	Don Elston
Vic Roznovsky	BAL A	Aug 26, 1966	9	BOS	Lee Stange
Boog Powell	BAL A	Aug 26, 1966	9	BOS	Lee Stange
Willie Crawford	LA N	Jul 23, 1975	9	STL	Bob Forsch
Lee Lacy	LA N	Jul 23, 1975	9	STL	Bob Forsch
Wayne Gross	BAL A	Aug 12, 1985	9	CLE	Jerry Reed
Larry Sheets	BAL A	Aug 12, 1985	9	CLE	Jerry Reed
Oddibe McDowell	TEX A	Sep 1, 1986	9	BOS	Steve Crawford
Darrell Porter	TEX A	Sep 1, 1986	9	BOS	Steve Crawford
Mackey Sasser	NY N	May 4, 1991	9	SF	Jeff Brantley
Mark Carreon	NY N	May 4, 1991	9	SF	Jeff Brantley

Two Pinch-Hit Home Runs in One Game, AL

Player	Team	Date	Opp.
Billy Sullivan	CLE	May 26, 1937	PHI
Bruce Campbell	CLE	May 26, 1937	PHI
Bob Cerv	NY	Jul 23, 1955	KC
Elston Howard	NY	Jul 23, 1955	KC
Max Alvis	CLE	Aug 15, 1965	MIN
Leon Wagner	CLE	Aug 15, 1965	MIN
Vic Roznovsky	BAL	Aug 26, 1966	BOS
Boog Powell	BAL	Aug 26, 1966	BOS
Wayne Comer	DET	Aug 11, 1968	BOS
Gates Brown	DET	Aug 11, 1968	BOS

Two Pinch-Hit Home Runs in One Game, AL (*cont.*)

Player	Team	Date	Opp.
Jim Pagliaroni	SEA	Aug 2, 1969	NY
Don Mincher	SEA	Aug 2, 1969	NY
Bob Allison	MIN	Jul 31, 1970	DET
Chuck Manuel	MIN	Jul 31, 1970	DET
Rod Carew	MIN	Jul 28, 1974	CAL
Harmon Killebrew	MIN	Jul 28, 1974	CAL
Bob Stinson	SEA	Apr 27, 1979	NY
Dan Meyer	SEA	Apr 27, 1979	NY
Lamar Johnson	CHI	Jul 6, 1980	OAK
Greg Pryor	CHI	Jul 6, 1980	OAK
Dave Engle	MIN	May 16, 1983	OAK
Mickey Hatcher	MIN	May 16, 1983	OAK
John Shelby	BAL	May 5, 1984	TEX
Benny Ayala	BAL	May 5, 1984	TEX
Wayne Gross	BAL	Aug 12, 1985	CLE
Larry Sheets	BAL	Aug 12, 1985	CLE
Rick Leach	TOR	Jun 14, 1986	DET
Buck Martinez	TOR	Jun 14, 1986	DET
Oddibe McDowell	TEX	Sep 1, 1986	BOS
Darrell Porter	TEX	Sep 1, 1986	BOS
George Hendrick	CAL	Jun 28, 1987	CHI
Ruppert Jones	CAL	Jun 28, 1987	CHI

Two Pinch-Hit Home Runs in One Game, NL

Player	Team	Date	Opp.
Jimmie Wilson	PHI	May 30, 1925	NY
Hal Carlson	PHI	May 30, 1925	NY
Jim Bottomley	STL	Jul 21, 1930	BKN
George Puccinelli	STL	Jul 21, 1930	BKN
Stan Musial	STL	May 12, 1951	CIN
Bill Howerton	STL	May 12, 1951	CIN
Joe Garagiola	CHI	Jun 9, 1954	PHI
Bill Serena	CHI	Jun 9, 1954	PHI
Bobby Hofman	NY	Jun 20, 1954	STL
Dusty Rhodes	NY	Jun 20, 1954	STL
Hank Sauer	SF	Jun 4, 1958	MIL
Bob Schmidt	SF	Jun 4, 1958	MIL
Rip Repulski	PHI	Aug 13, 1958	PIT
Bob Bowman	PHI	Aug 13, 1958	PIT
Choo Choo Coleman	NY	Aug 15, 1962	PHI
Jim Hickman	NY	Aug 15, 1962	PHI
Frank Howard	LA	Aug 8, 1963	CHI
Bill Skowron	LA	Aug 8, 1963	CHI
Joe Hicks	NY	Sep 17, 1963	PHI
Frank Thomas	NY	Sep 17, 1963	PHI

Two Pinch-Hit Home Runs in One Game, NL (*cont.*)

Player	Team	Date	Opp.
Johnny Stephenson	NY	Aug 4, 1966	SF
Ron Swoboda	NY	Aug 4, 1966	SF
Jim Lyttle	MON	Jul 13, 1973	ATL
Hal Breeden	MON	Jul 13, 1973	ATL
Jim Tyrone	CHI	Sep 10, 1974	PIT
Carmen Fanzone	CHI	Sep 10, 1974	PIT
Willie Crawford	LA	Jul 23, 1975	STL
Lee Lacy	LA	Jul 23, 1975	STL
Champ Summers	CHI	Aug 23, 1975	HOU
Rick Monday	CHI	Aug 23, 1975	HOU
Rick Monday	LA	Aug 27, 1982	CHI
Mike Marshall	LA	Aug 27, 1982	CHI
Jeffrey Leonard	SF	Sep 28, 1987	SD
Chili Davis	SF	Sep 28, 1987	SD
Mackey Sasser	NY	May 4, 1991	SF
Mark Carreon	NY	May 4, 1991	SF

Home Runs by First Three Batters in Game

Player	Team	Date	Opp.	Opp. Pitcher
Marvell Wynne	SD N	Apr 13, 1987	SF	Roger Mason
Tony Gwynn	SD N	Apr 13, 1987	SF	Roger Mason
John Kruk	SD N	Apr 13, 1987	SF	Roger Mason

Home Runs by First Two Batters in Game, AL

Player	Team	Date	Opp.	Opp. Pitcher
Boze Berger	CHI	Sep 2, 1937	BOS	Johnny Marcum
Mike Kreevich	CHI	Sep 2, 1937	BOS	Johnny Marcum
Barney McCosky	DET	Jun 22, 1939	PHI	Lynn Nelson
Earl Averill	DET	Jun 22, 1939	PHI	Lynn Nelson
Hank Bauer	NY	Apr 27, 1955	CHI	Virgil Trucks
Andy Carey	NY	Apr 27, 1955	CHI	Virgil Trucks
Bill Tuttle	KC	Sep 18, 1958	BOS	Ted Bowsfield
Roger Maris	KC	Sep 18, 1958	BOS	Ted Bowsfield
Lenny Green	MIN	May 10, 1962	CLE	Jim Perry
Vic Power	MIN	May 10, 1962	CLE	Jim Perry
Luis Aparicio	BOS	May 1, 1971	MIN	Jim Perry
Reggie Smith	BOS	May 1, 1971	MIN	Jim Perry
Graig Nettles	CLE	Jun 19, 1971	DET	Dean Chance
Vada Pinson	CLE	Jun 19, 1971	DET	Dean Chance
Rick Miller	BOS	Jun 20, 1973	MIL	Bill Parsons
Reggie Smith	BOS	Jun 20, 1973	MIL	Bill Parsons
Don Money	MIL	Jul 29, 1975	BOS	Diego Segui
Darrell Porter	MIL	Jul 29, 1975	BOS	Diego Segui
Rick Burleson	BOS	Jun 17, 1977	NY	Catfish Hunter

Home Runs by First Two Batters in Game, AL *(cont.)*

Player	Team	Date	Opp.	Opp. Pitcher
Fred Lynn	BOS	Jun 17, 1977	NY	Catfish Hunter
Rickey Henderson	OAK	Sep 9, 1983	TOR	Jim Clancy
Mike Davis	OAK	Sep 9, 1983	TOR	Jim Clancy
Darryl Motley	KC	May 3, 1984	MIL	Don Sutton
Pat Sheridan	KC	May 3, 1984	MIL	Don Sutton
Dwight Evans	BOS	Sep 5, 1985	CLE	Neal Heaton
Wade Boggs	BOS	Sep 5, 1985	CLE	Neal Heaton
Kirby Puckett	MIN	Jul 18, 1986	BAL	Scott McGregor
Gary Gaetti	MIN	Jul 18, 1986	BAL	Scott McGregor
Lou Whitaker	DET	Aug 5, 1986	CLE	Jose Roman
Alan Trammell	DET	Aug 5, 1986	CLE	Jose Roman
Ken Gerhart	BAL	Jun 23, 1988	TOR	Jim Clancy
Fred Lynn	BAL	Jun 23, 1988	TOR	Jim Clancy
Devon White	TOR	Aug 18, 1991	DET	Bill Gullickson
Roberto Alomar	TOR	Aug 18, 1991	DET	Bill Gullickson
Brady Anderson	BAL	Jul 9, 1992	MIN	Scott Erickson
Mike Devereaux	BAL	Jul 9, 1992	MIN	Scott Erickson

Home Runs by First Two Batters in Game, NL

Player	Team	Date	Opp.	Opp. Pitcher
Roy Johnson	BOS	Aug 6, 1937	CHI	Tex Carleton
Rabbit Warstler	BOS	Aug 6, 1937	CHI	Tex Carleton
Pete Coscarart	PIT	Jul 6, 1945	BOS	Don Hendrickson
Jim Russell	PIT	Jul 6, 1945	BOS	Don Hendrickson
Grady Hatton	CIN	Apr 19, 1952	PIT	Mel Queen
Bobby Adams	CIN	Apr 19, 1952	PIT	Mel Queen
Whitey Lockman	SF	Jul 6, 1958	STL	Jim Brosnan
Willie Kirkland	SF	Jul 6, 1958	STL	Jim Brosnan
Curt Flood	STL	Aug 17, 1958	LA	Sandy Koufax
Gene Freese	STL	Aug 17, 1958	LA	Sandy Koufax
Chuck Hiller	SF	May 27, 1964	STL	Bob Gibson
Duke Snider	SF	May 27, 1964	STL	Bob Gibson
Pete Rose	CIN	Apr 7, 1969	LA	Don Drysdale
Bobby Tolan	CIN	Apr 7, 1969	LA	Don Drysdale
Pete Rose	CIN	Aug 17, 1969	PIT	Steve Blass
Bobby Tolan	CIN	Aug 17, 1969	PIT	Steve Blass
Pete Rose	CIN	Jun 28, 1970	HOU	Don Wilson
Bobby Tolan	CIN	Jun 28, 1970	HOU	Don Wilson
Omar Moreno	PIT	Jul 5, 1982	HOU	Joe Niekro
Johnny Ray	PIT	Jul 5, 1982	HOU	Joe Niekro
Juan Samuel	PHI	Jul 29, 1984	MON	Bill Gullickson
Von Hayes	PHI	Jul 29, 1984	MON	Bill Gullickson
Gary Redus	PHI	Jul 7, 1986	ATL	David Palmer
Juan Samuel	PHI	Jul 7, 1986	ATL	David Palmer

Home Runs by First Two Batters in Game, Other Leagues

Player	Team	Date	Opp.	Opp. Pitcher
Tom Brown	BOS AA	Jun 25, 1891	BAL	Sadie McMahon
Bill Joyce	BOS AA	Jun 25, 1891	BAL	Sadie McMahon
Jim McTamany	PHI AA	Aug 21, 1891	BOS	Darby O'Brien
Henry Larkin	PHI AA	Aug 21, 1891	BOS	Darby O'Brien

Four Consecutive Home Runs, Team

Player	Team	Date	Inn.
Eddie Mathews	MIL N	Jun 8, 1961	7
Hank Aaron	MIL N	Jun 8, 1961	
Joe Adcock	MIL N	Jun 8, 1961	
Frank Thomas	MIL N	Jun 8, 1961	
Woodie Held	CLE A	Jul 31, 1963	6
Pedro Ramos	CLE A	Jul 31, 1963	
Tito Francona	CLE A	Jul 31, 1963	
Larry Brown	CLE A	Jul 31, 1963	
Tony Oliva	MIN A	May 2, 1964	11
Bob Allison	MIN A	May 2, 1964	
Jimmie Hall	MIN A	May 2, 1964	
Harmon Killebrew	MIN A	May 2, 1964	

Three Consecutive Home Runs, Team, AL

Player	Team	Date	Inn.
Nap Lajoie	CLE	Jun 30, 1902	6
Piano Legs Hickman	CLE	Jun 30, 1902	
Bill Bradley	CLE	Jun 30, 1902	
Tilly Walker	PHI	May 2, 1922	4
Cy Perkins	PHI	May 2, 1922	
Bing Miller	PHI	May 2, 1922	
Bob Meusel	NY	Sep 10, 1925	4
Babe Ruth	NY	Sep 10, 1925	
Lou Gehrig	NY	Sep 10, 1925	
Babe Ruth	NY	May 4, 1929	7
Lou Gehrig	NY	May 4, 1929	
Bob Meusel	NY	May 4, 1929	
Al Simmons	PHI	Jun 18, 1930	5
Jimmie Foxx	PHI	Jun 18, 1930	
Bing Miller	PHI	Jun 18, 1930	
Bob Johnson	PHI	Jul 17, 1934	4
Jimmie Foxx	PHI	Jul 17, 1934	
Pinky Higgins	PHI	Jul 17, 1934	
Ben Chapman	CLE	Jun 25, 1939	7
Hal Trosky	CLE	Jun 25, 1939	
Jeff Heath	CLE	Jun 25, 1939	
Ted Williams	BOS	Sep 24, 1940	6
Jimmie Foxx	BOS	Sep 24, 1940	

Three Consecutive Home Runs, Team, AL (cont.)

Player	Team	Date	Inn.
Joo Cronin	BOS	Sep 24, 1940	
Joe DiMaggio	NY	May 23, 1946	5
Nick Etten	NY	May 23, 1946	
Joe Gordon	NY	May 23, 1946	
Roy Cullenbine	DET	Apr 23, 1947	8
Dick Wakefield	DET	Apr 23, 1947	
Hoot Evers	DET	Apr 23, 1947	
Charlie Keller	NY	May 13, 1947	6
Joe DiMaggio	NY	May 13, 1947	
Johnny Lindell	NY	May 13, 1947	
Stan Spence	BOS	Apr 19, 1948	2
Vern Stephens	BOS	Apr 19, 1948	
Bobby Doerr	BOS	Apr 19, 1948	
Ted Williams	BOS	Jun 6, 1948	6
Stan Spence	BOS	Jun 6, 1948	
Vern Stephens	BOS	Jun 6, 1948	
Larry Doby	CLE	Jul 28, 1950	3
Al Rosen	CLE	Jul 28, 1950	
Luke Easter	CLE	Jul 28, 1950	
Harry Simpson	CLE	Sep 2, 1951	1
Al Rosen	CLE	Sep 2, 1951	
Luke Easter	CLE	Sep 2, 1951	
Clint Courtney	STL	Jul 16, 1953	5
Dick Kryhoski	STL	Jul 16, 1953	
Jim Dyck	STL	Jul 16, 1953	
Harvey Kuenn	DET	Jul 7, 1956	7
Earl Torgeson	DET	Jul 7, 1956	
Charlie Maxwell	DET	Jul 7, 1956	
Don Buddin	BOS	Sep 7, 1959	2
Jerry Casale	BOS	Sep 7, 1959	
Pumpsie Green	BOS	Sep 7, 1959	
Jim Gentile	BAL	Apr 30, 1961	7
Gus Triandos	BAL	Apr 30, 1961	
Ron Hansen	BAL	Apr 30, 1961	
Norm Cash	DET	May 23, 1961	9
Steve Boros	DET	May 23, 1961	
Dick Brown	DET	May 23, 1961	
Gene Green	WAS	Jun 27, 1961	1
Willie Tasby	WAS	Jun 27, 1961	
Dale Long	WAS	Jun 27, 1961	
Jerry Kindall	CLE	Jun 17, 1962	2
Bubba Phillips	CLE	Jun 17, 1962	
Jim Mahoney	CLE	Jun 17, 1962	
Gino Cimoli	KC	Aug 19, 1962	7
Wayne Causey	KC	Aug 19, 1962	
Billy Bryan	KC	Aug 19, 1962	
Lee Thomas	LA	Aug 28, 1962	4

Three Consecutive Home Runs, Team, AL (*cont.*)

Player	Team	Date	Inn.
Leon Wagner	LA	Aug 28, 1962	
Buck Rodgers	LA	Aug 28, 1962	
Brooks Robinson	BAL	Sep 10, 1965	8
Curt Blefary	BAL	Sep 10, 1965	
Jerry Adair	BAL	Sep 10, 1965	
Tony Oliva	MIN	Jun 9, 1966	7
Don Mincher	MIN	Jun 9, 1966	
Harmon Killebrew	MIN	Jun 9, 1966	
Bobby Richardson	NY	Jun 29, 1966	3
Mickey Mantle	NY	Jun 29, 1966	
Joe Pepitone	NY	Jun 29, 1966	
Frank Howard	WAS	Jul 2, 1966	6
Don Lock	WAS	Jul 2, 1966	
Ken McMullen	WAS	Jul 2, 1966	
Ted Kubiak	OAK	Jun 22, 1969	3
Reggie Jackson	OAK	Jun 22, 1969	
Sal Bando	OAK	Jun 22, 1969	
Bobby Murcer	NY	Aug 10, 1969	6
Thurman Munson	NY	Aug 10, 1969	
Gene Michael	NY	Aug 10, 1969	
Frank Robinson	BAL	Sep 4, 1969	9
Boog Powell	BAL	Sep 4, 1969	
Brooks Robinson	BAL	Sep 4, 1969	
Duke Sims	CLE	Aug 22, 1970	6
Graig Nettles	CLE	Aug 22, 1970	
Eddie Leon	CLE	Aug 22, 1970	
Jim Northrup	DET	Apr 17, 1971	7
Norm Cash	DET	Apr 17, 1971	
Willie Horton	DET	Apr 17, 1971	
Aurelio Rodriguez	DET	Jun 27, 1972	1
Al Kaline	DET	Jun 27, 1972	
Willie Horton	DET	Jun 27, 1972	
George Mitterwald	MIN	Jul 15, 1973	8
Joe Lis	MIN	Jul 15, 1973	
Jim Holt	MIN	Jul 15, 1973	
Al Kaline	DET	Jul 29, 1974	1
Bill Freehan	DET	Jul 29, 1974	
Mickey Stanley	DET	Jul 29, 1974	
Bobby Bonds	CAL	May 11, 1977	2
Don Baylor	CAL	May 11, 1977	
Ron Jackson	CAL	May 11, 1977	
Fred Lynn	BOS	Jul 4, 1977	8
Jim Rice	BOS	Jul 4, 1977	
Carl Yastrzemski	BOS	Jul 4, 1977	
George Scott	BOS	Aug 13, 1977	6
Butch Hobson	BOS	Aug 13, 1977	
Dwight Evans	BOS	Aug 13, 1977	

Three Consecutive Home Runs, Team, AL (cont.)

Player	Team	Date	Inn.
Eddie Murray	BAL	May 8, 1979	6
Lee May	BAL	May 8, 1979	
Gary Roenicke	BAL	May 8, 1979	
Tony Perez	BOS	May 31, 1980	6
Carlton Fisk	BOS	May 31, 1980	
Butch Hobson	BOS	May 31, 1980	
Dave Revering	OAK	Jun 3, 1980	9
Mitchell Page	OAK	Jun 3, 1980	
Tony Armas	OAK	Jun 3, 1980	
Cecil Cooper	MIL	May 28, 1982	6
Don Money	MIL	May 28, 1982	
Gorman Thomas	MIL	May 28, 1982	
Robin Yount	MIL	Jun 5, 1982	7
Cecil Cooper	MIL	Jun 5, 1982	
Ben Oglivie	MIL	Jun 5, 1982	
Ron Washington	MIN	Jun 7, 1982	8
Tom Brunansky	MIN	Jun 7, 1982	
Kent Hrbek	MIN	Jun 7, 1982	
Cecil Cooper	MIL	Sep 12, 1982	3
Ted Simmons	MIL	Sep 12, 1982	
Ben Oglivie	MIL	Sep 12, 1982	
Steve Henderson	SEA	Aug 2, 1983	3
Dave Henderson	SEA	Aug 2, 1983	
Domingo Ramos	SEA	Aug 2, 1983	
Carlton Fisk	CHI	Sep 9, 1983	1
Tom Paciorek	CHI	Sep 9, 1983	
Greg Luzinski	CHI	Sep 9, 1983	
Reggie Jackson	CAL	Apr 14, 1984	4
Brian Downing	CAL	Apr 14, 1984	
Bobby Grich	CAL	Apr 14, 1984	
Willie Upshaw	TOR	Apr 26, 1984	6
George Bell	TOR	Apr 26, 1984	
Jesse Barfield	TOR	Apr 26, 1984	
Don Mattingly	NY	May 29, 1984	6
Don Baylor	NY	May 29, 1984	
Dave Winfield	NY	May 29, 1984	
Oscar Gamble	NY	Jun 3, 1984	4
Steve Kemp	NY	Jun 3, 1984	
Toby Harrah	NY	Jun 3, 1984	
Andre Thornton	CLE	Jun 29, 1984	5
Mel Hall	CLE	Jun 29, 1984	
Jerry Willard	CLE	Jun 29, 1984	
Darryl Motley	KC	Aug 19, 1984	7
Frank White	KC	Aug 19, 1984	
Steve Balboni	KC	Aug 19, 1984	
Rudy Law	CHI	Aug 24, 1985	9
Ron Kittle	CHI	Aug 24, 1985	

Three Consecutive Home Runs, Team, AL (*cont.*)

Player	Team	Date	Inn.
Harold Baines	CHI	Aug 24, 1985	
Cal Ripken	BAL	Sep 16, 1985	8
Eddie Murray	BAL	Sep 16, 1985	
Fred Lynn	BAL	Sep 16, 1985	
Kirk Gibson	DET	Jul 8, 1986	4
Lance Parrish	DET	Jul 8, 1986	
Darrell Evans	DET	Jul 8, 1986	
George Brett	KC	Sep 28, 1986	4
Frank White	KC	Sep 28, 1986	
Jamie Quirk	KC	Sep 28, 1986	
Johnny Grubb	DET	Jun 28, 1987	9
Matt Nokes	DET	Jun 28, 1987	
Bill Madlock	DET	Jun 28, 1987	
Ernie Whitt	TOR	Sep 12, 1987	8
Jesse Barfield	TOR	Sep 12, 1987	
Kelly Gruber	TOR	Sep 12, 1987	
Dan Pasqua	CHI	Jul 9, 1988	4
Greg Walker	CHI	Jul 9, 1988	
Daryl Boston	CHI	Jul 9, 1988	
Jose Canseco	OAK	May 16, 1990	4
Mark McGwire	OAK	May 16, 1990	
Ron Hassey	OAK	May 16, 1990	
Candy Maldonado	CLE	Jun 17, 1990	7
Brook Jacoby	CLE	Jun 17, 1990	
Cory Snyder	CLE	Jun 17, 1990	
Rickey Henderson	OAK	Jul 6, 1990	3
Carney Lansford	OAK	Jul 6, 1990	
Jose Canseco	OAK	Jul 6, 1990	
Alan Trammell	DET	Apr 20, 1992	3
Cecil Fielder	DET	Apr 20, 1992	
Mickey Tettleton	DET	Apr 20, 1992	

Three Consecutive Home Runs, Team, NL

Player	Team	Date	Inn.
Frank Shugart	STL	May 10, 1894	7
Doggie Miller	STL	May 10, 1894	
Heinie Peitz	STL	May 10, 1894	
Bill Terry	NY	Aug 13, 1932	4
Mel Ott	NY	Aug 13, 1932	
Freddie Lindstrom	NY	Aug 13, 1932	
Paul Waner	PIT	Jun 10, 1935	8
Arky Vaughan	PIT	Jun 10, 1935	
Pep Young	PIT	Jun 10, 1935	
Tony Cuccinello	BOS	Jul 9, 1938	3
Max West	BOS	Jul 9, 1938	
Elbie Fletcher	BOS	Jul 9, 1938	

Three Consecutive Home Runs, Team, NL (cont.)

Player	Team	Date	Inn.
Burgess Whitehead	NY	Jun 6, 1939	4
Manny Salvo	NY	Jun 6, 1939	
Joe Moore	NY	Jun 6, 1939	
Alex Kampouris	NY	Aug 13, 1939	4
Bill Lohrman	NY	Aug 13, 1939	
Joe Moore	NY	Aug 13, 1939	
Phil Cavarretta	CHI	Aug 11, 1941	5
Stan Hack	CHI	Aug 11, 1941	
Bill Nicholson	CHI	Aug 11, 1941	
Walker Cooper	STL	Jun 11, 1944	8
Whitey Kurowski	STL	Jun 11, 1944	
Danny Litwhiler	STL	Jun 11, 1944	
Grady Hatton	CIN	Aug 11, 1946	8
Max West	CIN	Aug 11, 1946	
Ray Mueller	CIN	Aug 11, 1946	
Johnny Mize	NY	Jun 20, 1948	8
Williard Marshall	NY	Jun 20, 1948	
Sid Gordon	NY	Jun 20, 1948	
Whitey Lockman	NY	Jun 4, 1949	6
Sid Gordon	NY	Jun 4, 1949	
Willard Marshall	NY	Jun 4, 1949	
Roy Campanella	BKN	Apr 19, 1952	7
Andy Pafko	BKN	Apr 19, 1952	
Duke Snider	BKN	Apr 19, 1952	
Ralph Kiner	PIT	Sep 27, 1952	7
Joe Garagiola	PIT	Sep 27, 1952	
Gus Bell	PIT	Sep 27, 1952	
Wes Westrum	NY	Sep 4, 1953	4
Al Corwin	NY	Sep 4, 1953	
Whitey Lockman	NY	Sep 4, 1953	
Bobby Hofman	NY	Jun 20, 1954	6
Wes Westrum	NY	Jun 20, 1954	
Dusty Rhodes	NY	Jun 20, 1954	
Gus Bell	CIN	Aug 15, 1954	9
Ted Kluszewski	CIN	Aug 15, 1954	
Jim Greengrass	CIN	Aug 15, 1954	
Randy Jackson	CHI	Apr 16, 1955	2
Ernie Banks	CHI	Apr 16, 1955	
Dee Fondy	CHI	Apr 16, 1955	
Jerry Lynch	PIT	Jul 6, 1955	6
Frank Thomas	PIT	Jul 6, 1955	
Dale Long	PIT	Jul 6, 1955	
Eddie Mathews	MIL	May 30, 1956	1
Hank Aaron	MIL	May 30, 1956	
Bobby Thomson	MIL	May 30, 1956	
Gus Bell	CIN	May 31, 1956	9
Ted Kluszewski	CIN	May 31, 1956	

Three Consecutive Home Runs, Team, NL (*cont.*)

Player	Team	Date	Inn.
Frank Robinson	CIN	May 31, 1956	
Duke Snider	BKN	Jun 29, 1956	9
Randy Jackson	BKN	Jun 29, 1956	
Gil Hodges	BKN	Jun 29, 1956	
Hank Thompson	NY	Jul 8, 1956	4
Daryl Spencer	NY	Jul 8, 1956	
Wes Westrum	NY	Jul 8, 1956	
Frank Thomas	PIT	Apr 21, 1957	3
Paul Smith	PIT	Apr 21, 1957	
Dick Groat	PIT	Apr 21, 1957	
Hank Aaron	MIL	Jun 26, 1957	5
Eddie Mathews	MIL	Jun 26, 1957	
Wes Covington	MIL	Jun 26, 1957	
Bob Skinner	PIT	May 7, 1958	5
Ted Kluszewski	PIT	May 7, 1958	
Frank Thomas	PIT	May 7, 1958	
Hank Aaron	MIL	May 31, 1958	1
Eddie Mathews	MIL	May 31, 1958	
Wes Covington	MIL	May 31, 1958	
Hank Aaron	MIL	Jun 18, 1961	3
Joe Adcock	MIL	Jun 18, 1961	
Frank Thomas	MIL	Jun 18, 1961	
	NY	Apr 28, 1962	6
Charlie Neal	NY	Apr 28, 1962	
Gil Hodges	NY	Apr 28, 1962	
Willie Mays	SF	Aug 27, 1963	3
Orlando Cepeda	SF	Aug 27, 1963	
Felipe Alou	SF	Aug 27, 1963	
Ken Boyer	STL	Jul 18, 1964	8
Bill White	STL	Jul 18, 1964	
Tim McCarver	STL	Jul 18, 1964	
Dave Marshall	SF	Aug 5, 1969	5
Ron Hunt	SF	Aug 5, 1969	
Bobby Bonds	SF	Aug 5, 1969	
Dave Marshall	NY	May 18, 1970	8
Joe Foy	NY	May 18, 1970	
Jerry Grote	NY	May 18, 1970	
Bob Robertson	PIT	Aug 1, 1970	7
Willie Stargell	PIT	Aug 1, 1970	
Jose Pagan	PIT	Aug 1, 1970	
Nate Colbert	SD	Jul 16, 1974	9
Willie McCovey	SD	Jul 16, 1974	
Dave Winfield	SD	Jul 16, 1974	
George Theodore	NY	Jul 20, 1974	5
Rusty Staub	NY	Jul 20, 1974	
Cleon Jones	NY	Jul 20, 1974	
Larry Biittner	CHI	May 17, 1977	5

Three Consecutive Home Runs, Team, NL (cont.)

Player	Team	Date	Inn.
Bobby Murcer	CHI	May 17, 1977	
Jerry Morales	CHI	May 17, 1977	
Greg Luzinski	PHI	Sep 30, 1977	2
Richie Hebner	PHI	Sep 30, 1977	
Garry Maddox	PHI	Sep 30, 1977	
Gary Matthews	ATL	Aug 14, 1978	3
Jeff Burroughs	ATL	Aug 14, 1978	
Bob Horner	ATL	Aug 14, 1978	
Tony Perez	MON	Jun 17, 1979	4
Gary Carter	MON	Jun 17, 1979	
Ellis Valentine	MON	Jun 17, 1979	
Jerry Turner	SD	Jul 11, 1979	1
Dave Winfield	SD	Jul 11, 1979	
Gene Tenace	SD	Jul 11, 1979	
Ken Griffey	CIN	May 27, 1980	3
George Foster	CIN	May 27, 1980	
Dan Driessen	CIN	May 27, 1980	
Reggie Smith	SF	Jul 11, 1982	2
Milt May	SF	Jul 11, 1982	
Champ Summers	SF	Jul 11, 1982	
Enos Cabell	HOU	Jun 24, 1984	5
Phil Garner	HOU	Jun 24, 1984	
Jose Cruz	HOU	Jun 24, 1984	
Juan Samuel	PHI	Aug 17, 1985	7
Glenn Wilson	PHI	Aug 17, 1985	
Mike Schmidt	PHI	Aug 17, 1985	
Gary Carter	NY	Jul 27, 1986	3
Darryl Strawberry	NY	Jul 27, 1986	
Kevin Mitchell	NY	Jul 27, 1986	
Marvell Wynne	SD	Apr 13, 1987	1
Tony Gwynn	SD	Apr 13, 1987	
John Kruk	SD	Apr 13, 1987	
Milt Thompson	PHI	Jul 26, 1987	8
Von Hayes	PHI	Jul 26, 1987	
Mike Schmidt	PHI	Jul 26, 1987	
Tim Teufel	NY	May 1, 1988	5
Keith Hernandez	NY	May 1, 1988	
Darryl Strawberry	NY	May 1, 1988	
	NY	Apr 17, 1989	3
Kevin McReynolds	NY	Apr 17, 1989	
Keith Hernandez	NY	Apr 17, 1989	
Chris Sabo	CIN	Jun 16, 1990	5
Barry Larkin	CIN	Jun 16, 1990	
Eric Davis	CIN	Jun 16, 1990	
Mariano Duncan	CIN	Sep 14, 1991	4
Hal Morris	CIN	Sep 14, 1991	
Paul O'Neill	CIN	Sep 14, 1991	

Three Consecutive Home Runs, Team, NL (cont.)

Player	Team	Date	Inn.
Dave Justice	ATL	Sep 20, 1992	6
Brian Hunter	ATL	Sep 20, 1992	
Ron Gant	ATL	Sep 20, 1992	

Three Consecutive Home Runs, Team, Other Leagues

Player	Team	Date	Inn.
George Gore	NY P	May 31, 1890	8
Buck Ewing	NY P	May 31, 1890	
Roger Connor	NY P	May 31, 1890	

Most Home Runs in One Inning, Team, AL

Player	Team	Date	Inn.
Rich Rollins	MIN	Jun 9, 1966	7
Zoilo Versalles	MIN	Jun 9, 1966	
Tony Oliva	MIN	Jun 9, 1966	
Don Mincher	MIN	Jun 9, 1966	
Harmon Killebrew	MIN	Jun 9, 1966	
Ted Williams	BOS	Sep 24, 1940	6
Jimmie Foxx	BOS	Sep 24, 1940	
Joe Cronin	BOS	Sep 24, 1940	
Jim Tabor	BOS	Sep 24, 1940	
Dizzy Trout	DET	Jun 23, 1950	4
Gerry Priddy	DET	Jun 23, 1950	
Vic Wertz	DET	Jun 23, 1950	
Hoot Evers	DET	Jun 23, 1950	
Gene Mauch	BOS	May 22, 1957	7
Ted Williams	BOS	May 22, 1957	
Dick Gernert	BOS	May 22, 1957	
Frank Malzone	BOS	May 22, 1957	
Norm Zauchin	BOS	Aug 26, 1957	7
Ted Lepcio	BOS	Aug 26, 1957	
Jimmy Piersall	BOS	Aug 26, 1957	
Frank Malzone	BOS	Aug 26, 1957	
Woodie Held	CLE	Jul 31, 1963	6
Pedro Ramos	CLE	Jul 31, 1963	
Tito Francona	CLE	Jul 31, 1963	
Larry Brown	CLE	Jul 31, 1963	
Tony Oliva	MIN	May 2, 1964	11
Bob Allison	MIN	May 2, 1964	
Jimmie Hall	MIN	May 2, 1964	
Harmon Killebrew	MIN	May 2, 1964	
Andy Etchebarren	BAL	May 17, 1967	7
Sam Bowens	BAL	May 17, 1967	
Boog Powell	BAL	May 17, 1967	
Davey Johnson	BAL	May 17, 1967	
Al Kaline	DET	Jul 29, 1974	1

Most Home Runs in One Inning, Team, AL (*cont.*)

Player	Team	Date	Inn.
Bill Freehan	DET	Jul 29, 1974	
Mickey Stanley	DET	Jul 29, 1974	
Ed Brinkman	DET	Jul 29, 1974	
Rick Burleson	BOS	Jun 17, 1977	1
Fred Lynn	BOS	Jun 17, 1977	
Carlton Fisk	BOS	Jun 17, 1977	
George Scott	BOS	Jun 17, 1977	
Fred Lynn	BOS	Jul 4, 1977	8
Jim Rice	BOS	Jul 4, 1977	
Carl Yastrzemski	BOS	Jul 4, 1977	
George Scott	BOS	Jul 4, 1977	
Dave Stapleton	BOS	May 31, 1980	4
Tony Perez	BOS	May 31, 1980	
Carlton Fisk	BOS	May 31, 1980	
Butch Hobson	BOS	May 31, 1980	
Dave Engle	MIN	May 16, 1983	9
Bobby Mitchell	MIN	May 16, 1983	
Gary Gaetti	MIN	May 16, 1983	
Mickey Hatcher	MIN	May 16, 1983	
Chet Lemon	DET	Sep 10, 1986	4
Mike Heath	DET	Sep 10, 1986	
Kirk Gibson	DET	Sep 10, 1986	
Darnell Coles	DET	Sep 10, 1986	
Shane Mack	MIN	May 2, 1992	5
Kirby Puckett	MIN	May 2, 1992	
Kent Hrbek	MIN	May 2, 1992	
Randy Bush	MIN	May 2, 1992	

Most Home Runs in One Inning, Team, NL

Player	Team	Date	Inn.
Harry Danning	NY	Jun 6, 1939	4
Frank Demaree	NY	Jun 6, 1939	
Burgess Whitehead	NY	Jun 6, 1939	
Manny Salvo	NY	Jun 6, 1939	
Joe Moore	NY	Jun 6, 1939	
Del Ennis	PHI	Jun 2, 1949	8
Andy Seminick	PHI	Jun 2, 1949	
Willie Jones	PHI	Jun 2, 1949	
Schoolboy Rowe	PHI	Jun 2, 1949	
Andy Seminick	PHI	Jun 2, 1949	
Orlando Cepeda	SF	Aug 23, 1961	9
Felipe Alou	SF	Aug 23, 1961	
Jim Davenport	SF	Aug 23, 1961	
Willie Mays	SF	Aug 23, 1961	
John Orsino	SF	Aug 23, 1961	
Jake Stenzel	PIT	Jun 6, 1894	3

Most Home Runs in One Inning, Team, NL (*cont.*)

Player	Team	Date	Inn.
Denny Lyons	PIT	Jun 6, 1894	
Lou Bierbauer	PIT	Jun 6, 1894	
Jake Stenzel	PIT	Jun 6, 1894	
Cliff Heathcote	CHI	May 12, 1930	7
Hack Wilson	CHI	May 12, 1930	
Charlie Grimm	CHI	May 12, 1930	
Clyde Beck	CHI	May 12, 1930	
Zeke Bonura	NY	Aug 13, 1939	4
Alex Kampouris	NY	Aug 13, 1939	
Bill Lohrman	NY	Aug 13, 1939	
Joe Moore	NY	Aug 13, 1939	
Erv Dusak	STL	Jun 6, 1948	6
Red Schoendienst	STL	Jun 6, 1948	
Enos Slaughter	STL	Jun 6, 1948	
Nippy Jones	STL	Jun 6, 1948	
Davey Williams	NY	May 28, 1954	8
Alvin Dark	NY	May 28, 1954	
Monte Irvin	NY	May 28, 1954	
Billy Gardner	NY	May 28, 1954	
Willie Mays	NY	Jul 8, 1956	4
Hank Thompson	NY	Jul 8, 1956	
Daryl Spencer	NY	Jul 8, 1956	
Wes Westrum	NY	Jul 8, 1956	
Eddie Mathews	MIL	Jul 8, 1961	7
Hank Aaron	MIL	Jul 8, 1961	
Joe Adcock	MIL	Jul 8, 1961	
Frank Thomas	MIL	Jul 8, 1961	
Joe Torre	MIL	Jun 8, 1965	10
Eddie Mathews	MIL	Jun 8, 1965	
Hank Aaron	MIL	Jun 8, 1965	
Gene Oliver	MIL	Jun 8, 1965	
Ivan Murrell	SD	Jul 10, 1970	9
Ed Spiezio	SD	Jul 10, 1970	
Dave Campbell	SD	Jul 10, 1970	
Clarence Gaston	SD	Jul 10, 1970	
Mike Lum	ATL	Jun 21, 1971	8
Hal King	ATL	Jun 21, 1971	
Hank Aaron	ATL	Jun 21, 1971	
Darrell Evans	ATL	Jun 21, 1971	
Andre Dawson	MON	Jul 30, 1978	3
Larry Parrish	MON	Jul 30, 1978	
Dave Cash	MON	Jul 30, 1978	
Andre Dawson	MON	Jul 30, 1978	
Juan Samuel	PHI	Aug 17, 1985	7
Glenn Wilson	PHI	Aug 17, 1985	
Mike Schmidt	PHI	Aug 17, 1985	
Darren Daulton	PHI	Aug 17, 1985	
Andre Dawson	MON	Apr 29, 1986	4

Most Home Runs in One Inning, Team, NL (*cont.*)

Player	Team	Date	Inn.
Hubie Brooks	MON	Apr 29, 1986	
Tim Wallach	MON	Apr 29, 1986	
Mike Fitzgerald	MON	Apr 29, 1986	
Dave Justice	ATL	Sep 20, 1992	6
Brian Hunter	ATL	Sep 20, 1992	
Ron Gant	ATL	Sep 20, 1992	
Mark Lemke	ATL	Sep 20, 1992	

Most Home Runs by Team, Game, AL

Player	Team	Date	HR	Score	Opp.
Ernie Whitt	TOR	Sep 14, 1987	3	18–3	BAL
George Bell	TOR	Sep 14, 1987	2		
Rance Mulliniks	TOR	Sep 14, 1987	2		
Fred McGriff	TOR	Sep 14, 1987	1		
Rob Ducey	TOR	Sep 14, 1987	1		
Lloyd Moseby	TOR	Sep 14, 1987	1		
Total			10		
Babe Dahlgren	NY	Jun 28, 1939	2	23–2	PHI
Joe DiMaggio	NY	Jun 28, 1939	2		
Bill Dickey	NY	Jun 28, 1939	1		
Joe Gordon	NY	Jun 28, 1939	1		
Tommy Henrich	NY	Jun 28, 1939	1		
George Selkirk	NY	Jun 28, 1939	1		
Total			8		
Harmon Killebrew	MIN	Aug 29, 1963	2	14–2	WAS
Vic Power	MIN	Aug 29, 1963	2		
Bernie Allen	MIN	Aug 29, 1963	1		
Bob Allison	MIN	Aug 29, 1963	1		
Jimmie Hall	MIN	Aug 29, 1963	1		
Rich Rollins	MIN	Aug 29, 1963	1		
Total			8		
Fred Lynn	BOS	Jul 4, 1977	2	9–6	TOR
George Scott	BOS	Jul 4, 1977	2		
Carl Yastrzemski	BOS	Jul 4, 1977	1		
Jim Rice	BOS	Jul 4, 1977	1		
Butch Hobson	BOS	Jul 4, 1977	1		
Bernie Carbo	BOS	Jul 4, 1977	1		
Total			8		
Jimmy Dykes	PHI	Jun 3, 1921	2	15–9	DET
Frank Welch	PHI	Jun 3, 1921	2		
Tilly Walker	PHI	Jun 3, 1921	1		
Cy Perkins	PHI	Jun 3, 1921	1		
Joe Dugan	PHI	Jun 3, 1921	1		
Total			7		

Most Home Runs by Team, Game, AL (*cont.*)

Player	Team	Date	HR	Score	Opp.
Lou Gehrig	NY	Jun 3, 1932	4	20–13	PHI
Tony Lazzeri	NY	Jun 3, 1932	1		
Earle Combs	NY	Jun 3, 1932	1		
Babe Ruth	NY	Jun 3, 1932	1		
Total			7		
Clyde Vollmer	WAS	May 3, 1949	2	14–12	CHI
Mark Christman	WAS	May 3, 1949	1		
Gil Coan	WAS	May 3, 1949	1		
Eddie Robinson	WAS	May 3, 1949	1		
Al Evans	WAS	May 3, 1949	1		
Bud Stewart	WAS	May 3, 1949	1		
Total			7		
Bobby Doerr	BOS	Jun 8, 1950	3	29–4	STL
Ted Williams	BOS	Jun 8, 1950	2		
Walt Dropo	BOS	Jun 8, 1950	2		
Total			7		
Sherm Lollar	CHI	Apr 23, 1955	2	29–6	KC
Bob Nieman	CHI	Apr 23, 1955	2		
Walt Dropo	CHI	Apr 23, 1955	1		
Jack Harshman	CHI	Apr 23, 1955	1		
Minnie Minoso	CHI	Apr 23, 1955	1		
Total			7		
Mickey Mantle	NY	May 30, 1961	2	12–3	BOS
Roger Maris	NY	May 30, 1961	2		
Bill Skowron	NY	May 30, 1961	2		
Yogi Berra	NY	May 30, 1961	1		
Total			7		
Rocky Colavito	CLE	Jul 17, 1966	2	15–2	DET
Chuck Hinton	CLE	Jul 17, 1966	2		
Max Alvis	CLE	Jul 17, 1966	1		
Buddy Booker	CLE	Jul 17, 1966	1		
Leon Wagner	CLE	Jul 17, 1966	1		
Total			7		
Paul Blair	BAL	May 17, 1967	1	12–8	BOS
Sam Bowens	BAL	May 17, 1967	1		
Boog Powell	BAL	May 17, 1967	1		
Andy Etchebarren	BAL	May 17, 1967	1		
Davey Johnson	BAL	May 17, 1967	1		
Brooks Robinson	BAL	May 17, 1967	1		
Frank Robinson	BAL	May 17, 1967	1		
Total			7		

Most Home Runs by Team, Game, AL (cont.)

Player	Team	Date	HR	Score	Opp.
Ben Oglivie	MIL	Apr 29, 1980	2	14–1	CLE
Sal Bando	MIL	Apr 29, 1980	2		
Sixto Lezcano	MIL	Apr 29, 1980	1		
Paul Molitor	MIL	Apr 29, 1980	1		
Larry Hisle	MIL	Apr 29, 1980	1		
Total			7		
Gorman Thomas	SEA	Apr 11, 1985	3	14–6	OAK
Al Cowens	SEA	Apr 11, 1985	1		
Jim Presley	SEA	Apr 11, 1985	1		
Phil Bradley	SEA	Apr 11, 1985	1		
Dave Henderson	SEA	Apr 11, 1985	1		
Total			7		
Eddie Murray	BAL	Aug 26, 1985	3	17–3	CAL
John Shelby	BAL	Aug 26, 1985	1		
Floyd Rayford	BAL	Aug 26, 1985	1		
Gary Roenicke	BAL	Aug 26, 1985	1		
Rick Dempsey	BAL	Aug 26, 1985	1		
Total			7		
Darrell Porter	TEX	Sep 13, 1986	2	14–1	MIN
Rubin Sierra	TEX	Sep 13, 1986	2		
Pete O'Brien	TEX	Sep 13, 1986	1		
Pete Incaviglia	TEX	Sep 13, 1986	1		
Steve Buechele	TEX	Sep 13, 1986	1		
Total			7		
Mark McGwire	OAK	Jul 6, 1990	2	12–1	CLE
Rickey Henderson	OAK	Jul 6, 1990	2		
Carney Lansford	OAK	Jul 6, 1990	1		
Jose Canseco	OAK	Jul 6, 1990	1		
Jamie Quirk	OAK	Jul 6, 1990	1		
Total			7		

Most Home Runs by Team, Game, NL

Player	Team	Date	HR	Score	Opp.
Jim Pendleton	MIL	Aug 30, 1953	3	19–4	PIT
Eddie Mathews	MIL	Aug 30, 1953	2		
Del Crandall	MIL	Aug 30, 1953	1		
Jack Dittmer	MIL	Aug 30, 1953	1		
Johnny Logan	MIL	Aug 30, 1953	1		
Total			8		
Bob Thurman	CIN	Aug 18, 1956	3	13–4	MIL
Ted Kluszewski	CIN	Aug 18, 1956	2		
Frank Robinson	CIN	Aug 18, 1956	2		
Wally Post	CIN	Aug 18, 1956	1		
Total			8		

Most Home Runs by Team, Game, NL (*cont.*)

Player	Team	Date	HR	Score	Opp.
Willie Mays	SF	Apr 30, 1961	4	14–4	MIL
Jose Pagan	SF	Apr 30, 1961	2		
Felipe Alou	SF	Apr 30, 1961	1		
Orlando Cepeda	SF	Apr 30, 1961	1		
Total			8		
Larry Parrish	MON	Jul 30, 1978	3	19–0	ATL
Andre Dawson	MON	Jul 30, 1978	2		
Tony Perez	MON	Jul 30, 1978	1		
Dave Cash	MON	Jul 30, 1978	1		
Chris Speier	MON	Jul 30, 1978	1		
Total			8		
Jack Rowe	DET	Jun 12, 1886	2	14–7	STL
Sam Thompson	DET	Jun 12, 1886	2		
Charlie Bennett	DET	Jun 12, 1886	1		
Dan Brouthers	DET	Jun 12, 1886	1		
Sam Crane	DET	Jun 12, 1886	1		
Total			7		
Roger Connor	NY	May 9, 1888	3	18–4	IND
George Gore	NY	May 9, 1888	1		
Tim Keefe	NY	May 9, 1888	1		
Danny Richardson	NY	May 9, 1888	1		
Mike Tiernan	NY	May 9, 1888	1		
Total			7		
Lou Bierbauer	PIT	Jun 6, 1894	2	27–11	BOS
Jake Stenzel	PIT	Jun 6, 1894	2		
Denny Lyons	PIT	Jun 6, 1894	1		
Connie Mack	PIT	Jun 6, 1894	1		
Frank Scheibeck	PIT	Jun 6, 1894	1		
Total			7		
Joe Moore	NY	Jun 6, 1939	2	17–3	CIN
Harry Danning	NY	Jun 6, 1939	1		
Mel Ott	NY	Jun 6, 1939	1		
Frank Demaree	NY	Jun 6, 1939	1		
Manny Salvo	NY	Jun 6, 1939	1		
Burgess Whitehead	NY	Jun 6, 1939	1		
Total			7		
Frank Demaree	NY	Aug 13, 1939	2	11–2	PHI
Joe Moore	NY	Aug 13, 1939	1		
Bob Seeds	NY	Aug 13, 1939	1		
Zeke Bonura	NY	Aug 13, 1939	1		
Alex Kampouris	NY	Aug 13, 1939	1		
Bill Lohrman	NY	Aug 13, 1939	1		
Total			7		

Most Home Runs by Team, Game, NL (cont.)

Player	Team	Date	HR	Score	Opp.
Eddie Lake	STL	May 7, 1940	2	18–2	BKN
Johnny Mize	STL	May 7, 1940	2		
Stu Martin	STL	May 7, 1940	1		
Joe Medwick	STL	May 7, 1940	1		
Don Padgett	STL	May 7, 1940	1		
Total			7		
Ralph Kiner	PIT	Aug 16, 1947	3	12–7	STL
Hank Greenberg	PIT	Aug 16, 1947	2		
Billy Cox	PIT	Aug 16, 1947	2		
Total			7		
Wes Westrum	NY	Jun 24, 1950	3	12–2	CIN
Alvin Dark	NY	Jun 24, 1950	1		
Monte Irvin	NY	Jun 24, 1950	1		
Whitey Lockman	NY	Jun 24, 1950	1		
Hank Thompson	NY	Jun 24, 1950	1		
Total			7		
Joe Adcock	MIL	Jul 31, 1954	4	15–7	BKN
Eddie Mathews	MIL	Jul 31, 1954	2		
Andy Pafko	MIL	Jul 31, 1954	1		
Total			7		
Willie Mays	NY	Jul 8, 1956	2	16–1	PIT
Daryl Spencer	NY	Jul 8, 1956	2		
Wes Westrum	NY	Jul 8, 1956	2		
Hank Thompson	NY	Jul 8, 1956	1		
Total			7		
Frank Robinson	CIN	Jun 1, 1957	2	22–2	CHI
Ed Bailey	CIN	Jun 1, 1957	1		
Gus Bell	CIN	Jun 1, 1957	1		
Don Hoak	CIN	Jun 1, 1957	1		
Hal Jeffcoat	CIN	Jun 1, 1957	1		
Wally Post	CIN	Jun 1, 1957	1		
Total			7		
Adolfo Phillips	CHI	Jun 11, 1967	3	18–10	NY
Randy Hundley	CHI	Jun 11, 1967	2		
Ernie Banks	CHI	Jun 11, 1967	1		
Ron Santo	CHI	Jun 11, 1967	1		
Total			7		
Clete Boyer	ATL	Aug 3, 1967	2	10–3	CHI
Joe Torre	ATL	Aug 3, 1967	2		
Hank Aaron	ATL	Aug 3, 1967	1		
Tito Francona	ATL	Aug 3, 1967	1		
Denis Menke	ATL	Aug 3, 1967	1		
Total			7		

Most Home Runs by Team, Game, NL (*cont.*)

Player	Team	Date	HR	Score	Opp.
Bernie Carbo	CIN	Apr 21, 1970	2	13–8	STL
Johnny Bench	CIN	Apr 21, 1970	1		
Dave Concepcion	CIN	Apr 21, 1970	1		
Tony Perez	CIN	Apr 21, 1970	1		
Pete Rose	CIN	Apr 21, 1970	1		
Bobby Tolan	CIN	Apr 21, 1970	1		
Total			7		
Jim Hickman	CHI	Aug 19, 1970	2	12–2	SD
Glenn Beckert	CHI	Aug 19, 1970	1		
Johnny Callison	CHI	Aug 19, 1970	1		
Ferguson Jenkins	CHI	Aug 19, 1970	1		
Joe Pepitone	CHI	Aug 19, 1970	1		
Billy Williams	CHI	Aug 19, 1970	1		
Total			7		
Henry Cruz	LA	May 5, 1976	2	14–12	CHI
Bill Buckner	LA	May 5, 1976	1		
Ron Cey	LA	May 5, 1976	1		
Bill Russell	LA	May 5, 1976	1		
Ed Goodson	LA	May 5, 1976	1		
Steve Yeager	LA	May 5, 1976	1		
Total			7		
Larry Biittner	CHI	May 17, 1977	2	23–6	SD
Steve Ontiveros	CHI	May 17, 1977	1		
Gene Clines	CHI	May 17, 1977	1		
Bobby Murcer	CHI	May 17, 1977	1		
Jerry Morales	CHI	May 17, 1977	1		
Dave Rosello	CHI	May 17, 1977	1		
Total			7		
Dusty Baker	LA	May 25, 1979	1	17–6	CIN
Rick Sutcliffe	LA	May 25, 1979	1		
Steve Garvey	LA	May 25, 1979	1		
Gary Thomasson	LA	May 25, 1979	1		
Joe Ferguson	LA	May 25, 1979	1		
Derrel Thomas	LA	May 25, 1979	1		
Davey Lopes	LA	May 25, 1979	1		
Total			7		
Dave Parker	CIN	Sep 15, 1987	2	21–6	ATL
Barry Larkin	CIN	Sep 15, 1987	1		
Terry McGriff	CIN	Sep 15, 1987	1		
Buddy Bell	CIN	Sep 15, 1987	1		
Lloyd McClendon	CIN	Sep 15, 1987	1		
Leo Garcia	CIN	Sep 15, 1987	1		
Total			7		

Most 40-Home Run Hitters, AL

Player	Team	Year	HR
Babe Ruth	NY	1927	60
Lou Gehrig	NY	1927	47
Babe Ruth	NY	1930	49
Lou Gehrig	NY	1930	41
Babe Ruth	NY	1931	46
Lou Gehrig	NY	1931	46
Roger Maris	NY	1961	61
Mickey Mantle	NY	1961	54
Rocky Colavito	DET	1961	45
Norm Cash	DET	1961	41
Rico Petrocelli	BOS	1969	40
Carl Yastrzemski	BOS	1969	40

Most 40-Home Run Hitters, NL

Player	Team	Year	HR
Davey Johnson	ATL	1973	43
Darrell Evans	ATL	1973	41
Hank Aaron	ATL	1973	40
Duke Snider	BKN	1953	42
Roy Campanella	BKN	1953	41
Gil Hodges	BKN	1954	42
Duke Snider	BKN	1954	40
Ted Kluszewski	CIN	1955	47
Wally Post	CIN	1955	40
Orlando Cepeda	SF	1961	46
Willie Mays	SF	1961	40
Johnny Bench	CIN	1970	45
Tony Perez	CIN	1970	40

Most 30-Home Run Hitters, AL

Player	Team	Year	HR
Charlie Keller	NY	1941	33
Tommy Henrich	NY	1941	31
Joe DiMaggio	NY	1941	30
Harmon Killebrew	WAS	1959	42
Jim Lemon	WAS	1959	33
Bob Allison	WAS	1959	30

Most 30-Home Run Hitters, AL (cont.)

Player	Team	Year	HR
Harmon Killebrew	MIN	1963	45
Bob Allison	MIN	1963	35
Jimmie Hall	MIN	1963	33
Harmon Killebrew	MIN	1964	49
Bob Allison	MIN	1964	32
Tony Oliva	MIN	1964	32
Jim Rice	BOS	1977	39
George Scott	BOS	1977	33
Butch Hobson	BOS	1977	30
Gorman Thomas	MIL	1982	39
Ben Oglivie	MIL	1982	32
Cecil Cooper	MIL	1982	32
Cory Snyder	CLE	1987	33
Brook Jacoby	CLE	1987	32
Joe Carter	CLE	1987	32
Kent Hrbek	MIN	1987	34
Tom Brunansky	MIN	1987	32
Gary Gaetti	MIN	1987	31
Cecil Fielder	DET	1992	35
Rob Deer	DET	1992	32
Mickey Tettleton	DET	1992	32

Most 30-Home Run Hitters, NL

Player	Team	Year	HR
Steve Garvey	LA	1977	33
Reggie Smith	LA	1977	32
Dusty Baker	LA	1977	30
Ron Cey	LA	1977	30
Chuck Klein	PHI	1929	43
Lefty O'Doul	PHI	1929	32
Don Hurst	PHI	1929	31
Johnny Mize	NY	1947	51
Willard Marshall	NY	1947	36
Walker Cooper	NY	1947	35
Gil Hodges	BKN	1950	32
Duke Snider	BKN	1950	31
Roy Campanella	BKN	1950	31
Duke Snider	BKN	1953	42
Roy Campanella	BKN	1953	41
Gil Hodges	BKN	1953	31

Most 30-Home Run Hitters, NL (*cont.*)

Player	Team	Year	HR
Frank Robinson	CIN	1956	38
Wally Post	CIN	1956	36
Ted Kluszewski	CIN	1956	35
Joe Adcock	MIL	1961	35
Hank Aaron	MIL	1961	34
Eddie Mathews	MIL	1961	32
Willie McCovey	SF	1963	44
Willie Mays	SF	1963	38
Orlando Cepeda	SF	1963	34
Willie Mays	SF	1964	47
Orlando Cepeda	SF	1964	31
Jim Ray Hart	SF	1964	31
Eddie Mathews	MIL	1965	32
Hank Aaron	MIL	1965	32
Mack Jones	MIL	1965	31
Hank Aaron	ATL	1966	44
Joe Torre	ATL	1966	36
Felipe Alou	ATL	1966	31
Willie Mays	SF	1966	37
Willie McCovey	SF	1966	36
Jim Ray Hart	SF	1966	33
Johnny Bench	CIN	1970	45
Tony Perez	CIN	1970	40
Lee May	CIN	1970	34
Davey Johnson	ATL	1973	43
Darrell Evens	ATL	1973	41
Hank Aaron	ATL	1973	40

Most 20-Home Run Hitters, AL

Player	Team	Year	HR
Roger Maris	NY	1961	61
Mickey Mantle	NY	1961	54
Bill Skowron	NY	1961	28
Yogi Berra	NY	1961	22
Elston Howard	NY	1961	21
Johnny Blanchard	NY	1961	21
Harmon Killebrew	MIN	1964	49
Bob Allison	MIN	1964	32
Tony Oliva	MIN	1964	32

Most 20-Home Run Hitters, AL (*cont.*)

Player	Team	Year	HR
Jimmie Hall	MIN	1964	25
Don Mincher	MIN	1964	23
Zoilo Versalles	MIN	1964	20
Darrell Evans	DET	1986	29
Kirk Gibson	DET	1986	28
Lance Parrish	DET	1986	22
Alan Trammell	DET	1986	21
Darnell Coles	DET	1986	20
Lou Whitaker	DET	1986	20
Joe DiMaggio	NY	1938	32
Lou Gehrig	NY	1938	29
Bill Dickey	NY	1938	27
Joe Gordon	NY	1938	25
Tommy Henrich	NY	1938	22
Jimmie Foxx	BOS	1940	36
Joe Cronin	BOS	1940	24
Ted Williams	BOS	1940	23
Bobby Doerr	BOS	1940	22
Jim Tabor	BOS	1940	21
Leon Wagner	LA	1961	28
Ken Hunt	LA	1961	25
Lee Thomas	LA	1961	24
Earl Averill	LA	1961	21
Steve Bilko	LA	1961	20
Jim Rice	BOS	1977	39
George Scott	BOS	1977	33
Butch Hobson	BOS	1977	30
Carl Yastrzemski	BOS	1977	28
Carlton Fisk	BOS	1977	26
Fred Lynn	BOS	1979	39
Jim Rice	BOS	1979	39
Butch Hobson	BOS	1979	28
Dwight Evans	BOS	1979	21
Carl Yastrzemski	BOS	1979	21
Reggie Jackson	CAL	1982	39
Doug DeCinces	CAL	1982	30
Brian Downing	CAL	1982	28
Don Baylor	CAL	1982	24
Fred Lynn	CAL	1982	21
Gorman Thomas	MIL	1982	39
Ben Ogilvie	MIL	1982	34
Cecil Cooper	MIL	1982	32

Most 20-Home Run Hitters, AL (cont.)

Player	Team	Year	HR
Robin Yount	MIL	1982	29
Ted Simmons	MIL	1982	23
Tony Armas	BOS	1984	43
Dwight Evans	BOS	1984	32
Jim Rice	BOS	1984	28
Mike Easler	BOS	1984	27
Rich Gedman	BOS	1984	24
Gary Gaetti	MIN	1986	34
Kirby Puckett	MIN	1986	31
Kent Hrbek	MIN	1986	29
Tom Brunansky	MIN	1986	23
Roy Smalley	MIN	1986	20
Darrell Evans	DET	1987	34
Matt Nokes	DET	1987	32
Alan Trammell	DET	1987	28
Kirk Gibson	DET	1987	24
Chet Lemon	DET	1987	20
Cecil Fielder	DET	1991	44
Mickey Tettleton	DET	1991	31
Rob Deer	DET	1991	25
Lou Whitaker	DET	1991	23
Travis Fryman	DET	1991	21

Most 20-Home Run Hitters, NL

Player	Team	Year	HR
Hank Aaron	MIL	1965	32
Eddie Mathews	MIL	1965	32
Mack Jones	MIL	1965	31
Joe Torre	MIL	1965	27
Felipe Alou	MIL	1965	23
Gene Oliver	MIL	1965	21
Bobby Thomson	NY	1953	26
Hank Thompson	NY	1953	24
Alvin Dark	NY	1953	23
Monte Irvin	NY	1953	21
Daryl Spencer	NY	1953	20
Frank Robinson	CIN	1956	38
Wally Post	CIN	1956	36
Ted Kluszewski	CIN	1956	35
Gus Bell	CIN	1956	29
Ed Bailey	CIN	1956	28

Most 20-Home Run Hitters, NL (*cont.*)

Player	Team	Year	HR
Ernie Banks	CHI	1958	47
Walt Moryn	CHI	1958	26
Lee Walls	CHI	1958	24
Bobby Thomson	CHI	1958	21
Dale Long	CHI	1958	20
Willie McCovey	SF	1963	44
Willie Mays	SF	1963	38
Orlando Cepeda	SF	1963	34
Ed Bailey	SF	1963	21
Felipe Alou	SF	1963	20
Ron Cey	LA	1979	28
Steve Garvey	LA	1979	28
Davey Lopes	LA	1979	28
Dusty Baker	LA	1979	23
Joe Ferguson	LA	1979	20

Best Home Run Trios, Season, AL

Player	Team	Year	HR
Roger Maris	NY	1961	61
Mickey Mantle	NY	1961	54
Bill Skowron	NY	1961	28
Total			143
Babe Ruth	NY	1927	60
Lou Gehrig	NY	1927	47
Tony Lazzeri	NY	1927	18
Total			125
Jimmie Foxx	PHI	1932	58
Al Simmons	PHI	1932	35
Mickey Cochrane	PHI	1932	23
Total			116
Harmon Killebrew	MIN	1963	45
Bob Allison	MIN	1963	35
Tony Oliva	MIN	1963	33
Total			113
Harmon Killebrew	MIN	1964	49
Bob Allison	MIN	1964	32
Tony Oliva	MIN	1964	32
Total			113
Joe DiMaggio	NY	1937	46
Lou Gehrig	NY	1937	37
Bill Dickey	NY	1937	29
Total			112

Best Home Run Trios, Season, AL (*cont.*)

Player	Team	Year	HR
Hank Greenberg	DET	1938	58
Rudy York	DET	1938	33
Charlie Gehringer	DET	1938	20
Total			111
Frank Robinson	BAL	1966	49
Boog Powell	BAL	1966	34
Brooks Robinson/	BAL	1966	23
Curt Blefary			
Total			106
Fred Lynn	BOS	1979	39
Jim Rice	BOS	1979	39
Butch Hobson	BOS	1979	28
Total			106
Harmon Killebrew	WAS	1959	42
Jim Lemon	WAS	1959	33
Bob Allison	WAS	1959	30
Total			105
Rocky Colavito	DET	1961	45
Norm Cash	DET	1961	41
Al Kaline	DET	1961	19
Total			105
Norm Cash	DET	1962	39
Rocky Colavito	DET	1962	37
Al Kaline	DET	1962	29
Total			105
Rico Petrocelli	BOS	1969	40
Carl Yastrzemski	BOS	1969	40
Reggie Smith	BOS	1969	25
Total			105
Carl Yastrzemski	BOS	1970	40
Tony Conigliaro	BOS	1970	36
Rico Petrocelli	BOS	1970	29
Total			105
Gorman Thomas	MIL	1982	39
Ben Oglivie	MIL	1982	34
Cecil Cooper	MIL	1982	32
Total			105
Ben Oglivie	MIL	1980	41
Gorman Thomas	MIL	1980	38
Cecil Cooper	MIL	1980	25
Total			104

Best Home Run Trios, Season, AL (*cont.*)

Player	Team	Year	HR
Tony Armas	BOS	1984	43
Dwight Evans	BOS	1984	32
Jim Rice	BOS	1984	28
Total			103
Jim Rice	BOS	1977	39
George Scott	BOS	1977	33
Butch Hobson	BOS	1977	30
Total			102
Mark McGwire	OAK	1987	49
Jose Canseco	OAK	1987	31
Mike Davis	OAK	1987	22
Total			102
George Bell	TOR	1987	47
Jesse Barfield	TOR	1987	28
Lloyd Moseby	TOR	1987	26
Total			101
Cecil Fielder	DET	1991	44
Mickey Tettleton	DET	1991	31
Rob Deer	DET	1991	25
Total			100

Best Home Run Trios, Season, NL

Player	Team	Year	HR
Davey Johnson	ATL	1973	43
Darrell Evans	ATL	1973	41
Hank Aaron	ATL	1973	40
Total			124
Johnny Mize	NY	1947	51
Willard Marshall	NY	1947	36
Walker Cooper	NY	1947	35
Total			122
Johnny Bench	CIN	1970	45
Tony Perez	CIN	1970	40
Lee May	CIN	1970	34
Total			119
Willie McCovey	SF	1963	44
Willie Mays	SF	1963	38
Orlando Cepeda	SF	1963	34
Total			116

Best Home Run Trios, Season, NL (*cont.*)

Player	Team	Year	HR
Duke Snider	BKN	1953	42
Roy Campanella	BKN	1953	41
Gil Hodges	BKN	1953	31
Total			114
Ted Kluszewski	CIN	1955	47
Wally Post	CIN	1955	40
Gus Bell	CIN	1955	27
Total			114
Willie Mays	SF	1965	52
Willie McCovey	SF	1965	39
Jim Ray Hart	SF	1965	23
Total			114
Hank Aaron	ATL	1966	44
Joe Torre	ATL	1966	36
Felipe Alou	ATL	1966	31
Total			111
Eddie Mathews	MIL	1959	46
Hank Aaron	MIL	1959	39
Joe Adcock	MIL	1959	25
Total			110
Willie Mays	SF	1962	49
Orlando Cepeda	SF	1962	35
Felipe Alou	SF	1962	25
Total			109
Willie Mays	SF	1964	47
Orlando Cepeda	SF	1964	31
Jim Ray Hart	SF	1964	31
Total			109
George Foster	CIN	1977	52
Johnny Bench	CIN	1977	34
Joe Morgan	CIN	1977	22
Total			108
Willie Mays	SF	1966	37
Willie McCovey	SF	1966	36
Jim Ray Hart	SF	1966	33
Total			106
Hank Aaron	MIL	1960	40
Eddie Mathews	MIL	1960	39
Joe Adcock	MIL	1960	25
Total			104

Best Home Run Trios, Season, NL (*cont.*)

Player	Team	Year	HR
Orlando Cepeda	SF	1961	46
Willie Mays	SF	1961	40
Willie McCovey	SF	1961	18
Total			104
Darryl Strawberry	NY	1987	39
Howard Johnson	NY	1987	36
Kevin McReynolds	NY	1987	29
Total			104
Hank Aaron	MIL	1962	45
Joe Adcock	MIL	1962	29
Eddie Mathews	MIL	1962	29
Total			103
Andre Dawson	CHI	1987	49
Leon Durham	CHI	1987	27
Keith Moreland	CHI	1987	27
Total			103
Joe Adcock	MIL	1961	35
Eddie Mathews	MIL	1961	32
Hank Aaron	MIL	1961	34
Total			101
Lee May	CIN	1969	38
Tony Perez	CIN	1969	37
Johnny Bench	CIN	1969	26
Total			101
Billy Williams	CHI	1970	42
Jim Hickman	CHI	1970	32
Ron Santo	CHI	1970	26
Total			100

Best Home Run Duos, Season, AL (25 or more each)

Player	Team	Year	HR
Roger Maris	NY	1961	61
Mickey Mantle	NY	1961	54
Total			115
Babe Ruth	NY	1927	60
Lou Gehrig	NY	1927	47
Total			107
Jimmie Foxx	PHI	1932	58
Al Simmons	PHI	1932	35
Total			93

Best Home Run Duos, Season, AL (25 or more each) (cont.)

Player	Team	Year	HR
Babe Ruth	NY	1931	46
Lou Gehrig	NY	1931	46
Total			92
Hank Greenberg	DET	1938	58
Rudy York	DET	1938	33
Total			91
Babe Ruth	NY	1930	49
Lou Gehrig	NY	1930	41
Total			90
Rocky Colavito	DET	1961	45
Norm Cash	DET	1961	41
Total			86
Joe DiMaggio	NY	1937	46
Lou Gehrig	NY	1937	37
Total			83
Frank Robinson	BAL	1966	49
Boog Powell	BAL	1966	34
Total			83
Ted Williams	BOS	1949	43
Vern Stephens	BOS	1949	39
Total			82
Mickey Mantle	NY	1956	52
Yogi Berra	NY	1956	30
Total			82
Babe Ruth	NY	1928	54
Lou Gehrig	NY	1928	27
Total			81
Babe Ruth	NY	1929	46
Lou Gehrig	NY	1929	35
Total			81
Harmon Killebrew	MIN	1964	49
Tony Oliva	MIN	1964	32
Total			81
Harmon Killebrew	MIN	1963	45
Bob Allison	MIN	1963	35
Total			80
Carl Yastrzemski	BOS	1969	40
Rico Petrocelli	BOS	1969	40
Total			80

Best Home Run Duos, Season, AL (25 or more each) (*cont.*)

Player	Team	Year	HR
Mark McGwire	OAK	1987	49
Jose Canseco	OAK	1987	31
Total			80
Mickey Mantle	NY	1960	40
Roger Maris	NY	1960	39
Total			79
Ben Oglivie	MIL	1980	41
Gorman Thomas	MIL	1980	38
Total			79
Jimmie Foxx	PHI	1934	44
Bob Johnson	PHI	1934	34
Total			78
Lou Gehrig	NY	1936	49
Joe DiMaggio	NY	1936	29
Total			78
Frank Howard	WAS	1969	48
Mike Epstein	WAS	1969	30
Total			78
Reggie Jackson	OAK	1969	47
Sal Bando	OAK	1969	31
Total			78
Fred Lynn	BOS	1979	39
Jim Rice	BOS	1979	39
Total			78
Harmon Killebrew	MIN	1962	48
Bob Allison	MIN	1962	29
Total			77
Norm Cash	DET	1962	39
Rocky Colavito	DET	1962	37
Total			76
Carl Yastrzemski	BOS	1970	40
Tony Conigliaro	BOS	1970	36
Total			76
Mark McGwire	OAK	1990	39
Jose Canseco	OAK	1990	37
Total			76
Babe Ruth	NY	1932	41
Lou Gehrig	NY	1932	34
Total			75

Best Home Run Duos, Season, AL (25 or more each) (*cont.*)

Player	Team	Year	HR
Hank Greenberg	DET	1937	40
Rudy York	DET	1937	35
Total			75
Harmon Killebrew	MIN	1961	46
Bob Allison	MIN	1961	29
Total			75
Jim Rice	BOS	1983	39
Tony Armas	BOS	1983	36
Total			75
Tony Armas	BOS	1984	43
Dwight Evans	BOS	1984	32
Total			75
George Bell	TOR	1987	47
Jesse Barfield	TOR	1987	28
Total			75
Cecil Fielder	DET	1991	44
Mickey Tettleton	DET	1991	31
Total			75
Hank Greenberg	DET	1940	41
Rudy York	DET	1940	33
Total			74
Gorman Thomas	MIL	1980	45
Ben Oglivie	MIL	1980	29
Total			74
Jose Canseco	OAK	1988	42
Mark McGwire	OAK	1988	32
Total			74
Jimmie Foxx	PHI	1930	37
Al Simmons	PHI	1930	36
Total			73
Gorman Thomas	MIL	1982	39
Ben Oglivie	MIL	1982	34
Total			73
Al Rosen	CLE	1953	43
Larry Doby	CLE	1953	29
Total			72
Jim Rice	BOS	1977	39
George Scott	BOS	1977	33
Total			72

Best Home Run Duos, Season, AL (25 or more each) *(cont.)*

Player	Team	Year	HR
Rocky Colavito	CLE	1959	42
Woodie Held	CLE	1959	29
Total			71
Jesse Barfield	TOR	1986	40
George Bell	TOR	1986	31
Total			71
Hal Trosky	CLE	1936	42
Earl Averill	CLE	1936	28
Total			70
Jim Lemon	WAS	1960	38
Harmon Killebrew	WAS	1960	31
Total			69
Boog Powell	BAL	1970	37
Frank Robinson	BAL	1970	32
Total			69
Graig Nettles	NY	1977	37
Reggie Jackson	NY	1977	32
Total			69
Reggie Jackson	CAL	1982	39
Doug DeCinces	CAL	1982	30
Total			69
Darrell Evans	DET	1985	40
Kirk Gibson	DET	1985	29
Total			69
Jose Canseco	OAK	1991	44
Dave Henderson	OAK	1991	25
Total			69
Juan Gonzalez	TEX	1992	43
Dean Palmer	TEX	1992	26
Total			69
Norm Cash	DET	1962	39
Al Kaline	DET	1962	29
Total			68
Dave Kingman	OAK	1984	35
Dwayne Murphy	OAK	1984	33
Total			68
Dave Kingman	OAK	1986	35
Jose Canseco	OAK	1986	33
Total			68

Best Home Run Duos, Season, AL (25 or more each) (*cont.*)

Player	Team	Year	HR
Al Simmons	PHI	1929	34
Jimmie Foxx	PHI	1929	33
Total			67
Boog Powell	BAL	1964	39
Brooks Robinson	BAL	1964	28
Total			67
Ron Kittle	CHI	1983	35
Greg Luzinski	CHI	1983	32
Total			67
Cecil Fielder	DET	1992	35
Rob Deer/	DET	1992	32
Mickey Tettleton			
Total			67
Babe Ruth	NY	1933	34
Lou Gehrig	NY	1933	32
Total			66
Hal Trosky	CLE	1934	35
Earl Averill	CLE	1934	31
Total			66
Jimmie Foxx	BOS	1939	35
Ted Williams	BOS	1939	31
Total			66
Larry Hisle	MIL	1978	34
Gorman Thomas	MIL	1978	32
Total			66
Don Baylor	CAL	1979	36
Bobby Grich	CAL	1979	30
Total			66
Steve Balboni	KC	1985	36
George Brett	KC	1985	30
Total			66
Darrell Evans	DET	1987	34
Matt Nokes	DET	1987	32
Total			66
Kent Hrbek	MIN	1987	34
Tom Brunansky	MIN	1987	32
Total			66
Fred McGriff	TOR	1990	35
Kelly Gruber	TOR	1990	31
Total			66

Best Home Run Duos, Season, AL (25 or more each) (*cont.*)

Player	Team	Year	HR
Al Rosen	CLE	1950	37
Luke Easter	CLE	1950	28
Total			65
Roy Sievers	WAS	1958	39
Jim Lemon	WAS	1958	26
Total			65
Gary Gaetti	MIN	1986	34
Kirby Puckett	MIN	1986	31
Total			65
Cory Snyder	CLE	1987	33
Brook Jacoby	CLE	1987	32
Total			65
Jimmie Foxx	PHI	1935	36
Bob Johnson	PHI	1935	28
Total			64
Charlie Keller	NY	1941	33
Tommy Henrich	NY	1941	31
Total			64
Joe DiMaggio	NY	1948	39
Tommy Henrich	NY	1948	25
Total			64
Walt Dropo	BOS	1950	34
Vern Stephens	BOS	1950	30
Total			64
Harmon Killebrew	MIN	1966	39
Tony Oliva	MIN	1966	25
Total			64
Mark McGuire	OAK	1992	42
Jose Canseco	OAK	1992	22
Total			64
Joe Gordon	CLE	1948	32
Ken Keltner	CLE	1948	31
Total			63
Larry Doby	CLE	1952	32
Luke Easter	CLE	1952	31
Total			63
Roger Maris	NY	1962	33
Mickey Mantle	NY	1962	30
Total			63

Best Home Run Duos, Season, AL (25 or more each) (cont.)

Player	Team	Year	HR
Leon Wagner	LA	1962	37
Lee Thomas	LA	1962	26
Total			63
Mickey Mantle	NY	1964	35
Joe Pepitone	NY	1964	28
Total			63
Dick Stuart	BOS	1964	33
Felix Mantilla	BOS	1964	30
Total			63
Carlton Fisk	CHI	1985	37
Ron Kittle	CHI	1985	26
Total			63
Wally Joyner	CAL	1987	34
Brian Downing	CAL	1987	29
Total			63
Rocky Colavito	KC	1964	34
Jim Gentile	KC	1964	28
Total			62
Bobby Bonds	CAL	1977	37
Don Baylor	CAL	1977	25
Total			62
Mike Pagliarulo	NY	1987	32
Don Mattingly	NY	1987	30
Total			62
Larry Parrish	TEX	1987	32
Ruben Sierra	TEX	1987	30
Total			62
Joe DiMaggio	NY	1938	32
Lou Gehrig	NY	1938	29
Total			61
Joe DiMaggio	NY	1940	31
Joe Gordon	NY	1940	30
Total			61
Jackie Jensen	BOS	1958	35
Ted Williams	BOS	1958	26
Total			61
Norm Cash	DET	1966	32
Al Kaline	DET	1966	29
Total			61

Best Home Run Duos, Season, AL (25 or more each) (*cont.*)

Player	Team	Year	HR
Willie Horton	DET	1968	36
Norm Cash/ Bill Freehan	DET	1968	25
Total			61
Ron Kittle	CHI	1984	32
Harold Baines	CHI	1984	29
Total			61
Don Mattingly	NY	1985	35
Dave Winfield	NY	1985	26
Total			61
Larry Sheets	BAL	1987	31
Eddie Murray	BAL	1987	30
Total			61

Best Home Run Duos, Season, NL (25 or more each)

Player	Team	Year	HR
Hack Wilson	CHI	1930	56
Gabby Hartnett	CHI	1930	37
Total			93
Willie Mays	SF	1965	52
Willie McCovey	SF	1965	39
Total			91
Johnny Mize	NY	1947	51
Willard Marshall	NY	1947	36
Total			87
Ted Kluszewski	CIN	1955	47
Wally Post	CIN	1955	40
Total			87
Orlando Cepeda	SF	1961	46
Willie Mays	SF	1961	40
Total			86
Eddie Mathews	MIL	1959	46
Hank Aaron	MIL	1959	39
Total			85
Willie Mays	SF	1962	49
Orlando Cepeda	SF	1962	35
Total			84
Davey Johnson	ATL	1973	43
Darrell Evans	ATL	1973	41
Total			84

Best Home Run Duos, Season, NL (25 or more each) (*cont.*)

Player	Team	Year	HR
George Foster	CIN	1977	52
Johnny Bench	CIN	1977	31
Total			83
Gil Hodges	BKN	1954	42
Duke Snider	BKN	1954	40
Total			82
Willie McCovey	SF	1963	44
Willie Mays	SF	1963	38
Total			82
Hank Aaron	ATL	1971	47
Earl Williams	ATL	1971	33
Total			80
Hank Aaron	ATL	1966	44
Joe Torre	ATL	1966	36
Total			80
Hank Aaron	MIL	1960	40
Eddie Mathews	MIL	1960	39
Total			79
Hack Wilson	CHI	1929	39
Rogers Hornsby	CHI	1929	39
Total			78
Willie Mays	SF	1964	47
Orlando Cepeda/ Jim Ray Hart	SF	1964	31
Total			78
Willie McCovey	SF	1969	45
Bobby Bonds	SF	1969	32
Total			77
Greg Luzinski	PHI	1977	39
Mike Schmidt	PHI	1977	38
Total			77
Ralph Kiner	PIT	1947	51
Hank Greenberg	PIT	1947	25
Total			76
Ted Kluszewski	CIN	1954	49
Jim Greengrass	CIN	1954	27
Total			76
Hank Aaron	MIL	1957	44
Eddie Mathews	MIL	1957	32
Total			76

Best Home Run Duos, Season, NL (25 or more each) (*cont.*)

Player	Team	Year	HR
Andre Dawson	CHI	1987	49
Leon Durham/ Keith Moreland	CHI	1987	27
Total			76
Chuck Klein	PHI	1929	43
Lefty O'Doul	PHI	1929	32
Total			75
Duke Snider	BKN	1956	43
Gil Hodges	BKN	1956	32
Total			75
Joe Adcock	MIL	1956	38
Eddie Mathews	MIL	1956	37
Total			75
Lee May	CIN	1969	38
Tony Perez	CIN	1969	37
Total			75
Darryl Strawberry	NY	1987	39
Howard Johnson	NY	1987	36
Total			75
Duke Snider	BKN	1954	42
Roy Campanella	BKN	1954	32
Total			74
Hank Aaron	MIL	1962	45
Eddie Mathews/ Joe Adcock	MIL	1962	29
Total			74
Billy Williams	CHI	1970	42
Jim Hickman	CHI	1970	32
Total			74
Willie Stargell	PIT	1971	48
Bob Robertson	PIT	1971	26
Total			74
Gil Hodges	BKN	1951	40
Roy Campanella	BKN	1951	33
Total			73
Ernie Banks	CHI	1958	47
Walt Moryn	CHI	1958	26
Total			73

Best Home Run Duos, Season, NL (25 or more each) (*cont.*)

Player	Team	Year	HR
Willie Mays	SF	1966	37
Willie McCovey	SF	1966	36
Total			73
Hank Aaron	ATL	1970	38
Orlando Cepeda	ATL	1970	34
Total			72
Mike Schmidt	PHI	1975	38
Greg Luzinski	PHI	1975	34
Total			72
Wally Post	CIN	1956	36
Ted Kluszewski	CIN	1956	35
Total			71
Dale Murphy	ATL	1987	44
Ozzie Virgil	ATL	1987	27
Total			71
Johnny Mize	NY	1948	40
Sid Gordon	NY	1948	30
Total			70
Ted Kluszewski	CIN	1953	40
Gus Bell	CIN	1953	30
Total			70
Joe Adcock	MIL	1961	35
Hank Aaron	MIL	1961	34
Total			69
Andy Pafko	CHI	1950	36
Hank Sauer	CHI	1950	32
Total			68
Eddie Mathews	MIL	1955	41
Hank Aaron	MIL	1955	27
Total			68
Bobby Bonds	SF	1973	39
Willie McCovey	SF	1973	29
Total			68
Bob Horner	ATL	1980	35
Dale Murphy	ATL	1980	33
Total			68
Dale Murphy	ATL	1982	36
Bob Horner	ATL	1982	32
Total			68

Best Home Run Duos, Season, NL (25 or more each) (cont.)

Player	Team	Year	HR
Kevin Mitchell	SF	1990	35
Matt Williams	SF	1990	33
Total			68
Fred McGriff	SD	1992	35
Gary Sheffield	SD	1992	33
Total			68
Willie Mays	NY	1954	41
Hank Thompson	NY	1954	26
Total			67
Duke Snider	BKN	1957	40
Gil Hodges	BKN	1957	27
Total			67
Frank Robinson	CIN	1962	39
Gordy Coleman	CIN	1962	28
Total			67
Billy Williams	CHI	1965	34
Ron Santo	CHI	1965	33
Total			67
Willie McCovey	SF	1970	39
Bobby Bonds	SF	1970	28
Total			67
Nate Colbert	SD	1970	38
Clarence Gaston	SD	1970	29
Total			67
Ryne Sandberg	CHI	1990	40
Andre Dawson	CHI	1990	27
Total			67
Mel Ott	NY	1932	38
Bill Terry	NY	1932	28
Total			66
Lee May	CIN	1971	39
Johnny Bench	CIN	1971	27
Total			66
Darryl Strawberry	NY	1988	39
Kevin McReynolds	NY	1988	27
Total			66
Frank Robinson	CIN	1965	33
Deron Johnson	CIN	1965	32
Total			65

Best Home Run Duos, Season, NL (25 or more each) (*cont.*)

Player	Team	Year	HR
Hank Aaron	ATL	1967	39
Clete Boyer	ATL	1967	26
Total			65
Steve Garvey	LA	1977	33
Reggie Smith	LA	1977	32
Total			65
Howard Johnson	NY	1989	36
Darryl Strawberry	NY	1989	29
Total			65
Barry Bonds	PIT	1990	33
Bobby Bonilla	PIT	1990	32
Total			65
Hank Aaron	MIL	1965	32
Eddie Mathews	MIL	1965	32
Total			64
Deron Johnson	PHI	1971	34
Willie Montanez	PHI	1971	30
Total			64
Gil Hodges	BKN	1950	32
Roy Campanella/ Duke Snider	BKN	1950	31
Total			63
Frank Robinson	CIN	1961	37
Gene Freese	CIN	1961	26
Total			63
Billy Williams	CHI	1964	33
Ron Santo	CHI	1964	30
Total			63
Mike Schmidt	PHI	1987	35
Juan Samuel	PHI	1987	28
Total			63
Eric Davis	CIN	1987	37
Kal Daniels	CIN	1987	26
Total			63
Matt Williams	SF	1991	34
Will Clark	SF	1991	29
Total			63
Willie Stargell	PIT	1966	33
Roberto Clemente	PIT	1966	29
Total			62

Best Home Run Duos, Season, NL (25 or more each) (*cont.*)

Player	Team	Year	HR
Ernie Banks	CHI	1968	32
Billy Williams	CHI	1968	30
Total			62
Hank Aaron	ATL	1972	34
Earl Williams	ATL	1972	28
Total			62
Eddie Mathews	MIL	1958	31
Hank Aaron	MIL	1958	30
Total			61
Gary Carter	NY	1985	32
Darryl Strawberry	NY	1985	29
Total			61
Pedro Guerrero	LA	1985	33
Mike Marshall	LA	1985	28
Total			61

Home Run Duos, Career, AL

Player	Team	First	Last	HR
Babe Ruth	NY	1925	1934	424
Lou Gehrig	NY	1925	1934	348
Total				772
Jim Rice	BOS	1974	1989	382
Dwight Evans	BOS	1974	1989	355
Total				737
Harmon Killebrew	WAS	1958	1970	476
Bob Allison	MIN	1958	1970	256
Total				732
Mickey Mantle	NY	1951	1963	419
Yogi Berra	NY	1951	1963	283
Total				702
Norm Cash	DET	1960	1974	373
Al Kaline	DET	1960	1974	274
Total				647
Ted Williams	BOS	1939	1951	323
Bobby Doerr	BOS	1939	1951	216
Total				539
Boog Powell	BAL	1961	1974	303
Brooks Robinson	BAL	1961	1974	234
Total				537

Home Run Duos, Career, AL (cont.)

Player	Team	First	Last	HR
Carl Yastrzemski	BOS	1963	1976	308
Rico Petrocelli	BOS	1963	1976	210
Total				518
Hank Greenberg	DET	1934	1945	250
Rudy York	DET	1934	1945	239
Total				489
Jose Canseco	OAK	1986	1992	231
Mark McGwire	OAK	1986	1992	220
Total				451
George Brett	KC	1973	1990	281
Frank White	KC	1973	1990	160
Total				441
Kent Hrbek	MIN	1981	1990	223
Gary Gaetti	MIN	1981	1990	201
Total				424
Reggie Jackson	KC	1967	1975	254
Sal Bando	OAK	1967	1975	165
Total				419

Home Run Duos, Career, NL

Player	Team	First	Last	HR
Hank Aaron	MIL	1954	1966	442
Eddie Mathews	ATL	1954	1966	421
Total				863
Willie Mays	SF	1959	1971	430
Willie McCovey	SF	1959	1971	370
Total				800
Duke Snider	BKN	1947	1961	384
Gil Hodges	LA	1947	1961	361
Total				745
Billy Williams	CHI	1960	1973	376
Ron Santo	CHI	1960	1973	337
Total				713
Johnny Bench	CIN	1971	1981	277
George Foster	CIN	1971	1981	244
Total				521
Mike Schmidt	PHI	1972	1980	283
Greg Luzinski	PHI	1972	1980	220
Total				503

Home Run Duos, Career, NL (*cont.*)

Player	Team	First	Last	HR
Dale Murphy	ATL	1978	1986	264
Bob Horner	ATL	1978	1986	215
Total				479
Willie Stargell	PIT	1962	1972	277
Roberto Clemente	PIT	1962	1972	175
Total				452
Ron Cey	LA	1971	1982	228
Steve Garvey	LA	1971	1982	210
Total				438
Mel Ott	NY	1926	1936	275
Bill Terry	NY	1926	1936	138
Total				413
Frank Robinson	CIN	1958	1965	257
Vada Pinson	CIN	1958	1965	147
Total				404
Ken Boyer	STL	1955	1963	218
Stan Musial	STL	1955	1963	183
Total				401

Most Home Runs by Team, Season, AL

Team	Year	HR
NY	1961	240
MIN	1963	225
DET	1987	225
MIN	1964	221
MIL	1982	216
TOR	1987	215
BAL	1985	214
BOS	1977	213
DET	1962	209
DET	1991	209
DET	1985	205
BOS	1970	203
MIL	1980	203

Most Home Runs by Team, Season, NL

Team	Year	HR
NY	1947	221
CIN	1956	221
CHI	1987	209
BKN	1953	208
ATL	1966	207
ATL	1973	206
SF	1987	205
SF	1962	204
BKN	1955	201

Most 100-RBI Hitters, AL

Player	Team	Year	RBI
Lou Gehrig	NY	1936	152
Joe DiMaggio	NY	1936	125
Tony Lazzeri	NY	1936	109
George Selkirk	NY	1936	107
Bill Dickey	NY	1936	107

Most 100-RBI Hitters, AL (cont.)

Player	Team	Year	RBI
Ken Williams	STL	1922	155
Marty McManus	STL	1922	109
George Sisler	STL	1922	105
Baby Doll Jacobson	STL	1922	102
Lou Gehrig	NY	1927	175
Babe Ruth	NY	1927	164
Bob Meusel	NY	1927	103
Tony Lazzeri	NY	1927	102
Lou Gehrig	NY	1931	184
Babe Ruth	NY	1931	163
Ben Chapman	NY	1931	122
Lyn Lary	NY	1931	107
Lou Gehrig	NY	1932	151
Babe Ruth	NY	1932	137
Tony Lazzeri	NY	1932	113
Ben Chapman	NY	1932	107
Hank Greenberg	DET	1934	139
Charlie Gehringer	DET	1934	127
Goose Goslin	DET	1934	100
Billy Rogell	DET	1934	100
Goose Goslin	DET	1936	125
Charlie Gehringer	DET	1936	116
Al Simmons	DET	1936	112
Marv Owen	DET	1936	105
Joe DiMaggio	NY	1939	126
Joe Gordon	NY	1939	111
Bill Dickey	NY	1939	105
George Selkirk	NY	1939	101
Jimmie Foxx	BOS	1940	119
Ted Williams	BOS	1940	113
Joe Cronin	BOS	1940	111
Bobby Doerr	BOS	1940	105
Jim Rice	BOS	1977	114
Butch Hobson	BOS	1977	112
Carlton Fisk	BOS	1977	102
Carl Yastrzemski	BOS	1977	102
Cecil Cooper	MIL	1982	121
Robin Yount	MIL	1982	112
Gorman Thomas	MIL	1982	110
Ben Oglivie	MIL	1982	102

Most 100-RBI Hitters, NL

Player	Team	Year	RBI
Glenn Wright	PIT	1925	121
Clyde Barnhart	PIT	1925	114
Pie Traynor	PIT	1925	106
Kiki Cuyler	PIT	1925	102
Hack Wilson	CHI	1929	159
Rogers Hornsby	CHI	1929	149
Riggs Stephenson	CHI	1929	110
Kiki Cuyler	CHI	1929	102
Chuck Klein	PHI	1929	145
Don Hurst	PHI	1929	125
Lefty O'Doul	PHI	1929	122
Pinky Whitney	PHI	1929	115

Most Runs in One Inning, Team, AL

Team	Date	R	Inn.	Opp.
BOS	Jun 18, 1953	17	7	DET
NY	Jul 6, 1920	14	5	WAS
BOS	Jul 4, 1948	14	7	PHI
CLE	Sep 21, 1950	14	1	PHI
CLE	Jul 7, 1923	13	6	BOS
PHI	Jun 15, 1925	13	8	CLE
DET	Jun 17, 1925	13	6	NY
CHI	Sep 26, 1943	13	4	WAS
NY	Jun 21, 1945	13	5	BOS
KC	Apr 21, 1956	13	2	CHI
CLE	Apr 10, 1977	13	8	BOS
CAL	Sep 14, 1978	13	9	TEX
MIL	Jul 8, 1990	13	5	CAL
PHI	Jul 8, 1902	12	6	BOS
CLE	Apr 14, 1925	12	8	STL
WAS	Jul 10, 1926	12	8	STL
PHI	May 22, 1929	12	5	BOS
NY	May 27, 1933	12	8	CHI
BOS	May 6, 1934	12	4	DET
BOS	Jul 25, 1936	12	5	DET
PHI	Aug 29, 1937	12	1	CHI
CLE	Jul 2, 1943	12	4	NY
BOS	Aug 4, 1945	12	4	WAS
NY	Sep 11, 1949	12	3	WAS
PHI	Sep 23, 1950	12	6	WAS
CHI	Jun 10, 1952	12	4	PHI
BOS	May 4, 1962	12	5	CHI
BOS	Aug 10, 1965	12	5	BAL
CAL	Apr 30, 1966	12	8	BOS

Most Runs in One Inning, Team, AL (*cont.*)

Team	Date	R	Inn.	Opp.
TEX	Jul 3, 1983	12	15	OAK
BOS	Aug 21, 1986	12	6	CLE

Most Runs in One Inning, Team, NL

Team	Date	R	Inn.	Opp.
CHI	Sep 6, 1883	18	7	DET
BOS	Jun 18, 1894	16	1	BAL
HAR	May 13, 1876	15	4	NY
BKN	May 21, 1952	15	1	CIN
CLE	Aug 7, 1889	14	3	WAS
CIN	Jun 18, 1893	14	1	LOU
BAL	Apr 24, 1894	14	9	BOS
CHI	Aug 25, 1922	14	4	PHI
CIN	Aug 3, 1989	14	1	HOU
PRO	Jun 22, 1882	13	3	DET
NY	Sep 8, 1883	13	3	PHI
NY	Jul 19, 1890	13	2	CLE
CHI	Aug 16, 1890	13	5	PIT
BOS	Jul 25, 1900	13	1	STL
NY	May 13, 1910	13	1	STL
BKN	Aug 8, 1954	13	8	CIN
SF	May 7, 1966	13	3	STL
ATL	Sep 20, 1972	13	2	HOU
PRO	May 15, 1878	12	8	BOS
NY	Jun 7, 1887	12	3	PHI
CHI	May 8, 1890	12	6	CIN
PIT	Apr 22, 1892	12	1	STL
PIT	Jun 6, 1894	12	3	BOS
CHI	Jul 17, 1895	12	4	PHI
CIN	Jun 16, 1897	12	2	BKN
BKN	Sep 21, 1897	12	1	BOS
PHI	Oct 2, 1897	12	2	NY
PHI	Jul 21, 1923	12	6	CHI
CHI	May 28, 1925	12	7	CIN
NY	Sep 3, 1926	12	5	BOS
STL	Sep 16, 1926	12	3	PHI
NY	Jun 1, 1930	12	3	BOS
CHI	Aug 21, 1935	12	6	PHI
CHI	May 5, 1938	12	8	PHI
CIN	May 4, 1942	12	4	NY
BKN	May 24, 1953	12	8	PHI
BKN	Aug 30, 1953	12	7	STL
SF	Aug 23, 1961	12	9	CIN
HOU	May 31, 1975	12	8	PHI
CIN	Apr 25, 1977	12	5	SD
MON	Sep 24, 1985	12	5	CHI

Most Runs in One Inning, Team, Other Leagues

Team	Date	R	Inn.	Opp.
PHI P	Jun 26, 1890	14	6	BUF
WAS AA	Jun 17, 1891	14	1	BAL
STL AA	May 12, 1887	12	5	BAL
STL AA	Jun 19, 1887	12	4	CIN
STL AA	Aug 25, 1889	12	3	BAL
NY P	May 31, 1890	12	8	PIT

Most Runs by Team, Game, AL

Team	Date	R	Opp.
BOS	Jun 8, 1950	29	STL
CHI	Apr 23, 1955	29	KC
CLE	Jul 7, 1923	27	BOS
CLE	Aug 12, 1948	26	STL
CLE	May 11, 1930	25	PHI
NY	May 24, 1936	25	PHI
PHI	May 18, 1912	24	DET
NY	Sep 28, 1923	24	BOS
CLE	Jul 29, 1928	24	NY
PHI	May 1, 1929	24	BOS
BOS	Sep 27, 1940	24	WAS
TOR	Jun 26, 1978	24	BAL
CAL	Aug 25, 1979	24	TOR
BOS	Aug 21, 1986	24	CLE
BOS	May 2, 1901	23	PHI
CLE	Sep 2, 1902	23	BAL
BOS	Aug 26, 1937	23	CHI
NY	Jun 28, 1939	23	PHI
BOS	Jun 18, 1953	23	DET
KC	Apr 6, 1974	23	MIN
PHI	Jul 8, 1902	22	BOS
CLE	Aug 7, 1923	22	WAS
NY	Jul 26, 1931	22	CHI
NY	May 2, 1939	22	DET
BOS	Jun 29, 1950	22	PHI
NY	Aug 12, 1953	22	WAS
CHI	May 31, 1970	22	BOS
MIL	Aug 28, 1992	22	TOR

Most Runs by Team, Game, NL since 1900

Team	Date	R	Opp.
STL	Jul 6, 1929	28	PHI
CIN	Jun 4, 1911	26	BOS
CHI	Aug 25, 1922	26	PHI
NY	Apr 30, 1944	26	BKN
PHI	Apr 11, 1985	26	NY
NY	Jun 9, 1901	25	CIN
BKN	Sep 23, 1901	25	CIN

Most Runs by Team, Game, NL since 1900 (*cont.*)

Team	Date	R	Opp.
CIN	May 13, 1902	24	PHI
PIT	Jun 22, 1925	24	STL
NY	Sep 2, 1925	24	PHI
CHI	Jul 3, 1945	24	BOS
PIT	Apr 27, 1912	23	CIN
PHI	Aug 25, 1922	23	CHI
STL	Sep 16, 1926	23	PHI
NY	Jul 11, 1931	23	PHI
CIN	Jun 8, 1940	23	BKN
BKN	Jul 10, 1943	23	PIT
CIN	Jul 6, 1949	23	CHI
CHI	Apr 17, 1954	23	STL
MIL	Sep 2, 1957	23	CHI
CIN	Apr 25, 1977	23	ATL
CHI	May 17, 1977	23	SD
PHI	May 17, 1979	23	CHI
NY	Aug 16, 1987	23	CHI
SF	Jun 8, 1990	23	ATL
NY	Jun 5, 1912	22	CIN
STL	Jul 27, 1918	22	BKN
NY	Jun 1, 1923	22	PHI
NY	Sep 10, 1924	22	BOS
BKN	Sep 6, 1930	22	PHI
BKN	Jul 29, 1936	22	STL
CHI	Aug 13, 1937	22	CIN
BKN	Sep 23, 1939	22	PHI
CIN	Jun 1, 1957	22	CHI
PIT	Sep 16, 1975	22	CHI
CHI	May 17, 1979	22	PHI
CHI	Jun 3, 1987	22	HOU

Most Runs by Team, Game, NL before 1900

Team	Date	R	Opp.
CHI	Jun 29, 1897	36	LOU
CHI	Jul 24, 1882	35	CLE
CHI	Jul 3, 1883	31	BUF
CHI	Jul 22, 1876	30	LOU
BOS	Jun 9, 1883	30	DET
CIN	Jun 18, 1893	30	LOU
BOS	Jun 20, 1883	29	PHI
NY	Jun 15, 1887	29	PHI
PHI	Aug 17, 1894	29	LOU
HAR	May 13, 1876	28	NY
PRO	Aug 21, 1883	28	PHI
BOS	Aug 27, 1887	28	PIT
CHI	Aug 25, 1891	28	BKN

Most Runs by Team, Game, NL before 1900 (*cont.*)

Team	Date	R	Opp.
BOS	Aug 21, 1894	28	CIN
BOS	Sep 3, 1896	28	STL

Most Runs by Team, Game, Other Leagues

Team	Date	R	Opp.
PHI P	Jun 26, 1890	30	BUF
STL AA	Apr 30, 1887	28	CLE
PHI AA	Apr 23, 1888	28	CLE
BKN P	Jul 12, 1890	28	BUF
CIN AA	Sep 11, 1883	27	PIT
LOU AA	Aug 12, 1886	27	BKN
LOU AA	May 26, 1887	27	BKN
BAL AA	Jun 30, 1887	27	NY

Most Stolen Bases by Team, Season, AL

Team	Year	SB
OAK	1976	341
NY	1910	288
WAS	1913	287
CHI	1901	280
DET	1909	280
DET	1911	276
WAS	1912	274
NY	1911	270
DET	1912	270
CHI	1902	265
PHI	1912	258
MIL	1992	256
NY	1914	251

Most Stolen Bases by Team, Season, NL

Team	Year	SB
BAL	1899	364
NY	1911	347
NY	1912	319
STL	1985	314

Most Stolen Bases by Team, Season, NL (*cont.*)

Team	Year	SB
CIN	1910	310
NY	1913	296
NY	1905	291
CIN	1911	289
NY	1906	288
NY	1904	283
CHI	1906	283
NY	1910	282
CIN	1909	280
BKN	1900	274
BKN	1903	273
BKN	1899	271
CHI	1908	270
CHI	1905	267
NY	1903	264
PIT	1907	264
CHI	1905	263
STL	1986	262
PIT	1977	260
CHI	1903	259
BAL	1898	250
NY	1908	250

Best Stolen Base Duos, Season, AL

Player	Team	Year	SB
Rickey Henderson	OAK	1982	130
Davey Lopes	OAK	1982	28
Total			158

Best Stolen Base Duos, Season, AL (cont.)

Player	Team	Year	SB
Rickey Henderson	OAK	1983	108
Mike Davis	OAK	1983	32
Total			140
Clyde Milan	WAS	1913	75
Danny Moeller	WAS	1913	62
Total			137
Ty Cobb	DET	1915	96
Donie Bush	DET	1915	35
Total			131
Ty Cobb	DET	1909	76
Donie Bush	DET	1909	53
Total			129
Billy North	OAK	1976	75
Bert Campaneris	OAK	1976	54
Total			129
Rickey Henderson	OAK	1980	100
Dwayne Murphy	OAK	1980	26
Total			126
Ty Cobb	DET	1911	83
Donie Bush	DET	1911	42
Total			125
Clyde Milan	WAS	1912	88
Danny Moeller	WAS	1912	30
Total			118
Ty Cobb	DET	1910	65
Donie Bush	DET	1910	49
Total			114
Willie Wilson	KC	1979	83
Amos Otis	KC	1979	30
Total			113
Fritz Maisel	NY	1914	74
Roger Peckinpaugh	NY	1914	38
Total			112
Rickey Henderson	NY	1988	93
Claudell Washington	NY	1988	15
Total			108

Best Stolen Base Duos, Season, AL (*cont.*)

Player	Team	Year	SB
Dave Collins	TOR	1984	60
Damaso Garcia	TOR	1984	46
Total			106
Rickey Henderson	NY	1985	80
Bobby Meacham	NY	1985	25
Total			105
Mickey Rivers	CAL	1975	70
Jerry Remy	CAL	1975	34
Total			104
Eddie Collins	PHI	1912	63
Frank Baker	PHI	1912	40
Total			103
Ray Chapman	CLE	1917	52
Braggo Roth	CLE	1917	51
Total			103
Eddie Collins	PHI	1910	81
Frank Baker	PHI	1910	21
Total			102
Ty Cobb	DET	1912	61
Sam Crawford	DET	1912	41
Total			102
Rickey Henderson	NY	1986	87
Willie Randolph	NY	1986	15
Total			102
Amos Otis	KC	1971	52
Freddie Patek	KC	1971	49
Total			101
Rudy Law	CHI	1983	77
Julio Cruz	CHI	1983	24
Total			101
Harold Reynolds	SEA	1987	60
Phil Bradley	SEA	1987	40
Total			100

Best Stolen Base Duos, Season, NL

Player	Team	Year	SB
Vince Coleman	STL	1985	110
Willie McGee	STL	1985	56
Total			166

Best Stolen Base Duos, Season, NL (*cont.*)

Player	Team	Year	SB
Ron LeFlore	MON	1980	97
Rodney Scott	MON	1980	63
Total			160
Vince Coleman	STL	1987	109
Ozzie Smith	STL	1987	43
Total			152
Lou Brock	STL	1974	118
Bake McBride	STL	1974	30
Total			148
Vince Coleman	STL	1986	107
Ozzie Smith	STL	1986	31
Total			138
Vince Coleman	STL	1988	81
Ozzie Smith	STL	1988	57
Total			138
Maury Wills	LA	1962	104
Willie Davis	LA	1962	32
Total			136
Marquis Grissom	MON	1991	76
Delino DeShields	MON	1991	56
Total			132
Omar Moreno	PIT	1980	96
Phil Garner	PIT	1980	32
Total			128
Marquis Grissom	MON	1992	78
Delino DeShields	MON	1992	46
Total			124
Frank Taveras	PIT	1977	70
Omar Moreno	PIT	1977	53
Total			123
Bob Bescher	CIN	1910	70
Dode Paskert	CIN	1910	51
Total			121
Juan Samuel	PHI	1984	72
Von Hayes	PHI	1984	48
Total			120
Maury Wills	LA	1965	94
Willie Davis	LA	1965	25
Total			119

Best Stolen Base Duos, Season, NL (*cont.*)

Player	Team	Year	SB
Bob Bescher	CIN	1911	81
Dick Egan	CIN	1911	37
Total			118
Gene Richards	SD	1980	61
Ozzie Smith	SD	1980	57
Total			118
Omar Moreno	PIT	1978	71
Frank Taveras	PIT	1978	46
Total			117
Tim Raines	MON	1982	78
Andre Dawson	MON	1982	39
Total			117
Tim Raines	MON	1983	90
Andre Dawson	MON	1983	25
Total			115
Jimmy Sheckard	BKN	1903	67
Sammy Strang	BKN	1903	46
Total			113
Josh Devore	NY	1911	61
Fred Snodgrass	NY	1911	51
Total			112
Art Devlin	NY	1905	59
Sam Mertes	NY	1905	52
Total			111
Vince Coleman	STL	1990	77
Ozzie Smith	STL	1990	32
Total			109
Frank Chance	CHI	1906	57
Johnny Evers	CHI	1906	49
Total			106
Tim Raines	MON	1986	70
Mitch Webster	MON	1986	36
Total			106
Otis Nixon	ATL	1991	72
Ron Gant	ATL	1991	34
Total			106
Cesar Cedeno	HOU	1977	61
Jose Cruz	HOU	1977	44
Total			105

Best Stolen Base Duos, Season, NL (*cont.*)

Player	Team	Year	SB
Honus Wagner	PIT	1907	61
Tommy Leach	PIT	1907	43
Total			104
Alan Wiggins	SD	1984	70
Tony Gwynn	SD	1984	33
Total			103
Bob Bescher	CIN	1912	67
Armando Marsans	CIN	1912	35
Total			102
Dave Collins	CIN	1980	79
Ken Griffey	CIN	1980	23
Total			102
Tim Raines	MON	1984	75
Miguel Dilone	MON	1984	27
Total			102
Tim Raines	MON	1981	71
Rodney Scott	MON	1981	30
Total			101
Ryne Sandberg	CHI	1985	54
Davey Lopes	CHI	1985	47
Total			101
Frank Chance	CHI	1903	67
Jimmy Slagle	CHI	1903	33
Total			100
Red Murray	NY	1910	57
Josh Devore	NY	1910	43
Total			100
Joe Morgan	CIN	1972	58
Bobby Tolan	CIN	1972	42
Total			100
Joe Morgan	CIN	1975	67
Dave Concepcion	CIN	1975	33
Total			100
Omar Moreno	PIT	1982	60
Lee Lacy	PIT	1982	40
Total			100

Most .300 Hitters, Season, AL (300 AB each)

Player	Team	Year	AB	BA
Al Simmons	PHI	1927	406	.392
Ty Cobb	PHI	1927	490	.357
Mickey Cochrane	PHI	1927	432	.338
Jimmy Dykes	PHI	1927	417	.324
Sammy Hale	PHI	1927	501	.313
Joe Boley	PHI	1927	370	.311
Walter French	PHI	1927	326	.304
Charlie Gehringer	DET	1934	601	.356
Hank Greenberg	DET	1934	593	.339
Mickey Cochrane	DET	1934	437	.320
Marv Owen	DET	1934	565	.317
Jo Jo White	DET	1934	384	.313
Goose Goslin	DET	1934	614	.305
Gee Walker	DET	1934	347	.300
Tris Speaker	CLE	1920	552	.388
Joe Evans	CLE	1920	489	.321
Charlie Jamieson	CLE	1920	370	.319
Elmer Smith	CLE	1920	456	.316
Larry Gardner	CLE	1920	597	.310
Ray Chapman	CLE	1920	435	.303
Harry Heilmann	DET	1921	602	.394
Ty Cobb	DET	1921	507	.389
Bobby Veach	DET	1921	612	.338
Lu Blue	DET	1921	585	.308
Johnny Bassler	DET	1921	388	.307
Bob Jones	DET	1921	554	.303
Ty Cobb	DET	1922	526	.401
Harry Heilmann	DET	1922	455	.356
Bobby Veach	DET	1922	618	.327
Johnny Bassler	DET	1922	370	.323
Lu Blue	DET	1922	584	.300
Topper Rigney	DET	1922	536	.300
Marty McManus	STL	1924	439	.333
Ken Williams	STL	1924	398	.324
Gene Robertson	STL	1924	439	.319
Baby Doll Jacobson	STL	1924	1024	.318
Hank Severeid	STL	1924	428	.308
George Sisler	STL	1924	636	.305
Al Simmons	PHI	1925	658	.384
Bill Lamar	PHI	1925	568	.356
Sammy Hale	PHI	1925	391	.345
Mickey Cochrane	PHI	1925	420	.331
Jimmy Dykes	PHI	1925	465	.323
Bing Miller	PHI	1925	474	.319

Most .300 Hitters, Season, AL (300 AB each) (cont.)

Player	Team	Year	AB	BA
Al Simmons	PHI	1928	464	.351
Bing Miller	PHI	1928	510	.329
Jimmie Foxx	PHI	1928	400	.328
Ty Cobb	PHI	1928	353	.323
Max Bishop	PHI	1928	472	.316
Sammy Hale	PHI	1928	510	.309
Goose Goslin	WAS	1928	456	.379
Sam Rice	WAS	1928	616	.328
Joe Judge	WAS	1928	542	.306
Bobby Reeves	WAS	1928	353	.303
Red Barnes	WAS	1928	417	.302
Sammy West	WAS	1928	378	.302
Al Simmons	PHI	1929	581	.365
Jimmie Foxx	PHI	1929	517	.354
Bing Miller	PHI	1929	556	.335
Mickey Cochrane	PHI	1929	514	.331
Jimmy Dykes	PHI	1929	401	.327
Mule Haas	PHI	1929	578	.313
Heinie Manush	WAS	1930	356	.362
Sam Rice	WAS	1930	593	.349
Joe Cronin	WAS	1930	587	.346
Sammy West	WAS	1930	411	.328
Joe Judge	WAS	1930	442	.326
Buddy Myer	WAS	1930	541	.303
Lou Gehrig	NY	1930	581	.379
Babe Ruth	NY	1930	518	.359
Earle Combs	NY	1930	532	.344
Bill Dickey	NY	1930	366	.339
Ben Chapman	NY	1930	513	.316
Tony Lazzeri	NY	1930	571	.303
Babe Ruth	NY	1931	534	.373
Lou Gehrig	NY	1931	619	.341
Bill Dickey	NY	1931	427	.327
Earle Combs	NY	1931	563	.318
Ben Chapman	NY	1931	600	.315
Joe Sewell	NY	1931	484	.302
Bill Dickey	NY	1936	423	.362
Lou Gehrig	NY	1936	579	.354
Joe DiMaggio	NY	1936	637	.323
Red Rolfe	NY	1936	568	.319
George Selkirk	NY	1936	493	.308
Jake Powell	NY	1936	324	.306

Most .300 Hitters, Season, NL (300 AB each)

Player	Team	Year	AB	BA
George Watkins	STL	1930	391	.373
Frankie Frisch	STL	1930	540	.346
Chick Hafey	STL	1930	446	.336
Jimmie Wilson	STL	1930	362	.318
Sparky Adams	STL	1930	570	.314
Jim Bottomley	STL	1930	487	.304
Charley Gelbert	STL	1930	513	.303
Taylor Douthit	STL	1930	664	.303
Kiki Cuyler	PIT	1925	617	.357
Max Carey	PIT	1925	542	.343
George Grantham	PIT	1925	359	.326
Clyde Barnhart	PIT	1925	539	.325
Pie Traynor	PIT	1925	591	.320
Earl Smith	PIT	1925	329	.313
Glenn Wright	PIT	1925	614	.308
Freddie Lindstrom	NY	1928	646	.358
Shanty Hogan	NY	1928	411	.333
Bill Terry	NY	1928	568	.326
Mel Ott	NY	1928	435	.322
Lefty O'Doul	NY	1928	354	.319
Andy Reese	NY	1928	406	.308
Jimmy Welsh	NY	1928	476	.307
Rogers Hornsby	STL	1921	592	.397
Austin McHenry	STL	1921	574	.350
Jack Fournier	STL	1921	574	.343
Jack Smith	STL	1921	411	.328
Verne Clemons	STL	1921	341	.320
Milt Stock	STL	1921	587	.307
Frank Snyder	NY	1922	318	.343
Ross Youngs	NY	1922	559	.331
Irish Meusel	NY	1922	617	.331
George Kelly	NY	1922	592	.328
Frankie Frisch	NY	1922	514	.327
Dave Bancroft	NY	1922	651	.321
Ross Youngs	NY	1924	526	.356
Frankie Frisch	NY	1924	603	.328
George Kelly	NY	1924	571	.328
Irish Meusel	NY	1924	549	.310
Travis Jackson	NY	1924	596	.302
Frank Snyder	NY	1924	354	.302
Edd Roush	CIN	1924	483	.348
Rube Bressler	CIN	1924	383	.347
Hughie Critz	CIN	1924	413	.322

Most .300 Hitters, Season, NL (300 AB each) (cont.)

Player	Team	Year	AB	BA
Babe Pinelli	CIN	1924	510	.306
Bubbles Hargrave	CIN	1924	312	.301
Curt Walker	CIN	1924	397	.300
Zack Wheat	BKN	1925	359	.359
Jack Fournier	BKN	1925	545	.350
Dick Cox	BKN	1925	434	.329
Milt Stock	BKN	1925	615	.328
Zack Taylor	BKN	1925	352	.310
Eddie Brown	BKN	1925	618	.306
Rogers Hornsby	NY	1927	568	.361
George Harper	NY	1927	483	.331
Bill Terry	NY	1927	580	.326
Travis Jackson	NY	1927	469	.318
Fred Lindstrom	NY	1927	562	.306
Edd Roush	NY	1927	570	.304
Pie Traynor	PIT	1929	540	.356
Lloyd Waner	PIT	1929	662	.353
Paul Waner	PIT	1929	596	.336
Adam Comorosky	PIT	1929	473	.321
George Grantham	PIT	1929	349	.307
Dick Bartell	PIT	1929	610	.302
Chick Hafey	STL	1929	517	.338
Taylor Douthit	STL	1929	613	.336
Frankie Frisch	STL	1929	560	.334
Ernie Orsatti	STL	1929	346	.332
Jimmie Wilson	STL	1929	394	.325
Jim Bottomley	STL	1929	560	.314
Lefty O'Doul	PHI	1929	638	.398
Chuck Klein	PHI	1929	616	.356
Pinky Whitney	PHI	1929	612	.327
Fresco Thompson	PHI	1929	623	.324
Don Hurst	PHI	1929	589	.304
Barney Friberg	PHI	1929	455	.301
Bill Terry	NY	1930	633	.401
Shanty Hogan	NY	1930	389	.389
Fred Lindstrom	NY	1930	609	.379
Mel Ott	NY	1930	521	.349
Travis Jackson	NY	1930	431	.339
Freddy Leach	NY	1930	544	.327
Chuck Klein	PHI	1930	648	.386
Lefty O'Doul	PHI	1930	528	.383
Pinky Whitney	PHI	1930	606	.342
Barney Friberg	PHI	1930	331	.341

Most .300 Hitters, Season, NL (300 AB each) (*cont.*)

Player	Team	Year	AB	BA
Don Hurst	PHI	1930	391	.327
Spud Davis	PHI	1930	329	.313
Bill Terry	NY	1931	611	.349
Chick Fullis	NY	1931	302	.328
Travis Jackson	NY	1931	555	.310
Freddy Leach	NY	1931	515	.309
Shanty Hogan	NY	1931	396	.301
Fred Lindstrom	NY	1931	303	.300
Chuck Klein	PHI	1932	650	.348
Don Hurst	PHI	1932	579	.339
Spud Davis	PHI	1932	402	.336
Kiddo Davis	PHI	1932	576	.309
Dick Bartell	PHI	1932	614	.308
Hal Lee	PHI	1932	595	.303

.300-Hitting Outfields, AL

Player	Team	Year	BA
Patsy Dougherty	BOS	1902	.342
Chick Stahl	BOS	1902	.323
Buck Freeman	BOS	1902	.309
Tris Speaker	BOS	1911	.327
Harry Hooper	BOS	1911	.311
Duffy Lewis	BOS	1911	.307
Ty Cobb	DET	1919	.384
Bobby Veach	DET	1919	.355
Ira Flagstead	DET	1919	.331
Tris Speaker	CLE	1920	.388
Charlie Jamieson	CLE	1920	.319
Elmer Smith	CLE	1920	.316
Baby Doll Jacobson	STL	1920	.355
Jack Tobin	STL	1920	.341
Ken Williams	STL	1920	.307
Baby Doll Jacobson	STL	1921	.352
Jack Tobin	STL	1921	.352
Ken Williams	STL	1921	.349
Harry Heilmann	DET	1921	.394
Ty Cobb	DET	1921	.389
Bobby Veach	DET	1921	.338
Ken Williams	STL	1922	.332
Jack Tobin	STL	1922	.331
Baby Doll Jacobson	STL	1922	.317

.300-Hitting Outfields, AL (*cont.*)

Player	Team	Year	BA
Ty Cobb	DET	1922	.401
Harry Heilmann	DET	1922	.356
Bobby Veach	DET	1922	.327
Babe Ruth	NY	1923	.393
Whitey Witt	NY	1923	.314
Bob Meusel	NY	1923	.313
Harry Heilmann	DET	1923	.403
Ty Cobb	DET	1923	.340
Heinie Manush	DET	1923	.334
Tris Speaker	CLE	1923	.380
Charlie Jamieson	CLE	1923	.345
Homer Summa	CLE	1923	.328
Sam Rice	WAS	1923	.316
Nemo Leibold	WAS	1923	.305
Goose Goslin	WAS	1923	.300
Ken Williams	STL	1923	.357
Jack Tobin	STL	1923	.317
Baby Doll Jacobson	STL	1923	.309
Bing Miller	PHI	1924	.342
Bill Lamar	PHI	1924	.330
Al Simmons	PHI	1924	.308
Bibb Falk	CHI	1924	.352
Harry Hooper	CHI	1924	.328
Johnny Mostil	CHI	1924	.325
Al Simmons	PHI	1925	.384
Bill Lamar	PHI	1925	.356
Bing Miller	PHI	1925	.319
Harry Rice	STL	1925	.359
Baby Doll Jacobson	STL	1925	.341
Ken Williams	STL	1925	.331
Harry Heilmann	DET	1925	.393
Ty Cobb	DET	1925	.378
Al Wingo	DET	1925	.370
Goose Goslin	WAS	1926	.354
Sam Rice	WAS	1926	.337
Earl McNeely	WAS	1926	.303
Bibb Falk	CHI	1926	.345
Johnny Mostil	CHI	1926	.328
Bill Barrett	CHI	1926	.307

.300-Hitting Outfields, AL (*cont.*)

Player	Team	Year	BA
Heinie Manush	DET	1926	.378
Harry Heilmann	DET	1926	.367
Bob Fothergill	DET	1926	.367
Babe Ruth	NY	1927	.356
Earl Combs	NY	1927	.356
Bob Meusel	NY	1927	.337
Al Simmons	PHI	1927	.392
Ty Cobb	PHI	1927	.357
Walter French	PHI	1927	.304
Al Simmons	PHI	1928	.351
Bing Miller	PHI	1928	.329
Ty Cobb	PHI	1928	.323
Goose Goslin	WAS	1928	.379
Sam Rice	WAS	1928	.328
Red Barnes	WAS	1928	.302
Harry Heilmann	DET	1928	.328
Bob Fothergill	DET	1928	.317
Harry Rice	DET	1928	.302
Al Simmons	PHI	1929	.365
Bing Miller	PHI	1929	.335
Mule Haas	PHI	1929	.313
Harry Heilmann	DET	1929	.344
Roy Johnson	DET	1929	.314
Harry Rice	DET	1929	.304
Heinie Manush	WAS	1930	.362
Sam Rice	WAS	1930	.349
Sammy West	WAS	1930	.328
Dick Porter	CLE	1930	.350
Earl Averill	CLE	1930	.339
Charlie Jamieson	CLE	1930	.301
Babe Ruth	NY	1931	.373
Earle Combs	NY	1931	.318
Ben Chapman	NY	1931	.315
Sammy West	WAS	1931	.333
Sam Rice	WAS	1931	.310
Heinie Manush	WAS	1931	.307
Earl Averill	CLE	1931	.333
Joe Vosmik	CLE	1931	.320
Dick Porter	CLE	1931	.312

.300-Hitting Outfields, AL (*cont.*)

Player	Team	Year	BA
Doc Cramer	PHI	1932	.336
Al Simmons	PHI	1932	.322
Mule Haas	PHI	1932	.305
Earl Averill	CLE	1932	.314
Joe Vosmik	CLE	1932	.312
Dick Porter	CLE	1932	.308
Gee Walker	DET	1936	.353
Al Simmons	DET	1936	.327
Goose Goslin	DET	1936	.315
Joe DiMaggio	NY	1936	.323
George Selkirk	NY	1936	.308
Jake Powell	NY	1936	.306
Beau Bell	STL	1937	.340
Sammy West	STL	1937	.328
Joe Vosmik	STL	1937	.325
Rip Radcliff	CHI	1937	.325
Dixie Walker	CHI	1937	.302
Mike Kreevich	CHI	1937	.302
George Case	WAS	1938	.305
Sammy West	WAS	1938	.302
Al Simmons	WAS	1938	.302
Ben Chapman	BOS	1938	.340
Joe Vosmik	BOS	1938	.324
Doc Cramer	BOS	1938	.301
Joe DiMaggio	NY	1939	.381
Charlie Keller	NY	1939	.334
George Selkirk	NY	1939	.306
Ted Williams	BOS	1940	.343
Doc Cramer	BOS	1940	.303
Dom DiMaggio	BOS	1940	.301
Dom DiMaggio	BOS	1950	.328
Al Zarilla	BOS	1950	.325
Ted Williams	BOS	1950	.317
Hoot Evers	DET	1950	.323
Vic Wertz	DET	1950	.308
Johnny Groth	DET	1950	.306
Dave Winfield	NY	1988	.322
Claudell Washington	NY	1988	.308
Rickey Henderson	NY	1988	.305

.300-Hitting Outfields, NL

Player	Team	Year	BA
Paul Hines	PRO	1878	.358
Dick Higham	PRO	1878	.320
Tom York	PRO	1878	.309
King Kelly	CHI	1884	.354
George Gore	CHI	1884	.318
Abner Dalrymple	CHI	1884	.309
Mike Tiernan	NY	1889	.335
Jim O'Rourke	NY	1889	.321
George Gore	NY	1889	.305
Billy Hamilton	PHI	1892	.330
Ed Delahanty	PHI	1892	.306
Sam Thompson	PHI	1892	.305
Elmer Smith	PIT	1893	.346
George Van Haltren	PIT	1893	.338
Patsy Donovan	PIT	1893	.317
Billy Hamilton	PHI	1893	.380
Sam Thompson	PHI	1893	.370
Ed Delahanty	PHI	1893	.368
Joe Kelley	BAL	1894	.393
Steve Brodie	BAL	1894	.366
Willie Keeler	BAL	1894	.361
Hugh Duffy	BOS	1894	.438
Tommy McCarthy	BOS	1894	.349
Jimmy Bannon	BOS	1894	.336
Sam Thompson	PHI	1894	.404
Ed Delahanty	PHI	1894	.400
Billy Hamilton	PHI	1894	.399
Mike Griffin	BKN	1894	.365
Oyster Burns	BKN	1894	.361
George Treadway	BKN	1894	.328
Elmer Smith	PIT	1894	.356
Jake Stenzel	PIT	1894	.354
Patsy Donovan	PIT	1894	.302
Jimmy Ryan	CHI	1894	.360
Walt Wilmot	CHI	1894	.330
Bill Lange	CHI	1894	.328
Bill Hassamaer	WAS	1894	.322
Charlie Abbey	WAS	1894	.314
Kip Selbach	WAS	1894	.306

.300-Hitting Outfields, NL (*cont.*)

Player	Team	Year	BA
Willie Keeler	BAL	1895	.391
Joe Kelley	BAL	1895	.365
Steve Brodie	BAL	1895	.348
Ed Delahanty	PHI	1895	.404
Sam Thompson	PHI	1895	.392
Billy Hamilton	PHI	1895	.389
Jake Stenzel	PIT	1895	.374
Patsy Donovan	PIT	1895	.308
Elmer Smith	PIT	1895	.302
Elmer Smith	PIT	1896	.362
Jake Stenzel	PIT	1896	.361
Patsy Donovan	PIT	1896	.319
Tom McCreery	LOU	1896	.351
Fred Clarke	LOU	1896	.325
Ollie Pickering	LOU	1896	.303
Chick Stahl	BOS	1897	.354
Billy Hamilton	BOS	1897	.343
Hugh Duffy	BOS	1897	.340
Willie Keeler	BAL	1897	.424
Joe Kelley	BAL	1897	.362
Jake Stenzel	BAL	1897	.353
Jesse Burkett	CLE	1897	.383
Ollie Pickering	CLE	1897	.352
Louis Sockalexis	CLE	1897	.338
John Anderson	BKN	1897	.325
Mike Griffin	BKN	1897	.316
Fielder Jones	BKN	1897	.314
Ed Delahanty	PHI	1898	.334
Duff Cooley	PHI	1898	.312
Elmer Flick	PHI	1989	.302
Charlie Dexter	LOU	1898	.314
Fred Clarke	LOU	1898	.307
Dummy Hoy	LOU	1898	.304
Ed Delahanty	PHI	1899	.410
Elmer Flick	PHI	1899	.342
Roy Thomas	PHI	1899	.325
Willie Keeler	BKN	1900	.368
Joe Kelley	BKN	1900	.319
Fielder Jones	BKN	1900	.309

.300-Hitting Outfields, NL (*cont.*)

Player	Team	Year	BA
Jesse Burkett	STL	1900	.363
Patsy Donovan	STL	1900	.316
Emmet Heidrick	STL	1900	.301
Ed Delahanty	PHI	1901	.354
Elmer Flick	PHI	1901	.336
Roy Thomas	PHI	1901	.309
Jesse Burkett	STL	1901	.382
Emmet Heidrick	STL	1901	.339
Patsy Donovan	STL	1901	.303
Ginger Beaumont	PIT	1901	.332
Fred Clarke	PIT	1901	.324
Lefty Davis	PIT	1901	.313
Patsy Donovan	STL	1902	.315
Homer Smoot	STL	1902	.311
George Barclay	STL	1902	.300
Jack Dalton	BKN	1914	.319
Zack Wheat	BKN	1914	.319
Casey Stengel	BKN	1914	.316
Edd Roush	CIN	1921	.352
Pat Duncan	CIN	1921	.308
Rube Bressler	CIN	1921	.307
Walt Cruise	BOS	1921	.346
Billy Southworth	BOS	1921	.308
Ray Powell	BOS	1921	.306
Turner Barber	CHI	1921	.314
George Maisel	CHI	1921	.310
Max Flack	CHI	1921	.301
Zack Wheat	BKN	1922	.335
Hy Myers	BKN	1922	.317
Tommy Griffith	BKN	1922	.316
Curt Walker	PHI	1922	.337
Cliff Lee	PHI	1922	.322
Cy Williams	PHI	1922	.308
Kiki Cuyler	PIT	1925	.357
Max Carey	PIT	1925	.343
Clyde Barnhart	PIT	1925	.325
Zack Wheat	BKN	1925	.359
Dick Cox	BKN	1925	.329
Eddie Brown	BKN	1925	.306

.300-Hitting Outfields, NL (*cont.*)

Player	Team	Year	BA
Billy Southworth	STL	1926	.317
Taylor Douthit	STL	1926	.308
Ray Blades	STL	1926	.305
Cuckoo Christensen	CIN	1926	.350
Edd Roush	CIN	1926	.323
Curt Walker	CIN	1926	.306
Cy Williams	PHI	1926	.345
Freddy Leach	PHI	1926	.329
Johnny Mokan	PHI	1926	.303
Paul Waner	PIT	1927	.380
Lloyd Waner	PIT	1927	.355
Clyde Barnhart	PIT	1927	.319
Riggs Stephenson	CHI	1927	.344
Hack Wilson	CHI	1927	.318
Earl Webb	CHI	1927	.301
Mel Ott	NY	1928	.322
Lefty O'Doul	NY	1928	.319
Jimmy Welsh	NY	1928	.307
Lloyd Waner	PIT	1928	.353
Paul Waner	PIT	1928	.336
Adam Comorosky	PIT	1928	.321
Riggs Stephenson	CHI	1929	.362
Kiki Cuyler	CHI	1929	.360
Hack Wilson	CHI	1929	.345
Chick Hafey	STL	1929	.338
Taylor Douthit	STL	1929	.336
Ernie Orsatti	STL	1929	.332
Lefty O'Doul	PHI	1929	.398
Chuck Klein	PHI	1929	.356
Denny Sothern	PHI	1929	.306
Babe Herman	BKN	1929	.381
Johnny Frederick	BKN	1929	.328
Rube Bressler	BKN	1929	.318
George Watkins	STL	1930	.373
Chuck Hafey	STL	1930	.336
Taylor Douthit	STL	1930	.303
Riggs Stephenson	CHI	1930	.367
Hack Wilson	CHI	1930	.356
Kiki Cuyler	CHI	1930	.355

.300-Hitting Outfields, NL (cont.)

Player	Team	Year	BA
Chuck Klein	PHI	1932	.348
Kiddo Davis	PHI	1932	.309
Hal Lee	PHI	1932	.303
Chuck Klein	PHI	1933	.368
Wes Schulmerich	PHI	1933	.334
Chick Fullis	PHI	1933	.309
Kiki Cuyler	CHI	1934	.338
Babe Herman	CHI	1934	.304
Chuck Klein	CHI	1934	.301
Woody Jensen	PIT	1935	.324
Paul Waner	PIT	1935	.321
Lloyd Waner	PIT	1935	.309
Ernie Koy	STL	1940	.310
Enos Slaughter	STL	1940	.306
Terry Moore	STL	1940	.304
Pete Reiser	BKN	1941	.343
Joe Medwick	BKN	1941	.318
Dixie Walker	BKN	1941	.311
Goody Rosen	BKN	1945	.325
Luis Olmo	BKN	1945	.313
Dixie Walker	BKN	1945	.300
Tommy Holmes	BOS	1948	.325
Jeff Heath	BOS	1948	.319
Mike McCormick	BOS	1948	.303
Bobby Thomson	NY	1949	.309
Willard Marshall	NY	1949	.307
Whitey Lockman	NY	1949	.301
Carl Furillo	BKN	1953	.344
Duke Snider	BKN	1953	.336
Jackie Robinson	BKN	1953	.329
Felipe Alou	SF	1962	.316
Willie Mays	SF	1962	.304
Harvey Kuenn	SF	1962	.304
Rico Carty	MIL	1964	.330
Hank Aaron	MIL	1964	.328
Lee Maye	MIL	1964	.304
Matty Alou	PIT	1966	.342
Roberto Clemente	PIT	1966	.317
Willie Stargell	PIT	1966	.315

.300-Hitting Outfields, NL (*cont.*)

Player	Team	Year	BA
Pete Rose	CIN	1969	.348
Alex Johnson	CIN	1969	.315
Bobby Tolan	CIN	1969	.305
Roberto Clemente	PIT	1969	.345
Matty Alou	PIT	1969	.331
Willie Stargell	PIT	1969	.307
Pete Rose	CIN	1970	.316
Bobby Tolan	CIN	1970	.316
Bernie Carbo	CIN	1970	.310
Vic Davalillo	PIT	1972	.318
Roberto Clemente	PIT	1972	.312
Al Oliver	PIT	1972	.312
Bake McBride	STL	1974	.309
Reggie Smith	STL	1974	.309
Lou Brock	STL	1974	.306
Al Oliver	PIT	1974	.321
Richie Zisk	PIT	1974	.313
Willie Stargell	PIT	1974	.301
Ken Griffey	CIN	1976	.336
Cesar Geronimo	CIN	1976	.307
George Foster	CIN	1976	.306
Garry Maddox	PHI	1976	.330
Jay Johnstone	PHI	1976	.318
Greg Luzinski	PHI	1976	.304
Dan Gladden	SF	1984	.351
Chili Davis	SF	1984	.315
Jeffrey Leonard	SF	1984	.302

.300-Hitting Outfields, Other Leagues

Player	Team	Year	BA
Jim O'Rourke	NY P	1890	.360
George Gore	NY P	1890	.318
Mike Slattery	NY P	1890	.307
Jimmy Ryan	CHI P	1890	.340
Hugh Duffy	CHI P	1890	.320
Tip O'Neill	CHI P	1890	.302
Benny Kauff	IND F	1914	.370
Vin Campbell	IND F	1914	.318
Al Scheer	IND F	1914	.306

.300-Hitting Outfields, Other Leagues (*cont.*)

Player	Team	Year	BA
Steve Evans	BKN F	1914	.348
Al Shaw	BKN F	1914	.326
George Anderson	BKN F	1914	.316

Teammates Who Finished 1–2 in Batting, AL

Player	Team	Year	AB	H	BA
Ty Cobb	DET	1907	605	212	.350
Sam Crawford	DET	1907	582	188	.323
Ty Cobb	DET	1908	581	188	.324
Sam Crawford	DET	1908	591	184	.311
Ty Cobb	DET	1919	497	191	.384
Bobby Veach	DET	1919	538	191	.355
Harry Heilmann	DET	1921	603	237	.394
Ty Cobb	DET	1921	507	197	.389
Ted Williams	BOS	1942	522	186	.356
Johnny Pesky	BOS	1942	620	205	.331
Ted Williams	BOS	1958	411	135	.328
Pete Runnels	BOS	1958	568	183	.322
Harvey Kuenn	DET	1959	561	198	.353
Al Kaline	DET	1959	511	167	.327
Norm Cash	DET	1961	535	193	.361
Al Kaline	DET	1961	586	190	.324
George Brett	KC	1976	645	215	.333
Hal McRae	KC	1976	527	175	.332
Rod Carew	MIN	1977	616	239	.388
Lyman Bostock	MIN	1977	592	199	.336
Don Mattingly	NY	1984	603	207	.343
Dave Winfield	NY	1984	567	193	.340

Teammates Who Finished 1–2 in Batting, NL

Player	Team	Year	AB	H	BA
George Gore	CHI	1880	322	116	.360
Cap Anson	CHI	1880	356	120	.337
King Kelly	CHI	1886	451	175	.388
Cap Anson	CHI	1886	504	187	.371
Cap Anson	CHI	1888	515	177	.344
Jimmy Ryan	CHI	1888	549	182	.332

Teammates Who Finished 1–2 in Batting, NL (cont.)

Player	Team	Year	AB	H	BA
Billy Hamilton	PHI	1893	355	135	.380
Sam Thompson	PHI	1893	600	222	.370
Honus Wagner	PIT	1903	512	182	.355
Fred Clarke	PIT	1903	427	150	.351
Rogers Hornsby	STL	1923	424	163	.384
Jim Bottomley	STL	1923	523	194	.371
Rogers Hornsby	STL	1925	504	203	.403
Jim Bottomley	STL	1925	619	227	.367
Bubbles Hargrave	CIN	1926	326	115	.353
Cuckoo Christensen	CIN	1926	329	115	.350
Chuck Klein	PHI	1933	606	223	.368
Spud Davis	PHI	1933	495	173	.349
Joe Medwick	STL	1937	633	237	.374
Johnny Mize	STL	1937	560	204	.364
Willie Mays	NY	1954	565	195	.345
Don Mueller	NY	1954	619	212	.342

Teammates Who Finished 1–2 in Batting, Other Leagues

Player	Team	Year	AB	H	BA
Fred Dunlap	STL U	1884	449	185	.412
Orator Shaffer	STL U	1884	467	168	.360
Guy Hecker	LOU AA	1886	343	117	.341
Pete Browning	LOU AA	1886	467	159	.340
Dan Brouthers	BOS AA	1891	486	170	.350
Hugh Duffy	BOS AA	1891	536	180	.336

Most 200-Hit Batters, AL

Player	Team	Year	AB	H	BA
Gee Walker	DET	1937	635	213	.335
Charlie Gehringer	DET	1937	564	209	.371
Pete Fox	DET	1937	628	208	.331
Hank Greenberg	DET	1937	594	200	.337
Eddie Collins	CHI	1920	601	222	.369
Joe Jackson	CHI	1920	570	218	.382
Buck Weaver	CHI	1920	630	210	.333
George Sisler	STL	1920	631	257	.407
Baby Doll Jacobson	STL	1920	609	216	.355
Jack Tobin	STL	1920	593	202	.341

Most 200-Hit Batters, AL (*cont.*)

Player	Team	Year	AB	H	BA
Jack Tobin	STL	1921	671	236	.352
George Sisler	STL	1921	582	216	.371
Baby Doll Jacobson	STL	1921	599	211	.352
Dale Alexander	DET	1929	626	215	.343
Charlie Gehringer	DET	1929	634	215	.339
Roy Johnson	DET	1929	640	201	.314
Robin Yount	MIL	1982	635	210	.331
Cecil Cooper	MIL	1982	654	205	.315
Paul Molitor	MIL	1982	666	201	.302
Rafael Palmeiro	TEX	1991	631	203	.322
Ruben Sierra	TEX	1991	661	203	.307
Julio Franco	TEX	1991	589	201	.341

Most 200-Hit Batters, NL

Player	Team	Year	AB	H	BA
Lefty O'Doul	PHI	1929	638	254	.398
Chuck Klein	PHI	1929	616	219	.356
Fresco Thompson	PHI	1929	623	202	.324
Pinky Whitney	PHI	1929	612	200	.327
Kiki Cuyler	CHI	1930	642	228	.355
Woody English	CHI	1930	638	214	.335
Hack Wilson	CHI	1930	585	208	.356
Chuck Klein	PHI	1930	648	250	.386
Pinky Whitney	PHI	1930	606	207	.342
Lefty O'Doul	PHI	1930	528	202	.383
Bill Terry	NY	1935	596	203	.341
Hank Leiber	NY	1935	613	203	.331
Joe Moore	NY	1935	681	201	.295
Dick Groat	STL	1963	631	201	.319
Curt Flood	STL	1963	662	200	.302
Bill White	STL	1963	658	200	.304

Most Hits by Team, Game, AL

Team	Date	H	Opp.
CLE	Jul 10, 1932	33	PHI
MIL	Aug 28, 1992	31	TOR
NY	Sep 28, 1923	30	BOS
PHI	May 1, 1929	29	BOS
CLE	Aug 12, 1948	29	STL
CHI	Apr 23, 1955	29	KC
OAK	Jul 1, 1979	29	TEX

Most Hits by Team, Game, AL (cont.)

Team	Date	H	Opp.
DET	Sep 29, 1928	28	NY
BOS	Jun 8, 1950	28	STL
NY	Aug 12, 1953	28	WAS
PHI	Jul 8, 1902	27	BOS
NY	Aug 31, 1921	27	WAS
CLE	Jul 29, 1928	27	NY
CLE	May 11, 1930	27	NY
WAS	May 16, 1933	27	CHI
CLE	Apr 29, 1950	27	PHI
BOS	Jun 18, 1953	27	DET
BOS	Apr 24, 1960	27	WAS
BOS	Aug 5, 1979	27	MIL
PHI	May 18, 1912	26	DET
CLE	Aug 7, 1923	26	WAS
NY	Jun 20, 1932	26	PHI
PHI	Jun 21, 1932	26	CHI
CHI	Sep 11, 1936	26	PHI
KC	Jul 27, 1956	26	NY
CAL	Aug 25, 1979	26	TOR
MIL	May 5, 1901	25	CHI
DET	Jul 27, 1908	25	PHI
STL	Sep 12, 1909	25	DET
PHI	Sep 23, 1914	25	DET
CHI	May 3, 1918	25	DET
BOS	Sep 5, 1919	25	PHI
CHI	Aug 15, 1922	25	BOS
PHI	Jul 25, 1929	25	CLE
CLE	Jun 5, 1930	25	BOS
PHI	Jul 10, 1932	25	CLE
NY	Jun 6, 1934	25	BOS
DET	Jul 1, 1936	25	CHI
PHI	Jul 26, 1936	25	CLE
PHI	Jul 27, 1936	25	CHI
BOS	Jun 24, 1949	25	STL
CLE	Apr 29, 1952	25	PHI
OAK	Jun 14, 1969	25	BOS

Most Hits by Team, Game, NL since 1900

Team	Date	H	Opp.
NY	Jun 9, 1901	31	CIN
NY	Sep 2, 1925	30	PHI
BKN	Aug 22, 1917	28	PIT
NY	Jul 10, 1922	28	PIT
NY	Jun 15, 1929	28	PIT
STL	Jul 6, 1929	28	PHI
BKN	Jun 23, 1930	28	PIT

Most Hits by Team, Game, NL since 1900 (*cont.*)

Team	Date	H	Opp.
NY	Jul 11, 1931	28	PHI
CHI	Jul 3, 1945	28	BOS
MON	Jun 30, 1978	28	ATL
NY	Jul 4, 1985	28	ATL
PIT	Apr 27, 1912	27	CIN
NY	Aug 5, 1922	27	CHI
PIT	Aug 8, 1922	27	PHI
NY	Sep 10, 1924	27	BOS
PHI	Jul 23, 1930	27	PIT
NY	Sep 21, 1931	27	CHI
BKN	Sep 23, 1939	27	PHI
CIN	Jun 8, 1940	27	BKN
STL	Aug 5, 1957	27	BKN
SF	Jun 8, 1990	27	ATL
PIT	Jul 31, 1900	26	BKN
BKN	Jun 21, 1901	26	CIN
BKN	Sep 23, 1901	26	CIN
STL	Jul 27, 1918	26	BKN
CIN	Jul 13, 1923	26	PHI
CHI	Sep 12, 1923	26	CIN
NY	Jul 10, 1930	26	PHI
NY	Aug 10, 1930	26	PHI
NY	May 13, 1957	26	BKN
MIL	Sep 2, 1957	26	CHI
SF	May 13, 1958	26	LA
CHI	May 17, 1979	26	PHI
CIN	Aug 3, 1989	26	HOU
BOS	Apr 10, 1900	25	PHI
BKN	Jun 10, 1900	25	PHI
BOS	Jun 25, 1900	25	PHI
PHI	Jul 13, 1900	25	PIT
PHI	Jun 4, 1901	25	CIN
PHI	Jun 24, 1901	25	CIN
CIN	Jun 24, 1917	25	STL
PIT	Jun 9, 1921	25	BOS
NY	May 30, 1922	25	BOS
BKN	Jun 21, 1922	25	PIT
CHI	Aug 25, 1922	25	PHI
PHI	Aug 25, 1922	25	CHI
BKN	Jun 29, 1923	25	PHI
STL	Aug 24, 1924	25	BKN
PIT	Jun 20, 1925	25	BKN
PIT	Jun 12, 1927	25	PHI
PIT	Jun 12, 1928	25	PHI
NY	Sep 2, 1930	25	PHI
STL	Aug 9, 1932	25	PHI
PIT	Aug 25, 1936	25	STL

Most Hits by Team, Game, NL since 1900 (*cont.*)

Team	Date	H	Opp.
BKN	Jun 24, 1950	25	PIT
CIN	Aug 3, 1969	25	PHI
STL	Jun 27, 1973	25	PIT
HOU	May 30, 1976	25	ATL
HOU	Jul 2, 1976	25	CIN
MON	May 21, 1977	25	SD

Most Hits by Team, Game, NL before 1900

Team	Date	H	Opp.
PHI	Aug 17, 1894	36	LOU
CHI	Jul 3, 1882	32	DET
CHI	Jul 3, 1883	32	BUF
WAS	Jun 7, 1892	32	CIN
CIN	Jun 18, 1893	32	LOU
CHI	Jun 29, 1897	32	LOU
CHI	Jul 22, 1876	31	LOU
CHI	Sep 6, 1883	31	DET
NY	Jun 11, 1887	31	WAS
CHI	Jun 18, 1887	31	DET
HAR	May 13, 1876	30	NY
STL	Jun 1, 1895	30	NY
BOS	Sep 3, 1896	30	STL

Doubleheader Shutouts, AL

Player	Team	Date	Score	Opp.
Earl Moore	CLE	Sep 3, 1901	1–0	BOS
Bill Cristall	CLE	Sep 3, 1901	4–0	BOS
Rube Waddell	PHI	Aug 13, 1902	8–0	DET
Bert Husting	PHI	Aug 13, 1902	9–0	DET
Earl Moore	CLE	Sep 1, 1902	10–0	WAS
Bill Bernhard	CLE	Sep 1, 1902	8–0	WAS
Cy Young	BOS	Jun 28, 1903	1–0	STL
Long Tom Hughes	BOS	Jun 28, 1903	3–0	STL
Cy Young	BOS	Aug 22, 1904	8–0	STL
Norwood Gibson	BOS	Aug 22, 1904	3–0	STL
Doc White	CHI	Sep 6, 1905	2–0	DET
Frank Smith	CHI	Sep 6, 1905	15–0	DET
Jack Chesbro	NY	Jul 6, 1906	4–0	BOS
Doc Newton	NY	Jul 6, 1906	8–0	BOS
Slow Joe Doyle	NY	Aug 25, 1906	2–0	CLE
Walter Clarkson	NY	Aug 25, 1906	2–0	CLE
Walter Clarkson	NY	Sep 4, 1906	7–0	BOS
Al Orth	NY	Sep 4, 1906	1–0	BOS
Jack Powell	STL	Sep 26, 1906	5–0	PHI
Harry Howell	STL	Sep 26, 1906	0–0	PHI
Tacks Neuer	NY	Sep 9, 1907	10–0	WAS

Doubleheader Shutouts, AL *(cont.)*

Player	Team	Date	Score	Opp.
Jack Chesbro	NY	Sep 9, 1907	2–0	WAS
Long Tom Hughes	WAS	Aug 28, 1908	2–0	CLE
Walter Johnson	WAS	Aug 28, 1908	8–0	CLE
Bill Burns	CHI	Jul 31, 1909	1–0	WAS
Frank Smith	CHI	Jul 31, 1909	4–0	WAS
Chief Bender	PHI	Sep 25, 1909	5–0	CLE
Cy Morgan	PHI	Sep 25, 1909	3–0	CLE
Smoky Joe Wood	BOS	Sep 16, 1911	6–0	CLE
Buck O'Brien	BOS	Sep 16, 1911	3–0	CLE
Jim Scott	CHI	Sep 22, 1911	5–0	STL
Frank Lange	CHI	Sep 22, 1911	1–0	STL
Joe Bush	PHI	Sep 22, 1913	4–0	DET
Eddie Plank	PHI	Sep 22, 1913	1–0	DET
Chief Bender	PHI	Jul 3, 1914	2–0	NY
Bob Shawkey	PHI	Jul 3, 1914	1–0	NY
Mellie Wolfgang	CHI	Aug 11, 1914	2–0	CLE
Eddie Cicotte	CHI	Aug 11, 1914	2–0	CLE
Rube Bressler	PHI	Aug 25, 1914	9–0	STL
Herb Pennock	PHI	Aug 25, 1914	1–0	STL
Rube Foster	BOS	Jul 5, 1915	4–0	WAS
Babe Ruth	BOS	Jul 5, 1915	6–0	WAS
Jim Scott	CHI	May 28, 1916	2–0	CLE
Red Faber	CHI	May 28, 1916	2–0	CLE
Lefty Williams	CHI	Jul 10, 1916	4–0	BOS
Reb Russell	CHI	Jul 10, 1916	3–0	BOS
Nick Cullop	NY	May 30, 1917	6–0	PHI
Slim Love	NY	May 30, 1917	2–0	PHI
Ernie Shore	BOS	Jun 23, 1917	4–0	WAS
Dutch Leonard	BOS	Jun 23, 1917	5–0	WAS
Harry Harper	WAS	Sep 15, 1917	5–0	PHI
Walter Johnson	WAS	Sep 15, 1917	4–0	PHI
Joe Bush	BOS	Jul 17, 1918	7–0	STL
Babe Ruth	BOS	Jul 17, 1918	4–0	STL
Joe Bush	BOS	Jul 22, 1918	1–0	DET
Carl Mays	BOS	Jul 22, 1918	3–0	DET
Herb Pennock	BOS	Sep 11, 1919	4–0	STL
Allan Russell	BOS	Sep 11, 1919	6–0	STL
Dave Keefe	PHI	Jul 7, 1920	6–0	BOS
Scott Perry	PHI	Jul 7, 1920	1–0	BOS
Waite Hoyt	BOS	Aug 21, 1920	12–0	CLE
Herb Pennock	BOS	Aug 21, 1920	4–0	CLE
Duster Mails	CLE	Jul 10, 1921	10–0	PHI
Guy Morton	CLE	Jul 10, 1921	1–0	PHI
Alex Ferguson	BOS	Sep 2, 1922	3–0	WAS
Bill Piercy	BOS	Sep 2, 1922	1–0	WAS
Ted Wingfield	BOS	Sep 17, 1925	2–0	STL
Paul Zahniser	BOS	Sep 17, 1925	4–0	STL

Doubleheader Shutouts, AL (*cont.*)

Player	Team	Date	Score	Opp.
Bump Hadley	WAS	Sep 18, 1929	2–0	DET
Lloyd Brown	WAS	Sep 18, 1929	1–0	DET
Clint Brown	CLE	Jun 23, 1931	13–0	BOS
Willis Hudlin	CLE	Jun 23, 1931	10–0	BOS
Oral Hildebrand	CLE	Jun 18, 1933	7–0	BOS
Mel Harder	CLE	Jun 18, 1933	4–0	BOS
Lefty Stewart	WAS	Jul 15, 1933	1–0	STL
Bobby Burke	WAS	Jul 15, 1933	2–0	STL
Eldon Auker	DET	Sep 22, 1936	12–0	STL
Tommy Bridges	DET	Sep 22, 1936	14–0	STL
Ted Lyons	CHI	Jul 13, 1940	5–0	BOS
Jack Knott	CHI	Jul 13, 1940	7–0	BOS
Thornton Lee	CHI	Aug 19, 1941	4–0	PHI
John Humphries	CHI	Aug 19, 1941	1–0	PHI
Tex Hughson	BOS	Aug 23, 1942	2–0	PHI
Joe Dobson	BOS	Aug 23, 1942	7–0	PHI
Monk Dubiel	NY	Sep 4, 1944	10–0	PHI
Mel Queen	NY	Sep 4, 1944	14–0	PHI
Hal Newhouser	DET	May 6, 1945	3–0	STL
Al Benton	DET	May 6, 1945	1–0	STL
Bobo Newsom	PHI	Jul 12, 1945	4–0	STL
Jesse Flores	PHI	Jul 12, 1945	11–0	STL
Marino Pieretti	WAS	Aug 20, 1945	7–0	CLE
Alex Carrasquel	WAS	Aug 20, 1945	6–0	CLE
Mel Harder	CLE	May 15, 1946	3–0	PHI
Steve Gromek	CLE	May 15, 1946	5–0	PHI
Dick Fowler	PHI	May 30, 1947	1–0	NY
Joe Coleman	PHI	May 30, 1947	4–0	NY
Bill Wight	CHI	May 15, 1949	10–0	CLE
Al Gettel	CHI	May 15, 1949	2–0	CLE
Virgil Trucks	DET	Jun 19, 1949	9–0	WAS
Fred Hutchinson	DET	Jun 19, 1949	7–0	WAS
Ted Gray	DET	Jul 31, 1949	3–0	PHI
Fred Hutchinson	DET	Jul 31, 1949	6–0	PHI
Mel Parnell	BOS	Sep 25, 1950	8–0	PHI
Harry Taylor	BOS	Sep 25, 1950	3–0	PHI
Marv Grissom	CHI	May 25, 1952	1–0	DET
Joe Dobson	CHI	May 25, 1952	3–0	DET
Tom Gorman	NY	Sep 2, 1952	5–0	BOS
Ewell Blackwell	NY	Sep 2, 1952	4–0	BOS
Billy Pierce	CHI	Jun 14, 1953	6–0	BOS
Sandy Consuegra	CHI	Jun 14, 1953	1–0	BOS
Ed Lopat	NY	Jun 18, 1953	5–0	STL
Jim McDonald	NY	Jun 18, 1953	3–0	STL
Mickey McDermott	BOS	Jul 24, 1953	6–0	STL
Bill Henry	BOS	Jul 24, 1953	8–0	STL
Whitey Ford	NY	Aug 8, 1953	1–0	CHI

Doubleheader Shutouts, AL *(cont.)*

Player	Team	Date	Score	Opp.
Bob Kuzava	NY	Aug 8, 1953	2–0	CHI
Whitey Ford	NY	May 6, 1956	4–0	CHI
Rip Coleman	NY	May 6, 1956	4–0	CHI
Tom Brewer	BOS	Jul 17, 1956	10–0	KC
Bob Porterfield	BOS	Jul 17, 1956	4–0	KC
Herb Score	CLE	Jul 29, 1956	3–0	BAL
Hank Aguirre	CLE	Jul 29, 1956	4–0	BAL
Herb Score	CLE	Sep 18, 1956	1–0	WAS
Mike Garcia	CLE	Sep 18, 1956	6–0	WAS
Frank Lary	DET	Jun 15, 1958	2–0	NY
Jim Bunning	DET	Jun 15, 1958	3–0	NY
Dick Donovan	CHI	Jun 15, 1958	4–0	BAL
Jim Wilson	CHI	Jun 15, 1958	3–0	BAL
Ray Herbert	KC	Jul 9, 1959	5–0	DET
Johnny Kucks	KC	Jul 9, 1959	4–0	DET
Milt Pappas	BAL	Jul 9, 1959	8–0	WAS
Jerry Walker	BAL	Jul 9, 1959	5–0	WAS
Jack Fisher	BAL	Sep 11, 1959	3–0	CHI
Jerry Walker	BAL	Sep 11, 1959	1–0	CHI
Russ Kemmerer	CHI	Jun 5, 1960	2–0	KC
Frank Baumann	CHI	Jun 5, 1960	2–0	KC
Hoyt Wilhelm	BAL	Jun 19, 1960	2–0	DET
Milt Pappas	BAL	Jun 19, 1960	1–0	DET
Wynn Hawkins	CLE	May 21, 1961	9–0	MIN
Mudcat Grant	CLE	May 21, 1961	2–0	MIN
Dick Stigman	MIN	Jul 24, 1963	9–0	CLE
Jim Kaat	MIN	Jul 24, 1963	5–0	CLE
Jim Bouton	NY	Aug 27, 1963	5–0	BOS
Ralph Terry	NY	Aug 27, 1963	3–0	BOS
Bo Belinsky	LA	Jun 26, 1964	1–0	KC
Bob Meyer	LA	Jun 26, 1964	6–0	KC
Juan Pizarro	CHI	Jul 5, 1964	2–0	CLE
Joe Horlen	CHI	Jul 5, 1964	5–0	CLE
Luis Tiant	CLE	Sep 30, 1964	5–0	BOS
Sam McDowell	CLE	Sep 30, 1964	3–0	BOS
Jack Lamabe	CHI	May 30, 1966	1–0	BOS
John Buzhardt	CHI	May 30, 1966	4–0	BOS
Chuck Dobson	KC	Jun 9, 1967	2–0	CLE
Catfish Hunter	KC	Jun 9, 1967	6–0	CLE
Joe Horlen	CHI	Sep 10, 1967	6–0	DET
Cisco Carlos	CHI	Sep 10, 1967	4–0	DET
Jim Palmer	BAL	Apr 13, 1969	6–0	WAS
Tom Phoebus	BAL	Apr 13, 1969	9–0	WAS
Mickey Lolich	DET	May 23, 1971	5–0	WAS
Les Cain	DET	May 23, 1971	11–0	WAS
Catfish Hunter	OAK	Jun 4, 1972	2–0	BAL
Dave Hamilton	OAK	Jun 4, 1972	2–0	BAL

Doubleheader Shutouts, AL (cont.)

Player	Team	Date	Score	Opp.
Fritz Peterson	NY	Jul 21, 1972	6–0	CAL
Mel Stottlemyre	NY	Jul 21, 1972	3–0	CAL
Bill Lee	BOS	Jul 27, 1974	1–0	NY
Roger Moret	BOS	Jul 27, 1974	6–0	NY
Ross Grimsley	BAL	Sep 2, 1974	1–0	BOS
Mike Cuellar	BAL	Sep 2, 1974	1–0	BOS
Dave McNally	BAL	Sep 6, 1974	2–0	CLE
Mike Cuellar	BAL	Sep 6, 1974	1–0	CLE
Vida Blue	OAK	Sep 9, 1974	3–0	KC
Catfish Hunter	OAK	Sep 9, 1974	7–0	KC
Luis Tiant	BOS	Sep 26, 1975	4–0	CLE
Reggie Cleveland	BOS	Sep 26, 1975	4–0	CLE
Don Aase	BOS	Sep 5, 1977	8–0	TOR
Reggie Cleveland	BOS	Sep 5, 1977	6–0	TOR
Ron Guidry	NY	Sep 25, 1977	15–0	TOR
Ed Figueroa	NY	Sep 25, 1977	2–0	TOR
Charles Hudson	NY	Apr 19, 1987	5–0	KC
Pat Clements	NY	Apr 19, 1987	1–0	KC
Charlie Lea	MIN	Jun 26, 1988	11–0	OAK
Frank Viola	MIN	Jun 26, 1988	5–0	OAK

Doubleheader Shutouts, NL

Player	Team	Date	Score	Opp.
Harry Staley	PIT	Apr 13, 1888	4–0	BOS
Pud Galvin	PIT	Apr 13, 1888	6–0	BOS
George Haddock	BKN	Jul 19, 1892	1–0	STL
Ed Stein	BKN	Jul 19, 1892	3–0	STL
Zeke Wilson	CLE	Jul 21, 1896	2–0	WAS
Bobby Wallace	CLE	Jul 21, 1896	7–0	WAS
Billy Rhines	CIN	Sep 16, 1896	1–0	PIT
Frank Dwyer	CIN	Sep 16, 1896	4–0	PIT
Joe McGinnity	BAL	Jul 15, 1899	10–0	CLE
Frank Kitson	BAL	Jul 15, 1899	5–0	CLE
Sam Leever	PIT	Sep 26, 1899	5–0	CHI
Bill Hoffer	PIT	Sep 26, 1899	12–0	CHI
Jesse Tannehill	PIT	Jul 4, 1902	3–0	BKN
Jack Chesbro	PIT	Jul 4, 1902	4–0	BKN
Togie Pittinger	BOS	Sep 4, 1902	1–0	PIT
John Malarkey	BOS	Sep 4, 1902	0–0	PIT
Doc Scanlan	BKN	Sep 16, 1904	6–0	CIN
John Cronin	BKN	Sep 16, 1904	3–0	CIN
Jake Weimer	CHI	Sep 26, 1904	4–0	BKN
Buttons Briggs	CHI	Sep 26, 1904	1–0	BKN
Tom Walker	CIN	Oct 9, 1904	3–0	STL
Noodles Hahn	CIN	Oct 9, 1904	1–0	STL
Three Finger Brown	CHI	Jul 4, 1906	1–0	PIT

Doubleheader Shutouts, NL (*cont.*)

Player	Team	Date	Score	Opp.
Carl Lundgren	CHI	Jul 4, 1906	1–0	PIT
Three Finger Brown	CHI	Aug 3, 1906	1–0	PHI
Ed Reulbach	CHI	Aug 3, 1906	7–0	PHI
Doc Scanlan	BKN	Sep 3, 1906	8–0	PHI
Harry McIntire	BKN	Sep 3, 1906	10–0	PHI
Mal Eason	BKN	Sep 8, 1906	6–0	NY
Doc Scanlan	BKN	Sep 8, 1906	1–0	NY
Vic Willis	PIT	Sep 26, 1906	5–0	PHI
Lefty Leifield	PIT	Sep 26, 1906	8–0	PHI
Red Ames	NY	Oct 1, 1906	3–0	STL
George Ferguson	NY	Oct 1, 1906	1–0	STL
Vive Lindaman	BOS	Jul 8, 1907	2–0	CIN
Irv Young	BOS	Jul 8, 1907	4–0	CIN
Orval Overall	CHI	Aug 11, 1907	1–0	PHI
Jack Pfiester	CHI	Aug 11, 1907	1–0	PHI
Art Fromme	STL	Sep 2, 1907	6–0	CHI
Johnny Lush	STL	Sep 2, 1907	9–0	CHI
Orval Overall	CHI	Aug 23, 1908	2–0	BKN
Ed Reulbach	CHI	Aug 23, 1908	2–0	BKN
Bill Chappelle	BOS	Sep 7, 1908	1–0	BKN
Vive Lindaman	BOS	Sep 7, 1908	1–0	BKN
Ed Reulbach	CHI	Sep 26, 1908	5–0	BKN
Ed Reulbach	CHI	Sep 26, 1908	3–0	BKN
Nap Rucker	BKN	Jul 24, 1909	1–0	STL
George Bell	BKN	Jul 24, 1909	1–0	STL
Babe Adams	PIT	Sep 21, 1909	2–0	BOS
Howie Camnitz	PIT	Sep 21, 1909	5–0	BOS
Charlie Smith	CHI	Sep 17, 1911	4–0	BKN
Larry Cheney	CHI	Sep 17, 1911	5–0	BKN
Art Fromme	CIN	Sep 16, 1912	6–0	PHI
Rube Benton	CIN	Sep 16, 1912	1–0	PHI
Grover Alexander	PHI	Sep 26, 1912	7–0	BKN
Tom Seaton	PHI	Sep 26, 1912	11–0	BKN
Tom Seaton	PHI	Aug 5, 1913	1–0	BOS
Grover Alexander	PHI	Aug 5, 1913	0–0	BOS
Wilbur Cooper	PIT	May 31, 1915	1–0	CHI
Al Mamaux	PIT	May 31, 1915	1–0	CHI
Al Mamaux	PIT	Aug 7, 1915	9–0	PHI
Bob Harmon	PIT	Aug 7, 1915	6–0	PHI
Art Nehf	BOS	Aug 31, 1915	2–0	CIN
Tom Hughes	BOS	Aug 31, 1915	2–0	CIN
Tom Hughes	BOS	Oct 6, 1915	1–0	NY
Pat Ragan	BOS	Oct 6, 1915	1–0	NY
Slim Sallee	NY	Jul 31, 1916	7–0	PIT
Jeff Tesreau	NY	Jul 31, 1916	7–0	PIT
Jesse Barnes	BOS	Aug 7, 1916	2–0	CIN
Frank Allen	BOS	Aug 7, 1916	6–0	CIN

Doubleheader Shutouts, NL (*cont.*)

Player	Team	Date	Score	Opp.
Grover Alexander	PHI	Sep 1, 1916	3–0	BKN
Eppa Rixey	PHI	Sep 1, 1916	6–0	BKN
Frank Miller	PIT	Sep 4, 1916	7–0	STL
Wilbur Cooper	PIT	Sep 4, 1916	2–0	STL
Hippo Vaughn	CHI	Sep 9, 1916	3–0	PIT
Jimmy Lavender	CHI	Sep 9, 1916	2–0	PIT
Jeff Tesreau	NY	Sep 28, 1916	2–0	BOS
Ferdie Schupp	NY	Sep 28, 1916	6–0	BOS
Dick Rudolph	BOS	May 30, 1917	4–0	BKN
Lefty Tyler	BOS	May 30, 1917	2–0	BKN
Jeff Pfeffer	BKN	Aug 25, 1917	12–0	STL
Rube Marquard	BKN	Aug 25, 1917	4–0	STL
Oscar Horstmann	STL	Sep 1, 1917	1–0	PIT
Milt Watson	STL	Sep 1, 1917	1–0	PIT
Jesse Barnes	BOS	Sep 26, 1917	1–0	CIN
Art Nehf	BOS	Sep 26, 1917	3–0	CIN
Lefty Tyler	CHI	Jul 4, 1918	1–0	STL
Claude Hendrix	CHI	Jul 4, 1918	1–0	STL
Jimmy Ring	CIN	Jul 10, 1918	7–0	BKN
Mike Regan	CIN	Jul 10, 1918	5–0	BKN
Claude Hendrix	CHI	Aug 17, 1918	3–0	PHI
Lefty Tyler	CHI	Aug 17, 1918	2–0	PHI
Grover Alexander	CHI	Jul 23, 1919	3–0	BKN
Phil Douglas	CHI	Jul 23, 1919	6–0	BKN
Ray Fisher	CIN	Jul 31, 1919	5–0	BOS
Dolf Luque	CIN	Jul 31, 1919	2–0	BOS
Joe Genewich	BOS	Aug 20, 1924	2–0	CHI
Jesse Barnes	BOS	Aug 20, 1924	5–0	CHI
Carl Mays	CIN	Sep 1, 1924	5–0	STL
Rube Benton	CIN	Sep 1, 1924	9–0	STL
Bob Smith	BOS	Aug 7, 1926	2–0	PIT
Johnny Wertz	BOS	Aug 7, 1926	2–0	PIT
Carl Hubbell	NY	May 21, 1931	3–0	BOS
Bill Walker	NY	May 21, 1931	6–0	BOS
Dazzy Vance	BKN	Jul 4, 1931	4–0	NY
Watty Clark	BKN	Jul 4, 1931	5–0	NY
Flint Rhem	STL	Sep 6, 1931	3–0	CIN
Syl Johnson	STL	Sep 6, 1931	7–0	CIN
Carl Hubbell	NY	May 7, 1932	1–0	CIN
Hal Schumacher	NY	May 7, 1932	5–0	CIN
Carl Hubbell	NY	Jul 2, 1933	1–0	STL
Roy Parmelee	NY	Jul 2, 1933	1–0	STL
Heinie Meine	PIT	Sep 12, 1933	1–0	BKN
Waite Hoyt	PIT	Sep 12, 1933	2–0	BKN
Ray Benge	BKN	Sep 9, 1934	5–0	CIN
Van Lingle Mungo	BKN	Sep 9, 1934	3–0	CIN
Dizzy Dean	STL	Sep 21, 1934	13–0	BKN

Doubleheader Shutouts, NL (*cont.*)

Player	Team	Date	Score	Opp.
Paul Dean	STL	Sep 21, 1934	3–0	BKN
Curt Davis	PHI	Jul 21, 1935	4–0	CIN
Joe Bowman	PHI	Jul 21, 1935	2–0	CIN
Carl Hubbell	NY	Jul 28, 1935	6–0	BKN
Slick Castleman	NY	Jul 28, 1935	1–0	BKN
Larry French	CHI	Jun 28, 1936	3–0	NY
Bill Lee	CHI	Jun 28, 1936	6–0	NY
Frank Gabler	BOS	Jun 30, 1937	1–0	BKN
Guy Bush	BOS	Jun 30, 1937	7–0	BKN
Peaches Davis	CIN	Jul 11, 1937	6–0	STL
Al Hollingsworth	CIN	Jul 11, 1937	7–0	STL
Danny MacFayden	BOS	May 30, 1938	1–0	NY
Jim Turner	BOS	May 30, 1938	6–0	NY
Larry French	CHI	May 30, 1939	6–0	CIN
Vance Page	CHI	May 30, 1939	2–0	CIN
Bill Posedel	BOS	Jul 6, 1939	3–0	CIN
Joe Callahan	BOS	Jul 6, 1939	4–0	CIN
Luke Hamlin	BKN	Apr 19, 1941	8–0	BOS
Whit Wyatt	BKN	Apr 19, 1941	8–0	BOS
Jim Tobin	BOS	Aug 3, 1941	5–0	CIN
Johnny Hutchings	BOS	Aug 3, 1941	3–0	CIN
Johnny Vander Meer	CIN	Aug 20, 1941	2–0	PHI
Elmer Riddle	CIN	Aug 20, 1941	3–0	PHI
Ray Starr	CIN	May 10, 1942	1–0	STL
Bucky Walters	CIN	May 10, 1942	3–0	STL
Claude Passeau	CHI	Aug 23, 1942	3–0	CIN
Lon Warneke	CHI	Aug 23, 1942	3–0	CIN
Hank Gornicki	PIT	Sep 6, 1942	6–0	CHI
Luke Hamlin	PIT	Sep 6, 1942	5–0	CHI
Wally Hebert	PIT	May 2, 1943	3–0	CHI
Bob Klinger	PIT	May 2, 1943	1–0	CHI
Charlie Fuchs	PHI	May 20, 1943	3–0	CHI
Al Gerheauser	PHI	May 20, 1943	2–0	CHI
Hi Bithorn	CHI	Jul 25, 1943	2–0	NY
Claude Passeau	CHI	Jul 25, 1943	2–0	NY
Elmer Riddle	CIN	Sep 26, 1943	2–0	BOS
Johnny Vander Meer	CIN	Sep 26, 1943	1–0	BOS
Paul Erickson	CHI	Jun 11, 1944	5–0	PIT
Bob Chipman	CHI	Jun 11, 1944	1–0	PIT
Mort Cooper	STL	Jul 9, 1944	1–0	BOS
Harry Brecheen	STL	Jul 9, 1944	9–0	BOS
Paul Erickson	CHI	Jul 6, 1946	2–0	CIN
Hank Wyse	CHI	Jul 6, 1946	1–0	CIN
Jim Hearn	STL	Jul 6, 1947	3–0	CIN
Murry Dickson	STL	Jul 6, 1947	2–0	CIN
Larry Jansen	NY	Jul 31, 1949	10–0	CIN
Adrian Zabala	NY	Jul 31, 1949	9–0	CIN

Doubleheader Shutouts, NL (*cont.*)

Player	Team	Date	Score	Opp.
Larry Jansen	NY	Jun 22, 1950	3–0	STL
Dave Koslo	NY	Jun 22, 1950	5–0	STL
Bubba Church	PHI	Jul 25, 1950	7–0	CHI
Robin Roberts	PHI	Jul 25, 1950	1–0	CHI
Sal Maglie	NY	Aug 6, 1950	3–0	PIT
Larry Jansen	NY	Aug 6, 1950	5–0	PIT
Jim Hearn	NY	Sep 4, 1950	2–0	PHI
Sal Maglie	NY	Sep 4, 1950	9–0	PHI
Gerry Staley	STL	Sep 30, 1950	2–0	CHI
George Munger	STL	Sep 30, 1950	4–0	CHI
Jocko Thompson	PHI	Aug 27, 1951	2–0	CIN
Ken Johnson	PHI	Aug 27, 1951	3–0	CIN
Sal Maglie	NY	Apr 25, 1954	3–0	PHI
Johnny Antonelli	NY	Apr 25, 1954	5–0	PHI
Johnny Klippstein	CIN	Aug 2, 1955	2–0	PHI
Joe Nuxhall	CIN	Aug 2, 1955	4–0	PHI
Frank Sullivan	PHI	Apr 23, 1961	1–0	CHI
Art Mahaffey	PHI	Apr 23, 1961	6–0	CHI
Bob Purkey	CIN	Aug 16, 1961	8–0	LA
Jim O'Toole	CIN	Aug 16, 1961	8–0	LA
Jack Sanford	SF	Apr 29, 1962	7–0	CHI
Billy Pierce	SF	Apr 29, 1962	6–0	CHI
Larry Jackson	STL	Jun 27, 1962	4–0	CHI
Ray Sadecki	STL	Jun 27, 1962	8–0	CHI
Bob Hendley	SF	May 17, 1964	6–0	NY
Ron Herbel	SF	May 17, 1964	1–0	NY
Larry Jackson	CHI	Jul 11, 1965	6–0	STL
Cal Koonce	CHI	Jul 11, 1965	6–0	STL
Don Drysdale	LA	Jul 24, 1966	5–0	NY
Joe Moeller	LA	Jul 24, 1966	6–0	NY
Sandy Koufax	LA	Sep 11, 1966	4–0	HOU
Joe Moeller	LA	Sep 11, 1966	1–0	HOU
Joe Gibbon	SF	Jun 4, 1967	7–0	NY
Mike McCormick	SF	Jun 4, 1967	5–0	NY
Bill Singer	LA	Sep 15, 1967	1–0	PHI
Don Drysdale	LA	Sep 15, 1967	1–0	PHI
Jerry Koosman	NY	Sep 12, 1969	1–0	PIT
Don Cardwell	NY	Sep 12, 1969	1–0	PIT
Al Downing	LA	Sep 19, 1971	12–0	ATL
Don Sutton	LA	Sep 19, 1971	4–0	ATL
Jim Barr	SF	Jul 21, 1974	4–0	MON
John D'Acquisto	SF	Jul 21, 1974	2–0	MON
Ron Reed	STL	Jun 23, 1975	1–0	NY
John Denny	STL	Jun 23, 1975	4–0	NY
Don Carrithers	MON	Aug 5, 1975	7–0	NY
Dennis Blair	MON	Aug 5, 1975	7–0	NY
Jim Rooker	PIT	Oct 3, 1976	1–0	STL

Doubleheader Shutouts, NL (*cont.*)

Player	Team	Date	Score	Opp.
Jerry Reuss	PIT	Oct 3, 1976	1–0	STL
Joe Magrane	STL	Sep 29, 1987	1–0	MON
Greg Mathews	STL	Sep 29, 1987	3–0	MON

Most Lopsided Shutouts, AL

Team	Date	Score	Opp.	WP	LP
DET	Sep 15, 1901	21–0	CLE	Ed Siever	Jack Bracken
NY	Aug 13, 1939	21–0	PHI	Red Ruffing	Hal Pippen
BOS	Apr 30, 1950	19–0	PHI	Joe Dobson	Dick Fowler
CLE	May 18, 1955	19–0	BOS	Herb Score	Willard Nixon
DET	Apr 29, 1935	18–0	STL	Tommy Bridges	Bobo Newsom
NY	Jul 10, 1936	18–0	CLE	Red Ruffing	Lloyd Brown
BOS	Jul 11, 1954	18–0	PHI	Frank Sullivan	Bob Trice
MIL	Apr 16, 1990	18–0	BOS	Ted Higuera	Mike Boddicker
NY	Apr 24, 1909	17–0	WAS	Joe Lake	Walter Johnson
NY	Jul 6, 1920	17–0	WAS	Carl Mays	Eric Erickson
CHI	Sep 9, 1925	17–0	WAS	Ted Lyons	Tom Zachary
NY	Sep 17, 1931	17–0	STL	Red Ruffing	George Blaeholder
LA	Aug 23, 1963	17–0	WAS	Ken McBride	Steve Ridzik
BAL	Jul 27, 1969	17–0	CHI	Jim Hardin	Billy Wynne
CAL	Apr 23, 1980	17–0	MIN	Bruce Kison	Terry Felton
CHI	Jul 5, 1987	17–0	CLE	Scott Nielsen	Phil Niekro
DET	Jul 19, 1991	17–0	KC	Bill Gullickson	Tom Gordon

Most Lopsided Shutouts, NL

Team	Date	Score	Opp.	WP	LP
PRO	Aug 21, 1883	28–0	PHI	Larry Corcoran	Art Hagan
NY	May 27, 1885	24–0	BUF	Mickey Welch	Jim Galvin
PHI	Jun 28, 1887	24–0	IND	Charlie Ferguson	Hank Morrison
PIT	Sep 16, 1975	22–0	CHI	John Candelaria	Rick Reuschel
CHI	May 28, 1886	20–0	WAS	Jim McCormick	Cannonball Crane
PIT	Jul 15, 1893	19–0	WAS	Frank Killen	Jesse Duryea
PIT	Jul 7, 1896	19–0	WAS	Jim Hughey	Win Mercer
CHI	Jun 7, 1906	19–0	NY	Jack Pfeister	Christy Mathewson
PIT	Aug 3, 1961	19–0	STL	Harvey Haddix	Al Cicotte
CHI	May 13, 1969	19–0	SD	Dick Selma	Dick Kelley
LA	Jun 28, 1969	19–0	SD	Don Drysdale	Steve Arlin
MON	Jul 30, 1978	19–0	ATL	Woodie Fryman	Mickey Mahler
CHI	Jul 20, 1876	18–0	LOU	Al Spalding	Jim Devlin
BUF	Aug 4, 1884	18–0	DET	Jim Galvin	Frank Meinke
BOS	Oct 3, 1885	18–0	BUF	Bill Stemmeyer	Pete Conway
PHI	Jul 11, 1910	18–0	PIT	George McQuillan	Al Leifield
PHI	Aug 10, 1930	18–0	CIN	Claude Willoughby	Biff Wysong
PHI	Jul 14, 1934	18–0	CIN	Snipe Hansen	Don Brennan
STL	Jun 10, 1944	18–0	CIN	Mort Cooper	Bill Lohrman
CIN	Aug 8, 1965	18–0	LA	Jim Maloney	Don Drysdale

Most Lopsided Shutouts, NL (*cont.*)

Team	Date	Score	Opp.	WP	LP
STL	Jun 1, 1876	17–0	PHI	George Bradley	George Zettlein
CHI	Aug 11, 1881	17–0	DET	Fred Goldsmith	Frank Mountain
CHI	Sep 16, 1884	17–0	BOS	Larry Corcoran	Charlie Buffinton
BAL	May 7, 1894	17–0	WAS	Tony Mullane	Al Maul
BOS	Sep 17, 1897	17–0	NY	Kid Nichols	Mike Sullivan
PHI	Sep 4, 1899	17–0	WAS	Chick Fraser	Gus Weyhing
STL	Aug 24, 1924	17–0	BKN	Eddie Dyer	Jim Roberts
PHI	May 20, 1951	17–0	PIT	Russ Meyer	Murry Dickson
CIN	Sep 4, 1988	17–0	CHI	Danny Jackson	Calvin Schiraldi

Most Lopsided Shutouts, Other Leagues

Team	Date	Score	Opp.	WP	LP
CIN AA	Jul 6, 1883	23–0	BAL	Will White	Hardie Henderson
STL AA	May 7, 1889	21–0	COL	Silver King	Al Mays
CIN AA	Aug 10, 1889	20–0	BAL	Jesse Duryea	Frank Foreman
STL AA	Aug 15, 1886	19–0	BKN	Dave Foutz	Bill Terry
PIT AA	Jun 3, 1886	18–0	BKN	Ed Morris	Bill Terry
BOS P	Aug 29, 1890	18–0	PIT	Old Hoss Radbourn	Al Maul
NY AA	Jul 4, 1884	17–0	STL	Tim Keefe	Jumbo McGinnis
PIT AA	Jul 9, 1885	17–0	NY	Ed Morris	Dug Crothers
BKN AA	Oct 3, 1889	17–0	PHI	Bob Caruthers	Sadie McMahon

Longest Shutouts, AL

Team	Date	Inns.	Score	Opp.
OAK	Jul 9, 1971	20	1–0	CAL
DET	Jul 16, 1909	18	0–0	WAS
WAS	Jul 16, 1909	18	0–0	DET
WAS	May 15, 1918	18	1–0	CHI
WAS	Jun 8, 1947	18	1–0	CHI
CHI	Sep 13, 1967	17	1–0	CLE
BAL	Sep 27, 1974	17	1–0	MIL
CHI	Aug 4, 1910	16	0–0	PHI
PHI	Aug 4, 1910	16	0–0	CHI
STL	Jun 5, 1942	16	1–0	PHI
BAL	Sep 11, 1959	16	1–0	CHI
CAL	Sep 22, 1975	16	3–0	CHI
WAS	Aug 14, 1903	15	1–0	STL
BOS	May 11, 1904	15	1–0	DET
CHI	Apr 20, 1912	15	0–0	STL
STL	Apr 20, 1912	15	0–0	CHI
WAS	Jul 3, 1913	15	1–0	BOS
NY	May 30, 1917	15	2–0	PHI
WAS	Jul 25, 1918	15	1–0	STL
NY	Jul 4, 1925	15	1–0	PHI
WAS	Apr 13, 1926	15	1–0	PHI
CLE	Aug 24, 1935	15	2–0	PHI

Longest Shutouts, AL *(cont.)*

Team	Date	Inns.	Score	Opp.
CLE	Jun 4, 1948	15	5–0	WAS
CLE	May 14, 1961	15	1–0	BAL
LA	Apr 13, 1963	15	1–0	CHI
CHI	Jun 4, 1965	15	2–0	NY
NY	Aug 27, 1976	15	5–0	CAL
KC	May 23, 1981	15	1–0	MIN

Longest Shutouts, NL

Team	Date	Inns.	Score	Opp.
HOU	Apr 15, 1968	24	1–0	NY
LA	Aug 23, 1989	22	1–0	MON
PIT	Aug 1, 1918	21	2–0	BOS
SF	Sep 1, 1967	21	1–0	CIN
BKN	Sep 11, 1946	19	0–0	CIN
CIN	Sep 11, 1946	19	0–0	BKN
PRO	Aug 17, 1882	18	1–0	DET
NY	Jul 2, 1933	18	1–0	STL
NY	Oct 2, 1965	18	0–0	PHI
PHI	Oct 2, 1965	18	0–0	NY
PIT	Jun 7, 1972	18	1–0	SD
CHI	Sep 21, 1901	17	1–0	BOS
PIT	Aug 22, 1908	17	1–0	BKN
NY	Jul 16, 1920	17	7–0	PIT
SF	Aug 19, 1968	17	1–0	NY
HOU	Aug 23, 1980	17	1–0	CHI
MON	Sep 21, 1981	17	1–0	PHI
BKN	Jul 7, 1915	16	0–0	BOS
BOS	Jul 7, 1915	16	0–0	BKN
SF	Jul 2, 1963	16	1–0	MIL
PIT	Sep 30, 1964	16	1–0	CIN
HOU	Apr 21, 1976	16	1–0	LA
PHI	May 17, 1991	16	1–0	CHI
CIN	Sep 11, 1906	15	0–0	PIT
PIT	Sep 11, 1906	15	0–0	CIN
CIN	Jun 11, 1915	15	1–0	BKN
CIN	Jun 16, 1933	15	1–0	NY
PHI	Jun 22, 1944	15	1–0	BOS
PHI	Aug 7, 1951	15	1–0	BOS
NY	Jun 4, 1969	15	1–0	LA
LA	Apr 14, 1970	15	1–0	NY
SF	Jul 21, 1980	15	2–0	CHI

Teams with Four 20-Game Winners

Player	Team	Year	W
Red Faber	CHI A	1920	23
Lefty Williams	CHI A	1920	22

Teams with Four 20-Game Winners (*cont.*)

Player	Team	Year	W
Eddie Cicotte	CHI A	1920	21
Dickie Kerr	CHI A	1920	21
Dave McNally	BAL A	1971	21
Pat Dobson	BAL A	1971	20
Mike Cuellar	BAL A	1971	20
Jim Palmer	BAL A	1971	20

Teams with Three 20-Game Winners, AL

Player	Team	Year	W
Cy Young	BOS	1903	28
Bill Dinneen	BOS	1903	21
Long Tom Hughes	BOS	1903	20
Cy Young	BOS	1904	26
Bill Dinneen	BOS	1904	23
Jesse Tannehill	BOS	1904	21
Rube Waddell	PHI	1905	26
Eddie Plank	PHI	1905	25
Andy Coakley	PHI	1905	20
Bob Rhoads	CLE	1906	22
Addie Joss	CLE	1906	21
Otto Hess	CLE	1906	20
Wild Bill Donovan	DET	1907	25
Ed Killian	DET	1907	25
George Mullin	DET	1907	20
Doc White	CHI	1907	27
Ed Walsh	CHI	1907	24
Frank Smith	CHI	1907	23
Smoky Joe Wood	BOS	1912	34
Hugh Bedient	BOS	1912	20
Buck O'Brien	BOS	1912	20
Jim Bagby	CLE	1920	31
Stan Coveleski	CLE	1920	24
Ray Caldwell	CLE	1920	20
Lefty Grove	PHI	1931	31
George Earnshaw	PHI	1931	21
Rube Walberg	PHI	1931	20
Bob Feller	CLE	1951	22
Mike Garcia	CLE	1951	20
Early Wynn	CLE	1951	20

Teams with Three 20-Game Winners, AL (*cont.*)

Player	Team	Year	W
Early Wynn	CLE	1952	23
Mike Garcia	CLE	1952	22
Bob Lemon	CLE	1952	22
Bob Lemon	CLE	1956	20
Herb Score	CLE	1956	20
Early Wynn	CLE	1956	20
Mike Cuellar	BAL	1970	24
Dave McNally	BAL	1970	24
Jim Palmer	BAL	1970	20
Ken Holtzman	OAK	1973	21
Catfish Hunter	OAK	1973	21
Vida Blue	OAK	1973	20

Teams with Three 20-Game Winners, NL since 1900

Player	Team	Year	W
Jack Chesbro	PIT	1902	28
Deacon Phillippe	PIT	1902	20
Jesse Tannehill	PIT	1902	20
Joe McGinnity	NY	1904	35
Christy Mathewson	NY	1904	33
Dummy Taylor	NY	1904	21
Christy Mathewson	NY	1905	31
Red Ames	NY	1905	22
Joe McGinnity	NY	1905	21
Christy Mathewson	NY	1913	25
Rube Marquard	NY	1913	23
Jeff Tesreau	NY	1913	22
Fred Toney	NY	1920	21
Art Nehf	NY	1920	21
Jesse Barnes	NY	1920	20
Dolf Luque	CIN	1923	27
Pete Donohue	CIN	1923	21
Eppa Rixey	CIN	1923	20

Strikeout Duos, Season, AL

Player	Team	Year	SO
Nolan Ryan	CAL	1973	383
Bill Singer	CAL	1973	241
Total			624

Strikeout Duos, Season, AL (*cont.*)

Player	Team	Year	SO
Nolan Ryan	CAL	1976	327
Frank Tanana	CAL	1976	261
Total			588
Rube Waddell	PHI	1904	349
Eddie Plank	PHI	1904	201
Total			550
Sam McDowell	CLE	1968	283
Luis Tiant	CLE	1968	264
Total			547
Nolan Ryan	CAL	1974	367
Frank Tanana	CAL	1974	180
Total			547
Nolan Ryan	CAL	1977	341
Frank Tanana	CAL	1977	205
Total			546
Mickey Lolich	DET	1971	308
Joe Coleman	DET	1971	236
Total			544
Sam McDowell	CLE	1965	325
Sonny Siebert	CLE	1965	191
Total			516

Strikeout Duos, Season, NL

Player	Team	Year	SO
Sandy Koufax	LA	1965	382
Don Drysdale	LA	1965	210
Total			592
Sandy Koufax	LA	1963	306
Don Drysdale	LA	1963	251
Total			557
Sandy Koufax	LA	1966	317
Don Sutton	LA	1966	209
Total			526
Jim Bunning	PHI	1965	268
Chris Short	PHI	1965	237
Total			505
Nolan Ryan	HOU	1987	270
Mike Scott	HOU	1987	233
Total			503

Strikeout Duos, Season, NL (*cont.*)

Player	Team	Year	SO
Mike Scott	HOU	1986	306
Nolan Ryan	HOU	1986	194
Total			500

Best Lefty-Righty Duos

Player	Team	LH/RH	First	Last	W	L
Warren Spahn	BOS N	LH	1951	1963	264	158
Lew Burdette	MIL N	RH	1951	1963	179	120
Total					443	278
Hooks Wiltse	NY N	LH	1904	1914	138	85
Christy Mathewson	NY N	RH	1904	1914	297	120
Total					435	205
Eddie Plank	PHI A	LH	1903	1914	225	118
Chief Bender	PHI A	RH	1903	1914	191	103
Total					416	221
Lefty Gomez	NY A	LH	1930	1942	189	101
Red Ruffing	NY A	RH	1930	1942	219	120
Total					408	221
Hal Newhouser	DET A	LH	1939	1952	200	147
Dizzy Trout	DET A	RH	1939	1952	161	153
Total					361	300
Carl Hubbell	NY N	LH	1931	1942	204	121
Hal Schumacher	NY N	RH	1931	1942	154	116
Total					358	237
Curt Simmons	PHI N	LH	1948	1960	114	110
Robin Roberts	PHI N	RH	1948	1960	233	189
Total					347	299
Sandy Koufax	BKN N	LH	1956	1966	163	85
Don Drysdale	LA N	RH	1956	1966	177	134
Total					340	219
Wilbur Cooper	PIT N	LH	1912	1924	202	159
Babe Adams	PIT N	RH	1912	1924	134	105
Total					336	264
Doc White	CHI A	LH	1904	1913	143	108
Ed Walsh	CHI A	RH	1904	1913	190	121
Total					333	229
Jerry Koosman	NY N	LH	1967	1977	137	122
Tom Seaver	NY N	RH	1967	1977	189	110
Total					326	232

Best Lefty-Righty Duos (*cont.*)

Player	Team	LH/RH	First	Last	W	L
Bill Sherdel	STL N	LH	1920	1930	142	110
Jesse Haines	STL N	RH	1920	1930	166	127
Total					308	237
Dave McNally	BAL A	LH	1965	1974	164	94
Jim Palmer	BAL A	RH	1965	1974	129	69
Total					293	163
Eppa Rixey	CIN N	LH	1921	1929	155	120
Dolf Luque	CIN N	RH	1921	1929	125	137
Total					280	257
Jim Kaat	MIN A	LH	1963	1972	151	109
Jim Perry	MIN A	RH	1963	1972	128	90
Total					279	199
Johnny Vander Meer	CIN N	LH	1938	1948	108	101
Bucky Walters	CIN N	RH	1938	1948	160	107
Total					268	208
Mike Flanagan	BAL A	LH	1975	1984	125	87
Jim Palmer	BAL A	RH	1975	1984	139	83
Total					264	170
Paul Splittorff	KC A	LH	1974	1983	125	107
Dennis Leonard	KC A	RH	1974	1983	136	93
Total					261	200
Tommy Bridges	DET A	LH	1933	1942	155	100
Schoolboy Rowe	DET A	RH	1933	1942	105	62
Total					260	162
Herb Pennock	NY A	LH	1923	1930	135	75
Waite Hoyt	NY A	RH	1923	1930	119	73
Total					254	148
Lefty Grove	PHI A	LH	1928	1933	152	41
George Earnshaw	PHI A	RH	1928	1933	98	58
Total					250	99
Sid Fernandez	NY N	LH	1984	1992	93	72
Dwight Gooden	NY N	RH	1984	1992	142	66
Total					235	138
Ed Killian	DET A	LH	1904	1910	98	74
George Mullin	DET A	RH	1904	1910	136	114
Total					234	188
Mickey Lolich	DET A	LH	1963	1970	116	93
Denny McLain	DET A	RH	1963	1970	117	62
Total					233	155

Best Lefty-Righty Duos (*cont.*)

Player	Team	LH/RH	First	Last	W	L
Eppa Rixey	PHI N	LH	1912	1917	70	69
Grover Alexander	PHI N	RH	1912	1917	162	75
Total					232	144
Doc White	CHI A	LH	1904	1910	123	80
Frank Smith	CHI A	RH	1904	1910	108	81
Total					231	161
Ed Lopat	NY A	LH	1948	1954	109	51
Allie Reynolds	NY A	RH	1948	1954	112	57
Total					221	108
Jack Pfiester	CHI N	LH	1906	1911	69	41
Three Finger Brown	CHI N	RH	1906	1911	148	55
Total					217	96
Whitey Ford	NY A	LH	1955	1962	132	56
Bob Turley	NY A	RH	1955	1962	82	52
Total					214	108
Jim Kaat	WAS A MIN A	LH	1959	1966	98	83
Camilo Pascual	WAS A MIN A	RH	1959	1966	114	75
Total					212	158
Mel Parnell	BOS A	LH	1948	1956	121	72
Ellis Kinder	BOS A	RH	1948	1956	88	52
Total					209	124
Bob Veale	PIT N	LH	1964	1972	109	87
Steve Blass	PIT N	RH	1964	1972	100	67
Total					209	154
Larry French	CHI N	LH	1935	1940	97	86
Bill Lee	CHI N	RH	1935	1940	110	87
Total					207	173
Tom Zachary	WAS A	LH	1919	1925	86	87
Walter Johnson	WAS A	RH	1919	1925	120	80
Total					206	167
Harry Brecheen	STL N	LH	1943	1952	127	79
George Munger	STL N	RH	1943	1952	74	49
Total					201	128
Reb Russell	CHI A	LH	1913	1919	74	60
Eddie Cicotte	CHI A	RH	1913	1919	126	84
Total					200	144

Best Lefty-Righty Duos (*cont.*)

Player	Team	LH/RH	First	Last	W	L
Doc White	CHI A	LH	1903	1909	124	82
Frank Owen	CHI A	RH	1903	1909	76	75
Total					200	157

INDEX

●

Boldface entries indicate record holder.

Bahnsen, Stan
  Most Shutout Losses, Career, 184
  Most Wins, Career, 211
  Shutout with Most Hits Allowed, AL, 190
  Twenty Wins One Year, 20 Losses the Next,
    AL, 204
Bailey, Bob
  Grand Slam Home Runs, NL, 36, 37, 38, 39
  Pinch-Hit Grand Slams, NL, 53
Bailey, Ed
  Brother Batteries, NL, 336
  Grand Slam Home Runs, NL, 34, 35, 36
  Most Games Caught, Career, 296
  Most Home Runs by Team, Game, NL, 367
  Most Pinch-Hit Grand Slams, Career, 55
  Most Pinch-Hit Home Runs, Career, 48
  Most RBIs, Game, NL, 153
  Most 20-Home Run Hitters, NL, 373
  Pinch-Hit Grand Slams, NL, 52
  Three Home Runs in One Game, NL, 75
  Walked Twice in One Inning, NL, 105
Bailey, Jim
  Brother Batteries, NL, 336
Bailey, Mark
  Grand Slam Home Runs, NL, 43
  Switch-Hit Home Runs in One Game, NL, 84
Bailor, Bob
  .300 Average in Rookie Year Only, AL, 306
Baines, Harold
  Best Home Run Duos, Season, AL, 386
  Grand Slam Home Runs, AL, 19, 20, 23
  Home Run and Double in One Inning, AL,
    100
  Most Extra-Base Hits, Game, AL, 91
  Most RBIs in One Inning, AL, 150
  Retired Numbers, AL, 332
  Three Consecutive Home Runs, Team, AL,
    356
  Three Home Runs in One Game, AL, 72, 73
Bair, Doug
  Most Grand Slams Allowed, Career, 270
  Most Relief Wins, Career, 245
  Most Relief Wins, Season, NL, 248
Bakely, Jersey
  Most Consecutive Losses, NL, 243
Baker, Bill
  Grand Slam Home Runs, NL, 31
Baker, Dusty
  Grand Slam Home Runs, NL, 40, 41, 42
  Most Home Runs by Team, Game, NL, 368
  Most RBIs in One Inning, NL, 151
  Most 30-Home Run Hitters, NL, 370
  Most 20-Home Run Hitters, NL, 374
  Stole 2nd, 3rd, and Home in One Game, NL,
    161
Baker, Frank
  Cycle Hitters, AL, 126
  Grand Slam Home Runs, AL, 3
  Most Assists, 3rd Baseman, Game, 300
  Most Extra-Base Hits, Game, AL, 89
  Most Stolen Bases, Game, AL, 158
  Most Triples, Rookie, AL, 307
  Stolen Base Duos, Season, AL, 402
  Two Legs of Triple Crown, AL, 123
Baker, Frank
  Grand Slam Home Runs, AL, 16
Baker, Gene
  Grand Slam Home Runs, NL, 34

Balboni, Steve
  Best Home Run Duos, Season, AL, 383
  Best Home Run Ratio, Career, 65
  Club Leaders, Home Runs, Season, AL, 64
  Grand Slam Home Runs, AL, 19, 20, 21, 22
  Most Consecutive Times Struck Out, AL, 178
  Most Home Runs, Season, AL, 58
  Three Consecutive Home Runs, Team, AL, 355
  Worst Hitters, 131
Baldschun, Jack
  Most Relief Wins, Season, NL, 247
Baldwin, Lady
  Most Strikeouts, Season before 1900, 223
Baldwin, Mark
  Most Home Runs, Pitcher, Career, 273
  Most Strikeouts, Season before 1900, 223
  Most Wins, Career, 211
  Twenty Wins with Last-Place Team, NL, 206
  Two Complete Game Wins in One Day, NL
    before 1900, 257
Ball, Neal
  Unassisted Triple Plays, 286
Bancroft, Dave
  Cycle Hitters, NL, 128
  Most Hits, Game, NL, 110
  Most Assists, Shortstop, Game, 300
  Most .300 Hitters, Season, NL, 408
  No Home Runs, Season, NL, 81
  Walked Twice in One Inning, NL, 105
Bando, Chris
  Brothers with Most Home Runs, Career, 87
Bando, Sal
  Best Home Run Duos, Career, AL, 393
  Best Home Run Duos, Season, AL, 380
  Brothers with Most Home Runs, Career, 87
  Grand Slam Home Runs, AL, 14, 15, 16
  Most Home Runs by Position, Career, AL, 66
  Most Home Runs by Team, Game, AL, 365
  Most Times Walked, Game, 103
  Three Consecutive Home Runs, Team, AL, 354
Bankhead, Dan
  Home Run in First At-Bat in Majors, NL, 68
Banks, Ernie
  Best Home Run Duos, Season, NL, 388, 392
  Best Home Run Ratio, Career, 65
  Career Spent with One Team, 331
  Elected to Hall of Fame in First Year Eligible,
    333
  Grand Slam Home Runs, NL, 34, 35, 36, 37
  Great Players Who Never Played in a World
    Series, 332
  Home Run and Double in One Inning, NL, 100
  Most Consecutive Games Played, 174
  Most Extra-Base Hits, Game, NL, 93
  Most Grand Slams, Career, 47
  Most Grand Slams, Season, NL, 47
  Most Home Runs, Career, 62
  Most Home Runs, Season, NL, 59, 60, 61
  Most Home Runs by Position, Career, NL, 67
  **Most Home Runs by Position, Season, NL,
    67**
  Most Home Runs by Team, Game, NL, 367
  **Most Putouts in Nine Innings, First Base-
    man, 298**
  Most RBIs, Career, 147
  Most Triples, Game, NL, 99
  Most 20-Home Run Hitters, NL, 374
  Retired Numbers, NL, 333

David, Andre
  Home Run in First At-Bat in Majors, AL, 68
Davis, Alvin
  Grand Slam Home Runs, AL, 20, 21, 22, 23
  Most Grand Slams, Season, AL, 47
  **Most Putouts in Nine Innings, First Base-
  man, 298**
  Most RBIs, Game, AL, 152
  One Hundred or More RBIs, Rookie,AL, 308
Davis, Bud
  Most Walks in One Game, AL, 232
Davis, Chili
  Grand Slam Home Runs, NL, 42
  Pinch-Hit Grand Slams, NL, 54
  Switch-Hit Home Runs in One Game, AL, 84
  .300-Hitting Outfields, NL, 419
  Two Pinch-Hit Home Runs in One Game, NL,
    350
Davis, Curt
  Best Control Pitchers, Career, 258
  Best-Hitting Pitchers, Season, NL, 279
  Doubleheader Shutouts, NL, 432
  Grand Slam Home Runs, NL, 30
  Grand Slams, Pitcher, NL, 275
  Most Home Runs, Pitcher, Career, 273
  Most Wins, Career, 211
  Won Twenty and Hit .300 in Same Year, NL,
    272
Davis, Dick
  Grand Slam Home Runs, AL, 17, 18
Davis, Dixie
  Most Innings Pitched, Game, AL, 260
  Most Walks in One Game, AL, 233
Davis, Eric
  Best Home Run Duos, Season, NL, 391
  Cycle Hitters, NL, 128
  Grand Slam Home Runs, NL, 43
  Most Consecutive Times Struck Out, NL, 178
  Most Grand Slams, Season, NL, 47
  Most Home Runs, Season, NL, 61
  Most Runs, Game, NL, 146
  Most Stolen Bases, Game, NL, 160
  Most Stolen Bases, Season, NL, 155
  Most Times Struck Out, Game, NL, 108
  Thirty Home Runs with 30 Stolen Bases, Sea-
    son, NL, 85
  Three Consecutive Home Runs, Team, NL,
    359
  Three Home Runs in One Game, NL, 76
  Twenty Home Runs with 50 Stolen bases, Sea-
    son, 84
Davis, George
  Grand Slam Home Runs, NL, 25
  Longest Hitting Streaks, NL, 169
  Most Extra-Base Hits, Game, NL, 91
  Most Hits, Game, NL, 110
  Most Runs, Career, 141
  Most Runs Produced, Career, 149
  Most Stolen Bases, Game, AL, 157
  Most Triples, Game, NL, 98
  No-Hitters, NL, 194
  Two Doubles in One Inning, NL, 97
Davis, Glenn
  Three Home Runs in One Game, NL, 76
Davis, Harry
  Cycle Hitters, AL, 126
  Grand Slam Home Runs, AL, 3
  Two Grand Slams in One Game, AL, 346

Two Legs of Triple Crown, AL, 123
Davis, Jim
  Four Strikeouts in One Inning, NL, 225
Davis, Jody
  Grand Slam Home Runs, NL, 42, 43, 44
  Most Games Caught, Career, 296
  Most Games Caught, Season, 294
  Most Runs, Game, NL, 146
Davis, Jumbo
  Cycle Hitters, Other Leagues, 130
Davis, Kiddo
  Most Doubles, Rookie, NL, 307
  Most .300 Hitters, Season, NL, 410
  .300-Hitting Outfields, NL, 418
Davis, Lefty
  .300-Hitting Outfields, NL, 416
Davis, Mark
  Most Relief Losses, Season, NL, 250
  Most Saves, Season, NL, 253
  Most Wins Plus Saves, Season, NL, 254
Davis, Mike
  Best Home Run Trios, Season, AL, 376
  Home Runs by First Two Batters in Game,
    AL, 351
  Stolen Base Duos, Season, AL, 401
Davis, Peaches
  Doubleheader Shutouts, NL, 432
Davis, Ron
  Most Consecutive Strikeouts, AL, 243
  Most Relief Losses, Career, 248
  Most Relief Losses, Season, AL, 249
  Most Relief Wins, Season, AL, 245
  Most Saves, Season, AL, 252
  Most Saves, Career, 251
Davis, Spud
  Grand Slam Home Runs, NL, 28, 29
  Most Games Caught, Career, 295
  Most .300 Hitters, Season, NL, 410
  Teammates Who Finished 1-2 in Batting, NL,
    421
Davis, Storm
  Most Consecutive Wins, AL, 239
  Most Wins, Career, 213
Davis, Tommy
  Grand Slam Home Runs, AL, 16
  Grand Slam Home Runs, NL, 35, 36, 37
  Longest Hitting Streaks, NL, 173
  Most RBIs Season, NL, 147
  **.300 Batting Average as a Pinch Hitter, Ca-
  reer, 165**
Davis, Willie
  Grand Slam Home Runs, NL, 36, 38, 39
  Longest Hitting Streaks, NL, 170
  Most Hits, Game, NL, 111
  Stolen Base Duos, Season, NL, 403
Dawley, Bill
  Most Relief Wins, Season, NL, 248
Dawson, Andre
  Best Home Run Duos, Season, NL, 388, 390
  Best Home Run Trios, Season, NL, 378
  Club Leaders, Home Runs, Season, NL, 65
  Cycle Hitters, NL, 128
  Grand Slam Home Runs, NL, 42, 43, 44, 45
  Most Consecutive Hits, NL, 177
  Most Home Runs, Career, 63
  Most Home Runs, Season, NL, 59
  Most Home Runs in One Inning, Team, NL,
    362

Donohue, Jiggs
Most Putouts in Nine Innings, First Baseman, 298
Most Runs, Game, AL, 142
Donohue, Pete
Best Control Pitchers, Career, 258
Most Wins, Career, 211
Teams with Three 20-Game Winners, NL, 438
Won Twenty and Hit .300 in Same Year, NL, 272
Donohue, Red
Most Complete Games, Season, AL, 264, 265
Most Complete Games, Season, NL, 266
Most Consecutive Losses, NL, 243
Most Wins, Career, 210
No-Hitters, NL, 193
Donovan, Dick
Doubleheader Shutouts, AL, 428
Most Home Runs, Pitcher, Career, 272
Most Wins, Career, 212
No-Hitters Broken Up by Home Runs, AL, 200
Two Home Runs in One Game, Pitcher, AL, 273
Two Home Runs in One Game Twice in One Season, Pitcher, 274
Donovan, Patsy
Grand Slam Home Runs, NL, 25
.300-Hitting Outfields, NL, 414, 415, 416
Donovan, Wild Bill
Best Won-Lost Record, Season, AL, 203
Most Complete Games, Season, AL, 264, 265
Most Complete Games, Season, NL, 267
Most Innings Pitched, Game, NL, 260
Most Innings Pitched, Season, NL, 269
Most Shutouts, Career, 183
Most Strikeouts, Season, NL, 221
Most Wins, Career, 210
Pitchers Who Stole Home, AL, 277
Stole 2nd, 3rd, and Home in One Game, AL, 160
Teams with Three 20-Game Winners, AL, 437
Dooin, Red
Grand Slam Home Runs, NL, 26
Most Errors by Position, Season, NL, since 1900, 286
Most Games Caught, Career, 296
Doolan, Mickey
Worst Hitters, 131
Doran, Bill
Grand Slam Home Runs, NL, 44, 45
Dorgan, Mike
Grand Slam Home Runs, NL, 24
Dorish, Harry
Pitchers Who Stole Home, NL, 277
Dorner, Gus
Most Complete Games, Season, NL, 267
Most Walks in One Game, AL, 232
Doscher, Herm
Fathers and Sons in Baseball, 343
Doscher, Jack
Fathers and Sons in Baseball, 343
Dotson, Richard
Most Wins, Career, 213
No-Hitters Broken Up By Home Runs, AL, 200
Dotterer, Dutch
Grand Slam Home Runs, NL, 35

Dougherty, Patsy
Cycle Hitters, AL, 126
Highest Batting Average, Rookie, AL, 309
Most Triples, Game, AL, 98
No-Hit Spoilers—The Only Hit Most Often, 137
.300-Hitting Outfields, AL, 410
Douglas, Phil
Doubleheader Shutouts, NL, 431
Douthit, Taylor
Grand Slam Home Runs, NL, 28
Longest Hitting Streaks, NL, 171
Most Consecutive Hits, NL, 177
Most Runs, Game, NL, 144
Most .300 Hitters, Season, NL, 408, 409
.300-Hitting Outfields, NL, 417
Dowd, Tommy
Cycle Hitters, NL, 128
Dowling, Pete
Most Times Struck Out, Game, NL, 108
Downing, Al
Doubleheader Shutouts, NL, 433
Most Consecutive Strikeouts, NL, 244
Most Strikeouts, Rookie, AL, 313
Most Strikeouts, Season, AL, 218
Most Strikeouts per Nine Innings, Career, 237
Most Wins, Career, 212
Perfect Innings, AL, 226
Downing, Brian
Best Home Run Duos, Season, AL, 385
Fewest Errors by Position, Season, AL, 285
Grand Slam Home Runs, AL, 18, 19, 21, 23
Most Consecutive Errorless Games by Position, AL, 286
Most Leadoff Home Runs, Career, 78
Most Leadoff Home Runs, Season, 78
Most 20-Home Run Hitters, AL, 372
Three Consecutive Home Runs, Team, AL, 355
Two Grand Slams in One Game, AL, 346
Downs, Dave
Shutout in First Start in Majors, NL, 189
Doyle, Denny
Longest Hitting Streaks, AL, 167
Walked Twice in One Inning, NL, 105
Doyle, Jack
Most Errors by Position, Season, NL, since 1900, 286
Most Hits, Game, NL, 110
Doyle, Jess
Two Home Runs in One Game, Pitcher, AL, 273
Doyle, Larry
Grand Slam Home Runs, NL, 27
Most Steals of Home, Career, 161
Most Stolen Bases, Game, NL, 159
Doyle, Slow Joe
Doubleheader Shutouts, AL, 425
Shutout in First Start in Majors, AL, 187
Shutout in First Two Major League Starts, AL, 189
Drabowsky, Moe
Most Relief Wins, Season, AL, 246
Undefeated Seasons, 208
Drago, Dick
Most Consecutive Times Struck Out, AL, 178
Most Wins, Career, 213

Harper, Brian
  Grand Slam Home Runs, AL, 23
  Longest Hitting Streaks, AL, 169
Harper, George
  Grand Slam Home Runs, NL, 28
  Most .300 Hitters, Season, NL, 408
  Three Home Runs in One Game, NL, 73
Harper, Harry
  Doubleheader Shutouts, AL, 425
Harper, Jack
  Three Hundred or More Innings Pitched,
    Rookie, NL, 312
Harper, Terry
  Grand Slam Home Runs, NL, 43
Harper, Tommy
  Grand Slam Home Runs, AL, 15, 16
  Longest Hitting Streaks, NL, 172
  Most Leadoff Home Runs, Career, 78
  Most Leadoff Home Runs, Season, 78
  Most Stolen Bases, Career, 157
  Most Stolen Bases, Game, AL, 158
  Most Stolen Bases, Season, AL, 186
  Thirty Home Runs with 30 Stolen Bases, Sea-
    son, AL, 84
Harrah, Toby
  Grand Slam Home Runs, AL, 16, 18, 21
  Three Consecutive Home Runs, Team, AL,
    356
Harrelson, Bud
  Hardest to Double Up, Career, 116
  No Home Runs, Season, NL, 82
  Most Putouts, Shortstop, Game, 302
Harrelson, Ken
  Grand Slam Home Runs, AL, 14
  Most Home Runs, Season, AL, 58
  Three Home Runs in One Game, AL, 71
Harris, Bucky
  Best Double-Play Combinations, Season, 296
  Most Wins, Manager, Career, 333
  No Home Runs, Season, AL, 79
  Pennant-Winning Rookie Managers, AL, 315
  .300 Average in Rookie Year Only, AL, 304
Harris, Dave
  Grand Slam Home Runs, AL, 5
Harris, Greg W.
  Struck Out Twice in One Inning, NL, 107
  Worst-Hitting Pitchers, 281
Harris, Joe
  Most Consecutive Losses, AL, 241
  Most Innings Pitched, Game, AL, 260
  Most Shutout Losses, Season, AL, 186
Harris, Lenny
  Grand Slam Home Runs, NL, 45
Harris, Lum
  Most Consecutive Losses, AL, 241
Harris, Spence
  Grand Slam Home Runs, AL, 4
Harrison, Chuck
  Grand Slam Home Runs, NL, 37
Harshman, Jack
  Most Home Runs, Pitcher, Career, 272
  Most Home Runs, Pitcher, Season, 278
  Most Home Runs by Team, Game, AL, 364
  Most Strikeouts in Nine Inning Game, AL, 227
  Two Home Runs in One Game, Pitcher, AL,
    273
  Two Home Runs in One Game Twice in One
    Season, Pitcher, 274

Hart, Jim Ray
  Best Home Run Duos, Season, NL, 386
  Best Home Run Trios, Season, NL, 377, 378
  Cycle Hitters, NL, 130
  Grand Slam Home Runs, NL, 37
  Most Pinch-Hit Home Runs, Career, 47
  Most RBIs in One Inning, NL, 151
  Most 30-Home Run Hitters, NL, 370, 371
  Thirty or More Home Runs, Rookie, NL, 305
Hartley, Grover
  Two Doubles in One Inning, AL, 96
Hartnett, Gabby
  Best Home Run Duos, Season, NL, 386
  Grand Slam Home Runs, NL, 28, 29, 30
  Longest Hitting Streaks, NL, 170
  Most Game Caught, Career, 297
  Most Home Runs, Season, NL, 61
  Pennant-Winning Rookie Managers, NL, 316
Hartsel, Topsy
  Most Putouts, Outfielder, Game, 290
  Most Stolen Bases, Game, AL, 158
Hartung, Clint
  Most Walks in One Game, NL, 235
Hartzel, Roy
  Grand Slam Home Runs, AL, 3
  Home Run and Double in One Inning, AL, 99
  Most RBIs, Game, AL, 152
Harvey, Brian
  Most Saves, Career, 251
  Most Saves, Season, AL, 252
  Most Wins Plus Saves, Season, 256
Harvey, Ervin
  Most Hits, Game, AL, 109
Hassamaer, Bill
  Cycle Hitters, NL, 129
  Most Triples, Game, NL, 98
  .300-Hitting Outfields, NL, 414
Hassett, Buddy
  Longest Hitting Streaks, AL, 168
  Most Consecutive Hits, NL, 176
Hassey, Ron
  Home Run and Double in One Inning, AL, 99
  Most No-Hitters Caught, Career, 300
  Three Consecutive Home Runs, Team, AL, 357
Hassler, Andy
  Most Consecutive Losses, AL, 242
  Most Walks in One Game, AL, 233
Hatcher, Billy
  Grand Slam Home Runs, NL, 44
  Most Doubles, Game, NL, 96
  Most Extra-Base Hits, Game, NL, 93
Hatcher, Mickey
  Most Consecutive Hits, AL, 175
  Most Hits in Three Consecutive Games, AL, 118
  Most Home Runs in One Inning, Team, AL,
    361
  Two Pinch-Hit Home Runs in One Game, AL,
    349
  Two Pinch-Hit Home Runs in One Inning,
    Team, AL, 347
Hatton, Grady
  Grand Slam Home Runs, AL, 10
  Grand Slam Home Runs, NL, 32
  Home Runs by First Two Batters in Game,
    NL, 351
  Three Consecutive Home Runs, Team, NL, 357
Hauser, Joe
  Most Extra-Base Hits, Game, AL, 88

Best Won-Lost Record, Season, AL, 203
Doubleheader Shutouts, AL, 428, 429
Fewest Base Runners per Nine Innings, Career, 262
Most Complete Games, Season, AL, 265
Most Shutouts, Career, 182
Most Strikeouts, Career, 227
Most 20-Win Seasons, 208
Most Wins, Career, 209
No-Hitters, AL, 192
Perfect Games, 200
Retired Numbers, AL, 332
Teams with Three 20-Game Winners, AL, 438
Won 20 and Hit .300 in Same Year, AL, 272
Hurst, Bruce
  Most Wins, Career, 213
  No-Hitters Broken Up by Home Runs, NL, 201
Hurst, Don
  Grand Slam Home Runs, NL, 28
  Most 100-RBI Hitters, NL, 398
  Most .300 Hitters, Season, NL, 408, 409
  Most 30-Home Run Hitters, NL, 370
Husting, Bert
  Doubleheader Shutouts, AL, 426
Hutchings, Johnny
  Doubleheader Shutouts, NL, 432
Hutchinson, Bill
  Most Home Runs, Pitcher, Career, 273
  Most Home Runs, Pitcher, Season, 276
  Most Strikeouts, Season before 1900, 223
  Most Wins, Career, 210
  Two Complete Game Wins in One Day, NL before 1900, 255
Hutchinson, Fred
  Best-Hitting Pitchers, Career, 280
  Doubleheader Shutouts, AL, 427
  Pitchers Who Stole Home, AL, 277
  Retired Numbers, NL, 332
Hutto, Jim
  Grand Slam Home Runs, NL, 38
  Pinch Hit Grand Slams, NL, 53
Hutton, Tommy
  Most Pinch-Hits, Career, 164

Incaviglia, Pete
  Grand Slam Home Runs, AL, 21, 22, 23
  Most Home Runs by Team, Game, AL, 365
  Thirty or More Home Runs, Rookie, AL, 305
  Two Doubles in One Inning, AL, 97
Iorg, Dane
  Most Extra-Base Hits, Game, NL, 94
Irelan, Hal
  Grounded into Most Double Plays, Game, NL, 117
Irvin, Monte
  Grand Slam Home Runs, NL, 32, 33, 34
  Grounded into Most Double Plays, Game, NL, 117
  Most Home Runs in Final Season, 86
  Most Home Runs in One Inning, Team, NL, 362
  Most Home Runs by Team, Game, NL, 366
  Most 20-Home Run Hitters, NL, 373
Irwin, Arthur
  Most Putouts, Shortstop, Game, 300
Irwin, Charlie
  Grand Slam Home Runs, NL, 27

Ivie, Mike
  Grand Slam Home Runs, NL, 41, 42
  Most Pinch-Hit Grand Slams, Career, 55
  Pinch-Hit Grand Slams, NL, 53
  Two Doubles in One Inning, NL, 98

Jablonski, Ray
  Grand Slam Home Runs, NL, 35
  One Hundred or More RBIs, Rookie, NL, 309
  One Hundred or More RBIs with Fewer than 15 Home Runs (Since 1946), 150
Jackson, Bo
  Grand Slam Home Runs, AL, 21, 23
  Home Runs in Most Consecutive At-Bats, AL, 179
  Most Consecutive Times Struck Out, AL, 178
  Most Times Struck Out, Game, AL, 108
  Struck Out Twice in One Inning, AL, 106
  Three Home Runs in One Game, AL, 73
Jackson, Danny
  No-Hitters Broken Up by Home Runs, NL, 201
Jackson, Darrin
  Grand Slam Home Runs, NL, 45
Jackson, Grant
  Most Relief Wins, Career, 245
  Undefeated Seasons, 202
Jackson, Joe
  Highest Batting Average, Career, 133
  Grand Slam Home Runs, AL, 3
  Longest Hitting Streaks, AL, 167
  Most Seasons with 200 Hits, 135
  Most RBIs, Game, AL, 153
  Most Triples, Game, AL, 98
  Most 200-Hit Batters, AL, 421
  Stole 2nd, 3rd, and Home in One Game, AL, 160
  .300 Batting Average in Final Season, 102
Jackson, Larry
  Doubleheader Shutouts, NL, 434
  Most 1-0 Losses, Career, 202
  Most Shutouts, Career, 183
  Most Wins, Career, 211
  Twenty Wins One Year, 20 Losses the Next, NL, 205
Jackson, Randy
  Grand Slam Home Runs, NL, 33
  Grounded into Most Double Plays, Game, NL, 117
  Three Consecutive Home Runs, Team, NL, 358
Jackson, Reggie
  Best Home Run Duos, Career, AL, 393
  Best Home Run Duos, Season, AL, 381, 382
  Best Home Run Ratio, Career, 65
  Club Leaders, Home Runs, Season, AL, 64
  Easiest to Strike Out, Career, 122
  Elected to Hall of Fame, 333
  Grand Slam Home Runs, AL, 15, 16, 17, 18, 19, 20
  Home Runs in Most Consecutive Games, 78
  Most Consecutive Times Struck Out, AL, 178
  Most Grand Slams, Career, 46
  Most Grand Slams, Season, AL, 47
  Most Home Runs, Career, 62
  Most Home Runs, Season, AL, 56, 57
  Most Home Runs in Final Season, 84
  Most Pinch-Hit Grand Slams, Career, 55
  Most Pinch-Hit Home Runs, Career, 48
  Most RBIs, Career, 147

Johnson, Syl
  Doubleheader Shutouts, NL, 426
  Most Wins, Career, 211
Johnson, Tom
  Most Relief Wins, Season, AL, 244
Johnson, Wallace
  Most Pinch Hits, Season, NL, 164
  Most Pinch Hits, Career, NL, 164
Johnson, Walter
  Best-Hitting Pitchers, Season, AL, 279
  Best Lefty-Righty Duos, 442
  Best Won-Lost Record, Season, AL, 203
  Career Spent with One Team, 330
  Doubleheader Shutouts, AL, 426
  Fewest Base Runners per Nine Innings, Career,
    262
  Fewest Errors by Position, Season, AL,
    286
  Four Strikeouts in One Inning, AL, 224
  Grand Slam Home Runs, AL, 3
  Grand Slams, Pitcher, AL, 275
  Highest Percentage of Team's Wins, AL, 206
  Lowest ERA, Season, AL, 258
  Lowest ERA, Season, NL, 259
  Most Complete Games, Season, AL, 263, 264,
    265
  Most Complete 1-0 Wins, Career, 202
  Most Consecutive Wins, AL, 238
  Most Games with Ten or More Strikeouts, Ca-
    reer, 236
  Most Hits, Pitcher, Career, 277
  Most Home Runs, Pitcher, Career, 272
  Most Innings Pitched, Game, AL, 260
  Most Innings Pitched, Season, AL, 268, 269
  Most Losses, Career, 214
  Most 1-0 Losses, Career, 202
  Most Shutout Losses, Career, 183
  Most Shutout Losses, Season, AL, 184
  Most Shutouts, Career, 183
  Most Shutouts, Season, AL, 184, 185
  Most Strikeouts, Career, 226
  Most Strikeouts, Season, AL, 216, 217, 218,
    219
  Most Strikeouts in Extra-Inning Game, 231
  Most 20-Win Seasons, 207
  Most Wins, Career, 207
  Most Wins by Age, Season, AL, 215
  No Hits Allowed, Less than Nine Innings,
    197
  No-Hitters, AL, 189
  Shutout with Most Hits Allowed, AL, 192
  Thirty-Game Winners, AL, 207
  .300-Win Club, 214
  Triple-Crown Pitchers, AL, 257
  Twenty Wins One Year, 20-Losses the Next,
    AL, 204
  Twenty Wins and 20 Losses in Same Year,
    AL, 205
  Won 20 and Hit .300 in Same Year, AL, 269
Johnston, Doc
  Most Consecutive Hits, AL, 176
Johnston, Jimmy
  Cycle Hitters, NL, 130
  Longest Hitting Streaks, NL, 170
  Most Consecutive Hits, NL, 178
  Most Runs, Game, NL, 144
  Most Steals of Home, Career, 161
  Stole 2nd, 3rd, and Home in One Game, NL,
    161

Johnstone, Jay
  Grand Slam Home Runs, AL, 14, 17
  Most Pinch-Hit Home Runs, Career, 48
  Most Pinch Hits, Career, 164
  Pinch-Hit Grand Slams, AL, 50
  .300-Hitting Outfields, NL, 414
Jolley, Smead
  Longest Hitting Streaks, AL, 168
  One Hundred or More RBIs, Rookie, AL, 308
Jolly, Dave
  Most Relief Wins, Season, NL, 247
Jones, Barry
  Most Relief Wins, Season, AL, 246
Jones, Bobby
  Two Doubles in One Inning, AL, 97
Jonas, Bumpus
  No-Hitters, NL, 193
  Rookie No-Hitters, NL, 310
Jones, Charley
  Most Triples, Game, Other Leagues, 99
  Two Home Runs in One Inning, NL, 69
Jones, Charlie
  Grand Slam Home Runs, AL, 3
Jones, Cleon
  Grand Slam Home Runs, NL, 37
  Longest Hitting Streaks, NL, 171
  Three Consecutive Home Runs, Team, NL,
    359
  Most Times Walked in One Doubleheader,
    NL, 106
Jones, Dalton
  Most Pinch Hits, Career, 164
Jones, Davy
  Grand Slam Home Runs, NL, 25
Jones, Doug
  Most Relief Losses, Season, AL, 250
  Most Relief Wins, Season, NL, 248
  Most Saves, Career, 251
  Most Saves, Season, AL, 252
  Most Saves, Season, NL, 253
  Most Wins Plus Saves, Season, 251, 252
Jones, Fielder
  Grand Slam Home Runs, NL, 25
  Highest Batting Average, Rookie, NL, 309
  Most Extra-Base Hits, Game, AL, 88
  Most Runs, Game, AL, 141
  .300-Hitting Outfields, NL, 416
  Unassisted Double Plays, Outfielder, 291
Jones, Jake
  Grand Slam Home Runs, AL, 8
Jones, Jimmy
  Shutout in First Start in Majors, NL, 189
Jones, Mack
  Grand Slam Home Runs, NL, 37, 38
  Most Hits in First Game, 304
  Most 30-Home Run Hitters, NL, 371
  Most 20-Home Run Hitters, NL, 373
Jones, Nippy
  Most Home Runs in One Inning, Team, NL, 362
Jones, Odell
  Undefeated Seasons, 209
Jones, Oscar
  Most Complete Games, Rookie, NL, 314
  Most Complete Games, Season, NL, 265, 266
  Most Innings Pitched, Season, NL, 269
  Three Hundred or More Innings Pitched,
    Rookie, NL, 312
  Twenty Wins One Year, 20 Losses the Next,
    NL, 204

Leibrandt, Charlie
  Shutout in First Start in Majors, NL, 189
  Most Wins, Career, 212
Leifield, Lefty
  Doubleheader Shutouts, NL, 430
  Most Shutouts, Season, NL, 186
  Most Wins, Career, 212
  No Hits Allowed, Less than Nine Innings, 196
  Pitchers Who Stole Home, NL, 278
  Shutout in First Start in Majors, NL, 188
Lemaster, Denny
  Most Strikeouts per Nine Innings, Career, 237
Lemaster, Johnnie
  Home Run in First At-Bat in Majors, NL, 68
  Worst Hitters, 131
Lemke, Mark
  Most Home Runs in One Inning, Team, NL,
    363
Lemon, Bob
  Career Spent with One Team, 332
  Most Consecutive Wins, AL, 238
  Most Home Runs, Pitcher, Career, 272
  Most Home Runs, Pitcher, Season, 276
  Most Shutouts, Season, AL, 184
  Most 20-Win Seasons, 207
  Most Walks in One Game, AL, 233
  Most Wins, Career, 210
  No-Hitters, AL, 192
  No-Hitters Broken Up By Home Runs, AL,
    200
  Teams with Three 20-Game Winners, AL, 438
  Two Home Runs in One Game, Pitcher, AL,
    273
Lemon, Chet
  Grand Slam Home Runs, AL, 20
  Most Home Runs in One Inning, Team, AL,
    360
  Most 20-Home Run Hitters, AL, 371
Lemon, Jim
  Best Home Run Duos, Season, AL, 381, 383
  Best Home Run Ratio, Career, 66
  Best Home Run Trios, Season, AL, 374
  Grand Slam Home Runs, AL, 11
  Most Home Runs, Season, AL, 57
  Most RBIs in One Inning, AL, 151
  Most 30-Home Run Hitters, AL, 369
  Three Home Runs in One Game, AL, 70
  Two Home Runs in One Inning, AL, 67
Lemonds, Dave
  Most Consecutive Times Struck Out, AL, 177
Lenhardt, Don
  Grand Slam Home Runs, AL, 9
  Most Grand Slams, Season, AL, 46
Lennox, Ed
  Cycle Hitters, Other Leagues, 130
Leon, Eddie
  Three Consecutive Home Runs, Team, AL, 354
Leonard, Dennis
  Best Lefty-Righty Duos, 441
  Most Strikeouts, Season, AL, 217
  Most Wins, Career, 211
Leonard, Dutch
  Doubleheader Shutouts, AL, 426
  Lowest ERA, Season, AL, 258
  Most No-Hitters, Career, 199
  Most Wins, Career, 211
  No-Hitters, AL, 191
Leonard, Emil "Dutch"
  Most Wins, Career, 210

Leonard, Jeffrey
  Grand Slam Home Runs, AL, 22
  Grand Slam Home Runs, NL, 42, 43
  Most Times Struck Out, Game, AL, 108
  .300-Hitting Outfields, NL, 418
  Two Pinch-Hit Home Runs in One Game, NL,
    350
Lepcio, Ted
  Grand Slam Home Runs, AL, 10, 11, 12
  Most Home Runs in One Inning, Team, AL,
    360
Leppert, Don
  Home Run in First At-Bat in Majors, NL, 68
  Three Home Runs in One Game, AL, 70
Lerch, Randy
  Two Home Runs in One Game, Pitcher, NL,
    274
Lerchen, Dutch
  Fathers and Sons in Baseball, 344
Lerchen, George
  Fathers and Sons in Baseball, 344
Lersch, Barry
  Most Consecutive Losses, NL, 243
Leslie, Sam
  Cycle Hitters, NL, 129
  Grand Slam Home Runs, NL, 29
  Most Extra-Base Hits, Game, NL, 93
  Most Pinch Hits, Season, NL, 163
Leverenz, Walt
  Worst Won-Lost Record, Season, 202
Levsen, Dutch
  Two Complete Game Wins in One Day, AL,
    255
Lewis, Buddy
  **Most Hits in Four Consecutive Games, AL,
    120**
Lewis, Duffy
  Grand Slam Home Runs, AL, 3
  .300-Hitting Outfields, AL, 410
Lewis, Jack
  Most Triples, Game, Other Leagues, 100
Lewis, Ted
  Most Consecutive Wins, NL, 239
  Most Complete Games, Season, AL, 264
Lezcano, Sixto
  Grand Slam Home Runs, AL, 17, 18
  Most Home Runs by Team, Game, AL, 364
Libke, Al
  Longest Hitting Streaks, NL, 173
Liebhardt, Glenn
  Fathers and Sons in Baseball, 344
Liebhardt, Glenn (Jr.)
  Fathers and Sons in Baseball, 344
Lillie, Jim
  Grand Slam Home Runs, NL, 25
Lilliquist, Derek
  Two Home Runs in One Game, Pitcher, NL,
    274
Limmer, Lou
  Grand Slam Home Runs, AL, 9
Lind, Carl
  Most Doubles, Rookie, AL, 307
Lindaman, Vive
  Doubleheader Shutouts, NL, 430
  Most Complete Games, Rookie, NL, 314
  Most Shutout Losses, Season, NL, 187
  Shutout in First Start in Majors, NL, 188
  Three Hundred or More Innings Pitched,
    Rookie, NL, 312

Madlock, Bill (*cont.*)
  Grand Slam Home Runs, NL, 40, 42
  Most Hits, Game, NL, 111
  Most Home Runs in Final Season, 87
  Most Runs, Game, NL, 146
  Pinch-Hit Grand Slams, NL,, 53
  Three Consecutive Home Runs, Team, AL,
    355
  Three Home Runs in One Game, AL, 71
  Two Grand Slams in One Game, NL, 347
Magee, Lee
  Grand Slam Home Runs, NL, 27
  Most Assists, Outfielder, Game, 290
  Most Assists, Second Baseman, Game, 300
  Most Runs, Game, NL, 144
  Most Times Caught Stealing, Game, AL,
    161
Magee, Sherry
  Grand Slam Home Runs, NL, 27
  Most Extra-Base Hits, Game, NL, 92
  Most Steals of Home, Career, 161
  Most Stolen Bases, Career, 157
  Most Stolen Bases, Game, NL, 159
  No-Hit Spoilers—The Only Hit Most Often,
    136
  Two Legs of Triple Crown, NL, 125
Maggert, Harl
  Fathers and Sons in Baseball, 344
Maggert, Harl (Jr.)
  Fathers and Sons in Baseball, 344
  Pinch-Hit Grand Slams, NL, 52
  Two Grand Slams in One Game, NL, 346
Maglie, Sal
  Doubleheader Shutouts, NL, 432
  Most Consecutive Wins, NL, 240
  Most Wins, Career, 212
  No-Hitters, NL, 194
Magrane, Joe
  Doubleheader Shutouts, NL, 433
Maguire, Freddie
  No Home Runs, Season, NL, 81
Mahaffey, Art
  Doubleheader Shutouts, NL, 432
  Grand Slam Home Runs, NL, 36
  Grand Slams, Pitcher, NL, 276
  Most Strikeouts in Nine Inning Game, NL, 229
Mahler, Mickey
  Most Wins by Brothers, 340
  Pitching Brothers, Same Team, NL, 338
Mahler, Rick
  Most Wins by Brothers, 340
  No-Hitters Broken Up by Home Runs, NL,
    201
  Pitching Brothers, Same Team, NL, 338
Mahoney, Jim
  Three Consecutive Home Runs, Team, AL,
    353
Mails, Duster
  Doubleheader Shutouts, AL, 426
  Shutout with Most Hits Allowed, AL, 190
  Undefeated Seasons, 208
Main, Alex
  No-Hitters, Other Leagues, 196
Maisel, Fritz
  Most Steals of Home, Career, 161
  Most Stolen Bases, Game, AL, 158
  Most Stolen Bases, Season, AL, 155
  Most Times Caught Stealing, Game, AL,
    161

  Stole 2nd, 3rd, and Home in One Game, AL,
    160
  Stolen Base Duos, Season, AL, 401
Maisel, George
  300-Hitting Outfields, NL, 416
Majeski, Hank
  Grand Slam Home Runs, NL, 29
  Most Extra-Base Hits in a Doubleheader,
    AL, 95
  One Hundred or More RBIs with Fewer than
    15 Home Runs (Since 1946), 150
Malarkey, John
  Doubleheader Shutouts, NL, 429
Malay, Charlie
  Fathers and Sons in Baseball, 344
Malay, Joe
  Fathers and Sons in Baseball, 344
Maldonado, Candy
  Cycle Hitters, NL, 129
  Grand Slam Home Runs, NL, 44
  Most Pinch-Hit Home Runs, Career, 46
  Most Pinch Hits, Season, NL, 163
  Pinch-Hit Grand Slams, NL, 54
  Three Consecutive Home Runs, Team, AL, 355
Maler, Jim
  Grand Slam Home Runs, AL, 19
Malkmus, Bobby
  Grand Slam Home Runs, NL, 35
Mallon, Les
  .300 Average in Rookie Year Only, NL, 306
Malone, Pat
  Most Wins, Career, 211
Maloney, Bill
  Grand Slam Home Runs, NL, 27
Maloney, Jim
  Most Consecutive Strikeouts, NL, 243
  Most Games with Ten or More Strikeouts, Ca-
    reer, 236
  Most No-Hitters, Career, 199
  Most Strikeouts, Season, NL, 220, 221
  Most Strikeouts in Extra-Inning Game, NL,
    231
  Most Strikeouts in Nine Inning Game, NL, 229
  Most Strikeouts per Nine Innings, Career, 239
  Most Walks in One Game, NL, 235
  Most Wins, Career, 246
  No-Hitters, NL, 194
  No-Hitters Broken Up in Extra Innings, 197
Malzone, Frank
  Grand Slam Home Runs, AL, 10, 11
  Most Home Runs in One Inning, Team, AL,
    360
Mamaux, Al
  Doubleheader Shutouts, NL, 430
  Most Shutouts, Season, NL, 186
Mancuso, Gus
  Grand Slam Home Runs, NL, 30
  Most Games Caught, Career, 295
  Two Grand Slams in One Game, NL, 346
Mangual, Angel
  Grand Slam Home Runs, AL, 16
Mangual, Pepe
  Most Times Struck Out, Game, NL, 109
Mann, Les
  Grand Slam Home Runs, NL, 27
Manning, Jack
  Three Home Runs in One Game, NL, 73
Manning, Rick
  Grand Slam Home Runs, AL, 16, 18

McDonald, Ben
  Shutout in First Start in Majors, AL, 188
McDonald, Jim
  Doubleheader Shutouts, AL, 427
  Walked Twice in One Inning, AL, 105
McDougald, Gil
  Grand Slam Home Runs, AL, 9, 10
  Most RBIs in One Inning, AL, 151
McDowell, Jack
  No-Hitters Broken Up By Home Runs, AL,
    201
McDowell, Oddibe
  Back-to-Back Pinch-Hit Home Runs, Team,
    348
  Cycle Hitters, AL, 127
  Grand Slam Home Runs, AL, 21
  Leadoff Home Runs in two Consecutive
    Games, AL, 80
  Most Consecutive Hits, AL, 176
  Most Leadoff Home Runs, Career, 79
  Most Putouts, Outfielder, Game, 290
  Two Pinch-Hit Home Runs in One Game, AL,
    349
  Two Pinch-Hit Home Runs in One Inning,
    Team, AL, 347
McDowell, Roger
  Most Relief Wins, Career, 246
  Most Relief Wins, Season, NL, 247
  Most Saves, Career, 251
McDowell, Sam
  Doubleheader Shutouts, AL, 427
  Most Games with Ten or More Strikeouts, Ca-
    reer, 235
  Most Strikeouts, Career, 226
  Most Strikeouts, Season, AL, 216, 217
  Most Strikeouts in Nine Inning Game, AL,
    227, 228
  Most Strikeouts in Nine Inning Game, NL,
    229
  Most Strikeouts per Nine Innings, Career, 236
  Most Wins, Career, 211
  Strikeout Duos, Season, AL, 438
McElroy, Jim
  Worst Won-Lost Record, Season, 202
McFadden, Barney
  Most Walks in One Game, NL, 234
McFarland, Herm
  Grand Slam Home Runs, AL, 3
  Grand Slam Home Runs, NL, 25
  Most No-Hitters Caught, Career, 297
  Most Runs, Game, AL, 141
  Two Grand Slams in One Game, AL, 346
McFayden, Danny
  Most Strikeouts in Nine Inning Game, NL, 230
McFetridge, John
  Most Consecutive Losses, NL, 243
McGaffigan, Andy
  Undefeated Seasons, 208
  Worst-Hitting Pitchers, Career, 281
McGann, Dan
  Grand Slam Home Runs, NL, 25
  Most Stolen Bases, Game, NL, 159
McGarr, Chippy
  Cycle Hitters, Other Leagues, 130
McGeachey, Jack
  Grand Slam Home Runs, NL, 25
  Most Extra-Base Hits, Game, Other Leagues,
    95

McGee, Willie
  Cycle Hitters, NL, 129
  Grand Slam Home Runs, NL, 42
  Longest Hitting Streaks, NL, 172
  Most Walks, Season, 231
  Most Walks in One Game, NL, 234
  One Hundred or More RBIs with Fewer than
    15 Home Runs (Since 1946), 150
  Stolen Base Duos, Season, NL, 402
McGinn, Dan
  Most Relief Losses, Season, NL, 250
McGinnis, Jumbo
  Most Wins, Career, 213
McGinnity, Joe
  Best Won-Lost Record, Season, NL, 203
  Doubleheader Shutouts, NL, 429
  Fewest Base Runners per Nine Innings, Career,
    262
  Lowest ERA, Season, NL, 259
  Most Complete Games, Season, AL, 263
  Most Complete Games, Season, NL, 265, 266
  Most Consecutive Wins, NL, 239, 240
  Most Innings Pitched, Season, AL, 267
  Most Innings Pitched, Season, NL, 269, 270
  Most Shutouts, Season, NL, 185
  Most 20-Win Seasons, 207
  Most Wins, Career, 209
  Most Wins by Age, Season, NL, 215
  Pitchers Who Stole Home, NL, 278
  Teams with Three 20-Game Winners, NL, 438
  Thirty-Game Winners, NL, 207
  Twenty Wins One Year, 20 Losses the Next,
    Two Leagues, 205
  Twenty Wins and 20 Losses, Season, NL, 206
  Twenty Wins and 20 Losses in Same Year,
    AL, 206
  Two Complete Game Wins in One Day, NL,
    256
McGlothen, Lynn
  Perfect Innings, NL, 226
McGlynn, Stoney
  Most Consecutive Losses, NL, 243
  Most Innings Pitched, Season, NL, 269
  No Hits Allowed, Less than Nine Innings, 196
McGraw, John
  Grand Slam Home Runs, NL, 25
  Most Consecutive Years Managing One Club,
    335
  Most League Pennants Won, Manager, 335
  Most Stolen Bases, Season, NL, 156
  Most Wins, Manager, Career, 333
  Retired Numbers, NL, 333
McGraw, Tug
  Most Grand Slams Allowed, Career, 270
  Most Relief Losses, Career, 249
  Most Relief Wins, Career, 245
  Most Relief Wins, Season, NL, 248
  Most Saves, Career, 251
  Most Strikeouts per Nine Innings, Career, 236
McGregor, Scott
  Most Wins, Career, 211
McGriff, Fred
  Best Home Run Duos, Season, AL, 383
  Grand Slam Home Runs, AL, 22
  Grand Slam Home Runs, NL, 45
  Grand Slams in Two Consecutive Games, NL,
    46
  Most Home Runs, Season, AL, 57, 58

Most Home Runs, Season, NL, 62
Most Home Runs by Team, Game, AL, 362
McGriff, Terry
  Grand Slam Home Runs, NL, 44
  Most Home Runs by Team, Game, NL, 369
McGuire, Deacon
  Grand Slam Home Runs, AL, 3
  Most Games Caught, Career, 295
McGwire, Mark
  Best Home Run Duos, Season, AL, 379, 380,
  381
  Best Home Run Trios, Season, AL, 375
  Grand Slam Home Runs, AL, 22, 23
  Most Home Runs, Season, AL, 55, 56
  Most Home Runs by Team, Game, AL, 365
  Most Runs, Game, AL, 143
  One Hundred or More RBIs, Rookie, AL, 308
  **Thirty or More Home Runs, Rookie, AL,
  303**
  Three Consecutive Home Runs, Team, AL,
  356
  Three Home Runs in One Game, AL, 71
McHenry, Austin
  Most .300 Hitters, Season, NL, 408
McInnis, Stuffy
  Fewest Errors by Position, Season, AL, 287
  Grand Slam Home Runs, AL, 3
  Hardest to Strike Out, Career, 121
  Most Putouts in Nine Innings, First Baseman,
  298
  No Home Runs, Season, AL, 79
McIntire, Harry
  Doubleheader Shutouts, NL, 430
  Most Complete Games, Rookie, NL, 314
  Most Walks in One Game, NL, 234
  No-Hitters Broken Up in Extra Innings, 197
  Three Hundred or More Innings Pitched,
  Rookie, NL, 312
McKain, Archie
  Undefeated Seasons, 208
McKay, Dave
  Home Run in First At-Bat in Majors, AL, 67
  Two Doubles in One Inning, AL, 97
McKean, Ed
  Grand Slam Home Runs, NL, 26
McKechnie, Bill
  Most Times Caught Stealing, Game, NL, 162
  Most Wins, Manager, Career, 334
McKeon, Larry
  Most Strikeouts, Season before 1900, 223
  Most Strikeouts in Nine Inning Game, Other
  Leagues, 231
  No Hits Allowed, Less than Nine Innings, 196
McKinnon, Alex
  Grand Slam Home Runs, NL, 25
McKnight, Jeff
  Fathers and Sons in Baseball, 344
McKnight, Jim
  Fathers and Sons in Baseball, 344
McLain, Denny
  Best Lefty-Righty Duos, 440
  Best Won-Lost Record, Season, AL, 203
  Fewest Base Runners per Nine Innings, Career,
  262
  Most Consecutive Strikeouts, AL, 243
  Most Innings Pitched, Season, AL, 268, 269
  Most Shutouts, Season, AL, 184
  Most Strikeouts, Season, AL, 216

Most Wins, Career, 211
Thirty-Game Winners, AL, 207
McMahon, Don
  Most Relief Losses, Career, 249
  Most Relief Wins, Career, 245
  Most Saves, Career, 250
McMahon, Sadie
  Most 20-Win Seasons, 208
  Most Wins, Career, 211
  Twenty Wins with Last-Place Team, NL, 206
McManus, Marty
  Grand Slam Home Runs, AL, 4
  Grand Slam Home Runs, NL, 29
  Most 100-RBI Hitters, AL, 394
  Most .300 Hitters, Season, AL, 396
McMillan, Norm
  Grand Slam Home Runs, NL, 28
McMillan, Roy
  Best Double-Play Combinations, Season, 291,
  293
  Most Consecutive Games Played, 173
  Most Double Plays, Shortstop, Season, NL,
  290
McMullen, Ken
  Grand Slam Home Runs, AL, 13
  Grand Slam Home Runs, NL, 36, 40
  Most Assists, Third Baseman, Game, 300
  Pinch-Hit Grand Slams, NL, 53
  Three Consecutive Home Runs, Team, AL 353
McMurtry, Craig
  Worst-Hitting Pitchers, Career, 283
McNair, Eric
  Grand Slam Home Runs, AL, 5
  Longest Hitting Streaks, AL, 168
McNally, Dave
  Best Lefty-Righty Duos, 441
  Best Won-Lost Record, Season, AL, 203
  Doubleheader Shutouts, AL, 428
  Fewest Base Runners per Nine Innings, Career,
  262
  Grand Slam Home Runs, AL, 14
  Grand Slam, Pitcher, AL, 275
  Most Strikeouts, Season, AL, 219
  Most Wins, Career, 210
  Shutout in First Start in Majors, AL, 188
  Teams with Four 20-Game Winners, 437
  Teams with Three 20-Game Winners, AL, 438
McNamara, John
  Most Wins, Manager, Career, 334
McNeely, Earl
  .300-Hitting Outfields, AL, 411
McNertney, Jerry
  Grand Slam Home Runs, AL, 13
McPhee, Bid
  Cycle Hitters, Other Leagues, 132
  Grand Slam Home Runs, NL, 25
  Most Runs, Career, 140
  Most Triples, Game, NL, 99
McQuery, Mox
  Cycle Hitters, NL, 129
McQuillan, George
  ERA Under 2.00, Rookie NL, 312
  Lowest ERA, Season, NL, 259
  Most Complete Games, Rookie, NL, 314
  Most Complete Games, Season, NL, 266
  Most Innings Pitched, Season, NL, 269
  Most Shutout Losses, Season, NL, 187
  Most Shutouts, Rookie, NL, 314

Merriman, Lloyd
  Most Putouts, Outfielder, Game, 290
Merritt, Jim
  Most Consecutive Strikeouts, AL, 243
Mertes, Sam
  Cycle Hitters, NL, 129
  Grand Slam Home Runs, NL, 27
  Leadoff Home Runs in Two Consecutive
    Games, NL, 80
  Most Times Walked, Game, NL, 103
  Stolen Base Duos, Season, NL, 404
  Unassisted Double Plays, Outfielder, 291
Merullo, Lennie
  Grand Slam Home Runs, NL, 31
Mesner, Steve
  Grand Slam Home Runs, NL, 31
  No Home Runs, Season, NL, 82
Messersmith, Andy
  Fewest Base Runners per Nine Innings, Career,
    262
  Most Strikeouts, Season, AL, 218
  Most Strikeouts, Season, NL, 221
  Most Strikeouts per Nine Innings, Career, 237
  Most Wins, Career, 215
Metovich, Catfish
  Longest Hitting Streaks, AL, 166
  Most Runs, Game, AL, 143
Metzger, Butch
  Most Consecutive Wins, NL, 241
  Most Relief Wins, Season, NL, 247
Metzger, Roger
  No Home Runs, Season, NL, 83
  Worst Hitters, 131
Meusel, Bob
  Best-Hitting Brothers, 342
  Brothers with Most Home Runs, Career, 87
  Cycle Hitters, AL, 127
  Grand Slam Home Runs, AL, 3, 4
  Most Assists, Outfielder, Game, 291
  Most Doubles, Rookie, 307
  Most 100-RBI Hitters, AL, 395
  Stole 2nd, 3rd, and Home in One Game, AL,
    160
  Three Consecutive Home Runs, Team, AL,
    351
  .300-Hitting Outfields, AL, 410, 411
  Two Legs of Triple Crown, AL, 124
Meusel, Irish
  Best-Hitting Brothers, 341
  Brothers with Most Home Runs, Career, 87
  Grand Slam Home Runs, NL, 27, 28
  Most .300 Hitters, Season, NL, 408
Meyer, Bob
  Doubleheader Shutouts, AL, 428
Meyer, Billy
  Retired Numbers, NL, 333
Meyer, Dan
  Grand Slam Home Runs, AL, 17
  Longest Hitting Streaks, AL, 168
  Two Pinch-Hit Home Runs in One Game, AL,
    348
  Two Pinch-Hit Home Runs in One Inning,
    Team, AL, 347
Meyer, Joey
  Most Times Struck Out, Game, AL, 108
Meyers, Chief
  Cycle Hitters, NL, 129
  Grand Slam Home Runs, NL, 27

Michael, Gene
  Three Consecutive Home Runs, Team, AL,
    355
Michaels, Cass
  Best Double-Play Combinations, Season, 293
  Grand Slam Home Runs, AL, 9, 10
  Most Double Plays, Second Baseman, Season
    AL, 289
Milacki, Bob
  Combined No-Hitters, 198
Milan, Clyde
  Career Spent with One Team, 331
  Most Consecutive Games Played, 175
  Most Stolen Bases, Career, 157
  Most Stolen Bases, Game, AL, 167
  Most Stolen Bases, Season, AL, 155
  Stole Base Duos, Season, AL, 401
Milbourne, Larry
  Grand Slam Home Runs, AL, 17
  Switch-Hit Home Runs in One Game, AL,
    84
Millan, Felix
  Grand Slam Home Runs, NL, 37
  Most Hits, Game, NL, 111
  Most RBIs in One Inning, NL, 151
Miller, Bing
  Longest Hitting Streaks, AL, 166
  Most .300 Hitters, Season, AL, 406, 407
  Three Consecutive Home Runs, Team, AL,
    352
  .300-Hitting Outfields, AL, 410, 411
  Two Doubles in One Inning, AL, 97
Miller, Bob
  Most At-Bats with No Hits, Pitcher, Season,
    279
  Most Consecutive Losses, NL, 242
  Worst Won-Lost Record, Season, 202
Miller, Doc
  Most Pinch Hits, Season, NL, 163
Miller, Doggie
  Grand Slam Home Runs, NL, 25
  Three Consecutive Home Runs, Team, NL,
    356
Miller, Dots
  Grand Slam Home Runs, NL, 27
Miller, Dusty
  Most Assists, Outfielder, Game, 291
Miller, Eddie
  Best Double-Play Combinations, Season, 294
  Grand Slam Home Runs, NL, 29, 30, 31
  Most Double Plays, Shortstop, Season, NL,
    290
  Most Putouts, Shortstop, Game, 300
Miller, Elmer
  Struck Out Twice in One Inning, AL, 106
Miller, Frank
  Doubleheader Shutouts, NL, 431
Miller, Hack
  Grand Slam Home Runs, NL, 27
  Home Run in First At-Bats in Majors, AL, 68
  Most Extra-Base Hits, Game, NL, 92
Miller, John
  Home Run in First At-Bat in Majors, AL, 68
Miller, Norm
  Grand Slam Home Runs, NL, 37
Miller, Ox
  Grand Slam Home Runs, NL, 32
  Grand Slams, Pitcher, NL, 275

Most Strikeouts, Season, NL, 221, 222
Most Strikeouts in Nine-Inning Game, NL, 230
Most 20-Win Seasons, 208
Most Wins, Career, 209
Most Wins by Brothers, 339
Most Wins Since Age 40, 271
No-Hitters, NL, 195
Pitching Accomplishments in AL and NL, 271
Pitching Brothers, Same Team, AL, 337
Shutouts with Most Hits Allowed, AL, 190
300-Win Club, 214
Perry, Gerald
  Grand Slam Home Runs, AL, 23
Perry, Jim
  Best Lefty-Righty Duos, 441
  Most Wins, Career, 209
  Most Wins by Brothers, 339
  Pitching Brothers, Same Team, AL, 337
Perry, Scott
  Doubleheader Shutouts, AL, 426
  ERA Under 2.00, Rookie, AL, 312
  Highest Percentage of Team's Wins, AL, 206
  Most Complete Games, Rookie, AL, 313
  Most Complete Games, Season, AL, 265
  Most Innings Pitched, Season, AL, 268
  Most Times Struck Out, Game, AL, 107
  Three Hundred or More Innings Pitched, Rookie, AL, 312
  Twenty or More Wins, Rookie, AL, 311
  Twenty Wins with Last-Place Team, AL, 205
Pesky, Johnny
  Best Double-Play Combinations, Season, 294
  Highest Batting Average, Rookie, AL, 309
  Longest Hitting Streaks, AL, 166
  Most Consecutive Hits, AL, 175
  Most Runs, Game, AL, 141
  Most Seasons with 200 Hits, 135
  No Home Runs, Season, AL, 80
  Teammates Who Finished 1-2 in Batting, AL, 420
  Two Hundred or More Hits, Rookie, AL, 305
Peters, Gary
  Grand Slam Home Runs, AL, 14
  Grand Slams, Pitcher, AL, 275
  Most Consecutive Wins, AL, 238
  Most Home Runs, Pitcher, Career, 272
  Most Strikeouts, Rookie, AL, 313
  Most Strikeouts, Season, AL, 218
  Most Wins, Career, 212
  No-Hitters Broken Up by Home Runs, AL, 200
Peters, Rick
  Grand Slam Home Runs, AL, 18
Peterson, Fritz
  Best Control Pitchers, Career, 257
  Doubleheader Shutouts, AL, 429
  Fewest Base Runners per Nine Innings, Career, 263
  Most Consecutive Wins, AL, 239
  Most Shutout Losses, Career, 184
  Most Wins, Career, 212
Peterson, Kent
  Worst-Hitting Pitchers, Career, 281
Petralli, Geno
  Most Pinch-Hit Home Runs, Career, 48
Petrocelli, Rico
  Best Home Run Duos, Season, AL, 379

Best Home Run Trios, Season, AL, 375
Grand Slam Home Runs, AL, 13, 14, 15, 16
Home Run Duos, Career, AL, 393
Most 40-Home Run Hitters, AL, 369
Most Grand Slams, Season, AL, 47
Most Home Runs, Season, AL, 57
Most Home Runs by Position, Season, AL, 67
Petry, Dan
  Most Wins, Career, 212
Pettis, Gary
  Grand Slam Home Runs, AL, 20
  Most Putouts, Outfielder, Game, 288
Pfeffer, Big Jeff
  Most Complete Games, Season, NL, 266
  Most Wins by Brothers, 339
  No-Hitters, NL, 194
Pfeffer, Fred
  Grand Slam Home Runs, NL, 24
  Most Extra-Base Hits, Game, NL, 91
  No-Hit Spoilers—The Only Hit Most Often, 137
Pfeffer, Jeff
  Doubleheader Shutouts, NL, 431
  ERA Under 2.00, Rookie, NL, 312
  Most Complete Games, Season, NL, 266, 267
  Most Innings Pitched, Game, NL, 260
  Most Innings Pitched, Season, NL, 270
  Most Wins, Career, 211
  Most Wins by Brothers, 339
  Three Hundred or More Innings Pitched, Rookie, NL, 312
  Twenty or More Wins, Rookie, NL, 311
Pfiester, Jack
  Best Lefty-Righty Duos, 442
  Doubleheader Shutouts, NL, 430
  ERA Under 2.00, Rookie, NL, 312
  Lowest ERA, Season, NL, 259
  Most Strikeouts in Extra-Inning Game, NL, 231
  Twenty or More Wins, Rookie, NL, 311
Phelps, Babe
  Grand Slam Home Runs, NL, 30
Phelps, Ken
  Grand Slam Home Runs, AL, 20
  Most Pinch-Hit Home Runs, Career, 48
Philley, Dave
  Grand Slam Home Runs, AL, 10
  Longest Hitting Streaks, AL, 169
  Most Consecutive Pinch Hits, 165
  Most Pinch Hits, Career, 164
  Most Pinch Hits, Season, AL, 162
  Most Pinch Hits, Season, NL, 163
  No Home Runs, Season, AL, 80
Phillippe, Deacon
  Best Control Pitchers, Career, 257
  Fewest Base Runners per Nine Innings, Career, 261
  Grand Slam Home Runs, NL, 26
  Grand Slams, Pitcher, NL, 275
  Most Complete Games, Season, NL, 266, 267
  Most Consecutive Wins, NL, 240
  Most Innings Pitched, Game, NL, 260
  Most 20-Win Seasons, 207
  Most Wins, Career, 210
  No-Hitters, NL, 193
  Rookie No-Hitters, NL, 310
  Teams with Three 20-Game Winners, NL, 438

Robinson, Wilbert (*cont.*)
Most Wins, Manager, Career, 334
Rodgers, Andre
Grand Slam Home Runs, NL, 34, 36
Most Consecutive Pinch Hits, 165
Rodgers, Buck
Grand Slam Home Runs, AL, 12
Most Games Caught, Career, 294
Three Consecutive Home Runs, Team, AL, 354
Rodriguez, Aurelio
Grand Slam Home Runs, AL, 16
Home Run and Double in One Inning, AL, 100
Three Consecutive Home Runs, Team, AL, 354
Rodriguez, Ed
Undefeated Seasons, 208
Roe, Preacher
Best Won-Lost Record, Season, NL, 203
Most Consecutive Wins, NL, 241
Most Wins, Career, 212
Roebuck, Ed
Most Relief Wins, Career, 245
Struck Out Twice in One Inning, NL, 107
Roenicke, Gary
Brothers with Most Home Runs, Career, 87
Grand Slam Home Runs, AL, 17, 19, 20
Most Home Runs by Team, Game, AL, 365
Three Consecutive Home Runs, Team, AL, 355
Roenicke, Ron
Brothers with Most Home Runs, Career, 87
Roettger, Wally
Grand Slam Home Runs, NL, 28, 29
Rogell, Billy
Best Double-Play Combinations, Season, 293
Most 100-RBI Hitters, AL, 395
Most Times Walked, Game, AL, 102
No Home Runs, Season, AL, 80
Rogers, Steve
ERA Under 2.00, Rookie, NL, 312
Most Shutouts, Career, 183
Most Strikeouts, Season, NL, 222
Most Wins, Career, 211
No-Hitters Broken Up by Home Runs, NL, 201
Rogodzinski, Mike
Most Pinch Hits, Season, NL, 164
Rogovin, Saul
Grand Slam Home Runs, AL, 9
Grand Slams, Pitcher, AL, 275
Rohr, Billy
Shutout in First Start in Majors, AL, 188
Rojas, Cookie
Best Double-Play Combinations, Season, 293
Grand Slam Home Runs, AL, 15, 16
Grand Slam Home Runs, NL, 37
Rojek, Stan
No Home Runs, Season, NL, 82
Rolfe, Red
Most Extra-Base Hits, Game, AL, 90
Most .300 Hitters, Season, AL, 407
Rollins, Rich
Grand Slam Home Runs, AL, 13, 14
Most Home Runs in One Inning, Team, AL, 360
Most Home Runs by Team, Game, AL, 363
Roman, Bill
Home Run in First At-Bat in Majors, AL, 68

Pinch-Hit Home Run in First At-Bat in Majors, AL, 55
Romano, Johnny
Grand Slam Home Runs, AL, 12, 13
Longest Hitting Streaks, AL, 167
Rommel, Eddie
Highest Percentage of Team's Wins, AL, 206
Most Relief Wins, Career, 245
Most Wins, Career, 210
Romine, Kevin
Grand Slam Home Runs, AL, 23
Romo, Enrique
Grand Slam Home Runs, NL, 41
Grand Slams, Pitcher, NL, 276
Roof, Phil
Grand Slam Home Runs, AL, 16
Rooker, Jim
Doubleheader Shutouts, NL, 432
Most Wins, Career, 213
Two Home Runs in One Game, Pitcher, AL, 273
Roomes, Rolando
Most Putouts, Outfielder, Game, 288
Root, Charlie
Most Home Runs, Pitcher, Career, 273
Most Wins, Career, 210
Roque, Jorge
Grand Slam Home Runs, NL, 39
Rosar, Buddy
Cycle Hitters, AL, 127
Grand Slam Home Runs, AL, 7
Most No-Hitters Caught, Career, 297
Rose, Don
Home Run in First At-Bat in Majors, AL, 68
Home Run on First Pitch in Majors, AL, 68
Rose, Pete
Batted .300 after Age 40, 140
Fewest Games Missed, 174
Grand Slam Home Runs, NL, 36
Home Runs by First Two Batters in Game, NL, 351
Leadoff Home Runs in Two Consecutive Games, NL, 79
Longest Hitting Streaks, NL, 169, 170, 171, 173
Most Combined Hits and Walks, Season, NL, 114
Most Consecutive Games Played, 174
Most Consecutive Hits, NL, 177
Most Games with Five or More Hits, Career, 112
Most Home Runs by Team, Game, NL, 368
Most Leadoff Home Runs, Career, 78
Most Runs, Career, 141
Most Runs Produced, Career, 149
Most Seasons with 200 Hits, 134
Rookies of the Year Who Later Won MVP or Cy Young Awards, 314
Stole 2nd, 3rd, and Home in One Game, NL, 161
Switch-Hit Home Runs in One Game, NL, 83
Three Home Runs in One Game, NL, 76
.300-Hitting Outfields, NL, 419
3,000 Hit Club, 133
3,000th Hit, 134
Two Doubles in One Inning, NL, 98
Roseboro, Johnny
Grand Slam Home Runs, NL, 35, 36

Snyder, Frank
  Grand Slam Home Runs, NL, 27
  Most Games Caught, Career, 295
  Most .300 Hitters, Season, NL, 408
Snyder, Russ
  Grand Slam Home Runs, AL, 14
Sockalexis, Louis
  .300-Hitting Outfields, NL, 415
Soderholm, Eric
  Grand Slam Home Runs, AL, 15, 16, 18
Solaita, Tony
  Most Runs, Game, AL, 143
  Three Home Runs in One Game, AL, 72
Solters, Moose
  Cycle Hitters, AL, 127
  Grand Slam Home Runs, AL, 6
  Three Home Runs in One Game, AL, 70
Sosa, Elias
  Most Relief Wins, Career, 245
Sosa, Jose
  Home Run in First At-Bat in Majors, NL, 68
Sosa, Sammy
  Most Times Struck Out, Game, AL, 108
Sothern, Denny
  Grand Slam Home Runs, NL, 28
  Most Doubles, Game, NL, 96
  Most Extra-Base Hits, Game, NL, 92
  Most Runs, Game, NL, 144
  .300-Hitting Outfields, NL, 417
Soto, Mario
  Fewest Base Runners per Nine Innings, Career,
    262
  Four Strikeouts in One Inning, NL, 225
  Most Games with Ten or More Strikeouts,
    Career, 236
  Most Strikeouts, Season, NL, 220, 221
  Most Strikeouts in Nine-Inning Game, NL, 231
  Most Strikeouts per Nine Innings, Career, 236
  Most Wins, Career, 214
  No-Hitters Broken Up by Home Runs, NL,
    201
Souchock, Steve
  Pinch-Hit Grand Slams, AL, 49
Southern, Denny
  Grand Slam Home Runs, NL, 28
Southworth, Billy
  Grand Slam Home Runs, NL, 28
  Most Extra-Base Hits, Game, NL, 92
  Most Wins, Manager, Career, 334
  No-Hit Spoilers—The Only Hit Most Often,
    138
  .300-Hitting Outfields, NL, 416, 417
Sowders, Bill
  Three or More Brothers in Baseball, 338
Sowders, John
  Three or More Brothers in Baseball, 338
Sowders, Len
  Three or More Brothers in Baseball, 338
Spade, Bob
  Shutout in First Start in Majors, NL, 188
Spahn, Warren
  Best Lefty-Righty Duos, 440
  Fewest Base Runners per Nine Innings, Career,
    263
  Most Complete 1-0 Wins, Career, 202
  Most Consecutive Wins, NL, 240, 241
  Most Hits, Pitcher, Career, 277
  Most Home Runs, Pitcher, Career, 272

Most Home Runs by Position, Career, NL,
  67
Most Losses, Career, 214
Most No-Hitters, Career, 199
Most Shutouts, Career, 183
Most Strikeouts, Career, 226
Most Strikeouts in Extra-Inning Game, NL,
  231
Most Strikeouts in Nine-Inning Game, NL, 230
Most 20-Win Seasons, 207
Most Wins, Career, 209
Most Wins by Age, Season, NL, 216
Most Wins Since Age 40, 271
No-Hitters, NL, 194
Retired Numbers, NL, 333
300-Win Club, 214
Won 20 and Hit .300 in Same Year, NL, 272
Spalding, Al
  Most Consecutive Wins, NL, 240
  Most Shutouts, Season, NL, 185
  Shutout in First Start in Majors, NL, 188
  Shutout in First Two Major League Starts, NL,
    190
Sparks, Tully
  Most Consecutive Wins, NL, 240
  Most Innings Pitched, Game, NL, 260
  Most Wins, Career, 221
Speaker, Tris
  Cycle Hitters, AL, 127
  Grand Slam Home Runs, AL, 4
  Hardest to Strike Out, Career, 121
  Highest Batting Average, Career, 133
  Longest Hitting Streaks, AL, 165, 167, 168,
  Most Combined Hits and Walks, Season, AL,
    113, 114
  Most Consecutive Hits, AL, 175
  Most Grand Slams, Season, AL, 47
  Most RBIs, Career, 147
  Most Runs, Career, 141
  Most Runs, Game, AL, 142
  Most Runs Produced, Career, 149
  Most Seasons with 200 Hits, 135
  Most Steals of Home, Career, 161
  Most Stolen Bases, Career, 157
  Most .300 Hitters, Season, AL, 406
  Most Times Caught Stealing, Game, AL,
    161
  Most Times Walked, Game, AL, 102
  .300-Hitting Outfields, AL, 410, 411
  3,000th Hit, 134
  3,000th Hit Club, 133
  Unassisted Double Plays, Outfielder, 289
  Walked Twice in One Inning, AL, 104
Spehr, Tim
  Grand Slam Home Runs, AL, 23
Speier, Chris
  Cycle Hitters, NL, 130
  Grand Slam Home Runs, NL, 39, 44
  Most Extra-Base Hits, Game, NL, 94
  Most Home Runs by Team, Game, NL, 366
  Most RBIs, Game, NL, 153
Spence, Stand
  Most Hits, Game, AL, 109
  Three Consecutive Home Runs, Team, AL, 353
Spencer, Daryl
  Grand Slam Home Runs, NL, 33, 35
  Most Home Runs in One Inning, Team, NL,
    362

Strief, George (cont.)
Most Triples, Game, Other Leagues, 99
Stripp, Joe
Grand Slam Home Runs, NL, 29
Strom, Brent
Worst-Hitting Pitchers, Career, 281
Stroud, Ed
Most Extra-Base Hits, Game, AL, 90
Stroud, Sailor
Shutout in First Start in Majors, AL, 187
Stuart, Dick
Best Home Run Duos, Season, AL, 385
Best Home Run Ratio, Career, 65
Easiest to Strike Out, Career, 122
Grand Slam Home Runs, AL, 12
Grand Slam Home Runs, NL, 34, 35, 36
Most Grand Slams, Season, AL, 47
Most Home Runs, Season, AL, 57
Most Home Runs, Season, NL, 62
Most Pinch-Hit Home Runs, Career, 48
Three Home Runs in One Game, NL, 75
Stuart, Johnny
Two Complete Game Wins in One Day, NL,
259
Stubbs, Franklin
Grand Slam Home Runs, AL, 23, 24
Grand Slam Home Runs, NL, 44
Sudakis, Bill
Grand Slam Home Runs, AL, 16
Grand Slam Home Runs, NL, 37
Suder, Pete
Grand Slam Home Runs, AL, 8, 9
Sudhoff, Willie
Most Complete Games, Season, AL, 265
Most Wins, Career, 213
Suggs, George
Most Wins, Career, 214
Suhr, Gus
Most Consecutive Games Played, 174
Most Times Walked, Game, NL, 103
One Hundred or More RBIs, Rookie, NL,
309
Sullivan, Billy
Fathers and Sons in Baseball, 345
Most Games Caught, Career, 296
Worst Hitters, 131
Sullivan, Billy (Jr.)
Fathers and Sons in Baseball, 345
Two Pinch-Hit Home Runs in One Game, AL,
348
Sullivan, Frank
Doubleheader Shutouts, NL, 433
Sullivan, Haywood
Fathers and Sons in Baseball, 345
Sullivan, Marc
Fathers and Sons in Baseball, 345
Sullivan, Marty
Most Triples, Game, NL, 98
Summa, Homer
Grand Slam Home Runs, AL, 4
.300-Hitting Outfields, AL, 411
Summers, Champ
Grand Slam Home Runs, AL, 18
Grand Slam Home Runs, NL, 40
Most Pinch-Hit Grand Slams, Career, 55
Most Pinch-Hit Home Runs, Career, 47
Most Pinch Hits, Season, NL, 164
Pinch-Hit Grand Slams, NL, 53, 54

Three Consecutive Home Runs, Team, NL,
359
Two Pinch-Hit Home Runs in One Game, NL,
350
Summers, Ed
ERA Under 2.00, Rookie, AL, 311
Most Innings Pitched, Game, AL, 260
Most Shutouts, Rookie, AL, 314
Three Hundred or More Innings Pitched,
Rookie, AL, 312
Twenty or More Wins, Rookie, AL, 310
Two Complete Game Wins in One Day, AL,
255
Two Home Runs in One Game, Pitcher, AL,
273
Sunday, Billy
Unassisted Double Plays, Outfielder, 289
Sundberg, Jim
Fewest Errors by Position, Season, AL, 285
Grand Slam Home Runs, AL, 16, 18, 21
Grand Slam Home Runs, NL, 44
Longest Hitting Streaks, AL, 167
Most Games Caught, Career, 295
Most Games Caught, Season, 294
Pinch-Hit Grand Slams, NL, 54
Sundra, Steve
Most Consecutive Wins, AL, 238
No-Hitters Broken Up by Home Runs, AL,
200
Surhoff, B. J.
Grand Slam Home Runs, AL, 22, 23
Surkont, Max
Most Consecutive Strikeouts, NL, 244
Susce, George
Fathers and Sons in Baseball, 345
Susce, George (Jr.)
Fathers and Sons in Baseball, 345
Sutcliffe, Rick
Most Consecutive Wins, NL, 239
Most Home Runs by Team, Game, NL, 368
Most Strikeouts in Nine-Inning Game, NL, 231
Most Wins, Career, 211
Pitchers Who Stole Home, NL, 278
Rookies of the Year Who Later Won MVP or
Cy Young Awards, 314
Sutter, Bruce
Most Relief Losses, Career, 248
Most Relief Losses, Season, NL, 250
Most Relief Wins, Career, 245
Most Saves, Career, 250
Most Saves, Season, NL, 253
Most Wins Plus Saves, Season, 254
Perfect Innings, NL, 226
Worst-Hitting Pitchers, Career, 281
Sutton, Don
Doubleheader Shutouts, NL, 433
Fewest Base Runners per Nine Innings, Career,
262
Most Games with Ten or More Strikeouts,
Career, 236
Most Grand Slams Allowed, Career, 270
Most Losses, Career, 219
Most Shutouts, Career, 183
Most Shutouts, Season, NL, 185
Most Strikeouts, Career, 226
Most Strikeouts, Rookie, NL, 313
Most Strikeouts, Season, NL, 221, 222
Most Wins, Career, 209

Taylor, Carl
  Grand Slam Home Runs, NL, 38
  Most Pinch Hits, Season, NL, 163
  Pinch-Hit Grand Slams, NL, 53
Taylor, Danny
  Grand Slam Home Runs, NL, 29
  Unassisted Double Plays, Outfielder, 290
Taylor, Dummy
  Most Complete Games, Season, NL, 265
  Most Innings Pitched, Season, NL, 269
  Most Wins, Career, 213
  Teams with Three 20-Game Winners, NL, 438
Taylor, Harry
  Doubleheader Shutouts, AL, 427
Taylor, Hawk
  Grand Slam Home Runs, NL, 37
  Pinch-Hit Grand Slams, NL, 53
Taylor, Jack
  Fewest Base Runners per Nine Innings, Career,
    262
  Lowest ERA, Season, NL, 259
  Most Complete Games, Season, NL, 265, 266,
    267
  Most Innings Pitched, Games, NL, 260
  Most Innings Pitched, Season, NL, 269, 270
  Most Shutouts, Season, NL, 186
  Most Wins, Career, 211
  Twenty Wins One Year, 20 Losses the Next,
    NL, 205
  Undefeated Seasons, 208
Taylor, Jack
  Most Wins, Career, 212
Taylor, Tony
  Grand Slam Home Runs, NL, 38
  Most Pinch Hits, Season, NL, 163
Taylor, Zack
  Most .300 Hitters, Season, NL, 409
  Grand Slam Home Runs, NL, 28
Tebbetts, Birdie
  Grand Slam Home Runs, AL, 6, 7, 8
  Most Games Caught, Career, 296
Tekulve, Kent
  Most Relief Losses, Career, 248
  Most Relief Losses, Season, NL, 250
  Most Relief Wins, Career, 244
  Most Relief Wins, Season, NL, 247, 248
  Most Saves, Career, 250
  Most Saves, Season, NL, 253
  Most Wins Plus Saves, Season, 254
  Worst-Hitting Pitchers, Career, 281
Temple, Johnny
  Best Double-Play Combinations, Season, 291,
    293
  Grand Slam Home Runs, NL, 33, 34
  No Home Runs, Season, NL, 82
Templeton, Garry
  Grand Slam Home Runs, NL, 42, 44
  Most Runs, Game, NL, 145
Tenace, Gene
  Best Home Run Ratio, Career, 66
  Easiest to Strike Out, Career, 122
  Grand Slam Home Runs, AL, 15, 16
  Grand Slam Home Runs, NL, 40
  More Walks than Hits, Season, AL, 135
  More Walks than Hits, Season, NL, 135
  Most Grand Slams, Season, AL, 47
  Three Consecutive Home Runs, Team, NL,
    359

Tenney, Fred
  Most Hits, Game, NL, 110
  Most Times Walked, Game, NL, 103
Terrell, Jerry
  Grounded into Most Double Plays, Game, AL,
    117
Terrell, Walt
  Most Wins, Career, 213
  Two Home Runs in One Game, Pitcher, NL,
    274
Terry, Adonis
  Home Run and Double in One Inning, NL, 100
  Most No-Hitters, Career, 199
  No-Hitters, Other Leagues, 196
Terry, Bill
  Best Home Run Duos, Season, NL, 390
  Cycle Hitters, NL, 130
  .400 Average and 20 Home Runs, Season, 133
  .400 Hitters, NL, 132
  Grand Slam Home Runs, NL, 28
  Highest Batting Average, Career, 133
  Home Run Duos, Career, NL, 394
  Most Combined Hits and Walks, Season, NL,
    114
  Most Extra-Base Hits, Game, NL, 92
  Most Hits, Season, 133
  Most Putouts in Nine Innings, First Baseman,
    298
  Most Seasons with 200 Hits, 134
  Most .300 Hitters, Season, NL, 408, 409, 410
  Most 200-Hit Batters, NL, 422
  Pennant-Winning Rookie Managers, NL, 316
  Retired Numbers, NL, 333
  Three Consecutive Home Runs, Team, NL,
    356
  Three Home Runs in One Game, NL, 74
Terry, Ralph
  Doubleheader Shutouts, AL, 428
  Fewest Base Runners per Nine Innings, Career,
    262
  Most Wins, Career, 213
Terwilliger, Wayne
  Grand Slam Home Runs, AL, 9
  Most Consecutive Hits, NL, 177
Tesreau, Jeff
  Doubleheader Shutouts, NL, 430, 431
  ERA Under 2.00, Rookie, NL, 312
  Fewest Base Runners per Nine Innings, Career,
    262
  Most Shutouts, Season, NL, 186
  Most Wins, Career, 212
  No-Hitters, NL, 194
  Rookie No-Hitters, NL, 310
  Teams with Three 20-Game Winners, NL, 438
Tettleton, Mickey
  Best Home Run Duos, Season, AL, 381, 383
  Best Home Run Trios, Season, AL, 376
  Grand Slam Home Runs, AL, 23, 24
  Most 30-Home Run Hitters, AL, 370
  Most 20-Home Run Hitters, AL, 373
  Pinch-Hit Grand Slams, AL, 51
  Switch-Hit Home Runs in One Game, AL, 83
  Three Consecutive Home Runs, Team, AL,
    356
Teufel, Tim
  Grand Slam Home Runs, NL, 43, 44, 45
  Most Extra-Base Hits, Game, NL, 94
  Most Pinch-Hit Home Runs, Career, 48